Public Administration

Random House Series in Political Science

STEPHEN J. WAYNE
George Washington University
General Editor

Public Administration

UNDERSTANDING MANAGEMENT, POLITICS, AND LAW IN THE PUBLIC SECTOR

SECOND EDITION

David H. Rosenbloom
Syracuse University

With the assistance of
Deborah D. Goldman, J.D., M.P.A.
Member of the New York State Bar
Syracuse, New York

RANDOM HOUSE
New York

To Ricky, our all-time favorite bureaucrat

Second Edition
987654321
Copyright © 1986, 1989 by Random House, Inc.

Library of Congress Cataloging-in-Publication Data

Rosenbloom, David H.
    Public administration.

    Includes bibliographies and index.
    1. Public administration.   2. United States—
Politics and government.   I. Goldman, Deborah D.
II. Title.
JF1351.R56   1988   350   88-11542
ISBN 0-394-38301-X

Manufactured in the United States of America

Chapter-opening photo credits:
Chapter 1: Bruce Davidson/Magnum; **Chapter 2:** AP/Wide World Photos; **Chapter 3:** Meyer Rangell/The Image Works; **Chapter 4:** Roger Malloch/Magnum; **Chapter 5:** Neal Boenzi/NYT Pictures; **Chapter 6:** Bob Adelman/Magnum; **Chapter 7:** Courtesy of Brookhaven Town Board; **Chapter 8:** Mark Godfrey/Archive; **Chapter 9:** Cary Wolinsky/Stock, Boston; **Chapter 10:** Elizabeth Crews; **Chapter 11:** Bruce Roberts/Photo Researchers; **Chapter 12:** W. Keith McManus/Archive; **Chapter 13:** Howard Dratch/The Image Works.

Preface to the Second Edition

When Deborah Goldman and I began working on the first edition of this book, we wanted to provide a useful framework for organizing the field of public administration, to produce a work that would be comprehensive, informative, and above all intellectually engaging. We started with some general ideas, a rudimentary outline, and a supportive publisher. The response has been gratifying. In 1987, *Public Administration Review* published a review, by Eleanor V. Laudicina, of seven recent public administration texts.[1] It is a pleasure to quote her at length:

> Rosenbloom presents a simple but powerful conceptualization of contemporary public administration. Of all the new texts, Rosenbloom's articulates the most lucid, coherent, and comprehensive framework for understanding the current state of public administration as a discipline and as a practice. He takes the constitutional separation of powers as a starting point and examines every aspect of the field as it is influenced by political, managerial, and legal demands and by the simultaneous interplay of the three. The distinctive framework effectively illuminates the fundamental conflicts, strains, and tensions within the field and facilitates organizing and presenting the substantive material.

Laudicina went on to note that the last section of the book "attempts to restore to a central focus some fundamental values" by reemphasizing the "importance of the public in public administration with an examination of the inevitable tensions between individual and state," by stressing "the moral responsibility of the administrator to uphold individual rights," and by considering "in detail the concept of democratic constitutionalism as a core for the profession." Overall, she found that the book "offers a clear focus and moral imperative for the prospective administrator. . . ."

Professor Laudicina also picked up on a point that requires some clarification: "If the text has a weakness, it lies in the author's effort to conclude many of the chapters with evidence of an emerging synthesis of the three competing values." The discussions of synthesizing the managerial, political, and legal perspectives on public administration should be taken as suggestive and illustrative of how these views might be usefully combined. They are not intended to present convincing evidence that the competing approaches have been synthesized in practice. The main objective of these sections is to find useful common ground in the three perspectives, lest, in our thinking, they remain forever separate and in conflict. The second edition is clearer than the first on these points.

A word should be said about the framework itself. We view it as grounded, for the United States, in the Constitution's definition and partial separation of executive, legislative, and judicial powers and roles. The Constitution provides each branch with a different focus: the executive is charged with executing the law, the legislature is a representative body, the judiciary adjudicates conflicting legal claims. But public administration must often combine these functions. It is a means of coordinating and bridging the separation of powers.

The idea that public administration includes executive, legislative, and judicial functions goes back at least as far as Alexander Hamilton's discussion in *Federalist* No. 72. He noted that "the administration of government, in its largest sense, comprehends all the operations of the body politic, whether legislative, executive, or judiciary," though he went on to emphasize that "in its most usual and perhaps in its most precise signification, it is limited to executive details" and falls within the province of the executive branch.[2] Leonard White's *Introduction to the Study of Public Administration* displayed interest in developing the larger Hamiltonian conception:

> Students of government are familiar with the traditional division of governmental activities into the legislative, executive, and judicial. It is important to understand that the work of the administration involves all three types of activity. . . . Administration more and more tends in fact to reach into the established fields of legislation and adjudication, raising important problems. . . .[3]

More recently, Robert Fried's *Performance in American Bureaucracy* presented a related discussion of three "basic performance ethics" in public administration: a work ethic, a democratic ethic, and a legal ethic.[4]

Public Administration: Understanding Management, Politics, and Law in the Public Sector builds upon this intellectual legacy by developing each of the perspectives further and emphasizing their relationships to one another in all the major areas of public administration in the United States. As Professor Laudicina put it, in words too kind not to reproduce, "Rosenbloom's skillful use of his tripartite framework enlivens the material and sharpens the political, managerial, and legal perspectives on the evolution and current status of public administration."

Given the favorable response to the first edition, I have cast the second in a fundamentally similar mold. It is divided into the same four parts. Part One introduces the book's intellectual framework and discusses the development of public administration in the United States. Part Two considers public administration's core areas: organization, personnel, budgeting, decision making, and policy analysis and evaluation. Part Three analyzes regulatory administration as an illustration of the interplay of the three perspectives. Part Four focuses on the "public" and the "public interest" in public administration.

But the book has been strengthened considerably throughout. It has been updated to include more on the Reagan presidency's impacts on public administration; more attention is paid to state and local administration; and much new material has been added. More specifically, Chapter 3, on federalism and intergovernmental relations, now includes a better discussion of different types of federalism and a section entitled "Relationships among Local Governments." Chapter 4, on organization, has been substantially improved by a more comprehensive discussion of the systems approach and by the presentation of new material on the environmental, ecological, network, agency-theory, and matrix approaches. A section on performance appraisal has been added to Chapter 5, on public personnel administration and collective bargaining. Chapter 6, on budgeting, addresses the impact of the Gramm-Rudman-Hollings Act and the pervasive concern with the federal deficit. Chapter 7, concerning decision making, now includes a discussion of "grid-regulations" as an administrative decision-making tool. Material on "utilizing evaluation" appears in Chapter 8, on policy analysis and evaluation. A stronger framework for analyzing regulatory policy, regulatory reform, and administration has been incorporated into Chapter 9. Part Four, like the rest of the book, has been updated in a variety of ways. The second edition is accompanied by a revised instructor's manual, which includes a test bank.

Turning the first edition into the second made me more aware of how much change has occurred in some areas of public administration—especially political-career administrative relationships, federalism, budgeting, and regulatory and "third-party" administration. But it is difficult to assess the long-term significance of many of these changes. California's Proposition 13, hailed as revolutionary back in 1978, turned out to have only a limited impact generally. The "Reagan revolution" is already considered by many to be "one that wasn't."[5] Deregulation has been far more limited than seemed likely to be the case in the early 1980s. Historically, the administrative state seems so universal and entrenched that the movement toward "privatization" could be considered merely a limited expedition into a backwater. But it, and other changes, may actually be fundamental. The future will definitely bring interesting times to public administration, but can we say more?

John Chubb, of the Brookings Institution, has given us a useful metaphor in likening the administrative state to a "fat cell" (which is far better than the cancer as which bureaucracy is so often portrayed!).[6] A fat cell will shrink when it is deprived of nourishment, but it will not disappear. It will always seek to be fed and will expand almost continuously when it is able to do so. Chubb argues that the institutional structure of the administrative state acts in a similar way. It can be put on a diet and forced to shrink, but its basic structure remains intact, and it will grow when the opportunity is present. One can point to relationships between legislative committees and administrative bureaus and to those between local administration and federal agencies as examples of institutional arrangements that have been constrained, but perhaps not fundamentally altered, during the Reagan years. As our discussion of public administration and the public in Chapter 10 indicates, there is strong public support, which may be nourished in the future, for *expansion* of the government's role in several areas of social life. The second edition reflects the caution of the fat cell perspective. We hope that there will be a third edition, and we will know more by then.

1. Eleanor V. Laudicina, "A Thousand Flowers Blooming: Recent Texts in Public Administration," *Public Administration Review*, 47 (May/June 1987): 272–275.
2. *The Federalist Papers*, ed. by Clinton Rossiter (New York: Mentor, 1961), p. 435.
3. Leonard D. White, *Introduction to the Study of Public Administration* (New York: Macmillan, 1926), chap. 1, as reprinted in Jay Shafritz and Albert Hyde, eds., *Classics of Public Administration*, 2d ed. (Chicago: Dorsey, 1987), pp. 58–59.
4. Robert C. Fried, *Performance in American Bureaucracy* (Boston: Little, Brown, 1976), pp. iv–v.
5. Peter Kilborn, "Where the Reagan Revolution Went Awry," *New York Times*, November 8, 1987, sec. 4, p. 1.
6. John Chubb, "Centralization, Federalism, and the Constitution: An Institutional Perspective," presented at the conference, The Constitution and the American Political Process, University of Illinois, December 6–8, 1987, Urbana.

Preface to the First Edition

Public Administration: Understanding Management, Politics, and Law in the Public Sector appears sixty years after the publication of the first major American public administration textbook, Leonard D. White's *Introduction to the Study of Public Administration* (1926). White viewed public administration as "the heart of the problem of modern government."[1] He tried not only to explain and cover his subject matter comprehensively but also to frame the discipline of public administration and its discourse. I have sought to remain within the tradition of public administration texts begun by White. *Public Administration: Understanding Management, Politics, and Law in the Public Sector* agrees with White that public administration is central to modern government. It also presents an intellectual framework that can be a device for developing a deep and comprehensive understanding of contemporary public administration in all its complexity. I believe that this framework can provide a basis for further fruitful discourse and development in the discipline and practice of public administration. Ironically—but not really surprisingly—the most succinct description of the intellectual framework employed here is Dwight Waldo's, rather than my own. With reference to my essay introducing the framework,[2] Waldo remarked:

> . . . David Rosenbloom has set forth the structure of the problem before us. For each of the three constitutional branches, he points out, there is a body of doctrine, set of values, collection of instruments, and repertoire of procedures. For the executive branch this "cluster" is administrative, managerial, bureaucratic, and the emphasis is upon effectiveness and efficiency. For the legislative branch the cluster is political and policy making and the emphasis is upon the values of representativeness and responsiveness. For the judicial branch the cluster is legal, and the emphasis is on constitutional integrity on one side and substantive and procedural protections for individuals on the other.
>
> Realistically our public administration does consist of varying mixtures of these three approaches or clusters. It is not just undesirable, it is impossible to narrow the concerns of public administration to any one of them. Our task is to find the proper way to put the three together.[3]

These clusters (I call them *approaches* or *perspectives*) are an outgrowth of the constitutional separation of powers; they are inherent in our political culture and institutions. As public administration is central to contemporary American government, these approaches are central to our contemporary public administration.

Waldo called this framework, "both an excellent analysis and an excellent prescription."[4] *Public Administration: Understanding Management, Politics, and Law in the Public Sector* engages the task of putting the three approaches together. I hope the reader will find this effort worthwhile and participate in it. Together we may be able to help resolve the problem of modern government; certainly we can improve our understanding and practice of public administration.

The book is divided into four parts. Part One introduces the book's intellectual framework and discusses the development of public administration in the United States. Part Two considers public administration's core functions: organization, personnel, budgeting, decision making, and policy analysis and evaluation. Each of these areas is analyzed from the perspectives of management, politics, and law. Efforts are made to synthesize these three perspectives with regard to each core function. Part Three analyzes regulatory administration as an illustration of the interplay of management, politics, and law in the public sector. Part Four focuses on the place of the "public" and the "public interest" in public administration. Chapters are devoted to public administration and the public, public administration and democratic constitutionalism, and accountability and ethics. The concluding chapter is devoted to the prospects for building a new "administrative culture."

The book is accompanied by an instructor's manual, which includes a test bank.

In many respects, *Public Administration: Understanding Management, Politics, and Law in the Public Sector* differs from other texts in the field. It addresses the complexity of public administration in theory and practice. It provides a comprehensive intellectual framework. It emphasizes *understanding* public administration in its presentation of information, description, theory, and interpretation. It is an ambitious book. I hope you find it rewarding.

1. Leonard D. White, *Introduction to the Study of Public Administration* (New York: Macmillan, 1926), Preface.
2. David H. Rosenbloom, "Public Administrative Theory and the Separation of Powers," *Public Administration Review*, 43 (May/June 1983), pp. 219–227.
3. Brack Brown and Richard J. Stillman, "A Conversation with Dwight Waldo: An Agenda for Future Reflections," *Public Administration Review*, 45 (July/August 1985), pp. 463–464.
4. *Ibid.*, p. 464.

ACKNOWLEDGMENTS

A book of this scope can generate intellectual and professional debts too numerous to acknowledge fully. The second edition rests upon the first and continues to be informed by those who were acknowledged in the earlier volume. But special thanks are again due to Bertrand Lummus of Random House, Inc., whose enthusiasm, encouragement, and support continue to be a source of inspiration. Mark Emmert, Ralph Shangraw, and David Nachmias generously assisted me with the revisions of Chapters 4, 7, and 8, respectively. The revisions also benefited from several anonymous reviews. The Maxwell School of Citizenship and Public Affairs, Syracuse University, provided an excellent environment in which to complete the second edition. Sole responsibility for any shortcomings the book may contain remains with the author.

D. H. R.
Syracuse, N.Y.

Contents in Brief

Contents in Detail

PART ONE | *Introduction:*

Definitions, Concepts, and Setting

CHAPTER 1

The Practice and Discipline of Public Administration:

Competing Concerns

This chapter develops a definition of public administration. It considers what distinguishes *public* administration from the administration and management of private enterprises, focusing on the roles of the Constitution, the public interest, economic market forces, and sovereignty. The tendency for public administration to provide both *service* and *regulation* is explored. The bulk of this chapter discusses three general and competing approaches to public administration. One sees public administration as essentially management, another emphasizes its political nature, and the third, its legalistic concerns and processes. Each perspective favors a different set of values, offers distinctive organizational approaches for maximizing these values, and each considers the individual in different ways.

Public administration, like many human endeavors, is difficult to define. Nonetheless we all have a sense of what it is, though we may disagree profoundly about how it should be carried out. In part, this is because public administration covers such a vast amount of activity. Public administrative jobs range from the exploration of outer space to sweeping the streets. Some public administrators are highly educated professionals, who may be at the forefront of their fields of specialization; others possess few skills that differentiate them from the mass of the citizenry. Some public administrators make policies that have a nationwide impact and may benefit millions of people; others have virtually no responsibility for policy making at all and simply carry out the mundane governmental tasks of typing, word processing, filing, and recordkeeping. Public administrators are doctors, lawyers, scientists, engineers, accountants, budgeters, personnel officers, managers, clerks, typists, manual laborers, and individuals engaged in a host of other occupations and functions. But knowing what public administrators *do* does not resolve the problem of defining what public administration *is*.

At first glance, one might be inclined to ignore the problem of defining public administration. After all, it was pointed out some time ago that any one-paragraph or even one-sentence definition of public administration is bound to prove temporarily mind-paralyzing.[1] This is because public administration as a category is so abstract and varied that it can only be described in vague, general, amorphous, and somewhat competing terms. Yet some attention to definition is important. First, it is necessary to establish the general boundaries and to convey the major concerns of the discipline and practice of public administration. Second, the definition of public administration helps to place the field in a broader political, economic, and social context. Third, consideration of the leading definitions of public administration reveals that there are three distinct underlying approaches to the field. For years the tendency of scholars and practitioners to stress one or another of these approaches has promoted confusion, since each approach tends to emphasize different values, different organizational arrangements, different methods of developing information, and radically distinct views of the individual citizen.

SOME DEFINITIONS

One can find a wide variety of definitions of public administration, but the following are among the most serious and influential efforts to define the field.

1. "Public administration . . . is the action part of government, the means by which the purposes and goals of government are realized."[2]
2. "Public administration as a field is mainly concerned with the means for implementing political values. . . ."
3. ". . . Public administration can be best identified with the executive branch of government."
4. "Public administration differs from political science in its emphasis on bureaucratic structure and behavior and in its methodologies. Public

administration differs from administrative science in the evaluative techniques used by nonprofit organizations, and because profit-seeking organizations are considerably less constrained in considering the public interest in their decision-making structures and the behavior of their administrators."

5. "The process of public administration consists of the actions involved in effecting the intent or desire of a government. It is thus the continuously active, 'business' part of government, concerned with carrying out the law, as made by legislative bodies (or other authoritative agents) and interpreted by the courts, through the processes of organization and management."

6. Public administration: (a) is a cooperative group effort in a public setting; (b) covers all three branches—executive, legislative, and judicial—and their interrelationships; (c) has an important role in the formulation of public policy, and is thus part of the political process; (d) is different in significant ways from private administration; and (e) is closely associated with numerous private groups and individuals.

What conclusions can be drawn from the variety of definitions of public administration and their myriad nuances? One, of course, is that definitions of public administration are indeed mind-paralyzing. Another conclusion is that there is really no such subject as "public administration," but rather that public administration means different things to different observers and lacks a significant common theoretical or applied meaning. However, this perspective has limited appeal because the problem is certainly not that there is no public administration—we not only know it's there, but often are acutely aware of its contributions or shortcomings. Thus, the fact that we cannot neatly define the substance and process of public administration is hardly an excuse for concluding that the phenomenon is nonexistent, especially at a time when almost every society is seeking to improve its public bureaucracy.

Ironically, another conclusion that can be drawn from the multiplicity of definitions is that, on the contrary, public administration is everywhere. Accordingly, some have argued that there is no field or discipline of public administration per se because the study of public administration overlaps a number of other disciplines, including political science, sociology, economics, psychology, and business administration. Although this approach contains a great deal of truth, in practical terms it is unsatisfactory because it leaves us without the ability to analyze coherently a major aspect of contemporary public life—indeed, one that many believe to be the central political development of the twentieth century, namely, the emergence of large and powerful governmental bureaucracies.

This book develops a less extreme approach to the problem of defining public administration. We conclude that all of the above definitions are helpful. Public administration does involve *activity*, it is concerned with *politics* and *policy making*, it tends to be concentrated in the *executive* branch of government, it does differ from private administration, and it is concerned with *implementing the law*. But we can be much more specific by offering a definition of our own: *Public administration is the use of managerial, political, and legal theories and processes to fulfill legislative, executive, and judicial governmental mandates for the provision of regulatory and service functions for the society as a whole or for some segments of it.* There are obviously several points here that require further elaboration.

EMPHASIZING THE PUBLIC IN PUBLIC ADMINISTRATION

First, public administration differs from private administration in significant ways. Although there are several aspects of public management that are *generic*, that is, they are similar in both public and private settings, on balance public administration is largely a separate endeavor. The reasons public administration differs from private are outlined in the following pages.

Constitutions

In the United States, the federal and state constitutions define the environment of public administration and place constraints upon it. First, constitutions fragment power and control over public administration. The separation of powers places public administration under three "masters." We have become accustomed to thinking of chief executives, such as the president, as being in control of public administration, but in practice legislatures often possess as much or more constitutional power over administrative operations than do the president or state governors. This is clearly true at the federal level, where Congress has the constitutional authority to create agencies and departments by law, fix their size in terms of personnel and budget, and determine their missions and legal authority, internal structures, locations, and establish personnel procedures. Similarly, courts often exercise considerable power and control over public administration. They help define the legal rights and obligations of agencies and those of the individuals and groups upon whom public administrators act. They also define the constitutional rights of public employees and the nature of their liabilities for breaches of law or the Constitution. In recent years, the judiciary has also been active in the restructuring of school systems, public mental health facilities, public housing, and prisons in an effort to make certain they comply with constitutional standards. In fact, one federal judge has written that the courts and public administrators are now "partners."[3] The extent of legislative and judicial authority over public administration leaves chief executives with only limited control over the executive branch, and far less authority than is commonly found in the hands of chief executive officers of private organizations, whether profit-seeking or not. Indeed, under the federal Constitution, the president's only specific powers over public administrators are the ability to appoint department heads with the advice and consent of the Senate and to ask these heads for their opinions in writing on various subjects. In practice, of course, chief executives in the public sector now often exercise power delegated to them by legislatures—but it is unusual for legislative bodies to abandon their powers altogether or to be uninterested in matters of public administration.

The separation of powers not only provides each branch with somewhat different authority over public administration but may also frustrate coordination among them. Basic political science tells us that chief executives, legislatures, and courts are responsive to different political pressures and constituencies. Contemporary constitutional law sometimes makes it difficult for legislatures and chief executives to participate jointly in the direction of administrative activity. For example, in *Immigration and Naturalization Service* v. *Chadha* (1983),[4] the Supreme Court held that Congress cannot constitutionally veto, at least by one house only, the exercise of authority it has delegated to the executive branch. The legislative veto was deemed to violate the constitutional system for passing legislation by both houses and presenting it to the president for approval or veto. In *Bowsher* v. *Synar* (1986),[5] the Court held that Congress could not constitutionally vest executive functions in the comptroller general, who is an employee of the legislative branch. Justice White's dissent in this case served to emphasize how important the separation of powers is to a majority of the Court: "The Court, acting in the name of separation of powers, takes upon itself to strike down the Gramm-Rudman-Hollings Act, one of the most novel and far-reaching legislative responses to a national crisis since the New Deal."[6]

The federal constitutional framework also creates a system of federalism that places serious constraints upon the nature of public administration at the state and local levels. It was once common to think of federalism in terms of clear distinctions between the federal and state governments, each having its own powers and programs. This approach is sometimes called the "layer cake" model of federalism. It implies that state-level public administration is separate from public administration at the federal level and not constrained or influenced by it. Today, however, it is more generally true that the Constitution is interpreted to allow an intermixing of state and federal administrative functions. This approach to federalism is sometimes visualized in terms of a marble cake. Often, for instance, the federal government will create a program and rely upon the states to implement it. Funding and authority may be shared. In practice, state agencies may be responsible to federal departments to a greater extent than they are to state governors or state legislatures. Moreover, the federal courts define the constitutional or legal rights of citizens as they are affected by governmental activity, further fragmenting authority over public administration. For example, a state director of mental health may find himself or herself compelled to go to a state legislature to request more funds to meet the requirements of mandates established by a federal department acting under the authority of Congress. The director may also be required to create conditions in the state's mental health facilities that satisfy a federal court's definition of the constitutional rights of the patients.

Constitutional concerns favoring the separation of powers and federalism create a very complex environment for contemporary public administration in the United States. This complexity of fragmented authority is generally not matched in the private sector. Legal restrictions and requirements affect private management, but they do not fragment authority over it in the same way or to the same extent. Nor do they provide so many parties with a legal right to participate in organizational matters.

Constitutional concerns are important in another way as well. They establish values in the public sector that frequently run counter to the values embodied in private management. We will have much more to say about this when we discuss the values inherent in the political and legal approaches to public administration. For now, however, it should be noted that efficiency in government is often subordinated to political principles such as representativeness, or to legalistic considerations like due process. Moreover, in the public sector, there is no genuine equivalent to the profit motive which is so central to private enterprise. This brings us to a second aspect of the "publicness" of public administration.

The Public Interest

The governmental obligation to promote the public interest distinguishes public administration from private management. In a moral and basic sense, it must serve "a higher purpose."[7] Although it is often difficult to say precisely what is in the public interest, there can be no dispute about the obligation of public administrators to consider it as a general guide for their actions. When they fail to do so, public administrators may rightly be criticized for placing personal or agency interests above those of the people as a whole. Indeed, in the view of some, such as Frederick Mosher, a central issue presented by contemporary public administration is assuring that public administrators represent the interests of the citizenry.[8] Otherwise, there can be no guarantee that democracy will prevail. Various regulations have been enacted over the years in an effort to assure that those exercising public power will not use it for narrow partisan or purely private gain or engage in subversion. Many public personnel systems in the United States and abroad place restrictions on the political activities of civil servants, some have very comprehensive conflict-of-interest regulations, and all are concerned with the loyalty of their employees.

This situation often stands diametrically opposed to practice in the private sector under prevailing capitalist ideology. Private firms are thought to best serve the general interest by vigorously pursuing their own economic interests. Their task is to be highly efficient and competitive in the marketplace. Profit is not only the bottom line, it is viewed as a positive social and economic good. Of course, private companies should not damage the health and safety of their workers or that of the general community. Nor should they damage or destroy the environment. By and large, however, it is assumed to be government's role to assure, through proper regulation, that the private sector does not harm society at large.

One way of summarizing this different perspective on the public interest is to think in terms of **externalities**—or aspects of the productive or service operations of organizations that do not enter into the agreement between buyer and seller. Pollution is a classic example of an externality. It is not accounted for in the sale of the product itself, that is, it is external to the market.

Historically, in the United States, private firms have not always felt a moral or other nonlegal obligation to avoid creating harmful externalities. Pollution, damage to the environment, and social damage caused by such practices as sweatshops, child labor, or abusive conditions in migrant labor were all viewed as costs to be passed off upon society as a whole. Eventually, governments took steps to regulate such practices. Today, there is pressure upon governments to regulate plant closings because of their devastating impact on communities. The main point, however, is that in contemporary public administration, there are few harmful externalities that government is not called upon to deal with in some fashion. This is true for the simple reason that when one government agency creates a problematic externality, the public interest will almost inevitably demand that another government agency be empowered to combat it. This contemporary perspective regarding externalities forces public administrators to take a wider view of their responsibilities, recognizing that harmful externalities should not simply be "someone else's problem." This is partly why it is plausible to hold that "public administration is not a kind of technology but a form of moral endeavor."[9]

The Market

A closely related distinction between public and private administration concerns the market. It is generally true that public agencies do not face free, competitive markets in which their services or products are sold.[10] For the most part, the price tags attached to governmental operations are established through budgetary routines rather than fixed at the market through free transactions between buyer and seller. Revenues are largely generated through taxation, although in some cases user fees are a substantial source of operating budgets. Even where such fees are important, however, the governmental agency may be operating as a legal monopoly, or be under a mandate to provide service to everyone at a fixed cost, no matter how difficult or expensive it may be to reach them. The U.S. Postal Service's mission regarding delivery of first-class mail is an example.

The main consequence of this kind of fiscal arrangement is that the market is less constraining in the public than in the private sector. In fact, the market becomes most salient for public agencies when governments, primarily cities, are under severe fiscal constraints. In the long run, excessive taxation of the public in support of undesired or inefficient governmental operations can erode tax bases to the extent that certain market pressures begin to develop. In such cases, individuals (the consumers of public administrative operations) may opt out of the system by moving to another jurisdiction or country. They may also seek to "privatize" some services such as trash collection. But the government in question is likely to remain in some form.

Private firms, however, typically face markets in a far more direct fashion. Under free-market conditions, if they fail to produce products or services at competitive prices, consumers turn to alternate sources and the company's income declines. Eventually the noncompetitive private firm will go out of business. In between the typical public agency and private firm is a gray area in which not-for-profit organizations and highly regulated industries, such as utilities, operate.

The remoteness of market forces from public administrative operations has profound consequences. First, it enables government to provide services and products that could not profitably be offered by private firms, which is another way of saying would not be provided by private enterprise at all. Some of these services and products are referred to as **public goods** or **collective goods.** Roads provide an excellent example. Society as a whole clearly benefits from the existence of a good network of modern highways. Therefore, society as a whole should bear the cost of the system. Moreover, it would not be feasible to make only direct users pay for the building and maintenance of all roads, because the fees would be too high. Public education and public welfare provide additional examples. These functions were once supplied exclusively by nongovernmental organizations, often by churches. Eventually, however, they were "secularized," with government taking the leading role in their provision on the theory that it was in the public interest to do so, and that universal education or welfare could not be provided successfully solely by private groups.

The remoteness of markets in the public sector also makes it difficult to assess or evaluate the worth and efficiency of public administrative operations. If government agencies produce a product that is not sold freely in open markets, then it is hard to determine what the product is worth. It is also difficult to determine the value of any given public administrator's contribution to it. This means that measuring performance and efficiency can be extremely difficult in the public sector. One way that governments try to get around this problem is to contract out some of their functions to private organizations. Theoretically, at least, private companies will compete against one another to obtain the public sector's business. But the range of activity that the public and their governments deem appropriate for contracting out is limited. Nor are the long-term economic and political implications of contracting out some traditional governmental functions, such as prison management, clear. Accordingly, for the most part, when taken together these factors make public administration substantially different from private enterprise.

Sovereignty

Sovereignty is the concept that somewhere in a political community there is an ultimate repository of supreme political power and authority. In the United States, sovereignty resides in the people, as a whole, who exercise it through a representative government. Public administration and public employment, in particular, are consequently considered to be a "public trust." As representatives of the sovereign people, public administrators are also placed in a position that differs considerably from that of managers and employees in the private sector. *Public administrators are engaged in the formulation and implementation of policies that allocate resources, values, and status in a fashion that is binding upon the society as a whole.* Their actions embody the will of the sovereign, which means that the actions of public administrators have the force of law and the coercive power of the government behind them. Private firms also make policies and they are engaged in activities that affect the lives of individuals in the society as a whole, but their actions are not binding in the same sense and they cannot be enforced through legitimate coercive physical power. Rather, the private sector must turn to the public sector's courts and police power for the enforcement of contracts.

Public administrators, being trustees of the sovereign, are inevitably engaged in matters of public policy making and implementation. From the 1880s to the late 1940s, public administrative theory in the United States held that administration and politics should be almost separate from one another. Perhaps this dichotomy between politics and administration was primarily concerned with eliminating partisan or electoral politics from the public service. But today it is broadly accepted that public administrators do have a legitimate role in all phases of the public policy cycle.* In other words, theory and practice now support the idea that the political system should take advantage of public administrators' expertise when it is appropriate to the identification of problems to which public policy ought to be addressed (agenda setting) and to the formulation, analysis, evaluation, and revision of policies. It is now also recognized that public administrators are often required to make policy choices while implementing statutes and executive orders. They exercise discretion because their mandates from legislatures are general (rather than specific) and/or because of a scarcity of resources that virtually requires the selective enforcement of the law. Of course, to say that public administrators *participate* in policy making is not to say that *all* policy is made by them or that all they do is to make policy.

Public administrators' involvement in the public policy cycle makes politics far more salient in the public sector than in private enterprise. Public administrators are perforce required to build and maintain political support for the policies and programs they implement. They must try to convince members of the legislature, chief executives, interest groups, private individuals, and the public at large that their activities and policies are desirable. This involves far more than the kind of advertising done in the private sector. It may involve the principle of quid pro quo, or the trading of political support or the modification of public policies and activities to win over the support of some particularly important group or individual.

Involvement in policy making and politics also raises the question of how it can be assured that those exercising a public trust will in fact be representative, in some sense, of the people as a whole. This is the concept of *representative bureaucracy*, which will be discussed at a later point. Here, however, it is important to note that federal policy has sought to make the federal bureaucracy representative by assuring that its work force is drawn from all social segments of the society and that it provides formal processes through which interested parties

---

* The notion of the public policy cycle is a conceptual tool that views public policy as moving through the following stages: agenda setting (identification of an issue), policy formulation, implementation, analysis/evaluation of impact or implementation process, and revision of some sort, including termination and succession.

can express their views on the adoption of administrative policies and rules.[11] In the past, the representative principle was applied to the public service through the widespread use of partisan patronage, which allowed the political party in power to select the vast majority of public employees. Once again, it is evident that concerns of this nature are less relevant in the private sector. Private enterprise is built around the principle of the profit motive, not that of providing representation to different groups and political parties. It would be ludicrous to think that a private company would institute a spoils system along the lines of that used in the federal government in the 1840s, where just about every four years almost the entire work force would be fired and replaced by supporters of another political party. Yet, when practiced in the public sector, spoils systems have some beneficial effects, such as enabling the growth of strong, competitive, and representative political parties.

Sovereignty also requires that much of the business of public administrators lies in the formulation and implementation of public policies that are very broad, ambitious, and sometimes rather amorphous and oriented toward change in the long run. Analyzing the effectiveness and costs of these policies is generally possible, but it is often much more difficult to evaluate the operations of public agencies than to assess those of private firms. Politics may require that the objectives of public programs be rather ill defined and vague. Indeed, often Congress will empower a federal agency to formulate policies affecting some area of public life with little more direction than to require that the agency promote the public interest. It is frequently easier to build a consensus around very general principles than around specifics, as is apparent in the typical political party platform. For instance, there has been very little disagreement over the objective of establishing equal employment opportunity, but the technique of affirmative action—that is, the use of goals for hiring and promoting members of minority groups and women—has been extremely controversial for almost two decades. Moreover, evaluating the full impact of public policies dealing with such matters as equality, nutrition, the environment, eliminating the federal budget deficit, and foreign affairs may require decades of observation.

In sum, any definition of public administration must lay heavy stress on the *public*. There are similarities between public and private administration, but these are often relatively unimportant in conveying the essence of each. Public administration is concerned with administration of the public interest, it is constrained by constitutions and relatively unconstrained by market forces, and it is considered a public trust exercised on behalf of the sovereign. Private administration, on the other hand, generally has a narrower concept of the public interest; profit-making firms are heavily constrained by market forces, and in no case except the U.S. Constitution's prohibition of slavery (Thirteenth Amendment) is purely private administration in the United States directly constrained by the Constitution. Moreover, private administration is not connected to the issue of sovereignty and is rarely considered to be a public trust of any kind. The lines between public and private administration may become blurred when government contracts out essentially public functions to not-for-profit organizations or other third parties. The same is sometimes true when public agencies are run like corporations. But the private sector is not dominated or characterized by not-for-profit organizations, nor is the public sector largely organized in corporate form. Substantial differences between the public and private sectors remain and, importantly, they promote reliance on different values and processes.

REGULATION AND SERVICE

In the discussion of sovereignty, it was mentioned that the activities of public administrators have a binding quality, that in general, they have the force of law and can rely upon the coercive physical power of the government for enforcement. This raises another point that is crucial to a satisfactory definition of public administration. Although we often think of public administration in terms of providing services to the public, it is also true that public administrators are engaged in *regulation* of the public. In fact, political conservatives opposed to governmental administration have long charged that the public service or the civil service is not a "service" at all, but rather an authoritarian regulatory force used to place constraints upon the public. In truth, one person's service often turns out to be another's constraint, and it is common to find regulation and service intertwined in governmental programs. For instance, welfare programs undeniably provide a service, but at the same time they place constraints upon the behavior of the recipients. In some cases, for example, a woman receiving welfare benefits for her children stands to lose these if a man sleeps in her dwelling because he may be a MARS (man assuming role of spouse). Drivers' licenses provide a service by promoting highway safety, but at the same time they keep those who cannot pass a driver's test off the roads and they place constraints on the behavior of drivers who stand to lose their right or privilege to drive legally if the license is suspended or revoked for infractions. Affirmative action provides a service to some but places a regulation upon public and private employers. One could go down the list of government functions and find that service after service turns out also to be a constraint. Public transportation services often preclude direct competition from private companies. Occupational licenses serve the public by assuring that doctors, hairdressers, and plumbers are competent, but they also regulate entry into those occupations. Food and drug regulations certainly constrain producers and serve consumers. It is sometimes true that agencies with the word "service" in their title are the most directly engaged in regulation. The Internal Revenue *Service* and the Selective *Service* System (former military drafting agency) are examples. Similarly, public *service* commissions are involved in the regulations of utilities.

In many cases, however, governmental regulation is billed as such. Thus, there is a Nuclear Regulatory Commission and a variety of other commissions to deal not only with utilities but also with consumer safety, securities and stocks, transportation, radio and television, and many other aspects of contemporary life. Regulatory activities also provide a service when they promote the public interest. The main point for the student of public administration, though, is to be continually cognizant of the fact that by exercising public power on behalf of the sovereign people, public *servants* are also frequently engaged in the business of placing constraints upon the behavior of individuals or corporations. The acceptability and constitutionality of these constraints are often a matter to be decided by the courts, bringing legal processes directly to bear upon public administration.

MANAGERIAL, POLITICAL, AND LEGAL APPROACHES

By now it should be evident that public administration involves a number of complex concerns and functions. It is not surprising, therefore, that as an intellectual discipline or body or theory, public administration lacks coherence. In fact, it is the overall view of this book that public administration contains three relatively distinct approaches that grow out of different perspectives on its functions. Some have viewed it as a managerial endeavor, similar to practices in the private sector. Others, stressing the "publicness" of public administration, have emphasized its political aspects. Still others, noting the importance of sovereignty, constitutions, and regulation in public administration, have viewed it as a distinctly legal matter. Each of these approaches tends to stress different values and procedural and structural arrangements for the operation of public administration, each views the individual citizen in a remarkably different way, and each adopts a different perspective on how to develop knowledge. It is very important to bear in mind that these approaches are embedded in our political culture. They reflect the constitutional separation of powers and assignment of functions to different branches. The managerial approach is associated with the executive branch's interest in faithful execution or implementation of the law. The political approach is associated with legislative policy-making concerns. The legal approach focuses on government's adjudicatory function and incorporates a juridical outlook.

Once we have presented the gist of these three approaches to public administration, we will have completed our definitional discussion. Then we can turn to an explanation of how each of these approaches is present in the various central activities of contemporary public administration.

The Managerial Approach to Public Administration

Those who define public administration in managerial terms and take a businesslike approach to it tend to minimize the distinctions between public and private administration. In their view, public administration is essentially the same as big business and ought to be run according to the same managerial principles and values. This view is strongly entrenched in some segments of American society, and is frequently found among elective political leaders who tend to resent the political influence exercised by civil servants. Indeed, nowadays it is unusual for a presidential election campaign not to stress the candidates' purported abilities to "manage" the "huge" federal bureaucracy and to make it more efficient.

But the roots of the managerial approach go back much farther. It was the nineteenth-century civil service reformers who first promoted the approach as a means of organizing the public service. The reformers' chief complaints were that political patronage appointments to the public services at all levels of government led to corruption, inefficiency, and the emergence of a class of politicians—"spoilsmen," as they were frequently called—who were fundamentally unfit to lead the nation. In fact, one well-known historian of the 1850s insisted that the federal service had become staffed by the nation's "refuse" (garbage).[12] In the reformers' view, "What civil service reform demand[ed], [was] that the business part of the government shall be carried on in a sound businesslike manner."[13] In order for it to become businesslike, it had to become nonpolitical. Consequently, appointments were to be made on the basis of "merit" and "fitness" rather than political partisanship. Many reformers thought that public employees should be prohibited from taking an active part in electoral politics, other than voting. Once politics was rejected as the basis for hiring and firing public administrators, the reformers believed that the selection and tenure of public servants could be based on their efficiency and performance.

In order to sustain this logic, the reformers had to insist that the vast majority of public administrators had no legitimate political or policy-making functions. Thus, much of their thinking and the logic of the managerial approach depended on the existence of a dichotomy between politics and administration. This aspect of the managerial approach was most influentially put forward by Woodrow Wilson, who in the 1880s, could be counted among the strong supporters of civil service reform. In Wilson's well-known words "administration lies outside the proper sphere of *politics*. Administrative questions are not political questions."[14] Rather, they are managerial questions, for as Wilson expressed it, public administration is "a field of business."

Just as politics involves certain values, such as representativeness, so does business or management. Wilson was also influential in his straightforward articulation of these: "It is the object of administrative study to discover, first, what government can properly and successfully do, and, secondly, how it can do these proper things with the utmost possible efficiency and at the least possible cost either of money or of energy."[15] In other words, according to the managerial approach, public administration is to be geared toward maximizing effectiveness, efficiency, and economy.

The advocacy of businesslike public administration eventually became the orthodox or classical view of how the public service should be run. Managers, not politicians, were to be in control, and efficiency was to be considered the ultimate "good," the "axiom number one in the value scale of administration."[16] Politics was to be eliminated because it produced inefficiency. Moreover, despite the growing regulatory activities of the public service, law was deemphasized because, as Leonard White's influential *Introduction to the Study of Public Administration* (1926) contended, "the study of administration should start from the base of management rather than the foundation of law, and is therefore more absorbed in the affairs of the American Management Association than in the decisions of the courts."[17] In fact, from the 1910s to the 1940s, a worldwide "scientific management" movement, based on the work of Frederick Taylor,[18] developed and advocated the premise that effective, efficient management could be reduced to a set of scientific principles. In the view of critics of this approach, the net result in terms of administrative values was that "the 'goodness' or 'badness' of a particular organizational pattern was a mathematical relationship of 'inputs' to 'outputs.' Where the latter was maximized and the former minimized, a moral 'good' resulted. Virtue or 'goodness' was therefore equated with the relationship of these two factors, that is, 'efficiency' or 'inefficiency.' Mathematics was transformed into ethics."[19] Wastefulness, through inefficiency, was considered immoral.

Organizational Structure   In an effort to maximize the attainment of these values, the managerial approach to public administration promotes an organizational structure that is universally identified as *bureaucratic*. This may strike the contemporary reader as odd, since today *bureaucratic* is often used as a synonym for *inefficient*. In Chapter 4, we will consider the complex reasons why bureaucratic organizations often develop inefficiencies. Nevertheless, it remains true that many of their organizational principles are *intended* to maximize the amount of output per unit of input. Bureaucracies stress the need for a division of labor that enables employees to specialize in the accomplishment of a given set of tasks. Specialization enables each worker to become expert at what he or she does, although the work of any individual may be only a small part of the organization's total activity. *Specialization* requires coordination, and bureaucracy relies upon *hierarchy* for this purpose. Hierarchy creates a chain of authority to manage and coordinate the work divided according to the principle of specialization. Hierarchy, in turn, requires that programs and functions be clearly assigned to specific organizational units. Otherwise there will be overlapping authorities that are likely to promote conflicts. Bureaucratic organizations are also organized along *formalistic* lines, which spell out precisely the functions and responsibilities of each employee. Positions are classified according to "scientific" principles and are organized into a rational scheme. The selection of employees is to be based on their ability to perform the tasks at hand, that is, upon their merit. Other factors, such as political affiliation, race, or sex, should not be taken into account. In conveying the core of the managerial approach toward administrative organization, Harold Seidman writes:

> Orthodox theory is preoccupied with the anatomy of Government organization and is concerned primarily with arrangements to assure that (1) each function is assigned to its appropriate niche within the Government structure; (2) component parts of the executive branch are properly related and articulated; and (3) authorities and responsibilities are clearly assigned.[20]

View of the Individual   The managerial approach to public administration promotes an impersonal view of individuals. This is true whether the individuals in question are the employees, clients, or the "victims" of public administrative agencies. One need not go so far as Max Weber (1864–1921), perhaps the foremost analyst of bureaucracy, in considering "dehumanization" to be the "special virtue" of bureaucracy or to view the bureaucrat as a "cog" in an organizational machine over which he or she has virtually no control.[21] Weber saw this as an advantage of bureaucracy because it meant that "irrational" emotions would not interfere with the bureaucrat's job performance. This perspective was promoted by the Scientific Management Movement and the managerial approach, which tend to turn the individual worker into an appendage to a mechanized means of production. The worker has to adapt to the machine; the machine is not engineered to suit an *individual* worker's physical, mental, social, and emotional idiosyncrasies (see Box 1–1). By 1920, this view of the employee was clearly embodied in the principles of position classification (that is, the description of duties and rank) in the public sector: "The individual characteristics of an employee occupying a position should have no bearing on the classification of the position." Indeed, the strong "position-orientation" of the managerial approach to public administration, which views organization in formalistic structural rather than human terms, continues to diminish the importance of the individual employee to the organization.

Clients, too, have been depersonalized and turned into cases in an effort to promote the managerial values of efficiency, economy, and effectiveness. Ralph Hummel explains:

> Bureaucracy is an efficient means for handling large numbers of people. "Efficient" in its own terms. It would be impossible to handle large numbers of people in their full depth and complexity. Bureaucracy is a tool for ferreting out what is "relevant" to the task for which bureaucracy was established. As a result, only those facts in the complex lives of individuals that are relevant to that task need to be communicated between the individual and the bureaucracy.
>
> To achieve this simplification, the modern bureaucrat has invented the "case." At the intake level of the bureaucracy, individual personalities are converted into cases. Only if a person can qualify as a case, is he or she allowed treatment by the bureaucracy. More accurately, a bureaucracy is never set up to treat or deal with persons: it "processes" only "cases."[22]

"Victims"[23] of public administrators' activities may be depersonalized to such an extent that they are considered subhuman, especially where physical force or coercion is employed, as in public mental health facilities, prisons, and police functions.

Other approaches to organization argue that reliance on impersonality tends to be counterproductive because it generates "bureaupathologies." These matters will be discussed in Chapters 4 and 10. Nevertheless, the impersonal view of individuals is deeply ingrained in the managerial approach, and is considered essential to the maximization of efficiency, economy, and effectiveness.

Cognitive Approach   The managerial approach emphasizes a scientific method in developing knowledge. The kernel of the idea that public administration

---

BOX 1–1 Scientific Management from Shoveling to Baseball

Shoveling: "There is a scientific fact. A first class shoveler ought to take twenty-one and one-half pounds on his shovel in order to work to the best possible advantage. You are not giving that man a chance unless you give him a shovel which will hold twenty-one pounds. . . .

"There is only one way to do it right. Put your forearm down onto the upper part of your leg, and when you push into the pile, throw your weight against it. That relieves your arm of work. You then have an automatic push, we will say, about eighty pounds, the weight of your body thrown on to it."

Baseball: ". . . I think this instance represents one of the best illustrations of the application of the principles of scientific management. I refer to the management of a first-class American baseball team. In such a team you will find almost all of the elements of scientific management.

"You will see that the science of doing every little act that is done by every player on the baseball field has been developed. Every single element of the game of baseball has been the subject of the most intimate, closest study of many men, and, finally, the best way of doing each act that takes place on the baseball field has been fairly well agreed upon and established as a standard throughout the country. The players have not only been told the best way of making each important motion or play, but they have been taught, coached, and trained to it through months of drilling. And I think that every man who has watched first-class play, or who knows anything of the management of the modern baseball team, realizes fully the utter impossibility of winning with the best team of individual players that was ever gotten together unless every man on the team obeys the signals or orders of the coach and obeys them at once. . . ."

SOURCES: Frederick Winslow Taylor, "The Principles of Scientific Management," in Jay Shafritz and Philip Whitbeck, eds., *Classics of Organization Theory* (Oak Park, Ill.: Moore, 1978), pp. 18–19; and "Scientific Management," in Jay Shafritz and Albert Hyde, eds., *Classics of Public Administration* (Oak Park, Ill.: Moore, 1978), p. 20.

---

could be a science was contained in Woodrow Wilson's 1887 call for "The Study of Administration."[24] By 1926, Leonard White noted that public administration was being transformed from an art into a science and, in 1937, Luther Gulick and L. Urwick could publish, most influentially, *Papers on the Science of Administration.*[25] The commitment to developing a science of public administration remains very strong—in fact, dominant—in contemporary American public administrative research and scholarship.

In practice, treating public administration as a science has promoted an effort to develop generalizations about administrative behavior. This involves the formulation of hypotheses that can be tested empirically. Data are gathered, aggregated, and statistically analyzed. The basic orientation is deductive; knowledge consists of statistically verifiable generalizations that can be applied, with caution, to specific cases.

The Political Approach to Public Administration

The political approach to public administration was perhaps most forcefully and succinctly stated by Wallace Sayre:

> Public administration is ultimately a problem in political theory: the fundamental problem in a democracy is responsibility to popular control; the responsibility and responsiveness of the administrative agencies and the bureaucracies to the elected officials (the chief executives, the legislators) is of central importance in a government based increasingly on the exercise of discretionary power by the agencies of administration.[26]

This approach grew out of the observations of scholars, such as Paul Appleby, that public administration during the New Deal and World War II was anything but devoid of politics. Indeed, Appleby considered administration to be a "political process,"[27] and numerous others have since called attention to the extent to which public administrators participate in public policy making. Thus, unlike the origin of the managerial approach, which stressed what public administration ought to be, the political approach developed from an analysis of an apparent practical reality.

Once public administration is considered a political endeavor, emphasis is inevitably placed on a different set of values than those promoted by the managerial approach. Efficiency, in particular, becomes highly suspect, because it has little to do with the larger questions of government (see Box 1–2). As Supreme Court Justice Louis Brandeis pointed out in dissent in *Myers* v. *United States* (1926):

> The doctrine of the separation of powers was adopted by the Convention in 1787, not to promote efficiency but to preclude the exercise of arbitrary power. The purpose was, not to avoid friction, but, by means of the inevitable friction incident to the distribution of governmental powers among these three departments, to save the people from autocracy.[28]

The political approach to public administration stresses the values of representativeness, political responsiveness, and accountability through elected officials to the citizenry. These are viewed as crucial to the maintenance of constitutional democracy and it is considered necessary to incorporate them into all aspects of government, including public management.

One can find many examples of governmental reforms aimed at maximizing the political values of representativeness, responsiveness, and accountability within public administration. For instance, the Federal Civil Service Reform Act of 1978 sought representativeness by making it "the policy of the United States . . . to provide a . . . Federal work force reflective of the Nation's diversity" by endeavoring "to achieve a work force from all segments of society." The Federal Advisory Committee Act of 1972 sought to make the use of advisory committees more representative. It declares that such committees "are frequently

---

BOX 1-2 The Supreme Court on "Efficiency"

In *Immigration and Naturalization Service* v. *Jagdish Rai Chadha* (1983), Chief Justice Warren Burger, on behalf of the Supreme Court, had occasion to observe:

[I]t is crystal clear from the records of the [Constitutional] Convention, contemporaneous writings and debates, that the Framers ranked other values higher than efficiency. . . .

The choices we discern as having been made in the Constitutional Convention impose burdens on governmental processes that often seem clumsy, inefficient, and even unworkable, but those hard choices were consciously made by men who had lived under a form of government that permitted arbitrary governmental acts to go unchecked. There is no support in the Constitution or decisions of this Court for the proposition that the cumbersomeness and delays often encountered in complying with explicit Constitutional standards may be avoided, either by the Congress or by the President. . . . With all the obvious flaws of delay, untidiness, and potential for abuse, we have not yet found a better way to preserve freedom than by making the exercise of power subject to the carefully crafted restraints spelled out in the Constitution.

462 U.S. 919, 958–959

---

a useful and beneficial means of furnishing expert advice, ideas, diverse opinions to the Federal Government" and requires that "the membership of advisory committee(s) . . . be fairly balanced in terms of the points of view represented. . . ." Earlier, the poverty and model cities programs of the 1960s sought to use citizen participation as a means of promoting political responsiveness in administrative operations. In addition, the quest for responsiveness has blended into a wide variety of attempts to promote the accountability of public administrators to the public and their elected officials, including the use of "sunshine" and "sunset" provisions.

It is important to note that the values sought by the political approach to public administration are frequently in tension with those of the managerial approach. For instance, efficiency in the managerial sense is not necessarily served through sunshine regulations that open aspects of public administration to public scrutiny and can dissuade public administrators from taking some courses of action, though they may be the most efficient. They can divert time and resources from program implementation to the deliverance of information to outsiders. Consultation with advisory committees and "citizen participants" can be time-consuming and costly. Since it is not chosen by merit alone, a socially representative public service may not be the most technically competent or efficient one. Accountability has a price. As Marver Bernstein reported long ago, "Many officials complain that they must spend so much time preparing for appearing at Congressional hearings and in presenting their programs before the

Bureau of the Budget and other bodies that it often leaves little time for directing the operations of their agencies."[29] Managerial effectiveness is often difficult to gauge, of course, but federal managers have long complained that their effectiveness is hampered by the large congressional role in public administration and the need to consult continually with a variety of parties having a legitimate concern with their agencies' operations.

Organizational Structure   Public administration organized around the political values of representativeness, responsiveness, and accountability also tends to be at odds with the managerial approach to organization. Rather than emphasizing clear lines of functional specialization, hierarchy, unity, and recruitment based on politically neutral administrative competence, the political approach stresses the extent and advantages of political **pluralism** within public administration. Thus, Seidman argues that "[e]xecutive branch structure is in fact a microcosm of our society. Inevitably it reflects the values, conflicts, and competing forces to be found in a pluralistic society. The ideal of a neatly symmetrical, frictionless organization structure is a dangerous illusion."[30] Norton Long makes a similar point: "Agencies and bureaus more or less perforce are in the business of building, maintaining, and increasing their political support. They lead and in large part are led by the diverse groups whose influence sustains them. Frequently they lead and are themselves led in conflicting directions. This is not due to a dull-witted incapacity to see the contradictions in their behavior but is an almost inevitable result of the contradictory nature of their support."[31] Roger Davidson finds a political virtue where those imbued with the managerial approach might see disorder: "In many respects, the civil service represents the American people more comprehensively than does Congress."[32]

The basic concept behind pluralism within public administration is that since the administrative branch is a policy-making center of government, it must be structured to enable competing groups to counteract each other by providing political representation to a comprehensive variety of the organized political, economic, and social groups that are found in society at large. To the extent that the political approach's organizational scheme is achieved, the structure of public administration becomes politicized, with different groups continually seeking representation. Overlapping missions and programs become common as the administrative structure comes to resemble a political party platform that promises something to almost everyone without establishing clear priorities for resolving conflicts among them. Agency becomes adversary of agency and the resolution of conflict is shifted to the legislature, the office of the chief executive, interagency committees, and the courts. Moreover, the number of bureaus and agencies tends to grow over time, partly in response to the political demands of organized interests for representation. This approach to administrative organization has been widely denounced as making government "unmanageable," "costly," and "inefficient," but as Seidman argues, it persists because administrative organization is frequently viewed as a political question heavily emphasizing political values.

View of the Individual   The political approach to public administration tends to aggregate the individual into a broad social, economic, or political group. It does not depersonalize the individual by turning him or her into a "case," as does the managerial approach, but rather identifies the individual's interests as being similar or identical to those of others considered to be within the same group or category. For example, affirmative action within the government service is aimed at specific groups such as blacks and women without inquiry as to the particular circumstances of any individual member of these broad and diverse groups. Similarly, farmers growing the same crops and/or located in the same national geopolitical subdivisions are considered alike, despite individual differences among them. The same is true in any number of areas of public administration that are engaged in implementing public policies. This is a tendency, of course, that fits the political culture well—politicians tend to think in terms of groups, e.g., the "black" vote, the "farm" vote, "labor," and so forth. Indeed, this approach is so strong that some consider it the central feature of government in the United States. Theodore Lowi argues that a central tenet of the contemporary American "public philosophy" is that "[o]rganized interests are homogeneous and easy to define, sometimes monolithic. Any 'duly elected' spokesman for any interest is taken as speaking in close approximation for each and every member."[33] In this view of the individual, then, personality exists, but it is addressed in collective terms.

Cognitive Approach   The political approach views science as an appropriate way of developing factual knowledge. However, it is so concerned with representativeness and responsiveness that it often bases decisions on the opinions of the public, interest groups, and the media. Elections, public opinion surveys, content analysis of constituents' letters and news coverage, and review of citizens' views expressed at hearings or in other ways are among the political approach's prime techniques for gaining the information it finds relevant. Consequently, the "proper" approach to serving the public interest through administration is not necessarily a question for resolution by experts or science. Rather, the public, or organized segments of it, ought to have a large role in determining what is in the collective interest. Informed public administration reflects public choice,[34] which may or may not coincide with generalizations that are scientifically derived.

The Legal Approach to Public Administration

In the United States, the legal approach to public administration has historically been eclipsed by the other approaches, especially the managerial. Nevertheless, it has a venerable tradition and has recently emerged as a full-fledged way of defining public administration. It views public administration as infused with legal and adjudicatory concerns. This approach is derived primarily from three interrelated sources. First is administrative law. As early as 1905, Frank Goodnow, a leading contributor to the development of public administrative theory generally, published a book entitled *The Principles of the Administrative Law of the United States.* He defined administrative law as "that part of the law which fixes the organization and determines the competence of the authorities which execute the law, and indicates to the individual remedies for the violation of his rights."[35] Others have found this broad conception of administrative law adequate for defining much of the work of public administrators and the nature of public agencies. For instance, Marshall Dimock writes:

> To the public administrator, law is something very positive and concrete. It is his authority. The term he customarily uses to describe it is "my mandate." It is "his" law, something he feels a proprietary interest in. It does three things: tells him what the legislature expects him to accomplish, fixes limits to his authority, and sets forth the substantive and procedural rights of the individual and group. Having a positive view of his mandate, the administrator considers himself both an interpreter and a builder. He is a builder because every time he applies old law to new situations he builds the law. Therefore law, like administration, is government in action.[36]

Taking a related view, Kenneth Davis argues that public agencies are best defined in terms of law: "An administrative agency is a governmental authority, other than a court and other than a legislative body, which affects the rights of private parties through either adjudication, rule-making, investigating, prosecuting, negotiating, settling or informally acting."[37]

A second source of the legal approach has been the movement toward the **judicialization** of public administration. Judicialization is the tendency for administrative processes increasingly to resemble courtroom procedures. Judicialization falls within the purview of Goodnow's definition of administrative law, but tends to concentrate heavily upon the establishment of procedures designed to safeguard individual rights. Dimock succinctly captures the essence of judicialization:

> Before the Administrative Procedure Act (1946) came into existence, decisions were made by the regular administrative staff, with the ultimate decision being entrusted to the head of the agency. Characteristically, it was a collective or institutional decision, each making his contribution and all checking each other. The decisions were made on the basis of statutory law, plus agency sublegislation, plus decided court cases. The system worked, and in most cases worked well. Then the idea arose of using "hearing examiners" in certain cases where hearings were long and technical, as in railroad cases coming under the Interstate Commerce Commission. . . .
>
> When the Administrative Procedure Act . . . was enacted, however, judicialization was speeded up, and now, like a spreading fog, it has become well-nigh universal. It began with hearing officers who were recruited by the U.S. Civil Service Commission and put in a pool, from which they were assigned to various agencies. . . . The idea of courtroom procedure was still further enlarged when [the government] created the office of "Administrative Judge," this being one who operates inside the agency instead of outside it, as in the case of the European administrative courts.
>
> . . . In actual practice . . . the longer the system has been in existence, the more frequently the [hearing examiner's] recommended decision becomes the final decision.[38]

Thus, judicialization brings not only law but legal procedure as well to bear upon administrative decision making. Agencies begin to function more like courts and consequently legal values come to play a greater role in their activities. During the 1980s, at least 29 federal agencies employed administrative law judges, who numbered more than a thousand.[39]

Constitutional law provides a third source of the contemporary legal approach to public administration. Since the 1950s, the federal judiciary has virtually redefined the procedural, equal protection, and substantive rights and liberties of the citizenry vis-à-vis public administrators. An old distinction between rights and privileges, which had largely made the Constitution irrelevant to individuals' rights regarding the receipt of governmental benefits, met its demise. There was also a vast expansion in the requirement that public administrators afford constitutional procedural due process, such as trial-like hearings, to the specific individuals whose governmental benefits, such as welfare or public education, were terminated through administrative action. A new stringency was read into the Eighth Amendment's prohibition of cruel and unusual punishment. Wholly new rights, such as the right to treatment and habilitation, were created, if not fully ratified by the Supreme Court, for those confined to public mental health facilities. The right to equal protection was vastly strengthened and applied in a variety of administrative matters ranging from public personnel recruitment systems to the operation of public schools and prisons. (These developments are addressed throughout the book. The place of constitutional values in public administration is the subject of Chapter 11.)[40]

The expansion of the constitutional rights of individuals vis-à-vis public administrators has been enforced primarily in two ways, both of which enhance the relevance of the legal approach to contemporary public administration. The courts have sought to force public administrators scrupulously to avoid violating individuals' constitutional rights by reducing public officials' once absolute immunity from civil suits for damages to a qualified immunity. In a remarkable development, discussed further in the next chapter, many public administrators are now liable for monetary damages if they "knew or reasonably should have known" that an action taken abridged someone's constitutional rights. This is one reason why the student and practitioner of public administration must have an understanding of some aspects of constitutional law. Indeed, public administrators who violate someone's constitutional rights may well find themselves personally responsible for paying damages to the injured individual. In the Supreme Court's view, this approach, "in addition to compensating victims, serves a deterrent purpose" that "should create an incentive for officials who may harbor doubts about the lawfulness of their intended actions to err on the side of protecting citizens' constitutional rights."[41] Consequently, the concept of administrative competence is expanded to include reasonable knowledge of constitutional law. In addition, in suits challenging the constitutionality or legality of public institutions such as schools, prisons, and mental health facilities, the courts have frequently decreed ongoing relief requiring institutional reforms that place the judges in the role of "partner" with public administrators. In some instances judges clearly become supervisors of vast administrative undertakings, and find themselves establishing such detailed administrative standards as how many mental patients there should be per shower or toilet and how hot or cold mental health facilities should be (see Box 1–3).

The constitutional law affecting public administration is continually changing as the judiciary applies the Constitution to new situations and revises its interpretations of older ones. Some rights that have not yet been established will be declared; the scope of others will be reduced. But constitutional law, and therefore the courts, will continue to define the rights of individuals vis-à-vis public administrative activity.

The legal approach to public administration embodies three central values. One is **procedural due process,** which is hard to define precisely because it has long been recognized that this value cannot be confined to any single set of requirements or standards. Rather, the term stands for the value of fundamental fairness and is viewed as requiring procedures designed to protect individuals from malicious, arbitrary, erroneous, capricious, or unconstitutional deprivation of life, liberty, or property at the hands of government. A second value concerns individual substantive rights and equal protection of the laws as embodied in evolving interpretations of the Bill of Rights and the Fourteenth Amendment. In general, the judiciary views the maximization of individual rights and liberties as a positive good and a necessary feature of the United States political system. Breaches of these rights may be tolerated by the courts when, on balance, some essential governmental function requires their abridgement. However, the usual presumption is against the government in such circumstances and, consequently, judicial doctrines place a heavy burden on official administrative action that infringes upon the substantive constitutional rights of individuals. Third, the judiciary values equity, a concept that like due process is subject to varying interpretation. However, in terms of public administration in general, equity stands for the value of fairness in the *result* of conflicts between private parties and the government. Equity includes the power to dispense with the harsh application of the law where it would be inappropriate. It militates against

---

BOX 1–3 **The Impact of Judicial Activity on Public Administration**

[I]n the last decade several thousand damage suits have been filed by Americans against hundreds of state and local governments and thousands of state and local government officials. The face amount of the damages claimed adds up to billions of dollars. In over half the states, one or more institutions—prisons, mental institutions, institutions for the retarded, juvenile homes—have been declared unconstitutional, as structured and administered. Many state and local government officials have found themselves subject to demands that they be held personally liable in money damages to individuals and organizations claiming they have been harmed by actions of these officials.

SOURCE: James D. Carroll, "The New Juridical Federalism and Alienation of Public Policy and Administration," *American Review of Public Administration*, 16 (Spring 1982): 89–105, at page 90.

arbitrary or invidious treatment of individuals and enables the courts to fashion remedies for individuals whose constitutional rights have been violated by administrative action.

One of the major features of the values of the legal approach to public administration is the downgrading of the cost-effectiveness reasoning associated with the managerial approach. The judiciary is not oblivious to the costs of its decisions, but its central focus tends to be on the nature of the individual's rights, rather than on the costs to society of securing those rights. This is especially evident in cases involving the reform of public institutions. As one court said, "Inadequate resources can never be an adequate justification for the state's depriving any person of his constitutional rights."[42]

Organizational Structure   As suggested in the discussion of judicialization, the preferred structure of the legal approach to public administration is one that will maximize the use of adversary procedure. The full-fledged judicial trial is the clearest model of this structure. Adversary procedure calls upon two opposing parties to marshal facts and arguments in support of their positions. These are brought before an impartial referee (e.g., a judge or a jury) who weighs them and ultimately decides which side is more correct. In public administration, however, adversary procedure is generally modified to allow greater flexibility in the presentation of "evidence" and interpretation. Juries are not used and hearing examiners often play a more active role than traditional judges in bringing out relevant information. Although this structure is often associated with regulatory commissions, it has broad presence in public administration. For example, it is heavily relied upon in contemporary public personnel management, especially in the areas of dismissals and disciplinary actions against employees, equal employment opportunity, and labor relations. It is also common in instances where governmental benefits, such as welfare or public school education, are being withheld or withdrawn from individuals. The precise structure varies from context to context, but the common element running through it is the relative independence and impartiality of the hearing examiner. To a large extent this independence undermines the managerial approach's reliance on hierarchy, especially in the sense of "unity of command." Hearing examiners stand outside administrative hierarchies in an important sense. Although they can be told what to do, that is, which cases to hear, they cannot be told how to rule or decide, where cases turn on matters of judgment. Moreover, for all intents and purposes, their rulings may be binding upon public agencies. This may introduce serious limitations on administrative coordination because the hearing examiner's interpretation of law and agency rules may differ from that of the agency's managerial hierarchy. Dimock summarizes the impact of the adjudicatory structure as follows:

> The hearing officers and administrative judges are on a different payroll. Moreover, unlike other officials in his department or agency, the executive is expressly forbidden to fire, discipline, or even communicate with the administrative judge except under very special circumstances, which usually means when the judge submits his proposed order. Under the old system, the entire resources of the agency could be relied upon

in making an institutional decision. Under the new system, the judge is isolated in the same manner as a judicial judge, for fear that improper influence will be brought to bear upon him.[43]

To a considerable extent, therefore, this model is at odds with all the values embodied in the other two approaches: it militates against efficiency, economy, managerial effectiveness, but also representativeness, responsiveness, and political accountability. It is intended, rather, to afford maximum protection of the rights of private parties against illegal, unconstitutional, or invidious administrative action.

View of the Individual   The legal approach's emphasis on procedural due process, substantive rights, and equity leads it to consider the individual as a unique person in a unique set of circumstances. The notion that every person is entitled to a "day in court" is appropriate here. The adversary procedure is designed to enable an individual to explain his or her unique and particular circumstances, thinking, motivation, and so forth to the governmental decision maker. Moreover, a decision may turn precisely upon such considerations, which become part of the "merits" of the case. There are some outstanding examples of this in the realm of public administration. For example, the Supreme Court has ruled that before a mandatory maternity leave could be imposed upon a pregnant public school teacher, she was entitled to an individualized medical determination of her fitness to continue on the job.[44] In *Wyatt v. Stickney* (1971),[45] a federal district court required that an individual treatment plan be developed for each person involuntarily confined to Alabama's public mental health facilities. Whether an individual's right to equal protection has been violated may depend not only on the administrative action taken but also upon the public administrators' *intent* or purpose in taking it.[46] Emphasis on the individual as an individual does not, of course, preclude the aggregation of individuals into a broader group, as in the case of class-action suits. However, while such a suit may be desirable to obtain widespread change, it does not diminish the legal approach's focus on the rights of specific individuals.

Cognitive Approach   The legal approach favors adjudication as the method of developing knowledge. Facts are established through adversary procedure and rules of evidence that screen the information that can be considered by the decision maker. Individuals' intentions or states of mind are treated as objective facts rather than as subjective conditions. Science is not rejected, but the legal approach is very wary about applying generalizations to individual cases. The adjudicatory method is frequently inductive. It relies on the specific elements of the case at hand to develop broad, general legal principles. The whole inquiry may be normative in seeking to choose between competing values. Because individual constitutional rights are intended to protect political, economic, and social minorities from a majoritarian government, the results of public opinion polls and elections are not necessarily of immediate import to adjudicators.

   One of the most striking differences between the intellectual orientation of the legal approach and the other two concerns the use of social classifications for the sake of analyzing and predicting individual behavior. The managerial approach's reliance on social science may involve the use of categories such as race or sex in analyzing behavior. The political approach, being concerned with representation and responsiveness in the distribution of governmental benefits and burdens, is frequently intensely interested in how programs affect women, blacks, and members of other social groups. By contrast, though, the legal approach views some social classifications as "suspect" because they are presumed to threaten the constitutional requirement of equal protection. Racial classifications are the preeminent example. Such classifications may be constitutional, depending on a number of factors (discussed in Chapter 11), but the courts review them with strict scrutiny to ensure that the government has a compelling need for their use.

CONCLUSION: PUBLIC ADMINISTRATION RECONSIDERED

Public administration is an extremely complex endeavor. It embodies at least the three major approaches just discussed. Each of these approaches emphasizes values, organizational arrangements, views of the individual, and intellectual orientations that are at odds with those of the other two approaches. The public administrator is called upon to be a manager, policy maker, and constitutional lawyer. He or she is stuck between the proverbial rock and a hard place when called upon to act in a fashion that will integrate three approaches that may defy successful integration. This is one reason why politicians and the society generally have become so critical of bureaucracy. It is virtually impossible to satisfy frequently all the managerial, political, and legal/constitutional demands placed upon public agencies and public administrators. Efficient management may preclude political representation and constitutional due process. Emphasizing one approach is certain to provoke criticisms from those who think the others are more important. And so public administrators, who are popularly viewed as entrenched and immovable, actually stand on very shaky ground that is always likely to crumble beneath them. Cave-ins, earthquakes, and erupting volcanoes are everywhere—in the press, legislative committee hearings, presidential and gubernatorial offices, and the courts. No doubt this is discouraging in some respects, but it also makes public administration challenging and even fascinating. Public administrators are called upon to help solve the nation's problems and improve its quality of life. However, there is little consensus on how they should proceed. They are both blessed and cursed by living in "interesting times."

NOTES

1. Dwight Waldo, "What Is Public Administration?" in Jay Shafritz and Albert Hyde, eds., *Classics of Public Administration* (Oak Park, Ill.: Moore, 1978), p. 171.
2. This and the next five definitions can be found in Richard Stillman, *Public Administration: Concepts and Cases* (Boston: Houghton Mifflin, 1978), pp. 2–4. They are

offered by John J. Corson and J. P. Harris; John Pfiffner and Robert Presthus; James W. Davis, Jr.; Nicholas Henry; Dwight Waldo; and Felix and Lloyd Nigro, respectively.

3. David Bazelon, "The Impact of the Courts upon Public Administration," *Indiana Law Journal*, 52 (1976): 101–110. See also David H. Rosenbloom, "Public Administrators and the Judiciary: The 'New Partnership,' " *Public Administration Review*, 47 (January/February 1987): pp. 75–83.

4. Immigration and Naturalization Service v. Chadha, 462 U.S. 919 (1983).

5. Bowsher v. Synar, 92 L. Ed. 2d 583 (1986).

6. Ibid., p. 617.

7. David K. Hart, "The Virtuous Citizen, the Honorable Bureaucrat, and 'Public' Administration," *Public Administration Review*, 44 (special issue, March 1984), p. 112.

8. Frederick Mosher, *Democracy and the Public Service*, 2nd ed. (New York: Oxford University Press, 1981).

9. Hart, "The Virtuous Citizen," p. 116.

10. See Anthony Downs, *Inside Bureaucracy* (Boston: Little, Brown, 1967).

11. These goals are embodied in the Civil Service Reform Act of 1978 (PL 95–454) and the Federal Advisory Committee Act of 1972 (PL 92–463).

12. James Parton, *The Life of Andrew Jackson* (Boston: Houghton Mifflin, 1887), vol. 3, p. 220.

13. Carl Schurz, *The Necessity and Progress of Civil Service Reform* (Washington, D.C.: Good Government, 1894), p. 3.

14. Woodrow Wilson, "The Study of Administration," *Political Science Quarterly*, 56 (December 1941): 494 (originally copyrighted in 1887).

15. Ibid., p. 481.

16. See *Papers on the Science of Administration*, ed. by Luther Gulick and L. Urwick (New York: Institute of Public Administration, 1937), pp. 192, 10. See also Alan Altshuler and Norman Thomas, eds., *The Politics of the Federal Bureaucracy* (New York: Harper & Row, 1977), pp. 2–17.

17. Leonard D. White, *Introduction to the Study of Public Administration* (New York: Macmillan, 1926), pp. vii–viii. See also Herbert J. Storing, "Leonard D. White and the Study of Public Administration," *Public Administration Review*, 25 (March 1965): 38–51.

18. Frederick Taylor, *The Principles of Scientific Management* (New York: Harper & Bros., 1917).

19. Robert Simmons and Eugene Dvorin, *Public Administration* (Port Washington, N.Y.: Alfred Publishing, 1977), p. 217.

20. Harold Seidman, *Politics, Position, and Power* (New York: Oxford University Press, 1970), p. 5.

21. Max Weber, *From Max Weber: Essays in Sociology*, trans. and ed. by H. H. Gerth and C. W. Mills (New York: Oxford University Press, 1958), pp. 196–244, at p. 228.

22. Ralph Hummel, *The Bureaucratic Experience* (New York: St. Martin's, 1977), pp. 24–25.

23. See Eugene Lewis, *American Politics in a Bureaucratic Age: Citizens, Constituents, Clients, and Victims* (Cambridge, Mass.: Winthrop, 1977).

24. Wilson, "The Study of Administration," pp. 481 and 482 noted that "the eminently practical science of administration is finding its way into college courses . . ." (p. 481). He also maintained that "the science of administration is the latest fruit of that study of politics."

25. White, *Introduction to the Study of Public Administration*, pp. vii–viii, 4; Gulick and Urwick, eds., *Papers on the Science of Administration*.

26. Wallace Sayre, "Premises of Public Administration: Past and Emerging," in Jay Shafritz and Albert Hyde, eds., *Classics of Public Administration* (Oak Park, Ill.: Moore Publishing, 1978), p. 201. Dwight Waldo, *The Administrative State* (New York: Ronald Press, 1948), demonstrates how the basic value choices of managerial public administration are ultimately statements of political preference.

27. Paul Appleby, *Policy and Administration* (University, Ala.: University of Alabama Press, 1949). See also Theodore J. Lowi, *The End of Liberalism* (New York: Norton, 1969).

28. Myers v. United States, 272 U.S. 52, 293 (1926).

29. Marver Bernstein, *The Job of the Federal Executive* (Washington, D.C.: Brookings, 1958), p. 30.

30. Seidman, *Politics, Position, and Power*, p. 13.

31. Norton Long, "Power and Administration," in Francis Rourke, ed., *Bureaucratic Power in National Politics* (Boston: Little, Brown, 1965), p. 18.

32. Roger Davidson, "Congress and the Executive: The Race for Representation," in A. DeGrazia, ed., *Congress: The First Branch of Government* (New York: Anchor, 1967), p. 383.

33. Lowi, *The End of Liberalism*, p. 71. See also Grant McConnell, *Private Power and American Democracy* (New York: Knopf, 1966), chaps. 4 & 5.

34. See Gordon Tullock, *The Politics of Bureaucracy* (Washington, D.C.: Public Affairs Press, 1965) and Vincent Ostrom, *The Intellectual Crisis in American Public Administration* (University, Ala.: University of Alabama Press, 1973).

35. Frank Goodnow, *The Principles of the Administrative Law of the United States* (New York: G. P. Putnam's Sons, 1905), p. 17.

36. Marshall Dimock, *Law and Dynamic Administration* (New York: Praeger, 1980), p. 31.

37. Kenneth Davis, *Administrative Law and Government* (St. Paul, Minn.: West, 1975), p. 6.

38. Dimock, *Law and Dynamic Administration*, p. 113. According to Charles Dullea, "Development of the Personnel Program for Administrative Law Judges," *Administrative Law Review*, 25 (Winter 1973): 41–47, the title administrative law judge was created by the U.S. Civil Service Commission rather than by Congress.

39. U.S. Senate, Committee on the Judiciary, Subcommittee on Administrative Practice and Procedure, Administrative Law Judge Corps Act, 98th Congress, 1st Session (1981).

40. See also David H. Rosenbloom, *Public Administration and Law* (New York: Marcel Dekker, 1983).

41. Carlson v. Green, 446 U.S. 14, 21 (1980); Owen v. City of Independence, 445 U.S. 622, 652 (1980); Harlow v. Fitzgerald, 457 U.S. 800, 819 (1982).

42. Hamilton v. Love, 328 F. Supp. 1182, 1194 (1971). See Rosenbloom, *Public Administration and Law*, for an extended discussion.

43. Dimock, *Law and Dynamic Administration*, p. 114.

44. Cleveland Board of Education v. LaFleur and Cohen v. Chesterfield Co. School Board, argued and decided together, 414 U.S. 632 (1974).

45. Wyatt v. Stickney, 325 F. Supp. 781 (1971); 334 F. Supp. 387 (1972).

46. Washington v. Davis, 426 U.S. 229 (1976); Baker v. St. Petersburg, 400 F.2d 294 (1968).

ADDITIONAL READING

GAWTHROP, LOUIS. *Public Sector Management, Systems, and Ethics.* Bloomington, Ind.: University of Indiana Press, 1984.

GOODNOW, FRANK. *The Principles of the Administrative Law of the United States.* New York: G. P. Putnam's Sons, 1905.

MOSHER, FREDERICK. *American Public Administration: Past, Present, and Future.* University, Ala.: University of Alabama Press, 1975.

OSTROM, VINCENT. *The Intellectual Crisis in American Public Administration.* University, Ala.: University of Alabama Press, 1974.

RABIN, JACK, AND JAMES S. BOWMAN, EDS. *Politics and Administration: Woodrow Wilson and American Public Administration.* New York: Marcel Dekker, 1984.

ROHR, JOHN A. *To Run A Constitution.* Lawrence, Kan.: University Press of Kansas, 1986.

ROSENBLOOM, DAVID, H. *Public Administration and Law.* New York: Marcel Dekker, 1983.

ROSENTHAL, STEPHEN, *Managing Government Operations.* Glenview, Ill.: Scott, Foresman, 1982.

SIMON, HERBERT. *Administrative Behavior,* 3rd ed. New York: Free Press, 1976.

WALDO, DWIGHT. *The Administrative State,* 2nd ed. New York: Holmes and Meier, 1984.

STUDY QUESTIONS

1. Consider public administrative operations with which you have recently dealt or are familiar. List all their functions that (a) provide services, (b) enforce regulations, or (c) provide a mix of service and regulation.

2. Think about some public administrative issue that has recently been in the news. Consider whether the three perspectives emphasized in this chapter are present in the general discussion of the issue. If so, are the proponents and opponents addressing each other's concerns?

CHAPTER 2 | *The Development of Public Administration in the United States*

The chapter begins by addressing how and why public administration became so important in the United States. It considers the nature of the political power of public administrative agencies. It addresses the ways in which various other political actors have tried to cope better with this power: the presidency, Congress, the judiciary, interest groups, the politically involved public, and political parties. These actors are part of public administration's political environment and affect the scope and nature of public administrators' activity.

Public administration is complex and problematic. Almost everywhere, including the United States, public bureaucrats are the butt of complaints, grievances, and jokes. They are denounced for their vast power on the one hand and their ineffectuality and lackadaisical performance on the other. Virtually everyone has had an unsatisfying and somewhat bizarre encounter with a bureaucrat. Presidents, members of Congress, and other elected officials routinely promise to do something about the perceived glut of public bureaucrats and expensive public administrative programs, but change has been slow and limited. What accounts for the tenacity of public administration?

In part the answer lies in the fact that American society is thoroughly dependent upon public administrators for the provision of services, regulation of the economy, and defense. Problems with public bureaucracy are easily identified, and often exaggerated, but alternatives to reliance on public administrators are often unavailable. Improvements in their performance are certainly possible and desirable, but whether we like it or not there is every reason to believe that the "administrative state" is here to stay. In fact, many countries, including the United States, are becoming more bureaucratic all the time. Every student and practitioner of public administration should appreciate the centrality of public administration to the nation's economic, political, and social life. Our review of the development of American public administration in this chapter is intended to impart precisely such an appreciation. But in order to understand contemporary public administration in the United States, we must first understand its origins.

THE RISE OF THE AMERICAN ADMINISTRATIVE STATE

Today, there are perhaps 15 million civilian public employees in the United States. The growth of this number in the twentieth century and the development of large administrative components in governments at all levels are generally referred to as the "rise of the administrative state" (see Boxes 2–1, 3–3). The term "administrative state" is intended to convey several realities of contemporary government: that a great deal of the society's resources are spent on the salaries and functions of public administrators; that public administrators are crucial to the operation of contemporary government; that, as a whole, they are politically powerful; and that the nation has decided upon a course of attempting to solve its problems and achieve its aims through the use of administrative action. The growth of administrative power is a worldwide phenomenon that affects the nature of governments in virtually all nations. Each of the approaches discussed in the previous chapter has contributed to the expansion of public administration in the United States.

The Political Roots of the American Administrative State

The constitutional government of the United States came into existence in 1789 with some clearly stated formal goals. These are found in the Preamble to the Constitution, which reads:

WE THE PEOPLE of the United States, in Order to form a more perfect Union, establish Justice, insure domestic Tranquility, provide for the common defence, promote the general Welfare, and secure the Blessings of Liberty to ourselves and our Posterity, do ordain and establish this CONSTITUTION for the United States of America.

In this passage can be found some of the classic purposes of almost all contemporary nations: the desire to provide for the defense of the political community, for law and order, and for the general welfare. The latter may seem too vague to convey anything of a specific nature, but generally it includes a commitment to economic development and to the provision of services by the government for the purpose of advancing the common good. The idea that the state should provide such services did not develop in western Europe until the 1660s, but now it is perhaps the most prominent feature of the administrative state. Thus, governments in the United States provide educational services, transportation services, communications services, and services intended to promote health and social and economic well-being in general.

BOX 2–1 Growth of Federal Employment

Year	Number of Employees
1791	4,479
1821	6,914
1831	11,491
1841	18,038
1851	26,274
1861	36,672
1871	51,020
1881	100,020
1891	157,442
1901	239,476
1911	395,905
1921	561,143
1931	609,746
1941	1,437,682
1951	2,482,666
1961	2,435,808
1971	2,862,926
1981	2,865,000
1985	3,020,531

SOURCES: Richard Stillman, *The American Bureaucracy* (Chicago: Nelson-Hall, 1987), p. 13, Figure 1.4. Through 1951, U.S. Bureau of the Census and Social Science Research Council, *Statistical History of the United States from Colonial Times to the Present* (Stamford, Conn.: Fairfield Publishers, 1965), p. 710. Figures for 1961 and 1971 are from U.S. Civil Service Commission, *Annual Report*, pp. 78, 88, appendix A. The U.S. Bureau of the Census is the source for 1981 and 1985.

The decision to pursue these purposes in the first place is political. So is the choice of a means for achieving them. Several alternatives to government sponsorship of such services do exist. Governments could rely heavily upon private resources and incentives to serve their purposes. For example, private armies of mercenaries were once a common means of waging war or promoting national defense. Education was once a private or church-related endeavor. Taking care of individuals' health and welfare needs was once left up to families and churches. Private action has frequently been augmented by the provision of governmental financial assistance to those individuals whose actions promote general national goals. For instance, at one time mentally retarded persons were "sold" to private individuals who would care for them at the least cost to the government, which was willing to pay for this service as part of its commitment to the common interest. Farm subsidies pay private farmers to use the nation's agricultural resources in the national interest. Governmental grants to promote a broad variety of private activities—including research, health care, training, education, and technological development—are common. Today, some economists, such as Milton Friedman, argue that education should be supplied by private organizations through a scheme in which the parents of school children would receive tuition vouchers from the government. These could be used at any school the parents felt best suited their children's educational needs. Such an approach, it is argued, would create a greater incentive for schools to operate efficiently and effectively and would also maximize the freedom of parents to choose among competing educational services. In the early 1980s, the Department of Housing and Urban Development tested a voucher system as a means of aiding people to obtain housing. Rather than build more housing units directly, the department's policy assumed that vouchers would make some housing units already available more affordable. It might also stimulate some growth in the number of housing units by increasing the demand for them. Similarly, various incentives can be built into the government's system of taxation to promote individual behavior deemed in the common interest. The federal tax structure has used a system of deductions and differential rates to promote investment and home owning by private individuals. Apparently, the tax code has been viewed as a tool for promoting social and political stability as well as economic growth. Thus, one way to make a house cheaper to own is to allow the owner to deduct interest payments on the mortgage from his or her federal tax return. When viewed in broad policy terms, this deduction also becomes one way through which the government can encourage the building of adequate housing for the population. (See the discussion of tax expenditures in Chapter 6.) There are now so many federal purposes sought through grants, direct loans, loan guarantees, tax expenditures, contracts, and other indirect means that the United States has a great deal of "third party government." In other words, "many of the newer or most rapidly growing tools of government action share a common characteristic: they are *indirect*, they rely upon a variety of non-federal 'third parties'—states, cities, banks, industrial corporations, hospitals, nonprofit organizations, etc.—for their operation."[1] But because the total scope of government activity has grown so dramatically, during the twentieth century governments have also sought to achieve many of their goals through direct public action. For instance, in the housing example, governments have also sought to assure that everyone is adequately housed by building and running public housing projects. They may also maintain shelters for those who remain homeless. Instead of paying private individuals to take care of the mentally retarded, governments build and operate mental health facilities for this purpose. Similarly, education, defense, and a host of other operations are undertaken by governments.

The essence of the administrative state and the need for large-scale public administration lie in the policy choice of governments to undertake organizational action themselves to achieve their ultimate political goals. It is commonly believed that the American Founding Fathers never anticipated that governments in the United States would become engaged in a great deal of administrative action. However, it is also clear that the Constitution itself indicates the preference for public action in some areas. For instance, it authorizes the federal government to establish post offices and post roads and to raise and direct an army and a navy. Even a brief review of the development of large-scale public administration in the United States during the past two centuries indicates the extent to which such direct administrative action has become increasingly commonplace.

In a thoughtful and succinct analysis, James Q. Wilson has identified several primary roots of the development of the contemporary American administrative state.[2] One was to provide a reliable postal service. The U.S. Post Office was not viewed as an end in itself but rather as a means of promoting economic development and national cohesion. It was also spurred by a desire for political patronage. Wilson observes that "from 1816 to 1861, federal civilian employment in the executive branch increased nearly eightfold (from 4,837 to 36,672), but 86 percent of this growth was the result of additions to the postal service."[3]

A second source of administrative growth has been the desire to promote economic development and social well-being through governmental action recognizing the needs of various sectors of the economy. For example, the Department of Agriculture was created in 1862 and the Departments of Commerce and Labor came into existence in 1913. More recently, the Department of Health, Education, and Welfare (now Health and Human Services) and the Departments of Housing and Urban Development, Transportation, Energy, and Education have been created to promote governmental goals in these economic and social areas of American life. Departments such as Agriculture, Labor, and Commerce are often called **clientele departments** because they deal largely with a relatively well-defined category of people who are generally assumed to have common economic interests. Clientele departments are often directly engaged in supplying services. For example, the Department of Agriculture tries to educate farmers in improved agricultural techniques and to provide direct economic assistance to them in a variety of ways. It has also undertaken projects to conserve soil, and it manages a system of national forests. Departments such as Health and Human Services, having a broader mission, also engage in direct action, such as research and disease control.

Another source of administrative growth has been defense. The Departments of War and Navy were created in the eighteenth century, but the military establishment did not emerge as the federal government's largest administrative operation until after World War II. Since that time, the Department of Defense has often employed one-third or more of all civilian federal workers. Interestingly, this means that more than half (61 percent in 1985) of all federal employees are employed in two agencies—Defense and the Postal Service.[4] The creation of a standing army, navy, and air force and a large civilian administrative component to manage the military reflects the government's view that providing for the common defense requires centralized planning for the procurement and deployment of weapons and personnel. No longer is it believed that private individuals can be trained quickly for military service at the outbreak of war, or that private industry can be rapidly converted for military defense. Here as in other areas, the government has increasingly moved away from relying upon private action alone.

In sum, the political roots of development of contemporary public administration in the United States lie primarily in two political choices made by the government and society. One was that government would exist to promote such objectives as the common defense, economic development, and the general welfare. At the national level, this was a choice first made back in the late 1780s and reinforced subsequently on many occasions. Second has been the more recent choice of placing heavy reliance upon direct provision of services and functions by the government as opposed to reliance solely upon the manipulation of subsidies for private action. In addition to these factors, the Constitution expresses a desire to promote domestic tranquility, which brings us to what can be considered the legal roots of the contemporary administrative state.

The Legal Origins of American Public Administration

Political communities seek to promote law and order within their jurisdictions. Otherwise, political, economic, and social conditions become chaotic and governmental stability and the achievement of purposes such as defense and economic development are threatened. Again, it is possible to promote law and order through private means. Private religious groups, social leaders, and private schools can imbue individuals with the sense of a moral and civic obligation to obey the law and avoid violating the rights of others. Social sanctions—such as excommunication, ostracism, and shunning—can act as powerful controls on individual behavior. However, governments have typically played a large role in promoting law and order through the creation of and enforcement of criminal and civil codes of law. These codes or bodies of law establish the obligations of individuals toward one another and toward the government. In less complex societies, law and order centers largely on the character of direct interaction between individuals and can be enforced by police, courts, and moral suasion. However, as societies become more complex, that is, as large organizations and institutions emerge as potential threats to the stability and welfare of society, governments typically strengthen their regulatory activities as a means of securing law and order. To do so, they create new administrative units to oversee the activities of these large organizations in an effort to protect the public from them and to protect the organizations from each other. Donald Warwick has explained this source of administrative growth as follows: As the concentration of power increases, "governmental bureaucracies arise to: (a) provide the political and economic stability needed to protect the investments of the corporate giants; (b) protect the interests of society against the corporations; (c) prevent political chaos by mediating between corporations and organized labor; or (d) act as agents to stimulate economic activity by corporations and channel it in constructive directions."[5]

Regulation   James Q. Wilson also points to regulatory activity as a source of administrative growth in the United States.[6] He indicates that regulatory agencies were created mainly during four periods, each having a common set of political features. The first period was 1887 to 1890, when the Interstate Commerce Commission (1887) was created to regulate transportation (primarily railroads) and the Sherman Act (1890) was passed as a rudimentary means of controlling the development of economic monopolies. During the second period, which was from 1906 to 1915, some of these regulatory activities were strengthened and the Pure Food and Drug Act (1906) and the Meat Inspection Act (1907) were passed to regulate the quality of these products being offered to consumers. Banks were regulated by the Federal Reserve Act (1913). Additional economic and trade practices were brought under regulatory administration by the Clayton and Federal Trade Commission Acts (1914). During the 1930s, a third period, a host of industries were added to the list of the federally regulated, including cosmetics, utilities, securities, airlines, and communications. Private sector labor relations also came under federal regulation at this time. Finally, during the 1960s, federal regulatory activities focused upon environmental and workplace safety concerns (in the Environmental Protection Agency and the Occupational Safety and Health Administration, respectively) and the protection of racial and ethnic minorities and women from discrimination in employment (in the Equal Employment Opportunity Commission).

Wilson points out that the political circumstances prevailing during each of these periods were relatively unusual, and this provides a clue to the reasons why regulatory administration has become highly legalistic. In Wilson's words:

> Each of these periods was characterized by progressive or liberal Presidents in office (Cleveland, T. R. Roosevelt, Wilson, F. D. Roosevelt, Johnson); one was a period of national crisis (the 1930s); three were periods when the President enjoyed extraordinary majorities of his own party in both houses of Congress; . . . and only the first period preceded the emergence of the national mass media of communication. These facts are important because of the special difficulty of passing any genuinely regulatory legislation. . . . Without special political circumstances . . . the normal barriers to legislative innovation . . . may prove insuperable.[7]

A major political problem with governmental regulatory activities is that while they do tend to promote law and order, they also are widely viewed as a breach of the government's commitment to secure the "blessings of liberty." Traditionally in the United States, liberty included the freedom to pursue one's economic interests free of wide-ranging governmental control. For the most part, the public and businesses were provided protection only through the common law, if at all. However, by the 1890s, it was evident that the common law would have to be augmented by administrative regulation. A major stimulus for change was conceptual and biological, as legal historian Lawrence Friedman explains:

> The discovery of germs, insidious, hidden in every spot of filth, had a profound effect on the legal system. To a much greater extent than before [the 1890s], goods—including food—were packaged and sent long distances, to be marketed impersonally, in bulk, rather than to be felt, handled, and squeezed at the point of purchase. This meant that a person was dependent on others, on strangers, on far-off corporations, for necessities of life, that society was more than ever a complex cellular organism; these strangers, these distant others had the capacity to inflict catastrophic irreparable harm.[8]

Society as a whole also needed protection against industrial pollution of the environment, such dangers as unsafe vehicles, and a host of products that could not sensibly be evaluated by the public. Harmful products and production practices, it was agreed, could best be controlled through governmental intervention.

To some extent, the political conflict over regulation is related to a much wider historical political tension between liberty and equality. This conflict has been a characteristic political problem in the United States since its founding. Liberty to pursue one's economic interests produces differences in individual wealth. These economic disparities can be translated into inequalities in terms of political influence and economic and social power. Government intervention, often generated by populist opposition to the power of big business, inevitably reduces economic liberty. Minimum wage and hours legislation and regulation of child labor are excellent examples of this phenomenon. Fearing the exploitation of workers by large corporations that can exercise great power over labor markets, government stepped in and limited how little a worker can be paid, how long he or she may be required to work per week, and how young or old he or she may be. Originally, such legislation was opposed by many, including the U.S. Supreme Court, on the grounds that it limited workers' liberty to contract out their services at their discretion, but nowadays the Fair Labor Standards Act is generally viewed as an important constraint on employers. Equal employment opportunity legislation presents another example of the tension between liberty and equality found in regulatory legislation. In the absence of statutes barring discrimination against members of minority groups and women, private employers would be free to exclude them from their work forces. But this would, and did, promote economic, social, and political inequality. On the other hand, requiring nondiscrimination or the use of affirmative action hiring goals for members of certain groups interferes with an employer's liberty to hire and fire as it pleases.

Because governmental regulation of the economic life of the nation is in tension with the stated constitutional goal of securing the blessings of liberty, far-reaching efforts have been made to assure that such governmental intervention is not arbitrary, capricious, or unduly violative of the economic liberty of individuals and businesses. These efforts have generally used law and legal processes as a check upon the activities of public administrators in this realm. Consequently, regulatory activities become law-bound, and the agencies engaging in regulation are structured to emphasize the values of the legal approach to public administration.

As mentioned earlier, there are a number of regulatory commissions in the federal government. Many more exist in state governments. Typically, regulatory commissions differ from other administrative agencies in the extent to which they combine legislative, executive, and judicial functions. In other words, they make rules for the regulation of some aspect of economic life, such as radio and television broadcasting or the fares and rates charged by railroads (a legislative function); they enforce these rules (an executive function); and they adjudicate issues arising out of the adoption or enforcement of these rules (a judicial function). The combination of these functions in single agencies seems to ignore the constitutional commitment to a system of checks and balances and to the separation of powers. Consequently, there has been a long-standing crisis of legitimacy associated with the operations of regulatory commissions.[9] To some extent efforts have been made to mitigate this crisis by placing a bipartisan group of commissioners at the head of each such agency. But this raises another problem; the commissioners are often people familiar with the industries being regulated, sometimes having been employed in them. These appointments reduce the opposition of businesses to regulation, but they promote a situation in which the regulatory commissions may speak more for industry interests than for the public. In fact, some industries such as the airlines (in the 1930s, but now "deregulated") actively sought to be regulated to save themselves from the chaos of uncontrolled competition.

The original idea behind the creation of regulatory commissions was that, as administrative bodies, they could develop a great deal of expertise in the area they were assigned to regulate. This expertise could be used to determine what the public interest was, and the definition of the public interest could be refined incrementally over time through adjudication. The latter process would enable the regulatory commissions to use the adversary procedure to determine the interests of all parties to disputes and to develop a body of precedent that would assure a relatively high degree of continuity in regulatory policies.

The Administrative Procedure Act   By the mid-1940s, however, Congress had come to believe that the regulatory process should afford greater protection to economic liberty from encroachments by administrative agencies. It enacted the Administrative Procedure Act (1946). Although the act, as amended, contains many exceptions, basically it affords the following protections to private parties being regulated:

- An agency must publish in the *Federal Register* descriptions of its organization, general method of operation, and procedural and substantive rules.

- Proposed changes in substantive rules must be published in the *Federal Register*, an opportunity for response by interested parties must be granted, and such responses are to be taken into account by the agency before adopting its final rule on the matter. The final rule must be published in the *Federal Register*, and not less than thirty days must elapse between its publication and its initial application. In some cases, called "formal rule making" or "rule making on the record," a judicial-like hearing is held before an administrative law judge or agency officials to determine the desirability of a new rule or rule change. (Box 2–2 on page 44 presents an example of a proposed rule.)

- Adjudicatory procedures within the agency must include the opportunity for aggrieved parties to be heard, to submit information and arguments on their behalf, and to have an initial recommendation for disposition of the case made by an impartial hearing examiner (administrative law judge).

- A right to judicial review is required for a person suffering legal wrong or adversely affected by agency actions. Judicial review is intended to check arbitrary or capricious abuses of discretion, violations of constitutional rights and statutes, breaches of procedural regularity, and agency decisions that are unwarranted by the facts of the case. There is also a model state administrative procedure act that recommends that many similar protections be afforded private parties being regulated by state administrative agencies.

Clearly, governmental regulatory activities have not only promoted the growth of public administration but also infused it with a legalistic character. A great deal of administrative time and resources at all levels of government are now devoted to regulatory hearings for the setting of rates charged by utilities and for the issuance of licenses to a host of economic endeavors and practitioners of a wide variety of occupations. In the view of many, such regulation has gone too far in diminishing economic liberty and has also led to a tremendous increase in the costs of providing regulated services. During the early 1980s, there was a broad move toward *deregulation*, as in the banking and airline industries, but it is still uncertain how far regulatory activity can be abandoned. There is little support among the public, for example, for the elimination of governmental regulation of the safety and purity of drugs and food. In fact, by 1987, some calls for "reregulation" of deregulated industries could be heard. For instance, economists Walter Adams and James Brock urged the Reagan administration to enforce the antitrust laws to stimulate competition among the airlines. They were also among many calling for greater regulation of flight safety.[10] We will have more to say about the operation of regulatory agencies in Chapter 9.

The Managerial Origins of the Contemporary American Administrative State

Public administration has developed and expanded in pursuit of broad political goals, including regulation of areas of the economy. The United States has sought to reach several goals, including economic development and better defense, through public administration. But the administrative activities of agencies assigned to achieve these substantive goals should not just follow a reasonably standardized and relatively fair set of procedures; they should also comply with the standards of good management. Goals and legal constraints aside, what are the values that should inform the day-to-day organizational operations of administrative agencies? The answer, as the reader has no doubt already guessed, is that agencies should be managed well, meaning they should be efficient and economical in their operations. Perhaps surprisingly, this too has been a source of the growth of the American administrative state.

Good management may immediately suggest getting more done for less money, which in turn might mean that fewer people would be employed in the public sector. Certainly it is true that well-managed agencies may realize such savings. It was very common during the period of rampant patronage in the nineteenth century (1841–1865) for superfluous employees to swell the rolls of post offices and customs houses in order to enrich the coffers of and strengthen support for the prevailing political party. But good management also requires the creation of **overhead agencies.** These are administrative units that perform services for other agencies or are engaged in overseeing aspects of their operations. The following are several examples at the federal level.

- The *General Services Administration* supplies other agencies' needs, ranging from rubber bands to the most sophisticated office technologies. It is involved in building facilities for agencies and renovating and altering them. It provides maintenance and policing functions for agency buildings and operates various food services within them. The GSA has about 26,000 employees and a budget of $392 million. Although scandals involving kickbacks and corrupt contracting have sometimes rocked the GSA, managerial theory generally contends that there are vast economies and efficiencies to be gained by centralizing the government's supply functions in a single agency. For instance, the GSA can buy products like paper clips in huge quantities at significant discounts. If each agency had to worry about procuring supplies directly from manufacturers or having its buildings built, the agencies would not only be distracted from their substantive missions but also lack the expertise to obtain the supplies economically or efficiently.

- The *Government Printing Office* is officially part of Congress. It publishes government documents, such as the *Federal Register*, and a massive variety of administrative reports. These range over everything from tips on controlling common garden insects to elaborate reports on substantive policy areas such as civil rights. The Government Printing Office also publishes

DEPARTMENT OF HEALTH AND HUMAN SERVICES

Public Health Service

42 CFR Part 59

Statutory Prohibition on Use of Appropriated Funds in Programs Where Abortion Is a Method of Family Planning; Standard of Compliance for Family Planning Services Projects

AGENCY: Public Health Service, DHHS.

ACTION: Proposed rules.

SUMMARY: The Public Health Service (PHS) proposes to amend the regulations governing the use of funds for family planning services under Title X of the Public Health Service Act in order to set specific standards for compliance with the statutory requirement that none of the funds appropriated under Title X may be used in programs where abortion is a method of family planning. This change is being proposed to bring the compliance requirements for programs using Title X funds into conformity with the statutory ban on such use of Title X appropriated funds. The proposed amendments should improve compliance by grantees with the statute and facilitate monitoring of compliance by PHS.

DATE: Comments must be in writing and be received by November 2, 1987. It is intended that final regulations will be promulgated within 45 days following the close of the above noted comment period.

ADDRESS: Comments should be sent to the Deputy Assistant Sec-retary for Population Affairs, Department of Health and Human Services, P.O. Box 23993, L'Enfant Plaza, Washington, DC 20026-3993.

FOR FURTHER INFORMATION CONTACT: Nabers Cabaniss at 202-245-0152.

SUPPLEMENTARY INFORMATION: On July 30, 1987, President Reagan announced that the Department of Health and Human Services would, within 30 days, publish draft regulations governing grants under Title X of the Public Health Service Act, 42 U.S.C. 300, *et seq.*, to give effect to the statutory prohibition on the use of Title X appropriated funds in programs that include abortion as a method of family planning. Set out below are the Department's proposed regulations, along with a statement of the basis and purpose of the amendments. The regulations proposed herein, when they become final, will automatically supersede the present Title X guidelines to the extent those guidelines are inconsistent with the final rules. After the final rules are issued, the Department intends to issue revised Title X guidelines in conformity therewith.

For the reasons set out in the preamble, it is hereby proposed to amend Subpart A of Part 59, 42 Code of Federal Regulations, as set forth below.

PART 59—[AMENDED]

1. The authority citation for Subpart A of 42 CFR Part 59 is revised to read as follows:
    Authority: 42 U.S.C. 300a-4.
    2. In 42 CFR 59.2, the following definitions are added:

§59.2 [Amended]

"Family planning" means the process of establishing objectives for the number and spacing of a family's children, and selecting the means (including natural family planning methods, adoption, infertility services and general reproductive health care, abstinence and contraception) by which those objectives may be achieved. As such, family planning does not include medical services or counseling related to pregnancy care after pregnancy is diagnosed (including prenatal or postpartum care or counseling), or abortion-related services. As it relates to the statutory prohibition on the inclusion of abortion as a method of family planning, proper family planning should reduce the incidence of abortion.

"Grantee" means the organization to which a grant is awarded under section 1001 of the Public Health Service Act.

"Organization," as applied to an applicant for or grantee of funds under section 1001 of the Public Health Service Act means any public or private nonprofit entity in a State. An organization may operate multiple family planning or related programs or projects.

"Program" and "project," which are used interchangeably in these regulations, both refer to the identified activity approved by the Secretary for support under section 1001 of the Public Health Service Act, unless the context indicates otherwise.

"Title X" means Title X of the Public Health Service Act, 42 U.S.C. 300, *et seq.*

BOX 2–2 *Continued*

§59.5 [Amended]

3. In 42 CFR 59.5, paragraph (a)(5) is removed and paragraphs (a)(6) through (a)(11) are redesignated as paragraphs (a)(5) through (a)(10) respectively.

§§59.7 through 59.13 [Redesignated as §§59.11 through 59.17]

4. In 42 CFR Part 59. §§59.7 through 59.13 are redesignated as §§59.11 through 59.17 respectively, and new §§59.7 through 59.10 are added to read as follows:

§59.7 Standards of compliance with prohibition on abortion.

A project may not receive funds under this subpart unless it provides assurance satisfactory to the Secretary that it does not include abortion as a method of family planning. Such assurance must include, at a minimum, representations (supported by documentary evidence where the Secretary requests) as to compliance with each of the requirements in §§59.8 through 59.10. A project supported under this subpart must comply with such requirements at all times during the project period.

§59.8 Prohibition on counseling and referral for abortion services; limitation of program services to family planning.

(a) In order to give effect to the statutory prohibition on the use of Title X appropriated funds in projects where abortion is a method of family planning, a project which provides counseling and referral for abortion services as a method of family planning is not eligible to receive funds under this subpart. In addition, because Title X funds are intended only for family planning, services related to pregnancy care after pregnancy is diagnosed may not be provided with Title X funds. Where appropriate, medical or social service referrals for non-Title X supported services shall be made by providing a full list of available health care providers of appropriate prenatal medical care and delivery services and/or social service agencies from which a family planning client may select. Such referrals may not, however, be used as an indicated means to encourage or promote abortion in violation of section 1008, such as consciously weighting the list of referrals in favor of health care providers and/or facilities which provide abortions. One effect of these regulations will be to insure the ability of otherwise eligible organizations or programs that refuse to engage in abortion-related activities to receive support under this subpart.

(b) *Examples.* (1) A pregnant client at a family planning clinic supported with Title X funds solicits prenatal care services. Clinic personnel are medically qualified to provide such services. Nonetheless, provision of such services is outside the scope of family planning supported by Title X.

(2) A client at a family planning clinic supported with Title X funds seeks pregnancy testing and infertility counseling and services. Clinic personnel provide the requested services and in the process thereof discover an ectopic pregnancy. The client is immediately provided a complete list of appropriate hospitals and physicians from which to choose. This service is within the scope of family planning supported by Title X.

(3) A childless husband and wife seek counseling and services relating to infertility and adoption. Such counseling and services are within the scope of family planning supported by Title X.

(4) Clients at a family planning clinic are given a brochure and shown a film about birth control methods that include sections on abortion. Because use of the film and the brochure depicts abortion as a method of family planning, the clinic would not be eligible to receive Title X funds.

§59.9 Separation of abortion-related services from family planning programs.

(a) A project supported under this subpart must be kept entirely separate and distinct, financially and physically, from any abortion-related activities. This requirement includes maintaining separate financial, accounting, personnel, and medical record systems and separately maintaining other project functions and physical facilities (including office space, equipment, stationary and the like) in such a manner as to clearly separate Title X-funded activities from abortion-related activities. This requirement prohibits, by way of example, common waiting, consultation, examination, and treatment areas; shared telephone numbers and receptionists; common names for eligible and ineligible programs; and common office entrances and exits. Although common street or mailing addresses will presumptively constitute a failure to separate ade-

BOX 2–2 *Continued*

quately Title X-funded programs from other programs which include abortion as a method of family planning, grant applicants may seek to establish the reasonableness of such arrangements in exceptional cases where, as in the example of a large metropolitan hospital with abortion and family planning services located in different wings, the fact of physical separation is otherwise established and no use of appropriate funds in an ineligible program is likely.

(b) *Examples.* (1) A nonprofit family planning organization operates abortion and family planning clinics simultaneously on Wednesdays and Fridays in the same one-story building. Nothing on the exterior of the building indicates the existence of two separate programs, although the programs are organized as legally separate entities. The clinics utilize a common parking lot adjacent to the building, a common entrance at the front of the building, and a common receptionist and reception area. The two clinics share the same executive director and financial manager, and the abortion clinic pays a management fee for the services of such personnel. Two other employees of the family planning clinic also work for the abortion clinic. The family planning clinic refers clients to the abortion clinic. The family planning clinic in this example is not "separate and distinct, financially and physically," from abortion-related activities.

(2) A nonprofit organization operates both abortion and family planning clinics at the same address. Both clinics are staffed by the same personnel, and the medical director for the family planning program generally performs the abortions for the abortion clinic as well. The programs, however, schedule clients at different times, with abortion clinic hours only in the mornings and family planning hours only in the afternoon. The schedules do not overlap. The programs use the same telephone number, and the same receptionist answers the phone and makes appointments for both. The programs use the same automobiles, office furnishings, and advertisements. The family planning program in this example is not "separate and distinct, financially and physically," from abortion-related activities.

(3) A private, nonprofit corporation operates a family planning program (Program A) and a program which includes abortion-related services (Program B). Both programs are operated as parts of the same corporate entity, with common directors and officers. Program A and Program B occupy office space leased under the terms of a common master lease, but the offices are in fact located in different sections of the city. Program A maintains entirely separate financial records and has no on-site personnel in common with Program B. The programs conduct no joint advertising and use separate furnishings and equipment. Program A is "separate and distinct, physically and financially," from Program B.

(4) A private, nonprofit organization operates both a family planning clinic that receives Title X funds and an abortion clinic. The clinics are physically separate, but their accounting and financial records are maintained jointly. Although the family planning clinic is separated physically from the abortion clinic, the joint financial records indicate that the family planning clinic is not "separate and distinct, financially and physically" from abortion-related activities.

(5) A private, nonprofit organization operates both a family planning clinic and an abortion clinic. Both clinics lease space in the same one-story building. The two clinics share a common waiting room. The family planning clinic has separate personnel and maintains separate financial records from the abortion clinic. The family planning clinic in this example is not "separate and distinct, physically and financially" from the abortion-related activities.

§59.10 **Prohibition on activities that encourage, promote or advocate abortion.**

(a) A project supported under this subpart may take no action which encourages, promotes, or advocates abortion as a method of family planning, or which assists a woman in obtaining an abortion as a method of family planning. Actions are considered to encourage, promote, or advocate abortion as a method of family planning if they in any way have the effect of facilitating obtaining abortion as a method of family planning. Such prohibited actions include the following:

BOX 2–2 *Continued*

---

(1) Lobbying for the passage of pro-abortion legislation, providing speakers to argue for abortion as a method of family planning, or paying dues to organizations that advocate abortion as a method of family planning;

(2) Using legal action to make available in any way abortion as a method of family planning;

(3) Developing, assisting in the development of, posting or disseminating in any way materials (including printed matter and audiovisual materials) that advocate abortion as a method of family planning;

(b) *Examples.* (1) A family planning clinic provides those of its clients who inquire concerning abortion with brochures advertising an abortion clinic. Such a service would "encourage, promote or advocate" abortion.

(2) A family planning clinic pays dues to an organization that devotes a substantial part of its activities to lobbying the Congress for liberalized abortion laws. This activity would "encourage, promote or advocate" abortion.

(3) A family planning clinic displays in its waiting room posters encouraging clients to write their legislative representatives to urge them to vote "pro choice" on pending legislation, and distributes post cards for the same purpose.

The clinic is engaged in "encouraging, promoting or advocating" abortion.

(4) A family planning clinic that receives Title X funds assists its clients in making appointments at abortion clinics. The provision of such services would violate section 1008.

(5) Personnel of a family planning project write their legislative representatives in support of pro-choice legislation, utilizing no project funds to do so. The eligibility of the project for Title X funds would be unaffected by their advocacy of abortion.

SOURCE: *Federal Register*, 52 (No. 169, September 1, 1987), pp. 33210–33215.

---

the *Government Manual*, which describes each federal agency's function and organization, making it an invaluable tool for students and practitioners of public administration.

- The *General Accounting Office* is also a part of the legislature. It was established in 1921 to facilitate Congress's ability to monitor the use of governmental funds by administrative agencies. In more recent years it has added to its concern with fiscal accountability an effort to evaluate the general quality of management of specific administrative agencies. It also evaluates the policies agencies are pursuing. Today, the GAO employs about 5,400.

- The *Office of Management and Budget* is part of the Executive Office of the President. It works with the president, his advisors, and federal agencies to prepare the annual budget submitted by the chief executive to the legislature. In formulating the budget, the OMB evaluates agency requests for funding and evaluates their activities. It also makes recommendations to the president when agencies seek new legislation or the issuance of presidential executive orders to aid them in fulfilling their functions. In practice, the OMB exercises a veto over such requests. It plays a similar role in overseeing the regulatory rules of executive branch agencies. Although less developed than its budgeting activities, the OMB also tries to advise agencies on good management practices and to evaluate their managerial operations. In 1985, OMB had about 570 employees on its staff.

- The *Office of Personnel Management* is an executive branch agency that oversees the federal personnel system. It broadly regulates the way agencies recruit, select, promote, transfer, dismiss, discipline, classify, pay, retire, and generally treat federal employees. It also provides some training services and has a role in promoting equal employment opportunity. In the past, the OPM and its predecessor, the Civil Service Commission, developed centralized merit examinations for entry into the general career structure of federal employment. Closely related to the OPM's activities are those of the Merit Systems Protection Board and the Federal Labor Relations Authority. The former is charged with assuring that the merit system is not violated and the latter regulates the process of collective bargaining in the federal government. The OPM is the largest of these three agencies. It employs about 6,000 people.

- The *Bureau of the Census* and the *Bureau of Labor Statistics* are examples of the classic managerial administrative function of gathering information as an aid to policy planning. Both of these agencies supply invaluable information to other agencies as well as to members of the public.

In sum, the quest for good management as well as the desire to promote various political and economic goals, while protecting the rights of private parties, has contributed to the growth of public administration in the United States. However, the essence of the administrative state is not characterized by the large number of administrative units and public employees alone. Its fundamental importance lies instead in the extent to which public administrative agencies exercise governmental power over the political, economic, and social life of the nation.

ADMINISTRATIVE POWER

We have been discussing the rise of the administrative state in terms of the development and growth of administrative units. But the phenomenon of the administrative state and what makes public administration so interesting goes well beyond simply counting the number of units, employees, or money spent. Contemporary public administration is problematic not only because it is large and expensive but also because it is politically powerful. It is sometimes difficult to imagine that public employees have emerged as a major—perhaps in some policy areas, the major—power center in complex political systems such as the United States. After all, what does a postal letter carrier, a government accountant, a personnel official, a recordkeeping clerk, or typist have to do with political power? Indeed, what kind of impact can even high-level officials have in administrative systems that are dominated by organizations rather than individuals, that are rule-bound, and that place major constraints on individual action? These questions hint at a paradox of contemporary public administration. Cumulatively, public administrators have a great deal of power, but individually they are often likened unto cogs in a machine over which they have very little control.[11] Each administrator's discretion is constrained by many forces, yet public administration has become a center for the development of policy choices for American society as a whole. The French writer Honoré de Balzac captured this irony by referring to bureaucracy as "giant power wielded by pygmies."[12]

One place to begin a consideration of the nature of administrative power is with a consideration of what public administrators do. As was discussed earlier, public administrators have become the vehicle through which society has chosen to carry out the public action aimed at securing political objectives, such as economic development and regulation to promote law and order. The scope of their activities is truly astounding. Indeed, it is difficult to find more than a few interests or concerns in the society that are not in some way addressed through administrative action (see Box 2–3). Births and deaths are recorded by administrators; so are marriages and divorces. They inspect food and drugs and regulate radio and television broadcasting. Entrance into a very wide variety of occupations—from the most manual to the most cerebral—requires an administrative stamp of approval. Transportation, housing, education, health service, banking, wages and hours for work, employment, and many, many more aspects of daily life are subject to some kind of administrative action. There is no denying that the contemporary administrative state is characterized by a high degree of penetration of the daily life of society.

The centrality of public administration does not automatically make it powerful. It is at least theoretically possible that public administrative action could be wholly directed by law and political arrangements to the extent that it simply carried out the will of the elected legislative and executive officials. But in practice it has considerable independence, for at least two reasons.

First, public administrators develop a great deal of expertise upon which the society becomes dependent. All the functional specialization, recordkeeping, and information gathering that goes on in public administration enable public administrators to develop expertise on some matters that cannot be matched elsewhere in society. For instance, who else but a bureaucrat is likely to know how much of a particular crop was produced in any given year, or how much of some product was imported, or how many people took an occupational licensing examination? Indeed, sometimes one is puzzled by the kind of information collected by public bureaucracies, but, in the end, the cumulative information held by public administrators becomes an important source of political power and influence. Organizational and policy specialization compound this situation. Not only do public administrators often know more about many aspects of national life than does anyone else, they also know more about how to accomplish programmatic ends than legislators or elected officials.

Second, elected officials frequently delegate decision-making authority to public administrators. In part this delegation flows from deference to adminis-

BOX 2–3 **The Reach of the Federal Bureaucracy—"Touching You, Touching Me"**

The *U.S. Government Manual* indicates that bureaucratic agencies deal with the following areas of American life: Abaca production and sale; adult education; the arts; consumer affairs; historic preservation; economic growth and stability; aeronautics; age discrimination and aging (there is an Office of Aging); agriculture, including the subsidization and regulation of the production of specific crops, marketing, and farmers in general; welfare; maintenance of an air force; various Alaskan projects; alcohol; drug abuse; mental health; tobacco; firearms; aliens; allergies and infectious diseases; battle monuments; Indians; Mexicans; the blind; transportation, technology; armed forces and defense, including the procurement of manpower and weaponry; astronomy; building of dams; reclamation of land; conservation of soil; arthritis; metabolism and digestive diseases; athletics; atomic energy; automobiles; Coast Guard; aviation; banks; standards and measures; biology; birds; bituminous coal; blood; boating safety; bonds; school breakfast and lunch programs; broadcasting; business; cable television; campaign financing; census; (Center for) Short-Lived Phenomena; chemistry; child development; children; environmental quality; cities; civil defense; civil rights; coins; colleges and community development; conservation; construction; corporations; cosmetics; cost of living; cotton; crime; dairy industry; day care; the deaf; Delaware River basin; disadvantaged persons; disaster assistance; discrimination; docks; earthquakes; economic development; the economy; education; electric power; emergencies; employment; unemployment; underemployment; the handicapped; energy; engineering; equal opportunity; exports; families; highways; radiation; railroads; fertilizer; fish, wildlife; fitness; fabrics; floods; food; gas; geographic names; patents; copyrights; grain; grazing; Great Lakes; hazardous substances; health; hospitals; housing; nutrition; hydroelectric power; icebreakers; immigration; imports; insects; intergovernmental relations; international affairs; irrigation; justice; juvenile delinquency; labeling; labor; land; law enforcement; libraries; livestock; loans; mail; manpower; maps; maritime activities; mediation; medical matters; minorities; Mississippi River; Missouri basin; motor vehicles; narcotics; outer space; national parks; water quality; national forests; naval matters; occupational health and safety; oceans; oil; minority business; outdoor recreation; passports; plants; police; pollution; postal service; power; prices; rat control; reading; refugees; rents; retirement; rivers; rubber; rural areas; safety; savings; scholarships; schools; science; screw threads; securities; small business; social security; subversive activities; sugar; tariffs and taxes; Tennessee Valley; textiles; trade; trademarks; veterans; visual disorders; vocational affairs; wages; war; water; waterways; weather; women; youth.

SOURCE: David Nachmias and David H. Rosenbloom, *Bureaucratic Government, USA* (New York: St. Martin's, 1980), p. 59.

trative expertise. It also stems from recognition that public administrative directives are actually more flexible than legislation in the sense that they can be redrafted or abolished through a far less elaborate process than enacting a statute. Thus, where the legislature feels that standards for regulation or for eligibility for various governmental benefits will have to be changed frequently, or applied in a great variety of circumstances, it may be apt to delegate power to administrative agencies. For instance, the Occupational Safety and Health Administration Act (1970) mandates that "so far as possible every working man and woman in the Nation [shall have] safe and healthful work conditions." Among other issues, implementing this mandate requires that somebody determine which levels of which substances used in manufacturing and other sectors are toxic. Given the vast number of production practices and potentially toxic chemicals used (not to mention their combination), it is unlikely that Congress *could* address every such danger through specific legislation. Instead, it has delegated its legislative authority to the Occupational Safety and Health Administration to make and enforce rules regarding workers' safety. Additionally, sometimes the legislature does not know what to do, or cannot agree on what to do in some policy area. In such a case, rather than do nothing at all—especially if the public and/or interest groups are clamoring for action—it may seek to delegate authority to an administrative agency to deal with the problem.

Delegations of legislative authority can be accomplished by clear and forceful legislative guidance. Frequently, however, the legislature places only the vaguest of conditions upon the exercise of powers it delegates to public administrators. For example, the Federal Communications Commission, which regulates radio and television broadcasting, is supposed to exercise the powers granted to it by Congress in "the public convenience, interest, or necessity." If you were chairperson of the FCC, what kind of guidance would you find in these words? Confronted with an equally unspecific charge, a chairman of the Civil Aeronautics Board, which regulated the airline industry, once said that the "philosophy of the [CAB] changes from day to day,"[13] something that could not occur if its powers were constrained by strict standards laid down by Congress. Delegations with little guidance generally result from the legislature's inability or unwillingness, for political reasons, to set clear standards for the use of the powers it delegates to administrative agencies. Sometimes the subject matter of the agency's jurisdiction is so complex that the legislature does not have the time or staff resources truly to master it. At other times, political expediency dictates that the legislature will not take a firm stand on an issue, which may be politically controversial, divisive, and lead to a loss of support among segments of the electorate. The net result of reliance on the expertise of public administrators and the scope and frequency of vague delegations is that public administrators, as a group, become influential policy makers. Today, there is no doubt that "the staffs of the executive branch agencies have come to exercise an important share of the initiative, the formulation, the bargaining, and the deciding in the process by which governmental decisions are taken."[14] They are consulted by committees in Congress, by officials in the Executive Office of the

President, and by the politically appointed department heads and their staffs. Moreover, despite the denunciations of "bureaucratic power" at election times, political officials often acknowledge the legitimacy of including agency administrators in the policy-making process.

Public administrators are even more powerful when it comes to choosing the means through which public policies will be implemented. As Wallace Sayre observes, "Great power also belongs naturally to those who carry out decisions of public policy. In this stage, the career staffs have had a paramount role. The choices of means, the pace and tone of governmental performance, reside largely in the hands of the federal service. . . . The civil servants have a position of distinct advantage in determining how public policies are executed."[15] It is very important to note that this choice of means can be as much a policy-making exercise as the choice of ends. Equal employment opportunity and affirmative action present an excellent example. The goal of equal employment opportunity is hardly controversial today. Political officials and the public overwhelmingly accept the principle, in the abstract at least, that no person should be discriminated against in most public or private employment as a result of his or her race, color, national origin, religion, or sex. This principle is the policy objective of federal equal employment opportunity programs. But what means should be chosen to attain it? Federal administrative agencies charged with implementing the EEO principle decided upon *affirmative action*. Affirmative action entails the establishment of goals and timetables for the hiring, promotion, and/or job training of members of certain minority groups and women. Affirmative action has been criticized by many—including Supreme Court justices, presidents, and members of Congress—for relying upon preferential treatment based on race, ethnicity, and sex. It has engendered a great deal more political controversy than EEO itself. Yet affirmative action is but a means, not an end in itself. And, to reemphasize the main point, it is a means that has been chosen by public administrators rather than by elected officials. (An interesting side issue is whether, given its controversiality, politically elected officials *could* have chosen it?)

Public administrative power in the United States today is evidenced in the volume of rule making by administrative agencies, which far exceeds the volume of legislation passed by the nation's legislatures; in the fact that even with very crowded judicial dockets, more adjudication, such as hearings, takes place in administrative agencies; and in the fact that despite the vast publicity given to presidential and gubernatorial policy initiatives, public administrative agencies remain a main source of ideas for new legislation. The power of individual agencies and officials varies with a variety of factors, a topic generally called *bureaucratic politics*. But, overall, administrative power has developed to such an extent that it has had a major impact on the nature of the other branches of government. Indeed, the rise of the administrative state is perhaps the most important governmental development in this century, because it transforms the nature of the political system as a whole. This is a point that no public administrator should ever forget.

RESPONSES TO THE RISE OF THE ADMINISTRATIVE STATE

Over the long run, a successful public administrator must have a deep understanding of the environment in which he or she operates. That environment includes many actors and the managerial, political, and legalistic approaches and values discussed in the first chapter. Among the leading actors are elected chief executives, legislatures, courts, interest groups, and the public at large. In some jurisdictions, where patronage is still a major influence on public administration, political parties are important as well. The successful practitioner of public administration may come to develop a feel for the way these actors influence public administration, for their values and objectives. The student of public administration, on the other hand, does not have the opportunity for daily interaction with the environment of public administration and consequently finds it necessary to rely on accounts of others. These accounts can be valuable, but it is of the utmost importance that they portray the reality of what is, and not some civics textbook notion of how things ought to be. In this section we will explain how the president, Congress, the federal judiciary, interest groups, the public, and to a lesser extent, political parties have responded to the rise of the administrative state. It should be borne in mind that although our discussion focuses on the federal government, the same patterns hold true at the state and local levels as well.

The President and Public Administration

The office of the President of the United States is surrounded by so much myth that it is sometimes very difficult even to begin to figure out what really goes on in the White House, much less in the president's mind. For some reason—a psychological need for a hero figure, perhaps—Americans have built up the image of the president in a way that simply does not correspond to reality. For example, ideas such as the following abound: "America is the hope of the world, and for that time given him, the president is the hope of America;"[16] "the President of the United States of America is, without question, the most powerful elected executive in the world";[17] "there is virtually no limit to what the President can do if he does it for democratic ends and by democratic means";[18] "the President's values, his qualities of character and intellect, his capacity for leadership, his political skills, his definition of his own role, and the way he performs it—these are fundamental determinants of the working of the American government and of American politics."[19] Really? Then why has the experience of recent presidents been so often characterized by an inability to achieve their stated goals and deliver on their promises to the public? At least some modern presidents might well have been the topic of a famous nineteenth-century essay on "Why Great Men Are Not Chosen Presidents"![20] More to the point, why have so many presidents come into office promising that they could do something constructive to control "the bureaucracy," only to leave office with questionable accomplishments and a sense of defeat at the hands of the bureaucrats? Indeed, even Jimmy Carter, who did introduce major reforms in the federal personnel system, eventually admitted that he was unable to overcome the entrenched force of the federal bureaucracy. Although his reforms were hailed as equal in importance to the adoption of a merit system in the 1880s and called the "centerpiece" of his efforts to reform government and make it more efficient and effective, Carter hardly mentions civil service reform in his memoirs, *Keeping Faith*. In some important ways, discussed later on in this section, President Ronald Reagan's administration was more successful than most in influencing the bureaucracy. But it also faced serious frustrations. Despite Reagan's vows to cut the federal bureaucracy's size, toward the end of his second term the budget deficit was larger than ever and, although some agencies had been shrunken, overall levels of federal employment were higher than when he took office. In fact, at times the Reagan administration was mired in bureaucratic politics, as was true of the scandal-rocked Environmental Protection Agency in the first term and during the Iran-Contra affair in the second. Perhaps even more telling, government spending continued to rise as a proportion of the gross national product (GNP).

It is obvious that the gap between the imaginary presidency and the real powers and influence available to the president is vast. Virtually all presidential administrations since the days of Franklin D. Roosevelt (1933–1945) have noted how difficult it is for the president to get things done. President Harry S Truman may have conveyed the limits of presidential power when he mused about General Dwight D. Eisenhower, president-elect, taking over: "He'll sit here, and he'll say, 'Do this! Do that!' *And nothing will happen.* Poor Ike—it won't be a bit like the Army. He'll find it very frustrating."[21] Years later, Richard Cheney, Chief of White House Staff in the Ford administration, commented on the same phenomenon:

> There's a tendency before you get to the White House or when you're just observing it from outside to say, "Gee, that's a powerful position that person has." The fact of the matter is that while you're here trying to do things, you are far more aware of the constraints than you are of the power. You spend most of your time trying to overcome obstacles getting what the President wants done.[22]

President Carter once exclaimed, "I can't even get a damn mouse out of my office," after its removal was delayed by a bureaucratic jurisdictional dispute between the Department of the Interior (White House grounds) and the General Services Administration (White House building)! More reflectively, Carter revealed that he had "underestimated the inertia or the momentum of the federal bureaucracy. . . . It is difficult to change."[23] Perhaps President Reagan's secretary of state, George Schultz, summed up the political environment in Washington, D.C., best: "Nothing ever gets settled in this town. You have to keep fighting every inch of the way."[24]

Presidential powers over public administration are particularly limited. It is customary to view the president as the chief executive, but almost all of his powers over the executive branch are shared with Congress and the courts. For example, under the Constitution, the president has only one explicit power over public administrators—he can ask for the opinions in writing of department heads! Presidential appointments are shared with the Senate. Dismissals, even of some presidential appointments such as the chairman of the FTC, have been constrained by constitutional and statutory law.[25] Funding for agencies and salaries must be authorized by Congress. Likewise, agencies must either be created by law or pursuant to a congressional delegation of power to the president. In either case, their creation requires at least the tacit approval of the legislature. Agency missions are rarely if ever established or significantly formally modified by the president alone. The federal personnel system is based on statute and consequently requires congressional involvement. Collective bargaining arrangements also place constraints upon what the president can do in terms of managing people in the executive branch. Presidential executive orders are subject to challenge in the federal courts. Nor can presidents refuse to spend money allocated by Congress without congressional approval.

So what are these presidential powers of which so many have so long been in awe? Some would point to the president's duty to faithfully execute the laws. Yet this and other significant powers are shared with the legislature and the courts—and that presents the crux of the president's problem vis-à-vis large-scale federal public administration. Stated concisely, the president is held responsible and accountable for the performance of the executive branch, but he does not have the powers necessary to control its performance. This has been a long-standing complaint of presidents who feel, in particular, that they are unable to influence the direction of the executive branch sufficiently because they are unable to make appointments and dismissals with a free hand. Ironically, many of the statutory constraints on the handling of federal personnel are derived from the managerial approach to public administration, which has stressed the need for public employees to be insulated from partisan political influences.

The gap between responsibility and authority faced by the president places severe strains upon him. In honest moments, a president might repeat the thoughts of Presidents Truman and Carter. But given the dynamics of getting elected to office and dealing with the media, generally such open admissions of frustration will not do. People expect results, in part because every candidate for the presidential office is sure to promise them. The Carter administration showed the risks of scaling down the image of the presidency. He may even have lost his bid for reelection in 1980 partly because "he reduced public expectations by being a president who was smaller rather than larger than real life."[26] Clearly, when it comes to management of the executive branch, no modern president is likely to throw up his hands in disgust—as Ulysses S. Grant is reputed once to have done—and declare that the whole public administrative mess is Congress's problem. Rather, presidential action is necessary—and increasingly it takes one very familiar form.[27]

Beginning in 1939, but escalating rapidly since the 1960s, there has been a tendency for presidents to try to use the Executive Office of the President to manage the executive branch (see Box 2–4). When the office was created in 1939, it was assumed that it would house a few close presidential aides who

BOX 2–4 **The Structure of the Presidency**

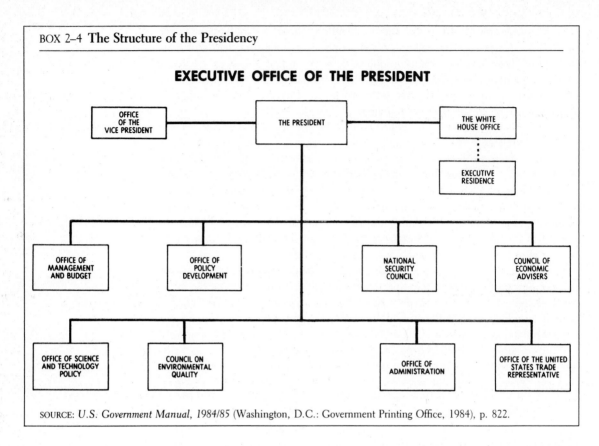

SOURCE: *U.S. Government Manual, 1984/85* (Washington, D.C.: Government Printing Office, 1984), p. 822.

would work behind the scenes to bring the president's influence to bear upon executive branch agencies. More recently, its size has fluctuated with presidential managerial and political philosophy, but it will clearly never return to either its initial size or role in the government.

The enlarged size of the EOP reflects its greater involvement and power in the executive branch. Today, its main units are the following:

1. the *White House Office*, which provides staff and managerial assistance to the president. Basically it serves to coordinate the activities of the executive branch, enable the president to exert greater influence on the executive branch, generate ideas for solutions to pressing problems, and deal with outsiders such as Congress, interest groups, and the media. The White House Office has grown from forty-five full-time employees in 1939 to about four or five hundred under recent presidents.
2. the *Office of Management and Budget*, created in 1970. It encompassed the old Bureau of the Budget, which was created in 1921, as an independent agency located in the Treasury Department, and moved to the

Executive Office in 1939. Its primary task is to prepare the federal budget and to suggest ways in which federal management can be improved. It serves as a clearinghouse for agency requests for legislation or executive orders to facilitate their operations. OMB has been very strong in dealing with executive branch agencies and has provided the presidential office with an important managerial tool.

During the Reagan presidency, OMB was given authority to review the proposed rules of executive branch departments and agencies prior to their release for public comment. In January 1985, its role in regulatory administration was strengthened by the requirement that departments and agencies submit a "draft regulatory program" before developing rules. Independent regulatory commissions, such as the Federal Communications Commission and the Securities and Exchange Commission, were not covered by the new requirement, but it did apply to independent executive branch agencies, including the Environmental Protection Agency and the Equal Employment Opportunity Commission. OMB's reliance on cost-benefit analysis in reviewing agencies' potential rule changing provoked considerable opposition, but its role in evaluating agencies' rules and proposed rules now seems well established. (See Chapter 9 for a discussion of regulatory reform.)

3. the *National Security Council*, established in 1947. The NSC seeks to advise the president on the integration of domestic, foreign, and military policies as they relate to national security. However, the NSC has sometimes been a competitor of the Departments of State and Defense in defining policy. During the Reagan administration, it became evident that the NSC was involved in covert operations that actually undercut State Department initiatives and positions regarding terrorism and the Persian Gulf war. In August 1987, President Reagan took steps to prohibit such activities in the future.[28]

4. the *Office of Policy Development*. A Domestic Council was established in 1970 to help integrate and develop domestic policy. It has since undergone several changes, including conversion to a Domestic Policy Staff. The Reagan administration reorganized the domestic policy function into the OPD. However, since so much of the Reagan domestic policy agenda involved budgetary and personnel reductions and greater oversight of regulatory administration, the OPD has not been very active in developing new legislative proposals.

When viewed in organizational terms, these four units can be seen as "superagencies" intended to make it possible to run a great deal of the executive branch directly out of the presidential office. The OMB deals with budgets, economic matters, and management. The National Security Council deals with foreign affairs, while the Office of Policy Development addresses domestic affairs. The operations of these specialized units are coordinated by the White House Office, which controls access to the president. Thus, the standard managerial principles of specialization and hierarchy are present, and the whole Executive Office of the President is intended to serve as a presidential tool for management and policy making in the executive branch.

From the administrative side, the EOP increases the number of actors to whom attention must be paid. No longer does the chain of command reach from the president to the career public administrators through the politically appointed agency heads and their assistants. Rather, the agency heads are for the most part in fact responsible and subordinate to people in the EOP. They rarely have direct access to the president, but rather must go through functionaries in the White House Office. Moreover, the OMB plays a critical role in many aspects of agency operations.

This arrangement *might* enable the president to gain authority more commensurate with the responsibilities thrust upon him or self-imposed. He has great freedom to make appointments to the White House Office since these functionaries do not require senatorial approval. Many of the operations of the Executive Office of the President can be cloaked in the secrecy afforded by the principle of executive privilege, which limits congressional inquiry into its affairs. But in practice the EOP has not wholly solved the presidential dilemma, primarily because it has grown too large to serve, in any simple sense, as a direct arm of the president. Somewhere along the line, the EOP developed some interests of its own. As Stephen Wayne summed up the problem:

> The growth of presidential policy making has encouraged the development of a large, specialized and highly structured White House, one that has become capable of assisting the president in more of his duties but one that also has become less amenable to his direct, personal control. . . .
>
> In the process of expansion, the White House aggregated considerable power. By the 1970s, it had clearly become more than the president's personal office.[29]

Perhaps the dilemma of choosing between managerial capacity and political control was best illustrated by the Iran-Contra affair (1986–1987). It dramatically showed some of the political and managerial problems inherent in the enlarged EOP. Rear Admiral John Poindexter, presidential advisor for national security, testified before Congress that he did not consider the president's staff bound by a law (the "Boland Amendment") that forbade aid to the Contras in Nicaragua. Presumably, he felt that the separation of powers limits the extent to which Congress can impose specific restrictions on the president's activity in foreign affairs. But if Poindexter did not consider himself bound by the law, neither did he think he was required to tell the president about the diversion of funds (from arms sales to Iran) to the Contras. He called the whole episode—which led to a U.S. naval build-up in the Persian Gulf and a loss of face with our European allies—a "detail," "a matter of implementation of the President's policy." In his words, he "was convinced that we could properly do it and that the President would approve if asked."[30] Later, though, the very same president asserted that he *should* have been informed. As Reagan saw it, "I had the right, the obligation, to make my own decision."[31] Ironically, the *stronger presidency* led to the image of a *weaker president*. In March 1987, a CBS/New York Times poll found that

66 percent of the public thought that "most of the time other people [than President Reagan] are really running the government."[32] This figure was up from 50 percent in December 1986, when the affair was first gaining publicity. Here, then, is not only an example of the problematic character of presidential power, but also a lesson in basic public administration in which organizational structure, accountability, information, decision making, and authority are central elements of governance.

The Iran-Contra affair notwithstanding, the Reagan administration was innovative and somewhat more successful than other recent presidencies in promoting its policies throughout the bureaucracy. It sought to augment the president's control of the executive branch by the creation of **cabinet councils.** By the end of Reagan's first term, there were seven such councils: Economic Affairs, Commerce and Trade, Human Resources, Natural Resources and Environment, Food and Agriculture, Legal Policy, and Management and Administration. They are subgroups of the cabinet and chaired by the president or a cabinet member in his absence. Like the organizational units in the EOP, the cabinet councils are used to coordinate and develop policy.

The Reagan administration also emphasized the use of **political executives**—that is, department heads, assistant secretaries, and other political appointees to executive agencies—as a means of bringing presidential policy direction to the bureaucracy. The president appoints about 650 top political executives to positions in the Executive Office and executive branch agencies. These include the cabinet members and about fifteen to twenty other individuals in each of the departments as well as approximately eleven appointees in each of the independent agencies, including their heads.[33] Additionally, there are roughly two thousand political appointees scattered throughout the upper and middle levels of the bureaucracy. These appointees are exceptions to the nonpartisan career service that overwhelmingly comprises these ranks. About seven hundred such political appointees are in the Senior Executive Service positions at the top of federal service and about 1,300 are in Schedule C slots in the middle levels.[34]

Traditionally, political executives and appointees have had a dual allegiance. On the one hand, they are presidential appointments and consequently are expected to express loyalty to the chief executive. On the other, political executives must be able to work with the top-ranking career staffs of the agencies to which they are assigned. This job is complicated by the likelihood that the political executive's tenure will be relatively short—two to three years on average—and that he or she will depend considerably upon the expertise of the career staffs to achieve policy objectives. Too often it is assumed that the hierarchy of an organizational chart actually conveys the authority necessary to manage a federal agency. Those public administrators who make it to the top career positions in their agencies necessarily develop a considerable network of supporters in the legislature and among interest groups. They are politically influential and cannot be effectively ordered around without considerable managerial and political skill. The politically appointed secretary depends upon them to a certain extent. Consequently, he or she not only represents the president's will to the agency, but must also represent the agency to the president. The fact that most political executives no longer enjoy direct access to the president complicates their jobs considerably. Let's take a look at what two political executives have observed about the problems they faced:

- In a real sense, delegation of authority to the operating manager of an entirely unfamiliar field means that the Secretary serves the bureau chiefs [career bureaucrats managing bureaus] rather than vice versa.

- The White House attitude is often bafflingly ambivalent. Thus, the staffer who is charged with relaying his own or the President's instructions to a cabinet officer usually expects unquestioning obedience. On the other hand, the President, when and if he has occasion to call on the Secretary to help, often expects him to enjoy at least the public image of independence.

- [The Secretary's] judgment on budget items is, of course, the most important decision he will make in his term in office and is the decision he is usually least well-equipped to make intelligently.

- The traditional answer of the busy executive to excessive workload—delegation of authority—is often a high-risk business in a political organization.[35]

The Reagan administration did somewhat better than other recent presidential administrations in using the EOP and political executives to control the bureaucracy, though the Iran-Contra episode was a failure of very major proportions. By and large, Reagan's appointees were characterized by considerable ideological and political unity. This strengthened their ability to coordinate policy and administration. Early on, Reagan indicated that his strategy would rest on "the appointment to top government positions of men and women who share my economic philosophy. We will have an administration in which the word from the top isn't lost or hidden in the bureaucracy."[36] Among his aims was to assure that his cabinet appointees would be "the managers of the national administration—not captives of the bureaucracy or the special interests they are supposed to direct."[37]

The administration also took great care in making appointments to political positions in the Senior Executive Service and to Schedule C jobs. In some cases, as part of a strategy to reduce the size and power of the bureaucracy, individuals who were opposed to the programs being administered by agencies were appointed to manage those agencies! This was true, for instance, in the Departments of Labor and Housing and Urban Development, the Commission on Civil Rights, the Equal Employment Opportunity Commission, and, in the early 1980s, the Environmental Protection Agency as well.

An interesting aspect of Reagan's relative success in relying on political appointees to control the career bureaucracy was how varied the patterns of influence and styles of management were. Similar political ideologies among his appointees did not necessarily yield parallel managerial styles. Some political executives were almost ruthless in their treatment of career civil servants, who were downgraded, transferred, dismissed in cutbacks, and prompted to resign. But others adopted a managerial style imbued with greater respect for the talent of the career staffs and more open to their participation in decision making.[38] The more systematic information contained in Box 2–5 indicates that Reagan's political executives generally held the career service in high regard, but less so than did political executives in other recent administrations.

Despite its relative success, the Reagan administration faced several common difficulties in seeking to use political executives to promote its policies. First, some talented individuals were deterred from pursuing or accepting governmental appointments by the pay, which is relatively low compared with that of the private sector, complex and costly conflict-of-interest regulations, high personal relocation costs, and the frustrating quality of the work. Second, high turnover, especially in the domestic agencies, made policy and program continuity difficult. Third, though not clearly linked to Reagan's appointment strategy, enough unethical and illegal behavior occurred among his political executives to enable the Democratic party to pin the label "sleaze" on the administration—and with some credibility.

Whether future presidents will want to follow Reagan's strategy with regard to political appointments is uncertain. As Stephen Wayne points out, it is more suitable for an administration seeking to reduce the size and power of the bureaucracy than one attempting to implement new policies and programs:

> . . . [F]rom a short-term perspective and on the basis of the administration's goals, the domestic policy apparatus seems to be working well. It has enabled Reagan to stay his course and his administration to appear to speak with a single voice. Internal dissent has been muted (albeit with the threat of polygraphs), and the "going-native" syndrome, whereby secretaries advocate their department's interests, has been contained (although not eliminated). The public understands the direction of the administration and the presidential force behind it. Reagan is seen as a strong leader despite his penchant to delegate and his tendency to wait for decisions to "perk up" to him. The contrasts with Ford and Carter are striking.
>
> From the perspective of effective administration and responsive governance, the verdict is less clear. A system in which most policymaking units do not generate new programs or do so marginally and reactively does not impress me as fulfilling the needs of the institution [the presidency] that has become the principal policymaker of our national government.[39]

Congress and the Administrative State

The response of legislatures to the rise of the contemporary administrative state has been complex and somewhat convoluted. Typically, unlike chief executives, their problem is not the lack of adequate constitutional or legal authority to control the actions of public administrative agencies. Rather, the problem is one of technical ability to exercise *oversight* (review) of public administrators and the political interest or will to do so. The United States Congress presents an excellent and well-researched example of how the growth of public administration affects the operation of legislatures.

Institutional Responses   It is sometimes said that it takes bureaucracy to control bureaucracy. This could be the motto of Congress, except that it is uncertain whether it really desires systematically to control the actions of public administrators at all. Beginning with a legislative reorganization in 1946, Congress has sought to deal with the burgeoning federal bureaucracy primarily with three tools. First, it has added a vast number of new staff. In 1947, there were 182 committee staff in the House and 222 in the Senate. By 1983, the number had reached 1,970 in the House and 1,075 in the Senate.[40] Committee staff are attached to congressional committees and subcommittees. Their primary tasks are to aid in the drafting of legislation, assist the members of Congress during committee hearings, and engage in the oversight of administrative agencies in the executive branch. Although committee staff hold no formal tenure, many of them remain in office for long periods of time and develop working relationships with bureau chiefs in the executive branch. Committee staff often write the reports that accompany bills, and these provide useful guidance for administrators seeking to understand the legislature's intent.

The personal staffs of members of Congress have also grown immensely— from 590 in the Senate and 1,449 in the House in 1947 to 4,059 and 7,606 respectively in 1983.[41] Personal staff are attached to members of Congress and can be used as the member sees fit. In practice, most members of Congress organize them according to similar functions, including administrative assistance, legislative assistance, and clerical. Personal staff assist the members of Congress in developing legislation, responding to constituents, and engaging in oversight. In 1983, the combined total of personal and committee staff was 14,710, or about 27.5 staff per member.

A second tool for dealing with public administration has been the strength-

---

BOX 2–5 **Presidential Appointees Rate the Career Bureaucrats**

Administration	Competence*	Responsiveness*
Johnson	92%	89%
Nixon	88%	84%
Ford	80%	82%
Carter	81%	86%
Reagan	77%	78%

* Positive ratings
SOURCE: National Academy of Public Administration, Presidential Appointees Project, *Leadership in Jeopardy: The Fraying of the Presidential Appointments System* (Washington: NAPA, 1985). The survey was mailed to all living presidential appointees in these administrations whose address was known. The response rate was 56 percent.

ening of administrative units that are part of Congress. These have a variety of functions, including making the legislature more effective in dealing with executive branch agencies. Although there is nothing new in the use of legislative administrative agencies for this purpose, in recent years Congress has placed greater reliance upon them by establishing the Congressional Budget Office and strengthening the General Accounting Office. There is also an Office of Technology Assessment and a Congressional Research Service, both of which have some importance vis-à-vis the executive branch. To an extent, the growth in size and importance of Congress's administrative units matches the expansion of the Executive Office of the President, and presents similar problems. The Congressional Budget Office has a staff of approximately 225; the General Accounting Office, about 5,400; the Office of Technology Assessment has about 139 staff and uses some 2,000 outside experts; and the Congressional Research Service employs about 850.[42] Given the influence of committee staff, personal staff, and administrative staff, it is not the least bit implausible to ask of Congress, "Who's in charge here?"[43]

The third tool employed by Congress as a response to the growth of federal administration has been to develop greater committee and subcommittee specialization. Committees and subcommittees are where the work of Congress is done. There are roughly 38 standing committees and 142 subcommittees of these in the legislature.[44] Their subject matter jurisdiction covers virtually all of the areas of life with which government deals. These range from matters of nationwide importance, such as economic policy and defense, to highly specialized areas such as the production of specific crops. In fact, as Harold Seidman observes, the committee structure of Congress tends to match the administrative specialization found in the executive branch.[45] For every executive branch bureau, there is likely to be a committee or subcommittee.

Political Responses   These tools, along with Congress's legal, constitutional authority, could place the legislature in a position to exercise a great deal of direction over executive branch agencies. But such direction is not exercised in any consistent manner because, individually and collectively, most members of Congress have little incentive to engage in forceful oversight. One or two, such as Senator Proxmire of Wisconsin, are able to make a career of oversight, but for most, greater rewards lie elsewhere. Somewhere along the line members of Congress came to realize that the executive branch bureaucracy could be used to promote their own incumbency. As Morris Fiorina explains:

> . . . [T]he growth of an activist federal government has stimulated a change in the mix of congressional activities. Specifically, a lesser proportion of congressional effort is now going into programmatic activities [that is, legislation and oversight] and a greater proportion into pork-barrel and casework activities. As a result, today's congressmen make relatively fewer enemies and relatively more friends among the people of their districts. . . .
>
> Congress does not just react to big government—it creates it. All of Washington prospers. More and more bureaucrats promulgate more and more regulations and

dispense more and more money. Fewer and fewer congressmen suffer electoral defeat.[46]

The **pork barrel** to which Fiorina refers is, of course, the spending of federal funds in the member of Congress's home district. These funds can be used for a number of capital improvement and public works (infrastructure) programs as well as for federal facilities. Roads, bridges, river and harbor improvement, new postal facilities, and defense installations are some classic examples. To a large extent, these are "gifts" that Congress as a whole gives to each of its members. But the gifts, delivered through the executive branch administrative agencies, may be provided with more or less vigor, depending in part upon a member of Congress's stance on something the agency is seeking. After an exhaustive analysis, R. Douglas Arnold reported in a somewhat overly cautious tone that:

> . . . bureaucrats appear to allocate benefits strategically in an effort both to maintain and to expand their supporting coalitions. When it furthers their purposes, they broaden their program's geographic scope and increase the number of shares of benefits so that more congressmen can be brought into their supporting coalitions. When necessary, they allocate extra shares of benefits to leaders and to those who are crucial coalition members.[47]

It is hardly any wonder, then, that in 1975 "fewer than 75 of the 435 members of the House of Representatives [did] *not* have a major defense plant or a military installation in their district."[48] Under these conditions, it is obvious that there would be insufficient interest in Congress in exercising forceful and systematic oversight.

As Fiorina explains, **casework** presents another facet of the legislature's ability to use the federal bureaucracy to promote its own incumbency. "Casework" refers to the service rendered by members of Congress to constituents having some sort of problem with a federal agency or with filling out forms and the like for federal grants or benefits. In essence, casework is used to cut through bureaucratic red tape. It has emerged as a major congressional activity. In 1977, members of the House estimated their casework load at 10,000 cases per year. Senators put theirs at 1,000 to 70,000, depending on their states' populations.[49] Members of Congress actually advertise their willingness and ability to engage in it. More personal staff have been assigned to this function in recent years. In fact, the proportion of personal staff assigned to the home district has grown partly in accordance with the increasing casework activities of members of Congress. Casework is important to the member's desire to be reelected because it provides a favor which may presumably be repaid with a vote. For example, when a member of Congress helps someone receive social security benefits, he or she is likely to win at least one vote—perhaps more, depending upon the recipient's garrulousness and the size of the recipient's family and circle of friends and acquaintances. (See Box 2–6 for a congressman's solicitation of casework.)

Thus, the legislative response to the growth of public administration is

BOX 2–6 **A Congressman's "Dear Postal Patron" Letter**

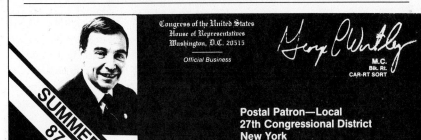

Congress of the United States
House of Representatives
Washington, D.C. 20515

Official Business

George C. Wortley

M.C.
Blk. Rt.
CAR-RT SORT

Postal Patron—Local
27th Congressional District
New York

Need Assistance? Have an Opinion?
I'm Eager to Listen and Help

Besides voting in Congress, one of my most important responsibilities is to help constituents solve problems that they encounter with any federal agency. . . .

Whenever you, members of your family, or friends have an opinion on any legislative issue or federal policy or program, please express your views in a letter to me and send it to my Washington office. **I'll give it my personal attention.**

Send your letter to:

Congressman George C. Wortley
229 Cannon House Office Building
Washington, D.C. 20515

Because my legislative duties require my presence in Washington on most weekdays throughout the year, the quickest way to get my help when experiencing any federal problem is to telephone, visit or write my district office in Syracuse. Should you experience a problem with the Internal Revenue Service, an undue delay in receiving a benefit check, or any difficulty with a federal agency, the members of my district staff are eager to try and solve your problems as quickly as possible.

Each member of my staff, in the 27th district and in Washington, is an authority in dealing with specific agencies. My staff helps constituents who encounter bureaucratic difficulties obtaining education grants, Social Security, pension and disability benefits. They help to resolve medicare, medicaid and workers' compensation claims. They provide advice to applicants seeking federal jobs, and assist veterans who are eligible for home loans and educational benefits. They help constituents in the military services to obtain emergency leaves and reassignments under certain hardship circumstances. Planning a visit to Washington? My staff can arrange White House and FBI tours. We fulfill requests for flags that have been flown over the U.S. Capitol as well as requests for federal documents. We also assist persons who seek small business loans and federal contracts.

If you live in Onondaga County and need assistance, please telephone or write my Syracuse district office. The telephone number is 423-5657. The office address is:

1269 Federal Building
Clinton Square
Syracuse, New York 13260

If you reside in Madison County, telephone 687-5027 or toll free, 1-800-462-8080. The address of my Madison County office is:

601 Lake Port Road
Chittenango, New York 13037

somewhat cynical and perverse. But that is often the reality of politics. Politicians, like most everyone, promote their own self-interest. Since the purpose of the constitutional system of checks and balances is to limit the extent to which they could successfully do this, such behavior should come as no surprise to Americans. Yet some may find the style in which Congress pursues its interests by using public bureaucracy to be troublesome. Leroy Rieselbach, author of *Congressional Reform*, provided the following reflection in 1986:

> For all the increased attention Congress has paid to gaining control of a "runaway" bureaucracy, it is not certain that much has been accomplished. More oversight activity—more hearings, more reports required, more legislative-bureaucratic contacts—has not necessarily meant more influence or at least not coordinated management of the executive agencies. This probably suits most members of Congress, who for policy or reelection reasons prefer power over some small segment of institutional control. It is not that members lack the capacity to exercise close oversight of the executive branch; rather they lack incentive to impair the cozy subgovernment relationships with executive agencies and interest groups, relationships that foster their electoral goals. . . .
>
> Constituency service, oversight, and other forms of nonpolicy representation afford electoral protection; policy analysis and innovation remain dangerous.[50]

The Courts: A Judicial Response to Contemporary Public Administration

The federal and state judiciaries have also reacted to the rise of public administrative power. It is common to find judges heavily involved in public administrative matters, such as the management of prisons, public mental health facilities, and schools. Judges have also begun to question public administrators' expertise and to second-guess their decisions with some frequency. To a very large extent, **judicial activism** of this kind has been decried as inappropriate, undemocratic, a threat to federalism and a breach of the separation of powers.[51] Yet it arises as a direct response to the growth of authority in the hands of public agencies.

One of the chief constitutional problems of the contemporary administrative state is that the separation of powers tends to collapse as more and more legislative and judicial activity takes place in public administrative agencies in the executive branch. In the abstract, to say that these agencies make rules, enforce their rules, and adjudicate challenges to those rules may hardly sound like a matter of grave constitutional concern. But when these powers are exercised over specific individuals or corporations, a sense of unfairness and injustice may be engendered. For example, suppose an agency makes rules for eligibility to receive welfare benefits, enforces these by holding predawn raids on the homes of recipients, and then adjudicates challenges to this method of enforcement.[52] Or suppose an agency makes rules for licensing cable TV, denies a license to a would-be broadcaster, and upon challenge holds that the agency does in fact have the authority to do exactly what it did?[53] Or, to take a final example, suppose a personnel agency refuses to hire a member of a minority group, who then challenges its personnel rules on the grounds that they are racially discriminatory, only to be told by the agency itself after it holds a hearing that the rules are valid and have been properly followed?[54] These are all based on actual cases, and when public administrators act as legislature, prosecutor, judge, and jury in ways that are harmful to individuals or businesses, the judiciary, which is often viewed as the constitutional guardian of individuals' rights, may find it difficult to sit idly by.

Yet, from the mid-1930s until the 1950s, this is largely what the courts did.[55] The federal judiciary, in particular, had been politically weakened by its opposition to the New Deal in the 1930s. After President F. D. Roosevelt threatened to "pack" the Supreme Court with justices more favorable to his approaches, the judiciary as a whole began to ignore the genuine constitutional problems posed by the vesting of legislative and judicial authority in executive branch administrative agencies.* By the 1950s, however, neither the power of public administrators over individual citizens nor the injustices they perpetrated could be ignored. For example, during the "Red scare" of the late 1940s and 1950s, there were cases of federal employees losing their jobs, accused of "disloyalty" for having been readers of the *New York Times*, favoring racial integration, believing in the desirability of sex before marriage, or even having intelligent or clever friends.[56] Until the 1960s and 1970s, welfare recipients were subject to all manners of harassments, and anyone seeking an occupational license seemed to be almost completely at the mercy of petty administrative tyrants.

Since the 1950s, when the federal courts rekindled their interest in the actions of public administrators, the judiciary as a whole has responded to the rise of administrative power primarily in four ways. It is extremely important that the public administrative student understand these, for they have a great deal to do with the contemporary legal approach and legal constraints on public administration, and they also explain how the courts have become a full-fledged partner in seeking to control the direction of the administrative state.[57]

The Strengthening and Articulation of Constitutional Rights   The federal judiciary has "created" or had occasion to declare new constitutional rights for individuals as they come into contact with public administrators in some contexts, and it has strengthened individuals' rights in others. Although treatises could be (and have been) written on these subjects, basically what the courts have done is to provide individuals greater constitutional protections when assuming the role of public employee or that of client of public administrative agencies. In both instances, the substantive, equal protection, and procedural constitutional rights of the individual have been strengthened considerably. Prior to the 1950s, clients' and public employees' rights were governed by the constitutional doctrine of privilege, which had the effect of denying them virtually any

---

* In *Bowsher* v. *Synar*, 92 L.Ed 2d 583 (1986), the Supreme Court did hold unconstitutional the vesting of executive functions in a legislative official (the comptroller of the currency).

protections against administrative infringements upon the civil rights and liberties normally held by United States citizens. If they wanted a public sector job or a benefit, such as public housing, they had to accept virtually any and all conditions attached to it. Individuals can no longer be denied welfare benefits because they do not meet an extended residency test, nor can they be denied unemployment compensation because their religious beliefs preclude their acceptance of work on Saturdays. They are also often entitled to "due process" when benefits are being withdrawn or denied. Similarly, the right of public employees to speak out in nonpartisan fashion on matters of political or administrative concern has been upheld, as has their right to belong (or not belong) to associations, including political parties and labor unions. Public employees also enjoy extensive constitutional procedural protections when facing dismissals for causes that would seriously damage their reputations, future employability, or infringe upon a property interest, such as tenure, that they hold in their jobs. The courts have also afforded greater protection to prisoners and to people confined to public mental health facilities. Indeed, the latter now have a constitutional right to treatment or training.[58]

Stricter Scrutiny of Administrative Decisions   Although this policy is somewhat haphazardly applied, the federal judiciary has begun to require public administrators to explain the basis of their policy-making decisions with greater precision. From the late 1930s until the 1970s, the courts tended to pay great deference to the expertise of public administrators and consequently rarely questioned their decisions on matters of a technical or policy matter. More recently, however, the judiciary has become somewhat dissatisfied with this approach. As Judge David Bazelon, a leading proponent of stricter judicial scrutiny of administrative decisions, explains:

> We stand on the threshold of a new era in the history of the long and fruitful collaboration of administrative agencies and reviewing courts. For many years, courts have treated administrative policy decisions with great deference, confining judicial attention primarily to matters of procedure. On matters of substance, the courts regularly upheld agency action, with a nod in the direction of the "substantial evidence" test, and a bow to the mysteries of administrative expertise. Courts occasionally asserted, but less often exercised, the power to set aside agency action on the ground that an impermissible factor had entered into the decision, or a crucial factor had not been considered. Gradually however, that power has come into more frequent use, and with it, the requirement that administrators articulate the factors on which they base their decisions.[59]

The United States Supreme Court followed this approach in *FTC* v. *Sperry & Hutchinson* (1972), when it set aside an FTC decision on the grounds that the agency's reasoning was illogical—one could not rationally proceed from its premise to its conclusion. The Court adhered to the same approach more recently in *Motor Vehicle Manufacturers Association* v. *State Farm* (1983).[60]

Public Law Litigation   In a far more complex development, the federal judiciary has altered the model of the traditional lawsuit in a fashion that makes it far easier for the courts to intervene in public administration. The new model is often called *public law litigation.*[61] Roger Cramton is among many who have noted its significance for public administration. He asks us to "consider in the context of the Leviathan [administrative] State two models of judicial review of administrative action."[62] One is "the traditional model . . . of a restrained and sober second look at what government has done that adversely affects a citizen. The controversy is bipolar in character, with two parties opposing each other; the issues are narrow and well-defined; and the relief is limited and obvious."[63] He views judicial review in this model as an essential corrective to the "tunnel vision in which particular values are advanced and others are ignored" by public administrators socialized into particular organizations and charged with implementing some possibly very narrow aspect of public policy. However, this model has been viewed by the judiciary as a whole as too limiting because it does not enable the courts to be proactive in their influence on public administration.

Consequently, as Cramton observes, a newer attitude toward public administration developed. As one federal judge expressed it, "If there is a serious problem, and the legislature and executive don't respond, the courts have to act."[64] In Cramton's words, this approach leads to:

> . . . a second model of judicial review that is growing in acceptance and authority. This model of the judicial role has characteristics more of general problem-solving than of dispute resolution. . . . [There is] a modern tendency to view courts as modern handymen—as jacks of all trades available to furnish the answer to whatever may trouble us. "What is life? When does death begin? How should we operate prisons and hospitals? Shall we build nuclear power plants, and if so, where? Shall the Concorde fly to our shores?"[65]

Three major features of the public law litigation model should be emphasized. First, it has been developed by the courts in conjunction with a relaxing of the requirements of *standing,* that is, the ability to bring a case. As a result, today many more individuals are in a position to challenge administrative action through litigation. In fact, Kenneth Davis, the dean of contemporary experts on administrative law, has observed that "[t]he present law of standing differs no more than slightly, if it differs at all, from the simple proposition that one who is hurt by governmental action has standing to challenge it."[66]

Second, the public law litigation model enables the judiciary to become directly involved in public management. For instance, in decreeing that public mental health facilities and prisons be brought up to constitutional standards, federal judges have used their powers to provide equitable relief to specify the maximum number of inmates or patients there can be per toilet and per shower; they have established minimum standards for square footage of space per individual in various rooms in such facilities; they have established permissible temperature ranges; they have directed the placement of guards; and, in one case, a judge even "ordered" that the management of the prison be improved immediately. The courts have also been heavily involved in public administration in other areas, including public schools.[67]

Third, judicial involvement in public administration has budgetary ramifications. Consequently, the public law litigation model enables judges to have an expanded impact on budgeting. For instance, in 1980, 48 percent of Boston's budgetary appropriations were "presided" over by federal and state judges seeking to reform aspects of public education, public housing, public personnel administration, jails, and care of the mentally retarded.[68]

The public law litigation model of judicial review is a powerful tool for enabling the judiciary to assume direction of many aspects of public administration. As Judge Bazelon has indicated, it helps place the judiciary in the role of partner with public administrators. Consequently, public administrators are likely to find themselves working with the judiciary in a way that was virtually unheard of only two decades ago. It is extremely important in appreciating this new development to bear in mind that the public law litigation model was not established by the legislature or executive branch; rather it was developed by the judiciary itself and is part of a broad concern with the power of public administrators.

Liability and Immunity   A final and equally dramatic aspect of the judiciary's response to the rise of the contemporary administrative state has been to reduce drastically public administrators' immunity from civil suits for damages arising out of the performance of their duties. Traditionally, under American common law and with some broad general support from constitutional law, public administrators were absolutely immune from such suits. The public administrator could not be sued for harming private parties in the course of his or her job— even if the harm were gratuitous or based upon a mistake. For example, a public administrator might libel a private individual, perhaps calling him dishonest, disloyal, or immoral. Under the doctrine of absolute immunity, the individual whose reputation and perhaps livelihood were damaged by such statements could not effectively seek some compensation from the public administrator through litigation. Similarly, a public administrator might abridge the constitutional rights of an individual, through racial discrimination, for instance. Again, the injured individual would have no effective suit for recompense against the public administrator. Or, as happens with some frequency, police, FBI, narcotics agents, and other law enforcement personnel might act in an overzealous manner, subjecting an individual to excessive brutality, humiliation, and invasion of privacy. Under the doctrine of absolute immunity, however, there would be virtually no effective recourse available to the injured party.

During the 1970s, the Supreme Court abandoned the prevailing approach of *absolute* immunity and substituted a *qualified* immunity. Although some public administrators—primarily those exercising judicial functions—still enjoy absolute immunity, today most public employees are potentially *personally* liable for any actions within the scope of their official duties that abridge the constitutional or federally protected legal rights of other individuals. In other words, the public administrator who unconstitutionally or illegally injures another person can be sued for damages, and if awarded, the public administrator is personally responsible for the settlement. It is important to grasp the connection between the changing presumption from immunity to liability and the creation of new constitutional rights for individuals vis-à-vis public administration, as discussed above. The Supreme Court has stated flatly that the greater liability of public administrators is a means of assuring that these officials will scrupulously avoid violating individuals' constitutional rights.[69] The Court has sought to assure that when in doubt, public administrators will err on the side of protecting constitutional rights. This approach is contained in the current standard for determining the scope of qualified immunity: in plain language, the public administrator is very likely to be personally liable if he or she knew or reasonably should have known that the official actions taken violated someone's constitutional or legal rights.[70]

The switch from a presumption of absolute immunity to a presumption of liability touched off a flurry of activity among public administrators. Nobody likes to be sued, or to pay damages out of his or her pocket. Many sought legal insurance. Some probably quit their jobs and sought private sector employment. Others have complained bitterly that this aspect of the judicial response to the administrative state has made their jobs almost impossible. They are afraid to take action and they are afraid to remain inactive. The problem is compounded by the severe economic plight of many agencies and political jurisdictions, which is coupled with the continuing requirement that they meet their obligations to various groups under federal law, whether these be schoolchildren, prisoners, mental patients, the handicapped, members of disadvantaged minority groups, or others. The Supreme Court is not oblivious to the problems involved, but it seems committed to the new standard of liability.

The public administrator is liable if he or she violates someone's constitutional rights. But constitutional rights, as they now exist, are not simply engraved in the Constitution. As former Supreme Court Justice Lewis Powell has pointed out, constitutional law is "what the courts say it is."[71] At any given time, individual constitutional rights are a reflection of the judiciary's values and interpretation of constitutional history. Standards of individual civil rights and liberties, equal protection, and due process are forever undergoing change. Prior to 1954, racial segregation in public schools was permissible, pupils could be expelled without any established or fair procedure, public employees could be fired for "wrong thoughts," mental patients and prisoners could be "warehoused" under incredibly harsh and brutal conditions, and citizens generally had little or no legal protection against public administrative action denying them various benefits or occupational licenses. Today, the picture has radically changed as a result of newer judicial views of what the Constitution requires. The courts have created the present standard of public administrators' liability to force public administrators to be responsive not only to declared constitutional law, but to constitutional values as well. The fact that there may be no specific precedent in the constitutional case law does not afford protection from liability today. The facts surrounding a public administrator's actions may never have arisen before.[72] They may never have been previously litigated. Or they may have been litigated at a time when the content of the constitutional law was clearly different. In such circumstances, the smart public administrator will not look simply to the most recent case, but rather will consider how the next one—the one he or she may be involved in—is likely to be decided. In order to do this effectively, public administrators must have a broad understanding of constitutional values and contemporary judicial philosophies. Public administrators must now be responsive to the judiciary's values, and therefore, the judiciary gains greater ability to exercise influence on the activities of the administrative state. (The relevance of constitutional values to public administration is discussed in Chapter 11.)

It should be evident that the judicial response to the rise of the contemporary administrative state considerably strengthens the legalistic approach to public administration. Public administrators find themselves working as partners with judges. They are under greater pressure to explain their decisions and actions to the courts. Knowledge of constitutional values, as expressed by the judiciary, becomes a positive job requirement for many public administrators. The partnership developed during the stewardship of Chief Justice Warren Burger, 1969–1986; and it is likely to persist even as the composition of the judiciary changes. It is grounded in the courts' institutional interest in maintaining influence over public administration and assuring that the actions of public administrators comport with the Constitution. All this while members of the chief executive's establishment are demanding sound management and members of the legislature are seeking favorable treatment for their constituents and districts. The job of the public administrator probably has never been more complicated.

Interest Groups

Organized interest groups have long been an important feature of American politics.[73] These organizations typically are established to represent the economic or social interests of a relatively well-defined group of people. There are literally thousands of such groups, representing everything from A (American Civil Liberties Union) to Z (zinc producers). Traditionally, they lobbied in the legislature in an effort to convince its members to sponsor or vote for a bill that would be of benefit to the group's members. Conversely, they might try to convince a legislator to oppose a policy that might be harmful to their interests. Although much criticism has been levied at lobbyists, essentially they exercise First Amendment rights to freedom of speech and association, and to petition the government for a redress of grievances. As long as bribery and other corruption does not take place, the activities of pressure groups can be viewed as valuable in informing policy makers of where important interests stand on any given matter.

Naturally, as public administrators became more involved in agenda setting and policy formulation, interest group lobbying became more common in the executive branch. Nowadays, public administrators interact with representatives of perhaps a thousand or so interest groups. In the early 1980s, about 970 "advisory committees," consisting of roughly 22,000 members and costing approximately $80 million, were attached to federal agencies.[74] While some of these had relatively broad concerns, the majority appear to have had a very narrow focus. For example, there was a Flue-Cured Tobacco Advisory Committee and a Distributors Advisory Committee for Georgia Peaches (see Box 2–7). The latter seems to have been dominated by the three largest shippers of that commodity.[75]

By 1972, the role of interest groups in pressing for their policy preferences was fully legitimized by the Federal Advisory Committee Act.[76] This statute

---

BOX 2–7 **Representation in Administration: Advisory Committees of the U.S. Department of Agriculture**

A comprehensive listing of the USDA's Advisory Committees is not feasible. But in 1976, Senator Patrick Leahy (D-VT) uncovered the following:

National Agricultural Research Planning Committee

Cascade Head Scenic Research Area Advisory Council

National Advisory Council on Safety in Agriculture

General Conference Committee of the National Poultry Improvement Plan

USDA Citizens' Advisory Committee on Civil Rights

National Advisory Council on Child Nutrition

National Arboretum Advisory Council

National Cotton Marketing Study Committee

Okanagan National Forest Grazing Advisory Board

Advisory Committee on State and Private Forestry

Expert Panel on Nitrates and Nitrosamines

Advisory Committee for the U.S. Meat Animal Research Center

Agricultural Research Policy Advisory Committee

Advisory Committee on Foreign Animal & Poultry Diseases

Advisory Committee on Grains, Wheat, Feed & Soybeans

Advisory Committee on Hog Cholera Eradication

Cattle Industry Advisory Committee

National Peanut Advisory Committee

National Tobacco Advisory Committee

National Rice Advisory Committee

Flue-Cured Tobacco Advisory Committee

National Cotton Advisory Committee

Hop Market Advisory Board

Raisin Advisory Board

SOURCE: Patrick J. Leahy, A Report on Advisory Committees in the Department of Agriculture and the Department of Defense (Washington, D.C.: Office of U.S. Senator Leahy, 1976).

---

started from the premise that such committees are a useful source of opinion and information. The main purpose of the act was to improve the quality of interest group interaction with public administrative agencies by assuring that the lobbying process was representative. An important part of this act was the requirement that the official meetings between advisory committees and public administrators be open to the public.

The evidence to date is sketchy, but it suggests that the Federal Advisory

Committee Act of 1972 has fallen short of its goals of assuring that the interaction of interest groups with public administrators be representative and open.[77] But the truly significant point is Congress's readiness to recognize that public administration should promote representativeness in its dealings with interest groups and, presumably, in its policy making. Traditionally, representation was the function of legislative bodies, such as the House of Representatives, not of executive branch agencies. This change captures the essence of the political approach to public administration that we discussed in the previous chapter. The lines between politics and administration become hopelessly blurred because "advisory committees are connected to administrative agencies, but they are established as frequently by Congress as by the agencies involved."[78] Moreover, as Henry Steck explains, "Congress and agencies look to advisory groups to introduce representational and participatory legitimacy into the administrative process."[79] Accordingly, "Advisory committees become a technique for reducing political uncertainty vis-à-vis clientele groups, stabilizing existing political relations, deflecting group opposition, securing group cooperation, and mobilizing political support."[80]

Interest groups not only interact with public administrators through the use of the advisory committee device, they also lobby outright and work indirectly through the legislature. In any event, however, the net result is often that the private interest group "captures" public power for its own use. Speaking of interest groups in general, Grant McConnell observed that an important

> . . . characteristic of American government is the conquest of segments of formal state power by private groups and associations. Although it would be impossible to state with any precision what proportion of the power of American government has been taken possession of in this way, it is certain that the proportion is substantial and that the control involved is considerable. . . .
>
> The pattern by which this condition has developed varies, but several steps in the process are common. Local elites have become organized nationally, usually on a federal basis, and have then been able to assume the exercise of public authority within significant areas of policy. The public agency with a particular clientele is a familiar phenomenon. However, it is but one of various types of administrative body that serve the purposes of narrow groups. . . . In return for special consideration of its interests, the private group supports and defends the agency from attack and from demands that the general executive policy be followed. . . .
>
> The function of policy-making is often turned over to the private group in what amounts to a delegation [of administrative power to it].[81]

Private interest groups capture public power by gaining an informal veto power over appointments to the political executive positions in administrative agencies. In practice, this means that the leadership of many agencies, especially regulatory commissions, will come directly from the industry being regulated. In some ways, this is necessary if the appointments are to be familiar with the industry in question, but it also tends to turn would-be regulation into "collusion," as Carol Greenwald observes.

A study of nine regulatory commissions [in the federal government] showed that between 1960 and 1975, 30 percent of the appointees came from the regulated industry; from 1970 to 1975, the figure increased to 50 percent. Personnel-industry ties are further reinforced by the practice of circular employment whereby regulatory employees learn the byways of government and then leave for lucrative jobs with the industry they once regulated. . . . Between 1960 and 1975, 37 percent of the eighty-five persons who left nine regulatory commissions went to work in the industries they had regulated. . . .

Inevitably human relationships turn regulation in the public interest into pro-tection of private interests. [82]

Greenwald's last point is especially important. [83] It suggests that public admin-istrators who interact with members of interest groups may have a difficult time in recognizing the wider public interest. McConnell also points out that this type of interaction with interest groups leads to discrimination against two types of interests. One is that of weak minorities, who are unable to organize and gain access to the system of representation through interaction with public adminis-trators. The other is the general public interest, which is too diffuse and not salient enough to any particular group to gather enough support to be actively promoted in this fashion.

The latter problem has been the target of *public interest groups*. A public interest group has been defined as "one that seeks a collective good, the achieve-ment of which will not selectively and materially benefit the membership or activists of the organization." [84] Yet when discussing public interest groups, it should not be forgotten that traditional interest groups often promote what they believe to be in the public interest. Therefore the distinction is not perfect. Among the organizations generally considered to be public interest groups are the Consumers Union, Common Cause, the League of Women Voters, and a variety of Public Interest Research Groups.

During the 1970s, public interest groups rapidly gained influence, often by working with public administrative agencies or for reform of administrative processes. They have employed the provisions of the Administrative Procedure Act of 1946 to gain access to bureaucratic decision making by filing views, data, and opinions concerning proposed agency rules and policy changes. They have also used the Freedom of Information Act of 1966 and the National Environ-mental Policy Act of 1969 as vehicles to influence and challenge the actions of public administrators. Although much of the process is technical, obscure, and highly legalistic, it is precisely through the day-to-day monitoring of the *Federal Register*, the submission of opinions, and the participation in public agency decision making that public interest groups can have a significant impact.

From the perspective of the public administrator, the interest group re-sponse to the rise of the administrative state has been to try, often with great success, to gain a voice in the policy-making activities of public agencies. Today, public agencies are viewed by interest groups as a focal point for representation. Indeed, it has been observed that "the bureaucracy is recognized by all interested groups as a major channel of representation to such an extent that Congress rightly feels the competition of a rival." [85]

Historically, interest groups, administrative agencies or bureaus, and congressional committees or subcommittees have frequently formed harmonious relationships called *iron triangles*, *cozy triangles*, and *subgovernments*.[86] These are considered the basic policy-making units for much of routine governance in the United States. In recent years, some of the "iron triangles" have been permeated by public interest groups and other outside parties concerned with very broad issues, such as the environment, nuclear power, civil rights, and aging policy. When this occurs, policy becomes influenced by "issue networks" of interested experts and organized groups. These networks subject administrative agencies and congressional (sub)committees to more diverse influences.

It is intriguing to consider whether the Reagan administration's emphasis on reducing domestic programs and shifting more of the responsibility for domestic matters to the states has deeply affected the roles of interest groups in public administration. One substantial study concluded that the "overall role of interest groups is unlikely to be weakened . . ."[87] but that more activity will shift to the state level in the future.

The Public

Promotion of the public interest is certainly a prime goal of contemporary public administration in the United States. But defining the public interest is often difficult. Public administrators, like all human beings, are limited in their ability to foresee all the immediate and long-term consequences of their policy choices. They are subject to a number of influences that may distort their perception and definition of the public interest. Public interest groups may come forth in an effort to correct this tendency, but they may also represent a rather select perspective. Their membership appears to be overwhelmingly composed of middle-class activists. So, the question arises, how can the public respond to the growth of administrative power?

To date the public's reaction to the rise of the administrative state appears to be partly one of recognition and resignation and partly one of finding new means of participating in government and influencing its directions. Chapter 10 is devoted to this subject. Here, it should be pointed out that public opinion regarding public administration is complex, divided, and perhaps even inconsistent. Despite political rhetoric that would suggest otherwise, public bureaucracy is by no means universally or consistently opposed. The public is aware that administrative agencies are now a powerful component of government and it recognizes that the citizenry is dependent upon them. Politically, the public seems to demand candidates who can "manage" bureaucracy. Sometimes it favors cutting back on public administrative activities. However, there is limited support for abandoning a host of regulatory functions intended to protect the public's safety, including aircraft and food and drug inspection, for example. As a practical matter, public administrators may accurately view public opinion as both a constraint on and a stimulus for a variety of administrative actions. This is precisely a point made by Woodrow Wilson, a century ago, in his famous essay entitled "The Study of Administration": "In order to make any advance at all we must instruct and persuade a multitudinous monarch called public opinion."[88]

Political Parties

Historically, there has been a strong link between political parties and public administration.[89] In many countries, including the United States, political parties promoted the growth of large-scale public administration as a means of creating and securing patronage positions for their members. During the nineteenth century, this **spoils system** was instrumental in both the development of American political parties and in the increasing size of several public agencies. However, patronage politics led to widespread political corruption and administrative inefficiency and mismanagement. In the effort to remove the pernicious effects of partisan politics from public administration through civil service reforms, political parties were weakened, in an organizational sense.

Civil service reforms mandating the use of merit systems were instituted in the federal government and some states and cities in the 1880s. The rationale behind these was that public administration was essentially a field of business, as Woodrow Wilson wrote in 1887, and consequently ought to be run according to businesslike, managerial principles. Whoever heard of a business firing its employees every four years on the grounds that they held their places long enough and ought to give someone else a turn, the reformers asked with indignation and derision. There is no doubt that merit-oriented reforms vastly improved the honesty, morality, efficiency, economy, and administrative effectiveness of public agencies. But they also weakened the political parties.

The parties' first response was to turn to the rising industrial sector for support. It seemed that patronage could be replaced by large-scale financial donations—in return for various policy and other considerations, of course. Soon the Senate became known as the millionaires' club and the politics associated with patronage and the "common man" of Andrew Jackson's day rapidly receded. Yet reliance on large monetary contributions also caused corruption, and from the turn of the century until the 1920s, several political reforms were inspired by the Progressive movement. Especially important among these was the institution of the primary election and the promotion of restrictions on the political activities of public employees. Such reforms were aimed at destroying political machines and political bossism. Although largely successful in this regard, they also further weakened the parties. Indeed, by the 1930s and 1940s, when the federal government passed the Hatch Acts, regulating the political activities of federal and some categories of state and local public employees, some members of Congress argued that limiting the participation of such employees in political conventions would lead to the total destruction of political parties.

Reforms along these lines have had the impact of not only weakening the political parties but also of freeing public administration from their influence and control. Merit systems prevent partisan intrusion in the selection, assignment, promotion, dismissal, and general treatment of public employees. In fact, it is actually illegal to ask a federal civil servant or an applicant for such a position what political party he or she belongs to. Political officials have long complained of the inability to take charge of administrative operations that results from the lack of power to make civil service assignments on a partisan basis. They feel that members of the opposition party are forever subverting their electoral mandates. In at least one sense, though, public administrators may be nonpartisan, as former President Gerald Ford explains: "There are bureaucratic fiefdoms out in the states or in various regions [that] have been disregarding Presidents for years, both Democratic and Republican."[90] Sometimes this leads politicians to engage in illegal maneuvers or questionable practices to get around "all the civil service restrictions." On balance, however, the political community has opted for politically neutral public personnel administration as opposed to pronounced partisan intrusion in public administration. It is interesting to note in this context that in the 1976 case of *Elrod* v. *Burns*[91] and later in *Branti* v. *Finkel* (1980)[92] the Supreme Court held that patronage dismissals from the public service can be unconstitutional infringements upon the public employee's First and Fourteenth Amendment rights and that the government bears the burden of showing that partisanship is positively related to on-the-job performance when seeking to make such dismissals (see Box 2–8). In this area, then, we see both the conflict and the congruence of managerial, political, and legal considerations pertaining to public administration.

Are the political parties totally powerless to influence public administration under these conditions? The answer is no, but their power is certainly limited. Recent reforms have been aimed at enabling political executives to exercise greater influence over top level career public administrators. (These reforms are discussed in Chapter 5.) Political parties also remain important in legislatures and may sponsor various administrative reorganizations. But when all is said and done, where strong merit systems prevail, political parties are a relatively weak channel for exercising control over public administration. Of course, in the places where political machines and bossism still prevail, parties would continue to maintain a heavy presence in administrative affairs.

CONCLUSION

The American administrative state has developed in response to a host of factors, including political, managerial, and legalistic concerns. There is no doubt that the growth of public administration has enabled governments to exercise greater influence over the society and the economy. However, contemporary public administration poses several problems. One is the question of according to which principles public administration should be organized—political, managerial, legal, or in what combination of these? Another problem is whether the administrative state can be adequately controlled by elected public officials or political processes in general. Yet another concerns the proper role of the judiciary in public administration and whether contemporary public administrators can harmoniously incorporate the judiciary's constitutional values. The presidential, legislative, and judicial responses to the rise of the administrative state have certainly enhanced their influence over it. But they have also promoted the development of a large Executive Office of the President that is hard to manage effectively, a proliferation of subcommittees and staff in Congress that has

---

BOX 2–8 **The "Unconstitutionalizing" of Political Patronage**

In *Elrod* v. *Burns* (1976), the Supreme Court held that patronage dismissals of rank-and-file employees of the Cook County, Illinois, Sheriff's Office were unconstitutional. Justice Brennan announced the judgment of the Court. He expressed the view that ". . . patronage dismissals severely restrict political belief and association. Though there is a vital need for government efficiency and effectiveness, such dismissals are on balance not the least restrictive means for fostering that end. There is also a need to insure that policies which the electorate has sanctioned are effectively implemented. That interest can be fully satisfied by limiting patronage dismissals to policy-making positions. . . . [A]ny contribution of patronage dismissals to the democratic process does not suffice to override their severe encroachment on First Amendment freedoms." In dissent, Justice Powell admonished that "history and long prevailing practice across the country support the view that patronage hiring practices make a sufficiently substantial contribution to the practical functioning of our democratic system to support their relatively modest intrusion on First Amendment interests. The judgment today unnecessarily constitutionalizes another element of American life. . . ." *Branti* v. *Finkel* (1980) went even further in making patronage dismissals unconstitutional. A majority of the Supreme Court held that since such dismissals infringe on First Amendment rights, ". . . the ultimate inquiry is not whether the label 'policymaker' or 'confidential' fits a particular position; rather, the question is whether the hiring authority can demonstrate that party affiliation is an appropriate requirement for the effective performance of the public office involved." The standard announced in *Branti* will be a tough one, for those who would practice patronage on a widespread basis, to meet.

---

fragmented the legislative process and made it difficult for the institution to act in a coordinated fashion, and a judiciary that is often heavily involved in the thicket of administrative micromanagement. Overarching all of these concerns is the major issue of the public's relationship to government in the contemporary administrative age. Finally, although not stressed here, the cost of running the administrative state has become increasingly problematic—hence the widespread desire to reduce taxes and deficits and to balance budgets.

If the political community knew how to solve some of these problems and were willing to do so, American politics would be considerably different. In truth, however, lasting solutions have been elusive and some of the problems consequently appear intractable. It is important that the student of public administration recognize this, because in large part it is these quandaries that make public administration both interesting and frustrating. Certainly public administration provides valuable services in efficient ways. But just as surely we must strive for ways to improve it further. The nation has recently entered into a period of seeking to reform the character of public bureaucracies, but reform is only advancing in a slow and incremental fashion.

NOTES

1. Lester Salamon, "The Rise of Third Party Government: Implications for Public Management," in Donald Kettl, *Third Party Government and the Public Manager* (Washington, D.C.: National Academy of Public Administration, 1987), p. 12.
2. James Q. Wilson, "The Rise of the Bureaucratic State," *The Public Interest*, 41 (Fall 1975): 77–103.
3. Ibid., p. 82.
4. In the mid-1980s there were about 1,085,000 employed in the Department of Defense and some 750,000 in the Postal Service. If the independent Veterans Administration were included in the defense establishment, approximately 250,000 employees would have to be added.
5. Donald Warwick, *A Theory of Public Bureaucracy* (Cambridge, Mass.: Harvard University Press, 1975), pp. 7–8.
6. Wilson, "The Rise of the Bureaucratic State."
7. Ibid., pp. 96–97.
8. Lawrence Friedman, *A History of American Law* (New York: Simon & Schuster, 1973), p. 458.
9. James Freedman, *Crisis and Legitimacy* (New York: Cambridge University Press, 1978).
10. Walter Adams and James Brock, "Why Flying Is Unpleasant," *New York Times*, August 6, 1987, p. 27A.
11. Max Weber, *From Max Weber: Essays in Sociology*, trans. and ed. by H. H. Gerth and C. W. Mills (New York: Oxford University Press, 1958), p. 228.
12. Honoré de Balzac, *Les Employées*, 1836; quoted in Martin Albrow, *Bureaucracy* (New York: Praeger, 1970), p. 18.
13. Quoted in Grant McConnell, *Private Power and American Democracy* (New York: Knopf, 1966), p. 286.
14. Wallace Sayre, ed., Introd., *The Federal Government Service* (Englewood Cliffs, N.J.: Prentice-Hall, 1965), p. 2.
15. Ibid.
16. Thomas E. Cronin, *The State of the Presidency* (Boston: Little, Brown, 1975), p. 23; quoting Daniel Patrick Moynihan.
17. Ibid., p. 27.
18. Ibid., p. 28.
19. Ibid., p. 30; quoting Burton Sapin, *The Making of the United States Foreign Policy* (Washington, D.C.: Brookings, 1966), p. 90.
20. James Bryce, *The American Commonwealth* (New York: Putnam, 1959 [originally published in 1888]).
21. Richard Neustadt, *Presidential Power* (New York: Wiley, 1969), p. 9.
22. Quoted in George C. Edwards III and Stephen J. Wayne, *Presidential Leadership* (New York: St. Martin's, 1985), p. 351.
23. Harold M. Barger, *The Impossible Presidency* (Glenview, Ill.: Scott, Foresman, 1984), pp. 144–145, 166.
24. Robert Pear, "The Policy Wars: Those to Whom 'Battle Royal' Is Nothing New," *New York Times*, July 28, 1987, p. A14.
25. Humphrey's Executor v. U.S., 295 U.S. 602 (1935), is the classic example.
26. Barger, *Impossible Presidency*, p. 28.
27. Cronin, *State of the Presidency*, Chap. 5, presents a valuable description of the growth of the EOP. See also David Nachmias and David H. Rosenbloom, *Bureaucratic Government, USA* (New York: St. Martin's, 1980), chap. 4. Margaret J.

Wyszomirski, "The De-Institutionalization of Presidential Staff Agencies," *Public Administration Review*, 42 (September/October 1982): 448–458, discusses flexible organizational arrangements in the EOP.

28. Steven Roberts, "Reagan Says Aides Had Duty to Tell Him of Fund Diversion," *New York Times*, August 13, 1987, pp. A1, A8.
29. Stephen Wayne, *The Legislative Presidency* (New York: Harper and Row, 1978), pp. 59–60.
30. As transcribed in the *New York Times*, July 16, 1987, pp. A1, A12.
31. Roberts, "Reagan Says . . . ," *New York Times*, August 13, 1987, p. A1.
32. CBS News/New York Times Poll, July 17, 1987 Release, question 12.
33. Edwards and Wayne, *Presidential Leadership*, p. 368.
34. Richard Nathan, "The Reagan Presidency in Domestic Affairs," in Fred I. Greenstein, ed., *The Reagan Presidency: An Early Assessment* (Baltimore: Johns Hopkins University Press, 1983), p. 71.
35. Joseph W. Bartlett and Douglas N. Jones, "Managing a Cabinet Agency: Problems of Performance at Commerce," *Public Administration Review*, 34 (January/February 1974): 63–64.
36. Nathan, "The Reagan Presidency" in Greenstein, ed., *The Reagan Presidency*, p. 71.
37. Ibid.
38. Ibid., pp. 48–81. See also Laurence Lynn, Jr., "The Reagan Administration and the Renitent Bureaucracy," in Lester Salamon and Michael Lund, eds., *The Reagan Presidency and the Governing of America* (Washington, D.C.: Urban Institute Press, 1985), pp. 339–370, especially pp. 345–348.
39. Stephen J. Wayne, "Politics Instead of Policy," in Salamon and Lund, eds., *The Reagan Presidency and the Governing of America*, p. 179. See also Hugh Heclo, *A Government of Strangers* (Washington, D.C.: The Brookings Institution, 1977), for a classic discussion of political executives in the pre-Reagan years.
40. Roger Davidson and Walter Oleszek, *Congress and Its Members*, 2d ed. (Washington, D.C.: CQ Press, 1985), p. 241.
41. Ibid.
42. Ibid., pp. 255–257.
43. Michael Malbin, "Congressional Committee Staffs: Who's in Charge Here," *The Public Interest*, 47 (Spring 1977): 36.
44. Davidson and Oleszek, *Congress and Its Members*, p. 210.
45. Harold Seidman, *Politics, Position, and Power*, 2nd ed. (New York: Oxford University Press, 1975), esp. pp. 38–68.
46. Morris Fiorina, *Congress—Keystone of the Washington Establishment* (New Haven, Conn.: Yale University Press, 1977), pp. 46, 49.
47. R. Douglas Arnold, *Congress and the Bureaucracy* (New Haven, Conn.: Yale University Press, 1979), p. 207.
48. Thomas Dye and L. Harmon Zeigler, *The Irony of Democracy*, 3rd ed. (North Scituate, Mass.: Duxbury Press, 1975), p. 331.
49. Davidson and Oleszek, *Congress and Its Members*, p. 134.
50. Leroy Rieselbach, *Congressional Reform* (Washington, D.C.: CQ Press, 1986), pp. 104, 122.
51. See David H. Rosenbloom, *Public Administration and Law* (New York: Marcel Dekker, 1983), and James D. Carroll, "The New Juridical Federalism and the Alienation of Public Policy and Administration," *American Review of Public Administration*, 16 (1982): 89–105.
52. See Parrish v. Civil Service Commission, 425 P.2d 233 (1967).
53. United States v. South Western Cable Co., 392 U.S. 157 (1968).

54. See Robert Vaughn, *The Spoiled System* (New York: Charterhouse, 1975), for an analysis of this problem.
55. Martin Shapiro, *The Supreme Court and Administrative Agencies* (New York: Free Press, 1968).
56. See David H. Rosenbloom, *Federal Service and the Constitution* (Ithaca, N.Y.: Cornell University Press, 1971), chap. 6.
57. The following discussion is based on Rosenbloom, *Public Administration and Law*, and his article "The Judicial Response to the Rise of the Administrative State," *American Review of Public Administration*, 15 (Spring 1981): 29–51.
58. See Rosenbloom, *Public Administration and Law*, and the following cases: Shapiro v. Thompson, 394 U.S. 618 (1969); Sherbert v. Verner, 374 U.S. 398 (1963); Hobbie v. Unemployment Appeals Commission, 55 Law Week 4208 (1987); Goldberg v. Kelly, 397 U.S. 254 (1970); Pickering v. Board of Education, 391 U.S. 563 (1968); Rankin v. McPherson, 55 Law Week 5019 (1987); Cleveland Board of Education v. Loudermill, 470 U.S. 532 (1985); Wyatt v. Stickney, 325 F. Supp. 781 (1971); Youngberg v. Romeo, 457 U.S. 307 (1982).
59. Environmental Defense Fund v. Ruckelshaus, 439 F2d 584, 597 (1971).
60. FTC v. Sperry & Hutchinson Co., 405 U.S. 233 (1972); Motor Vehicle Mfg. Ass'n. v. State Farm, 463 U.S. 29 (1983).
61. See Abram Chayes, "The Role of the Judge in Public Law Litigation," *Harvard Law Review*, 89 (1976): 1281–1316.
62. Roger Cramton, "Judicial Lawmaking and Administration in the Leviathan State," *Public Administration Review*, 36 (September/October 1976), p. 552.
63. Ibid.
64. Ibid., p. 554.
65. Ibid., p. 552.
66. Kenneth Culp Davis, *Administrative Law and Government* (St. Paul, Minn.: West, 1975), p. 72.
67. Rosenbloom, *Public Administration and Law*, chap. 5.
68. Robert Turner, "Governing from the Bench," *The Boston Globe Magazine*, November 8, 1981, pp. 12 ff.
69. Carlson v. Green, 446 U.S. 14, 21 (1980).
70. See Rosenbloom, *Public Administration and Law*, chap. 6, for a more detailed discussion.
71. Owen v. City of Independence, 445 U.S. 622, 669 (1980).
72. See Pembaur v. Cincinnati, 89 L. Ed. 2d 452 (1986), for an example.
73. See Carol Greenwald, *Group Power* (New York: Praeger, 1977), for a comprehensive discussion. See also Samuel Krislov and David H. Rosenbloom, *Representative Bureaucracy and the American Political System* (New York: Praeger, 1981).
74. Henry J. Steck, "Politics and Administration: Private Advice for Public Purpose in a Corporatist Setting," in Jack Rabin and James Bowman, eds., *Politics and Administration* (New York: Marcel Dekker, 1984), pp. 158, 160.
75. Krislov and Rosenbloom, *Representative Bureaucracy*, p. 95.
76. PL 92-463, 86 *Stat.* 770, Oct. 6, 1972.
77. Krislov and Rosenbloom, *Representative Bureaucracy*, pp. 93–97.
78. Steck, "Politics and Administration," in Rabin and Bowman, eds., *Politics and Administration*, p. 159.
79. Ibid., p. 161.
80. Ibid.
81. Grant McConnell, *Private Power and American Democracy*, pp. 162–163.

82. Greenwald, *Group Power*, p. 230.
83. Randall Ripley and Grace Franklin, *Congress, the Bureaucracy, and Public Policy*, 3d ed. (Homewood, Ill.: Dorsey Press, 1984), pp. 11–12 concur.
84. Jeffrey Berry, quoted in Krislov and Rosenbloom, *Representative Bureaucracy*, p. 170.
85. Norton Long, "Power and Administration," in Francis Rourke, ed., *Bureaucratic Power in National Politics* (Boston: Little, Brown, 1965), pp. 17–18.
86. Ripley and Franklin, *Congress, the Bureaucracy, and Public Policy*, 3rd ed., esp. pp. 10–12.
87. Harold Wolman and Fred Teitelbaum, "Interest Groups and the Reagan Presidency," in Salamon and Lund, eds., *The Reagan Presidency and the Governing of America*, p. 329.
88. Woodrow Wilson, "The Study of Administration," *Political Science Quarterly*, 56 (December 1941), p. 491. Originally published in 1887.
89. A thoughtful discussion in the U.S. context can be found in Herbert Storing, "Political Parties and the Bureaucracy," in Robert A. Goldwin, ed., *Political Parties, USA* (Chicago: Rand McNally, 1964).
90. Edwards and Wayne, *Presidential Leadership*, p. 360.
91. 427 U.S. 347 (1976).
92. 445 U.S. 506 (1980).

ADDITIONAL READING

JACOBY, HENRY. *The Bureaucratization of the World*. Berkeley, Calif.: University of California Press, 1973.

LOWI, THEODORE J. *The End of Liberalism*, 2nd ed. New York: Norton, 1979.

NACHMIAS, DAVID, AND DAVID H. ROSENBLOOM. *Bureaucratic Government, USA*. New York: St. Martin's Press, 1980.

RIPLEY, RANDALL, AND GRACE FRANKLIN. *Congress, the Bureaucracy, and Public Policy*, 3rd ed. Homewood, Ill.: Dorsey Press, 1984.

ROURKE, FRANCIS E., ED. *Bureaucratic Power in National Policy Making*, 4th ed. Boston: Little, Brown, 1986.

TAYLOR, CHARLES. *Why Governments Grow*. Beverly Hills, Calif.: Sage Publications, 1983.

WHITE, LEONARD D. *The Federalists; The Jeffersonians; The Jacksonians; The Republican Era*; paperback editions. New York: The Free Press, 1965.

WOLL, PETER. *American Bureaucracy*, 2nd ed. New York: Norton, 1977.

STUDY QUESTIONS

1. The current reach of public administration is considered too broad by some people. Can you identify public administrative functions and programs that you think deal with matters that should be left up to private individuals, families, and/or private groups? What distinguishes these activities from those you think are appropriately dealt with through public administration?

2. Are there areas of social or economic life that you believe require more governmental involvement through public administration?

3. Think about a recent political campaign with which you are familiar. Did the candidates express concern with matters of public administration? If so, from what perspectives? How might a practicing public administrator respond to their campaign statements?

CHIMAYO
COMMUNITY CENTER
A COOPERATIVE PROJECT WITH
N.M. NATURAL RESOURCE DEPT.
& U.S. DEPARTMENT OF INTERIOR
SANTA FE COUNTY COMMISSION
BENNIE CHAVEZ CHRMN.
JOHN SENA MEM.
J. MARTINEZ MEM.

CHAPTER 3

Federalism and Intergovernmental Relations:

The Structure of the American Administrative State

Governing the United States is one of the most complicated activities in the world. The nation has some 82,000 governments within its boundaries. Their relationships are sometimes cooperative, sometimes competitive, and sometimes even conflictual. Public administrators often face the challenging task of coordinating the programs of several governments with one another in a variety of related policy areas. This chapter explores federalism, intergovernmental relations, and the administrative structure of the major forms of governments found in the United States. The maze of governments form a substantial part of the political and legal environments in which public administrators work.

The complex and fragmented nature of the American administrative state is partly a response to the growing complexity of economic and social life but also has roots in the system of federalism itself. Patriotic spirits are fond of referring to the United States as the "land of the free and the home of the brave." But by generally accepted count, the land of the free is regulated and served by some 82,000 governments—and it does indeed take some bravery to support these governments financially and to find one's way through the maze of complicated interrelationships. Although we sometimes think of the separation of powers as being manifested in the division of governmental authority among legislative, executive, and judicial branches, authority and jurisdiction are also divided up among a national government, 50 state governments, over 3,000 counties, about 19,000 municipalities, 1,400 New England towns, 15,300 townships, 14,900 school districts, and 28,600 special districts.[1] Indeed, the management, politics, and laws of federalism and intergovernmental relationships are so perplexing that they have emerged as areas of activity and study to which some have devoted their working lives. The typical citizen escapes with a lesser burden—on average he or she works two months a year just to pay for state and local governments.[2] Obviously, governmental decentralization and fragmentation are key areas of concern for public administrators and a feature of governance that they sometimes find quite frustrating.

WHY FEDERALISM?

Federalism is a common feature of contemporary nation-states. It is the division of political authority between a central government and state or provincial governments. Canada, Australia, Nigeria, the Soviet Union, and the United States are leading examples. In each of these nations, there are states, provinces, or "republics" (as they are called in the USSR) that have a substantial measure of legal or constitutional **sovereignty** (supreme political authority). However, in each case, these units of government are also subordinate in many major legal/constitutional respects to a central government. Federalism stands in contrast to "unitary" political systems in which there are not quasi-sovereign governmental units interposed between citizenry and the national government. England and Israel are examples. In such nations, all sovereignty is exercised by the national government, which in democracies is viewed as the agent of the people, who are the sovereign. Unitary governments may delegate administrative and political authority to municipalities or other governmental bodies, but these bodies have no sovereignty and no authority other than that which is given to them by the national government. Delegations of this type constitute political and administrative "decentralization," but not federalism.

Federalism represents a political solution to a vexing political problem. There are obvious advantages to the formation of *large* nation-states, such as the United States and the Soviet Union. Such nations are likely to be powerful economically and militarily. They will be more likely to mobilize effectively large-scale human effort to pursue their vision of "the good life" and the just society. They are also likely to have a greater human and physical resource base than smaller nations. Their large scale may also enable them to develop more vigorous economies within their territories. There is also likely to be less internal strife among the units of a single nation than there would be if that nation were divided into separate countries having full sovereignty and autonomy. These points can be illustrated by imagining for a moment that the United States were not "one nation, indivisible," but rather fifty separate, fully autonomous, and fully sovereign nations, each with its own armed forces and system of tariffs. Clearly our economic, military, and civic lives would be radically different under such circumstances.

But for all the advantages that large size can bring to nation-states, it can also have some important drawbacks. The main ones concern representation and keeping the parts together. These two concerns are often related. Many federal nations are "compound" political communities, that is, they are made up of *territorially based* and heterogeneous ethnic, tribal, racial, religious, linguistic, or other social groups imbued with different cultural values. Canada is a familiar example. A majority of the population of the province of Quebec is ethnically French-Canadian and religiously Catholic. No other of Canada's ten provinces has a majority that uses the French language as its native tongue. The cultural values held by Québecois also differ markedly in some respects from those of other Canadians. No other province seems to identify so strongly with a previous period in Canadian history. No other province identifies so strongly with France and is inundated with French pop culture, such as films and music. Citizens of Quebec have often felt discriminated against when traveling or living in English-speaking Canadian provinces. All things being equal, therefore, one might expect Quebec to be a separate nation.

But all things are not equal. There are clear advantages to Canada as a whole, including Quebec, in forming a single large nation in a peaceful way and without cultural repression. The solution, therefore, is to create a federal system that allows Quebec a good deal of sovereignty and autonomy in representing its population and protecting and developing its particular culture. Thus, for instance, before bilingualism was the rule, Quebec made French its official provincial language. The province has control over its educational system, through which values are inculcated. At the same time, however, a federal system must provide the national government with enough authority to assure that the various provinces do not turn into separate nation-states. At a minimum, this requires that the national government have responsibility for defense, foreign affairs, and a good measure of economic integration of the nation as a whole. In practice, of course, finding the appropriate mix of national versus provincial or state sovereignty can be very difficult. For example, in the 1970s Quebec developed a politically important separatist movement that sought to secede from Canada or to have the nation's political structure revised to provide the province with far greater legal/constitutional authority. Moreover, as difficult as the Canadian case is, it is hardly as complex as the situation of the Soviet Union. There, a plethora of ethnic and religious groups are involved, including Russians, Ukrainians, Latvians, Lithuanians, Estonians, Georgians, and several Central Asian and

Turkish populations. A multitude of languages is spoken and, although the Soviet national government opposes it, a number of religions are practiced. To a large extent, these diverse groups are organized into Soviet Republics, which are the political subunits of the Soviet Union as a whole.

Federalism in compound nations provides a measure of representation and political autonomy for ethnic and other territorially based cultural groups. Yet a large nation might also turn to federalism as a means of providing representation to a homogeneous population or one whose heterogeneity is not territorially based. The United States is a leading example here. In large part the United States relies upon federalism, due to the historical pattern of its early settlement by Europeans. Thirteen colonies were carved out and chartered. Initially there was some important religious and linguistic diversity among them. But soon English became the common language and a sense of being "American" developed. During the Revolutionary War, a *confederal* government was formed. Under this approach, the former colonies, now *states*, had a great deal of independent authority. A few years after the conclusion of the war, the current federal government was established. The main impetus for moving away from the confederal government seems to have been economic and military: trade among the states faced a number of barriers and the national government seemed too weak to deal with military threats posed by various European nations and Indian tribes.

Even if the states had no history of independence from one another, the large geographic size of the territories claimed by the United States might have been a barrier to the formation of a unitary nation in 1789, when the present Constitution was put into effect. Communication and the exercise of national authority on a local level would have been difficult. But the Founding Fathers were also concerned with another problem. How could a large population be represented by a single government? To be responsive, and effective, it was thought, elected or appointed representatives must know the people they are representing. But how many people can one individual know? A single government seeking to represent a large population would be confronted with a dilemma. On the one hand, a large number of representatives could be elected. But then the national legislature would have to be very large, perhaps too large to be effective. Alternatively, a smaller number of representatives could be relied upon. This would make the legislature manageable, but it would also tend to detract from the quality of representation since one individual would be responsible for representing a large number of citizens.

In order to accommodate the entrenched belief in state sovereignty and to deal with the representational problem, the Framers invented a form of federalism incorporating three central features. First, the states would retain sovereignty in some spheres, and more states would eventually be created from the lands under national control. The Constitution expressly identifies the powers vested in the national government, and the Tenth Amendment, ratified in 1791, specifies that "The powers not delegated to the United States by the Constitution, nor prohibited by it to the States, are reserved to the States respectively, or to the people." Article IV protects the territorial integrity of the states by prohibiting their division or combination without the consent of their own legislatures (and Congress). (But the territory itself may be in dispute. See Box 3–1.) Second, a bicameral Congress was created in which one chamber, the Senate, provides each state with equal representation. The Senate also has the power to approve treaties, which is in part a vestige of the sovereignty of the states. Third, the national government would have direct power over citizens, rather than having to act upon them through the state governments; accordingly, the citizenry would be represented directly in the House of Representatives. (In yet another vestige of state sovereignty, prior to the ratification of the Seventeenth Amendment in 1913, the Senate was not directly elected by the population; instead, senators were appointed by the state legislatures.)

This arrangement goes a long way toward resolving the representational dilemma. By vesting a good deal of political authority in small governmental units (the states), it enhances the likelihood that governmental representatives will actually represent the will of the people on important matters. For example, the states have constitutional authority to provide public education, public safety, and roads. They have authority to tax, to zone, to define crimes and punishments, to charter corporations, and to engage in a great many other functions. Nowadays, some of these functions are provided in conjunction with the federal government. But historically, the solution to the representational problem was thought to be allowing local people to control the governance of local matters. Sometimes this idea is discussed in terms of "grass-roots" democracy and/or "public choice" theory. The idea that smaller political jurisdictions are better able than larger ones to respond to the preferences of their citizens has evoked great support throughout United States history. It is discussed further toward the end of this chapter. Interestingly, this approach would also provide a special cultural group with a considerable amount of autonomy if it were able to gain political dominance of a state. The Mormons in Utah are the leading example. However, since the national government can act directly on the people and seek to represent them, the chances for separatist movements to develop and be successful in a federal system such as the United States are reduced. This has been especially true since the adoption of the post-Civil War constitutional amendments. The Fourteenth and Fifteenth, in particular, promoted national integration by giving the national government direct responsibility for protecting the civil rights and liberties of individuals against infringement by the states.

ADMINISTRATIVE DECENTRALIZATION

Federalism is a form of *political* decentralization. It divides political authority and sovereignty between the national government and states, provinces, or similar governmental bodies. Hence, political authority is not centralized in the national government but shared by other governmental units. The reasons for this arrangement are overwhelmingly political, but they are also of administrative concern. Here, the managerial perspective on public administration exerts its influence.

BOX 3–1 **One Nation, Indivisible, with Many Borders**

[469 US 504]
UNITED STATES

v

MAINE et al. (Rhode Island and New York Boundary Case)

469 US 504, 83 L Ed 2d 998, 105 S Ct 992

[No. 35 Original]

Argued November 26, 1984. Decided February 19, 1985.

Decision: Long Island Sound and Block Island Sound held to constitute juridical bay under Convention on Territorial Sea and Contiguous Zone.

SUMMARY

The United States brought an action against the states that border the Atlantic Ocean, invoking the original jurisdiction of the United States Supreme Court, in order to determine whether the United States had exclusive rights to the seabed and subsoil underlying the ocean beyond 3 geographical miles from each state's coastline. That action resulted in a determination that the states held interests in the seabeds only to a distance of 3 geographical miles from their respective coastlines. Supplemental proceedings were subsequently instituted to determine the legal coastline of the United States in the area of Block Island Sound and the eastern portion of Long Island Sound. That determination turned on whether Long Island Sound and Block Island Sound constitute a juridical bay under the provisions of the Convention on the Territorial Sea and the Contiguous Zone, since to the extent the Sounds constitute a juridical bay, the waters of the bay are internal waters subject to the jurisdiction of the adjacent states and the line that closes the bay is coastline for purposes of fixing the seaward boundaries of the states. The Special Master appointed by the court concluded that the Sounds in part constitute a juridical bay and that the bay closes at the line drawn from Montauk Point, at the eastern tip of Long Island, to Watch Hill Point on the Rhode Island shore.

On exceptions to the report of the Special Master, the United States Supreme Court overruled the exceptions, adopted the recommendations of the Special Master, and confirmed his report. In an opinion by BLACKMUN, J., expressing the unanimous views of the court, it was held (1) that Long Island Sound and Block Island Sound together constitute a juridical bay, viewing Long Island as an exceptional case of an island which should be treated as an extension of the mainland and as constituting the southern headland of the bay; and (2) that Block Island, which is no closer than 11 miles from what would otherwise be the closing line of the bay, is too removed from the closing line to form multiple mouths and therefore does not affect the closing line.

Administrative decentralization occurs when administrative responsibility, authority, and discretion are delegated to administrative units having jurisdiction over at least one program or function in a subnational geographic territory. For instance, the existence of a field office, or regional office of an administrative agency, is evidence of administrative decentralization. So is a neighborhood school. Administrative decentralization can coincide with federalism—that is, states and provinces can be administrative districts of the national government—but it does not necessarily have to do so. There are a variety of managerial reasons for encouraging administrative decentralization that are largely independent of political concerns.

Traditional American public administrative theory recognizes that organization by "place" may be an appropriate basis for establishing administrative arrangements. This is perhaps particularly true in large nations, especially if their physical characteristics, such as climate, topography, and hydrology, vary widely. Under such circumstances, there is an ever-present likelihood that highly centralized administration, with authority and responsibility vested in an agency's national headquarters, usually in the capital, will fail to adapt to local or regional conditions. Instructions from headquarters may simply fail to fit situations in vastly different geographic settings. For instance, from the mid-1970s until 1987, the nationally imposed speed limit of 55 miles per hour had a differential impact in different areas of the United States. In a state like Nebraska or Kansas, it represented a serious constraint on commerce and travel. In New York City, Chicago, Vermont, West Virginia, and other places where traffic and terrain make it difficult to go much faster than 55 miles per hour, it had a lesser impact. Similarly, a requirement that tandem trucks be allowed on the roads has a different impact in urban settings than in sparsely populated and flat areas. In the worst cases, regulations of this kind not only fail to fit the local circumstances but can be counterproductive. To continue the example, if tandem trucks in New York City cause accidents and tie up traffic in endless gridlocks, it will hardly promote commerce or save energy. Administrative decentralization can be used to avoid problems of this kind by allowing the administrative units in the field to adapt national objectives to local conditions.

Centralized administration can also present the difficulty of becoming too extended and far-flung to assure responsibility and compliance with national directives by local administrators. Here the concept of the **span of control**—that is, the number of underlings directly reporting to a superordinate—becomes important. It has been recognized that there is a limit to the number of subordinates any given administrative official can effectively supervise. Generally, it is recommended that the span of control not exceed eight to twelve. Administrative decentralization is one means of keeping the span of control manageable by organizing on the basis of installations (local administrative units), the heads of which report to field offices, whose heads report to regional offices, whose heads report, in turn, to the agency's national headquarters. By interposing field and regional offices between local administrators and national headquarters, the number of administrators reporting directly to the headquarters can be sharply reduced. Thus, if there were 120 installations reporting, in groups of 10, to 12 field offices, which report, in groups of 2, to 6 regional offices, reporting, in turn, to agency headquarters, the span of control would presumably be functional and the situation in which 120 local administrators would report directly to headquarters would be avoided. At the same time, the regional, field, and installation levels might be able to adapt national guidelines to local conditions and to coordinate the activities of local administrators in the same geographical area.

Decentralization of this type can be by function or by agency, or it can be geographic, by *prefecture*. In the United States, the national system is organized overwhelmingly by agency, meaning that, for the most part, federal agencies have their own regional headquarters that supervise field and installation operations. In France, by contrast, the separate administrative units report to the administrative head of a district, or **prefect.** Such an official would have responsibility for overseeing the operations of several ministries in the district, including, for example, education, health, welfare, and employment. The great advantage of the prefect system is the coordination of administrative operations within a geographical area. Its drawback is that the administrative official in charge of the prefect is not likely to possess sufficient specialization in all areas of administrative operation to foster the highest possible level of efficiency and economy.

The United States federal government does not use the prefect system. It seeks to coordinate the activities of different units, such as the Departments of Education and Housing and Urban Development, within regions through interagency meetings and conferences. However, at the subnational level of government, something approaching the coordination of the prefect system may develop. Here, administrative and political decentralization overlap. Municipal governments, townships and counties are headed by managers, executives, or other officials or bodies. These officials seek to coordinate and oversee all the administrative activities of that particular unit of government (e.g., the county) within the geographic territory under its jurisdiction. However, since so many functions provided by these units of government overlap, sometimes the administrative arrangements seem to be irrational, fragmented, and uncoordinated. For example, jurisdictional overlaps or disputes among city police, county sheriffs, state police, and sometimes even the FBI are fairly common. A jail in a city may be overcrowded, while space in the county facility is available.

Federalism and administrative decentralization are different in purpose. One promotes political values (representation, economic development, and perhaps military strength). The other promotes managerial values of efficiency, economy, and administrative effectiveness. But there is another difference as well. Administrative decentralization does not convey sovereignty to the subnational administrative units, whereas federalism does carry with it the notion that some subnational political units (states or provinces) will be vested with a measure of sovereignty. We will return to these matters shortly.

THE QUEST FOR UNIFORMITY AMONG THE STATES

Federalism and administrative decentralization carry with them the possibility that the nature of individual rights and the enforcement and implementation of administrative programs will vary widely from place to place. Indeed, this is one of the advantages of these arrangements. But it can also be a drawback. For instance, adapting to local conditions can stand in the way of integration of the nation's economy and further economic development. It can also involve the violation of individual rights and standards of decency to which the political community, as a whole, is committed. In the United States, an example combining these two types of concerns was present prior to the adoption of the federal Civil Rights Act of 1964. In some states, by state law, blacks could be excluded from places of public accommodation, such as motels and restaurants. They were also subject to segregation on common carriers (buses, trains) and in public buildings. This was not only offensive to the national commitment of equal protection and decency but, as the Supreme Court reasoned in *Katzenbach* v. *McClung* (1964),[3] it impeded commerce by making it difficult for blacks to travel.

This is where the legal perspective enters the picture most forcefully. Law, including constitutional law, can be used to protect the most fundamental rights of individuals from infringement by states or administrative units. The idea that federalism can enable local majorities to have a good measure of political control over their lives is sound. But it does not necessarily protect minorities from tyranny by those local majorities. For instance, English-speaking Canadians may be subject to discrimination in Quebec; non-Mormons may suffer inequality in Utah. Consequently, it is often necessary that a line be drawn between local control and national protection. Typically, this line will be drawn on the basis of the determination that some rights are so fundamental that they must be given national recognition and protection. However, precisely what those rights will be varies over time and is often difficult to discern.

In the United States, the courts have often been called upon to address this question. Historically, it was generally thought that the Bill of Rights (the First, Fourth, Fifth, Sixth, and Eighth Amendments in particular) imposed restrictions on the federal government's treatment of individuals but did not place limitations on the states or their political subdivisions. During the twentieth century, however, constitutional theory has held that the Fourteenth Amendment's guarantee that no state shall deprive any individual of life, liberty, or property without due process of law "incorporates" much of the Bill of Rights. In other words, whereas at one time an individual's right to freedom of expression or free exercise of religion was protected from *federal* interference by the First Amendment, such rights were not necessarily protected from abridgement by the state governments or their political subdivisions. Protection at the state level would depend upon the state constitutions and state judicial decisions. This approach permitted many practices that would be considered anomalous today, including the establishment of religions by the states. Currently, the treatment of individuals by states is protected by the Bill of Rights as well as by the state constitutions. Incorporation of the Bill of Rights through the Fourteenth Amendment has expanded the civil rights and liberties of the citizenry immensely. At the same time, however, it has limited the states' ability to adjust their policies in some areas to their own peculiar circumstances. For example, in theory at least, high-crime states and low-crime states must adhere to the same standards of due process, pretrial detention, "speedy trials," and prison conditions.

The judiciary has also dramatically affected federalism by its interpretation of the *commerce clause*. In the past, many of their decisions turned on the question of whether, in seeking to impose uniformity upon commercial practices—such as the use of child labor—within the states, Congress had gone beyond its constitutional powers to regulate commerce. Today, however, the vast majority of commercial activity in the nation is considered to be within the scope of Congress's reach. Indeed, in *Wickard* v. *Filburn* (1942),[4] the Supreme Court held that even a crop grown and consumed on a single farm within one state was subject to congressional regulation. The Court reasoned that if a large number of farmers grew a crop, such as wheat, for consumption on their farms, it would have an impact on the national economy even though the crop itself never actually entered the commercial market directly.

In the wake of judicial interpretations expanding the reach of Congress under the *commerce clause* and imposing limitations on the states through incorporation of the Bill of Rights, the states appear to be left with limited vestiges of sovereignty. The Supreme Court has construed the Tenth Amendment narrowly. In *National League of Cities* v. *Usery* (1976),[5] it held that the states had sovereignty to set wages and hours for their own employees. However, in *Garcia* v. *San Antonio Metropolitan Transit Authority* (1985),[6] it overruled that decision and held that Congress did have the power under the Constitution's commerce clause to apply minimum-wage-and-hour regulations to state employees. The Court reasoned that ". . . the Framers chose to rely on a Federal system in which special restraints on Federal power over the states inhered principally in the workings of the national Government itself, rather than in discrete limitations on the objects of Federal Authority." In other words, the states' chief protection against federal intrusion into their affairs lies in the political process that affords the states representation in the Senate, rather than in constitutional limitations imposed on the power of the federal government.

MIXES OF FEDERALISM

Several mixes in the allocation of authority between national governments and those of states or provinces can develop in response to the political interests in federalism, administrative concerns with the impact of decentralization, and a nation's desire to establish uniformity in some areas of public policy and in the definition of rights. David Nice outlines the major models as follows:[7]

1. Nation-centered federalism establishes "the national government as the dominant source in a federal system." It emphasizes the desirability of a

national perspective on public policy, the uniform regulation of commerce, and broad national protection of individuals' rights and statuses.

2. State-centered federalism favors state dominance in the political system because "the states are seen as closer to the people and able to adapt to variations in problems or citizen preferences from one part of the country to another."

3. Dual federalism is a system in which "each level of government, national and state, is supreme within its areas of responsibility. According to this model, neither level is dominant, and neither level should interfere in the affairs of the other." For instance, exclusive authority might be vested in the states for education and labor law, whereas foreign affairs might be solely in the domain of the national government.

4. Interdependent models "are based on a sharing of power and responsibility, with the various participants working toward shared goals." These models seek to couple the resources of the national government with the states' respresentative and administrative capacities as a means of adapting and implementing general policies at the subnational level of government.

During the twentieth century, the United States moved from a system closer to dual federalism to one more aptly characterized as interdependent. During the past two decades, the character of interdependence has varied from the heavy reliance of President Lyndon B. Johnson's "Great Society" on national initiatives and control to President Ronald Reagan's emphasis on the states' relative independence under his "New Federalism" approach. However, despite shifts in emphasis, the states and the national government are now highly interdependent in a wide range of policy areas and fiscal matters. We will discuss state-national and other intergovernmental relationships after reviewing the major forms found within the United States' 82,000 governments.

AMERICAN GOVERNMENT: A BOTTOM-UP VIEW

The vast majority of people in the United States fall under the jurisdiction of several governments. The exact number and mix of functions these governments provide depend upon precisely where one lives. It is impossible to do justice to the wide range of variation among the 82,000 governments that exist in the United States. Box 3–2, displaying the relative proportions of expenditures allotted by different levels of government to general categories of functions, provides an idea of the activities with which the federal, state, and local governments are most concerned. Box 3–3 shows the size and growth of public employment in the states (including local governments) from 1954 to 1982. It leaves no doubt that much public administrative activity takes place at the subnational levels of government. Although there are great differences among governments at the subnational level, some commonalities can be described.

Municipalities   These are cities, towns, villages, or boroughs, legally defined as public corporations. Their object is to provide governance and public adminis-

BOX 3–2 **The Percent of Federal, State and Local Governmental Budgets Allocated to Various Functions, 1983**

	GOVERNMENT		
FUNCTION	Federal* Percent of Budget	State* Percent of Budget	Local* Percent of Budget
Defense	42.3%	0.0%	0.0%
Postal	4.5	0.0	0.0
Education	2.4	27.7	42.7
Hospital	1.2	8.1	5.9
Health	1.3	3.2	1.9
Highways	0.1†	11.8	5.4
Police	0.4	1.4	5.4
Corrections	0.1	3.2	1.1
Natural Resources	8.0	3.0	0.5
Sewage	0.0	0.2	3.9
Housing/Urban Renewal	1.6	0.3	2.9
General Control	0.4	2.2	2.7
Interest on Debt	21.0	5.2	4.2

* Columns do not sum to 100 percent because not all functions are included.

† Much federal highway spending is "off-budget" in the form of a trust fund. Consequently, the direct expenditure figure presented here understates federal spending on highways.

SOURCE: The Council of State Governments, *The Book of the States*, 1984–85 (Lexington, Ky.: Council of State Governments, 1985), p. 304.

tration to local areas. Cities typically provide a greater range of functions than other municipalities and may have special status under a state's constitution. At a minimum, all municipalities seek to provide for the public safety and some degree of public works. At a maximum, cities may provide not only these functions but also hospitals, libraries, elaborate zoning and planning, higher education, museums, jails, public parks, recreation, and various licensing and inspection functions.

Municipalities tend to fall into one of three types of governmental structure. The **mayor-council** form of government is found in about half the nation's cities and is especially prevalent in those with 500,000 or more residents. Here the mayor has primarily executive functions, while the council has both executive and legislative ones. In what has been dubbed the "weak-mayor" variant, the heads of the city's departments may be directly elected, thereby limiting the mayor's control over their selection and activity. The council in such a form of government may be directly involved in executive decision making. Under the "strong mayor" plan, department heads are directly appointed by the mayor, subject to council approval. Here, although the mayor and the council make

BOX 3–3 Bureaucratic Size and Growth in the American States, 1954 and 1982

	1954		1982		1954–1982	
State	No. of Public Employees*	Bureau- cratic Load†	No. of Public Employees	Bureau- cratic Load	% Increase in Bureau- cratic Size	% Increase in Bureau- cratic Load
Alabama	77,895	2.5	189,780	4.8	144	92
Alaska			35,918	8.2		
Arizona	28,787	3.8	134,868	4.7	369	24
Arkansas	43,318	2.3	103,683	4.5	139	97
California	438,772	4.1	1,097,501	4.4	150	8
Colorado	51,539	3.9	149,330	4.9	190	26
Connecticut			137,835	4.4		
Delaware	11,477	3.6	31,357	5.2	173	45
Florida	109,926	4.0	467,396	4.5	325	12
Georgia	89,680	2.6	301,682	5.4	236	106
Hawaii			49,457	5.0		
Idaho	21,143	3.6	45,194	4.7	114	30
Illinois	251,288	2.9	486,572	4.2	94	47
Indiana	120,725	3.1	237,357	4.3	97	40
Iowa	90,611	3.5	142,182	4.9	57	40
Kansas	69,235	3.6	127,560	5.3	84	47
Kentucky	66,326	2.3	149,038	4.1	125	77
Louisiana	92,148	3.4	224,451	5.2	144	51
Maine	30,926	3.4	50,602	4.5	64	31
Maryland	69,651	3.0	218,560	5.1	214	71
Massachusetts	167,521	3.6	256,758	4.4	53	23
Michigan	221,332	3.5	392,485	4.3	77	23
Minnesota	114,543	3.8	189,345	4.6	65	21
Mississippi	57,043	2.6	126,397	4.9	122	90
Missouri	108,851	2.8	220,696	4.5	103	59
Montana	22,248	3.8	42,439	5.3	91	39
Nebraska	51,601	3.9	89,617	5.7	74	45
Nevada	8,213	5.1	42,252	4.8	414	−6
New Hampshire	21,059	3.9	39,776	4.1	89	7
New Jersey	149,427	3.1	358,825	4.8	140	55
New Mexico	24,853	3.6	76,661	5.6	208	57
New York	540,075	3.6	963,387	5.5	78	52
North Carolina	108,903	2.7	288,310	4.8	165	77
North Dakota	24,905	4.0	33,583	5.0	35	25
Ohio	254,615	3.2	457,955	4.2	80	33
Oklahoma	76,676	3.4	168,398	5.3	120	56
Oregon	56,934	3.7	128,802	4.9	126	31
Pennsylvania	260,188	2.5	458,259	3.9	76	54
Rhode Island	22,836	2.9	43,666	4.6	91	57
South Carolina	58,783	2.8	156,181	4.9	166	74
South Dakota	25,308	3.9	34,101	4.9	35	27

BOX 3–3 *Continued*

State	1954		1982		1954–1982	
	No. of Public Employees*	Bureau-cratic Load†	No. of Public Employees	Bureau-cratic Load	% Increase in Bureau-cratic Size	% Increase in Bureau-cratic Load
Tennessee	87,188	2.6	213,794	4.6	145	77
Texas	230,232	3.0	727,233	4.8	216	59
Utah	28,604	4.2	68,919	4.4	141	5
Vermont	13,002	3.4	24,167	4.7	89	37
Virginia	96,109	2.9	266,713	4.7	178	68
Washington	94,193	4.0	192,491	4.5	104	13
West Virginia	50,600	2.5	94,415	4.8	87	94
Wisconsin	119,494	3.8	213,842	4.5	79	18
Wyoming	12,411	4.3	33,058	6.6	166	53

* Combined state and local.
† Bureaucratic load = number of public sector employees per 100 persons in the state population.

SOURCE: Data from The Council of State Governments, *The Book of the States*, 1954–56, 1984–85 (Lexington, Ky.: The Council of State Governments).

policy jointly, it is the mayor's legal responsibility to execute it. Most large cities rely on the strong-mayor approach. In practice, of course, each city is likely to have its own hybrid of the strong- and weak-mayor approaches. The mayor-council approach was created to assure a separation of executive and legislative powers and a system of checks and balances. Council members may be elected "at large," that is, citywide, or by wards.

At the other extreme, municipalities with populations of 5,000 or less sometimes rely upon the **commission plan** of governance. Here, a number of commissioners, frequently five, are elected at large, generally for a four-year term. One serves as chair of the commission. There is little in the way of a separation of powers; the commission is a deliberative legislative body, yet each commissioner has executive responsibility for the operations of a specific department. The plan is convenient in politically and socially homogeneous jurisdictions. However, where there is marked political conflict, the commission can become deadlocked and administrative operations may not be coordinated with one another.

The **council-manager** plan is the third common form of municipal governance. It is found in about half of all cities in the 10,000–500,000 population range. Historically, the council-manager approach was last to evolve and was a part of the broader effort at administrative reform that included the establishment of merit systems for the selection of civil servants.[8] The council-manager plan reflects the orthodox, managerial approach to public administration in many respects. It assumes that the main problems of cities are administrative, not political. This was often captured in the aphorism that "there is no Republican and no Democratic way to pave a street." It also assumes that although the managers of cities should be responsible to elected officials, administration itself should not be infused with electoral concerns. The council is generally elected at large on a nonpartisan basis. It has legislative authority for the city, passing ordinances, developing or sanctioning policy, and approving financial and budgetary proposals. Generally the council consists of five to nine members. It is presided over by a mayor, who may be one of its members. The mayor in this form of government has important ceremonial functions but no significant executive powers. The council hires a manager, who serves at its pleasure. The manager is the chief executive officer of the city and has the authority to appoint and dismiss the heads of administrative departments. The council, in turn, is barred from involvement in administrative matters other than the selection and retention of the manager. City managers are considered professionals and often hold advanced degrees in public administration. Their jobs may be extremely difficult because it is often impossible for the manager to avoid becoming involved in political disputes—or even the object of them.

Townships   These are found primarily in the Midwest and mid-Atlantic states. Originally they were used to identify sections of federal lands. Today, they often constitute civic units as well. They are characteristic in rural areas and provide a minimum of functions, sometimes having responsibility only for roads. Townships rely heavily upon the commission form of government.

Counties   These are a comprehensive, general form of government with a wide range of functions. Municipalities, townships, and other forms of government (school districts and special districts) are found within their boundaries. Counties are best considered to be arms of the state government for local administration and governance. Exceptions are in New England, where the states rely on "towns" more than counties; Louisiana, which uses "parishes"; and Alaska, where "boroughs" provide some of the functions supplied by counties elsewhere. Their number varies widely from state to state, as does their size. On average, there are sixty-five counties per state. Some are highly urbanized, such as New York County (Manhattan), whereas others are rural. Counties derive all their authority and powers from the state. They are unincorporated. Their functions vary widely, but with few if any exceptions, they include some law enforcement functions, tax functions, and recordkeeping. Many counties have important responsibilities for education, recreation, roads, and civic activities. The typical county is governed by a board of elected commissioners, which is also frequently called a board of supervisors. About two-thirds of the counties have boards of three to five members, but some have as many as thirty or more.[9] The board has policy and administrative functions. It oversees a number of appointive officials who carry out executive responsibilities. In addition to the board, voters typically elect a number of other county officials including sheriffs, judicial officers, clerks, treasurers, assessors, and coroners. Some counties have professional managers and/or elected executives. In rural areas, the county may be the main focus of governance. In more urban settings, the coexistence of counties and municipalities may lead to a patchwork of overlapping functions and haphazard relationships.

School Districts and Other Special Districts   Special districts are "single-purpose" governments. They deal primarily with such areas as water, sewage, recreation, highways, bridges, fire protection, cemeteries, libraries, and utilities.[10] School districts are a special case. They were established to give local communities control over the education of their children. In the past, the independence of school districts was a guarantee of diversity. Today, however, school systems must meet so many state and federal requirements that a good deal of educational uniformity exists. For the most part, school districts are governed by boards. About 80 percent of these are elected; the remainder are appointed by municipal or county officials.[11] Other special districts, sometimes called "authorities," are also headed by boards, but here a higher proportion of the members are appointed. Special districts often overlap several municipal and/or county governments, and the composition of the board may be composed of elected or appointed representatives of those units of government. Special districts frequently exercise considerable powers of taxation and authority to charge user fees and incur debt. For the most part, however, the average citizen seems unconcerned with their composition and operations—at least as long as the latter are satisfactory. Historically, special districts have been considered a way of taking particular functions, such as cemeteries, water, and libraries, out of the political arena and of making it possible to manage them in a "businesslike" manner. Sometimes, of course, school districts and special districts generally can become embroiled in political controversy.

States   In many respects, the *structure* of state governments tends to parallel that of the federal government. The executive branch in all states is headed by an elected governor. With the exception of Nebraska, all states use a bicameral legislature. The upper house is invariably called the *senate*, while the lower house may be called an *assembly* or *state house*. The states also provide for independent judiciaries having the power of judicial review. The highest court in most states is called the *state supreme court*. Despite these structural similarities, however, many states differ markedly from the pattern of politics and administrative arrangements found at the national level. They also differ from one another.

One of the striking differences is the nature of state constitutions. Only those of Massachusetts (adopted in 1780) and New Hampshire (adopted in 1784) have had the longevity of the U.S. Constitution, which was adopted in 1789. Most states have had more than one constitution. Louisiana has had eleven. Only those of Connecticut and Vermont are as concise as the federal Constitution. Many are much wordier. Most have also been amended more frequently than the U.S. Constitution. Some, such as those of California and South Carolina, have been changed more than 400 times.[12] These differences reflect the virtue of federalism in enabling each state to adapt its governmental powers and processes to its own economic, political, and social conditions and needs.

They also reflect the ability of organized pressure groups to advance their interests by having provisions written into the state constitutions. State constitutions are far more detailed than the federal Constitution, sometimes resembling ordinary legislation in spelling out provisions for roads, sewer systems, and even zoos.[13] Many of them are easier to amend, which accounts in part for the tendency to treat them as vehicles for the expression of substantive policy as well as statements of the procedures by which the state governments operate. In several states—including large ones such as California, Florida, Massachusetts, and Illinois—constitutional amendments can be initiated directly by the people.[14] All state constitutions provide for checks and balances, suffrage and elections, taxation and appropriations, local government, public education, state institutions, and law enforcement.[15]

The states also vary greatly in their administrative structures. Every governor is considered the head of state administrative operations, but the governor's power to appoint, engage in fiscal management, and supervise administrators varies considerably from one state to another. In several states six or more administrative officials are elected by the voters. Among those most frequently elected are attorneys general, lieutenant governors, treasurers, secretaries of state, auditors, and superintendents of education. Among additional elective state administrators are agricultural commissioners, controllers, and commissioners for insurance, land, labor, highways, railroads, corporations, and charities. University regents and others may also be elected.[16] Generally speaking, the greater the number of elected administrative officials, the less control the governor has over state public administration. Elected officials may be opposed to the governor's policies and administrative programs. The governor has no official role in selecting those officials and cannot fire them. Their responsibility is to the voters, who may see no problem in electing administrative executives who are opposed to one another. Moreover, elected administrators may tend to develop closer relationships with the legislature than with the governor.

The governor's ability to oversee administrative matters is also complicated by the unwieldly structures of many state governments. In 1978, on average, a governor had some eighty-five state agencies reporting directly to him or her. The number of separate agencies could reach well over one hundred.[17] In recent years, efforts have been undertaken in several states to reform these administrative structures by consolidating such agencies into a few departments, because from a managerial perspective, the governor's span of control is simply too large to be effective. In part, however, the fragmented administrative structures of the states reflect the competing concerns of public administration. Some independent boards and commissions are designed to exercise judicial functions and to be independent of the rest of the government to a considerable degree. Others provide political representation for the interests of distinct economic, social, or geographical groups. Still others are engaged in executive functions and are most likely to be placed more closely under the governor's control.

Since the 1920s, the job of preparing state budgets has increasingly been moved from the legislature to the governor. Today, the formulation of an **executive budget,** that is, one prepared by the governor or a budget agency in the executive branch, is the focus of much administrative activity. During the 1980s, as the states played a more active role in the provision of services and the application of constraints within their jurisdictions, the state budget has emerged as a major vehicle for state planning.

The states also vary widely in the degree to which their administrative operations are professionalized. In 1978, 56 percent of all state administrators had graduate educational degrees.[18] Between 1958 and 1980, the proportion of state employees under merit personnel systems rose from 51 to 75 percent.[19] Under federal law, some categories of state employees dealing with federal grant-in-aid programs must be removed from politics and patronage. In the remainder, some employees may be covered by similar state requirements. Recent Supreme Court decisions also cast doubt upon the constitutionality of most patronage dismissals (see Chapter 2). The Federal Equal Employment Opportunity Act of 1972 prohibits discrimination based on race, color, ethnicity, religion, and gender in state employment. It also promotes the use of affirmative action to overcome past discriminatory practices. Other federal statutes deal with age discrimination, fair labor standards, and handicapping conditions. The federal Intergovernmental Personnel Act of 1970 was aimed at promoting professionalization of state civil services, but the results have been mixed. These regulations and efforts to standardize state administration notwithstanding, there is often considerable divergence between the letter of personnel law and actual practices on the job. This is especially true where public employment remains infused with partisan politics. (Public personnel administration is discussed in Chapter 5.)

Finally, in discussing the states, it is necessary to note that there are widespread variations in the patterns of their party politics, the professionalization and strength of their legislatures, the scope of services and regulations they provide, and their mix of administrative responsibility among the counties, local jurisdictions, and the state governments themselves. When taken together, these differences can make administrative life in one state quite different from administrative life in another. They can also lead to serious complications in trying to draft federal legislation and programs that require state administration of a certain caliber. We will return to this problem after we briefly review the federal government's administrative structure.

The Federal Government   We have already mentioned many of the salient features of the federal government's administrative component in our discussion of the rise of the contemporary American administrative state (Chapter 2). This is not the place for a discourse on the nature of federal administration and politics, but a brief summary will provide the reader with a useful overview. It may be helpful to refer to Box 3–4 as we review the administrative structure of the federal government. Like the states, the federal administrative structure is fragmented. It consists of departments, agencies, commissions, corporations, and a number of miscellaneous units. Departments are generally considered the most important and comprehensive administrative units. They enjoy the highest formal status. Today, there are thirteen departments, although their number has

BOX 3–4 The Organization of the Government of the United States

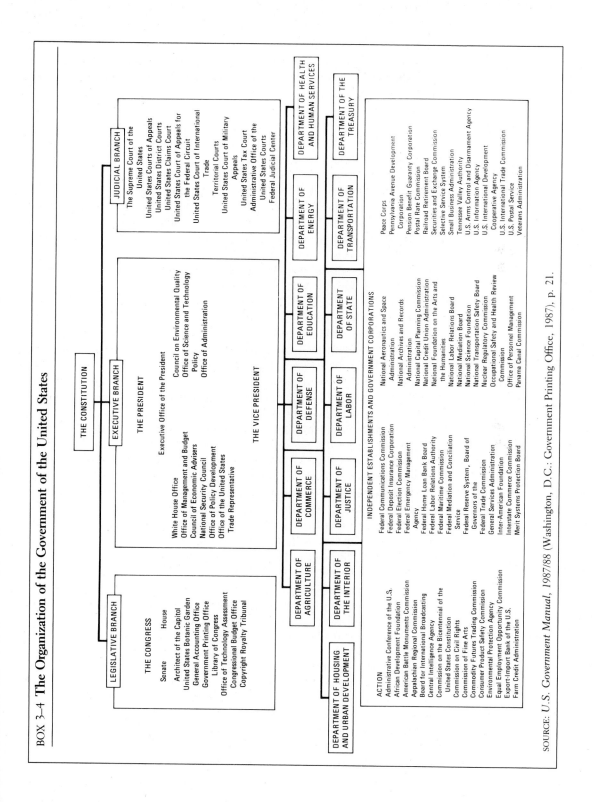

THE CONSTITUTION

LEGISLATIVE BRANCH

THE CONGRESS

Senate   House

Architect of the Capitol
United States Botanic Garden
General Accounting Office
Government Printing Office
Library of Congress
Office of Technology Assessment
Congressional Budget Office
Copyright Royalty Tribunal

EXECUTIVE BRANCH

THE PRESIDENT

Executive Office of the President

White House Office   Council on Environmental Quality
Office of Management and Budget   Office of Science and Technology
Council of Economic Advisers   Policy
National Security Council   Office of Administration
Office of Policy Development
Office of the United States
Trade Representative

THE VICE PRESIDENT

JUDICIAL BRANCH

The Supreme Court of the
United States
United States Courts of Appeals
United States District Courts
United States Claims Court
United States Court of Appeals for
the Federal Circuit
United States Court of International
Trade
Territorial Courts
United States Court of Military
Appeals
United States Tax Court
Administrative Office of the
United States Courts
Federal Judicial Center

DEPARTMENT OF HOUSING
AND URBAN DEVELOPMENT

DEPARTMENT OF
AGRICULTURE

DEPARTMENT OF
THE INTERIOR

DEPARTMENT OF
COMMERCE

DEPARTMENT OF
JUSTICE

DEPARTMENT OF
DEFENSE

DEPARTMENT OF
LABOR

DEPARTMENT OF
EDUCATION

DEPARTMENT
OF STATE

DEPARTMENT OF HEALTH
AND HUMAN SERVICES

DEPARTMENT OF
ENERGY

DEPARTMENT OF THE
TREASURY

DEPARTMENT OF
TRANSPORTATION

INDEPENDENT ESTABLISHMENTS AND GOVERNMENT CORPORATIONS

ACTION
Administrative Conference of the U.S.
African Development Foundation
American Battle Monuments Commission
Appalachian Regional Commission
Board for International Broadcasting
Central Intelligence Agency
Commission on the Bicentennial of the
  United States Constitution
Commission on Civil Rights
Commission of Fine Arts
Commodity Futures Trading Commission
Consumer Product Safety Commission
Environmental Protection Agency
Equal Employment Opportunity Commission
Export-Import Bank of the U.S.
Farm Credit Administration

Federal Communications Commission
Federal Deposit Insurance Corporation
Federal Election Commission
Federal Emergency Management
  Agency
Federal Home Loan Bank Board
Federal Labor Relations Authority
Federal Maritime Commission
Federal Mediation and Conciliation
  Service
Federal Reserve System, Board of
  Governors of the
Federal Trade Commission
General Services Administration
Inter-American Foundation
Interstate Commerce Commission
Merit Systems Protection Board

National Aeronautics and Space
  Administration
National Archives and Records
  Administration
National Capital Planning Commission
National Credit Union Administration
National Foundation on the Arts and
  the Humanities
National Labor Relations Board
National Mediation Board
National Science Foundation
National Transportation Safety Board
Nuclear Regulatory Commission
Occupational Safety and Health Review
  Commission
Office of Personnel Management
Panama Canal Commission

Peace Corps
Pennsylvania Avenue Development
  Corporation
Pension Benefit Guaranty Corporation
Postal Rate Commission
Railroad Retirement Board
Securities and Exchange Commission
Selective Service System
Small Business Administration
Tennessee Valley Authority
U.S. Arms Control and Disarmament Agency
U.S. Information Agency
U.S. International Development
  Cooperative Agency
U.S. International Trade Commission
U.S. Postal Service
Veterans Administration

SOURCE: *U.S. Government Manual, 1987/88* (Washington, D.C.: Government Printing Office, 1987), p. 21.

varied over the years. There are marked differences in their sizes and budgets. The Department of Defense (DOD) overshadows all others with some 1,085,000 employees. The largest share of the budget goes to defense ($280 billion) and Social Security and Medicare ($270 billion). On the other end of the scale, the Department of Education has only about 5,000 employees, and the Commerce Department's budget is relatively small ($2 billion). The structure of these departments also differs considerably. Some approach the pyramidal, hierarchical organizational form generally associated with bureaucracy. Others are conglomerates of separate, somewhat autonomous units and are best construed as "holding companies." The DOD is among the latter, being composed of the Army, Navy, and Air Force among other units (see Box 3–5). Typically, departments are distinguished from other units, such as agencies, by the comprehensiveness or national importance of their missions.

Independent agencies are administrative units outside the departments with responsibility for more limited areas of public policy. The Veterans Administration (VA), the Small Business Administration, and the National Aeronautics and Space Administration are examples. These agencies are called "independent" because they are not within departments. In practice, however, they may be tightly controlled by the president. Independent agencies may be quite large—the VA, with 247,000 employees, is larger than most departments.* However, the scope of their mission is often limited, focusing on a particular group of people or sector of the economy. Some independent agencies, such as the General Services Administration and the Office of Personnel Management, engage in overhead administrative functions, including supply, security, and personnel.

Independent regulatory commissions are another kind of unit. These commissions are intended to be autonomous and removed from direct presidential control. Among the better known regulatory commissions are the Interstate Commerce Commission, the Federal Communications Commission, the Securities and Exchange Commission, the National Labor Relations Board, and the Federal Trade Commission. Such commissions are headed by a bipartisan group of commissioners appointed by the president with the advice and consent of the Senate. They hold staggered terms and are not removable by the president except for specified kinds of causes. The president may disagree with them in terms of policy, but he cannot replace them for this reason until their terms expire. The regulatory commissions have quasi-legislative and quasi-judicial functions because they make rules for regulation of some sector of the economy and enforce those rules, which often requires judicial-style hearings. The basic idea behind the regulatory commission is that by taking an area out of legislative politics, it is possible to weigh competing perspectives on a matter, such as the rates common carriers can charge or what constitutes an unfair labor or trade practice, and to arrive at decisions that are judicious in their definition of the public interest. (Regulatory administration illuminates so much of public administration that Chapter 9 is devoted to it.)

---

* In 1987, President Reagan proposed to Congress that the VA be reorganized as a department.

BOX 3–5 The Organization of the Department of Defense

ARMED FORCES POLICY COUNCIL

SECRETARY OF DEFENSE
DEPUTY SECRETARY OF DEFENSE

OFFICE OF THE SECRETARY OF DEFENSE
UNDER SECRETARIES AND ASSISTANT SECRETARIES OF DEFENSE

JOINT CHIEFS OF STAFF

CHAIRMAN, JOINT CHIEFS OF STAFF
VICE CHAIRMAN, JOINT CHIEFS OF STAFF
CHIEF OF STAFF, ARMY
CHIEF OF NAVAL OPERATIONS
CHIEF OF STAFF, AIR FORCE
COMMANDANT, MARINE CORPS

THE JOINT STAFF

DEPARTMENT OF THE ARMY
SECRETARY OF THE ARMY
UNDER SECRETARY AND ASSISTANT SECRETARIES OF THE ARMY
CHIEF OF STAFF ARMY
ARMY MAJOR COMMANDS AND AGENCIES

DEPARTMENT OF THE AIR FORCE
SECRETARY OF THE AIR FORCE
UNDER SECRETARY AND ASSISTANT SECRETARIES OF THE AIR FORCE
CHIEF OF STAFF AIR FORCE
AF MAJOR COMMANDS AND AGENCIES

DEPARTMENT OF THE NAVY
SECRETARY OF THE NAVY
UNDER SECRETARY AND ASSISTANT SECRETARIES OF THE NAVY
CHIEF OF NAVAL OPERATIONS
COMMANDANT OF MARINE CORPS
NAVY MAJOR COMMANDS AND AGENCIES
MARINE CORPS MAJOR COMMANDS AND AGENCIES

INSPECTOR GENERAL

DEFENSE AGENCIES

DEFENSE COMMUNICATIONS AGENCY
DEFENSE MAPPING AGENCY
STRATEGIC DEFENSE INITIATIVE ORGANIZATION
DEFENSE NUCLEAR AGENCY
DEFENSE LEGAL SERVICES AGENCY
DEFENSE CONTRACT AUDIT AGENCY
DEFENSE SECURITY ASSISTANCE AGENCY
NATIONAL SECURITY AGENCY
DEFENSE INVESTIGATIVE SERVICE
DEFENSE LOGISTICS AGENCY
DEFENSE ADVANCED RESEARCH PROJECTS AGENCY
DEFENSE INTELLIGENCE AGENCY

UNIFIED COMMANDS

SPECIAL OPERATIONS COMMAND
EUROPEAN COMMAND
STRATEGIC AIR COMMAND
MILITARY AIRLIFT COMMAND
FORCES COMMAND

PACIFIC COMMAND
ATLANTIC COMMAND
CENTRAL COMMAND
TRANSPORTATION COMMAND

SOUTHERN COMMAND
SPACE COMMAND

SPECIFIED COMMANDS

SOURCE: *U.S. Government Manual, 1987/88* (Washington, D.C.: Government Printing Office, 1987), p. 173.

Federal corporations, such as the Tennessee Valley Authority (TVA) and the Federal Deposit Insurance Corporation (FDIC), differ from other federal units primarily in that they sell a product or service. (The organizational structure of the TVA is shown in Box 3–6.) The Postal Service corporation sells mail service; the TVA sells electricity; the FDIC sells insurance. Such administrative units can be run according to private sector methods. They are allowed to generate their revenues through sales, and as long as they do not run a deficit, need not rely on budgetary appropriations for their funds. When successful, this gives the corporations a large measure of financial independence from the legislature and budgetary process. In most other respects, however, the legal status of corporations is similar to that of other agencies.

In practice, federal administrative arrangements are somewhat more complicated than presented here. Hybrids can be found among the independent agencies and the regulatory commissions. There are a number of agencies called *boards*, and there are foundations, institutes, and institutions. Interagency com-

BOX 3–6 **The Organization of the Tennessee Valley Authority**

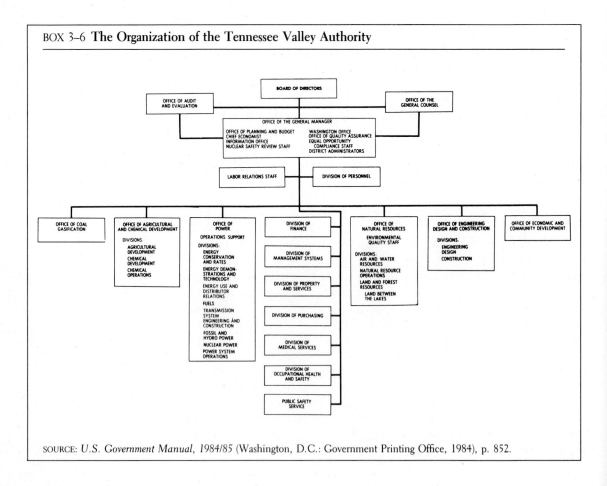

SOURCE: *U.S. Government Manual, 1984/85* (Washington, D.C.: Government Printing Office, 1984), p. 852.

mittees and advisory committees are plentiful. Some executive branch units are in the Executive Office of the President (EOP), such as the Office of Management and Budget, whereas others having related functions, such as the Office of Personnel Management, are outside the EOP. Many of the reasons for these organizational arrangements are discussed in Chapter 4. Basically, they reflect the competing managerial, political, and legalistic perspectives toward public administration. Their net result, however, is further governmental fragmentation and complexity in trying to coordinate governmental activity and policy. Not only does the American governmental and political structure make coordination among the different levels of government difficult, it also makes coordination within governments a considerable task. This can complicate intergovernmental relations greatly.

INTERGOVERNMENTAL RELATIONS

Federal and State Relations

Federalism requires coordination and cooperation of two major types. One is between the national government and state governments; the other is between or among the states. It also permits direct relationships between the national government and political subdivisions within the states. Historically, relationships between the national and state governments have preoccupied American thinking about federalism. The central question has always concerned the extent of state sovereignty in the federal system. What, precisely, are the powers reserved to the states by the Tenth Amendment? As early as the 1790s, Virginia and Kentucky argued that the states possessed the sovereignty to declare acts of the federal government to be void on the grounds that they violated the U.S. Constitution. The Virginia and Kentucky "resolves" were in response to the federal Naturalization, Alien, and Sedition Acts of 1798. They were wrapped up in electoral politics, but the fact that the Virginia resolves were drafted by James Madison, who played a leading role in the drafting and ratification of the U.S. Constitution, and that Kentucky's statement was written by Thomas Jefferson, gave this view of federalism some credibility. By the 1820s and 1830s, John Calhoun of South Carolina had developed a similar notion about the states' rights to nullify federal laws they viewed as unconstitutional. In 1832, South Carolina actually attempted to enforce this approach, but after President Jackson threatened to use military force against the state, a compromise was reached and the state repealed its nullification ordinance. The logical extension of this view of states' rights occurred at the time of the Civil War, when eleven states seceded from the federal union.

For the most part, the Civil War put to rest the theory that each state has an inherent right to define the scope of *federal* powers. Every now and then, however, a state governor may refuse to abide by a federal statute, sometimes involving civil rights, and may even make a dramatic show of the affair. These legal battles are fought out in the courts, and as noted earlier in connection with our discussion of the Tenth Amendment, the federal judiciary rarely sees things from the states' point of view—the Usery case being a short-lived modern exception.

Another fundamental question in federal-state relationships is equity. To what extent should each state be treated equally by the federal government? Should federal revenues to the states follow a strict formula? Should they be based on politics? Should they take state population, state size, and state need into account? One can ponder the philosophical concerns involved in these questions. As a practical matter, however, politics is frequently the motivating force behind federal allocations to states and their subdivisions. There is considerable variation in (1) the general federal presence in the states in the form of federal civilian and military employment, military bases, and federal allocation of contracts; and (2) the total federal spending per capita within states. Sometimes the politics involved in federal allocations depends heavily upon the memberships on various congressional committees and the relationship between these committees and the federal administrative units with which they deal. For instance, membership on the House Armed Services Committee has long been associated with disproportionately high military spending in one's district.[20]

As the concern with equity suggests, a great deal of contemporary federal-state relationships involve money. Indeed, the basic pattern of the expansion of federal relationships with state governments has involved federal grants to states as part of the federal government's attempt to achieve some national policy. This approach is not really new; the Morrill Act of 1862 provided federal aid to state land-grant colleges in an effort to further education, especially that involving agricultural techniques. The Federal Aid Road Act of 1916 made federal funds available to the states for highway construction as part of a policy intended to modernize road transportation in the wake of the growing utility of the automobile. What has changed in recent years is the scope of federal grants and the degree of cooperation and coordination that they require of the states. Box 3–7 presents total federal grant-in-aid outlays from 1950 to 1986.

In recent years, the federal government has relied heavily upon three types of grants to further national policies at the state level:

1. *Categorical grants* are provided for specific programs and are subject to strict federal regulations as to how they may be used. Welfare, airports, and highway programs are examples. Sometimes the states are required to participate in funding operations undertaken through such grants. The federal strings attached to such grants may reach matters that the states could legitimately consider to be within their sovereignty, such as speed limits, drinking age, public personnel, and collective bargaining regulations. However, since the states are not compelled to participate in these programs, prevailing constitutional logic has been that their rights as sovereign entities have not been violated.
2. *Block grants* are less tightly circumscribed by federal regulations. They

BOX 3–7 **Federal Grant-in-Aid Outlays to State and/or Local Government**

FEDERAL GRANT-IN-AID OUTLAYS,
1950–1986

Fiscal Year	Amount (In $ billions)	As Percentage of GNP
1950	2.3	0.9
1955	3.2	0.8
1960	7.0	1.4
1965	10.9	1.7
1970	24.0	2.3
1975	49.8	3.3
1980	91.5	3.6
1981	94.8	3.1
1982	88.2	2.9
1983 estimate	93.5	2.9
1984 estimate	95.9	2.7
1985 estimate	99.2	2.6
1986 estimate	102.5	2.5

SOURCE: Executive Office of the President, Office of Management and Budget, *Special Analysis, Budget of the United States Government, Fiscal Year 1984* (Washington, D.C.: Government Printing Office, 1983), p. H-16.

provide federal funding for a general policy area of governmental activity, such as community development, education, health services, and crime control, and leave a good deal of flexibility to the states in deciding how the funds should be used. This means that within the framework of general federal guidelines, each state can adapt the federal policy to its own circumstances.

3. *Revenue sharing* began in 1972 as a process in which the federal government disburses funds to state and local governments to use, generally, as they see fit. The major restriction is that the government must not engage in prohibited forms of discrimination. The amount of money transmitted to state and local governments through revenue sharing is predetermined by a complex formula. State governments were eliminated from the program in 1980. Funding that year was $4.6 billion. Most revenue-sharing funds were spent on equipment, streets, and roads rather than on social services and health programs. In part this was because such funds were so limited; but state and local officials were also apparently reluctant to use revenue-sharing grants in ways that would increase their political vulnerability and reduce their maneuverability in times of federal cutbacks.[21] This was good politics; general revenue sharing was phased out in 1987. (Box 3–8 displays the amount of all federal grants to states in fiscal year 1984.)

BOX 3–8 **Some Dimensions of Fiscal Federalism**

Federal Grants to State and Local Governments
Grants authorized to be given to each state and its local governments for the fiscal year 1984.

	Total grant (millions of dollars)	Total amount per capita		Total grant (millions of dollars)	Total amount per capita
Ala.	$ 1,634	$ 419	Neb.	$ 567	$ 354
Alaska	570	1,420	Nev.	316	395
Ariz.	910	337	N.H.	367	408
Ark.	929	404	N.J.	3,179	430
Calif.	10,355	439	N.M.	850	653
Colo.	1,174	405	N.Y.	11,185	636
Conn.	1,452	468	N.C.	2,083	353
Del.	281	468	N.D.	358	511
Fla.	3,078	317	Ohio	4,273	396
Ga.	2,344	426	Okla.	1,209	403
Hawaii	504	504	Ore.	1,185	456
Idaho	370	411	Pa.	5,144	432
Ill.	4,754	417	R.I.	590	655
Ind.	1,810	329	S.C.	1,202	388
Iowa	1,001	345	S.D.	359	513
Kan.	738	308	Tenn.	1,855	403
Ky.	1,622	438	Tex.	4,693	331
La.	2,031	484	Utah	670	447
Me.	554	504	Vt.	297	594
Md.	1,877	447	Va.	1,796	339
Mass.	2,844	499	Wash.	1,607	392
Mich.	4,071	438	W. Va.	887	467
Minn.	1,873	468	Wis.	2,094	446
Miss.	1,190	476	Wyo.	599	1,198
Mo.	1,803	368			
Mont.	468	585	U.S. TOTAL	$98,720	$ 436

SOURCE: Derived from the *New York Times*, December 20, 1983, p. B19.

Grants can also be classified according to how the funds are distributed.[22] *Formula grants* are based on a decision rule, such as *x* dollars per public school pupil in daily attendance. The rule is frequently written into the legislation creating the grant, though it could also be established by the administering agency. Members of Congress and their staffs often pay a great deal of attention to the effect any given formula will have on federal spending within their states or districts.

Project grants require jurisdictions seeking funds to submit applications describing how they intend to use the money. The administrative agency makes allocations with reference to these proposals from the total sum made available to the program area by the legislature. Consequently, project grants allow for considerable administrative discretion and promote politicking after the legislature has established the general parameters and scope of funding.

Matching grants require the recipient to contribute some of its own resources to the activity for which the funds are earmarked. Matching does not necessarily require that a state or local jurisdiction put up one dollar for each dollar it receives.

In thinking about grants, it is also important to note that while some are fixed, others are open-ended. In the latter case, the amount allocated will depend upon the number of individuals who are eligible for a program or treated by it or upon other factors such as reimbursible cost overruns.

The grant system is now a deeply entrenched feature of federalism. The Reagan administration sought to reorganize it in order to reduce paperwork, other administrative costs, and the federal budgetary deficit while at the same time encouraging the states to take on more responsibility. In particular, an effort was made to consolidate categorical grants into broad block grants, and general revenue sharing was terminated. However, despite some successes, Reagan's approach met considerable resistance in Congress. As an institution, the legislature demonstrated a powerful orientation toward protecting state, local, and private beneficiaries of existing programs funded by federal grants.

The grants approach also lies at the heart of third-party government (discussed in Chapter 1). Many federal objectives—including law enforcement, education, provisions for individuals' welfare, and the fostering of better administrative techniques—are now promoted through grants and dependent upon state and local governmental implementation. However, these subnational governments may, in turn, rely on not-for-profit organizations and privatization to achieve the specific goals. The system combines federalism and administrative decentralization in a way that is managerially, politically, and legally complicated. But it hardly describes the full complexity of contemporary intergovernmental relations in the United States.

Federal money can buy cooperation and coordination, but it is not the only means of achieving these objectives. Cooperation between the states and the national government can be voluntarily established. State governors can communicate with the state's representatives in Congress. An annual conference of governors also serves as a vehicle for expressing state concerns to the national government. Mayors engage in similar activities. There are also a number of organizations, such as the Council of State Governments and the National League of Cities, that engage in lobbying efforts to promote states' and cities' general interests. In drafting their regulations for the administration of grant programs, federal agencies may be sensitive to state and local governmental concerns.

However, where cooperation of this nature fails, coordination can also be imposed through congressional exercise of powers under the commerce clause. This can go a long way toward regulating the treatment of any person, product, or substance that crosses state lines. As noted earlier, even people, crops, or things that do not cross such lines may fall within Congress's power to regulate commerce.

There are three characteristics of federal-state relationships that bear further mention. One is the extent to which they make thinking about federalism in terms of states versus the national government inappropriate. States and the federal government may be opposed to one another on occasion, but the real focus now is on programs and the role public administrators at different levels of government will play in implementing them. Interdependency has replaced dual federalism. As Morton Grodzins, one of the preeminent analysts of federalism in the 1960s, observed, "In virtually no field does the complete body of law with respect to a given governmental activity have its source in one of these so-called levels of government. In a typical case a mixture of federal, state and local regulation covers an area of regulation or activity."[23] Grodzins punctuated the point with a description of a county health officer in a rural area of a border state. His delineation of this official's functions and responsibilities will give the student of public administration much to ponder:

> The sanitarian [health officer] is appointed by the state under merit standards established by the federal government. His base salary comes jointly from state and federal funds, the county provides him with an office and office amenities and pays a portion of his expenses, and the largest city in the county also contributes to his salary and office by virtue of his appointment as city plumbing inspector. It is impossible from moment to moment to tell under which governmental hat the sanitarian operates. His work of inspecting the purity of food is carried out under federal standards; but he is enforcing state laws when inspecting commodities that have not been in interstate commerce; and somewhat perversely he also acts under state authority when inspecting milk coming into the county from producing areas across the state border. He is a federal officer when impounding impure drugs shipped from a neighboring state; a federal-state officer when distributing typhoid immunization serum; a state officer when enforcing standards of industrial hygiene; a state-local officer when inspecting the city's water supply; and (to complete the circle) a local officer when insisting that the city butchers adopt more hygienic methods of handling their garbage. But he cannot and does not think of himself as acting in these separate capacities. All business in the county that concerns public health and sanitation he considers his business. Paid largely from federal funds, he does not find it strange to attend meetings of the city council to give expert advice on matters ranging from rotten apples to rabies control. He is even deputized as a member of both the city and county police forces.[24]

Grodzin's description of the sanitarian is helpful because it indicates the extent to which any given public administrator may perforce have to be concerned with the integration of the functioning of the various levels of government. It also shows how managerial, political, and legal concerns can bear upon the job of an individual public administrator. The sanitarian is selected according to a managerial approach, the merit system, he or she has to take legalistic concerns and court decisions into account when enforcing the law, and he or she cannot be oblivious to politics when attending meetings of the city council. No doubt sanitarians also want higher appropriations for their positions if these will make it possible to do a better job. Consequently, sanitarians are likely to be concerned with budgets—and the politics that surrounds them.

A second aspect of federal-state relationships that should be considered is the concept of **entitlements**—a large number of federal programs, administered with state and local personnel, that involve providing benefits to private individuals. Welfare, unemployment insurance, health, education, and public housing are some of the major policy areas in which this practice is found. A state's participation in these programs may be voluntary, but the private individual's eligibility for the benefits may be established under federal regulations. Thus, once a state is involved in such a program, it may be confronted with a number of people who are "entitled" to benefits. Moreover, their number may grow over the years, adding not just to the expense of funding the benefits but also to the cost of administering the program. Where states provide matching funds, the costs of a given program to the state may escalate rapidly. Yet the state is not free to reduce the number of beneficiaries at will by redefining eligibility. Moreover, under federal court rulings, it may be very difficult for a state to cut off an individual's benefits without affording that person a good measure of due process, sometimes culminating in a judicial-style hearing.[25] Due process also costs money and adds to the fiscal burdens upon the state. As a matter of popular administrative belief, it may even cost more than allowing ineligible people to continue to receive benefits!

There are several serious economic problems that entitlements pose for the states. They make it difficult to cut state budgets in some areas. They can also pass a heavy burden to the states when the federal government engages in reduced funding or program cuts. For example, if the federal government reduces welfare benefits, will the state have to make up the difference, if not as a matter of law, as a matter of political practice and humanity? If the state can also engage in program cuts, on what basis should it decide to reduce benefits or eligibility—and what will the federal courts say about this approach? These are hardly hypothetical issues. Under President Reagan's "New Federalism" program, federal grants to states, which constituted 26 percent of state and local spending in 1978, were reduced to only 20 percent of that spending in 1983.[26] This passed a considerable political, administrative, and financial burden to the states. What the individual views as an "entitlement," the state or local administrator may consider a federally imposed "mandate" for which the state bears the cost. This is a feature of federalism that state administrators find especially problematic.

Third, the huge growth of grant programs and funds since the 1960s created a qualitatively different relationship between the federal government and the nation's local governments, especially its large cities. Many of the "Great Society" programs of the Johnson presidency were oriented toward the urban poor. Cities—even neighborhoods—forged direct financial relationships with the federal government. Since that time, the famous **Dillon's rule**, which holds that local governments possess only those powers expressly allocated to them by the states, has frequently been circumvented, if not nullified, by direct federal funding of local administrative activities. The mayors and administrators of large cities may at times be more oriented toward federal agencies than those in their own state capitals.

Interstate Relations

Interstate relations are another aspect of American federalism that is of importance to public administration. The states not only need to get along with the federal government but, as quasi-sovereign entities, they must find ways of coordinating their activities with one another. They seek ways of cooperating in joint endeavors. When necessary, they must also attempt to resolve disputes in a satisfactory manner. The fact that, with the exception of Alaska and Hawaii, each state shares at least one border with another accentuates the need to develop harmonious and mutually beneficial relationships among the states. Indeed, the range of problems that can arise as a result of different state policies is enormous. Coordinating road construction, establishing uniform drivers' licensing and drinking-age regulations, agreeing on means of rebating sales taxes collected from out-of-state residents to the state in which they live, agreeing on the types of vehicles (large trucks) and equipment (studded snow tires) that can be operated on a state's roads, joint law enforcement activities and insect control programs, and many, many more matters are the stuff of everyday interstate relations. More exotic matters concern border disputes, one state's discrimination against residents or former residents of another state with regard to such matters as jobs, welfare benefits, public housing, higher education, the issuance of occupational licenses, and the granting of permits to engage in commercial exploitation of a state's natural resources. Clearly, interstate relations carry with them potential for chaos and disarray. In fact, that is one reason why the national government under the Articles of Confederation was abandoned and replaced by the present constitutional system.

The U.S. Constitution fosters coordination among the states in several areas. The main one is commerce, which was particularly problematic in colonial times and under the Articles of Confederation. Among the powers granted to the federal government are the authority to regulate commerce among the states, with foreign nations, and with Indian tribes. The federal government can also establish legal-tender money, levy tariffs, enact maritime law, grant patents and copyrights, and set standard weights and measures. These powers cut deeply into state sovereignty. Once the federal government takes action in any of these areas, state policies contrary to federal regulations are preempted and viewed as unconstitutional. Thus, now that the federal government has sought to regulate and penetrate the economic life of the nation to a large extent, a very wide range of state concerns must comply with federal law. These include occupational health, safety, compensation, and collective bargaining matters; banking regu-

lations; use of roads; transportation of products across state lines; and relationships with foreign nations and their political subdivisions, including Canada and
Mexico. In addition, as noted earlier, the Constitution's commerce clause has
been used as a vehicle for promoting civil rights through legislation prohibiting
discrimination in employment, in public accommodations, and on common
carriers.

The Constitution also promotes cooperation among the states. Here the
main means is the **full faith and credit clause.** It reads, "Full Faith and Credit
shall be given in each State to the public Acts, Records, and judicial Proceedings
of every other State," and that "A person charged in any State with Treason,
Felony, or other Crime, who shall flee from Justice, and be found in another
State, shall on Demand of the executive Authority of the State from which he
fled, be delivered up, to be removed to the State having Jurisdiction of the
Crime" (Article IV). Under this clause, one state is bound to recognize the legal
acts of another, even though their policies may differ. For instance, a marriage
that is legally performed in one state must be recognized by another, even
though the second state may have different health and age requirements. Similarly, a divorce decree of one state must be recognized as legal in another,
although the grounds for divorce vary considerably among the states. The same
is true of wills and other civil instruments. The extradition of persons accused or
convicted of crimes is also required.

However, the cooperation anticipated through Article IV has not been
perfect. When residents of one state go to another as migrants for the purpose of
gaining a divorce and then return to their native state, a jurisdictional issue may
arise. Even when a divorce granted in one state is recognized by a second state,
related child custody and property settlements may be subject to the jurisdiction
of the second state. Extradition is usually smooth, but sometimes a state governor
is reluctant or unwilling to return an individual to the state from which he or she
fled. What is a crime in one state may be an act of heroism and virtue in another,
as was true of civil rights protests in the 1960s. The unfair or harsh treatment that
one accused of a crime is likely to receive in the state seeking extradition may also
be a barrier to his or her return. Thus, while in most instances the full faith and
credit clause does promote cooperation, there have been enough exceptions to
generate a good deal of litigation and a whole area of study and adjudication
called "conflict of laws."[27]

The Fourteenth Amendment's **equal protection clause** is also of importance to interstate relations. It prohibits a state from discriminating against
nonresidents and new residents in some contexts. For instance, regulations
requiring substantial residency in a state before becoming eligible for state
welfare benefits have been challenged successfully under this amendment.[28]
Interestingly, in a leading case, a state made an administrative argument that
residency requirements facilitated budgetary planning and reduced fraud.[29]
The Supreme Court, however, was less impressed with these concerns than
with the free movement of individuals from one state to another and their
equal treatment under the law. Nevertheless, in some circumstances, includ-

ing public employment and higher education, states may treat established residents differently from nonresidents or newcomers. States may also require new residents and nonresidents to take occupational tests prior to being permitted to practice a trade or profession within their jurisdiction. The full faith and credit clause does not require one state to recognize occupational licenses granted by another. Lawyers, for example, may be required to take a bar examination in every state in which they seek to practice. Ultimately, it is for the federal judiciary to decide whether state policies having a discriminatory impact on newcomers or nonresidents are constitutional. Generally speaking, in reaching their conclusions, the courts weigh the state's rationale or interest in propounding regulations of this nature against their infringement on the equal protection of individuals.

Another form of cooperation among the states is anticipated by the Constitution. Article I, section 10, allows a state to enter into an "Agreement or Compact with another State," *provided* that Congress gives its consent. The Supreme Court has interpreted congressional consent to be pertinent only when such agreements or compacts increase the political power of the states and encroach upon the powers of the federal government.[30] Interstate compacts have been important means by which two or more states can tackle a common problem, such as pollution, health, the protection of natural resources and wildlife, and dealing with traffic congestion and transportation in a metropolitan area. Compacts may include the national government as a party. They sometimes create governmental "authorities," such as the Port of New York Authority, which was established by New York State and New Jersey in 1921. Authorities of this nature are single-purpose governments, although they can be quite extensive. The Port Authority, for instance, is involved in the operation of airports, trains, buses, bridges, tunnels, and land and sea terminals. While interstate authorities facilitate coordination among the states involved, they also fragment government responsibility and may make it difficult to coordinate the provision of municipal services.

States can also coordinate many of their policies without entering into formal compacts. For instance, in 1983 the governors of New York, New Jersey, New Hampshire, Connecticut, Massachusetts, Rhode Island, and Pennsylvania sought to coordinate state laws concerning the minimum drinking age.[31] They reasoned that a uniform drinking age would promote highway safety and save lives by reducing the number of people who drive from one state to another in search of a "legal beverage." The possibilities for states simply to agree to coordinate policies are virtually endless. However, different economic and cultural interests in the states often dictate disparate policies. For instance, independent-minded Vermont was notably uninvolved in the northeastern governors' efforts.

Another means of coordination among the states rests in the adoption of uniform laws. The most successful of these has been the Uniform Commercial Code, which covers a number of commercial transactions and is subscribed to by all the states, except Louisiana. Other attempts at uniformity in the face of the diversity anticipated by federalism have fared less well. However, it is of particular importance to public administrators that many states have adopted administrative procedure acts that more or less parallel the federal version.

Where it is envisioned that the states will need an ongoing organization to facilitate coordination, a regional commission may be established. There is an Appalachian Regional Commission, for economic development, and a New England Regional Commission, for river-basin planning.[32]

Relationships Among Local Governments

The overwhelming proportion of the 82,000 governments in the United States are below the state level. A typical large metropolitan area includes several municipalities, school districts, and special districts or public authorities. It may overlap county and state lines. (See Box 3–9.) Although there are clearly many common interests among adjacent local governments and those in close proximity to one another, there are also some aspects of their relationships that are almost inevitably competitive. Like states, municipalities compete with each other for business investments in offices, manufacturing facilities, shopping malls, and other forms of economic development. They also compete for federal and state grants and other public investments. They compete in the same labor markets for their public employees. Frequently, the actions of one jurisdiction will have problematic effects on its neighbors. For example, it is not uncommon for municipalities or counties to locate landfills at the edge of their boundaries, leaving their neighbors to cope with the pollution, health hazards, and damage to property values that they cause. Local zoning decisions can affect other jurisdictions. A shopping mall in a newer suburb may pose threats to the retailers in downtown areas of central cities and older suburbs. Sporting events, rock concerts, and other mass spectator activities can create traffic jams and congestion across municipal lines. Suburban strip development may impede the flow of traffic into central cities. According to one view, suburbs are able to exploit the specialization in central cities without paying for its social and other costs.[33]

At the same time, though, some of the activities in one jurisdiction are likely to have beneficial spillover effects on others. The same concert or sporting event that ties up traffic may bring patrons to the area's motels, restaurants, bars, and shops. The location of hospitals, universities, and theaters in one town may improve the quality of life and desirability of locating in nearby ones. Coordinating and managing these relationships is a major political and administrative concern.

The traditional managerial perspective on relationships among local governments has favored reduction of the number of independent municipalities through consolidation or the imposition of countywide or even regional governance.[34] The managerial perspective is particularly critical of the overlapping and duplicative functions performed by adjacent municipalities and the high overhead costs they incur. Economies of scale may be lost and coordination may be expensive. If regional problems are not treated on a regional basis, then

BOX 3-9 The Intergovernmental Maze: Counties, Cities, and Towns in the St. Louis Metropolitan Area

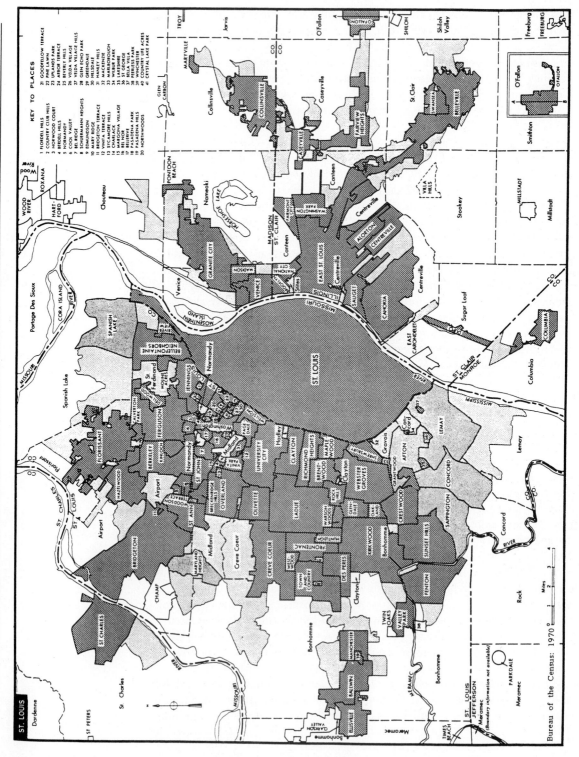

SOURCE: John L. Andriot, *Township Atlas of the United States* (McLean, Va.: Andriot Associates, 1979), p. 367.

resources may not be expended in the most cost-effective manner. Consolidation has sometimes been achieved by transferring municipal functions to the encompassing county. Annexation of smaller jurisdictions by central cities also reduces the number of independent governments in an area. In Florida, the Miami-Dade County Metropolitan Government has sought to reassign governmental functions in order to reduce costs and increase effectiveness.

The political perspective on the plethora of local governments is often quite different. It views small-scale governments as a means of enhancing political responsiveness and representativeness. Historically, general-purpose local governments were a manifestation of grass-roots democracy. The New England town meeting epitomizes the democratic and participatory self-government that can be achieved at the local level. Residents are afforded a meaningful opportunity to express their views in a public forum and to approve or disapprove of proposed governmental activities. Such government may be viewed as an end in itself, but the contemporary public-choice approach takes its logic further.[35] The multiplicity of municipalities in a large urban area may offer diverse combinations of public services. They may emphasize different educational, economic, developmental, crime control, and recreational points of view. If considered analogous to an economic market, individuals (that is, the consumers of public services) might choose to locate in those jurisdictions that suit their needs best. The presumed competition among municipalities for residents might impel them to be responsive to the public's demands for services. Moreover, since the "citizen-consumer" pays taxes, the competition might extend to the provision of such services in the most efficient fashion, thereby meeting the traditional managerial concerns head-on.

The dispute between the traditional administrative-management approach and the political/public-choice perspective remains unresolved. Those who support consolidation question the virtue of self-government that causes problems for neighboring jurisdictions. One town's "public choice" to locate its dump near the water supply of another, whose residents have no say in the matter, hardly appears democratic. How responsive a small government is to its voters depends upon a number of factors, including the citizens' interest in the local community, the degree of competition between candidates or parties, and the quantity of resources available. The extent to which individuals locate and *relocate* themselves in accordance with the mixes of services provided by different governments is generally unknown (and perhaps very limited). Therefore the validity of a fundamental premise of the public choice approach remains in doubt. On the other hand, large jurisdictions may not achieve the economies of scale predicted by those favoring consolidation.[36] Given these divergent perspectives and the practical impediments to consolidation, "interlocal" governmental relations are certain to remain an area of challenge to public administrators for some time to come.

Whatever the fate of consolidation, since 1954, the federal government has promoted the creation of regional councils as a means of coordinating the administrative activities of subnational governments. In 1980, there were some 650 such councils, virtually blanketing the country. They were involved in several policy areas, including planning, criminal justice, water quality, housing, and economic development. [37]

CONCLUSION

One can see many forces at work in the structuring of public administration in the United States. In fact, the nature of our 82,000 governments and their interrelationships are so complex that it is often difficult for governmental officials and citizens alike to keep track of administrative authority and responsibility. Perhaps the best way of understanding the contemporary American administrative state is to view it as a contest or tension between fragmentation and diversity on the one hand and coordination and uniformity on the other.

Political, as opposed to administrative, judgment stands largely on the side of fragmentation and diversity. It favors federalism as the solution to the problem of developing a representative government in a large territory. It also favors political decentralization as a means of affording the population a good measure of influence over matters of local governance. But it was also a political judgment to establish a *national* government as a means of coordinating activities among the states and of promoting uniform policies for economic development, military strength, and other purposes. This was accomplished through a constitution that clearly reflects the tensions between fragmentation and coordination. The Constitution protects state sovereignty in some respects and creates a national government that depends upon the states in several others, including representation in the Senate. But it also gives the national government considerable power over commerce and has been interpreted to require state protection of many rights that are thought to be too fundamental to vary from jurisdiction to jurisdiction. It must be noted that although constitutional law may promote uniformity in one sense, it frequently fosters diversity in another. Thus, when states are forbidden from abridging someone's free exercise of religion or freedom of speech, individual diversity is protected even though the same constitutional standard is imposed upon all the states.

For the most part, administrative judgment stands on the side of coordination and uniformity. Federal administrators devote a great deal of time, money, effort, and thought to seeking ways of implementing national programs in conjunction and coordination with state and local governments. But public administration in the United States is itself fragmented and decentralized. Coordinating activities among the agencies of one government can be difficult—from the lowest level to the highest. This is not a reflection of poor management. Rather it is a consequence of the mix of political, legal, and managerial approaches that dominate our public administrative theory and practice. Ironically, managerially based efforts to take the administration of many local matters, such as schools, cemeteries, and transportation, out of politics have contributed to further fragmentation and made coordination all the more difficult. This has made some yearn for the days of old, before administrative reforms got hold of our governments, when coordination was imposed by our political machines and strong political parties, relying heavily upon patronage. But must coordination come at the price of "dirty politics and corrupt government"?

Although historical analysis might lead one to answer with a resounding "yes," the student and practitioner of public administration should reject such a trade-off as inapt. The system can work, it *does* work, and it can work well. Of course, it can still be improved. But improvement depends in part upon public administrators who can learn to live with complexity and appreciate the opportunities it affords. The structure of the contemporary American administrative state presents the administrator with quite a challenge. He or she may be required to integrate the competing values and perspectives found in our public administration and to coordinate administrative activities among different levels of government. The system often depends upon such integration. Viewed in this context, the "sanitarian" mentioned earlier is neither a bureaucratic cog nor a pawn, but rather an inspiration.

NOTES

1. Robert Lorch, *State and Local Politics*, 2nd ed. (Englewood Cliffs, N.J.: Prentice-Hall, 1986), p. 221.
2. George E. Berkley and Douglas M. Fox, *80,000 Governments: The Politics of Subnational America* (Boston: Allyn & Bacon, 1978), p. 4.
3. Katzenbach v. McClung, 379 U.S. 294 (1964).
4. Wickard v. Filburn, 317 U.S. 111 (1942).
5. National League of Cities v. Usery, 426 U.S. 833 (1976).
6. Garcia v. San Antonio Metropolitan Transit Authority 469 U.S. 528 (1985).
7. David C. Nice, *Federalism: The Politics of Intergovernmental Relations* (New York: St. Martin's Press, 1987), pp. 4–9.
8. See Edward C. Banfield and James Q. Wilson, *City Politics* (Cambridge, Mass.: Harvard University Press and the M.I.T. Press, 1963), chaps. 11–13, for a classic discussion.
9. Daniel R. Grant and H. C. Nixon, *State and Local Government in America*, 3rd ed. (Boston: Allyn & Bacon, 1975), p. 380.
10. Berkley and Fox, *80,000 Governments*, p. 145.
11. Ibid., chap. 18.
12. Lorch, *State and Local Politics*, 2nd ed., p. 15.
13. Berkley and Fox, *80,000 Governments*, pp. 40–41. New York's Constitution has limited the width of certain ski trails.
14. Lorch, *State and Local Politics*, 2nd ed., p. 14.
15. Grant and Nixon, *State and Local Government in America*, 3d ed., p. 114.
16. Ibid., Table 12-1.
17. Berkley and Fox, *80,000 Governments*, p. 99.
18. Nice, *Federalism*, p. 92.
19. Ibid.
20. R. Douglas Arnold, *Congress and the Bureaucracy* (New Haven, Conn.: Yale University Press, 1979).
21. Nice, *Federalism*, p. 92.
22. See ibid., pp. 49–50.

23. Morton Grodzins, *The American System* (Chicago: Rand McNally, 1966), p. 80; quoted in Grant and Nixon, *State and Local Government in America*, 3d ed., pp. 37–38.

24. Morton Grodzins, "The Federal System," in *Goals for Americans*, ed. by the American Assembly (Englewood Cliffs, N.J.: Prentice-Hall, 1960), pp. 265–266; as quoted in Grant and Nixon, *State and Local Government in America*, 3d ed., pp. 37–38.

25. See David H. Rosenbloom, *Public Administration and Law* (New York: Marcel Dekker, 1983), chap. 3; Goldberg v. Kelly, 397 U.S. 254 (1970); Mathews v. Eldridge, 424 U.S. 319 (1976).

26. David Broder, "Reagan's Feat on Federalism," *Washington Post Weekly Edition*, vol. 1, no. 6 (December 12, 1983), p. 4.

27. See David D. Siegel, *Conflicts* (St. Paul, Minn.: West, 1982).

28. Shapiro v. Thompson, 394 U.S. 618 (1969).

29. Ibid.

30. Virginia v. Tennessee, 148 U.S. 503 (1893).

31. *New York Times*, December 6, 1983, p. 1.

32. Ann O'M. Bowman and Richard C. Kearney, *The Resurgence of the States* (Englewood Cliffs, N.J.: Prentice-Hall, 1986), p. 29.

33. Theodore J. Lowi, *The End of Liberalism* (New York: Norton, 1969), p. 197.

34. See Nice, *Federalism*, chap. 8.

35. See Robert Bish and Vincent Ostrom, *Understanding Urban Government* (Washington, D.C.: American Enterprise Institute, 1973), for a classic discussion.

36. Nice, *Federalism*, p. 188.

37. Bowman and Kearney, *The Resurgence of the States*, p. 162.

ADDITIONAL READING

BEER, SAMUEL. "Federalism, Nationalism, and Democracy in America," *American Political Science Review*, 72 (March 1978): 9–21.

BOWMAN, ANN O'M., AND RICHARD C. KEARNEY, *The Resurgence of the States*. Englewood Cliffs, N.J.: Prentice-Hall, 1986.

ELIZAR, DANIEL. *American Federalism: A View from the States*, 3rd ed. New York: Harper & Row, 1984.

GRODZINS, MORTON. *The American System: A New View of Government in the United States*. Chicago: Rand McNally, 1966.

HALE, GEORGE, AND MARIAN PALLEY. *The Politics of Federal Grants*. Washington, D.C.: Congressional Quarterly Press, 1981.

HOWITT, ARNOLD. *Managing Federalism*. Washington, D.C.: Congressional Quarterly Press, 1984.

NICE, DAVID C. *Federalism: The Politics of Intergovernmental Relations*. New York: St. Martin's Press, 1987.

RIKER, WILLIAM. *Federalism: Origin, Operation, Significance*. Boston: Little, Brown, 1964.

STUDY QUESTIONS

1. What seem to be the contemporary advantages and disadvantages for public administration of the kind of federalism found in the United States? Would the consolidation of the states into, say, ten regions be desirable? Why or why not?

2. How might public administration function today if the states were abolished altogether?

3. Some believe that the United States has too many governments in the sense that governmental authority is too fragmented and that the cost of redundancies and loss of coordination is too high. Would you favor abolishing any levels or kinds of government? Why or why not?

4. What are some of the externalities and spillover effects that public universities cause for the municipalities and counties in which they are located? How might universities and local governments deal with these?

PART TWO | *Core Functions*

CHAPTER 4 | Organization: Structure and Process

Organizations can be designed to achieve certain values and objectives. Since so much of contemporary life involves organizations, much attention has been paid to designing organizations appropriately. In public administration, bureaucratic organization is very common. Bureaucracy, a form of organization with several structural and procedural attributes, will be discussed in this chapter. Organization always involves relationships among employees, including supervisors. The "scientific management" and "human relations" approaches have defined the classic ways of structuring such relationships. At present, there are distinct managerial, political, and legal approaches to organizational structure and process. One possible way of synthesizing these approaches is through a more participatory form of public organization.

Public administration concerns *organized* activity aimed at the provision of services and the application of constraints to individuals and groups in the society. Consequently, public administration requires *organization*. But organization can take many different forms and can maximize many diverse values. The *structure* of an organization affects the behavior of the organization as a whole and of the individual members of it. The same is true of the *processes* through which organizations operate. By designing organizational structures and processes of one kind or another, different values can be maximized, different needs can be served, and different purposes can be achieved. Therefore, the organization of administrative activity ranks at the forefront of questions with which the student and practitioner of public administration must be concerned. As in other areas of public administration, though, there are few simple answers. Rather, there are competing responses to this basic issue: How should the public sector be organized?

ORGANIZATION THEORY

Organization is a form of coordination of human activity. Armies are a contemporary example that reaches back to antiquity. As human cultures developed from hunter-gatherer societies to the "postindustrial," technocratic ones found in some places today, greater reliance was placed on organizations as a means of achieving social, economic, and political purposes. The twentieth century has been characterized by the development of an "organizational society"[1]—that is, a society in which a great deal of our waking time is spent in organizations, such as schools, universities, workplaces, and places of worship, recreation, and health care. Although organizations have existed for centuries, contemporary organizations represent a qualitative change in the way we go about our lives. The crux of the modern organizational society is suggested in Amitai Etzioni's comprehensive yet succinct definition of organization:

> Organizations are social units (or human groupings) deliberately constructed and reconstructed to seek specific goals. Corporations, armies, schools, hospitals, churches, and prisons are included; tribes, classes, ethnic groups, friendship groups, and families are excluded. Organizations are characterized by: (1) divisions of labor, power, and communication responsibilities, divisions which are not random or traditionally patterned, but deliberately planned to enhance the realization of specific goals; (2) the presence of one or more power centers which control the concerted efforts of the organization and direct them toward its goals; these power centers also must review continuously the organization's performance and re-pattern its structure, where necessary, to increase its efficiency; (3) substitution of personnel, i.e., unsatisfactory persons can be removed and others assigned their tasks. The organization can also recombine its personnel through transfer and promotion.[2]

Inherent in modern organization is the assumption that organizations should be rationally designed to achieve their purposes effectively and efficiently. It is perhaps above all the commitment to rationality that separates contemporary organizational society from earlier periods in human history.

Unfortunately, the task of designing organizations that effectively and efficiently achieve their purposes can be extremely complicated. It is obvious that an "organizational society" may not mesh well with cultural and political values that emphasize individualism and individual rights. "The problem of modern organizations is thus how to construct human groupings that are as rational as possible, and at the same time produce a minimum of undesirable side effects and a maximum of satisfaction."[3] Working or participating in an organization can be frustrating and alienating. Rather than being tools for the rational attainment of goals, organizations can emerge as powerful masters that seek their own survival, aggrandizement, and maximization of power. Organizations can also infringe upon the human rights of individuals to privacy, to freedom of expression and association, to peace and even love. They can also stand at odds with individual efforts at further occupational, professional, and psychological self-development.

Efforts to come to grips with the rise of modern organization have led to the development of a self-conscious body of thought called "organization theory." Given its fragmented character, it might be more appropriate to speak in terms of *theories* of organization, but there are some premises that seem to underlie most of the thinking in this area.[4] Among these premises are the following: (1) the structure of an organization affects its behavior; (2) the structure of an organization affects the behavior of its workers, participants, and perhaps even casual members; (3) organizational processes also affect organizational and individual behavior; (4) organizations can be rationally (or scientifically) designed structurally and procedurally to achieve their goals in an effective and efficient manner; and (5) organizations can usefully be conceptualized as systems that respond to and affect their environments and seek to gain information about the efficacy of those responses. In general, organizational theory is "generic" in the sense that it does not make distinctions between public and private organizations. All organizations share some characteristics, and virtually all significant ones are regulated by governments in one way or another.[5] Nevertheless, by and large, public sector (or governmental) organizations face legal-constitutional, political, and market conditions that distinguish them from most private organizations. Consequently, some theorists concentrate on these distinctions in an effort to develop a theory and practice of the management of public organizations.[6] To date, organization theory has made some important strides; but it remains true, as Charles Perrow, a leading theorist, observed, that "[w]e have probably learned more, over several decades of research and theory, about the things that do *not* work (even though some of them obviously *should* have worked), than we have about things that do work."[7] What are some of the lessons we have learned?

COMMONALITIES IN PUBLIC ADMINISTRATIVE ORGANIZATION

Dwight Waldo, who has perhaps been the leading public administrative theorist in the United States since World War II, has observed that sometimes a theory is so commonplace and accepted that it becomes part of a society's culture.[8] There are certain aspects of organization theory that have acquired this status. They serve as a platform for the development of more specific theories about how public administration should be organized. Consequently, all leading theories of public administrative organization must respond to them.

Bureaucracy

Some aspects of the concept of bureaucracy and the attributes of that form of organization were already discussed in Chapter 1. But bureaucracy is so central to public administration that we must continually return to it. In fact, for some, "modern organization" is virtually synonymous with "bureaucracy." This is because so many organizations make use of structural and procedural elements that have been considered attributes of bureaucratic organization. These attributes were identified most influentially by Max Weber in his development of a general theory of bureaucracy.

Weber was a German sociologist (1864–1920) who used an "ideal-type" approach to identifying the structure, process, and behavior of bureaucratic organization.[9] The "ideal type" was not intended to be an observed reality. Rather, it is a mental construct that is intended to identify what would emerge if a phenomenon (such as bureaucracy) could develop into its purest form, that is, what it would be like if there were no militating forces to limit its full development. Thus, Weber does not purport to describe reality; but he does identify the essence of bureaucracy. (Examples of federal agencies that meet Weber's criteria are presented in Box 4–1.) In abridged form, bureaucracy in Weber's concept consists of the following structural elements:

1. Specialized jurisdictions, offices, and tasks; that is, a division of labor and authority regarding the achievement of the organization's goals.
2. A hierarchy of authority to coordinate the activities of the specialized offices and to integrate their jurisdictional authority. In the most rational bureaucratic design, the organization is headed by a single individual authority.
3. A career structure in which individual employees of the bureaucratic organization move through various specializations and ranks. Movement is based on merit and/or seniority.
4. A bureaucratic structure that tends to be permanent. It remains intact regardless of the flow of members in and out of it. Society becomes dependent upon the bureaucracy's functioning to the extent that chaos results if it is destroyed.
5. By implication, bureaucracies are large organizations.

Procedurally, bureaucracy is:

1. *Impersonal or dehumanizing.* This was considered by Weber to be bureaucracy's "special virtue" because it eliminates "irrational" emotional

Box 4.1 Bureaucratic Organization

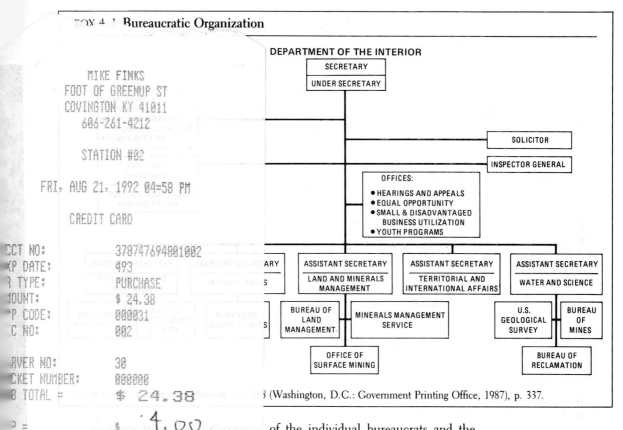

DEPARTMENT OF THE INTERIOR

(Washington, D.C.: Government Printing Office, 1987), p. 337.

of the individual bureaucrats and the organization as a whole.

2. *Impersonal.* Bureaucracy does not depend upon persons but rather upon offices (literally, "desks"). Virtually everything about its structure and operation is written down in a formal fashion. In addition, communication usually takes written form because it is between offices or persons in their capacity as officeholders and at least theoretically is independent of the actual persons who occupy those positions. Written documents are stored in files, access to which usually is carefully limited and is frequently a source of power.

3. *Rule-bound.* Bureaucracy operates according to formal rules that are in writing and can be learned. The object of the rules is to specify proper office procedure and to assure regularity in dealing with outsiders. These rules also seek to ensure impersonality and bolster hierarchical authority.

4. *Highly disciplined.* Individual bureaucrats are bound by the bureaucracy's rules and authority structure. They may be disciplined for rule infractions and insubordination.

As a result of these structural and procedural characteristics, bureaucracy is:

1. *Highly efficient.* Weber regarded bureaucracy as the most efficient form of organization. It acts with continuity, precision, rationality, expertise,

BOX 4–1 *Continued*

DEPARTMENT OF HEALTH AND HUMAN SERVICES

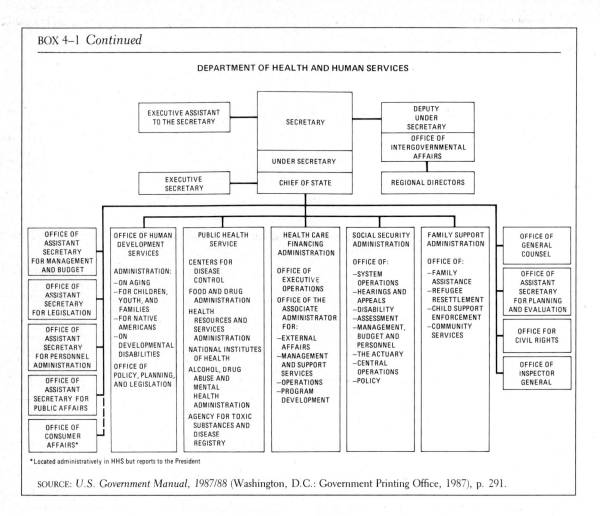

*Located administratively in HHS but reports to the President

SOURCE: *U.S. Government Manual, 1987/88* (Washington, D.C.: Government Printing Office, 1987), p. 291.

speed, and discipline. Its use of discretion is predictable, since it is structurally and procedurally constrained. Bureaucracy is reliable and reduces the emotional costs of attaining its goals. In Weber's view, bureaucracy compared with other forms of organization as did the machine with nonmechanical modes of production.

2. *Powerful*. Its power stems largely from its rationality, expertise, reliability, and continuity. Weber maintains that the well-developed bureaucracy is virtually uncontrollable by outsiders and that society becomes dependent upon it for the provision of services and the application of constraints. Thus, the organizational tool (bureaucracy) tends to emerge as the master of society.

3. *Ever-expanding*. Bureaucratic expansion is prompted not only by efficiency and power but also by the quantitative and qualitative growth of tasks requiring organized administration in a complex society. Indeed,

even as Weber described the advantages of bureaucracy, he admonished against its tendency to engulf society:

> It is horrible to think that the world could one day be filled with nothing but those little cogs [bureaucrats], little men clinging to little jobs and striving towards bigger ones. . . . This passion for bureaucracy . . . is enough to drive one to despair. . . . [W]hat can we oppose to this machinery in order to keep a portion of mankind free from this parcel-ling-out of the soul, from this supreme mastery of the bureaucratic way of life.[10]

Two additional points require emphasis. First, when Weber referred to individual bureaucratic employees as "cogs," he was recognizing the extent to which bureaucracy is dehumanizing and turns the individual into an appendage to a machinelike organization. The organization is not supposed to adapt to the individual's personal, emotional, psychological, mental, or even physical idiosyncrasies. Rather, the individual is *standardized*, dehumanized, to fit the particular organizational slot in which he or she is to be used. The organization revolves around positions and offices, not persons. Second, the power of bureaucratic organization is not derived just from its structural and procedural attributes but also flows from its *rationality*. People comply with bureaucratic orders and decisions because they accept them as legitimate. Their legitimacy is based on the belief that they are rational, reflect trained expertise and not irrational whim, and are regulated by law or official directive. In the ideal-type bureaucracy—although not, of course, in its real-world counterpart—an arbitrary, capricious, or personally discriminatory decision or order is an impossibility.

There has been a great deal of debate over the utility of Weber's concept and theory of bureaucracy. Although current consensus appears to be that Weber provided a brilliant and useful statement, four points of contention remain. First, that however bureaucracy might function as an ideal type, we live in a real world in which bureaucratic organizational behavior seems markedly at variance with Weber's ideas. Warren Bennis, a leading contemporary organizational theorist, seems to have captured this point best. He writes that real-world bureaucracy is characterized by:

- Bosses without (and underlings with) technical competence;

- arbitrary and zany rules;

- an underworld (or informal) organization which subverts or even replaces the formal apparatus;

- confusion and conflict among roles;

- cruel treatment of subordinates based not on rational or legal grounds but upon inhumanity.[11]

A second criticism is that Weber failed to understand the extent to which specialized expertise is inherently at odds with formal hierarchical authority. The point here is that the formal superordinate ("boss") becomes actually dependent upon subordinates who have greater specialized technical expertise in various areas of the bureaucracy's operation. As Victor Thompson observes:

> Whereas the boss-man [worker] relationship is *formally* unilateral with rights running in one direction from the boss to the man, the advance of personal specialization is converting the relationship *informally* into a unilateral one with ability running from the man to the boss. Authority is centralized, but ability is inherently decentralized because it comes from practice rather than from definition. Whereas the boss retains his full *rights* to make all decisions, he has less and less *ability* to do so because of the advance of science and technology.[12]

This growing gap between ability and authority can be the source of great stress for the "boss," who is responsible for operations over which he or she has far less than full control.

Third, as these two criticisms suggest, Weber may have overstated the extent to which bureaucrats can and do behave rationally. Herbert Simon, whose work in the 1940s and 1950s revolutionized public administrative thinking, reminded us that "human behavior in organizations is best described as 'intendedly rational. . . .' "[13] Complete rationality is frustrated by incomplete knowledge and information as well as by individuals' multiple, unranked preferences. Decision makers in organizations do not generally know what all the consequences of an important decision will be. Nor are they always able to determine which course of action suits their preferences most fully. The concept of "bounded rationality," as Simon's view has come to be called, is now an important aspect of the study of human behavior and decision making in organizations.

Finally, Weber's ideal-type analysis is widely considered of limited utility in designing real-world organizations because it fails to take into account the vast cultural differences among societies. For instance, whereas the authority and legitimacy of a bureaucrat in Germany, France, or Austria may be strengthened by the high social status accorded such functionaries, in other societies, such as the United States, the bureaucrat may be more or less an object of derision. Recognition of cultural variations that bear upon the operation of bureaucracies has prompted analysts to devote considerable attention to comparative public administration. It is hoped that by doing so, it will eventually be possible to analyze the effects of environmental factors on public bureaucracies.

Still, these criticisms should not be taken as rendering the Weberian analysis useless. All one needs to do is to belong to an organization, or better yet, try to form one, to realize how dependent American society is upon the principles of bureaucratic organization. Specialization (often by committee), hierarchy (for coordination, often by a governing board or council of some type), and formalized procedure (Robert's rules) are well-known attributes of contemporary organizations, whether they be social clubs or governmental units.

Scientific Management

Scientific management is a second aspect of organization theory that has worked its way into American culture. This approach developed, or at least was popularized, through the work of Frederick Taylor,[14] whose life span more or less coincided with Weber's. However, while Weber came to protest the transformation of employees into "cogs," Taylor embraced it as a prerequisite for scientifically finding the most efficient way of accomplishing any given task. By contemporary standards, much of what Taylor had to say appears naive, paternalistic, inaccurate, and sometimes just plain silly. However, Taylorism became a worldwide movement and continues to have an important legacy in the public sector in the United States. Taylor developed four core principles of scientific management:

1. Management should study the mass of traditional knowledge possessed by workmen and devise a way to accomplish each task, reducing it to a body of scientific laws of production. This requires time-and-motion studies that determine precisely the one best way of performing a specific work operation. For instance, Taylor developed a "science" of shovelling.
2. Workers should be scientifically selected according to physical, mental, and psychological attributes. For example, if the one best way of shovelling coal is to do it in twenty-one-pound loads, then a worker who has the physical strength and stamina to perform this operation would be selected. Equally important, Taylor stressed seeking workers who would "appreciate" management's help in making them more productive.
3. The worker should be scientifically motivated to do as management instructs. For the most part, Taylor stressed tying productivity to pay through "piece-rate" pay plans, in which the worker was paid according to how much he or she produced. Taylor also thought the frequency with which pay should be given could be scientifically determined in the interests of maximum motivation. He also recommended developing effective sanctions against workers who failed to do as they were told.
4. Work should be redivided so that management has more responsibility for designing work processes and work flow. This proposal fostered the rise of a "science" of efficiency engineering.

It was characteristic of Taylor's optimism that he assumed that scientific management would yield greater cooperation between workers and management. He believed his system would lead to greater productivity and therefore a higher standard of living for any society in the long run. The greater productivity would yield more profit to go around and therefore would reduce conflict over the distribution of revenues derived from the sale of products or services. Workers would lose some control over their work, but they would increase their standard of living.

In specific terms, Taylor's legacy has been pronounced in professionalized management, industrial engineering, industrial psychology, deskilled jobs, and a group of activities found in contemporary personnel administration. In the public sector, position classification and job design continue to reflect many of the attitudes and ideas of scientific management. More generally, Taylorism strongly reinforced the idea that the individual worker should be treated as an appendage to a machine, should perform only those functions that a machine or animal could not perform more cheaply, and should not be encouraged to participate in the designing of work processes and work flow, since these were matters for scientific managers. It also contributed to the still prevalent idea that productivity is the primary object of organization and that the "good" organization is the one that efficiently produces what it is intended to. In this view, the bottom line, so to speak, is output; what happens to the worker in the process—boredom, alienation, occupational disease—is of secondary concern. Work is to supply products and services, not to develop the full capability of workers.

Of course, when one lays bare the premises of Taylorism, it can sound dreadful. Yet as a society, the United States continues to define the workplace in terms of efficiency and productivity. The prevalent attitude is that good performance should be rewarded and inadequate productivity punished. Moreover, even on such emotionally wrenching issues as mandatory retirement, many prefer to enhance organizational efficiency rather than to reduce human costs.

The Human Relations Approach

The dehumanization explicit in Weber's ideal-type bureaucracy and implicit in Taylorism has been considered by some to be dysfunctional even in organizational terms because it runs counter to the needs of the human beings who actually make up the organization. Amitai Etzioni describes the problem posed by highly rational, dehumanizing organizations:

> Generally the less the organization alienates its personnel, the more efficient it is. Satisfied workers usually work harder and better than frustrated ones. Within limits, happiness heightens efficiency in organizations and, conversely, without efficient organizations much of our happiness is unthinkable. Without well-run organizations our standard of living, our level of culture, and our democratic life could not be maintained. Thus, to a degree, *organizational rationality and human happiness go hand in hand*. But a point is reached in every organization where happiness and efficiency cease to support each other. Not all work can be well-paid and gratifying, and not all regulations and orders can be made acceptable. Here we face a true dilemma.[15]

In large part, the object of the **human relations approach** has been to try to alleviate this dilemma by developing ways of making work in organizations more socially and psychologically acceptable to employees while at the same time enhancing or at least maintaining efficiency. Thus, the human relations approach accepts efficiency and productivity as the legitimate values of organization but seeks to maximize these by eliminating the dysfunctions caused by overspecialization, alienating hierarchical arrangements, and general dehumanization.

Ironically, the human relations approach grew out of a rather elaborate but standardly conceptualized set of experiments in the scientific management tradition. Elton Mayo, Fritz Roethlisberger, and others conducted studies at the

Hawthorne Works of the Western Electric Company in Chicago from 1927 to 1932.[16] The experiments started from the premise that the physical conditions at work would directly affect productivity in a linear fashion. For instance, it was hypothesized that an increase in illumination would lead to greater production per worker. This turned out to be the case, but as the experiment proceeded and lighting was reduced to the original level, it was observed that productivity remained higher than it had been before the study began. From a scientific management perspective this was puzzling indeed. Eventually, the experimenters concluded that to some extent the workers were actually responding to the experiment itself, that is, the attention being devoted to them, rather than to the levels of illumination. This phenomenon was dubbed the "Hawthorne Effect." In the context of organization, it stands for the premise that social and psychological factors can play a major role in determining the productivity of workers. This conclusion was a radical departure from the Weberian and Taylorist traditions emphasizing dehumanization because it asserted that human factors were key contributors to organizational efficiency. Put simply, the illumination experiment was taken to mean that if greater attention were paid to the worker as a person, the worker would feel a greater degree of self-esteem and happiness and would consequently be more productive.

As the Hawthorne studies continued, the researchers observed that workers socialize with one another and may form groups or informal organizations. As a result, workers tend to respond to changes in the work environment or formal organization as groups rather than as individuals. The responses could be functional in the sense of promoting greater productivity, or they could be dysfunctional, from the formal organization's perspective, by limiting productivity. A "functional" response would be, for example, that the production group would "cover" for a member who was having an off day and going slower than the norm. A "dysfunctional" response might be a mild, but symbolic, form of physical violence used against individual employees who exceed the group's norm for productivity. Such a collectively enforced limitation may be effectively imposed even though under the piece-rate pay plan it is in any given individual worker's economic interest to be as productive as possible.

Several very important conclusions were drawn from the Hawthorne experiments. These became the basis for further research and the development of the human relations approach to organization. Among them were that (1) productivity is strongly affected by social and psychological factors, not simply by physical ability and stamina; (2) noneconomic rewards and sanctions are significant determinants of workers' motivation and their level of job satisfaction; (3) the highest degree of specialization is not necessarily the most efficient approach to dividing labor; and (4) workers may react to management, the organization, and work itself as members of groups or informal organizations rather than as individuals. To the extent that these conclusions were accepted and acted upon, human relations became an explicit central facet of organizational theory and behavior. It is important to remember, however, that the human relations approach did not assert that the ultimate objective of an organization was to increase the workers' happiness—the end remained efficiency and productivity.

In short, the human relations approach conceptually put the human being back into the organization.

As this approach developed, organization theory placed greater emphasis on serving both the economic and noneconomic needs of workers and designing jobs to make them socially and psychologically satisfying. It also began to emphasize worker-management communication and worker participation in decision making concerning the way a product was to be manufactured or a service rendered. Perhaps especially important was the emergence of a new view of the complexity of the workers' motivation. Weber saw workers as cogs who were harnessed to a machine over which they had no control, while Taylor saw them as essentially one-dimensional and responsive only to economic rewards and sanctions. By the late 1930s, however, a new view found its way into print in Chester Barnard's very influential book entitled *The Functions of the Executive*.[17] Barnard was a successful manager of the New Jersey Bell Telephone Company and had a keen understanding of the complexities of human motivation at work. Barnard emphasized the obvious in reminding those imbued with the principles of scientific management that organization depended upon the willingness of its members to serve. Such willingness generally had to be induced and could be withdrawn by a participant at any time. Consequently, authority in organizations did not simply flow downward from the top; those on the bottom could also exercise power by refusing to cooperate. In Barnard's view, there was a "zone of indifference" in which workers would follow the directives of management without question. But orders beyond this zone would be questioned and perhaps opposed, subverted, or circumvented.

The zone of indifference is notably *personalized*. In theory, it can vary with each subordinate-superordinate relationship. The human relations approach followed through on this insight by dealing with personal and interpersonal behavior in organizations. A new dimension was added to organization theory, which had previously focused on the organization itself, rather than on the behavior of its members. Attention could now be more profitably turned to such key subjects as leadership and motivation.

Leadership

In *The Functions of the Executive*, Barnard called attention to the role of leadership in organizations. **Leadership** is a term that can be defined in several ways. However, at its core is the concept of consistent ability to influence people, to motivate them to serve a common purpose, and to fulfill the functions necessary for successful group action. The organization theory approach to leadership raises at least two broad concerns: What are the qualities of leadership? How is leadership exercised?

An early attempt to define the qualities of leadership focused on the personality traits of individuals who were clearly successful leaders. To an extent, this approach was derived from Max Weber's theorizing about "charismatic" authority.[18] According to Weber, some individuals are endowed with extraordinary qualities that induce others to follow their leadership. Religious leaders who are believed to be in contact with supernatural forces are a classic example. Some political leaders can also be considered "charismatic" in the technical Weberian sense. Many more have a kind of presence or charm that is now often called "charisma." And there is no doubt that many people are willing to follow their lead at least partly for this reason. Yet, when researchers have tried to pin down precisely the personality traits that contribute to leadership, they have been unable to come up with any consistent listing. Some leaders are introverted, shy, bland, and given to procrastination, whereas others are flamboyant, eccentric, and decisive.

Failure to identify a set of personality traits of leaders influenced some observers to view leadership as purely *situational*. In this view, circumstances external to the individual leader account for leadership. In other words, the corporation and the economy make the successful manager, rather than the other way around. Although the situational approach is valuable, it can also be too mechanistic. For instance, it would suggest that Ronald Reagan's personality had nothing to do with his historic landslide electoral victory in 1984. But throughout his presidency public opinion polls have shown that people tend to like Reagan more than they like his policies and more than they favor the Republican party. Clearly, the personal qualities of someone in a position of leadership can make a difference even though much of what leaders accomplish may be dictated by situational forces and circumstances.

Recent dissatisfaction with the strict situational approach has led to futher efforts to discover something about the personalities of leaders. One psychological approach is to study leaders' level of ego development.[19] Findings thus far suggest that as compared to most social groups that have been studied, managers have a higher awareness of self and inner feelings. They are also more likely to think in terms of contingencies and multiple possibilities, as opposed to dichotomous categories such as "right" and "wrong." Rather than view rules as fixed, they tend to see them as guidelines subject to change and challenge.

Leaving aside the disputed ground of personality traits, are there any qualities and skills that seem to be prerequisites for effective leadership in a wide variety and large number of situations? Among those qualities and skills often mentioned are:

1. *Belief in the possibility of success.* Leaders want to change or maintain some aspect of social, political, or economic life. They must believe that there is a significant, though possibly small, likelihood that their efforts will make a difference. Anyone who takes the stance that "there's nothing I can do about it anyway" is not very likely to influence others to work toward a common goal.
2. *Communications skills.* Leaders must communicate with followers. Generally, this requires substantial verbal skill. Followers must have a reasonably clear picture of what is expected of them if they are in fact to work in a coordinated way toward a desired common purpose.
3. *Empathy.* Leaders often have a deep understanding of the psychology, thought processes, aspirations, and fears of their followers. Empathy not

only facilitates communication but also enables the leader to find successful ways of influencing people. Empathy, of course, is not sympathy. The leader may remain detached or aloof yet still be able to enter the mental processes of the followers. Perhaps J. Edgar Hoover, former director of the FBI, is the most familiar example of this. Few would have found him "warm." Yet he was extremely effective in building the FBI into a strong federal police agency partly because he understood the outlook of a large number of Americans on crime, communism, and morality. By 1974, the FBI had a central file of some 159 million fingerprints, and the number was increasing by about three thousand per day. These were mostly supplied by state and local agencies and private employers. But due to his ability to dispel Americans' fears of a national police agency while playing upon their anxiety concerning communism, Hoover built the FBI into precisely such an agency with very little real opposition.[20]

4. *Energy.* Tales of the long hours put in by leaders are legion. The "workaholic" label probably fits many. To cite only a few examples, Eugene Lewis observes that Hyman Rickover, "father" of the U.S. nuclear Navy, and Robert Moses, who oversaw the building of more roads, bridges, tunnels, and parks than perhaps anyone in recent history, devoted tremendous time and attention to gaining detailed understanding of the projects and technologies that might be appropriate for their organizations.[21]

5. *Sound judgment.* Continuing leadership may depend substantially upon the exercise of sound, reasoned judgment. Emotional, arbitrary, or capricious responses to situations are not the hallmark of long-lasting leadership—at least where the followers are free to abandon the leader. History is rife with examples of the downfall of leaders who irrationally engaged in disasterous blunders. One of the problems leaders may face is developing a feeling of infallibility, which will make sound judgment all the more difficult. In organizational terms, it is generally considered important for leaders to maintain an unbiased, disinterested (but not uninterested) posture with regard to the organization's members. This helps the leader keep matters in perspective. One should always consider such questions as: How major or minor is an infraction or an individual's incompetence from the perspective of keeping an organization functioning toward the achievement of its goals? How serious a threat is some event or action occurring outside the organization? For instance, should scarce resources be expended to fight off every threat to a public administrative organization's jurisdiction, no matter how minor or remote?

There are a number of other qualities that leaders often possess but which appear to be less essential. Intelligence is one. Certainly the "best and the brightest" are often in a position of leadership. But many leaders are not the most intelligent people found in a society. Nor does it appear crucial that leaders have technical proficiency in the work performed by their organizations, though many of them do. Finally, leadership is sometimes defined in terms of decision making, but some effective leaders have avoided decisions whenever possible.

In view of the generality of contemporary knowledge about leadership, some have sought to learn more by studying the organizational careers of individuals who were exceptionally successful public administrative leaders. For instance, Eugene Lewis's book, *Public Entrepreneurship: Toward a Theory of Bureaucratic Political Power* (1984), considers in depth the "organizational lives" of Hyman Rickover, J. Edgar Hoover, and Robert Moses. These men were eccentric in many respects, but Lewis found some common keys to their leadership.

First, each saw organizations as tools for the achievement of his own goals. These goals were not simply rising to the top but rather accomplishing something substantive through the organization. Hoover created a national police force, Rickover brought the U.S. Navy into the atomic age by demonstrating the desirability and feasibility of submarines driven by nuclear power, and Moses pursued his vision of the public good by building parks and improving transportation in the greater New York City area.

Second, Lewis finds that "the [highly successful] public entrepreneur typically 'owns' all or some of the reality premises of the society in one or more areas of specialized concern."[22] Such entrepreneurs dominate media accounts, legislative hearings, and various meetings pertinent to their area of specialization and interest. In this way, the leader comes to "own" some aspect of public policy. Hoover "owned" statistics pertaining to crime. Rickover "owned" nuclear power in the Navy, Moses "owned" the construction of parks and bridges in metropolitan New York.

Third, rather than viewing the public service as hopelessly overrun by inefficient, ineffectual, and hidebound organizations and personnel, successful public administrative leaders grasp the potential impact that effective organizations can have. As Lewis puts it, "The public entrepreneur, somewhere during his career, comes to understand that *the large, complex public organization is the most powerful instrument for social, political, and economic change in the political universe.*"[23] Public organizations can provide a base of political power that protects the leader from opponents and serves as a lever for exercising influence on important external political actors, such as legislators. At the height of their influence, Hoover and Moses were untouchable by their political opponents.

Another important characteristic is that "each entrepreneur conveyed to his listeners the impression that he possessed a knowledgeability and a capacity to carry out monumental tasks that no other element in the political system seemed able to accomplish."[24] Rickover would introduce a new technology to submarine warfare that would make for a "true submarine," that is, one that could remain submerged for very extended periods of time. Hoover would control crime and subversion. Moses would mobilize the resources for huge projects, such as the Triboro Bridge. Robert Caro described the bridge, which connects the Bronx, Manhattan, and Queens, as follows: "Its anchorages, the masses of concrete in which its cables would be embedded, would be as big as any pyramid built by an Egyptian Pharaoh, its roadways wider than the widest roadways of the Caesars of Rome. . . . [It] would require enough concrete to pave a four-lane highway from

New York to Philadelphia, enough to reopen Depression-shuttered cement factories from Maine to Mississippi. . . . [F]urnaces would have to be fired up at no fewer than fifty separate Pennsylvania steel mills. . . . [A]n entire forest would have to crash on the Pacific Coast on the opposite side of the American continent."[25]

Finally, public entrepreneurs like Hoover, Rickover, and Moses expand their "ownership" of areas of public policy. They extend the boundaries of their organizations in order to bring more and more under their control. This reduces uncertainty and maximizes autonomy, though it may eventually undercut the democratic processes of representative government. Perhaps Hoover is the best example. He expanded the FBI's role in society from combatting narrowly-defined federal crimes to working with local police forces throughout the nation to combatting the alleged threat of subversion by communists and fellow travellers. The FBI grew from a small, ineffective adjunct of the Department of Justice to a virtually autonomous police agency with a presence throughout the nation. In theory, Hoover was subordinate to the president, the attorney general, and Congress. In practice, though, even when he was clearly out of touch with the nation's changing attitudes and concerns, he remained largely impervious to outside control. Indeed, Lewis observes that when Hoover died in office in 1972, it "was viewed by friend and foe alike as fortunate. . . ."[26]

Discovering some of the basic qualities associated with leadership does not suggest we should ignore the contributions of the situational approach. The qualities necessary to lead may depend on the situation or precisely what the job is. For instance, organizing a public celebration for the Bicentennial of the U.S. Constitution presents a different administrative situation from building a bridge or running a covert operation to destabilize or overthrow a government abroad. Similarly, providing public education differs from controlling crime, and processing motor vehicle license renewals presents a different situation than engaging in social work and family rehabilitation.

The situational approach emphasizes the importance of adopting the most effective leadership style for the organization and the job concerned. The root of this approach lies in Chester Barnard's insight that organizations depend upon individuals' willingness to serve and the extent of their zone of indifference. Using a related perspective, Amitai Etzioni has developed a useful scheme for organizing our thoughts about the appropriate leadership style in any given organization. He proposes that individual involvement in organizations can be based primarily on (1) a moral commitment to its goals and purposes (**moral involvement**); (2) a calculation that participating in the organization serves some individual need (**calculative involvement**); or (3) a belief that although the individual would rather not be associated with the organization, there is no viable alternative (**alienative involvement**).[27] Etzioni goes on to suggest that the appropriate kind of power used in organizations will depend on the nature of the involvement of most participants. In his view, normative power is most appropriate for organizations based on moral involvement, remunerative power for calculative involvement, and coercive power for alienative involvement. In short, the leadership style of voluntary organizations for the civic good should differ from the leadership style in a public bureau that processes applications for the renewal of drivers' licenses. Both should differ from the style in which a prison superintendent attempts to induce compliance from the prisoners.

Etzioni's perspective suggests that leadership styles can range from highly authoritarian through more democratic to laissez faire. Authoritarian leadership may be necessary when involvement is largely alienative. Here, even if physical coercion is unavailable, the leader can choose to keep organizational participants under a tight rein. Democratic leadership can be helpful where involvement is calculative because it can enable the leader to be more aware of the participants' personal reasons for willingness to serve in the organization. For instance, some may want status, others financial remuneration. Laissez-faire leadership, in which coordination and pursuit of group goals are organized almost entirely by the members, is potentially appropriate where involvement is moral. For instance, volunteers in building emergency sandbag dikes to prevent flooding of their hometown need materials and overall coordination, but they are not likely to require much supervision once they know how to fill, distribute, and place the bags.

A more thoroughly developed analysis of "How to Choose a Leadership Pattern" was presented by Robert Tannenbaum and Warren H. Schmidt in the *Harvard Business Review* in 1958. In 1973, they added a "Retrospective Commentary" to their classic article.[28] Like Etzioni, they emphasize the desirability of congruence between "forces" in the manager and those in the subordinates. The original article posited a continuum from a **boss-centered** leadership style to a **subordinate-centered** style. Although drawn more complexly in their article, the basic continuum was as follows, moving progressively from boss-centered to subordinate-centered leadership.

BOSS-CENTERED LEADERSHIP

1. The manager makes a decision and announces it.
2. The manager "sells" the decision to subordinates.
3. The manager presents ideas and invites questions.
4. The manager presents a tentative decision subject to change.
5. The manager presents a problem, obtains suggestions, and makes the decision.
6. The manager defines the restrictions pertinent to a decision and asks subordinates to make the decision as a group.
7. The manager permits subordinates to make decisions within broad limits defined by the manager.

SUBORDINATE-CENTERED LEADERSHIP

As the leadership style changed from highly boss-centered to more subordinate-centered, subordinates were given greater freedom and opportunities for participation in organizational decision making.

This scheme was modified by the authors in 1973, in response to a number of social and work-related changes that had occurred in the 1960s. Especially important were greater opposition to the exercise of hierarchical managerial authority, demands for participation in the workplace, and increasing concern with the quality of work life. In the 1973 version, subordinates were called "nonmanagers" and the labels on the continuum were changed. The boss-centered end was called "manager power and influence," while the other end was "nonmanager power and influence." There was also greater recognition that managers were dependent upon the willingness of nonmanagers to accept their decisions and that an organization's environment could impose constraints upon its decision making. For example, consumer groups and environmentalists might have to be taken into account.

Having posited these leadership styles, Tannenbaum and Schmidt reasoned that the most suitable one in any given context would depend upon the managers, the subordinates or nonmanagers, and the organizational situation. For managers, the main concerns would be their personal beliefs in the desirability of participation and their willingness to tolerate risk and uncertainty. For the subordinates, the main forces would be their willingness to participate in decision making, their understanding of and identification with the goals of the organization, and their tolerance for ambiguous direction as opposed to highly specific instruction from hierarchical authorities.

An important conclusion is that the leadership style should be determined by the congruence of forces in the manager and those in the subordinates. A subordinate-centered leadership style would be inappropriate where subordinates did not want to share authority and participate in decision making. Conversely, where the subordinates do want greater freedom and participation, a boss-centered leadership style would be inappropriate. Nor, of course, could a manager who is uneasy when exercising authority or one who is opposed to subordinate participation simply change his or her style to make it congruent with the outlook of the subordinates.

"Forces" in the situation stem from pressures on the organization, the nature of its work tasks, problems, and objectives. For instance, in work that routinely involves severe time pressures or a crisis atmosphere, such as fire-fighting, it is inappropriate to hold group discussions and reach group decisions while the work is going on. Decisions must be made and followed quickly. In some situations, workers are so widely dispersed and unsupervised that they must have a good deal of autonomy while they are doing their jobs. Police are a good example. The size of organizational units and the nature of technologies used are other situational forces that should be considered.

Whatever the leadership style, leaders generally perform some similar functions for organizations. Sometimes a conceptual distinction between two broad types of leadership is useful. **Expressive leaders** play a fundamental role in goal-setting and in gaining adherence to the norms and objectives of an organization. They also represent the organization to the outside world. **Instrumental leadership** involves maintenance of the organization in terms of securing the resources needed for its operation and assuring that they are distributed properly. Expressive leadership is embodied in the definition of leadership as "the capacity and will to rally men and women to a common purpose."[29] Instrumental leadership is better conveyed by the view that "leadership is the ability to provide those functions required for successful group action."[30] One individual can combine both types of leadership, though they are often separated. For instance, President Reagan best fit the "expressive" category, while some of his appointments to the White House staff, such as Donald Regan and Howard Baker were more in the instrumental category.

Expressive leaders are likely to be engaged in the roles of organizational spokesperson, nurturer of effective interpersonal relations within the organization, and developer of commitment to the organization. In the latter role leaders may also attempt to increase the motivation of the organization's members. Instrumental leaders tend to be more involved in the functions of coordination, motivation through the use of remunerative power, and procurement of resources. Either type of leader can be an innovator or manager of an organization in times of crisis. It should be noted again with emphasis, however, that these roles and functions are not likely to be wholly distinct. A leader does what is necessary for the effective functioning of an organization—and what is necessary at any moment varies very widely from organization to organization and from situation to situation. Moreover, based on Lewis's work on Rickover, Hoover, and Moses, one might suppose that very successful public administrative leaders are able to engage in expressive and instrumental leadership simultaneously.

Leadership is only part of an equation. There are those who are led, followers who are willing to serve. Consequently, any discussion of leadership must be complemented by a consideration of motivation.

Motivation

Scientific management theory assumed that workers were motivated by the manipulation of remunerative rewards and sanctions. Heavy emphasis was placed on piecework, under the assumption that if a worker could earn more by producing more, he or she would be motivated to work harder. Similarly, if productivity and pay could be increased by the introduction of highly specialized work tasks, this body of theory assumed the worker would perform them, however boring, mind-deadening, and physically uncomfortable they might be. This approach to motivation was dealt a severe blow by the Hawthorne experiments and the human relations approach. Initially the human relationists had a set of observations about workers' motivation, but they lacked a theory that could explain them.

An important breakthrough occurred in 1943, when Abraham Maslow introduced "A Theory of Human Motivation."[31] Maslow hypothesized that there is a hierarchy of human needs; that humans are satisfaction-seeking animals; and that they are therefore motivated in a never-ending quest for greater satisfaction of their needs. In Maslow's scheme, human beings first seek to satisfy their physiological needs, such as hunger and thirst; then, once these are met, they seek to fulfill safety and shelter needs. Next they focus upon social needs and seek a sense of belonging. At the fourth level of needs, they want self-esteem and social status; finally, they seek "self-actualization," or true self-fulfillment (see Box 4–2).

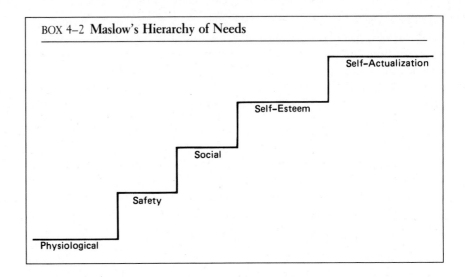

BOX 4–2 **Maslow's Hierarchy of Needs**

When viewed in the light of the human relations approach, it is not difficult to see some immediate implications of Maslow's theory. First, if the happy worker is the productive worker, then work should satisfy the workers' needs at whatever level they may be. If workers seek social activity, then the organization should provide opportunities for it. If they seek self-esteem or self-actualization, then they will probably need some control over the structuring of their jobs and some opportunity to participate in decision making. At the very least they cannot be ordered around like dumb beasts in the Taylorist tradition. In practical terms, this means that several elements of bureaucratic organization may be at odds with human needs. Certainly hierarchy and specialization militate against self-actualization, self-esteem, and the social needs of those who are denied control over their work processes and social interactions on the job—meaning virtually all employees except those at the top. The lack of opportunity to complete an entire unit of output, such as a report or an automobile, is also problematic in terms of self-esteem and self-actualization. Formalization and impersonality would seem seriously to undercut the fulfillment of social needs. The entire sense of being but a mere "cog" ought to be sufficient to deflate the self-esteem of even the most arrogant of individuals.

This has an important second implication: it may render bureaucratic organization somewhat out of date. It is possible that as a society develops economically and politically, the plurality of public employees may be seeking to satisfy needs at the top levels of Maslow's hierarchy. They may want meaningful work (status, self-esteem) and influence over the directions their agencies are taking (self-actualization through public policy making).[32] Unless bureaucracies can respond to these needs, their employees will be somewhat dissatisfied and organizational efficiency may consequently suffer. Those taking this general perspective have argued that therefore "democracy is inevitable"[33] in organizations and that traditional structural arrangements of bureaucracy will have to be modified. Perhaps it is not too much to say that according to this view we are in an "administrative revolution"[34] that will democratize our organizational life the way that political revolutions of the past brought much of the Western world from aristocracy to more democratic governments.

Despite the enthusiasm of some for Maslow's theory and its implications, others have remained unconvinced. At least two general criticisms are frequently directed at Maslow's hierarchy. First, although Maslow offered a theory that in principle could be empirically tested, it has been very hard to test it well. Consequently, it tends to remain inadequately tested. Moreover, some people find it counterintuitive. Many of us may be at the same level in our hierarchy of needs but nonetheless motivated by different stimuli. For instance, the *strength* of an individual's needs for self-esteem may vary in ways that do not seem to be explained by the hierarchy. Second, Maslow's categories are so broad that unless further refined they seem to offer little connection between the design of work and motivation in the workplace. This problem has been addressed by Frederick Herzberg and his associates.[35]

Herzberg hypothesized that job satisfaction was affected by two types of factors in the workplace. Hygiene factors included working conditions, supervisory relations, salary, and administrative policies. They were called **hygienes** after medical terminology to connote that they are environmental and contextual factors that could be attained by preventing undesirable conditions (like dirt in drinking water). Hygienes are considered to have the capacity to make workers dissatisfied if they are inadequately met. However, they do not lead to job satisfaction per se. On the other hand, **motivators,** including advancement, responsibility, the job itself, recognition, and achievement, could produce greater job satisfaction.

The implications of the Herzberg model are similar to those of Maslow's hierarchy. Motivation depends more on opportunities for advancement, responsibility, recognition, and achievement than on the type of hygiene factors that were of greater concern to the scientific management approach. Even more important, Herzberg turned attention to the nature of the job itself as a motivator. This led to the prospect that the highest degree of specialization, though seemingly productive, could dampen an employee's motivation. It also suggested that workers' motivation could be enhanced by allowing them to participate in the designing of jobs. Like Maslow's theory, however, Herzberg's approach has not won universal acceptance. Indeed, empirical tests of its propositions have led to different conclusions, and a debate continues as to its utility.

Some believe that cultural, social, economic, and psychological variation among a large work force make it unreasonable to assume that all workers can be motivated by fulfilling the same needs. For example, based on the work of David McClelland, there is reason to believe that some people are far more achievement-oriented than others. They will be motivated by the opportunity to achieve, while others, who are more or less at the same level of Maslow's hierarchy, will not.[36] The same could be true with regard to the other motivators identified by Herzberg.

Expectancy theory is an alternative approach that eliminates this problem.[37]

It assumes that workers have a variety of goals and that the strength of their preferences for them varies. Moreover, it proposes that their motivation on the job will depend upon the extent to which they expect a certain activity to lead to some degree of satisfaction of these goals. For instance, if they want higher pay and they think greater productivity will lead to it, the workers will be more productive. But the same is true if they want recognition or a sense of achievement and believe that these goals can be attained through greater productivity. According to this approach, the key to motivation is affording workers some opportunity to achieve their desired goals and making clear what activities or efforts on the job they can reasonably expect to lead to attainment of these goals.

Based on expectancy theory, organizations should emphasize recruiting personnel whose personal goals can be fulfilled while serving the needs of an organization itself. Additionally, rewards and sanctions must be clearly linked to an individual's performance. Although it is common to think in terms of rewarding productive, dynamic employees, Anthony Downs reminds us that some organizations prefer "conservers"—those who protect the status quo. There is no coherent body of theory about individual personality type and motivation in organizations. However, people do vary widely in their approach to work. Some possibilities are set forth in Box 4–3 on page 150.

Contemporary Approaches to Organization Theory

Today, organization theory is a diverse, interdisciplinary enterprise. If there is any unifying paradigm, it is methodological rather than substantive. Contemporary organization theory seeks to develop and test empirical propositions pertaining to all important aspects of organizational behavior, including structure, change, and psychology. Unlike some earlier approaches, it tries to separate facts from values and to use a modern social scientific method for determining relationships among observable aspects of organizational behavior. For the most part, it relies on systems theory to aid in the conceptualization of such relationships.

The systems approach can be quite elaborate, but at its core is the simple concept that an organization (or other functional entity) constitutes a system that is distinct from its environment.[38] It is a system because its parts are interrelated. The system responds to stimuli from the environment and obtains feedback (information) concerning the impact of its responses. A diagram of a basic systems model is presented in Box 4–4 on page 152.

Another way of thinking about a system is that it is an organization that converts inputs (stimuli) into outputs. For public agencies the inputs could be demands for the development or improvement of programs (e.g., crime control), while the conversion could be the combination of these demands into a change in public policy, such as more police patrols, which would be the output. The conversion process concerns how the organization responds to demands for changes in its programs and operations. Inputs can also be in the form of support for the organization and its policies and programs.

Some systems are treated as closed, which means it is assumed that everything is known about their internal functioning and their relationship to the environment. A heating device controlled by a thermostat is an example. The system puts out heat predictably with changes in the temperature of the environment. The environment responds to this output, the thermostat provides feedback on the response, and the outputs cease when a certain temperature is reached. Closed-systems theory tends to focus on stability (equilibrium), control mechanisms, and predictable responses. Some relatively simple public administrative operations can be viewed as closed systems. For instance, the operations of a motor vehicle bureau in renewing automobile registrations might be treated in this fashion. The registrant submits the required payment and documentation of insurance and inspection (inputs); the bureau processes these (conversion) and issues the registration (output). Should something in the environment change, such as the sale of the car, the bureau receives notification (feedback) and responds according to its regulations.

Open systems, by contrast, are viewed as too complex to be so predictable. It is recognized that the relationships between the parts of the system and the system and its environment are not fully understood. Both the environment and internal operations of the open system are viewed with an expectation of uncertainty. Many believe that the open-systems concept is more useful for analyzing most public organizations. By way of illustration, many of the operations of the U.S. Department of Agriculture fit this model. Inputs often depend upon such diverse and relatively unpredictable matters as the weather, pest control, consumer preferences, the relative strength of the dollar against other currencies, foreign policy, and the trade preferences of other nations. Feedback about the impact of outputs can be obscured by any of these factors as well. Conversion becomes more difficult where so much uncertainty and complexity prevail. Politics and individual preferences, as well as intraorganizational rivalries and other factors, come into play. Outputs can become highly unpredictable. The great benefit of the open-systems model is that it can help order our thoughts about the operations of public agencies or other organizations under such circumstances.

Open-systems theory has focused greater attention on organizational environments. Organizations can be seen as cooperating with and adapting to their environment. They adjust to its pressures, which enhances their ability to persist. For instance, public sector organizations are often required by legislators and political executives to take on new functions. How well they can assimilate and integrate new tasks is likely to have a bearing on the organization's long-term prospects for survival. The U.S. Civil Service Commission (1883–1979) is an excellent example of an organization that failed to adapt to a rapidly changing environment, and, consequently, was disbanded. Between 1965 and 1978, it struggled to combine new equal opportunity and affirmative action functions with traditional personnel administration. It also sought to be responsive to political appointees while protecting the somewhat competing interests of career civil servants. In 1973, these pressures led the commission's chairman, Robert Hampton, to ask, "What is our identity?" "What is our purpose?" And, "Why do we exist?"[39] By 1979, it didn't!

BOX 4–3 Organizational Personalities: A Sampling

According to Anthony Downs:

1. CLIMBERS—a "climber seeks to maximize his own power, income, and prestige, he always desires more of these goods." Climbers seek to increase the power, income, and prestige of their positions in ways that will create the least effective resistance.

2. CONSERVERS—"Conservers seek to maximize their security and convenience. . . . [They] are essentially change avoiders. In this respect, they are the opposite of climbers."

3. ZEALOTS—officials who "act as though pursuit of the public interest means promotion of very specific policy goals . . . regardless of the antagonism they encounter or the particular positions they occupy."

4. ADVOCATES—"are basically optimistic, and normally quite energetic. . . . [T]hey are strongly subject to influence by their superiors, equals, and subordinates. Nevertheless, they are often quite aggressive in pressing for what they believe best suits their organizations."

5. STATESMEN—are loyal to the nation or the society as a whole. They "can persist in maintaining a generalized outlook even when their responsibilities are quite particular. However, they do not like conflict situations and seek to reconcile clashes of particular viewpoints through compromises based upon their broad general loyalties."

According to Robert Presthus:

1. UPWARD-MOBILES—have "the capacity to identify strongly with the organization, permitting a nice synthesis of personal rewards and organizational goals." They make "special efforts to control situations and people." They "stress efficiency, strength, self-control, and dominance. [Their] most functional value is a deep respect for authority."

2. INDIFFERENTS—reject the values of status and prestige. Their "aspirations are based on a realistic appraisal of existing opportunities. Escaping the commitments of the 'true believer' and the anxiety of the neurotic striver, he receives big dividends in privacy, tranquility, and self-realization through his extravocational orientation."

3. AMBIVALENTS—have a fear of authority and an inability to accept the organization's collective goals, "which violate his need for personal autonomy. His 'tender minded' view of human relations disqualifies him for the 'universalistic' decision making required for success on organizational terms. Since his preferences include a desire for creativity and for a work environment that permits spontaneity and experiment, the structured personal relations, stereotyped procedures, and group decision making of big organization prove stifling. . . . If his values did not include prestige and influence, a happier accommodation might be possible. . . ."

According to Leonard Reissman:

1. FUNCTIONAL BUREAUCRATS—are "oriented towards and [seek] recognition from a given professional group outside of rather than within the bu-

BOX 4–3 *Continued*

reaucracy." For this group, bureaucracy is just another place to practice their profession.

2. SPECIALIST BUREAUCRATS —display "a greater awareness of an identification with the bureaucracy." They seek both professional and bureaucratic recognition and therefore can be "overly meticulous about the rules and regulations" of the organization.

3. SERVICE BUREAUCRATS— who enter "civil service primarily to realize certain personally-held goals which center about rendering service to a certain group." The service bureaucrat's task is using the bureaucratic mechanism to achieve these goals.

4. JOB BUREAUCRATS—are "immersed entirely within the structure" of the bureaucracy. They seek "recognition along departmental rather than professional lines," and strive for the "improvement of the operating efficiency of the bureau. His aspirations consist of achieving material rewards and increased status through promotions. He strongly adheres to the rules and the job constitutes his full center of attention and the end to be served."

According to Michael Maccoby:

1. THE CRAFTSMAN—displays "the work ethic, respect for people, concern for quality and thrift. . . . [H]is interest is in the process of making something; he enjoys building. . . . Although his virtues are admired by everyone, his self-containment and perfection do not allow him to lead a complex and changing organization."

2. THE JUNGLE FIGHTER —"The jungle fighter's goal is power. He experiences life and work as a jungle (not a game), where it is eat or be eaten, and the winners destroy the losers. . . . There are two subtypes of jungle fighters, lions and foxes. The lions are the conquerors who when successful may build an empire; the foxes make their nests in the corporate hierarchy and move ahead by stealth and politicking."

3. THE COMPANY MAN—is "the well-known organization man, or functionary whose sense of identity is based on being a part of the powerful, productive company. His strongest traits are his concern with the human side of the company, his interest in the feelings of the people around him and his commitment to maintain the organization's integrity."

4. THE GAMESMAN—is a new type. "His main interest is in challenge, competitive activity where he can prove himself a winner. . . . [H]e likes to take risks and to motivate others to push themselves beyond their normal pace. He responds to work and life as a game."

SOURCES: Anthony Downs, *Inside Bureaucracy* (Boston: Little, Brown, 1967), chap. 9; Robert Presthus, *The Organizational Society* (New York: Knopf, 1962), pp. 203, 218, 285–286; Leonard Reissman, "A Study of Role Conceptions in Bureaucracy," *Social Forces*, 27 (March 1949): 305–310; Michael Maccoby, *The Gamesman* (New York: Simon & Schuster, 1976), pp. 42–45, copyright © 1976 by Michael Maccoby, reprinted by permission of Simon & Schuster, Inc.

BOX 4–4 **A Systems Model of Politics**

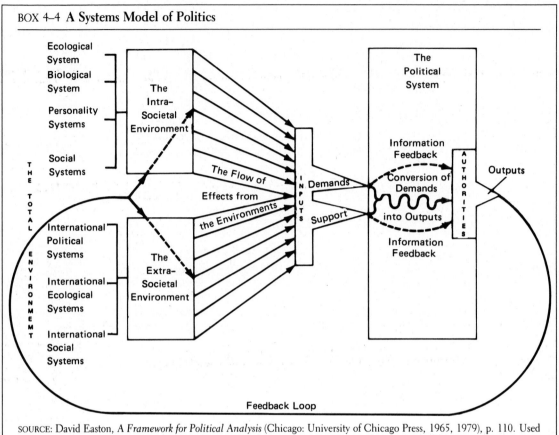

SOURCE: David Easton, *A Framework for Political Analysis* (Chicago: University of Chicago Press, 1965, 1979), p. 110. Used by permission of the University of Chicago Press and David Easton.

The concept that public organizations either adapt to their environment or perish fits the normative tenet of democratic constitutionalism that public administrators ought to be responsive to elected and politically appointed policy makers, including judges, and, perhaps in some areas, directly to constituencies and clientele groups as well. But organizational theorists such as Charles Perrow[40] and William Scott[41] argue that organizations may sometimes be more oriented toward *controlling* their environment than adapting to it. In Scott's words "organizations must ingest those necessary elements in their environment that enable them to survive. . . ."[42] Perrow reminds us that the environment can be conceptualized in strategic terms on the basis of network and ecological models.

Networks sort out the environment by identifying the external organizations with which an organization routinely deals *and* some of the other organizations that interact with those external organizations.[43] For example, organization A may deal with organizations B and C, which, in turn, deal with organizations D,

E, and F. Organization A might be a city bus system, whereas B and C might be transportation systems in the surrounding suburbs and counties. B and C might bring A a substantial number of its rush-hour riders. D and E might be the labor unions representing B and C's employees. F might be an organization that supplies B and C with new buses from time to time. Thinking about these relationships as networks makes it evident that A's ridership can be affected by B and C's operations, which depend upon D and E's activities to some extent. A has no direct relationship with D and E, but they can disturb its environment. Conceivably, A might be interested in supporting B and C in efforts to control or eliminate D and E. In any event, D and E are in A's network. F, on the other hand, is only very remotely related to A's functioning, because B and C are readily able to find substitutes for the buses it supplies.

The ecological model also considers the environment to be of critical importance to organizations. Its focus is change. As Perrow describes it,

> The ecological model identifies three stages in a process of social change. First is the occurrence of *variations* in behavior. They may be intended or unintended; it doesn't matter. In organizations, a production crew might gradually vary its techniques, or a shortage of gasoline might lead to a variation in truck-delivery practices. Second, natural *selection* occurs as some variations are eliminated because they are undesirable and others are reinforced because they work. The criterion of effectiveness is survival. Third, there is a *retention* mechanism that allows those "positively selected variations" to be retained or reproduced. Since nothing ever stands still, either for those in the organization or for its environment, over the long run positively selected variations that become stable activities will be subject to further variation.[44]

The systems approach has also enhanced analysis of the internal workings of organizations. It enables us to think in terms of "subsystems" and their relationships with one another as well as to the organization as a whole and the environment. Daniel Katz and Robert Kahn identify some common subsystems as "production subsystems," "supportive subsystems" (procurement, etc.), "maintenance subsystems" (personnel management), "adaptive subsystems" (concerned with organizational change), and "managerial subsystems" (controlling the other subsystems).[45] These subsystems are likely to have different and somewhat competing priorities and ideologies supporting them. The managerial subsystem seeks control, while a production subsystem may seek autonomy. In the public sector, it may be useful to think of programs or policy areas as the production subsystems of organizations. Recognizing subsystems' existence and interaction often yields a more sophisticated understanding of agencies and other organizations.

Contemporary organization theory includes both private and public organizations. However, there are some differences between the public and private sectors. When we focus specifically upon public agencies, the distinct perspectives of the managerial, political, and legal approaches to public administration should be considered in some detail.

MANAGERIAL PERSPECTIVES ON PUBLIC ORGANIZATION

The managerial approach to public organization grows largely out of the "classical" approaches of Weber and Taylor. It is sometimes considered an extension of those approaches, and with them is referred to as the public administrative "orthodoxy." It has been said that 1937 was the high noon of this orthodoxy—and that the clock stopped![46] It was in that year that the orthodoxy's principles were more or less codified in a volume called *Papers on the Science of Administration*, which was edited by Luther Gulick and Lyndall Urwick.[47] Gulick's own article, "Notes on the Theory of Organization," has been of particular importance in the managerial tradition.[48]

The managerial perspective emphasizes efficiency, economy, and effectiveness as the values that should inform the structure and process of public administrative organizations. It views the division of labor (specialization) as the fundamental key to economic rationality and productivity. But, once the work is divided, need it not be coordinated in some fashion? Gulick answers that coordination can be by (1) *organization*, "that is, by interrelating the subdivisions of work by allotting them to men who are placed in a structure of authority, so that the work may be coordinated by orders of superiors to subordinates, reaching from the top to the bottom of the entire enterprise,"[49] and (2) *idea*, "that is, the development of intelligent singleness of purpose in the minds and wills of those who are working together as a group, so that each worker will of his own accord fit his task into the whole with skill and enthusiasm."[50] Gulick thought that an enterprise could not be truly effective without utilizing both these bases of coordination, but he tended to stress organization for its reliability, predictability, and economy.

Gulick repeated many of Weber's observations, but he turned them into prescriptions. He believed that the organization coordinating the specializations should be hierarchical and culminate with "one master."[51] Hierarchical authorities should be in control in fact as well as in theory. Their control should be insured by limiting their span of control, that is, the number of subordinates who are directly responsible to any single superordinate. Gulick and others in this tradition believed that the appropriate span of control could be determined more or less scientifically. The work of executives was aimed at maintaining coordination and control. It consisted of "POSDCORB," an acronym that may well continue to describe the core curriculum of many public administrative master's degree programs today:

Planning: working out in broad outline the things that need to be done and the methods for accomplishing them

Organizing: establishing the formal structure of the enterprise

Staffing: the personnel function

Directing: decision making and communicating orders

COordinating: interrelating the various parts of the work

Reporting: supplying information through recordkeeping, research, inspection

Budgeting: fiscal planning, accounting and control

These POSDCORB activities were thought to include all functions of the chief executive and the heads of organizational subdivisions. Importantly, Gulick averred that some of them could be undertaken by *staff* employees, which are employees who are not in the *line* (or chain) of direct authority, but rather act as assistants to those in such positions. The distinction between line and staff became quite important in the orthodox tradition, which admonished that the two functions should not be mixed, as this blurs the assignment of responsibility.

Another extremely important feature of Gulick's organizational theory was the idea that there was essentially one most efficient way to organize any given governmental function. Thus, it could be organized by *purpose* (e.g., education, health, welfare); *process* (engineering, accounting); *clientele or materiel* (farmers, veterans, the poor, or a natural resource); or by *place* (state, region, city, rural areas). Each of these bases of organization had advantages and disadvantages in terms of the relevant organizational values of efficiency, economy, and effectiveness. A listing of these developed by the author is set out in Box 4–5.

The purpose/process/clientele/place scheme has been very influential in the thinking about government organization. Since it is somewhat abstract, a few examples may help to clarify its utility. Let's assume that every government agency uses lawyers in some capacity. How should these lawyers be selected, remunerated, directed, and so forth? One approach (by purpose) is to place a general counsel's office in every agency. Here lawyers are employed within the agency in which they function; they occupy some subdivision of it, and they are directed by its hierarchy. On the other hand, it would be possible to place all government lawyers in one department and assign them as needed to assist the various agencies and other departments in carrying out their organizational functions. In the latter case, the lawyers would be selected, remunerated, directed, and assigned by one department, such as a Department of Justice or Department of Legal Affairs. What would be the benefits and drawbacks of each approach? The second approach (by process) would tend to promote professionalism among the legal staff and to assure that the legal staff was fully up-to-date on matters of law. But, unlike the first, it might also lead to a situation where the lawyers were unresponsive to the needs of the agencies that they were assigned to assist. They might view the clarification and development of legal principles to be more important than the achievement of the missions of other agencies and thereby place process over purpose. So how would one choose?

Before addressing this question, another example is in order. Suppose we are organizing a poverty program. It would certainly simplify things if one agency could deal with the totality of problems facing poor people, ranging from health and housing to nutrition, family structure, education, job training and so on. This would make governmental service more accessible to the poor and would

BOX 4–5 **Scientific Administration: Advantages and Disadvantages of Different Organizational Bases**

Organization by Purpose (such as education, health, welfare):

Advantages:

- serves purpose better

- public prefers it

- elicits more energy and loyalty from employees

Disadvantages:

- requires substantial overlaps

- ignores new technologies

- loses sight of subordinate parts of work

Organization by Clientele or Materiel (farmers, the poor, veterans):

Advantages:

- simplifies and allows coordination of contact with consumer

- eliminates duplication

- centralizes information

Disadvantages:

- clientele may take over

- sacrifices specialization

- may be hard to apply (citizens fall into overlapping categories)

Organization by Process (teaching, law, engineering, accounting):

Advantages:

- utilizes technical skill maximally

- utilizes automation maximally

- permits coordination

- fosters professionalism, career service

Disadvantages:

- may be difficult to apply

- process may hinder purpose

- fosters arrogance, resistance to democratic control

Organization by Place (state, region, rural, urban areas):

Advantages:

- allows greater coordination

- adapts total program to area served

- cuts red tape in dealing with other governmental units (states, local)

- cuts costs for travel, etc.

Disadvantages:

- makes it difficult to maintain uniformity

- encourages short-sighted management geared to local problems

- may make it difficult to specialize

- may be vulnerable to local pressure groups

SOURCE: Compiled by the author, based on L. Gulick and L. Urwick, eds., *Papers on the Science of Administration* (New York: Institute of Public Administration, 1937).

reduce the paperwork involved in dealing with them. It might be especially important where poor people are deterred from seeking governmental assistance by all the impersonal red tape involved. Moreover, such an organizational scheme might make it easier to coordinate governmental dealing with the clientele group. But could such an agency provide the best health care or health advice? Could it provide the best available education or family counseling? According to common sense and the Gulick scheme, the answer appears to be probably not. Those who are specialists in the problems of the poor are not likely also to be specialists in health, housing, education, nutrition and other matters. So how does one decide?

To a very considerable extent, the scientific principles approach is only as good as its ability to answer this question on the basis of some body of thought more exacting than intuition, common sense, or judging from experience.

The purpose/process/clientele/place scheme has been severely criticized for not even approaching the level of scientific exactness that it purports to possess. The most devastating attack on the orthodoxy in this context came from Herbert Simon, who dismissed the purpose/process/clientele/place scheme as no more than proverbial.[52] And like proverbs, he argued, its premises come in twos. "Haste makes waste" is balanced out by "he who hesitates is lost." The scheme itself suggests that, for example, organization by process promotes professionalism on the one hand, and arrogant resistance to democratic control on the other.

Simon went on in *Administrative Behavior* to argue that there could be a science of administrative organization, but that it would have to separate out facts from values with great care. After so doing, it could develop a body of knowledge based on the factual context of administrative and organizational behavior.

In intellectual terms, the orthodox approach was dealt a devastating blow by Simon's critique. It was also impaled by Dwight Waldo's very influential work, *The Administrative State*.[53] Waldo attacked the classical approach on its own terms. He demonstrated that "efficiency" and "economy" could not be treated as values in an operational sense because they did not provide sufficient direction for public administrative action to be useful in practice. Moreover, far from being apolitical, Waldo showed that the traditional approach contained an implicit political theory. In fact, traditional theory, which stressed hierarchy and centralization, was at many points at odds with democratic political theory. This cast doubt upon the utility of the concept that there can be a strict separation of politics and administration.

Together, Simon and Waldo destroyed the intellectual underpinnings of the orthodox approach. Their critiques were successful in discrediting the earlier claims that orthodox theory was "scientific." Certainly none would deny that it contained a great deal of common sense; equally, however, few would continue to accept its advocates' claim to scientific, apolitical, and value-free knowledge of public administration. But as valuable as their critiques of the earlier theoretical paradigm was, Simon and Waldo were not successful in replacing it with a new one. Of course they are not to be faulted for this, since in the forty-odd years since they wrote their ground-breaking books, no one else has been able to develop a unified general public administrative or organization theory that has gained anywhere near the following that the orthodoxy once had.

One of the important consequences of the failure to develop a new theoretical paradigm for public organization theory has been a continuing reliance on the orthodox approach in practice. This obviously creates some serious difficulties for public administration. Practitioners and political leaders who must contend with actual public administrative practice on a day-to-day basis must have some body of thought and set of values to inform their actions. They must carry out public administration and they must have some reasons for doing what they do. They must also be able to articulate or rationalize these reasons in acceptable terms. Frequently, therefore, they fall back on the orthodoxy for its commonsense wisdom. It has been written that traditional "Public Administration Is Alive and Well—and Living in the White House"![54] Thus, presidents and presidential candidates frequently advance plans to reorganize the federal bureaucracy, redevelop its budgetary procedures, and reform its personnel system on the traditional grounds of efficiency and economy. Similar developments have been taking place at the state and local levels as well. Throughout the public sector, hierarchy is used to coordinate a consciously designed division of labor.

In fact, public organization theory, as actually practiced by some, is still reflected in the words of the Brownlow Committee's report on Administrative Management (1937) and the federal Reorganization Act of 1939, two of the core documents of the orthodox approach. The Brownlow report asserted that "real efficiency . . . must be built into the structure of government just as it is built into a piece of machinery."[55] The Reorganization Act, which has since been superseded by similar statutes, identified the main purposes of reorganizing the federal administrative structure as: (1) economy, (2) efficiency, (3) consolidation "according to major purposes," (4) reduction of the number of agencies, and (5) "elimination of overlapping and duplication of effort."[56]

Despite the difficulty of developing a more suitable managerially oriented general theory of public organization, the managerial perspective toward public administration continues to be distinguished by its commitment to productivity. The search for greater productivity in the public sector has led to two important developments in managerial thinking about organizations.

First, there has been a clearer focus on the organization and management of government operations. **Operations management** seeks to identify the specific operational responsibilities of government agencies and to design their organizations and work flows to maximize productivity.[57] This approach does not deny or belittle the importance of politics and law in the public sector. But it does concentrate on the obvious need to perform governmental functions productively within the parameters set by politics and law. Among the many functions of government that may be suitable for the operations management approach are such activities as the issuance of drivers' licenses and vehicular registrations, the maintenance of highways, roads, and other infrastructure, sanitation, water purification and supply, flood control, snow removal, and the provision of welfare benefits to eligible individuals.

One of the most useful tools of the operations management approach is the development of flow charts that map out and graphically display the relevant government operation in its entirety. Box 4–6 presents a simple example of how the process of applying for a government benefit might appear on a flow chart. Some operations would be much more complex and require far more elaborate, even mazelike, diagrams. It is often helpful to be able to visualize a government operation in its entirety in order to make it more efficient and productive. For example, the operations management approach can facilitate the elimination of unnecessary procedural steps or the combination of some procedures in order to simplify processes. Operations management also encourages the gathering of information about each step as a means of planning workloads and allocating the organization's resources more efficiently. Coupled with the analysis of organizational networks, it can also identify potential disturbances in the environment.

Philosophically, operations management is related to a variety of contemporary managerial organizational techniques. Perhaps **management by objectives,** or **MBO,** is the most common of these. MBO has been outlined by Chester Newland as follows:

1. Setting goals, objectives, and priorities in terms of results to be accomplished in a given time;
2. Developing plans for accomplishment of results;
3. Allocating resources; . . .
4. Involving people in implementation of plans, with emphasis on communications for responsiveness and on broad sharing in [establishing] authoritative goals and objectives;
5. Tracking or monitoring of progress toward goals and objectives, with specific intermediate milestones;

BOX 4–6 **Flow Chart for Processing Welfare Applications**

INPUT		PROCESSING STEPS	
	1	2	3
Eligible Client Referred to Welfare Office ⟶	Client Completes Application ⟶	Application Checked for Errors ⟶	Client Interviewed by Intake Worker ⟶

			OUTPUT
4	5	6	
Welfare Payment Determined ⟶	Payment Authorized ⟶	Check Printed and Mailed ⟶	Client Gets Check

SOURCE: Adapted from Stephen R. Rosenthal, *Managing Government Operations* (Glenview, Ill.: Scott, Foresman, 1982), p. 41.

6. Evaluating results in terms of effectiveness, . . . efficiency, and economy;
7. Generating and implementing improvements in objectives and results. . . .[58]

PERT, or **program evaluation and review technique,** is another approach that should be mentioned in this context. In some ways, PERT is like operations management, but it is done in advance. It involves deciding what functions should be performed and what activities will be necessary to address all aspects of the function, and estimating the resources that will be necessary to accomplish the function. The PERT chart would resemble a work-flow chart, mapping out the sequence and timing of all the steps necessary to accomplish the function.

MBO, PERT, and similar techniques are appropriate where the goals of government programs are clear. But even when, as is often the case in the public sector, goals and objectives are a matter of controversy, these techniques can help clarify the issues. At the very least, they provide a useful service by attaching estimated price tags to government functions and programs.

A second important development stemming from the quest for greater productivity has been the emergence of a wide-ranging debate in managerial theory concerning "organizational humanism." In *The Human Side of Enterprise,* Douglas McGregor developed a contrast between two managerial approaches.[59] "Theory X" assumed the average worker was indolent, found work distasteful, lacked ambition, lacking in creativity, largely indifferent to organizational needs, and in favor of close and continuous supervision. On the other hand, "Theory Y" assumed that people can find work natural and enjoyable, can be creative and exercise self-control, and that "[t]he motivation, the potential for development, the capacity for assuming responsibility, the readiness to direct behavior towards organizational goals are all present in people. Management does not put them there. *It is the responsibility of management to make it possible for people to recognize and develop these human characteristics for themselves.*"[60]

McGregor and other proponents of Theory Y argue that its application increases productivity and satisfies workers at the same time. Rensis Likert describes "the kind of organization created by the most successful managers" in the organizational humanist vein:

> This human system is made up of interlocking work groups with a high degree of group loyalty among members and favorable attitudes and trust between supervisors and subordinates. Sensitivity to others and relatively high levels of skill in personal interaction and the functioning of groups also are present. These skills permit effective participation in decisions on common problems. . . . Responsibility for the organization's success is felt individually by the members and each initiates action, when necessary, to assure that the organization accomplishes its objectives. Communication is efficient and effective. . . . The leadership in the organization has developed what might well be called a highly effective social system for interaction and mutual influence.[61]

Likert argues that organization along these lines, which he calls "System 4," is a key to financial success in the private sector.

Critics of the organizational humanism approach argue that many workers fit the assumptions of Theory X more than those of Theory Y. Additionally, critics such as H. Roy Kaplan and Curt Tausky charge that organizational humanism lacks empirical grounding.[62] Consequently, some view Theory Y as highly ideological. Yet ideologies as well as technological and scientific developments have the potential to change relationships in the workplace. Moreover, as indicated in the conclusion to this chapter, there is reason to believe that there is growing interest in extending employee participation in organizations.

THE POLITICAL APPROACH TO PUBLIC ORGANIZATION

Since the end of World War II, several observers have noted the extent to which politics is central to the organization of public bureaucracies. Today this may sound obvious—but it must be remembered that ever since the 1880s, theorists of public administration in the United States had been claiming that politics should be kept almost totally distinct from administration. Those who view public organization as a question of politics start off from three premises.

First, it is assumed that government is different from private organization. In other words, the prospects for generic organization theory are limited and consequently distinctions must be made between public organization and private organization. Perhaps Paul Appleby was the first student of public administration to assert this effectively. In *Big Democracy* (1945), he wrote that, "In broad terms the governmental function and attitude have at least three complementary aspects that go to differentiate government from all other institutions and activities: breadth of scope, impact, and consideration; public accountability; political character."[63]

Second, whereas orthodox theory is concerned with hierarchical authority in an administrative sense, the political approach emphasizes the development, maintenance, and location of political power—that is, the authority to make political decisions concerning policies, means of implementation, and general operations of public administrative agencies. According to the political approach, power is a central facet of administrative organization and public agencies can be neither efficient nor effective without cultivating it. Norton Long drew attention to this in a 1949 essay entitled "Power and Administration":

The lifeblood of administration is power. Its attainment, maintenance, increase, dissipation, and loss are subjects the practitioner and student can ill afford to neglect. . . .

The power resources of an administrator or agency are not disclosed by a legal search of titles and court decisions or by examining appropriations or budgetary allotments. Legal authority and a treasury balance are necessary but politically insufficient bases of administration. Administrative rationality requires a critical evaluation of the whole range of complex and shifting forces on whose support, acquiescence, or temporary impotence the power to act depends. . . .

It is clear that the American system of politics does not generate enough power at any focal point of leadership to provide the conditions for an even partially successful divorce of politics from administration. Subordinates cannot depend on the formal chain of command to deliver enough political power to permit them to do their jobs. Accordingly they must supplement the resources available through the hierarchy with those they can muster on their own, or accept the consequences in frustration. . . . [A]dministrative rationality demands that objectives be determined and sights set in conformity with a realistic appraisal of power position and potential.[64]

The third premise of the political approach is that representation is a major force behind the organization of public agencies. Long wrote that "the bureaucracy is recognized by all interested groups as a major channel of representation. . . ."[65] Consequently, in practice a great deal of effort is exerted by groups, political officials, and others who want to see a particular set of values represented in the missions and programs of public agencies. This often makes for an untidy situation in which agencies have highly diverse, overlapping, and conflicting goals. Yet, to the extent that representation is actually present, it has been noted that "[e]xecutive branch structure is in fact a microcosm of our society. Inevitably it reflects the values, conflicts, and competing forces to be found in a pluralistic society. The ideal of a neatly symmetrical, frictionless organization structure is a dangerous illusion."[66]

The political approach's interest in representation also leads it to consider the public sector work force in a radically different way than does the managerial approach. The concept of **representative bureaucracy**[67] holds that the social backgrounds and statuses of public administrators can affect their performance on the job. Members of the middle and lower classes, or men and women, may have disparate perspectives based on their experience and socialization. These different outlooks can lead them to define problems and design solutions in dissimilar ways. The concept also specifies that the social composition of government agencies is related to their legitimacy among members of the public. For example, an all-white police force might be considered less legitimate in black neighborhoods than would an all-black or racially integrated one.

The concept of representative bureaucracy, which is now ingrained in public personnel administration in the United States, is discussed further in the following chapter. Here, however, it should be noted how starkly the notion that public services can be made into representative organizations through their personnel contrasts with the view, espoused by Weber and Taylor, that workers ought to be molded into impersonal cogs for the sake of efficiency.

In emphasizing these three factors, the political approach to public organization holds that "established organization doctrine [the orthodoxy], with its emphasis on structural mechanics, manifests incomplete understanding of our constitutional system, institutional behavior, and tactical and strategic uses of organization structure as an instrument of politics, position, and power. Orthodox theories are not so much wrong when applied to the central issues of executive branch organization as largely irrelevant."[68] Here again, then, we find that to an extent the political and managerial approaches, starting from different premises, end up talking past one another.

The political approach is less focused than the managerial perspective. It certainly does not contain a unified body of theory. Rather, it starts from the premises listed above and proceeds to develop a number of observations that are not necessarily linked to each other in a coherent fashion. Among these are the following.

Pluralism

The organization of public agencies and governmental executive branches should be pluralistic. In other words, they should be highly representative of the competing political, social, and economic groups in the society as a whole. Agencies should provide representation to these interests and public policy should be made through the competition among agencies. This approach requires that organizational missions be compound rather than unified or that there be many separate organizations. Overall, the public sector must address a number of different concerns without establishing any formal set of priorities. The mission statement of the U.S. Department of the Interior may present the best example (Box 4–7). Diverse missions of this kind generate broad support for agencies and enable administrators to shift emphasis from one aspect of their program to others in conjunction with the need to maintain and strengthen support among their constituencies and to minimize opposition. Pluralism is also generated by overlapping missions among agencies. Perhaps the best current example is found in federal personnel administration. Each of the following is directly involved, but each has a different focus, as their names imply: the Office of Personnel Management, the Merit Systems Protection Board, the Federal Labor Relations Authority, and the Equal Employment Opportunity Commission.

As Harold Seidman notes, in practice,

Federal programs are likely to have multiple purposes. Disagreements as to priorities among diverse and sometimes conflicting objectives are a major source of current

---

BOX 4–7 Objectives of the Department of the Interior

In formulating and administering programs for the management, conservation, and develpment of natural resources, the Department pursues the following objectives: the encouragement of efficient use; the improvement of the quality of the environment; the assurance of adequate resource development in order to meet the requirements of national security and an expanding national economy; the maintenance of productive capacity for future generations; the promotion of an equitable distribution of benefits from nationally-owned resources; the discouragement of wasteful exploitation; the maximum use of recreational areas; and the orderly incorporation of Indian and Alaska Native people into our national life by creating conditions which will advance their social and economic adjustment.

SOURCE: *United States Government Manual, 1972/73* (Washington, D.C.: Government Printing Office, 1973), p. 251.

controversies. Is the major purpose of the food stamp program to dispose of surplus agricultural commodities or to feed the poor? Is mass transportation a transportation or an urban development program? Are loans for college housing a housing or education function? Should the Federal water pollution control program have as its principal objective health protection, or should it be concerned more broadly with the development of water resources?

Major purposes cannot be ascertained by scientific or economic analysis. Determination of major purpose represents a value judgment, and a transitory one at that.[69]

Organizational pluralism also requires the representation of constituencies and clientele groups. At the federal level, this has been spelled out in formal terms in the Federal Advisory Committee Act of 1972, which, as noted in Chapter 2, seeks to enhance the representative potential of agency decision making.[70] The subject matter of these committees comes close to matching the breadth of governmental programs. There seems to be little question that advisory committees do influence administrative decision making. But they do not provide comprehensive representation to all interests or even their own members. The "clientele" agencies, mentioned in Chapter 2, also provide representation to occupational and social groups.

Autonomy

Pluralism requires that government structure reflect the diverse interests of the society. Representation further demands that there be a high degree of autonomy among the many organizational units in a governmental administrative structure. Autonomy enables different units to focus on providing representation to their constituencies or clienteles. Sometimes autonomy evolves under political pressure and administrative leadership; at other times it is built into law. The latter is not only true of independent agencies and regulatory commissions, but also of such units as the Federal Aviation Administration, which have special (and protective) legal status within the departments in which they are housed.[71] Organizational autonomy may be politically desirable to emphasize the potential for representation, but it also makes unified action and executive control of public administration difficult.

The Legislative Connection

The political approach to public organization also stresses the connection between legislative committees and administrative agencies. In fact, many consider legislative committees and subcommittees to be the key adjuncts of public agencies. According to this view, organizational hierarchy within the executive branch does not encompass the actual hierarchy of authority, which would have to include at the very least the chairpersons of committees and subcommittees in the legislature and their staffs. To a large extent the organizational structure of the federal executive branch and that of Congress in terms of committees and subcommittees are directly related. The proliferation of executive branch organizational units goes hand in hand with the growth of subcommittees. Moreover, agencies and subcommittees develop mutually supportive relationships over time. Consequently, a public administrator may very well feel accountable, and psychologically and politically responsible to members of the legislature, as well as to political executives and others in the executive branch.

Decentralization

The orthodox approach to public organization addresses the question of centralization versus decentralization from the perspective of efficiency and economy. Decentralization in the sense of establishing field offices and regional offices is considered useful in making government services available to the citizenry. But decentralization also complicates coordination and control of administrative units. Hence, a balance must be struck at some point. This is often dictated by the span of control, among other considerations. Herbert Simon aptly summed up the orthodox wisdom on the centralization/decentralization issue as that, "on the one hand, centralization of decision-making function is desirable; on the other hand, there are definite advantages in decentralization."[72] Once again, the political approach asks a different question and reaches a different conclusion.

From the political perspective, decentralization cannot be considered separately from representation. For instance, Herbert Kaufman observes that "while [decentralization] is sometimes defended on grounds of efficiency, it is more frequently justified in terms of effective popular participation in government."[73] In fact, Kaufman believes that during the 1960s, "the most sweeping expression of the unrest over lack of representativeness [was] the growing demand for extreme administrative decentralization, frequently coupled with insistence on local clientele domination of the decentralized organizations. Dramatic manifestations of this movement occurred in the antipoverty program and in education."[74]

The last point is worth exploring. At the federal level, only about 10 percent of all employees are located in the metropolitan Washington, D.C., area. The others are located in agency field and regional offices, domestic or abroad. There is a certain logical order in the location of federal agencies' regional offices in ten major cities, including San Francisco, Denver, Boston, New York, and Atlanta (see Box 4–8). But the location of field offices for various administrative operations often appears haphazard. Indeed, within a given region, the separate bureaus of a single department may locate their field offices in different cities. Thus, if an individual wants to deal with one administrative unit in the field he or she may have to go to a different city than if he or she wants to deal with another unit of the same department. Some departments, such as agriculture, may have as many as twenty or more "regional maps," that is, ways of dividing up the country in terms of the location and jurisdiction of the field offices of their various bureaus.

A major explanation for this approach to organizational decentralization is political. As Kaufman points out, representation may be facilitated by it.[75]

BOX 4–8 **Standard Federal Regions**

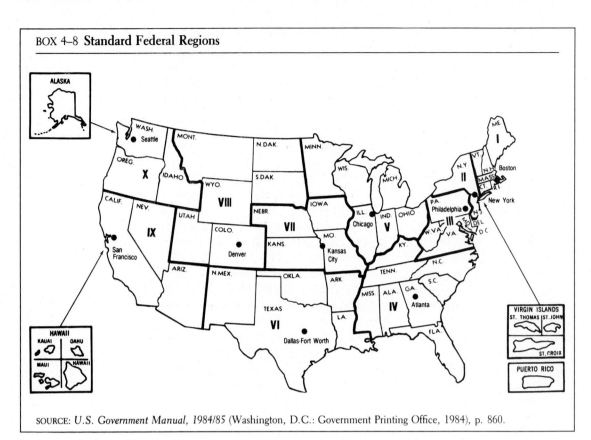

SOURCE: *U.S. Government Manual, 1984/85* (Washington, D.C.: Government Printing Office, 1984), p. 860.

Another factor is the relationship between a bureau and a member of the legislature. It may well be helpful to place a field office in the home district of a legislator with whom the bureau wants particularly to cooperate. The gerrymandering of field office jurisdictions may also reflect an effort to develop a harmonious relationship with particular members of the legislature. Here, the bureaus (agency subsystems) seek to adapt to or control their environment in ways that detract from the organization's overall coherence.

A Checklist of Political Questions on Administrative Organization

Harold Seidman has examined the political approach to public organization in great detail in his book, *Politics, Position, and Power: The Dynamics of Federal Organization.*[76] In his conclusion he provides a checklist of the issues that must be addressed in any proposed reorganization. His questions serve as a useful summary of the considerations discussed above. They can be paraphrased or quoted as follows:

1. "What is the nature of the constituency that is being created or acquired, and to what extent will it be able to influence policies and program administration?"

2. How broad is the constituency? Does it represent narrow interests opposed to some aspects of the administrative program?
3. What committees in Congress will have jurisdiction over the administrative program, and what is their attitude likely to be in view of their constituencies?
4. What is the tradition of the department in which a program is to be placed? Will it be supportive, hostile, or indifferent?
5. "What are the constituencies to whom the administering agency responds? Would there be any obvious conflicts of interest?"
6. "Where are the loci of power with respect to program administration: the President, the agency head, the bureaus, congressional committees, professional guilds, interest groups. . . ?"
7. What are the limitations on access to those with decision-making responsibility for the program?
8. "Does the program design foster dominance by a particular professional perspective and will this result in distortion of program goals?"
9. Will the organization of the program be designed so as to facilitate cooperation with other governmental units having overlapped or related responsibilities?
10. "What safeguards are provided to assure that no group or class of people is excluded from participation in the program and an equitable share in program benefits?"
11. Will the form of organization engender status, visibility, and public support to the extent appropriate for the program function?
12. How do the structural and procedural arrangements affect the definition of responsibility and accountability for the program? Do they encourage "buck passing"?[77]

To Seidman's list could be added questions about the supervision of the program within the executive branch. Of particular interest would be whether the political executives in charge of it will require senatorial confirmation, whether they will be appointed directly by the president, or whether they will be appointed by department heads. No doubt additional issues could also be raised. However, these considerations should provide a reasonably comprehensive guide to the political approach to organization.

THE LEGAL APPROACH TO PUBLIC ORGANIZATION

The legal approach to public organization is rarely discussed as a coherent body of principles and premises. Rather, it must more or less be defined from the writings of scholars, decisions of judges, and relevant legislative enactments. Its main thrust is to establish a structure in which an adversary adjudicatory process can take place. Such a structure must enable opposing sides to be given notice of the issues to be contested; to be afforded an opportunity to present evidence or information supporting their interpretation of rules or laws, and to have an opportunity to explain their behavior and intentions. But most importantly, perhaps, adversary procedure must afford each side a fair forum in which to challenge the evidence and information presented by the other. Although that is the essence of the legal approach to organization structure, it would take a volume or more to explicate all its facets. Here, we will have to be content with a brief review.

Independence

It has long been asserted by those supportive of the legal approach to public organization that administrative agencies exercising adjudicatory functions must enjoy a good deal of independence from the rest of the government. Indeed, as early as 1900, Frank Goodnow, who was among the first American scholars to pay substantial attention to administrative law, addressed this matter in a book called *Politics and Administration*.[78] Goodnow argued that there were two functions to government: the operations necessary for the expression of the will of the body politic, and the operations necessary for the execution of that will. Public administration was most concerned with execution and was to be largely free of political interference. This was especially the case where agencies engaged in a quasijudicial function such as rate setting or regulation. Some legal scholars thought that any adjudication by administrative agencies was "executive justice" and, consequently, "one of those reversions to justice without law."[79] But at the time, the evolving concept was that administrative adjudication could be vested safely in independent regulatory commissions. At the federal level, the first of these, the Interstate Commerce Commission, was created in 1887 and authorized to regulate transportation, especially the railroads, in the public interest. Over the years several other independent regulatory commissions, boards, and agencies were created largely under the rationale that "just as we want our judges to be independent of political influence, so we want agencies that exercise judicial functions to be similarly independent. The larger the judicial function, the stronger the reasons for independence."[80] In other words, where agency operations are concerned with adjudication, they should be insulated from partisan and other political pressures. The effort to establish such independence involves several structural arrangements.

The Commission Format

Frequently agencies that exercise quasijudicial functions are headed by a board of commissioners rather than a single political executive or other hierarchical authority, as would generally be dictated by orthodox managerial approaches to public organization. As Kenneth C. Davis explains, "just as we want appellate courts to be made up of plural members, to protect against the idiosyncracies of a single individual, we want agencies that exercise judicial power to be collegial. So the ICC has eleven members, the FCC seven, and the FTC five."[81] Moreover, since the missions of these agencies are defined as regulation in the *public* interest, necessity, or convenience, they should not be controlled by one political party or another. Rather they should be allowed to develop a long-term, nonpartisan perspective. Thus, there are typically limits on the number of commissioners who can belong to the same political party. Such arrangements guarantee minority party members some degree of participation and an opportunity to voice their opinions. If necessary, they may file dissenting opinions. In addition, commissioners who are typically appointed by the chief executive with legislative consent, generally hold their offices during staggered, fixed terms and are protected from removal solely on political grounds. This prevents the president or a governor from replacing all the commissioners at will.

Depending upon the context, the commission format may reach deep into the administrative structure of such an agency. Staff may be responsible and accountable to individual commissioners, thereby fragmenting authority. The commission may also become politically divided along partisan or policy lines. An organizational chart of the ICC is presented in Box 4–9; notice that several offices are directly responsible to the chairman rather than the managing director.

BOX 4–9 **The Oldest Federal Regulatory Commission (1887–   )**

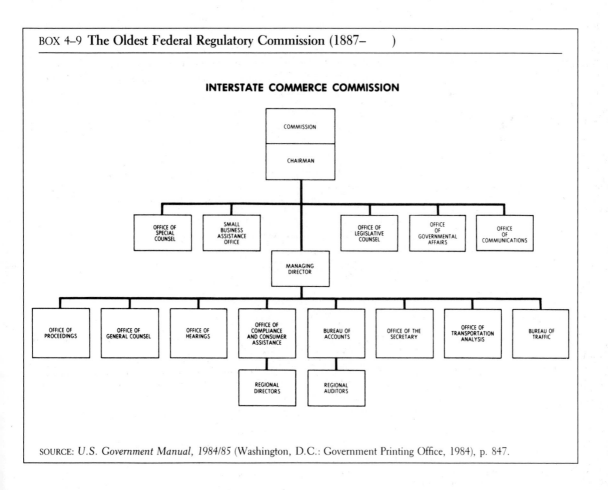

SOURCE: *U.S. Government Manual, 1984/85* (Washington, D.C.: Government Printing Office, 1984), p. 847.

Insulation from Ex Parte *Influences*

It stands to reason that if the commissioners of an agency with judicial functions are to be independent in their decision making, they must be insulated from pressures applied by the legislature and perhaps other groups. Yet it appears equally true that the views of legislators and others may be helpful in determining what is in the public interest. The legal approach tries to solve this dilemma by encouraging widespread participation in the *rule-making* procedures of such agencies, while at the same time prohibiting one-sided contacts with agency decision makers when they are engaged in adjudication. Such one-sided contacts are called "**ex parte,**" and they are considered an unfair breach of the adversary approach's requirement that each side have a fair opportunity to present its case. The legal approach has been so insistent upon this that in at least one case, *D.C. Federation of Civil Associations* v. *Volpe* (1972),[82] a federal Court of Appeals ordered a district court to require the Secretary of the Department of Transportation to establish a decision-making process that would enable it to act free "from extraneous pressures unrelated to the merits of the question."[83] The point of such procedures was to exclude pressure from a member of Congress!

Independent Hearing Examiners/Administrative Law Judges

Just as the legal approach considers that the heads of agencies exercising judicial functions should be independent and free from *ex parte* communications, it holds that others making adjudiciary decisions within the agency should be similarly autonomous. Again, this approach stands in stark contrast to the managerial insistence on hierarchy. It also contravenes the emphasis on representation and widespread participation encouraged by the political approach to public organization. Hearing examiners, who are also called administrative law judges, preside over administrative hearings involving issues of compliance with agency rules and laws, eligibility for benefits, license granting, some forms of rule making, and rate setting. At the federal level, the Administrative Procedure Act of 1946, as amended, provides the central personnel agency, now the Office of Personnel Management, with an important role in the selection, assignment, and removal of administrative law judges.[84] In principle, contrary to the notion of specialization found in managerial approaches, these civil servants are to be rotated from agency to agency so as not to become overly supportive of the policy perspectives of one agency or another.

In addition to these provisions for independence, the *ex parte* rule is strictly interpreted. Officials in the agency to which a hearing examiner is assigned are prohibited from discussing matters under adjudication with the hearing examiner. So are agency employees performing prosecutorial and investigatory functions except as part of the hearing.

These provisions for independence would make little sense if the agency were free to override the hearing examiner's recommended decision with impunity. Consequently, through custom, practice, and law, a tendency has developed for the administrative law judge's opinion to be upheld unless it appears to

"(1) be flatly unjustifiable in light of the facts; (2) be obviously contrary to and disruptive of agency policy objectives; (3) have been reached in a procedurally reckless manner destined to elicit court review; (4) be unnecessarily harsh on a party; and (5) be likely to attract unwanted political reprisals."[85] However, in order to guard against a misguided decision by a single hearing examiner, procedures may provide for an appeal within an agency. This adds another adjudicatory process and structure to the agency's organization.

Staffing for Adjudication

The legal approach toward public administration holds that the adjudicatory activities of public agencies will follow trial-like procedures. This approach is buttressed by constitutional requirements for procedural due process under certain circumstances. The adjudicatory model contains an implicit structure that goes beyond the existence of independent hearing examiners. It also includes other kinds of organizational positions, including investigatory and prosecutorial units. Investigators have been identified as key functionaries in many regulatory contexts.[86] Since they must exercise a good deal of discretion, their supervision and training become critical considerations for the proper functioning of the agency. This introduces the need for hierarchical positions to oversee their behavior and staff units to keep them fully cognizant of changes in agency policy, law, and technique. Prosecutors also require supportive arrangements, including staff to do research, analyze private parties' requests for rate increases, licenses, and other benefits, and help prepare cases and briefs for adjudication.

In sum, there is a legal approach to public organization that differs substantially from the managerial and political approaches. It emphasizes independence, rather than hierarchy; procedural fairness and regularity, rather than efficiency; and individual rights rather than group representation. Although it probably achieves many of its goals, it is not surprising that the legal approach to public organization is frequently attacked by those seeking to promote managerial and political objectives. Once again, therefore, we find the tendency for public administrative practices to confirm Miles's law: "Where one stands depends on where one sits." What are the prospects for a synthesis of the three approaches to public organization?

PARTICIPATIVE ORGANIZATION: FUTURE SYNTHESIS OR WISHFUL THINKING?

Many believe that public organizations of the future will look considerably different from those reflecting the managerial, political, or legal perspectives of today. But it is possible that they will synthesize many of the characteristics of contemporary organizations based upon these approaches. Whether the new form of organization is an emerging reality or merely wishful thinking is unclear, but there are widespread tendencies toward change in some of the more fundamental aspects of organizations that remain based upon traditional managerial concepts.[87] For the most part, these changes can be subsumed under the label of **participative organization.** The view that such organizations are in fact the organizations of the future rests on a set of assumptions requiring some identifiable structural changes.

Fundamental Assumptions

At the root of the general claim that public organization will look quite different in the future is the notion that contemporary administrative agencies are rapidly becoming outmoded. For a variety of reasons they are unable to adapt to the rapid pace of change in contemporary life. According to this assumption, agencies today are authoritarian, rigid, defensive, unable to utilize effectively their human resources, alienating, and repressive. In short, they simply lack the flexibility to keep up with the constantly changing technological, political, economic, and social environments with which they must interact. Hierarchy, in particular, is unable to tap the full talents and utilize the perspectives of employees in the lower and even the middle ranks. Moreover, it tends to overemphasize the authority and overstate the ability of those at the top in an age when a person's "knowledge and approach can become obsolete before he has even begun the career for which he was trained."[88] In this view, the era is rapidly passing when a "great leader," dominated by a single idea—such as assembly-line production—can effectively run an organization over a decade or so. Similarly, one might observe that the use of relatively static representational devices, such as advisory committees, creates structures of privilege that are too resistant to change to be sufficiently adaptive.[89] Adjudication, too, might be criticized for emphasizing adversary relationships rather than seeking to promote cooperation and problem solving in complex areas of public policy such as the regulation of utility rates. It also tends to emphasize procedure over substance.

What is needed for the future, therefore, is an organizational structure that is adaptive and, according to advocates of participative organization, this requires democracy. *"Democracy becomes a functional necessity whenever a social system is competing for survival under conditions of chronic change."*[90] Democracy in this view will include:

1. Full and free *communication*, regardless of rank and power.
2. A reliance on *consensus*, rather than the more customary forms of coercion or compromise to manage conflict.
3. The idea that *influence* is based on technical competence and knowledge rather than on the vagaries of personal whims or prerogatives of power.
4. An atmosphere that permits and even encourages emotional *expression* as well as task-oriented acts.
5. A basically *human* bias, one that accepts the inevitability of conflict between the organization and the individual, but which is willing to cope with and mediate this conflict on rational grounds.[91]

Moreover, a scientific attitude of inquiry and experimentation will prevail, loyalty to organizations per se will decline as those who are less committed are likely to be more able to take advantage of change, and structural arrangements will be flexible and task-oriented, rather than based on fixed specializations, rigid jurisdictions, and sharply defined levels of hierarchical authority.

Employee Participation

Participative organizations, according to this look into the future, will encourage the participation of employees at all levels in decisions affecting their work and, perhaps, in the formulation of broad agency policies. The rationale here has been summarized as follows: "Such participation has 'involving,' motivating effects which improve worker performance. Participation also increases the quality of organizational decisions by decentralizing them to those points in the organization where the real expertise and best information are located. Participative doctrine also takes the position that members at the lowest levels of the organization possess resources of creativity and capabilities for making worthwhile contributions to the management of the organization."[92] Some have even concluded that worker self-management, in which workers take responsibility for all the POSDCORB functions traditionally performed by management, is likely to be a feature of participative organizations of the future.[93]

The idea of employee participation is not new. As we have seen, in the 1930s, Chester Barnard argued that organizations depend upon individuals' willingness to serve in an organization, that is, to participate in it. Contemporary "agency theory," which grows out of economic assumptions concerning individuals' proclivity toward "self-regarding" behavior directed at maximizing their utilities (preferences), develops Barnard's insight further. Agency theory "assumes that social life is a series of contracts. Conventionally, one member, the 'buyer' of goods or services, is designated the 'principal,' and the other, who provides the goods or services, is the 'agent'. . . . The principal-agent relationship is governed by a contract specifying what the agent should do and what the principal must do in return (e.g., . . . pay a wage and benefits. . .)."[94] In the abstract, each employee of an organization could be considered an agent, free to attempt to write the terms of his or her contract with it. This ignores collective bargaining and some other aspects of personnel law, but it does call attention to the prospect that self-regarding behavior will lead to shirking and other forms of cheating.

One response to such potential behavior is to try to minimize the organizational characteristics that would foster undesirable self-regarding activity. Charles Perrow identifies some of these characteristics as follows:

- *"The measurement of individual effort or contribution is encouraged.* . . . It is a continuing legacy of nineteenth-century individualism, celebrating individual rather than cooperative effort."

- *"A preference for leadership stability and generalized authority dominates. . ."* as opposed to a practice of alternating "leadership tasks according to the skills of the individuals, thus avoiding stable patterns of dependency in subordinates and self-fulfilling assumptions of expertise in leaders."

- *"Tall hierarchies are favored* . . . based on unequal rewards and notions that coordination must be achieved by giving orders."[95]

Minimizing these characteristics in the public sector would "debureaucratize" organizations and transform the exercise and distribution of authority within them. In other words, greater equality and participation among employees in running an organization could check undesirable self-regarding behavior to an extent.

How would employee participation actually work? Here the advocates of participative organization tend to be less certain. Presumably, however, in large organizations participation will be among groups of workers or workers' committees or "quality circles." In some countries, notably Yugoslavia, widespread use of such committees is made in the management of industrial organizations. Elsewhere, especially in Scandinavia, participative management involving the structuring of work tasks is well developed. Japanese firms appear to rely on more participatory management doctrines that reduce undesirable self-regarding behavior. In the United States there has also been some successful experimentation with greater worker participation, especially in the form of quality circles that involve workers in the organization and design of work.[96] Still, the precise scope and structure of employee participation necessarily remains vague when we engage in speculation about the future. One aspect does seem certain, however, such participation, if it occurs at all, will go well beyond collective bargaining as presently constituted.

Advocacy Administration

Public administration in the future may include an increased reliance on **advocacy administration,** which involves "the passionate commitment of those with professional skills and official standing to use these assets on behalf of the least powerful and wealthy members of the community."[97] Advocacy can take at least three forms: (1) advocacy from outside the government, which we will discuss in the next section; (2) "advocacy from within a government agency established to act in a manner adversary to other public agencies and programs, as in the Office of Economic Opportunity advocacy law program";[98] and (3) advocacy by administrative officials on behalf of their clientele or constituency groups.

At the root of the advocacy concept is the belief that the adversary model of adjudication can be generalized to provide effective representation to all elements of the political community, including those who face special difficulties in organizing. Governmental structure will continue to be pluralistic, but in order to provide comprehensive representation, government may have to organize disadvantaged groups or, at least, place spokespersons who can effectively identify and represent their interests within the governmental structure. It may be possible to accomplish the latter by making public services socially representative of the society's composition as a whole. Special counsels, as in the Federal Merit Systems Protection Board (see Chapter 5), may also be used to advocate the rights of some group of individuals.

Advocacy administration also will require a changed view of hierarchical authority. Advocates' right to advocate, that is, to oppose the policies and programs of administrative hierarchies, must be protected. The notion of "insubordination" has little relevance in this context; nor does the managerial approach's desire to eliminate duplication, overlap, and conflictual lines of authority and responsibility. Yet advocacy would differ from adjudication in that the policy decisions would be made by elected bodies and political executives, rather than independent hearing examiners. Evidence would be political as well as factual, and advocacy would not be bound by the rules of trial-like adversary procedure.

Citizen Participation

Citizen participation, a form of advocacy from outside the government that is a longstanding feature of public administration in the United States, may become an even more important factor in the future. Such participation can be through advisory committees, citizen boards, or similar arrangements. For instance, according to Lewis Mainzer, there is a "national network of some 30,000 elective farmer committees" that participate in public administration.[99] Citizen participation can also be directly built into administrative decision making. This approach has been evident in the controversial use of "community action programs" which "offer citizen participation in and control of public administration. Local neighborhood representatives are held to be more truly spokesmen of the disadvantaged citizens, of the spirit of the local community, than the politicians of city hall and city council."[100] Community action approaches may be used to control or influence schools, public housing developments, zoning, police conduct, and other aspects of local, neighborhood administration. In some cases, citizen participation may be facilitated by the governmental provision of professional planners, lawyers, or others to the citizen groups. New York State's Department of Environmental Conservation employs full-time "citizen participation specialists" whose job is to facilitate citizen involvement in environmental policy decision making. Finally, citizen participation can be encouraged through open hearings on matters being considered by administrative agencies, such as changes in utility rates, zoning changes, and the building of roads or housing developments. Such hearings are often sparsely attended, but they afford public administrators an opportunity to hear what some citizens have to say.

Citizen participation is obviously based on the notion that one does not need to be an expert in technical matters of public policy to be able to form a valuable opinion about the desirability of pursuing one course or another. As the "policy consumer," the average citizen is considered an adequate judge of the desirability and problems of public policies. This approach poses a threat to hierarchy, specialization, and the belief that trained expertise should provide the dominant basis for participation in public policy making. In some forms, such as open hearings and community action programs, it also tends to challenge the political perspective's reliance on established groups and formal organizations as the basis for representing the views of the citizenry in public administration. (The public and public administration is the subject of Chapter 10.)

CONCLUSION: WILL ALL THE PIECES FIT TOGETHER?

Whether all these elements of participative organization can be harmoniously combined remains to be seen. Some are inclined to dismiss the whole discussion of such organizations as "mushy-headed idealism" and the already archaic notions of the 1960s. Nevertheless, there have been developments at the federal level that suggest slow change in the direction of more participative organization. First, evidence exists that management styles are becoming quite participative in the upper levels and that, consequently, high-ranking and middle-level federal bureaucrats are consulted on aspects of their jobs and agency policies.[101] At the lower levels, collective bargaining provides a rudimentary basis for more participation. Second, advocacy from within has been facilitated by new constitutional interpretations and legal rights to engage in "whistleblowing" and to speak out on matters of public policy. Third, the quest for equal employment opportunity has been defined partly in terms of making the federal work force socially representative of the nation's population as a whole. To some extent, policy makers believe that this will enable public administrators to be more representative of the interests of various social groups, especially the disadvantaged, in the society.[102] Fourth, certain forms of citizen participation are now well established. Experience with community action has been problematic and, in the view of many, a failure. Nevertheless, the idea that those citizens most affected by public administrative policies and programs should be consulted about their development and implementation seems to have gained considerable credence. In fact, William T. Gormley concludes that there has been a "representation revolution" in state-level regulatory administration that has promoted "substantive representation" of the public in regulatory decision making.[103]

Synthesizing changes along these lines within one organization may prove difficult. However, **matrix organizations** offer a potential prototype. These combine the advantages of traditional organization by function, such as police and fire protection, with those of organizing by projects, such as revitalizing a declining downtown area. Specialists from the various functional departments are recruited by the project manager to form a team for achieving the project's goals. This enables the project to utilize the diverse skills of specialists in the departments. The matrix organization violates the traditional principle of unity of command because both the department heads and the project manager supervise employees associated with the project. This arrangement creates complexities but also enhances flexibility and motivation. As Cole Graham and Steven Hays note,

In addition to enabling managers to coordinate specialists more effectively, matrix organizations have achieved a reputation for creating work environments that are highly motivating and productive of innovations. These qualities emerge from the interchange of ideas that occurs when diverse specialists interact, as well as from the inherent excitement of intensely purposive activity. In addition, matrix organizations are commonly used to deal with challenging and difficult tasks, so their members are selected on the basis of very competitive criteria; thus, they provide a rich professional environment which is conducive to creativity and productivity. Many of the technological achievements of the National Aeronautics and Space Administration (NASA) were forged in matrix organizations. . . .[104]

It is not difficult to envision an emphasis on employee participation within the matrix format. Depending on the project's goals, advocacy administration and citizen participation might also be encouraged. Nor is there any reason to think that the contemporary interest in equal opportunity and affirmative action would be reduced in such organizations. Moreover, unless the operations of the functional departments are severely disrupted by the administration of projects, matrix organization should not impair the achievement of traditional managerial interests in efficiency, economy, and effectiveness.

We have discussed theories and practices at present that point to a future form of public organization. But the future of public administration is not something that just arrives, it can be fostered by public administrators themselves. What is the future *you* want?

NOTES

1. Amitai Etzioni, *Modern Organizations* (Englewood Cliffs, N.J.: Prentice-Hall, 1964), p. 1.
2. Ibid., p. 3.
3. Ibid., p. 2.
4. A classic volume on organization theory is James G. March, ed., *Handbook of Organizations* (Chicago: Rand McNally, 1965).
5. Barry Bozeman, *All Organizations Are Public* (San Francisco: Jossey Bass, 1987).
6. Harold Gortner, Julianne Mahler, and Jeanne Nicholson, *Organization Theory: A Public Perspective* (Chicago: Dorsey, 1987).
7. Jay M. Shafritz and Philip Whitbeck, eds., *Classics of Organization Theory* (Oak Park, Ill.: Moore, 1978), p. 322.
8. Dwight Waldo, "Organization Theory: An Elephantine Problem," *Public Administration Review*, 21, no. 4 (1961): 210–225, at p. 220.
9. Max Weber, *From Max Weber: Essays in Sociology* (New York: Oxford University Press, 1958), trans. and ed. by H. H. Gerth and C. W. Mills, especially chap. 8; Max Weber, *The Theory of Social and Economic Organization* (New York: Free Press, 1947), trans. and ed. by A. M. Henderson and Talcott Parsons, especially chap. 3.
10. Quoted in Reinhard Bendix, *Max Weber: An Intellectual Portrait* (Garden City, N.Y.: Doubleday, 1962), p. 464.
11. Warren Bennis, "Beyond Bureaucracy," *Transaction*, 2 (July/August 1965): 32.
12. Victor Thompson, *Modern Organization* (New York: Knopf, 1961), p. 47.
13. Herbert Simon, *Models of Man* (New York: Wiley, 1957), p. 196.
14. See Frederick Winslow Taylor, "The Principles of Scientific Management," in Shafritz and Whitbeck, eds., *Classics of Organization Theory*, pp. 9–23. For a fuller discussion see Frederick W. Taylor, *Principles of Scientific Management* (New York: Norton, 1911).

15. Etzioni, *Modern Organizations*, p. 2.
16. For a good review, see George C. Homans, "The Western Electric Researches," in Amitai Etzioni, ed., *Readings on Modern Organizations* (Englewood Cliffs, N.J.: Prentice-Hall, 1969), pp. 99–114.
17. Chester I. Barnard, *The Functions of the Executive* (Cambridge, Mass.: Harvard University Press, 1938).
18. Max Weber, *From Max Weber*, chap. 9.
19. See Alon Gratch, "The Personality of the Corporate Leader: Testing for Traits That Make a Manager," *New York Times*, February 3, 1985, p. F3.
20. Eugene Lewis, *Public Entrepreneurship: Toward a Theory of Bureaucratic Political Power* (Bloomington: Indiana University Press, 1984), p. 109.
21. Ibid.
22. Ibid., p. 238.
23. Ibid.
24. Ibid., p. 240.
25. Robert A. Caro, *The Power Broker* (New York: Random House, 1975), p. 386; quoted in ibid., p. 201.
26. Lewis, *Public Entrepreneurship*, p. 153.
27. Amitai Etzioni, *Complex Organizations* (New York: Free Press, 1961), pp. 8–16.
28. Robert Tannenbaum and Warren H. Schmidt, "How to Choose a Leadership Pattern," *Harvard Business Review*, 36 (March/April 1958): 95–101; Tannenbaum and Schmidt, "Retrospective Commentary," *Harvard Business Review*, 51 (May/June 1973): 1–10.
29. J. D. Williams, *Public Administration: The People's Business* (Boston: Little, Brown, 1980), p. 136.
30. Ibid.
31. Abraham Maslow, "A Theory of Human Motivation," *Psychological Review*, 50 (July 1943): 370–396.
32. See Cary Hershey, *Protest in the Public Service* (Lexington, Mass.: Lexington Books, 1973), for further theoretical development and examples.
33. Philip E. Slater and Warren Bennis, "Democracy Is Inevitable," *Harvard Business Review*, 42 (March/April 1964): 51–59. See also George Berkley, *The Administrative Revolution* (Englewood Cliffs, N.J.: Prentice-Hall, 1971).
34. Berkley, *The Administrative Revolution*.
35. Frederick Herzberg, B. Mausner, and B. Snyderman, *The Motivation to Work* (New York: Wiley, 1959); Frederick Herzberg, *Work and the Nature of Man* (Cleveland, Ohio: World Publishing, 1966).
36. See David McClelland, *The Achieving Society* (Princeton, N.J.: Van Nostrand, 1961); David McClelland, "That Urge to Achieve," in Walter E. Natemeyer, ed., *Classics of Organizational Behavior* (Oak Park, Ill.: Moore, 1978), pp. 88–94.
37. John P. Campbell, Marvin A. Dunnette, Edward Lawler, III, and Karl E. Weick, Jr., *Managerial Behavior, Performance, and Effectiveness* (New York: McGraw-Hill, 1970); V. H. Vroom, *Work and Motivation* (New York: Wiley, 1964).
38. David Easton, *A Framework for Political Analysis* (Englewood Cliffs, N.J.: Prentice-Hall, 1965); James D. Thompson, *Organizations in Action* (New York: McGraw-Hill, 1967); Daniel Katz and Robert L. Kahn, *The Social Psychology of Organizations*, 2nd ed. (New York: Wiley, 1978).
39. Robert Hampton, "The Basic Question," *Civil Service Journal*, 13 (January–March 1983), pp. 2–5.
40. Charles Perrow, *Complex Organizations*, 3rd ed. (New York: Random House, 1986).

41. William Scott, "Organicism: The Moral Anesthetic of Management," *Academy of Management Review*, 4, no. 1 (1979): 21–28.
42. Ibid., p. 23.
43. Perrow, *Complex Organizations*, 3rd ed., pp. 192–208.
44. Ibid., p. 210.
45. Katz and Kahn, *The Social Psychology of Organizations*, 2nd ed., p. 52.
46. Harold Seidman, *Politics, Position, and Power* (New York: Oxford University Press, 1970), p. 9.
47. Luther Gulick and Lyndall Urwick, eds., *Papers on the Science of Administration* (New York: Institute of Public Administration, 1937).
48. Ibid., pp. 3–13.
49. Ibid.
50. Ibid.
51. Ibid.
52. Herbert Simon, *Administrative Behavior*, 2nd ed. (New York: Free Press, 1957), pp. 20–36 (originally published in 1947).
53. Dwight Waldo, *The Administrative State* (New York: The Ronald Press, 1948); see also Waldo, "Development of the Theory of Democratic Administration," *American Political Science Review*, 46 (March 1952): 81–103.
54. David R. Beam, "Public Administration Is Alive and Well—And Living in the White House," *Public Administration Review*, 38 (January/February 1978): 72–77.
55. President's Committee on Administrative Management, *Report of the Committee* (Washington, D.C.: Government Printing Office, 1937), "Introduction."
56. 53 Stat. 36 (1939).
57. See Stephen R. Rosenthal, *Managing Government Operations* (Glenview, Ill.: Scott, Foresman, 1982).
58. Chester A. Newland, "Policy/Program Objectives and Federal Management: The Search for Government Effectiveness," *Public Administration Review*, 36 (January/February 1976): 20–27, at p. 26.
59. Douglas McGregor, *The Human Side of Enterprise* (New York: McGraw-Hill, 1960); see also Douglas McGregor, *The Professional Manager* (New York: McGraw-Hill, 1967).
60. Douglas McGregor, "The Human Side of Enterprise," in H. J. Leavitt and L. R. Pondy, *Readings in Managerial Psychology* (Chicago: University of Chicago Press, 1973), p. 748.
61. Rensis Likert, "Human Organizational Measurements: Key to Financial Success," in Natemeyer, ed., *Classics of Organization Behavior*, pp. 293–297, at pp. 294–295. See also Rensis Likert, *The Human Organization* (New York: McGraw-Hill, 1967).
62. H. Roy Kaplan and Curt Tausky, "Humanism in Organizations: A Critical Perspective," *Public Administration Review*, 37 (March/April 1977): 171–180.
63. Paul Appleby, *Big Democracy* (New York: Knopf, 1945); the quoted passage can be found in Jay Shafritz and Albert Hyde, eds., *Classics of Public Administration* (Oak Park, Ill.: Moore, 1978), p. 105.
64. Norton Long, "Power and Administration," *Public Administration Review*, 9 (Autumn 1949): 257–264. As quoted from Long's essay, "Power and Administration," as it appears in Francis E. Rourke, ed., *Bureaucratic Power in National Politics* (Boston: Little, Brown, 1965), pp. 14–16.
65. Ibid., pp. 17–18.
66. Seidman, *Politics, Position, and Power*, p. 13.
67. Samuel Krislov and David H. Rosenbloom, *Representative Bureaucracy and the American Political System* (New York: Praeger, 1981).

68. Seidman, *Politics, Position, and Power*, p. 13.
69. Ibid., pp. 19–20.
70. 86 Stat. 770, October 6, 1972.
71. Seidman, *Politics, Position, and Power*, 2nd ed. (1975), p. 142.
72. Simon, *Administrative Behavior*, 2nd ed., p. 35.
73. Herbert Kaufman, "Administrative Decentralization and Political Power," in Shafritz and Hyde, eds., *Classics of Public Administration*, p. 356. Originally published in *Public Administration Review*, 29 (January/February 1969): 3–15.
74. Shafritz and Hyde, eds., *Classics of Public Administration*, p. 354.
75. Ibid., pp. 353–356.
76. Seidman, *Politics, Position, and Power*.
77. Ibid., 1st ed., pp. 284–285, and Harold Seidman and Robert Gilmour, *Politics, Position, and Power*, 4th ed. (New York: Oxford University Press, 1986), p. 340.
78. Frank Goodnow, *Politics and Administration* (New York: Macmillan, 1900); see also Frank Goodnow, *The Principles of the Administrative Law of the United States* (New York: Putnam, 1905).
79. Roscoe Pound, "Justice According to Law," *Columbia Law Review*, 14 (1914): 1.
80. Kenneth Culp Davis, *Administrative Law and Government*, 2nd ed. (St. Paul, Minn.: West, 1975), p. 17.
81. Ibid.
82. 459 F.2d 1231 (1972). For a discussion, see Kenneth F. Warren, *Administrative Law in the American Political System* (St. Paul, Minn.: West, 1982), p. 211.
83. As quoted in Warren, *Administrative Law*, p. 212.
84. 60 Stat. 237 (1946); 5 *U.S. Code*, sections 3105, 7521, 5362, 3344, 1305.
85. Warren, *Administrative Law*, p. 289.
86. Eugene Bardach and Robert Kagan, *Going by the Book* (Philadelphia: Temple University Press, 1982), especially chaps. 5 and 6. See also Pietro S. Nivola, *The Urban Service Problem* (Lexington, Mass.: Lexington Books, 1979).
87. Marvin Meade, " 'Participative' Administration—Emerging Reality or Wishful Thinking?" in Alan Altshuler and Norman Thomas, eds., *The Politics of the Federal Bureaucracy*, 2nd ed. (New York: Harper & Row, 1977), pp. 102–112.
88. Slater and Bennis, "Democracy Is Inevitable," as it appears in Shafritz and Whitbeck, *Classics of Organization Theory*, p. 306.
89. Krislov and Rosenbloom, *Representative Bureaucracy*, chap. 3; Theodore J. Lowi, *The End of Liberalism* (New York: Norton, 1969); Grant McConnell, *Private Power and American Democracy* (New York: Knopf, 1966).
90. Slater and Bennis, "Democracy Is Inevitable," in Shafritz and Whitbeck, eds., *Classics of Organization Theory*, p. 305.
91. Ibid., p. 304.
92. Meade, " 'Participative' Administration," in Altshuler and Thomas, *Politics of the Federal Bureaucracy*, 2nd ed., p. 103.
93. See Dick Olufs, "Workers' Self-Management in the Public Service," in David H. Rosenbloom, ed., *Public Personnel Policy: The Politics of Civil Service* (Port Washington, N.Y.: Associated Faculty Press, 1985).
94. Perrow, *Complex Organizations*, 3rd ed., p. 224.
95. Ibid., p. 233.
96. Berkley, *The Administrative Revolution*.
97. Lewis C. Mainzer, *Political Bureaucracy* (Glenview, Ill.: Scott, Foresman, 1973), p. 132.
98. Ibid.
99. Ibid., p. 136.

100. Ibid., p. 139.
101. David Nachmias, "Determinants of Trust Within the Federal Bureaucracy," in Rosenbloom, ed., *Public Personnel Policy*, pp. 133–145.
102. See U.S. Commission on Civil Rights, *The Federal Civil Rights Enforcement Effort—1974* (Washington, D.C.: Commission on Civil Rights, 1975), vol. 5, p. 6.
103. William T. Gormley, "The Representation Revolution: Reforming State Regulation Through Public Representation," *Administration and Society*, 18 (August 1986): 190.
104. Cole Graham and Steven Hays, *Managing the Public Organization* (Washington, D.C.: C. Q. Press, 1986), p. 92.

ADDITIONAL READING

ALBROW, MARTIN. *Bureaucracy*. New York: Praeger, 1970.

DENHARDT, ROBERT. *Theories of Public Organization*. Monterey, Calif.: Brooks/Cole, 1984.

FISCHER, FRANK, AND CARMEN SIRIANNI, EDS. *Critical Studies in Organization and Bureaucracy*. Philadelphia: Temple University Press, 1984.

GORTNER, HAROLD, JULIANNE MAHLER, AND JEANNE NICHOLSON. *Organization Theory: A Public Perspective*. Chicago: Dorsey Press, 1987.

GULICK, LUTHER, AND LYNDALL URWICK, EDS. *Papers on the Science of Administration*. New York: Institute of Public Administration, 1937.

HARMON, MICHAEL. *Action Theory for Public Administration*. New York: Longman, 1981.

HUMMEL, RALPH. *The Bureaucratic Experience*, 3rd ed. New York: St. Martin's Press, 1987.

KATZ, DANIEL, AND ROBERT KAHN. *The Social Psychology of Organizations*, 2nd ed. New York: John Wiley and Sons, 1978.

MARCH, JAMES G., ED. *Handbook of Organizations*. Chicago: Rand McNally, 1965.

PERROW, CHARLES. *Complex Organizations*, 3rd ed. New York: Random House, 1986.

SEIDMAN, HAROLD, AND ROBERT GILMOUR. *Politics, Position, and Power*, 4th ed. New York: Oxford University Press, 1986.

STUDY QUESTIONS

1. Consider the university or college that you attend from an organizational design perspective. What values does its organizational form emphasize? What objectives appear to be promoted by these values and the design? Are there any values or objectives that you think are appropriate to the institution, but suffer as a result of its organizational design? Does the organizational design cause you any problems personally?

2. Can you identify some public administrative organizations that should not be considered "bureacratic" from a Weberian perspective?

3. Choose any public administrative function with which you are familiar. How could it be organized to *maximize* efficiency, representativeness, and equity?

4. In terms of the future work life you would like, does participative organization seem appropriate? Why or why not?

5. Regardless of your response to question 4, do you foresee specific political advantages and/or disadvantages to participative organizations?

CHAPTER 5 | *Public Personnel Administration and Collective Bargaining*

This chapter discusses the history of public personnel administration in the United States, emphasizing how the three major historical phases of public personnel administration maximized certain values but failed to deal adequately with others and revealing how these failures subsequently led to reforms. The historical phases have been (1) the era of "gentlemen" (1789–1829), (2) the "spoils system" (1829–1882), and (3) the "merit system" (as it has evolved since 1883). The Federal Civil Service Reform of 1978 is discussed. The chapter then explores the managerial, political, and legal perspectives toward public personnel administration. The process and politics of public sector collective bargaining are also examined. The chapter concludes by considering how contemporary public sector labor relations can facilitate a synthesis of management, politics, and law in the area of public personnel administration.

There are about 15 million people employed by the 82,000 governments in the United States. If you were in charge of managing them, according to what criteria and under what organizational arrangements would you select, assign, train, discipline, promote, and pay these civil servants? How would you motivate them to provide the highest levels of performance? How would you assure their loyalty to the nation and their willingness to cooperate with their jurisdictions' political leadership? Would you engage in collective bargaining with them? These are among the central questions of contemporary public personnel management. They raise issues that seem to defy permanent resolution and remain quite perplexing. To a very large extent, the nation's ability to achieve its goals through public administrative action depends upon the performance, honesty, and motivation of public employees. Although we think in terms of institutions and principles, in the final analysis organizations and governments are not charts and words on pieces of paper; they are made up of people and it is necessary somehow to organize the conditions of their employment. Today, no one seriously disputes the importance of public personnel administration. As in other areas of public administration, personnel policy can be analyzed from the different perspectives provided by the managerial, political, and legal approaches.

HISTORICAL BACKGROUND

Sometimes public personnel administration seems to be in such a mess that we are tempted to ask how it ever arrived at such a state. In the 1960s and 1970s, a popular view was that civil servants were "uncivil" and that the merit system was "meritless."[1] But such charges were hardly novel; public personnel administration's historical development in the United States has been largely in response to successive calls for reform. In this area of public administration, therefore, it is particularly necessary to understand the past in order to comprehend the present and anticipate the future.[2]

Public Personnel Administration According to "Gentlemen"

It is possible to divide the evolution of public personnel practice in the United States into three broad periods. Each was characterized by a different style of politics, of which public personnel was an integral part. First was the era of "gentlemen," which began with Washington's first administration in 1789 and ended with the inauguration of President Jackson in 1829. President Washington considered public personnel to be of great importance and he wanted to get the fledgling administrative system off to a sound start. He realized the importance of his administration in setting precedents. For Washington, the primary criterion in making appointments was "fitness of character." Fit characters were those with high standing in the community and personal integrity. In practice, they tended to be members of the upper class. Sometimes they lacked any apparent technical qualifications of competence for the jobs to which they were appointed, but they did bring a measure of greater prestige to the new government.

They were also capable of learning what they needed to know on the job. At the time, public administration was relatively simple and many of its tasks could be effectively achieved by anyone with a modest degree of literacy.

Washington hoped his fit characters would perform honestly and efficiently, but he also sought effectiveness, and this brought forth another and somewhat competing criterion for selection. By 1795, when the division between the Hamiltonian and Jeffersonian visions of government was emerging, Washington realized that politics could be important in the selection and assignment of public personnel. He considered appointing a public administrator who opposed his policies to be a sort of "political suicide."[3] In other words, he sought political loyalty as well as social and administrative fitness.

Washington's precedents were indeed carried forward by his successors, though with a differing emphasis. President John Adams began to stress politics to a greater extent, although he still made appointments from the upper class. In addition, the regime's first political dismissals have been attributed to him. It was Jefferson, however, who first developed a reasonably clear theory about the role politics should play in public personnel administration.

Upon entering office, Jefferson complained that Adams had stocked the federal government's administrative apparatus with members of the opposition Federalist party. He thought that this situation could be remedied primarily in two ways. First, he sought to forbid federal administrators from taking any active part in electioneering. This was the federal government's earliest attempt to develop *political neutrality* in the administrative branch. By taking federal employees out of politics, Jefferson would be neutralizing the Federalist influence that could be waged against his Republican party. But his vision of political neutrality may have gone well beyond that. He argued that electioneering was inconsistent with the spirit of the Constitution and the administrative officials' responsibility to it. Public administrators were seen as exercising a public trust in the public interest rather than a partisan political role.

Like Washington, however, Jefferson recognized that public administrators did have a political role in terms of public policy. Consequently, he sought to appoint Republicans until the balance between them and Federalists in the administrative branch roughly matched the balance between the two parties among the electorate at large. In other words, he sought to make the federal service politically *representative* of the partisanship of the nation as a whole. At the same time, perhaps in self-contradiction, Jefferson also wanted to prohibit offensive displays of that *partisanship*. In practice, however, Jefferson overwhelmingly appointed Republicans throughout his tenure.

Presidents Adams and Jefferson differed more politically than socially. Although Jefferson paid lip service to making some appointments from outside the upper class, in practice he and Adams continued the tendency established by Washington of equating fitness with high social status. Presidents Madison, Monroe, and John Quincy Adams did little to alter this approach. Moreover, with the exception of the second Adams, who was philosophically opposed to making appointments and dismissals based on politics, these presidents inherited a federal service that matched their political outlook, and they found no reason to make many political removals. A partial consequence of this stability was that the tenure of federal administrators became secure and several remained in their jobs well into old age. There was even a tendency for civil service positions to be informally "bequeathed" to the incumbent's heirs when death made the ultimate removal. The federal service during this period was well managed, honest, efficient, and effective. Historical consensus holds that it reflected the highest ethical standards in the nation's history.

Public Personnel Administration According to "Spoils"

All this was changed by the inauguration of President Jackson in 1829. There has been historical debate as to whether it was really Jefferson or Jackson who made the first significant patronage dismissals and patronage appointments.[4] However, the fact of the matter is that it was Jackson who institutionalized the *spoils system* by developing a politically convincing rationale for it. Upon becoming president, Jackson declared that public sentiment was strongly in favor of "reform" of federal personnel administration. Why? What was wrong with public personnel during the era of "gentlemen"? Jackson's views were as follows:

1. The long tenure of federal administrators in office divorced them from the people and from an appreciation of the public interest. In Jackson's well-known words, "The duties of all public officers are, or at least admit of being made, so plain and simple that men of intelligence may readily qualify themselves for their performance; and I cannot but believe that more is lost by the long continuance of men in office than is generally to be gained by their experience."[5]

2. The upper-class bias of the federal service was intolerable in a democratic (republican) nation such as the United States. Jackson represented a different constituency than any of the earlier presidents, and he looked to this constituency for support. They were more likely to be from the western and frontier areas and to be of middle- or lower-class status. They were largely without formal education and a high proportion were illiterate. In fact, it is reputed that Jackson himself was unable to read fluently. Jackson thought such people ought to have an opportunity to participate in government by becoming public administrators. As he put it, "in a free government the demand for moral qualities should be made superior to that of talents."[6] By making appointments from among his constituents, Jackson would be able to reward his loyal supporters and strengthen himself politically. However, he may also have believed that "rotation" in office constituted "a leading principle of the republican creed" and was good for the political system.[7] To this end, he proposed that most administrators should not hold their positions for more than four years.

3. The long tenure of federal administrators had contributed to a serious problem of superannuation (old age) in the public service. Jackson felt that the elderly gentlemen were simply unable to rise to the tasks at hand and, consequently, the government was not functioning as well as it might. Related to this was the notion that a government job was a kind of property to which the incumbent civil servant had a right. Jackson and his political following found this position to be wholly antithetical to democratic principles.

Jackson's reforms were straightforward. He sought to establish a maximum term of four years in office for federal administrators. Previously, the Tenure of Office Act of 1820 set a four-year term for some federal employees, but it allowed their appointments to be renewed, and few removals were made. Jackson's proposed term would coincide with presidential administrations, thereby allowing the newly elected president to distribute "the spoils of victory"[8] among his supporters without facing the unpleasant necessity of actually dismissing incumbents, whose appointments would simply expire as a matter of law and/or custom. Unlike Jefferson, no pretense of creating partisan balance would be made. The victorious political party would simply feast upon the jobs in the federal administrative branch.

Jackson's program was severely opposed by the opposition party, the Whigs, until 1840. In that year, sometimes called the year of the great "Whig sellout," the Whigs embraced the spoils system with a vengeance.[9] From then on until the administration of President Andrew Johnson (1865–1869), the spoils system thrived. Among its chief effects were:

1. *A serious decline in administrative ethics, efficiency, and performance.* The spoils period was racked with scandals, petty and large. A plethora of superfluous administrative jobs were created to pay off the party faithful. Incumbents, recognizing their limited tenure, often sought to make the most of their positions through embezzlement, bribery, and extortion.

2. *A thorough intermixing of public administration and partisan politics.* Sometimes administrative appointments had nothing to do except engage in partisan acts and electioneering. Some never showed up at their federal offices, being assigned in practice to party headquarters. One of the more notorious practices was for the parties to levy "political assessments" of roughly 1 to 6 percent on the salaries of federal administrators. This practice, called an "indirect robbery" of the federal treasury, enabled the finances of the government and the political party in power to merge to an extent.

3. *A high degree of political competition.* This is something of a mystery, since one would assume that the advantages accruing to the party in power would be sufficient to assure its victory in future elections. Logically, spoils should have encouraged the development of a one-party state. In practice, however, the partisanship of the president changed in 1841, 1845, 1849, and 1853. In 1857 there was a marked change in the dominant faction within the Democratic party and in 1860 the modern Republican party achieved its first presidential victory with the election of Abraham Lincoln. The twenty years from 1841 to 1861 were a period of great popular participation (at least among the eligible electorate) in politics and very vigorous partisan competition. One explanation is that the party in power could only distribute so many jobs and inevitably made enemies by disappointing some of its supporters; on the contrary, the party out of power could generate a great deal of support by promising a massive amount of patronage should it be elected (only to cause disappointments later). Pres-

ident after president complained of being besieged by office seekers, and inaugurations became gala events attended by as many as a hundred thousand partisans, many of whom were seeking office. It is reported that Lincoln once said, upon being stricken with smallpox, "Tell all the office seekers to come in at once, for now I have something I can give to all of them!"[10]

4. A *reduction in the social class status of federal administrators.* The federal service became more representative of the social class composition of the population as a whole. This was a very important change, ending the possibility of the development of an elite civil service. Some consider it a great administrative strength to have a civil service representative of the nation's social composition.[11]

Public Personnel Administration According to "Merit"

It is evident that public personnel administration through the spoils system can have several valuable political effects. This is a lesson the student of public administration should always bear in mind, for the creation of strong political parties may be more valuable in some circumstances than "efficient" public administration. However, in the United States, the development of the administrative state spelled the doom of spoils, at least in terms of formal theory and practice, if not in each and every jurisdiction. In fact, patronage dismissals have fallen so out of favor under contemporary public personnel and constitutional theory that in 1976 and again in 1980, the Supreme Court handed down decisions that make such firings unconstitutional in the vast majority of circumstances.[12]

The commitment to a merit system began to develop at the federal level in the 1860s and 1870s. By 1883, it had been written into law—a law, the Pendleton Act (Civil Service Act), that was not superseded until the enactment of the Civil Service Reform Act of 1978. From the 1880s to the turn of the century, several states and cities followed suit in adopting "merit" as the basis of public personnel administration. The last serious challenge to the merit system seems to have been in the election of 1896, when Populist candidate William Jennings Bryan echoed President Jackson in declaring that "a permanent office-holding class is not in harmony with our institutions. A fixed term in appointive offices . . . would open the public service to larger numbers of citizens without impairing its efficiency."[13] Bryan's statement provides a clue as to the issues behind the adoption of "merit."

We have been using the term "merit" in quotation marks because in some respects it is a misnomer. The cornerstone of the merit system has been the open, competitive examination as a tool for selecting public servants. There have been important political and administrative reasons for the heavy reliance placed upon such devices. However, it is crucial to note at the outset that many merit examinations remain inadequately validated, which means that it cannot be demonstrated that they predict much, if anything, about a candidate's on-the-job performance. At the same time, such exams frequently exhibit a harsh bias against applicants who are members of minority groups, including blacks and Hispanics. In the view of some, therefore, the merit system is really a barrier to equal employment opportunity and primarily a means of keeping minorities out of the public service. We will have much more to say about this issue shortly. First, though, it is desirable to review briefly the chief causes and arguments for the adoption of the merit system as part of the civil service reform of the 1880s.

The civil service reformers of the 1870s and 1880s have been persistently misunderstood by those concerned with public personnel administration. In part, this is because the reformers themselves made somewhat misleading statements. Misinterpretation is also due to a peculiar situation in which the public personnel profession has come to treat as an end in itself what to the reformers was merely a means. The reformers had major political ambitions and viewed the adoption of the merit system as a means of bringing about political change. In their more candid moments, they were quite frank about this. Although they generally couched their arguments for reform in terms of efficiency and morality, these always remained secondary considerations to the leading reformers. For instance, the reformer Carl Schurz admitted that "the question whether the Departments at Washington are managed well or badly is, in proportion to the whole problem, an insignificant question."[14] The "whole problem" was the character of patronage politics, which tended to prevent middle-class political activists, like the reformers themselves, from obtaining elective and appointive positions of political leadership. The spoils politicians tended to be responsive to lower-class and ethnic interests—the urban poor and immigrants were the mainstay of the most powerful political machines. In order to displace such politicians and assume what the reformers considered to be their own place of natural leadership in the society, it would be necessary to destroy the spoils system. In the revealing words of Dorman B. Eaton, another leading reformer, "We have seen a class of politicians become powerful in high places, who have not taken (and who by nature are not qualified to take) any large part in the social and educational life of the people. Politics have tended more and more to become a trade, or separate occupation. High character and capacity have become disassociated from public life in the popular mind."[15] Schurz was even more blunt in claiming that the point of civil service reform was to "rescue our political parties, and in great measure the management of our political affairs, from the control of men whose whole statesmanship consists in the low arts of office mongering, and many of whom would never have risen to power had not the spoils system furnished them with the means and opportunity for organizing gangs of political followers as mercenary as themselves."[16]

Like Jackson's introduction of the spoils system, then, the introduction of civil service reform was premised largely on the desire to attain political change. But that does not mean that the reform movement was devoid of administrative objectives. By the 1880s, the spoils system had become a relatively easy target for change.

The spoils system was tolerable at an earlier time when the federal government played a minimal role in regulating the economic life of the nation and when the economy was based overwhelmingly on agriculture rather than manufacture. However, after the Civil War, the United States entered into a phase of rapid industrialization, which, as noted in Chapter 2, is associated with the rise of the administrative state. By the 1880s, the spoils system was rapidly becoming viewed as anachronistic—a harmful legacy of simpler times. In his inimitable style, Schurz squarely addressed this matter: "There are certain propositions so self-evident and so easily understood that it would appear like discourtesy to argue them before persons of intelligence. Such a one it is, that as the functions of government grow in extent, importance and complexity, the necessity grows of their being administered not only with honesty, but also with trained ability and knowledge."[17] Thus, as the government became more heavily engaged in regulatory policy and administration, it seemed inevitable that the spoils system would have to be replaced.

The spoils system was also vulnerable as a result of the harmful effect of its corruption on industrialization. In its heyday, spoils turned the nation's custom houses into hotbeds of corruption. Vast overstaffing, bribery, and extortion were common. By the late 1870s, the rising industrialists and proponents of industrialization had become opposed to patronage politics because it was harming international commerce. Thus, in 1877, an official federal commission studying the impact of spoils on the customs house in New York City concluded that patronage was "unsound in principle, dangerous in practice, demoralizing in its influence on all connected with the customs service, and calculated to encourage and perpetuate the official ignorance, inefficiency and corruption which, perverting the powers of Government to personal and party ends, have burdened the country with debt and taxes, and assisted to prostrate the trade and industry of the nation."[18]

There is a persistent thread running through this opposition to the spoils system. Both the reformers and the industrialists stood to gain by the diminishing impact of the lower-class and immigrant population in politics. The reformers thought the participation of these groups in machine politics tended to reduce the influence of middle-class Anglo-Americans—a category to which many of the reformers belonged. The industrialists were fearful of the rise of "socialist" labor unions and political parties, which in all likelihood would be led by and find their chief support among immigrant workers. In addition, the politically perceptive industrialist might have understood that once the political parties were denied "assessments" and could no longer count on patronage as a means of winning votes and inducing political participation, they would inevitably turn to the wealthy sector of society to finance their operations and campaigns. It has long been noted by political historians that popular participation in politics crested in the 1890s and at the same time the U.S. Senate began to emerge as a "millionaires' club."[19] In fact, the political system is still trying to cope with low electoral turnouts and the role of money in politics. Politically, there is no doubt that the chief battle lines concerning reform were drawn between industrialists and upper middle-class Anglo-Americans on the one hand, and the lower-class and immigrant populations and spoils politicians on the other. In some ways, this split was part of an even more acute division lasting until the 1910s between the Progressive movement, which was antiurban, antimachine, and xenophobic, and Populist sentiment, which tried to forge a national political party out of agrarian and immigrant interests.

Politics aside, however, the spoils system did have serious administrative drawbacks. In the reformers' view, these could be remedied by adopting the following public personnel program:

1. *Selection of public employees based on open competitive examination.* Open exams can be taken by anyone with the requisite background qualifications, such as literacy and citizenship. They prevent politicians from selecting a group of the party faithful and administering the exam to them only. Competitive exams require that appointments be made in the order of exam scores, that is, those who score highest are appointed first. This also prevents politicians from making placements based upon politics.

   Open, competitive examinations are a highly effective means of preventing patronage appointments, but they also have an administrative logic. Assuming that the examination scores are an adequate predictor of the level of on-the-job performance, which is not always the case, such exams promise to select the most competent and efficient applicants for the public service. As the spoils system receded into the political past, this was viewed by public personnel administrators as the chief virtue of the merit system. The exams are relatively cheap to administer and use as selection devices; it is also widely believed that they produce the best, that is, the most efficient civil servants.

2. *Depoliticization of the public service.* The reformers believed that the fundamental principle behind the operation of the public service should be politically neutral competence. Public employees were to function on the basis of their trained ability to accomplish the governmental tasks at hand. Their authority and legitimacy were to be based upon their professional and technical competence rather than upon their partisan activities. Importantly, this line of reasoning required the reformers to insist that the vast majority of administrative positions were not political, either in a partisan or policy-making sense. The public service should be organized like a business, according to this view. Consequently, the public service should be in the service of the whole public, not just the part of it belonging to the political party in power. The Civil Service Act of 1883 contained some provisions aimed at abolishing political assessments and political coercion.

3. *Tenure in office.* The spoils system was based on the premise that the rotation of public servants in and out of office was a desirable practice in a democratic nation. Reformers, on the other hand, preferred tenure to be based upon the competence of public employees and not subject to political or partisan considerations. Originally, the reformers thought this could be accomplished by merit selection. This would deprive hiring officials of the opportunity to engage in political favoritism, which, in the reformers' view, would eliminate the incentive for making dismissals based on political grounds. In practice, however, beginning in the 1890s it was

viewed as desirable to provide public employees with a measure of legally protected tenure. After some earlier efforts, the Lloyd-La Follette Act was passed in 1912, assuring that dismissals from the federal service would only be for such cause as would promote the efficiency of the service.[20] Some procedural protections were included in the act, but by today's standards, they were rather limited.

4. A *civil service commission.* The reformers thought that public personnel administration should be supervised by a central personnel agency, such as a civil service commission. A strong, independent agency could protect the public service against incursions by patronage-oriented politicians. The Civil Service Act of 1883 provided for a three-person, bipartisan Civil Service Commission (CSC) appointed by the president with the advice and consent of the Senate. The act gave the commission rule-making and investigative authority.

The reformers achieved lasting success in 1883, with the passage of the Pendleton Act (Civil Service Act) which was largely written by Dorman B. Eaton. Two factors determined the timing of its enactment. First, President Garfield was assassinated by a disappointed office seeker in 1881, and public opinion was quick to blame the spoils system rather than the demented assassin. Second, the Republican party suffered substantial setbacks in the congressional elections of 1882 and was seeking to protect itself against the Democrats' spoils, should that party go on to win the presidency in 1884.[21] Although these events were of great importance in the timing of the Pendleton Act, there is little doubt that reform-oriented public personnel administration would have been adopted sooner or later in any event. Several cities, including New York, Albany, Buffalo, Syracuse, Chicago, Evanston, and Seattle, introduced merit systems during the 1880s and 1890s. New York was the first state to adopt such a program (1883), but it was another two decades before the next state, Massachusetts, followed suit. Today, some merit provisions exist in the overwhelming number of jurisdictions. However sometimes merit systems are still only a thin veneer on more traditional political patronage practices.

The reform of 1883 established an institutional framework for federal personnel administration that lasted until 1978. During that period, several personnel concepts were developed and implemented within this institutional framework. By the 1920s, federal personnel officers had become less obsessed with combatting patronage and more concerned with achieving greater efficiency in the public service. Prior to the 1930s, the CSC was primarily an examining agency. In 1931, it embarked on a program of centralizing personnel functions under its authority. Soon the commission had taken on responsibilities for position classification, efficiency ratings, and retirement administration. As it became a more centralized personnel agency, the commission retained its "policing" outlook, though now this was aimed at other agencies as well as at politicians.

By the late 1930s, the CSC had come to be viewed as an obstacle to effective personnel management because it was so concerned with enforcing restrictive rules and statutes. In 1938, President Franklin D. Roosevelt issued an executive order that decentralized federal personnel management somewhat by requiring each agency to establish a division of personnel supervision and management. The vast expansion of the federal service during the 1940s made even greater decentralization desirable. In 1947, President Truman issued an executive order that placed much more responsibility for personnel management in the individual departments and agencies. Truman's decentralized approach was written into the Classification Act of 1949. Subsequently, agencies became responsible for position classification, evaluation, promotion, and many other personnel functions.

Decentralization of federal personnel administration changed the role of the CSC. Many viewed its continuing concern with "policing" as inappropriate, but the CSC had difficulty in changing its focus from enforcement and inspection to the development of broad policies for the improvement of federal personnel management. Ironically, the commission became involved in aiding the president with the selection of political executives. By the 1970s, many personnel specialists, political executives, and some members of Congress considered it an inappropriate administrative structure for contemporary personnel management. The commission format also lost favor at the state and local levels. Many of these governments moved to place the major personnel functions in a department or division directly responsible to the chief executive. This approach was followed by the federal government in the Civil Service Reform Act of 1978.

MANAGEMENT, POLITICS, AND LAW IN PUBLIC PERSONNEL ADMINISTRATION

Each of the three approaches to public administration discussed in the first chapter can be found in the historical development of public personnel administration. Managerial principles and premises were most evident in the period of administration by "gentlemen" and in the reform program. Assignments were to be made on the basis of fitness and merit; tenure was to be during good behavior and competent, efficient performance. The public service was viewed as largely nonpolitical and in the service of the nation as a whole. Efficiency, honesty, and morality were highly valued. Although some political removals were made, there was no widespread practice of spoils or rotation in office. Politics was most clearly manifested in the spoils system. Here, it was believed that the public service should be politically and socially representative of the dominant political party first, and technically competent second. Representation and political responsiveness rather than efficiency and economy were the fundamental values behind public personnel practices at this time. Rotation in office was valued as a means of promoting popular participation in government. Legal considerations were most clearly evident in the reform movement, although as a means of promoting managerially oriented personnel administration. The Pendleton Act and subsequent reform-oriented practices place much public personnel management in a law-bound environment. Complaints have often been heard that public personnel administration has become so legalistic that it is too rigid to be effective and that political executives lack the flexibility to handle personnel in a productive way. This is precisely the state of affairs that the reformers sought. As George William Curtis, perhaps the leading reformer, put it, "What we want is to intrench the principle and practice of Washington in the law."[22] Another reformer explained that, "We consider that fixed rules, however imperfect, are better than arbitrary power."[23] More recently, the judiciary has placed constitutional restraints upon the handling of public personnel as a means of preventing abuses derived from the arbitrary exercise of power. This approach favors fairness of procedure and equality of treatment, and often turns public personnel management into an adversary, legalistic procedure.

Historically, the chief problem of public personnel administration in the United States has been that it has tended to be organized according to one or another of the managerial, political, or legalistic approaches, and that a satisfactory combination of the three has proved elusive. Certainly the spoils system went overboard on the political dimension, but reform understated the importance of politics in the public service and especially the desire to have a public service that is representative, in some sense, of the general population. Similarly, contemporary personnel practices are frequently so legalistic and protective of employees' rights that it becomes very difficult for managers to discipline or to motivate their work forces. For the same reason political executives may find it hard to gain adequate action on their policy initiatives. It is extremely important to note that these conflicts are hardly moot. Today the perceived conflict between managerial personnel administration in the form of the merit system and political considerations in the form of representation (Equal Employment Opportunity/Affirmative Action) is one of the most persistent and pressing domestic political issues facing the nation. Similarly, drawing a proper line between the legal rights of employees and the needs of political responsiveness and managerial flexibility has resulted in a great deal of litigation. A major effort was made to resolve these conflicts in the federal civil service reform of 1978. An analysis of its content is valuable, not only because this reform act is something of a model for state and local personnel systems, but also because it was the first major revision of public personnel practice and theory in almost a century.

Civil Service Reform, 1978

The Civil Service Reform Act of 1978 was hailed by President Carter as the centerpiece of his efforts to reorganize the federal government to make it more manageable, efficient, effective, and politically responsive.[24] His administration was candid in proclaiming that the act had both managerial and political goals. The president himself said that "there is not enough merit in the merit system. There is inadequate motivation because we have too few rewards for excellence and too few penalties for unsatisfactory work."[25] Alan Campbell, chairman of the Civil Service Commission, which was established by the 1883 reform and phased out of existence by the 1978 reform, put forward the political perspective: "Every new administration feels the negative aspects of the bureaucracy's pressure for continuity. New policy makers arrive with mandates for change and find that though they can change structures and appearances, it is very difficult to make dramatic changes in direction."[26] But how could managerial and political goals be achieved simultaneously? And could this be accomplished without wholesale reduction of the legal rights of federal employees?

The enactment of the reform act was accompanied by massive politicking in Congress. Employee unions, veterans' groups, civil rights and minority interest groups, congressional committees and subcommittees, and officials in the presidential office brought a variety of perspectives to bear on the question of what should be done to improve federal personnel management. The net outcome was somewhat different from what Carter had proposed, but the basic outlines remained roughly similar. No one doubted the legitimacy of the claims of any of these political actors to participate in personnel policy making, for in this respect the public sector is radically different from private personnel administration. But given the diversity of perspectives, the final statute would necessarily be a compromise.

The major conceptual achievement of the reform act was the separation of many of the managerial, political, and legal aspects of federal personnel administration from one another. The effort made by the Civil Service Commission to combine these diverse perspectives was a major contribution to its lack of direction and ultimate demise. Under the reform, to a considerable extent, separate functions were housed in separate agencies. Thus, starting with the clearest case first, a Merit Systems Protection Board (MSPB) was created to deal with many of the legalistic concerns of federal personnel management (see Box 5–1). The MSPB includes an Office of the Special Counsel. Its function is to assure that personnel laws and regulations are followed and that merit system principles and requirements are not violated. The Special Counsel can investigate the activities of agencies and federal managers or officials. The MSPB can levy sanctions against federal employees who violate personnel regulations. The agency also hears appeals of adverse actions, such as demotions or dismissals, against federal employees. It is considered the watchdog of the federal merit system and protector of the legal rights of federal employees. The MSPB has specific authority to protect "whistleblowers," who expose waste, fraud, or abuse, against reprisals.

A second agency created by the reform, the Federal Labor Relations Authority (FLRA), also embodies the legalistic approach to public personnel. It oversees the process of collective bargaining in the federal service. The FLRA makes a variety of rulings concerning fair and unfair labor relations practices and the aspects of employment that can be collectively bargained. It also has authority to resolve questions concerning the representation of federal employees by labor unions and can play a role in the resolution of disputes between unions and the government. We will have more to say about collective bargaining in the public sector later in this chapter. Here, however, it is desirable to note that collective bargaining combines the legalistic, political, and managerial approaches. The procedures for collective bargaining are highly legalistic and the FLRA, like regulatory commissions generally and especially like the National

BOX 5–1 **The Merit Systems Protection Board**

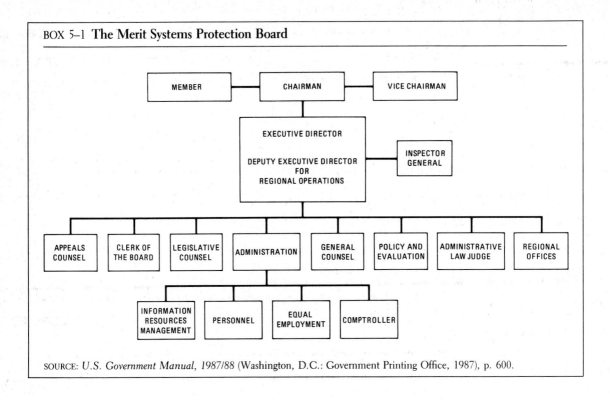

SOURCE: *U.S. Government Manual, 1987/88* (Washington, D.C.: Government Printing Office, 1987), p. 600.

Labor Relations Board, its counterpart for the private sector, holds adjudicatory hearings and makes rulings having the force of law. However, the actual practice of collective bargaining—that is, the give and take of bargaining sessions, as well as the actual substance of rulings—is often highly political in content. At the same time, though, many aspects of collective bargaining reflect managerial concerns, particularly limiting the scope of bargaining to protect managerial authority.

A more clearly political mission was vested in the Equal Employment Opportunity Commission. The EEOC was created by the Civil Rights Act of 1964, but it did not have authority over federal employment practices at that time. The federal equal employment opportunity (EEO) function was vested in a number of agencies, including the CSC. The decision to give the EEOC this authority for federal EEO was highly political, made at the urging of civil rights and minority groups who believed that the EEO program could not successfully be implemented under a personnel agency that viewed its primary mission in managerial terms. In their view, allowing those who make public personnel rules to enforce antidiscrimination measures was tantamount to allowing "the fox to watch the chickens." They saw a conflict because the merit system and merit exams emerged as major barriers to the achievement of a high degree of minority employment in the upper levels of federal service. The 1978 reform act actually declared that it is the policy of the United States to develop a federal service that is socially representative of the nation's work force as a whole. The act also defines "underrepresentation" of EEO target groups and outlines procedures for overcoming it. Part of the EEOC's mission is to promote the representation of minorities and women in the federal work force. Although much of the EEO process is legalistic, the ultimate objective of representation is highly political. Today, this is pursued primarily through the process of "affirmative action," as will be discussed below.

The reform act assigned the CSC's managerial functions to an Office of Personnel Management (see Box 5–2). This agency is designed to serve as the president's arm for positive, effective personnel management. It inherited from the CSC such managerial functions as responsibility for testing, training, operating a retirement system, and general oversight of the personnel operations of federal agencies. In addition to placing the managerially oriented personnel agency closer to the president than was the more independently organized bipartisan CSC, the reform act mandated the use of some new management tools, including a merit pay system and a performance appraisal system, which are discussed below.

Another central feature of the reform act bears mention here. The top career managerial positions in the federal service were largely converted into a

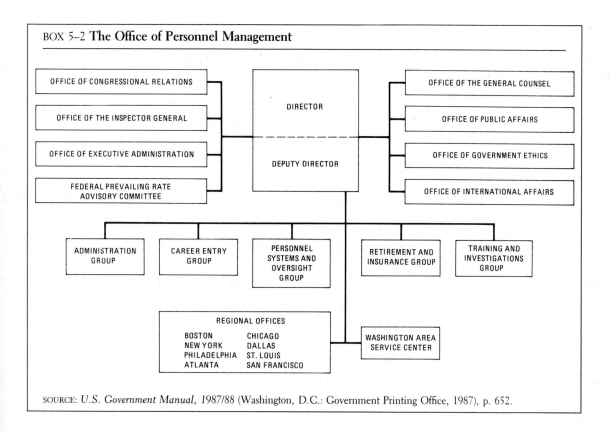

BOX 5–2 **The Office of Personnel Management**

OFFICE OF CONGRESSIONAL RELATIONS		OFFICE OF THE GENERAL COUNSEL
OFFICE OF THE INSPECTOR GENERAL	DIRECTOR	OFFICE OF PUBLIC AFFAIRS
OFFICE OF EXECUTIVE ADMINISTRATION		OFFICE OF GOVERNMENT ETHICS
FEDERAL PREVAILING RATE ADVISORY COMMITTEE	DEPUTY DIRECTOR	OFFICE OF INTERNATIONAL AFFAIRS

| ADMINISTRATION GROUP | CAREER ENTRY GROUP | PERSONNEL SYSTEMS AND OVERSIGHT GROUP | RETIREMENT AND INSURANCE GROUP | TRAINING AND INVESTIGATIONS GROUP |

REGIONAL OFFICES

BOSTON   CHICAGO
NEW YORK   DALLAS
PHILADELPHIA ST. LOUIS
ATLANTA   SAN FRANCISCO

WASHINGTON AREA SERVICE CENTER

SOURCE: *U.S. Government Manual, 1987/88* (Washington, D.C.: Government Printing Office, 1987), p. 652.

Senior Executive Service (see Box 5–3). Previously these positions (along with some others) were called the "supergrades." The theory behind the SES is largely an effort to combine the political and managerial approaches to public administration. It rests on the belief that: (1) There is a body of skill or professionalism called "public management" that can be transferred from organizational setting to organizational setting; (2) it is politically desirable for top federal managers to move among administrative units in order to develop a more comprehensive view of the public interest; and (3) political executives need greater flexibility in assigning and directing these top career officials in order to be able to fulfill their policy mandates. A major issue concerning the SES is whether it will inevitably be politicized, or whether the managerial aspects will be able to withstand the pressures of transition from one presidential administration to another. If the transition from the Carter to the Reagan administration serves as a model, a large number of senior executive servants can be expected to resign when a partisan change in the presidency occurs. There are about 7,000 positions in the SES.

The SES consists of four types of appointees. **Noncareer** appointments can constitute up to 10 percent of the total number of positions allocated to the SES. These are political appointees who assist the political executives at the top levels of departments and agencies, implementing their policies and programs. **Limited term** appointments can also be purely political. They can serve nonrenewable terms of one to three years. In 1983, there were seventy of these appointees in the SES. **Career** appointees constitute the largest group in the SES. These federal servants have often spent many years in the bureaucracy and may have worked their way up the ranks to the top of the career service. **Limited emergency** appointments are the fourth category, but to date one that has not been important. In addition to the four types of appointments, there are two types of positions, **career reserved** and **general.** Only career appointees can be assigned to the former; any type of appointee can be placed in the latter.

During its first two or three years, the SES was characterized by low morale and high turnover. By March 1983, more than 40 percent of those career appointees who joined the SES in 1979 had left the government. A major reason for dissatisfaction with the SES was the reduction in the opportunity to earn higher pay that resulted from limits placed on the allocation of bonuses for superior performance and on the top salary one could earn. At the beginning of the Reagan administration, it appeared that the career SES was being subject to unbridled political pressure. For instance, there were some highly publicized geographical reassignments of career SES staff, seemingly for partisan reasons. However, of the approximately 2,330 executive reassignments within the SES during 1982 and 1983, only about 15 percent involved geographic moves, and it no longer appears that reassignments are being used to force career appointees out of the SES. But there is no doubt that the Reagan administration, which stressed ideological unity in its political appointees to the bureaucracy, was able to use the SES in its effort to exert substantial control over federal administration.[27]

Finally, the Civil Service Reform Act provided for "personnel research programs and demonstration projects." It allows the OPM to suspend the appli-

BOX 5–3 Conditions of Employment for Career SES Executives

ASSIGNMENT	PERFORMANCE APPRAISAL	COMPENSATION AND BENEFITS	ACCOUNTABILITY	MOBILITY
• No grades in SES.	• Organizational and personal goals will be set annually in collaboration with supervisor.	• Base pay rate will be set by the appointing authority.	• Less than fully successful performance appraisal can lead to removal from SES.	• Cannot be involuntarily transferred between agencies, but OPM will facilitate voluntary mobility.
• May serve in any position in SES for which qualified.	• Performance Review Board will rate executives according to established goals.	• Base pay rate may be raised or lowered once a year. May be increased any number of rates, but reduced only one rate per year.	• May have informal public hearing for removal from SES based on performance.	• Can be reassigned within agency to any SES position for which qualified.
• Can accept Presidential appointment and retain "fallback" rights to SES position.	• Performance Review Board must have a career majority.	• Will be eligible each year for bonus pay up to 20% of base pay rate.	• If removed from SES, entitled to a position at GS-15 level or above and will retain SES salary.	• Cannot be involuntarily reassigned within 120 days after the appointment of a new agency head or noncareer supervisor.
• Retention in SES is based upon performance.	• "Fully Successful" rating is basis of eligibility for bonus pay and rank award.	• Will be eligible for a $10,000 rank award and a $20,000 rank award once every five-year period.	• Entitled to same protections and appeals in cases of adverse actions as non-SES members. (Removal from SES for performance is not an adverse action.)	• Must receive 15 days' notice in advance of reassignment to another SES position in an agency.
	• Less than fully successful ratings may be basis for removal from SES.	• Total compensation ceiling at Executive Level 1.	• When eligible, can elect discontinued service retirement if removed from SES for performance.	
	• Performance evaluation cannot take place within 120 days after beginning of a new administration.	• Can accumulate unused annual leave which is convertible to cash at time of leaving government.	• If removed from SES for performance, can reenter it at later date, but only competitively.	
		• Will be provided with executive development opportunities.		

SOURCE: U.S. Office of Personnel Management, *Senior Executive Service* (Washington, D.C.: Government Printing Office, February 1980), p. 16.

cation of many personnel regulations in order to experiment with new approaches and techniques. Projects can involve up to five thousand employees (not including any who may be in a control group) and last up to five years. They can be undertaken in most federal agencies, though not in security agencies, government corporations, or the General Accounting Office. One of the major experiments to date was at the Naval Weapons Center (China Lake, California) and the Naval Ocean Systems (San Diego, California) installations. It sought to test more flexible approaches to designing jobs and paying employees. Depending on the conclusions drawn, once analysis of the experiments is complete, the federal service may begin to implement similar changes on a permanent basis in several agencies.[28] Such research is invaluable because it enables personnel theories to be tested empirically. By designing sound experiments, public personnel specialists should learn much more about what works as intended under a given set of circumstances.

The passage of the Civil Service Reform Act of 1978 is a landmark in the development of public personnel administration in the United States. It is an effort to satisfy the three dominant approaches to public administration in the realm of one important aspect of governmental operations. Its long-term success or failure will be determined through the interaction of the OPM, MSPB, FLRA, and EEOC. Each of these agencies tends to emphasize a specific perspective. OPM is primarily managerial, MSPB and FLRA are legalistic, and the EEOC is political to the extent it seeks a socially representative federal service.

The reform program offers both great promise and serious potential pitfalls. Combining perspectives always runs the risk that an agency or program largely organized according to one approach, such as management, will ignore the values inherent in the other perspectives. However, creating different agencies to represent each of these values may do much to promote conflict and little to foster an integrated approach to an area such as public personnel administration. For instance, the EEOC and OPM have already been in considerable conflict over the use of merit examinations. OPM has opposed several MSPB decisions regarding employees' rights.[29] It has also been at odds with the FLRA on some aspects of collective bargaining. One of the great risks inherent in the reform program is that few of the actors in the personnel policy area will remain committed to a coherent personnel program. Rather, labor may favor greater collective bargaining rights; minorities greater EEO and affirmative action; career employees a stronger MSPB and better legal protection of their job tenure; and the presidential establishment and OPM, greater presidential authority over the public personnel system. In other words, the coalition that supported reform may fail to form or retain a consensus on public personnel policy.

We have discussed the historical development of public personnel administration in the United States and the conceptual problems presented by its organization in some detail so that the reader will not fall victim to a pervasive tendency to place "technique over purpose" in the area of public personnel.[30] Having tried to supply an overview by addressing the major and persisting issues concerning personnel policy, we now turn to a more techniques-oriented review of the major public personnel functions. This discussion is organized according to our threefold categorization of public administration into managerial, political, and legalistic approaches.

MANAGERIAL PUBLIC PERSONNEL ADMINISTRATION

Managerial public personnel administration seeks to maximize the values of efficiency, economy, and administrative effectiveness through the recruitment, selection, placement, pay, and general treatment of public employees at work. Today, the underlying assumption behind managerial public personnel administration is that the public service should largely be a career service. Employees should be selected, placed, promoted, and paid on the basis of their competence to perform the governmental tasks at hand. There should be adequate protection of the career service from political encroachments. Career growth and development through training should be emphasized. Employees should be appraised periodically as a means of indicating how their performance could be improved. Finally, career employees should have adequate benefits in their retirement. Each of these functions is valuable and each contains some controversial aspects.

Position Classification

Position classification is one of the most important aspects of contemporary public personnel management. In a sense, the entire personnel program rests upon it. Position classification is the system of designing jobs, organizing them into useful managerial and career categories, and establishing their rates of pay. A good position classification system provides a convenient inventory of everything that government workers do. The "position" is the work actually done, and according to rules established as early as 1923, the classification system should be based on the following principles:

1. Positions and not individuals should be classified. In other words, unlike the military, rank is vested in the position itself, not in the individual who happens to occupy that position. Membership in the SES is a major exception to this rule at the federal level.
2. The duties and responsibilities pertaining to a position constitute the outstanding characteristics that distinguish it from or make it similar to other positions. Among the classification factors frequently used are: the nature and variety of the work; the nature of supervision received by whoever is occupying the position; the nature of available guidelines for performance of the work (that is, is the work routine or does it require flexible responses to ever-changing situations?); the originality required; the purpose and nature of person-to-person work relationships; the scope and nature of decision making; the nature and extent of supervision over other employees; and the qualifications required. Sometimes, these considerations are grouped into four categories: the difficulty of duties, super-

visory responsibility, nonsupervisory responsibility, and requisite qualifications.

3. The individual characteristics of an employee occupying a position should have no bearing on the classification of the position.
4. Persons holding positions in the same class (level of position and kind of duties and responsibilities) should be considered equally qualified for any other position in that class.

In trying to grasp what is involved in position classification it may prove useful to think in terms of categories of positions, such as executive; administrative, professional, and technological; clerical, office machine operator, and technician; and trade, crafts, and manual labor. Within each of these broad categories would be a number of positions such as receptionist, typist, file clerk or stenographer. Each of these positions would bear a classification and a rank. The rank would be related to pay. For instance, the federal government has a position classified as "Supply Clerk GS-3." There is a position description explaining what a supply clerk at this level does (answers telephone inquiries, posts information from order contracts to order cards, determines replenishment needs through mathematical formulas—and three pages more of description). The supply clerk position is part of a general series of supply positions. The "GS-3" stands for General Schedule, grade 3. A more senior supply clerk might be a GS-4 or higher and would have broader responsibilities. In theory, unless a special security clearance is required, any supply clerk GS-3 in one agency would be suitable for employment in the same class of positions in another agency. To take the matter one step further, each of the grades in the General Schedule would be paid at a different rate. Thus, GS-1's, who are at the bottom of this classification system, receive the lowest rates of pay, and GS-15's, who are now in the highest general grade, receive the highest. In practice, there are pay steps within the grades and some employees at a lower level may actually be paid at a somewhat higher rate than those immediately above them. We will return to problems of pay shortly.

There is no doubt that position classification is a valuable managerial tool. How else might a 2.9 million employee work force be organized? Classification tells managers and employees what the occupants of positions are supposed to do. It makes it possible to design career ladders for advancement. It facilitates testing applicants for competence. It provides a basis for evaluating the performance of government workers. At the same time, however, position classification can be problematic. Among the most serious complaints about the practice of position classification is that it is dehumanizing for the employee. In essence, the job is designed and classified without regard to the employee who holds it. The organization is viewed as a set of positions (specializations) that are coordinated in some fashion, typically through hierarchy. An employee may be able to contribute more to the organization than the position he or she is in allows. For example, a typist may have the ability and willingness to take shorthand dictation, but that would require classification as a stenographer and higher pay. Hence allowing a typist to function as a stenographer would be prohibited by position classification principles. The employee can neither go beyond the level of work required in the position nor fall short of it. Thus, as Max Weber observed, the employee is treated as a cog that is forced into a machine, not as an individual human being who forms part of an organization.

Position classification practices, which were associated with Frederick Taylor's Scientific Management (see Chapter 4), have also tended to design jobs in a stultifying fashion (see Box 5–4). They have stressed the need for order and conformity in governmental positions, sometimes at the expense of the interest the job could possibly hold for the incumbent. This has led to boredom and alienation among employees. Nowadays, there is growing concern that job design take the following considerations into account:

1. Job rotation, that is, developing a classification and career system that enables employees to move through several positions. This enables the employee to use several skills and avoid the boredom that comes with the repetitious performance of routine tasks.
2. Job enlargement, or placing more tasks within a position description.
3. Job enrichment, or vesting greater authority, responsibility, and autonomy in positions.

In the view of some, however, no amount of tinkering can eliminate the dehumanization inherent in organizing around positions rather than persons.

Another problem with position classification is that position descriptions can become rapidly outdated as technology and the work of governmental agencies change. Position classifiers may not be able to keep pace with all the constant changes; but agency managers are not likely to favor limiting the introduction of new technologies and tasks in order to enable the classifiers to catch up. Then, too, there has been a problem of "grade creep," or a tendency for positions constantly to be reclassified at a higher level. The average grade for all General Schedule white-collar employees increased from 8.1 in 1982 to 8.58 in 1983, despite the Reagan administration's orientation toward reducing grade creep.[31] Collective bargaining also presents a problem for position classification. Unions contend that classification levels and pay should be subject to bargaining and that more positions should be created to take account of workers' increased seniority. For example, to return to the case of Supply Clerk GS-3, a union might want to see a classification system that would create a position of Senior Supply Clerk GS-4 (or higher) so that someone who has held the position for, let's say, fifteen years would not be paid at the same rate as a newcomer (even though they do the same work). Finally, as a practical matter, position classification systems are seldom as neat in practice as they are in theory. For instance, the federal government has not only a General Schedule, but also a wage board system for industrial-type jobs, a foreign service classification system, a postal classification system, the SES, and an executive-level system for political executives. In state and local systems, position classification often falls victim to partisan politics and is subject to a number of abuses.[32]

BOX 5–4 **Position Classification Standards**

Series	Grade
GS-305	3

FILE CLERK GS-3

Duties

Works in a file organization which provides service to an office concerned with processing claims.

—Receives all types of incoming mail, segregates and arranges in proper working order associating materials by case number with proper file folder, and assigning proper designation to assure priority of processing.

—Locates appropriate folders in files, identifies both folder and file with name and file number; records charge-out date, destination, and initials charge card; and dispatches folder to the proper operating element.

—Recharges folder file when moved from one operating element to another for control purposes; maintains suspense file of actions to be taken by operating elements at future dates; and initiates search for folders not in file, using charge cards and knowledge of work flow in operating elements.

—Performs a variety of related duties such as sequence checks, pulling files designated for retirement or transfer, assuring protection of contents of files, expanding or contracting file storage as necessary, and participating in records inventories and record reconciliations.

Factor 1, Knowledge Required by the Position

—Knowledge of functions and work flow within and among operating elements.

—Knowledge of terminal digit (numerical) system and filing procedures.

—Knowledge of subject matter and processing procedures for standardized material.

Recruitment, Selection, and Promotion

Recruitment, selection, and promotion are among the core functions of public personnel management. The managerial approach to them dictates that efficiency and economy be the ultimate values in performing these functions. Efficiency stresses the need to obtain the most productive and capable employees; economy demands that this be accomplished as inexpensively as possible. The rallying cry of the managerial approach in this regard has been that "only the best shall serve the state," and the chief vehicle for attempting to assure this result has been the open, competitive examination for selection and promotion. Recruitment has also been conditioned by these values. Although in the abstract the logic of stressing efficiency and economy appears to be unassailable, as in other areas of public administration, the competing claims of politics and law present formidable challenges to what has emerged as the traditional merit system.

Series	Grade
GS-305	3

Factor 2, Supervisory Controls

Assigned work is performed independently following established procedures. Supervisor is available to resolve unusual problems. Work is reviewed for accuracy and promptness by systematic spotchecks.

Factor 3, Guidelines

Procedures are well established. Written and oral guides provide specific instructions for processing material. A substantial portion of these instructions may be memorized and there is little interpretation necessary. When instructions do not apply, problems are referred to the supervisor.

Factor 4, Complexity

Performs a variety of related duties including searching, filling requests for files, association of materials, establishing priorities, etc., which require consideration of the differences among cases processed by operating units.

Factor 5, Scope and Effect

The purpose of the work is to provide prompt service in the daily flow of materials to and from operating units. The work affects the general efficiency of the serviced units.

Factor 6, Personal Contacts

There are recurring contacts with personnel in various operating units of the organization.

Factor 7, Purpose of Contacts

Contacts are for the purpose of obtaining and exchanging factual information regarding cases being processed.

Factor 8, Physical Demands

Work requires a great deal of standing, walking, stooping, reaching and pulling typically involved in filing activities.

Factor 9, Work Environment

Work is performed in an office setting.

SOURCE: U.S. Civil Service Commission, *Position Classification Standards* (Washington, D.C.: Civil Service Commission, May 1977), TS-27.

Recruitment is the process of encouraging individuals to apply for government positions. It can be accomplished in a passive or active fashion. The passive approach was heavily relied on until the 1950s and still may constitute the main way of doing business in some jurisdictions. However, toward the end of the 1950s and especially in the early 1960s, the federal government and some state and local governments appeared unable to attract personnel with the kinds of talent necessary to manage and run the contemporary administrative state. Consequently, instead of relying on a passive approach of simply announcing civil service examinations from time to time, these governments began to publicize actively the benefits and virtues of a career in the public service. Simultaneously, they also simplified the examination process and adjusted it more to the needs of the types of individuals being sought. In particular, governments began to advertise and send recruiters to college campuses and adjust the timing of examinations to the schedules of graduating students. Under the managerial approach, which has dictated most practice in this area, the best future civil servants, who could be economically recruited, were sometimes thought to be those graduating from large and/or prestigious institutions. There was a tendency to neglect recruiting at institutions that were smaller or whose student bodies were largely composed of members of minority groups. Ironically, some research has shown that government employment has historically carried more prestige with members of minority ethnic or racial groups;[33] consequently the effort to change the image of the public service, making it more prestigious generally, may have tended to produce a greater number of highly qualified nonminority applicants. Currently, however, more attention is paid to recruiting members of minority groups in an effort to assure that governments are equal opportunity employers.

The critical elements of a successful managerially oriented recruitment program aimed at procuring the most efficient, effective employees consists of (1) governmental efforts to upgrade the image of public employment; (2) efforts to recruit for careers rather than single jobs; (3) efforts to give examinations at convenient times and convenient places; (4) the elimination of pointless background requirements, such as age or non-job-related training requirements; and (5) efforts to reach all segments of the population. Of course, the value of economy dictates that government spending on these functions vary with its actual needs for personnel.

Selection is the process of choosing among applicants. In the United States a very wide variety of approaches is used, but there is a dominant pattern stemming from the managerial approach. This is reliance on an open, competitive examination of some kind, which can potentially generate the greatest degree of competition among applicants. Competitive examinations are those in which the hiring of individual test takers is in accordance with their exam scores. In a purely competitive examination the person who achieved the highest score would be hired first, while the person who scored the lowest passing grade would be hired last if enough positions were available. In practice, however, most jurisdictions modify this approach by allowing selection from among groups of applicants, such as those obtaining the three or ten highest scores. The latter approaches are called the "rule of three" or "ten" or any other number. The rationale for them is to provide the hiring authority with some discretion in making selections but nevertheless assure that the selection process is open and competitive.

Selection by examination generally involves the use of an **eligibles register**. This is simply a list of those who passed an examination, ranked in the order of their scores. Under the "rule of three" approach, for example, if a vacancy occurred, the appropriate eligibles register would be consulted and selection would be from among the top three scorers on the list. If another vacancy occurred, selection would be from among the remaining two highest scorers, plus whoever scored fourth highest (that is, ranked fourth on the eligibles register). If someone is passed over a number of times (typically three) he or she will be deleted from the register, despite his or her score. Computerization makes it possible to create an eligibles register for any particular job from among applicants who have passed a relevant examination. Sometimes this procedure is called a "person search," which is a flexible means of generating eligibles registers as they are needed.

Examinations can be **assembled** or **unassembled.** Assembled exams are those in which the applicants assemble in a room or set of rooms at the same time to take the test. Unassembled exams are taken individually. Sometimes the latter are really nothing more than the completing of forms that subsequently become the basis of a "rating" or scoring process. Within these two categories, there are a variety of possibilities:

1. *Performance examinations.* These are devices intended to determine whether the applicant can perform the tasks required in the position for which someone is being hired. Typing and equipment operation are functions in which performance exams are generally used. In such an instance, the exam might be, for example, to determine how many words a minute a person can process accurately.

2. *Written examinations.* These may stress achievement, aptitude, or both. They are typically of the multiple-choice, machine-scored variety. Some jurisdictions purchase them commercially, rather than developing their own. A major virtue of such examinations is that they are inexpensive to administer.

3. *Oral examinations.* These are often considered more practical for upper-level positions involving discretionary authority or positions for which there are few applicants. Generally, an oral exam is administered by a panel who have an established set of criteria for making a judgment. The candidate may appear before the panel alone or with a group of other applicants.

4. *Assessment centers.* Assessment centers try to duplicate some of the approaches of performance examinations, but for positions in which the tasks are less concrete and evaluated more subjectively. Individuals may be put through a series of activities that simulate some of the critical aspects of the job for which someone is being hired. Such activities may consist of getting along with others, engaging in leadership, or exercising discretion. Ratings are generally made by a panel, with predetermined criteria for assessment.

No matter which kind of examination is used, it is critical to the managerial approach that the selection device be *valid*. In other words, score on the exam must be predictive of the likely level of performance on the job. Yet for many positions this is difficult to achieve and demonstrate. The chief problems in validating examinations are threefold. First, it is difficult to construct an exam that truly reflects on-the-job conditions. This is especially true for positions involving the exercise of interpersonal skills, policy making, and discretion. However, it can also be a problem in performance examinations, since the environment in which an individual works can affect productivity. Sometimes this problem is addressed by distinguishing between **job proficiency**, that is, the actual ability to do the work, and **job performance**, which is the reality of how much work gets done. A simple example is a typist who, although proficient, performs far better in a room alone than in a pool with ten or twenty other typists. Although it may be possible to test for this, it may also be very expensive or impractical to do so. Aspects of the work environment, such as noise, degree of privacy, and the extent of time pressures, that can affect performance are called **situational factors.**

A second problem is that there may be very little variation in the scores of those who are actually selected for governmental positions. The dynamics of contemporary selection are such that there are typically many more applicants than position openings. Indeed, there have been cases of some 15,000 individuals applying for less than 100 jobs. Under such circumstances it is highly likely that those selected will have virtually the same scores on the exams, and their scores are likely to be very high. When this occurs, it is difficult to validate an examination simply because there is no way of knowing how well someone with a much lower score would have performed. Those with lower scores cannot be hired, of course, because of the rule of three or similar approach. It is important to note that the problem is that the exam cannot be satisfactorily validated, not that it is necessarily invalid. In other words, the exam may be valid, but there is no convincing way of demonstrating this statistically.

Third, in order to validate an examination, the level of performance by employees who took it must be measured. Again the object is to show a relationship between exam score and performance level on the job. If the latter cannot be measured well, then validity cannot be demonstrated. Performance appraisal is possible for some jobs, but extremely difficult in any systematic fashion in others. We will have more to say about this momentarily.

Despite these problems, there is a well-developed set of approaches to merit examination validation. The best is the **criterion-related** approach. It seeks to relate exam score to on-the-job performance in one of two ways. First, it may be **predictive,** that is, it takes the actual scores of those selected and associates them statistically with these employees' on-the-job performance at some later time. Predictive validation is very difficult to establish for the reasons discussed above. **Concurrent validation** is a technique that administers the exam to those already employed and then seeks to determine the statistical relationship between their scores and their performance appraisals. The chief virtue here is that there may be more variation in score among those taking the examination. However, performance remains difficult to measure objectively, and this approach also runs the risk that extraneous factors may contribute to both an employee's score and performance level. For instance, an employee who is well liked personally and consequently has a high degree of self-esteem may obtain both a higher score and higher performance appraisal than one who is isolated in and alienated from the workplace—even though under neutral social conditions both might score or perform equally.

Other types of validation do not technically seek to relate job performance to examination scores. **Content validation** merely seeks to establish whether the contents of the exam match the contents of the job, that is, does the exam reflect the knowledge, skills, abilities, and aptitudes necessary to perform well on the job. This runs into the problem of proficiency versus performance. **Construct validation** seeks to determine whether the exam ascertains the existence of "psychological constructs," such as honesty, reliability, or tact. It does not seek to show how these constructs are related to on-the-job performance. Finally, **face validity** simply addresses the question of whether the exam appears reasonable on its surface. For example, an examination that tests the current events or historical knowledge of applicants for the position of garbage collector or dogcatcher may appear ridiculous and therefore lack face validity. Interestingly, however, the many exams that have tested precisely for such knowledge in the past were premised on a very different concept of public servant—one who was imbued with civic virtue and knew much about public affairs.

We have dwelt upon examinations and validation at some length because they are currently areas of crisis in public personnel administration. Far too frequently, so-called merit examinations have had a harsh racial or ethnic impact, which has made it all the more difficult for members of some minority groups to gain public employment. The exams' discriminatory impact stems in part from the inequality of opportunity in society at large, especially in education. Such an impact thus flies in the face of equal opportunity and the political approach's emphasis on representative government, and can be tolerated only if the exams truly are highly predictive of job performance—and perhaps not even then. Indeed, two of the major federal examinations administered to college graduates for general administrative careers, the Federal Service Entrance Exam and the Professional and Administrative Career Exam (PACE), which replaced it, have been abandoned largely because of their negative impact on the employment of blacks and Hispanics. Under contemporary civil rights law, once an adverse racial or ethnic impact has been established, the burden of demonstrating that a civil service selection procedure has a high degree of validity generally falls upon the employer. However, as our discussion indicates, this is often very difficult, because even if the exam is highly predictive of on-the-job performance, it may be impossible to demonstrate the relationship statistically in a satisfactory fashion. (Box 5–5 presents sample questions from the PACE.)

The managerial approach also stresses efficiency and productivity as the basis for *promotion*. According to this approach, promotions are generally made on the basis of written examinations and/or performance appraisals. The promotional examination resembles the merit entrance examination except that it is open only to those employees who qualify for consideration for promotion. Performance appraisals are discussed below.

Promotions remain a controversial aspect of public personnel management. The plain hard fact is that, in hierarchical organizations, there are fewer positions at the top than at the bottom. Therefore there is a limit on how high up an employee can rise. Most employees will always be lower down in the organization's ranks. Therefore, promotions tend to be "zero-sum," that is, one employee's gain (promotion) is another's lost opportunity. The competition can be fierce

BOX 5–5 Sample Questions from the Professional and Administrative Career Examination*

1. The function of business is to increase the wealth of the country and the value and happiness of life. It does this by supplying the material needs of men and women. When the nation's business is successfully carried on, it renders public service of the highest value.

The paragraph best supports the statement that:

A) all businesses which render public service are successful

B) human happiness is enhanced only by the increase of material wants

C) the value of life is increased only by the increase of wealth

D) the material needs of men and women are supplied by well-conducted business

E) business is the only field of activity which increases happiness

2. Subsume means most nearly:

A) understate
B) absorb
C) include
D) belong
E) cover

3. Determine what the pattern of these letters is and decide which alternative gives the next letter in the series.

b c d b d e b c f b d g

A) b   B) c   C) h   D) i   E) e

4. Seventy 58-inch × 34-inch desks must be stored in a warehouse. If as many desks as possible are stored on the floor of a 14-foot, 8-inch × 24-foot, 6-inch room, how many desks will still require storage?

A) 46
B) 25
C) 45
D) 44
E) None of the above.

5. Pick the symbol that would create the same analogy as exists between the figures in the first group.

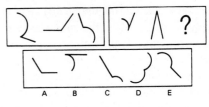

The exam is no longer given, but these questions may be considered typical of those found on merit exams for a wide variety of administrative and professional positions. The first edition of this text generated many requests for the answer to question 5. According to OPM, it is "B": "The similarity between the sets is that all the symbols are made up of lines which form an angle. Since some symbols in both sets are composed of both straight and curved lines, this is not helpful in determining the specific variation of the common characteristic that leads to the correct answer. The symbols in the first set are all made up of lines whose intersection forms an obtuse angle (greater than 90 degrees). The lines of symbols in the second set all form acute angles (less than 90 degrees). This difference indicates the variation of the common characteristic found only in the symbols of the second set. The analogy is defined by this similarity (lines forming angles) and difference (acute vs. obtuse angles). Alternative B is the only symbol which consists of two lines forming an acute angle, thus sharing the characteristic common among all the symbols (two lines forming an angle) and maintaining the same variation of the characteristic as the symbols in the second set (lines forming an acute angle)."

SOURCE: *Washington Post National Weekly Edition*, March 11, 1985, p. 33. The questions were distributed by the U.S. Civil Service Commission in 1975. OPM's answer appeared in the *Washington Post*, March 6, 1987, p. A21.

and lead to discord among employees. This is one of the virtues of a written promotional examination. As long as the exam is accepted as legitimate and fair, it settles the issue without any possibility of favoritism or office politics playing a role. Similarly, promotion by seniority, which is a principle often stressed by unions in collective bargaining, tends to minimize discord. However, seniority is not necessarily the best indicator of productivity and consequently the managerial approach tends to discourage it. Sometimes merit-oriented promotion and seniority are combined by restricting the opportunity for promotion to those who have been on the job for a given number of years.

Performance Appraisal

Performance appraisals have recently gained greater attention as part of the 1978 federal civil service reform, where they are part of a merit pay program. Although there is a wide variety of performance appraisal techniques, evaluating employee productivity remains problematic. The main difficulties are that appraisals reflect varying degrees of subjectivity, that it is often impossible to quantify the output of public employees in any meaningful fashion, and that there tends to be very limited variability in the level of appraisal. Indeed, prior to the 1978 reform, some 98 percent of all federal employees obtained a "satisfactory" efficiency rating. Today, many performance appraisal techniques stress a combination of self appraisals, peer ratings, and group or external ratings. Of course, the more tangible the employee's work product, the greater the probability of designing a performance appraisal approach that truly serves to indicate the level of an employee's productivity.

To some extent, public sector performance appraisal is a "process in search of a technique."[34] Typically, appraisals are concerned with the performance factors and employee traits displayed in Box 5–6. However, there are several ways of assessing these characteristics. Appraisals are generally done by supervisors, peers, the employees themselves, by groups, by external evaluators, or by some combination of these. The techniques strive for objectivity, but where an employee's work is essentially qualitative (e.g., writing reports, supervising others, evaluating grant applications, procuring weaponry), appraisal will inevitably contain subjective judgments. Among the major techniques are:

1. *Rating scales*, as in Box 5–6, which are easy to administer, relatively inexpensive, clear, and in widespread use.
2. *Essay reports* focusing on an employee's need for further training and his or her potential and ability to obtain results. This technique is time-consuming.
3. *Checklists* consisting of statements about the employee's performance. The rater checks the most appropriate statements. Some of these may be given greater weight than others in reaching an overall appraisal.
4. *Critical incidents*, an approach requiring the supervisor to keep a log of employees' performance, indicating incidents of both good and poor performance.

BOX 5–6 **Performance Appraisal by Graphic Rating Scale**

Person evaluated_____ Position_____

Location_____

PERFORMANCE FACTORS	Out-standing	Very Good	Good	Satis-factory	Unsatis-factory	Un-known
1. Effectiveness						
2. Use of time and materials						
3. Prompt completion of work						
4. Thoroughness						
5. Initiative						
6. Perseverance						

ETHICAL CONSIDERATIONS

	Out-standing	Very Good	Good	Satis-factory	Unsatis-factory	Un-known
7. Loyalty to department						
8. Loyalty to peers						
9. Loyalty to subordinates						

	Out-standing	Very Good	Good	Satis-factory	Unsatis-factory	Un-known
10. Sense of ethics						
11. Cooperativeness						
12. Responsibility						
13. Commitment of service						
14. Open-mindedness						

ABILITIES, SKILLS, AND FACULTIES

	Out-standing	Very Good	Good	Satis-factory	Unsatis-factory	Un-known
15. Technical skills						
16. Communication skills						
17. Judgment						
18. Analytical ability						
19. Ability to organize						
20. Ability to inspire and influence staff						
21. Ability to inspire and influence others than staff						
22. Flexibility and adaptability						
23. Imaginativeness and creativity						
24. Ability to develop subordinates						
25. Breadth of concepts						

Date evaluated_____ Evaluator_____

The above appraisal was reviewed with me on_____

_____

(Signature of Person Evaluated)

Comments _____

5. *Forced choice* requires supervisors to rate employees on the basis of descriptive statements. The statements are constructed so that the supervisor cannot be certain which ones are most indicative of employee performance that the personnel office will deem most desirable. An example is presented in Box 5–7. Forced choice enhances objectivity but results in evaluations that are difficult for supervisors and employees to interpret and use as a means of improving performance.
6. *Ranking* or comparing employees to one another.
7. *Forced Distribution* requires the rater to place employees in categories such as top 5 percent, next 10 percent, next 25 percent, and so on.

All of these techniques have pros and cons in terms of objectivity, usefulness, cost, and ease of administration. None is best for all positions and circumstances. The search for better performance appraisal techniques retains a high priority in the managerial approach.

Pay

The managerial approach also stresses economy and productivity in determining the pay levels of public employees. Pay systems are typically linked to position classification systems, but they tend to be problematic and controversial for a variety of reasons. First, it is currently held that pay systems should seek to motivate employees to be more productive. The federal merit pay arrangements for employees in grades GS 13–15 seek to establish a clear link between an employee's performance rating and his or her level of pay. In some jurisdictions, efforts are made to grant increases in the pay of public employees largely on the basis of increased productivity. The major difficulties in this regard seem to be

---

BOX 5–7 **Performance Appraisal by the Forced-Choice Technique**

Person Evaluated_____

Position_____

Organization Unit_____

Date_____

Evaluator_____

Instructions: Please place a check on the line to the left of the statement that best describes this employee.

This employee___a. is loyal to his or her supervisor___b. uses imagination and creativity___c. is thorough and dependable___d. accepts responsibility willingly

This employee___a. completes work promptly and on time___b. pays much attention to detail___c. works well under pressure___d. works well without supervisory guidance

This employee___a. always looks presentable___b. shows initiative and independence___c. works well with others in groups___d. produces work of high quality

twofold. On the one hand, merit pay or pay for greater productivity is most suitable to positions where the worker's output is tangible and measurable. Collecting garbage is an example. The total tons collected per employee or team per workday is measurable, as is the geographic area covered by a sanitation crew. Typing and a variety of other governmental jobs also lend themselves to productivity measurement. But jobs involving a qualitative output and the exercise of discretion tend to be unsuitable to meaningful productivity measurement. For instance, how would you measure the productivity of a police officer? By the number of tickets issued, the number of arrests made, the number of domestic disputes settled, the number of endangered lives saved? Clearly, these all say something about the officer's performance, but so does the crime rate on his or her beat and the feeling of security or insecurity that residents there have. One could argue that arrests are a poor indicator of productivity, because they signify that the officer has failed to deter crime. But it would be equally ludicrous to hold a single officer responsible for the crime rate in any particular area. Similarly, how can the productivity of a public employee exercising judicial functions be evaluated? Administrative law judges and hearing examiners make decisions in individual cases. Although we could measure the time it takes them to reach and write opinions, what we are really interested in is the quality of those decisions in terms of justice and the public interest. Within broad limits, we care very little whether one such employee hears more cases per year than another. A promising approach for resolving some of these difficulties is for an employee and his or her supervisor to discuss appropriate performance goals and ways of assessing progress toward them. Various peer review systems also help assess performance.

Pay is also complicated by the desire to make it comparable with pay in the private sector. In other words, it is generally held that an employee in the public sector should earn what he or she would earn if doing the same work in the private sector. In the federal government, **comparability** is assessed on the basis of a survey done by the Bureau of Labor Statistics. The survey presents some challenging technical problems, but the main difficulty is that there are no true private equivalents for a large number of public sector jobs. Again the problem is the qualitative aspect. Many of the features of a typical bureau chief's job can be compared to those of private sector executives—but the public sector job is ultimately different because it involves qualitative questions about public policy and the public interest.[35] To pay a bureau chief based on the number of employees he or she supervises rather than on the basis of his or her development and implementation of effective public policies in the public interest is to miss the main dimension of the job. Comparability also runs into difficulties with regional differences in pay levels. Suppose wages and salaries are lower in one region of the nation or of a state. Should the government contribute to this disparity by paying its employees less because they work in those regions? This could be viewed as perpetuating economic inequalities. On the other hand, by paying more, the government might place a difficult burden on private employers competing in the same labor market.

Comparability refers to wage and salary rates among different employers.

Comparable worth concerns the pay rates for different occupations by the same employer. The Equal Pay Act of 1963 prohibits pay differentials based on sex for employees performing similar jobs under similar working conditions for an employer. However, it does not prohibit different rates of pay to men and women if they are not in the same jobs. The concept of comparable worth seeks to extend the principles of comparability and equal pay to situations where men and women are performing dissimilar jobs that nonetheless are work that could be considered of equal value to an employer. The concept of comparable worth is especially important to an employer that has a high degree of occupational segregation, by sex, in its work force. Many public employers are characterized by such segregation because they employ individuals in a broad range of occupations. For instance, in 1981, 32.5 percent of all women in the federal General Schedule worked in occupations that were at least 90 percent female. About 55 percent of all General Schedule employees filled positions in which at least 80 percent of the other employees in the same positions were of the same sex.[36] Typically, under these sex-segregated conditions, "women's occupations" are paid at lower rates than what seem to be comparable "male occupations." "Comparable" in this sense can be assessed in terms of required level of education, skill, responsibility, and so forth.

The advocates of establishing pay based on comparable worth argue that women are discriminated against because the occupations into which they are segregated are underpaid. In their view, the labor market reflects social discrimination and stereotyping in establishing pay for occupations such as nursing. Los Angeles and the states of Minnesota, New York, New Mexico, Iowa, and South Dakota are among the jurisdictions that have instituted comparable worth. Opponents of comparable worth argue that if women, such as nurses, are dissatisfied with their pay, they should go into other occupations or try to raise their wages through collective bargaining. (One opponent, Clarence Pendleton, Jr., chairman of the U.S. Commission on Civil Rights, called the concept the "looniest idea since Looney Tunes came on the screen.") However, the key to comparable worth may lie less in the desirable trend of opening opportunities for women in what were once considered "male occupations" than in desegregating all occupations. Social factors still play an important role in occupational choice, and that is why Johnny is still not very likely to grow up to be a nurse. The Equal Employment Opportunity Act of 1972 can be used as a basis for seeking to obtain comparable worth through litigation. In such suits it is necessary to show that pay scales were depressed due to intentional sex discrimination.

Determining levels of public sector pay is complicated much further by politics. In recent years, politicians' electoral campaigns and taxpayers' dissatisfactions with government have often focused on the "bloated, unproductive" public sector. When inflation is rampant or budgets seem to defy balance or cities tread on the verge of bankruptcy, freezing or cutting the pay of public employees has become almost a reflexive response. Such freezes or reductions serve as indicators of the politicians' toughness and seem to offer the taxpayers some relief. Yet it is unclear why public employees should bear the brunt of fighting inflation or be penalized for providing services—such as police and fire protection and education—that are clearly in the public's interest. Whatever the sensibility of the "bash the bureaucrat" syndrome, however, public employees' pay remains an easy target in difficult economic times.

Sometimes the comparability principle is also violated by placing "caps" on public employees' level of pay. At the federal level, for instance, it is generally believed that career executives are relatively underpaid because Congress does not favor allowing them to earn more than members of the legislature itself—and when Congress votes itself a raise, it is always politically problematic. The collective bargaining process may also affect pay levels to reflect the relative power of unionized employees rather than equity or comparability.

Finally, in considering the pay of public employees, attention must be paid to fringe benefits and pensions, both of which are often substantially greater in the public sector than among comparably salaried employees in the private sector. Recent presidents have favored basing public employees' comparability on "total compensation," which includes fringe benefits.

Cutbacks

During the late 1970s, and early 1980s, the desire to reduce the public sector payroll in an effort to reduce taxes, balance budgets, and stimulate economic growth in the private sector led to widespread reductions-in-force (RIFs) in the public service. The managerial approach stresses the need to cut the least productive employees and services first and to abandon functions that can be supplied as well or better by the private sector. A dramatic illustration of work-force reductions occurred in New York City from 1975 to 1977, when the city was in the midst of a protracted economic/budgetary crisis. Some of the city's departments lost a quarter of their personnel.

Like promotions, cutbacks are controversial and problematic because there are clear winners and losers. Although the managerial approach of applying what amounts to a "demerit" procedure makes sense on its own terms and from its own value perspectives, it is generally in competition with other values and approaches. At present, the main approaches to cutbacks involve: (1) providing some employees with greater protection than others, such as veterans or more senior employees; (2) relying upon attrition, that is, the retirement of employees, their voluntary separation from the public sector, or their disability or death, without refilling their positions; (3) offering "early" retirements as an incentive for employees to leave the public sector voluntarily; and (4) employing "across-the-board" cuts among all levels of employees and all governmental functions. Recently, "job sharing," or splitting one position between two or more part-time employees, has also gained attention. As the managerial approach argues, the main problem with these processes is that they may not lead to cuts where they are most desirable from an organizational standpoint. Indeed, there have been instances where early retirements have led to the separation of highly valued and necessary employees who subsequently had to be replaced, netting the government very little, if any, savings.

Political Neutrality

Running throughout the managerial approach to public personnel administration is the concept that the civil service should be politically neutral in a partisan sense. Managerially oriented public administration holds that to a very large extent the public sector faces the same kinds of organizational and managerial conditions and problems as the private sector and that partisanship has no legitimate place in the vast majority of public personnel and managerial decisions. The notion that functions such as street paving and sanitation are inherently nonpartisan is illustrative. The functions of the public sector in this view have much to do with the public interest and very little to do with the immediate electoral interests of political parties. To a very large extent, the contemporary concept of political neutrality grew out of the nineteenth-century civil service reform movement and was a reaction to the abuses of the spoils system. However, not only can the mixing of partisanship and personnel be seen to impede efficiency and foster corruption, but it can also symbolize a perversion of the public interest, leading the citizenry to believe that the public service is engaged in the promotion of its own narrow partisan interests.

Contemporary regulations for political neutrality are embodied in the Hatch Acts of 1939 and 1940. The first Hatch Act applied to federal employees. The act allows federal servants to express opinions on political subjects and candidates for office, but it forbids them from taking an active part in partisan political management or in partisan political campaigns. The second Hatch Act applies similar restrictions to state and local employees whose salaries are derived in part from federal funds or who are engaged in spending such funds. Many states and local governments also have political neutrality regulations.

The main difficulty with the Hatch Acts and similar regulations is that they do not specify precisely what they prohibit. Some of the restrictions are clear, but it is not always evident when a political statement becomes part of an active partisan campaign. For instance, federal employees have been disciplined for such behavior as stating "unsubstantiated facts about the ancestry of a candidate" (calling him an S.O.B.?) failing to "discourage a spouse's political activity," and voicing "disapproval of treatment of veterans while acting as a Legion officer at a closed [American] Legion meeting."[37] Consequently, these restrictions may tend to inhibit public employees' freedom of speech more than is necessary to promote the value of partisan neutrality in the public service. On the other hand, some of the restrictions are well established: federal employees are prohibited from actively raising funds for partisan candidates; becoming a partisan candidate for, or campaigning for a partisan candidate for, public office; initiating or circulating partisan nominating petitions; soliciting votes for a partisan candidate for public office; or acting as a delegate, alternate, or proxy to a political party convention. It is important to note that while these kinds of regulations place substantial limitations on public employees' political rights, they also protect employees from being coerced by elected officials and political executives to engage in partisan activities.

Despite their interference with the public employee's constitutional rights under the First and Fourteenth Amendments, the Supreme Court has upheld the constitutionality of regulations for political neutrality in no uncertain terms.[38] In its view, legislatures have the power to establish such restrictions because they promote the legitimate objectives of creating and maintaining an efficient and nonpartisan civil service. Partly in response to pressure from unions representing public employees, Congress periodically develops an interest in liberalizing or repealing the Hatch Acts. In the mid-1970s, such an effort was vetoed by President Ford. In 1987, Congress took up the issue again, despite a threatened veto by President Reagan. (As of this writing, the act remains intact.)

THE POLITICAL APPROACH TO PUBLIC PERSONNEL ADMINISTRATION

The political approach to public personnel stresses radically different values than the managerial approach and leads to emphasis on different techniques and considerations. Perhaps its underlying value is to maximize the responsiveness of the public sector work force to political officials and to the public at large. The political approach deemphasizes the analogy between public and private employment and stresses the extent to which the public service is *public*. According to this approach, what is most significant about the public sector is that it makes and implements public policy, that it provides public goods and services that cannot or should not be supplied by the private sector, and that it is an integral part of a constitutional system of government.

Responsiveness

The quest for *responsiveness* has taken several forms. Underlying most of them, however, is the idea that public employees should not use their positions to subvert the general political goals being pursued by the elected component of government and the political community as a whole. This concern was evident from the outset of constitutional government in the United States. Concern with responsiveness reflects the view that public administration is not simply a politically neutral, technical, managerial endeavor, but rather has to be considered in terms of the political choices facing the nation.

The most outstanding effort to assure responsiveness is reliance on the widespread use of political patronage in recruiting, selecting, and promoting public employees. The primary function of patronage has probably been to sustain political parties—and the demise of patronage has coincided with the decline of parties in the United States. But there is another logic as well, and one that assures the responsiveness of public administrators to the public: The people elect political officials who espouse a political program outlined in a party platform and then the elected officials appoint public administrators who are sympathetic to the party's policies. This promotes administrative responsiveness to elected officials and, by extension, to the public. Moreover, in patronage systems, the ability of the elected officials to fire, reassign, or promote public administrators virtually at will comes very close to assuring that the administrators will not act in ways that subvert the programs of the political officials. In other words, patronage can be used to instill accountability.

Some of the arrangements of the federal Civil Service Reform Act of 1978 seek responsiveness in this fashion. The Senior Executive Service is composed predominantly of top-ranking career civil servants. By law, 10 percent of allocated positions in the SES can be purely political (patronage) appointees. Members of the SES can be reassigned, voluntarily transferred from agency to agency, given different kinds of work, and reduced in grade with far greater flexibility than most federal career servants. They are subject neither to the position classification system nor the normal adverse action system for demotions based on poor performance. The rationale behind the SES was in very large part to make these high-ranking administrative officials responsive to political executives. In addition, it was thought that moving SES members from bureau to bureau and possibly from agency to agency would enable them to develop a broader concept of the public interest, one that was not overly supportive of the aims of any particular narrow interest group. Aside from affording these administrators new opportunities and challenges, the act made them eligible for large financial bonuses in return for sacrificing some of the security they had previously held. It is interesting to note that the reform act seeks to assure some continuity in the higher civil service by prohibiting the involuntary reassignment of members of the SES within 120 days of the appointment of a new political executive in a supervisory position over them. The act also requires that 70 percent of all positions in the SES be filled with individuals with not less than five years of current, continuous administrative service.

The effort to assure responsiveness has also led to various other kinds of ideological and political screening. At various times in the nation's history, for instance, the loyalty of public employees to the United States has been the subject of investigation. The most elaborate loyalty-security program existed in the late 1940s and early 1950s, a period generally referred to as "McCarthyism" after Senator Joseph McCarthy of Wisconsin. During part of that time, the loyalty of *every* federal employee and applicant was subject to question. Loyalty was defined largely in terms of adhering to an uninformed anticommunism, which was a rather conservative, limited political vision. Loyalty-security hearings probed employees on such things as whether they read the *New York Times* or Tom Paine, whether they believed in racial integration, peace, freedom, and civil liberties, whether they provided religious training for their children, and whether they engaged in or believed in premarital sex. One federal employee was even asked if he sympathized with the underprivileged![39] In retrospect, had not so many lives been damaged by the program and had not the creativity of the federal service suffered so badly, the fetish with loyalty-security would be easily dismissed as aberrant. After all, seeking social equity, engaging in premarital sex, supporting racial integration, supporting the recognition of "red" (mainland) China, and reading high-quality newspapers are usually no longer considered even remote indicators of disloyalty. However, at the time there was a very real fear in Congress and the society at large that federal employees were not responsive to the dominant values of the American political community and that they would use their positions to undermine the goals being sought by elected officials.

The effort to assure the responsiveness of public administrators also forms the basis for much legislative activity vis-à-vis public personnel administration. Legislatures, including the U.S. Congress, frequently have committees that deal with matters pertaining to the civil service and public personnel. Other legislative committees become involved in personnel from time to time in the course of their exercise of oversight of administrative programs. These legislative activities not only concern the general quality and legality of agencies' personnel management, they also serve as a focal point for groups seeking changes in public personnel arrangements. For example, labor unions representing public employees and organizations seeking to promote the equality of various social groups, such as blacks and women, frequently appear at legislative hearings dealing with public personnel policy. They may also actively lobby members of the relevant legislative committees as a means of promoting their objectives.

Legislative involvement in public personnel administration sometimes results in programs and policies that are in conflict with the objectives of the managerial approach. Veteran preference is an outstanding example. The logic of the merit system makes no provision for awarding preferential treatment to those who have served in the nation's armed forces. Yet at the federal level and in the overwhelming majority of the states, some veterans are provided with such a benefit. Typically, a number of points are added to a preference recipient's score (usually five or ten). In some cases, recipients of veterans preference are placed at the top of the eligibles register. In either case, veteran preference can have profound effects on the order in which individuals are selected for the civil service. Sometimes veterans preference makes a shambles of ordinary merit hiring practices, and it has had a very adverse effect on the employment of women. Veterans may also be granted preferences in retention during reductions in force.

Another example of legislative involvement in public personnel administration in response to interest groups tending to undermine the logic of the managerial approach occurs in statutes authorizing collective bargaining in the public sector. We will have much more to say about this subject later in this chapter. Here, however, it should be pointed out that labor relations statutes may authorize collective bargaining over such matters as position classification, promotion, and pay—all of which are central to the managerial program for public personnel.

Representativeness

The political approach to public administration stresses the value of *representativeness*. Public bureaucracies are considered to be political, policy-making institutions that exercise public power. One line of thought is that this power can be controlled and channelled in the public interest if the bureaucrats and agencies are representative of the political community at large. Representativeness is related to responsiveness because it is assumed that a representative bureaucracy will have similar perspectives on questions of public policy as the majority in the legislature and in the electorate.[40] In terms of public personnel administration, the quest for representativeness has historically centered on the need to select public administrators who are socially and/or politically representative of the nation's general population. The Pendleton Act of 1883 even included a provision for apportioning civil service appointments in the District of Columbia by the appointees' state of residency and according to the relative size of the states' populations. The political approach's emphasis on representation sometimes brings it into conflict with the managerial perspective.

Today, the quest for representativeness in public bureaucracies is manifested to the greatest extent in a concern with equal employment opportunity and affirmative action (EEO/AA). One justification for such programs is that equal opportunity contributes to distributive and social justice; EEO is fair and ought to be practiced for that reason alone. Another justification stresses the supposed connection between the social representativeness of a public bureaucracy and its representativeness in a political and policy sense. Although the links between social background and policy behavior of public administrators have yet to be understood fully, some governmental policy makers have based the effort to establish greater social representation in the federal bureaucracy on the assumption that there is a close connection between the two.[41] Another aspect of the theory of representative bureaucracy stresses that the allegiance of various social groups to the government can be enhanced by including their members in all institutions of public power, including public bureaucracies. Finally, it is sometimes argued that government serves as an example (or model employer) for the society at large and that therefore its behavior has widespread ramifications for private personnel practices and the general treatment of groups. Whatever the intellectual and empirical viability of these approaches, it is clear that the federal government and many states have expressed a policy commitment to a socially representative work force and that EEO/AA has emerged as a central element of public personnel administration.

Equal employment opportunity began to emerge as a major personnel concern in the 1940s, when the first program for nondiscrimination was established in the federal government. The program was introduced against a background of rampant racial discrimination and segregation in the federal service. Although progress was uneven and a true commitment seemed to be lacking, by the 1960s EEO was a central programmatic effort in the personnel field. The Civil Rights Act of 1964 placed the policy of establishing EEO in federal personnel management on the basis of statute. The Equal Employment Opportunity Act of 1972 strengthened this commitment and extended it to state and local governments, many of which were under their own programs earlier. The federal Civil Service Reform Act of 1978 further strengthened the commitment to EEO by making a socially representative federal work force a policy objective.

The main reason why an EEO program is necessary is that managerially oriented public personnel administration neither produced socially representative bureaucracies nor prevented racial, ethnic, gender, and religious discrimination. The managerial quest for efficiency and a smoothly functioning public administration sometimes served as a rationale for blatant discrimination. Thus, when Woodrow Wilson extended the practice of racial segregation in the federal service, he claimed that it would reduce social "friction" that interfered with administrative operations.[42] More importantly, as we have seen earlier, merit examinations for a wide range of careers, including police, fire, sanitation, and general administration, have all too frequently manifested an adverse disparate impact against blacks, Hispanics, and perhaps Native Americans. In fact, many civil rights activists have considered the merit system to be the chief contemporary barrier to equal opportunity and a socially representative public work force.

That contemporary merit practices sometimes tend to be at odds with the objectives of EEO is clear, but precisely why remains elusive. Part of the reason is that there is not equal opportunity in United States society to gain the skills, knowledge, abilities, and perhaps aptitudes that the merit system considers predictors of efficient and economical on-the-job performance. Second, the merit system has not in fact prevented discrimination. The rule of three, for example, has sometimes been used to pass over qualified minority, handicapped, and female candidates. Fairness in promotions seems especially to have been lacking for members of these groups. Moreover, frequently they have been victims of the "last hired, first fired"* syndrome in times of reductions in force. Third, to an extent, women and members of minority groups appear to have had less exposure to government recruitment networks. In the past, jobs were not advertised in places where they were likely to learn about them. They also had limited access to word-of-mouth networks disseminating information about public sector jobs. In addition, job counseling and advising too often steered members of these groups into stereotypic "black" or "female" jobs. The latter has been a particularly invidious aspect of racism and sexism in the United States.

Since the 1960s public personnel programs have made a commitment to and efforts at establishing greater EEO. For the most part, this commitment is manifested in personnel activities intended to (1) reach all segments of the population in recruitment efforts; (2) eliminate artificial barriers to equal opportunity, such as height and weight requirements; (3) eliminate a harsh racial or ethnic bias from merit examinations; (4) establish upward-mobility training programs for minority and female employees; and (5) eliminate all vestiges of discriminatory thinking and practice from the entire gamut of personnel actions, including promotions, assignments, position classifications, and the like. Although these principles are generally focused most on women and members of minority groups (primarily blacks, Hispanics, indigenous North American peoples, Asian-Americans, and Pacific Islanders), they also apply to handicapped persons.

Furthermore, two broad techniques have emerged to achieve these objectives. One is the EEO Complaint System and related opportunities for litigation before the courts. Today, complaint systems seek to provide a quick resolution of

---

* Also called "last in, first out," or LIFO.

problems related to prohibited discrimination. They stress informal resolution and corrective action. However, where neither of these is forthcoming, a complaint system is likely to provide for elaborate adjudicatory hearings at which both sides can present evidence, testify, and seek to rebut the other. To be credible, complaint systems must also offer sufficient remedies, including back pay, promotion, desired training, and other personnel actions. Moreover, discriminatory supervisors must be disciplined.

Although in the abstract complaint systems often appear eminently fair, in practice they tend to be problematical and to generate anxiety. The most vexing difficulty has been resolving complaints on a timely basis. Supervisors also complain that they are inadequately protected against frivolous or misguided complaints and they cannot do their jobs under the threat of such actions. Complainants, on the other hand, have frequently voiced the view that complaint systems are not truly impartial, but rather tend to favor management.[43]

The second technique for achieving EEO has been the use of **affirmative action**.[44] This has been far more controversial and continues to divide American society. Philosophically, affirmative action represents a departure from traditional concepts of equal opportunity. Rather than seeking to assure equal opportunity to compete for civil service positions, affirmative action seeks to assure equality in the outcome of the competition for those positions. It seeks a kind of proportional representation of various social groups in public administrative posts at all levels and in all the nation's governments. The groups toward which affirmative action policies are most directly aimed are blacks, Hispanics, Native Americans, Asian-Americans, Pacific Islanders, and women. Each has suffered from a great deal of discrimination in public personnel administration. (Box 5–8 shows their average grade levels in the federal service.) The employment of blacks in the postal service was once banned by federal law (1809–1865). Unequal pay and blatant discrimination based on gender was also authorized by federal statute in the past. Proponents of affirmative action generally argue that at the very least, those who have been discriminated against so rampantly in the past should be entitled to special, compensatory treatment until effects of past practices have been eliminated. Such preferences may include special recruitment efforts, preferential allocation of training opportunities, and even reevaluation of position classification systems to facilitate the upward mobility of people belonging to those groups.

The crux of the controversy over affirmative action is whether the goals established for the employment and promotion of members of the various social groups are really quotas and whether, as such, they conflict with the merit system. Under contemporary guidelines propounded by the Equal Employment Opportunity Commission and OPM, goals should be established to assure that the employment of women and minorities in public personnel systems is proportionate to their numbers in the work force in the area from which these governments recruit their employees. The objective is to establish proportional representation at all levels and in all occupations within public agencies. However, once a goal is established its relationship to the merit system may be unclear.

BOX 5–8 **The Average General Schedule Grade of Various Groups, 1976 and 1983**

Group	1976 Average Grade	1983 Average Grade	1976–1983 Change
White Males*	—	10.58	—
Asian Males	10.16	10.09	-.07
American Indian Males	7.52	9.20	1.68
Hispanic Males	5.23	8.80	3.57
Black Males	5.58	8.07	2.49
Asian Females	6.62	7.11	0.49
White Females*	—	6.82	—
Black Females	6.26	6.32	0.06
Hispanic Females	6.93	6.18	-0.75
American Indian Females	4.79	5.94	1.15

*Other than Hispanic.

SOURCE: U.S. Equal Employment Opportunity Commission, *Annual Report on the Employment of Minorities, Women, and Handicapped Individuals in the Federal Government*, FY 83 (Washington, D.C.: Government Printing Office, 1986), Sect. 9244-10.1 (Women and Minorities), Table 1-7, p. 30, for 1983 data; 1976 data are from U.S. Office of Personnel Management, "Summary of Full-Time Employment for Women and Minority Government-wide, 1970–1980," unpublished.

Merit seeks to select the most qualified applicants, qualification being defined in nonpartisan and ostensibly socially neutral terms. Affirmative action seeks to take social characteristics into account in undertaking public personnel actions and to give at least a temporary preference to the members of some social groups. In practice, the two conflict when candidates for employment or promotion with higher merit system credentials are passed over in favor of individuals with lower merit scores who receive an affirmative action preference. To some this may be seen as sexist, racist, immoral, and inefficient; to others the affirmative action preference is merely the removal of an unfair advantage that was previously held by nonminority men. In addition, the merit approach looks primarily at individual qualifications, whereas affirmative action takes a more collectivist approach in addressing the needs of whole social groups. Eventually, the controversy may be resolved as the merit system is improved to eliminate some of its racial, ethnic and gender bias and as society makes greater strides toward social equality. However, this underlying tension between the managerial orientation (merit) and the political approach (representativeness) predates the controversy over affirmative action and is likely to outlive it.

At present, the Supreme Court considers hiring and promotional quotas to be constitutional as a remedy for past proven illegal and/or unconstitutional discrimination.[45] Quotas favoring minorities in layoffs and reductions in force are likely to be illegal and/or unconstitutional because of the burden they place on nonminority employees (who are dismissed according to racial or ethnic criteria in violation of the Equal Protection Clause of the Fourteenth Amendment).[46] The Court has upheld the legality of affirmative action that is voluntary (that is, not imposed as a remedy for past proven discrimination) in promotions.[47] (Chapter 11 considers the Constitution's equal protection requirement in greater detail.)

THE LEGAL APPROACH TO PUBLIC PERSONNEL ADMINISTRATION

The legal approach to public personnel administration places the constitutional relationship between citizen and government above the relationship between public employer and employee. It focuses on and values highly the rights and liberties of individual public employees and applicants for civil service jobs. It particularly stresses the need for fair and equitable procedures in adverse personnel actions or other situations in which an employee or applicant stands to lose or be denied something valuable to him or her. Moreover, the legal approach emphasizes the need for equal protection of the law and consequently opposes racial, ethnic, gender, and some other forms of discrimination. By and large, this approach to public personnel administration stands in contrast to the managerial and political approaches. Its expansive view of employee rights and due process tends to undercut the managerial approach's reliance on hierarchical control and direction of public employees. Similarly, recent Supreme Court decisions have created constitutional barriers to patronage dismissals, undercutting a basic value asserted by the political approach. The courts have also handed down decisions making loyalty-security programs, such as those of the 1940s and 1950s, difficult to establish within constitutional grounds. At some points, however, the political and legal approaches are in greater agreement, such as in the realm of EEO/AA and equal protection. In reviewing the main thrust of the legal approach as it concerns public personnel, it is extremely important to bear in mind that virtually all the important developments in this area occurred within the past three decades. Consequently, it is only recently that the courts have emerged as a primary participant in the formulation of public personnel policy and practice.

The Constitutional Rights of Public Employees and Applicants

In the early 1950s some federal civil servants were dismissed from their employment on the grounds that a reasonable doubt existed as to their loyalty to the United States. Ostensibly, at least, as noted above, this doubt was created by behavior labeled "un-American," which sometimes included absurdities such as having intelligent friends! Prior to dismissal, an employee might have gone through a hearing before a "Loyalty Review Board." The members of the board would be furnished, by the FBI or the Civil Service Commission, with information impugning the loyalty of the employee. The information would come from informants unknown to the board and their statements might be unsworn.

The employee was not afforded a right to confrontation and cross-examination of these adverse "witnesses." In one case that reached the Supreme Court, part of the evidence against an employee labeled disloyal was that she had written a letter to the Red Cross protesting the segregation of blood by race. A lower court decision, which was affirmed by an equally divided Supreme Court, held that although justice seemed to have been compromised, "the plain hard fact" was that there was no constitutional prohibition on the dismissal of public employees because of their political beliefs, activities, or affiliations.[48] In other words, public employees had few constitutionally protected civil rights and liberties, and consequently, it was not required to develop elaborate procedures to protect them against misguided and damaging dismissals.

The constitutional doctrine prevailing at the time is generally called the **doctrine of privilege.** It held that since public employment was voluntarily accepted by the employee and because no one had a "right" to a government job, the government was free to set virtually any conditions it saw fit with regard to public service. Even though these conditions infringed upon the ordinary constitutional rights that employees held as citizens, they were not necessarily unconstitutional because the employee accepted them voluntarily and because, technically, employees always retained their constitutional rights, they just lost their jobs for exercising them. Justice Holmes once captured the essence of the doctrine of privilege in his famous statement that "the petitioner may have a constitutional right to talk politics, but he has no constitutional right to be a policeman."[49] Such reasoning was obviously facile and ill suited to a large-scale administrative state in which some 15 percent of the work force was in public employment. Additionally, the doctrine applied to others seeking governmental benefits or largess, such as welfare and licenses of various types. By the late 1950s it was becoming increasingly clear to the courts that the doctrine of privilege condoned too many abuses and tended to erode the the fundamental constitutional rights of too large a segment of the United States population. Consequently, dramatic constitutional change was in the offing.

By the 1970s the Supreme Court indicated that it had "fully and finally" rejected "the concept that constitutional rights turn upon whether a governmental benefit is characterized as a 'right' or as a 'privilege.' "[50] It also called the distinction between rights and privileges "wooden."[51] Instead, the Court declared that public employees do indeed have constitutional rights and that these cannot be "chilled," abridged, violated, or denied simply because the individual works for the civil service (see Chapter 11). Where there is some infringement on the constitutional rights of public employees today, such as in the area of political neutrality, the government is required to demonstrate that such limitations are directly related to the necessities of the workplace or serve some overriding value, such as good, nonpartisan government.

A comprehensive treatment of the contemporary constitutional rights of public employees as they affect public personnel management would take volumes. Here, we will just identify some of the most outstanding instances of judicial involvement in public personnel. One of these is in the area of procedural due process, which addresses the fairness of the procedures under which a public employee is subjected to an adverse personnel action. Today, public employees are likely to have a *constitutional* (not just statutory or administrative) right to a hearing in adverse actions if (1) the basis of those actions is the exercise of an ordinary constitutional right, such as freedom of association; (2) the action is likely to damage the employee's reputation, such as labeling him or her dishonest or immoral; (3) there is something about the employee (age perhaps) or the job (possibly highly specialized) that would drastically reduce the civil servant's future employability if dismissed; or (4) the employee holds a contractual, tenure, or other "property interest" in the job.[52] The legal approach to public personnel administration places a strong emphasis on adversary procedure. Hearings are generally before impartial examiners and may be so elaborate as to resemble actual courtroom procedure. Employee and employer (supervisor) are pitted against one another at the hearing, yet at the same time, or in the future, they may have to work together. In some respects, elaborate hearings are inappropriate from the managerial perspective. They seriously compromise control and direction through the exercise of hierarchical authority and they exaggerate the adversity of relations between superordinates and subordinates. The extent to which the legal approach now dominates the procedure for dismissals is indicated by the chart in Box 5–9, which displays OPM's outline of the standard federal procedure. The chart indicates that managers need to build up their cases for dismissal, rather than just assert that in their judgment dismissal is warranted. It also indicates that removals can be complicated by EEO antidiscrimination regulations and by grievance procedures negotiated through collective bargaining.

Freedom of expression is an additional area in which the courts have dramatically changed the nature of public personnel administration. Today public employees have a broad constitutional right to engage in "whistleblowing," that is, they are relatively free to speak out about waste, abuse, fraud, corruption, or misguided policy in the public service. Their right to disseminate such information to the public is protected even if their statements are inaccurate (as long as the employee didn't display a reckless disregard for truth or falsity). The right to "whistleblow" recognizes that the public employee's ultimate loyalty should be to the public rather than to a specific agency or manager. Consequently, it places strains on efforts to promote efficiency through loyalty to the organization and strict obedience to agency leadership.[53]

Other forms of speech on matters of public concern are also constitutionally protected. In an outstanding example, the Supreme Court upheld the right of an employee in a constable's office to remark, upon hearing of an attempt on President Reagan's life, "if they go for him again, I hope they get him."[54] A majority of the Court reasoned that since the employee's comment was to a friend in the office, rather than public, and because she had very limited public contact or authority, her statement was not a basis for dismissal.

Developments in the area of freedom of association have also been revolutionary. There the courts have declared that public employees have a constitutional right to join organizations, including labor unions. This reversed a policy followed by some states that outlawed public sector labor organizations.

BOX 5–9 OPM's Outline of the Federal Demotion and Dismissal Process

l. Appeals and Grievances

The employee can generally appeal a removal or reduction in grade to the Merit Systems Protection Board, or if he or she is in the bargaining unit, can grieve the action under the negotiated grievance procedures unless the negotiated procedure excludes these types of actions. The employee has to choose between the two and cannot do both. Here is an outline of the procedures for reductions in grade and removals based on unacceptable performance, taken under Part 432 of Title 5, Code of Federal Regulations, and reassignment or demotion for unsatisfactory performance as a manager or supervisor under Subpart l of Part 315.

REDUCTIONS IN GRADE AND REMOVAL BASED ON UNACCEPTABLE PERFORMANCE

Beginning of appraisal cycle	Employee given critical elements and performance standards in writing.
Informal steps to improve performance deficiencies	
Performance becomes acceptable?	**YES** No action necessary.

NO

Formal period to show acceptable performance	1. Tell employee, preferably in writing, the critical elements involved in the unacceptable performance and the expected performance.
	2. Notify employee in writing of period to demonstrate acceptable performance and agency assistance in doing it.
	3. Tell employee of consequences of failure to improve.
Performance becomes acceptable?	**YES** No action necessary.

NO   Employee may be reassigned. Unacceptable rating may be given.

Moreover, it fostered the development of elaborate collective bargaining in the public sector—a development that radically changes public personnel management, as we will soon consider. The Supreme Court has also held that public

BOX 5–9 *Continued*

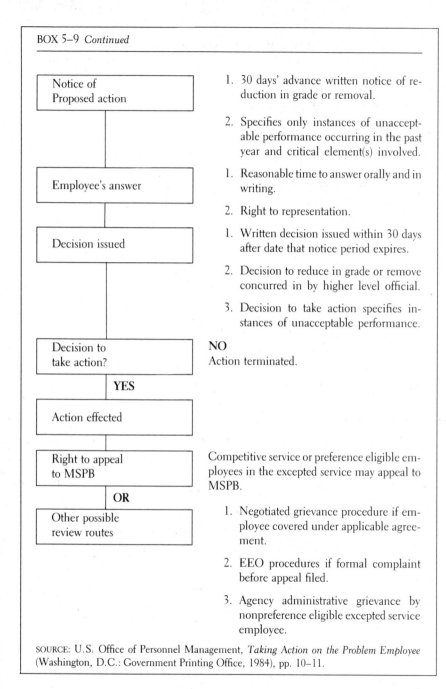

Notice of Proposed action	1. 30 days' advance written notice of reduction in grade or removal. 2. Specifies only instances of unacceptable performance occurring in the past year and critical element(s) involved.
Employee's answer	1. Reasonable time to answer orally and in writing. 2. Right to representation.
Decision issued	1. Written decision issued within 30 days after date that notice period expires. 2. Decision to reduce in grade or remove concurred in by higher level official. 3. Decision to take action specifies instances of unacceptable performance.
Decision to take action?	**NO** Action terminated.

YES

Action effected

Right to appeal to MSPB	Competitive service or preference eligible employees in the excepted service may appeal to MSPB.

OR

Other possible review routes	1. Negotiated grievance procedure if employee covered under applicable agreement. 2. EEO procedures if formal complaint before appeal filed. 3. Agency administrative grievance by nonpreference eligible excepted service employee.

SOURCE: U.S. Office of Personnel Management, *Taking Action on the Problem Employee* (Washington, D.C.: Government Printing Office, 1984), pp. 10–11.

employees cannot constitutionally be compelled to join organizations, including political parties and labor unions.

The judiciary has also handed down a number of decisions that protect the broad constitutional liberties of public employees. Among the most important of these are those dealing with mandatory maternity leaves. The traditional managerially oriented practice required a woman to begin a maternity leave well before the expected date of birth of her child. This made it possible to plan for a replacement employee for her and also was thought to assure that her physical condition would not interfere with her ability to perform the functions of her job. However, the Supreme Court found such rationales to be unsatisfactory.[55] It held that unless the maternity leave is geared to the woman's individual medical condition, that is, her ability to do her job, or begins very late in the term of a normal pregnancy, it constitutes an unconstitutional infringement on a woman's liberty to choose whether to have a child.

The legal approach has also had an important impact on equal employment opportunity. The judiciary has played a significant role in establishing standards for determining what kinds of personnel practices constitute unconstitutional violations of the right to equal protection of the laws. Today, under Supreme Court rulings, a personnel practice having an adverse impact against a specific social group will *not* be unconstitutional unless it is intentionally discriminatory. Even where some intent to treat people differently is evident, as in the case of mandatory retirement regulations, the judiciary may find them acceptable if they are based upon a rational approach to achieving a necessary or desirable governmental objective. However, where courts have found discriminatory treatment to be unconstitutional, they have sometimes responded with far-reaching intervention in public personnel administration. They have found several merit examinations to be unacceptable and have imposed such remedies as hiring and promotion based upon racial quotas.[56] Importantly, even where an intent to discriminate cannot be proven, civil rights and EEO *legislation* has formed the basis of such remedies.

At present, the role of the courts in public personnel administration is illustrated by the drug-testing controversy. Virtually all sides and parties involved believe that the judiciary will eventually establish the constitutional limits, under the Fourth and Fourteenth Amendments, to such testing.

The Liability and Immunity of Public Employees

It is important to emphasize that the mere declaration of constitutional or legal rights does not assure their enforcement. Independent enforcement mechanisms may be necessary where new legal or constitutional rights have been established. This is especially true where these rights stand in contravention of longstanding administrative, political, or social practice. The recently created constitutional barrier to patronage dismissals is a good example in the realm of public personnel administration. Thus far, the judiciary has tended to promote the enforcement of the employee's constitutional rights through two types of approaches. One, as discussed earlier, is the requirement of procedural due process in adverse actions. The other can be described briefly but has very far-reaching ramifications.

In the 1970s the Supreme Court expanded the scope of public employees' liability in civil suits for damages resulting from the violation of an individual's constitutional rights through an employee's action within the sphere of his or her official duties. But the individual whose rights have been violated and who is bringing the suit may be another public servant. At the state and local levels, if a supervisor, public personnel administrator, or other official violates a subordinate's constitutional rights, the latter may file a civil suit seeking damages.[57] The same is true of applicants whose constitutional rights have been violated. The suit may be against the official as an individual and may seek punitive damages, that is, more money than the actual amount of damage caused by the unconstitutional action. For instance, a supervisor who fires a subordinate for joining a union or other association may be vulnerable to such a suit. So may an official whose actions are unconstitutionally discriminatory. The standard by which such liability is determined today is whether it was reasonable (in the reviewing court's judgment) for the official to be aware that his or her actions were in violation of the Constitution.[58] Where the official should have known that the actions were unconstitutional he or she is liable, regardless of intent. The point of liability is not only to compensate individuals for wrongs done to them, but as the Supreme Court has declared, also to deter public officials from violating individuals' constitutional rights. Consequently, it becomes an important enforcement mechanism that strongly encourages public officials scrupulously to avoid abridging the constitutional rights of others. In *Bush* v. *Lucas* (1983), the Supreme Court held that federal employees cannot sue supervisors for damages for breach of their First Amendment rights because Congress had established an elaborate alternative protective scheme, including appeals to the MSPB.[59] This decision recognizes another remedy; it does not increase or reduce the scope of federal employees' constitutional rights.

In passing, it should be noted that municipalities may also be found liable in suits where their policies result in the violation of constitutional rights. Here, the standard is not whether the municipality reasonably should have known, in some sense, that its policies were unconstitutional. Rather, the sole issue is whether its policies did in fact lead to an unconstitutional abridgement of individual rights.[60] In public personnel management examples of such suits can be found in dismissals without adequate due process, mandatory maternity leaves, and violation of equal protection.

SEARCHING FOR A SYNTHESIS: THE RISE OF CODETERMINATION THROUGH COLLECTIVE BARGAINING

It is evident that the managerial, political, and legal approaches to public personnel administration stress different values and frequently conflict with one another. This has the tendency to fragment personnel practice, making it somewhat incoherent. For instance, merit, EEO, and veteran preference coexist on uneasy terms, as does traditional hierarchical managerial authority and constitutional procedural due process. According to contemporary constitutional interpretation, political patronage and the rights of public employees clash even more directly. These tensions and conflicts raise the question running throughout much public administration of whether it is possible to synthesize or combine the three approaches in some fashion. At the moment, in terms of public personnel administration, the answer is, "to some extent, but not completely." For the most part, progress toward this end has been made through the rise of a new model of public personnel administration—one that stresses **codetermination** of policy through the process of collective bargaining.

Until the 1960s, collective bargaining in the public sector was frequently considered antithetical to constitutional democracy in the United States. It was thought absurd that organized public employees could bargain with the government as a coequal, or that matters of public policy would be determined in any forum other than the legislature, elected executive, or courts. In particular, strikes were feared because they represented a breakdown of the public order and could lead to chaos. Many states viewed collective bargaining as a threat to sovereignty, and the federal government had no general policy or practice for collective bargaining by its employees.

All of this changed with remarkable rapidity. In large part, the rise of collective bargaining has been related to the growth of public employment and the political pressures exerted by unions. Many unions viewed the public sector as a promising recruiting ground in the face of declining private sector union membership. In any event, today public sector collective bargaining is found in the federal government and almost all states. Yet to a very large extent it remains a patchwork of practices. There is no national law on the subject, and state laws and practices vary widely in their coverage and content. Nonetheless, a common pattern is emerging. Public personnel policy is now largely determined through a framework of collective bargaining procedures that incorporate substantial parts of the managerial, political, and legal approaches to personnel administration. (Boxes 5–10 and 5–11 present union membership by governmental jurisdiction and occupation.)

The basic pattern consists of the following: employees in the same occupations (teachers, police, firefighters, clerks, etc.) or performing similar kinds of work (general administrative work, for instance) organize into **bargaining units.**

BOX 5–10 **Percentage of Organized Full-Time Employees, by Type Government, October 1980**

TYPE GOVERNMENT	FULL-TIME EMPLOYEES ORGANIZED (%)
School districts	59.9
Municipalities	53.9
States	40.5
Special districts	35.9
Counties	34.9
Total organized:	48.8%

SOURCE: U.S. Bureau of the Census (1981), *Labor-Management Relations in State and Local Governments: 1980*, Series GSS No. 100 (Washington, D.C.: U.S. Government Printing Office, 1981).

BOX 5–11 **Percentage of Organized Full-Time Employees, by Function, October 1980**

FUNCTION	FULL-TIME EMPLOYEES ORGANIZED (%)
Firefighters	70.6
Teachers	61.3
Police	52.8
Welfare	42.4
Sanitation	40.2
Highways	37.6
Hospitals	29.4

SOURCE: U.S. Bureau of the Census (1981), *Labor-Management Relations in State and Local Governments: 1980*, Series GSS No. 100 (Washington, D.C.: U.S. Government Printing Office, 1981).

Through an election or submission of union membership cards to the employer, a majority of the employees in the unit can designate a single union to bargain on behalf of all the employees in the unit. This is called **exclusive recognition** (of the union). Precisely what can be bargained over is called the **scope of bargaining.** This may be relatively comprehensive and include wages, hours, fringe benefits, position classification, promotion procedures, training, discipline, grievances, holidays, sick leave, seniority preferences, overtime assignments, and other working conditions. Conversely, it may be narrow and confined largely to matters of discipline and the issuance of safety clothing, coffee breaks, and parking spaces. It is useful to think of the scope of bargaining in terms of items over which bargaining is mandatory, items over which it is permitted, and items over which it is prohibited. Where labor and management cannot reach agreement on matters that are subject to mandatory bargaining, an impasse results. Resolution of the impasse can take many forms, including mediation, fact finding, and arbitration. Once there is agreement among the parties or an arbitration award is handed down, a contract is signed and goes into effect. Some states have permissive policies toward public employee strikes for resolving impasses (see Box 5–12). Again, depending upon the scope of bargaining, this may amount to codetermination by labor and management of the conditions of employment.

The collective bargaining approach outlined above readily takes advantage of managerial, political, and legal perspectives. It is no accident that the first federal executive order on the subject declared that labor-management relations could foster both efficiency and democracy.[61] From a managerial perspective, the emergent collective bargaining model promotes the following. First, it clearly defines the rights of management and makes these nonbargainable. Examples would be the right to direct employees and determine the budget of an agency. Second, it facilitates communication between management and employees, which provide supervisors and other officials with valuable information as to how efficiency and economy can be improved. A closely related benefit is that it

BOX 5–12   **State Permissive Strike Policies: A Sampling**

Alaska	All public employees except teachers	Right to strike for semiessential and nonessential workers. Police, firefighters, and hospital employees may not strike. Limited strike right for public utilities, sanitation, snow removal, and schools, after exhaustion of mediation. Other workers may strike upon majority vote.
California	All public employees	Under a 1985 California State Supreme Court ruling, strikes are legal "unless or until it is clearly demonstrated that such a strike creates a substantial and imminent threat to the health or safety of the public."*
Hawaii	All public employees	Strike permitted after exhaustion of impasse-resolution procedures and sixty days after issue of fact-finding report. Ten days' notice by union is required. Strikes endangering public health and safety are illegal, as determined by PERB (Public Employment Relations Board) and courts.
Minnesota	All public employees	Strikes prohibited except where employer refuses request for binding arbitration or refuses to submit to arbitration or to an arbitration award. Teachers have right to strike following expiration of contract, sixty days of mediation, and ten days' notice. Nonteaching local employees and state employees may strike after expiration of contract, forty-five days of mediation, and ten days' notice.
Montana	All public employees	Strikes permitted. Nurses must give thirty days' notice; no other nurses' strike may occur within 150 miles.

facilitates the participation of employees in determining the conditions under which they work. Within limits, such participation may create greater job satisfaction, loyalty to the organization, and, therefore, efficiency. Finally, the employee grievance system (discussed below) negotiated through collective bargaining serves to alert management to serious problems and unfit supervisors. Yet collective bargaining is not primarily a management tool and it clearly presents challenges to managers who cling to traditional practices and doctrines of hierarchical authority.

The political approach is also evident in the emergent collective bargaining model. On the one hand, the value of representation is fundamental to public sector collective bargaining. Part of the purpose of organized labor relations is to

BOX 5–12 *Continued*

Ohio	Public employees in jurisdictions of 5,000 or more, except police, fire, and related employees	Ten days' notice of intent to strike must be supplied to state Employment Relations Board. Employer can seek court order against strikes presenting a clear and present danger to the health and safety of the public. The order automatically expires after sixty days.
Oregon	All public employees except police, fire-fighters, and correctional institutional guards	Strikes permitted unless it creates a clear and present danger of threat to the public health, safety, or welfare. Mediation, fact finding, and thirty-day cooling-off period must be exhausted; ten days' notice must be given.
Pennsylvania	All public employees except prison guards or court employees	Strike permitted after exhaustion of impasse-resolution procedures, unless strike presents clear and present danger to public health, safety, or welfare.
Vermont	All local public employees except guards or court employees	Strikes permitted thirty days after fact-finding report where parties have not agreed to arbitration and there is no danger to public health, safety, or welfare. Teacher strike may be prohibited by courts if it endangers a sound program of education.
Wisconsin	Local public employees	Strike permitted if both parties withdraw their final offer, and ten days' notice is given by union. Strike is illegal if it poses imminent threat to public health, safety, or welfare.

* County Sanitation District No. 2 v. Los Angeles County Employees Association, L.A. 31850, May 13, 1985.

SOURCE: Richard C. Kearney, *Labor Relations in the Public Sector* (New York: Marcel Dekker, 1984), pp. 220–221. *IMPA News*, October 1983, pp. 7–8 (for Ohio). *Public Administration Times*, June 1, 1985, pp. 1, 4 (for California). Idaho and Illinois also allow public employees to strike under some circumstances.

provide civil servants with a voice in determining the nature of working conditions in government employment. Apart from actual bargaining sessions, public employees are to be represented by unions in many personnel matters and unions are frequently consulted on changes in public policy that may affect their jobs.

At the same time, however, the political approach demands that public sector collective bargaining practices serve the public interest and do not undermine the responsiveness of government to the electorate. Consequently, certain limitations have been placed on public sector labor relations that make the collective bargaining process quite different from private sector practices. Most notably in this context are serious restrictions on the scope of bargaining and the prohibition of strikes. Many jurisdictions have enacted a strong management rights clause that severely limits the items over which collective bargaining can take place. Frequently, agency missions, budgets, public policies, technologies, recruitment, selection, and sometimes the basis for disciplinary proceedings are outside the scope of bargaining. Within the ambit of these limitations lie some very fundamental conditions of work. For instance, in some jurisdictions teachers cannot bargain over the number of pupils per class or the school calendar; similarly, police may not be able to bargain over deployment (one- or two-person patrols), weapons, and defensive gear. Some employees, including most non-postal workers in the federal government, are prohibited from bargaining over wages and hours. These restrictions are a legacy of the concept of sovereignty, that is, the idea that government is the supreme representative of the citizenry and cannot be compelled to capitulate to or share its authority with private organizations. The main point of a limited scope of bargaining is to assure that matters of public policy are determined by representative governmental institutions rather than through a special process that entitles a group of individuals (public employees) to assert its will.

Some prohibitions on the right to strike are found in all the states and in the federal government. Although not always effective, these restrictions raise the cost of strikes to employees and unions and probably serve as a deterrent to them. Many view the strike as fundamental to any serious collective bargaining process. However, by and large the political approach to public administration has ruled it out not only because it could lead to chaos or anarchy, but because it tends to provide organized public employees with a means of undercutting the responsiveness of government to the citizenry. For example, teachers and parents have an interest in school calendars and curriculum. Providing teachers with the right to bargain over these matters and use the strike in an effort to compel the government (school board) to accept their will gives the teachers leverage over public policy that is not available to parents. The parents can neither collectively bargain nor strike. They can vote for school board members and lobby, but so can teachers. According to the political approach, if government is to be responsive to the public interest, then public policy cannot be the outcome of labor negotiations and strikes. The public interest cannot be held hostage by striking public employees or bargained over in negotiating sessions.

It is problematic whether these restrictions on the emergent public sector collective bargaining model reduce its coherence and limit its effectiveness. It is clear that the model cannot work well or be meaningful if the scope of bargaining is too narrow to serve as a vehicle for employees to affect their working conditions. It may also be true that management will not take public employees seriously in bargaining sessions unless the employees have a weapon such as the strike. Indeed, the absence of the right to strike requires some other means of resolving impasses. This brings us to the legal approach.

Overwhelmingly, the emergent public sector collective bargaining model is moving in the direction of arbitration as a means of resolving impasses. **Arbitration** can be over *interests* such as wages and hours or over *grievances* involving the mistreatment of an employee or other violation of a contract. It can take many forms. The most forceful interest arbitration is compulsory and binding.

This compels the parties to enter into arbitration when an impasse occurs and requires them to accept the arbitrators' award. Arbitration is a judicial-style process. The individual arbitrator or panel hears the views and proposals of both sides in what amounts to an adversary proceeding. The facts are then weighed, principles according to which a judgment will be made are considered, and a decision is handed down.

A similar approach is used in arbitrating grievances. Grievance arbitration is often quite similar to adverse action hearings and may even come to resemble courtroom procedure. It is extremely common and places new challenges and constraints upon public managers, who now find their flexibility in dealing with employees to be severely limited. (Box 5–13 presents some examples of grievance arbitration decisions in the federal service.)

Interest and grievance arbitration make much of the emergent collective bargaining model look like a judicial process. It appears that by regulating strikes the public sector model has taken conflict off the streets and away from the collective bargaining table and placed its resolution in the hands of arbitrators who act like judges. But the influence of the legal approach is felt in other ways as well.

Comprehensive programs for collective bargaining provide for Public Employment Relations Boards (PERB) or equivalent agencies, such as the Federal Labor Relations Authority. These agencies adjudicate or oversee the adjudication of unfair labor practice charges, disputes over the authorized scope of bargaining, the appropriateness of the bargaining units that employees seek to organize, and other matters. PERBs may also have rule-making authority regarding labor relations.

The judiciary's concern with constitutional rights and values has led it to hand down a number of decisions that have had a major impact on public sector collective bargaining. One, already mentioned, is that public employees have the right to join unions, though there is still no constitutional right actually to engage in collective bargaining. Another is that the "union shop," that is, an arrangement whereby all employees in a collective bargaining unit must join the exclusively recognized union, has been thought to be an unconstitutional abridgment of public employees' right to freedom of association.[62] However, an "agency shop," requiring all employees to pay fees to a union for its services as collective bargaining agent, is permissible. But just how far the legal approach penetrates collective bargaining is evident from the Supreme Court's holding in *Chicago Teachers Union* v. *Hudson* (1986), that "the constitutional requirements for the Union's collection of agency fees include an adequate explanation of the basis for the fee, a reasonably prompt opportunity to challenge the amount of the fee before an impartial decisionmaker, and an escrow for the amounts reasonably in dispute while such challenges are pending."[63] The Supreme Court has also refused to allow the principle of exclusive recognition to stifle the ability of public employees to express their views on matters of public policy in public forums.[64]

But the impetus of judicial decisions goes even farther. In one case, the Supreme Court articulated the premise that "the federal court is not the appropriate forum in which to review the multitude of personnel decisions that are

BOX 5–13 **Grievance Arbitration Decisions in the Federal Service: Some Examples**

10004 Did the agency have just cause for demoting the grievant for reporting to work while intoxicated?

Yes, but grievant must be paid the differential rate for all work performed in the higher classification. Demotion for the offense was within the range of discipline penalties. When management reduces the employee's classification, the arbitrator reasoned, it must assign duties within the confines of the new (lower) classification, and cannot require the employee to perform duties within the higher classification at the lower rate of pay.

10007 Was the change of grievant's work location a violation of the agreement?

Yes. Grievant should have been provided a work area which would diminish her embarrassment caused by the profanity and physical exposure of patients, and possible health hazards. Although management has a right to assign work to employees, the working conditions of the job must be considered in the assignment.

10015 Were the changes in the basic workweek of the aggrieved employees

instituted by the agency in violation of the agreement?

Yes. Management was required to pay each grievant the difference between the overtime rate and amount actually paid at the straight time rate for each Saturday and Sunday actually worked. The Shipyard management was not faced with an emergency when the decision to change the workweek was made. Further, management failed to consult properly with the union.

10023 Did management have just cause for imposing a three-day suspension on the grievant for his use of profane language?

No. The disciplinary action was stricken from the grievant's record and the grievant was made whole for three days lost pay. Although grievant did use profane language, he did not do so with knowledge that his broadcast lines were open and that he was transmitting. Further, due to lax enforcement by management of regulations against use of profanity, the arbitrator concluded that it was reasonable for the grievant to believe that such violations were tolerated by management.

SOURCE: U.S. Civil Service Commission, *Digest of Labor Arbitration Awards in the Federal Service* (Washington, D.C.: U.S. Civil Service Commission, March 1978).

made daily by public agencies" and that "numerous individual mistakes are inevitable in the day-to-day administration of our affairs. . . . The United States Constitution cannot feasibly be construed to require federal judicial review for every such error."[65] But what is the appropriate forum that the court had in mind? One obvious possibility is the collective bargaining process, including grievance proceedings. If this is true, then not only do the Court's decisions affect the collective bargaining process, but the existence of collective bargaining also has an influence on the judiciary's decisions.

CONCLUSION

The last point suggests why the emergent collective bargaining model *can* synthesize the managerial, political, and legal approaches to public personnel administration. It not only takes some of its features from each approach, but it also influences the approaches themselves. Thus, managing *organized* public employees through collective bargaining has become a matter of concern to theorists of public management and has affected managerial thinking, especially in the areas of employee participation, motivation, and discipline. The political view of public administration has also been affected by collective bargaining. Today, for instance, strict adherence to the concept of sovereignty and adherence to a traditional model of political control of public employees have given way to a more flexible view that stresses the desirability of providing public employees with representation in matters of public personnel administration and sees the codetermination of many matters of personnel policy as fully acceptable. Finally, the legal approach lends judicialized procedures to collective bargaining, especially in terms of arbitration and adjudication of charges of unfair labor practices. It also seems to take the existence of the collective bargaining forum into account in addressing the rights of public employees. Where appropriate, it appears that the Supreme Court is willing to allow public employment conditions affecting some of the rights of civil servants to be determined in the collective bargaining forum.[66]

In summing up, it is important to emphasize that public sector collective bargaining is not simply a new process tacked on to an existing personnel system. Rather, it creates a new system and represents a new chance to synthesize the three dominant approaches. It reaches almost every aspect of personnel administration and asserts values that stand in contrast with earlier personnel arrangements.

It is still too soon to conclude that synthesis of the managerial, political, and legal approaches in the area of public personnel administration *will* occur through collective bargaining. No doubt, the tensions among the approaches will remain dynamic and changes of at least an incremental type will be made on an almost continual basis. Yet it is the effort to combine the values and outlooks of these approaches that presents public administration with so many intellectual and practical challenges, and the emergent collective bargaining model serves as a framework for synthesizing them and a valuable example of what can be gained through their combination.

NOTES

1. David Sanford, "Our Uncivil Servants," *The New Republic*, April 6, 1968, pp. 8–9; and E. Savas and S. Ginzburg, "The Civil Service: A Meritless System?" *The Public Interest*, 32 (Summer 1973):70–85.
2. There are several excellent histories of the federal service that emphasize personnel administration. See Frederick Mosher, *Democracy and the Public Service*, 2nd ed.

(New York: Oxford University Press, 1982); Paul P. Van Riper, *History of the United States Civil Service* (Evanston, Ill.: Row, Peterson, 1958); Leonard D. White's four volume series, *The Federalists, The Jeffersonians, The Jacksonians,* and *The Republican Era* (New York: Free Press, 1965), paperback editions; and Stephen Skowronek, *Building A New American State* (Cambridge, England: Cambridge University Press, 1982).

3. David H. Rosenbloom, *Federal Service and the Constitution* (Ithaca, N.Y.: Cornell University Press, 1971), p. 36.

4. See ibid., pp. 38–41, and chap. 2 for a discussion of Jefferson's appointment policy and that of Jackson.

5. Quoted in ibid., p. 49.

6. Ibid., p. 56.

7. Ibid., p. 49.

8. See Jay M. Shafritz et al., *Personnel Management in Government* (New York: Marcel Dekker, 1978), p. 16.

9. Rosenbloom, *Federal Service and the Constitution*, p. 55.

10. Shafritz, et al., *Personnel Management in Government*, p. 33.

11. Paul P. Van Riper, *History of the United States Civil Service.*

12. Elrod v. Burns, 427 U.S. 347 (1976); Branti v. Finkel, 445 U.S. 506 (1980).

13. Quoted in Rosenbloom, *Federal Service and the Constitution*, pp. 70–71, note 1.

14. Quoted in ibid., p. 71. Many of the civil service reformers' statements were published in books and pamphlets that are now difficult to obtain. The referencing here is to a source that discusses their ideas in a historical context.

15. Quoted in ibid., p. 73.

16. Ibid.

17. Ibid., p. 71.

18. Ibid., p. 67.

19. Matthew Josephson, *The Politicos* (New York: Harcourt, Brace & World, n.d.), p. 438.

20. 37 Stat. 413 (August 23, 1912).

21. Ari Hoogenboom, *Outlawing the Spoils* (Urbana: University of Illinois Press, 1961).

22. Rosenbloom, *Federal Service and the Constitution*, p. 80.

23. Ibid.

24. *New York Times*, March 3, 1978, p. 1 and ff. See also David H. Rosenbloom, ed., "Public Administration Forum: Civil Service Reform, 1978: Some Issues," *Midwest Review of Public Administration*, 13 (September 1979):171–188.

25. *New York Times*, March 3, 1978, p. 10.

26. Alan K. Campbell, "Civil Service Reform: A New Commitment," *Public Administration Review*, 38 (March/April 1978): 102.

27. See Edie N. Goldenberg, "The Permanent Government in an Era of Retrenchment and Redirection," in Lester M. Salamon and Michael S. Lund, eds., *The Reagan Presidency and the Governing of America* (Washington, D.C.: The Urban Institute, 1985), pp. 381–404.

28. For a brief discussion, see Lois Friss and Gilbert Siegal, "Policy Issues in Pay Administration—A Symposium: Introduction," *Review of Public Personnel Administration*, 7 (Summer 1987), pp. 1–15.

29. U.S. Office of Personnel Management, Office of Employee, Labor, and Agency Relations, "Employee and Labor Relations Critical Cases, Report No. 2," (Washington, D.C.: Office of Personnel Management [mimeograph], March 6, 1987).

30. Wallace Sayre, "The Triumph of Techniques over Purpose," *Public Administration Review*, 8 (Spring 1948):134.

31. U.S. Equal Employment Opportunity Commission, *Annual Report on the Employment of Minorities, Women, and Handicapped Individuals in the Federal Government, FY 1983* (Washington, D.C.: Government Printing Office, 1986), section 9244–10.1, table I-4, p. 30.

32. See Jay M. Shafritz et al., *Personnel Management in Government*, 2nd ed. (New York: Marcel Dekker, 1981), chap. 4.

33. Leonard D. White, *The Prestige Value of Public Employment in Chicago* (Chicago: University of Chicago Press, 1929), and *Further Contributions to the Prestige Value of Public Employment* (Chicago: University of Chicago Press, 1932); Franklin P. Kilpatrick, et al., *The Image of the Federal Service* (Washington, D.C.: Brookings Institution, 1964).

34. Charlie B. Tyer, "Employee Performance Appraisal: Process in Search of a Technique," in Steven Hays and Richard Kearney, eds., *Public Personnel Administration* (Englewood Cliffs, N.J.: Prentice-Hall, 1983), pp. 118–136. The discussion in this paragraph is based on Tyer's essay.

35. See, among others, Paul Appleby, *Policy and Administration* (University, Ala.: University of Alabama Press, 1949).

36. See Joy Grune and Nancy Reder, "Addendum—Pay Equity," *Public Personnel Management* 13 (Spring 1984): 70–80, for a discussion of occupational segregation by sex.

37. National Association of Letter Carriers v. Civil Service Commission, 346 F. Supp. 578 (1972), at 581.

38. Civil Service Commission v. National Association of Letter Carriers, 413 U.S. 548 (1973).

39. See Rosenbloom, *Federal Service and the Constitution*, chap. 6.

40. See Samuel Krislov and David H. Rosenbloom, *Representative Bureaucracy and the American Political System* (New York: Praeger, 1981), for a comprehensive discussion.

41. See U.S. Commission on Civil Rights, *The Federal Civil Rights Enforcement Effort—1974*, vol. 5 (Washington, D.C.: Commission on Civil Rights, 1975), p. 6.

42. Arthur Link, *Wilson: The New Freedom* (Princeton, N.J.: Princeton University Press, 1965), p. 251.

43. See David H. Rosenbloom, *Federal Equal Employment Opportunity* (New York: Praeger, 1977), pp. 126–138. See also Robert Vaughn, *The Spoiled System* (New York: Charterhouse, 1975); and M. Weldon Brewer, *Behind the Promises* (Washington, D.C.: Public Interest Research Group, 1972).

44. See Rosenbloom, *Federal Equal Employment Opportunity*, chap. 5, for a discussion.

45. United States v. Paradise, 55 Law Week 4211 (1987).

46. Wygant v. Jackson, 90 L.Ed.2d 260 (1986).

47. Johnson v. Transportation Agency, 55 Law Week 4379 (1987).

48. Bailey v. Richardson, 182 F2d 46, 59 (1950); 341 U.S. 918 (1951).

49. McAuliffe v. New Bedford, 155 Mass. 216, 220 (1892).

50. Sugarman v. Dougall, 413 U.S. 634, 644 (1972).

51. Board of Regents v. Roth, 408 U.S. 564, 571 (1972).

52. Ibid. See also Cleveland Board of Education v. Loudermill, 470 U.S. 532 (1985).

53. See Robert Vaughn, "Statutory Protection of Whistleblowers in the Federal Executive Branch," *University of Illinois Law Review*, 1982 (No. 3, 1982), pp. 615–667; and "Public Employees and the Right to Disobey," *Hastings Law Journal*, 29 (November 1977): 261–295.

54. Rankin v. McPherson, 55 Law Week 5019 (1987).

55. Cleveland Board of Education v. LaFleur, 414 U.S. 632 (1974); argued and decided with Cohen v. Chesterfield County School Board.
56. See David H. Rosenbloom and Carole C. Obuchowski, "Public Personnel Examinations and the Constitution," *Public Administration Review*, 37 (January/ February 1977): 9–18; United States v. Paradise, 55 Law Week 4211 (1987).
57. This is true at present for state and local public employees under 42 U.S. Code section 1983. It does not apply to federal employees whose right of freedom of speech has been abridged; it may not apply in instances of violation of other constitutional rights of federal employees. See Bush v. Lucas, 462 U.S. 367 (1983).
58. Harlow v. Fitzgerald, 457 U.S. 800 (1982).
59. 462 U.S. 367.
60. See Owen v. City of Independence, 445 U.S. 622 (1980).
61. Executive Order 10988 (January 17, 1962), 27 *Federal Register* 551.
62. Abood v. Detroit Board of Education, 430 U.S. 209 (1977).
63. Chicago Teachers Union v. Hudson, 89 L.Ed. 2d 232 (1986).
64. City of Madison, Joint School District No. 8 v. Wisconsin Employment Relations Commission, 429 U.S. 167 (1976).
65. Bishop v. Wood, 426 U.S. 341, 349–50 (1976).
66. See Kelley v. Johnson, 425 U.S. 238 (1976), for an example of where collective bargaining may have been more appropriate than litigation.

ADDITIONAL READING

INGRAHAM, PATRICIA, AND CAROLYN BAN, EDS. *Legislating Bureaucratic Change: The Civil Service Reform Act of 1978*. Albany, N.Y.: State University of New York Press, 1984.

KEARNEY, RICHARD. *Labor Relations in the Public Sector*. New York: Marcel Dekker, 1984.

MOSHER, FREDERICK. *Democracy and the Public Service*, 2nd ed. New York: Oxford University Press, 1982.

ROSENBLOOM, DAVID H. *Federal Equal Employment Opportunity*. New York: Praeger, 1977.

ROSENBLOOM, DAVID H. *Federal Service and the Constitution*. Ithaca, N.Y.: Cornell University Press, 1971.

ROSENBLOOM, DAVID H., AND JAY M. SHAFRITZ. *Essentials of Labor Relations*. Reston, Va.: Reston, 1985.

SHAFRITZ, JAY M., ALBERT HYDE, AND DAVID H. ROSENBLOOM. *Personnel Management in Government*, 3rd ed. New York: Marcel Dekker, 1986.

THOMPSON, FRANK J. *Personnel Policy in the City*. Berkeley, Calif.: University of California Press, 1975.

VAN RIPER, PAUL P. *History of the United States Civil Service*. Evanston, Ill.: Row, Peterson, 1958.

STUDY QUESTIONS

1. Affirmative action has been an important issue in public personnel administration for almost two decades. To what extent do the proponents and opponents of "merit" and those of "affirmative action" seem to be talking to each other? To what extent are they talking past each other?

2. The issue of whether public employees should be allowed to strike has been a concern of public personnel administration. Do you think all strikes by public employees should be prohibited? Why or why not? If you favor a right to strike, should any limitations be placed on it? What would these be, if any? Why?

3. Having read the chapter on personnel, what aspects of the contemporary nature of public personnel management would attract you to the public sector? Which, if any, would you find objectionable?

CHAPTER 6 | *Budgeting*

Governmental budgets are currently an area of general concern and controversy. As governmental activity has consumed a greater proportion of society's resources, considerable attention has been paid to taxation and other sources of government revenues. The federal budget not only funds governmental activities but is also used as a tool to help regulate the economy's business cycles. The federal budget process, which is exceedingly complex, will be discussed at some length. This chapter will also present theories about how budgets should be formulated and executed, analyzing the strengths and weaknesses of the various approaches. As do other aspects of public administration, budgets involve managerial, political, and legal concerns, which in this case may come into sharp, almost unresolvable, conflict.

Budgeting is a public administrative activity of preeminent importance. Along with personnel, organization, and decision making, it is at the core of public administration. And, like those other subjects, it is generally surrounded by controversy and calls for reform. It appears that in view of the competing perspectives on public administration, no single budgetary process can satisfy everyone. Moreover, budgeting is so complex in its political and economic ramifications that in some respects it defies control and even understanding. But, of course, that is part of what makes public administration challenging and interesting.

In essence, a governmental budget is a statement of revenues and expenditures. It indicates how much money a government proposes to raise and spend. Equally important, it provides a record of past expenditures. But this definition is a bit too simple. The budget is also intimately related to taxation. Will revenues be generated through taxes? If so, what kinds? Sales taxes, income taxes, corporate taxes, value-added taxes, property taxes, excise taxes, luxury taxes? What will the mix be? Will funds also be raised through borrowing? If so, how? On the expenditure side, budgets indicate how governmental activity will be conceptualized. Will expenditures be categorized by "objects," such as equipment, supplies, and salaries of government employees? Will they be categorized by function, such as health or defense? By program, such as equal employment? Other critical questions are: What will the actual amounts of allocation be? How will these decisions be made? What considerations will be brought to bear upon them? These are the chief concerns of the budgetary process, and it is easy to see from them that budgeting can be quite perplexing. While we cannot provide all the answers in this chapter (indeed, no one can do so even in volumes), we can at least help the reader to understand the theoretical and practical considerations that are pertinent to the formulation of budgets and the selection of various budgetary strategies or techniques. We will start by mapping out some general considerations and then proceed to a discussion of managerial, political, and legal approaches to budget making.

THE SIZE AND GROWTH OF BUDGETS

Governmental spending is an indicator of the extent of governmental intervention in the life of society. But like the administrative state generally, its scope is difficult to comprehend. How does one make a budget of some $1,080 billion, as in the federal government, seem concrete? Some seek to do so by indicating that such a budget requires the spending of over $34,000 per second every second of the year. Others tell us the weight and length of these billions in $1 bills. Still others suggest that the best indicator of the size of the budget is the proportion of all spending in the society that is governmental. This latter measure is generally expressed as the percent of the GNP that is spent by the government. Today, the combined spending of all governments in the United States is about one-third of the GNP. In 1929, by contrast, it was only about 10 percent. The federal government's budget alone accounts for about 23 percent of the GNP (see Box 6–1). Such figures

BOX 6–1 Federal Finances and the Gross National Product, 1967–88 (dollar amounts in billions)

FISCAL YEAR	GROSS NATIONAL PRODUCT	BUDGET RECEIPTS Amount	Percent of GNP	OUTLAYS Total Amount	Percent of GNP	On-budget under current law Amount	Percent of GNP	Off-budget under current law* Amount	Percent of GNP	SURPLUS OR DEFICIT(-) Total Amount	Percent of GNP	On-budget under current law† Amount	Percent of GNP	FEDERAL DEBT, END OF YEAR Total Amount	Percent of GNP	Held by the public Amount	Percent of GNP
1967	777.3	148.8	19.1	157.5	20.3	157.5	20.3			-8.6	1.1	-8.6	1.1	341.3	43.9	267.5	34.4
1968	831.3	153.0	18.4	178.1	21.4	178.1	21.4			-25.2	3.0	-25.2	3.0	369.8	44.5	290.6	35.0
1969	910.6	186.9	20.5	183.6	20.2	183.6	20.2			3.2	0.4	3.2	0.4	367.1	40.3	279.5	30.7
1970	968.8	192.8	19.9	195.6	20.2	195.6	20.2			-2.8	0.3	-2.8	0.3	382.6	39.5	284.9	29.4
1971	1,031.5	187.1	18.1	210.2	20.4	210.2	20.4			-23.0	2.2	-23.0	2.2	409.5	39.7	304.3	29.5
1972	1,128.8	207.3	18.4	230.7	20.4	230.7	20.4			-23.4	2.1	-23.4	2.1	437.3	38.7	323.8	28.7
1973	1,252.0	230.8	18.4	245.7	19.6	245.6	19.6	0.1	‡	-14.9	1.2	-14.8	1.2	468.4	37.4	343.0	27.0
1974	1,379.4	263.2	19.1	269.4	19.5	267.9	19.4	1.4	0.1	-6.1	0.4	-4.7	0.3	486.2	35.3	346.1	25.1
1975	1,479.9	279.1	18.9	332.3	22.5	324.2	21.9	8.1	0.5	-53.2	3.6	-45.2	3.1	544.1	36.8	396.9	26.8
1976	1,640.1	298.1	18.2	371.8	22.7	364.5	22.2	7.3	0.4	-73.7	4.5	-66.4	4.0	631.9	38.5	480.3	29.3
1977	1,862.8	355.6	19.1	409.2	22.0	400.5	21.5	8.7	0.5	-53.6	2.9	-44.9	2.4	709.1	38.1	551.8	29.6
1978	2,091.3	399.7	19.1	458.7	21.9	448.4	21.4	10.4	0.5	-59.0	2.8	-48.6	2.3	780.4	37.3	610.9	29.2
1979	2,357.7	463.3	19.7	503.5	21.4	491.0	20.8	12.5	0.5	-40.2	1.7	-27.7	1.2	833.8	35.4	644.6	27.3
1980	2,575.8	517.1	20.1	590.9	22.9	576.7	22.4	14.2	0.6	-73.8	2.9	-59.6	2.3	914.3	35.5	715.1	27.8
1981	2,885.9	599.3	20.8	678.2	23.5	657.2	22.8	21.0	0.7	-78.9	2.7	-57.9	2.0	1,003.9	34.8	794.4	27.5
1982	3,046.0	617.8	20.3	745.7	24.5	728.4	23.9	17.3	0.6	-127.9	4.2	-110.7	3.6	1,147.0	37.7	929.4	30.5
1983	3,221.4	600.6	18.6	808.3	25.1	796.0	24.7	12.4	0.4	-207.8	6.4	-195.4	6.1	1,381.9	42.9	1,141.8	35.4
1984	3,581.0	666.5	18.6	851.8	23.8	841.8	23.5	10.0	0.3	-185.3	5.2	-175.4	4.9	1,576.7	44.0	1,312.6	36.7
1985 estimate	3,868.5	736.9	19.0	959.1	24.8	946.6	24.5	12.5	0.3	-222.2	5.7	-209.8	5.4	1,841.1	47.6	1,514.0	39.1
1986 estimate	4,198.5	793.7	18.9	973.7	23.2	972.2	23.2	1.5	‡	-180.0	4.3	-178.5	4.3	2,074.2	49.4	1,686.6	40.2
1987 estimate	4,550.4	861.7	18.9	1,026.6	22.6	1,029.9	22.6	-3.2	-0.1	-164.9	3.6	-168.2	3.7	2,308.3	50.7	1,850.8	40.7
1988 estimate	4,921.7	950.4	19.3	1,094.8	22.2	1,099.1	22.3	-4.3	-0.1	-144.4	2.9	-148.7	3.0	2,546.4	51.7	1,994.4	40.5

* Proposed to be included on-budget.
† The off-budget deficits under current law are equal to the off-budget outlays under current law but with the opposite sign.
‡ 0.05% or less.

SOURCE: The United States Budget in Brief, Fiscal Year 1986 (Washington, D.C.: Office of Management and Budget, 1985), p. 77.

convey the fact that governments now raise and spend a great deal of money and that the scope of governmental activity has been increasing; but such huge amounts of money necessarily remain difficult to grasp.

Some greater clarity could be achieved by looking at how the money is spent. But here we run into a fundamental problem. Should we report on expenditures in terms of such things as the number of pencils, pens, and paper clips bought by governments? The miles of highway built? Or, the broad categories of governmental activity, such as transportation? Shall we include "tax expenditures," which, as explained in Box 6–2, are government spending only in the sense that they are funds not collected in the first place due to special provisions in the tax code? It is evident that any number of categorizations of spending are possible, and this has been a subject of considerable controversy over the years. We will return to this problem later in the chapter. For now, however, it may prove helpful to mention the relative proportion of federal, state, and local budgetary expenditures that go to broad, general functions. Despite a good deal of overlap, governments in the United States are somewhat specialized. The federal government allocates a large proportion of its budget to defense, income security, and health programs (Social Security and Medicare in particular), the states spend a higher proportion on highways and education; local governments spend the greatest proportion of their funds on education and utilities.[1] If we looked at the outlay of funds in different terms, we would find that the proportion budgets allocated to the salaries of public employees is highest at the local level and lowest at the federal level, with the states falling somewhere in between. Box 6–3 presents a broad categorization of the proportion of federal revenues coming from different sources and expenditures going to different functions. Box 6–4 shows similar information for the states.

These figures and comparisons provide some idea of the size of governmental budgets in the United States, but they do not tell us about the causes of growth of governmental expenditure. In general, it is believed that government spending grows as a result of the same factors that give rise to the administrative state (see Chapter 2). As the society and economy become more complex, government intervenes in an effort to protect and promote the public interest. Antisocial behavior and harmful economic practices are regulated; governmental services are provided to enable individuals to contribute to continued economic development. Yet it is an inescapable fact that budgets tend to be wrapped up in electoral politics as well. Funds are sometimes allocated to help incumbents with reelection or, less commonly, to unseat them. For instance, so-called pork barrel projects are undertaken to bring funds, jobs, and capital improvements to a legislator's district.[2] It is also politically easier to allocate more funds rather than less to functions supported by powerful interest groups or important constituencies and voting blocs. As in the area of personnel, cutbacks and decline are painful, while growth can be used to resolve or smooth over conflicts. As we will see, it is especially for these political reasons that some politicians and analysts believed that the federal budget process had gotten out of control and that severe reforms were necessary if the political community were to cure its tendency toward deficit spending.

BOX 6–2 Tax Expenditures

Tax expenditures are features of the individual and corporation income tax laws that provide special benefits or incentives in comparison with what would be permitted under the general provisions of the Internal Revenue Code. They arise from special exclusions, exemptions, or deductions from gross income or from special credits, preferential tax rates, or deferrals of tax liability.

Tax expenditures are so designated because they are one means by which the federal government carries out public policy objectives; in many cases they can be considered as alternatives to direct expenditures. For example, investment in capital equipment is encouraged by the investment tax credit; a program of direct capital grants could also achieve this objective. Similarly, state and local governments benefit from both direct grants and the ability to borrow funds at tax-exempt rates.

Because tax expenditures can be viewed as alternatives to direct federal spending programs, it is desirable that estimates of tax expenditure items be comparable to outlay programs. Thus, tax expenditures are shown as outlay equivalents, that is, the amount of budget outlays required to provide the same level of after-tax benefits by substituting a direct spending program for the tax expenditure. The accompanying table displays estimates of tax expenditures classified by function.

Tax Expenditures Estimated as Outlay Equivalents
(*In billions of dollars*)

FUNCTION	1986	1987	1988
National defense	2.5	2.4	2.2
International affairs	4.6	4.7	4.4
General science, space, and technology	3.9	3.5	3.0
Energy	1.4	0.7	0.5
Natural resources and environment	3.3	3.1	3.4
Agriculture	1.2	0.6	0.8
Commerce and housing credit	219.6	163.7	130.1
Transportation	0.2	0.1	0.2
Community and regional development	1.1	1.3	1.7
Education, training, employment, and social services	31.8	22.8	20.0
Health	37.9	34.8	35.6
Income security	107.9	90.4	78.9
Social security	18.4	17.9	16.6
Veterans benefits and services	2.3	2.1	1.9
General government	0.2	0.1	—
General purpose fiscal assistance	36.3	31.2	27.6
Net interest	0.8	0.8	0.7

SOURCE: *The United States Budget in Brief, Fiscal Year 1986* (Washington, D.C.: Office of Management and Budget, 1985), p. 57, and ibid., *Fiscal Year 1988*, p. 88.

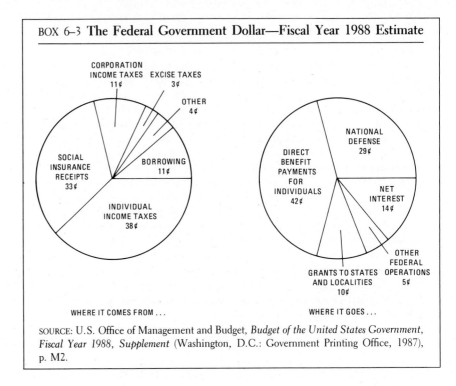

BOX 6–3 **The Federal Government Dollar—Fiscal Year 1988 Estimate**

WHERE IT COMES FROM . . .   WHERE IT GOES . . .

SOURCE: U.S. Office of Management and Budget, *Budget of the United States Government, Fiscal Year 1988, Supplement* (Washington, D.C.: Government Printing Office, 1987), p. M2.

Sources of Revenues

Governments have to obtain the money they spend from somewhere. They cannot simply print as much as they want and expect it to retain its value. They can borrow funds from private parties, but unless loaning the government money is compulsory, interest will have to be paid. In any case, borrowing causes debt, which must eventually be repaid. The options of printing money and unlimited borrowing notwithstanding, funds must be generated through other means. Taxation ranks foremost among these. A wide variety of taxes has been developed over the years, though Americans are probably most familiar with three types.

Individual and Corporate Income Taxes   Taxes levied on the income individuals earn from wages, salaries, and some forms of investment are called **income taxes.** Such taxes can be progressive, that is, they tax people with greater incomes at a higher rate than those with lesser incomes. They may also be flat-rate, taxing everyone at the same percentage of income regardless of the amount of income any given individual earns. For example, in a progressive system, someone making $100,000 per year might be taxed at 50 percent, whereas someone making $5,000 might be taxed at 5 percent. In a flat-rate system both would pay the same percentage, such as 20 percent. An income tax can also be regressive if it taxes people with lesser incomes at a higher rate than those with greater incomes. Under the federal Tax Reform Act of 1986, two progressive rates are

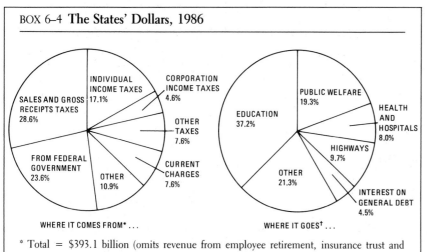

BOX 6–4 **The States' Dollars, 1986**

WHERE IT COMES FROM* ...   WHERE IT GOES† ...

* Total = $393.1 billion (omits revenue from employee retirement, insurance trust and unemployment programs; also from utility and liquor store operations).
† Total = $376.1 billion.

SOURCE: U.S. Census Bureau, as reported in the *Washington Post*, November 4, 1987, p. A21.

intended to prevail, 15 percent and 28 percent, with about 80 percent of all taxpayers falling into the lower bracket.[3] It should be immediately evident that there are several concerns that must be addressed in taxing income. Equity is important, as is incentive. Most Americans would probably find an income-tax system to be unfair if it didn't tax the incomes of the very wealthy *at all*. Stories about millionaires who pay no taxes routinely make the first page of newspapers. Equally evident, however, is the fact that if people were taxed close to 100 percent of their income, they would have no economic incentive to work. But between these extremes, what is equitable in the setting of rates, and where do incentives to work fall off intolerably? These are questions that are inherently debatable, but the answers arrived at by a society at any given time do set limits on the utility of the income tax. High rates place a premium on reducing one's *taxable* income through deductions and practices such as bartering. Consequently, actual tax rates may be considerably lower than nominal ones. The federal government places heavy reliance on the personal income tax, which accounts for about 38 percent of its revenues. It also levies a corporate income tax, accounting for about 11 percent of its revenues. Almost all the states also use income taxes.

Sales Taxes   Taxes levied on the sale of goods and services in states and/or local jurisdictions are called **sales taxes.** Currently, in states using them, sales-tax rates typically range from 3 to 8 percent. Sales taxes can generate a great deal of revenue, and they are easy to collect. They are also flexible in the sense that the jurisdiction in question can exempt certain items, such as food purchased at grocery stores. Such exemptions can reflect the values of any given community. For instance, Connecticut exempts clothing for young children from sales taxes. On the other hand, sales taxes have some potential drawbacks that must be taken into account. First, they are highly visible, since they are added to the bill for almost everything one buys. This makes it politically difficult to raise their level. Second, the sales tax can become counterproductive when individuals have alternative jurisdictions with lower rates in which they can purchase goods and services. For instance, the combined state and local sales-tax rate in New York City is 8¼ percent, whereas some of its suburbs have a rate of 5 percent or lower. At some point a rate that is too high in a jurisdiction will drive consumers to another area or out of the market altogether, and consequently the economic health of the jurisdiction may decline. Third, the sales tax is regressive in the sense that those with low incomes are likely to pay a higher proportion of their incomes in sales taxes than those with higher incomes. Whether this becomes an issue in any given state or community depends on the prevailing view of what equity requires.

Real Property Taxes   Taxes on real estate of various kinds are called **property taxes**—the mainstay of local governmental revenues. But as in the case of sales taxes, there is considerable variation among local governments in the extent to which they rely upon property taxes. In some states, such as those in New England, almost all local governmental revenues may come from property taxes. Elsewhere, it is typical for local governments to raise only about half or less of their revenues in this fashion (Alabama, Louisiana). Again, there may be competition among jurisdictions with regard to property tax rates. Where the rates in one city or town are high compared to neighboring jurisdictions, some people may locate in those jurisdictions in order to seek lower rates. This can lead to a stagnant or declining tax base in the place with higher rates and could eventually be a factor in a serious financial crisis. Of course, local jurisdictions with high property tax rates may provide better services, including education, public safety, and sanitation. Among the major problems with the property tax is the tendency for it to be inequitably administered over time. The tax assessments on similar dwellings may vary considerably, especially if one has been bought and sold more frequently during periods of high inflation. Sometimes, too, the property tax acts as a deterrent to improving one's house. The addition of rooms, porches, swimming pools, etc., can lead to a higher tax assessment. It is also possible that when property values and tax assessments rise, families or individuals with stable incomes will find the increasing tax burden too great. Property taxes are also regressive, as richer people tend to spend a lower proportion of their wealth on housing than do poorer people. Additionally, as the value of real property—such as farmland near urban and suburban areas—increases, so too may the tax on it, even though the incomes of those living on or farming the land remain relatively constant.

Additional Taxes and Sources of Revenue   There is also a variety of other sources of governmental revenues, including *excise taxes, motor fuel taxes,* *business taxes, capital-gains taxes, license fees, user fees, lotteries, sale of utilities,* such as water or electricity, and the *operation of liquor stores.* Governments can also borrow money through the sale of bonds and other forms of loans. The sources of federal revenues are displayed in Box 6–3; those of the states, in Box 6–4.

It is evident that in considering raising governmental revenues several general concerns must be taken into account. Equity is one. An inequitable taxing arrangement can promote a popular tax revolt, as was witnessed in California through Proposition 13 (1978), in Massachusetts through Proposition 2½ (1980), and elsewhere. Equity is related to political feasibility, which is another consideration. Some forms of taxation are simply too unpopular with the general public or with powerful constituencies to be applied or raised beyond certain levels. For example, it has been urged by some sober voices that the federal government should place a heavy tax upon the sale of gasoline—perhaps as much as a dollar a gallon. This would raise the cost and presumably encourage conservation, as well as raise funds that could be used for the development of other energy sources and cheaper means of transportation. However, in the absence of a very prolonged petroleum shortage, the political feasibility of such a high tax is low.

The administrative feasibility of different forms of taxation must also be considered. Can a particular tax be administered, or will it be evaded on a widespread basis? For instance, property taxes that base assessments on aspects of the interiors of houses may be difficult to apply. To do so, assessors would have to gain entrance to dwellings and be able to snoop around in them. Aside from questions of individual privacy and taxpayer resentment of administrative intrusion, such a system could take a great deal of time to administer on an equitable basis. It would be much easier to base assessments on the exteriors of houses, their last sales price, or their assumed market value. Similarly, in societies where cash registers are not generally used, applying the sales tax can be difficult. Income taxes can be problematical in some service areas of the economy, where payment of fees in cash may be the norm. Taxing tips has been a long-standing problem. Administrative feasibility is also concerned with the efficiency with which revenues can be raised. For instance, it is generally more efficient to collect taxes through withholding than by billing individuals once or twice a year.

Governments must also consider the elasticity of a means of raising revenue. As noted above, some forms of taxation can be counterproductive, that is, raising the tax or user fee may actually provide less revenue, since it will encourage individuals to move from one jurisdiction to another, shop elsewhere, or avoid publicly provided services such as transportation that are considered too costly. Eventually, of course, all tax and revenue-raising devices can reach their limits of efficacy by draining too much from the private sector and reducing private initiative to work. Although we are sometimes accustomed to believe that governments can raise as much money as they want, in truth there are substantial limitations on the ability of the public sector to finance itself. These limits must be taken into account in developing governmental budgets if political and economic crises are to be avoided. This brings us to a consideration of some fundamental concerns involved in public sector budgeting.

Countercyclical Governmental Fiscal Policy

For the most part, state and local governments cannot run substantial budgetary deficits for any length of time. Many are constitutionally or legally required to have balanced operating budgets. They can fund developmental projects through capital budgets, which do permit long-term debt. But they do not typically treat these budgets as a tool for encouraging or discouraging short-term economic growth. By contrast, however, the federal government can and does plan for deficits as a means of managing the nation's economy. This is another development that coincides with the expansion of the contemporary administrative state. Prior to the 1930s, the balanced budget was sacrosanct. A federal budget that *planned* to spend more than it anticipated in revenues would have been taken as a sign that the government was profligate and out of control. The government's credit, or at least so it was thought, would falter and an economic panic might ensue. Such deficits as did occur were unplanned. (A history of the federal budget appears in Box 6–5.) By the mid-1930s, however, another approach began to emerge. This is frequently called the **Keynesian approach** after the British economist who developed it, Lord John Maynard Keynes.[4] In its simplest form, Keynesian economics holds that once the government's role in the economic life of a capitalist society becomes substantial, government spending can be used to counteract the normal boom-and-bust tendencies of the business cycle. In other words, if governmental spending is a considerable proportion of a nation's GNP, then government should have substantial leverage over the business cycle fluctuations in that nation. Deficit spending—that is, spending more than is raised in revenues—can be used to stimulate the economy out of recession or depression. A government surplus—that is, raising more revenues than are to be spent—can be used as a means of regulating economic growth and limiting inflation.

To the extent that a government subscribes to the Keynesian approach, it is evident that budgeting has great ramifications for the economy. It is no longer simply a consideration of deciding what kinds of activities government should engage in, what they will cost, and how revenues may be raised to finance them. Rather, the budgetary process must also take into account the government's role in trying to keep the economy on an even keel. This being the case, governmental spending and revenue raising must be related to the economy generally as opposed to the funding of governmental programs alone. In the United States, this role for government was placed on a legal footing by the Employment Act of 1946, which created a policy that the federal government should promote full employment to the extent "practicable" in the society. This statute is often considered a landmark in the political and economic development of the United States because it signified the demise of an ideology of laissez-faire capitalism and called for governmental intervention in the economy.

Despite the Employment Act, however, Keynesian economics remains in dispute. The main problem *may* be less in the theory itself than in practice; it is difficult to apply. First, it is hard to analyze the economy and coordinate the analysis with a lengthy budget-making process. It now takes eighteen months or longer to formulate a federal budget for one year. The fiscal assumptions upon which a budget is built may fail to match a fast-changing economy. Second, the politics of the budgetary process make it difficult to generate surpluses—required by the Keynesian countercyclical approach when needed to curtail economic growth. The electoral interests of members of Congress generally dictate heavy federal spending on projects in their districts in election years and it is particularly painful for many legislators to have to campaign in a district with high levels of unemployment.[5] But the absence of political discipline can be costly. Deficit spending tends to be inflationary, which can create pressures for interest rates to rise. Higher rates, in turn, dampen borrowing for business investment and can slow down economic growth. Slower growth is likely to have a negative impact on the government's ability to raise revenues through income taxes. Consequently, in such a scenario, reducing the deficit or balancing the budget becomes even more difficult. Countercyclical fiscal policy requires delicate economic balancing that has often been upset by the real world of electoral politics.

Largely as a result of these difficulties, the Keynesian approach in the United States has laid the groundwork for the development of huge budgetary deficits. Box 6–5 indicates that there have been deficit budgets in all but eight years since 1931. The federal debt is now approaching 2.4 trillion dollars. Economists and political scientists are uncertain of the impact of a national debt of this size.[6] It amounts to some 40 percent of the annual GNP and costs the government about $150 billion a year in net interest payments. It also promotes high interest rates, which may make the dollar strong against other currencies and thereby contribute to problems in international trade. Still, from a comparative perspective it may not be as burdensome or damaging as the national debts of some other countries.

Whatever the actual problems posed by deficit spending and the national debt, however, many believe that the government should be required to balance the budget on an annual basis. In fact, some members of Congress have introduced a constitutional amendment for this purpose. Although the amendment does not appear likely to be approved and ratified, it represents a real concern over whether governmental spending is simply out of control. In fact, the deficit problem spurred both a political movement and a far-reaching revision of the federal budget process.

Supply-Side Economics

The election of Ronald Reagan to the presidency in 1980 brought greater credibility and interest to **supply-side economics.** This approach argues for a reduced government role in the economy—less regulation, lower taxes, and limited, if any, countercyclical spending. The basic concept is that governmental intervention in the economy is less efficient than free-market competition in

BOX 6–5 **A History of the Federal Budget**

BUDGET RECEIPTS AND OUTLAYS, 1789–1990[*]
(in millions of dollars)

Fiscal year	Budget receipts	Budget outlays	Budget surplus or deficit(−)	Fiscal year	Budget receipts	Budget outlays	Budget surplus or deficit(−)
1789–1849 ...	1,160	1,090	+70	1945	45,159	92,712	−47,553
1850–1900 ...	14,462	15,453	−991	1946	39,296	55,232	−15,936
1901–1905 ...	2,797	2,678	+119	1947	38,514	34,496	4,018
1906–1910 ...	3,143	3,196	−52	1948	41,560	29,764	11,796
1911–1915 ...	3,517	3,568	−49	1949	39,415	38,835	580
1916–1920 ...	17,286	40,195	−22,909	1950	39,443	42,562	−3,119
1921–1925 ...	20,962	17,323	+3,639	1951	51,616	45,514	6,102
1926	3,795	2,930	+865	1952	66,167	67,686	−1,519
1927	4,013	2,857	+1,155	1953	69,608	76,101	−6,493
1928	3,900	2,961	+939	1954	69,701	70,855	−1,154
1929	3,862	3,127	+734	1955	65,451	68,444	−2,993
1930	4,058	3,320	+738	1956	74,587	70,640	3,947
				1957	79,990	76,578	3,412
1931	3,116	3,577	−462	1958	79,636	82,405	−2,769
1932	1,924	4,659	−2,735	1959	79,249	92,098	−12,849
1933	1,997	4,598	−2,602	1960	92,492	92,245	247
1934	3,015	6,645	−3,630				
1935	3,706	6,497	−2,791				
1936	3,997	8,422	−4,425	1961	94,388	97,723	−3,335
1937	4,956	7,733	−2,777	1962	99,676	106,821	−7,146
1938	5,588	6,765	−1,177	1963	106,560	111,316	−4,756
1939	4,979	8,841	−3,862	1964	112,613	118,528	−5,915
1940	6,548	9,468	−2,920	1965	116,817	118,228	−1,411
				1966	130,835	134,532	−3,698
1941	8,712	13,653	−4,941	1967	148,822	157,464	−8,643
1942	14,634	35,137	−20,503	1968	152,973	178,134	−25,161
1943	24,001	78,555	−54,554	1969	186,882	183,640	3,242
1944	43,747	91,304	−47,557	1970	192,812	195,649	−2,837

allocating goods and services, directing investment, and generating economic growth. High taxation, in particular, is viewed as unhealthy because it removes money from the private sector, which supply-siders view as the productive sector, and places it in the hands of government, which allegedly uses it in an economically unproductive fashion. Inherent in the Reagan approach to supply-side economics was an effort to reduce the "disproportionate" tax burdens of the wealthy. One of the president's major successes was the 1986 Tax Reform Act, which reduced the top personal income tax from 50 percent to 28 percent

BOX 6–5 *Continued*

BUDGET RECEIPTS AND OUTLAYS, 1789–1990*
(in millions of dollars)

Fiscal year	Budget receipts	Budget outlays	Budget surplus or deficit(−)	Fiscal year	Off-budget under current law Outlays	On-budget under current law Outlays	Surplus or deficit(−)
1971	187,139	210,172	−23,033				
1972	207,309	230,681	−23,373				
1973	230,799	245,707	−14,908	1973	60	245,647	−14,849
1974	263,224	269,359	−6,135	1974	1,447	267,912	−4,688
1975	279,090	332,332	−53,242	1975	8,088	324,245	−45,154
1976	298,060	371,779	−73,719	1976	7,307	364,473	−66,412
TQ‡	81,232	95,973	−14,741	TQ†	1,785	94,187	−12,956
1977	355,559	409,203	−53,644	1977	8,700	400,504	−44,945
1978	399,740	458,729	−58,989	1978	10,359	448,370	−48,630
1979	463,302	503,464	−40,161	1979	12,467	490,997	−27,694
1980	517,112	590,920	−73,808	1980	14,245	576,675	−59,563
1981	599,272	678,209	−78,936	1981	21,005	657,204	−57,932
1982	617,766	745,706	−127,940	1982	17,331	728,375	−110,609
1983	600,562	808,327	−207,764	1983	12,357	795,969	−195,407
1984	666,457	851,781	−185,324	1984	9,966	841,815	−175,358
1985 est	736,859	959,085	−222,226	1985 est.	12,459	946,626	−209,767
1986 est	793,729	973,725	−179,996	1986 est.	1,501	972,224	−178,495
1987 est	861,676	1,026,625	−164,949	1987 est	−3,240	1,029,865	−168,189
1988 est	950,376	1,094,761	−144,385	1988 est	−4,334	1,099,095	−148,719
1989 est	1,029,934	1,137,390	−107,456	1989 est	−5,307	1,142,698	−112,764
1990 est	1,107,673	1,190,030	−82,357	1990 est	−6,764	1,196,795	−89,122

Data for 1789–1939 are for the administrative budget; data for 1940 and all following years are for the unified budget.
*Includes outlays (and deficits) that are off-budget under current law and proposed to be included on-budget. These transactions began in 1973.
†In calendar year 1976, the Federal fiscal year was converted from a July 1–June 30 basis to an Oct. 1–Sept. 30 basis. The TQ refers to the transition quarter from July 1 to Sept. 30, 1976.
SOURCE: *The United States Budget in Brief, Fiscal Year 1986* (Washington, D.C.: Office of Management and Budget, 1985), p. 79.

(actually, 33 percent during a phase-in period) while eliminating or reducing a number of deductions to partially offset the decrease.[7]

In economic terms, the supply-side approach either failed or was not adequately tested, depending upon one's point of view. Beyond a doubt, the Reagan administration ran up the largest federal deficits in the nation's history. The federal debt more than doubled during the Reagan years, as government spending continued to grow. Unemployment reached a low of 5.4 percent (as compared with 5.5 percent under President Carter), and inflation was kept at low levels. But the economy grew at a rate of 2.6 percent, the same as it had during the last half of the 1970s. In summing up supply-siders' general disappointment, William Niskanen, a former member of the Council of Economic Advisers under Reagan, said, "We have a bigger government, with higher spending. We've slowed regulation down, but we haven't reversed it. In other words, there was no Reagan revolution."[8]

But the supply-side movement has mobilized political pressure to prevent or reduce growth in the size of government and governmental work forces. Governmental programs involving regulation and redistribution are particularly under attack. In fact, some believe that the supply-side mentality threatens to "dismantle" America.[9] In addition, many local governments are exploring the economics and politics of "privatizing" services such as sanitation (garbage collection) and even prison construction and administration and fire protection. Whether private companies will be able to supply such services efficiently, equitably, and satisfactorily in the long run remains unclear. However, public administrators at all levels of government are now paying much greater attention to the possibilities of privatization. In fact, although no one appears to know the exact figure, it is often alleged that about one-third of the work of federal agencies is now contracted out to private research and policy analysis firms.

THE FEDERAL BUDGETARY PROCESS

Concern with the rising federal deficit and the size of the federal debt also prompted a major revision of the federal budgetary process. In 1985, the Balanced Budget and Emergency Deficit Control Act, better known as the Gramm-Rudman-Hollings Act, was passed. It superseded parts of the Budget and Impoundment Control Act of 1974 in creating a timetable and process for establishing the government's annual budget. Unlike earlier budgetary processes, though, Gramm-Rudman contained a schedule for reducing the deficit to zero (by 1991). Under its provisions and those remaining from earlier statutes, the

Reprinted by permission of Robbin Troy Armstrong and The Daily Orange Corporation.

"Prioritizing."

budget process is very complicated and its language is highly specialized. There-fore, throughout the discussion that follows, it may prove helpful to refer to the glossary of budgetary terms appearing in Box 6–6.

The development of the contemporary federal budgetary process has its roots back in 1921 when the Bureau of the Budget was created as a unit within the Treasury Department. Prior to that time, the budget was a somewhat hap-hazard and largely congressional function. There was little coordination in the process and no rigorous effort was made to connect revenues to expenditures in the budget itself. In 1939, as part of the development of the modern presidency, the Bureau of the Budget was placed in the newly created Executive Office of the President. This reorganization solidified the president's roles as administrator in chief and manager of the economy through countercyclical fiscal policy. It also emphasized the president's responsibility for developing a comprehensive budget for transmittal to Congress. In 1970, the Bureau of the Budget's functions were expanded to include greater responsibility for the way federal agencies were managed, and it was accordingly renamed the Office of Management and Budget (OMB). Throughout this time, the federal government has adhered to an annual budget. However, in 1974 it was decided to begin the fiscal year on October 1, rather than July 1. (The fiscal year [FY] is numbered according to the year in which it ends, i.e., FY 1990 ends on September 30, 1990.) In 1974, Congress created the Congressional Budget Office (CBO) to provide it with an independent source of information about the economy and the assumptions involved in the president's budgetary proposal. In a sense, the CBO was intended to balance the influence of OMB. This demonstrated the tendency to try to control one agency with another, giving testimony to the continuing relevance of the separation of powers and the application of checks and balances.

One of the problems with the budget process after the 1974 reforms was the development of "multiple budgets."[10] The president had one, but so did Con-gress. Disagreement between the two sometimes led to the failure to enact a budget by the beginning of the fiscal year. Instead, "continuing resolutions" were passed to maintain government funding. In addition, supplemental appropria-tions, future obligations, and projected expenditures were used in ways that threatened the concept of an annual budget.

The hallmark of the federal budgetary process is complexity. There are several things going on at once. The budget for one year is being executed; the budget for the next may be under legislative consideration; the budget for the year after the one being considered by Congress is simultaneously being devel-oped in the executive branch; and, in many instances, agencies are engaged in a consideration of the likely costs of their programs five years into the future. But these activities only begin to tap the surface of the budgetary activity that is going on. The Council of Economic Advisers, some officials in OMB, some of the president's aides on fiscal policy, and parts of the Treasury and Labor Depart-ments are trying to develop information and projections that will accurately describe the performance of the economy during the fiscal year for which the budget is being developed. This is necessary if revenues are to be estimated accurately and spending is to be matched to the business cycle. At the same time,

BOX 6–6 **Glossary of Budgetary Terms**

AUTHORIZING LEGISLATION—Legislation enacted by the Congress to set up or continue the operation of a Federal program or agency. Authorizing legislation is normally a prerequisite for subsequent appropriations, but does not usually provide budget authority (see below).

BUDGET—A plan of proposed receipts and spending for the coming fiscal year. By law the President's budget for the Federal Government must be transmitted to Congress within fifteen days after Congress convenes, which is usually in early January. However, the budget transmittal date can be extended by a joint resolution of the Congress.

BUDGET AUTHORITY (BA)—Authority provided by law to enter into obligations that will result in immediate or future outlays. It may be classified by the period of availability, by the timing of congressional action, or by the manner of determining the amount available. The basic forms of budget authority are:

Appropriations—Authority that permits Federal agencies to incur obligations and to make payments.

Authority to borrow—Authority that permits Federal agencies to incur obligations and to borrow money to make payments.

Contract authority—Authority that permits Federal agencies to enter into contracts or incur other obligations in advance of an appropriation.

BUDGET RECEIPTS—Income, net of refunds, collected from the public by the Federal Government through the exercise of its governmental or sovereign powers. Budget receipts also include gifts and contributions. Excluded are amounts received from business-type transactions (such as sales, interest, or loan repayments) and payments be-

tween Government accounts. (See offsetting receipts.)

BUDGET SURPLUS OR DEFICIT—Differences between budget receipts and outlays.

CONCURRENT RESOLUTION ON THE BUDGET—A resolution passed by both Houses of the Congress, but not requiring the signature of the President, setting outlay and receipt targets for the Congress.

CONTINUING RESOLUTION—Legislation enacted by the Congress to provide budget authority for specific ongoing activities when a regular appropriation for those activities has not been enacted by the beginning of the fiscal year.

CREDIT BUDGET—A plan of proposed direct loan obligations and guaranteed loan commitments. Budget authority and outlays associated with the credit budget are included in the budget totals.

CURRENT SERVICES ESTIMATES—Estimates of receipts, outlays and budget authority for coming fiscal years that assume no policy changes from the year in progress. The estimates include the effects of anticipated changes in economic conditions (such as unemployment or inflation), beneficiary levels, pay increases, and changes required under existing law.

DEFERRAL—Executive branch action that temporarily delays the obligation of budget authority. Deferrals may be overturned at any time by an act of the Congress.

FEDERAL FUNDS—Amounts collected and used by the Federal Government for the general purposes of the Government. There are four types of Federal fund accounts: the general fund, special funds, public enterprise revolving funds, and intragovernmental funds. The major Federal fund is the

BOX 6–6 *Continued*

general fund, which is derived from general taxes and borrowing. The other forms of Federal funds involve earmarked collections, such as those generated by and used to finance a continuing cycle of business-type operations.

FISCAL YEAR—The Federal Government's yearly accounting period, which begins on October 1 and ends on the following September 30. The fiscal year is designated by the calendar year in which it ends; e.g., fiscal year 1986 begins on October 1, 1985, and ends on September 30, 1986. (From 1844 to 1976 the fiscal year began on July 1 and ended on the following June 30.)

IMPOUNDMENT—Any action or inaction by an officer or employee of the Federal Government that precludes the obligation or expenditure of budget authority provided by the Congress (see deferral and rescission).

OBLIGATIONS—Amounts of orders placed, contracts awarded, services received, or similar legally binding commitments made by Federal agencies during a given period that will require outlays during the same or some future period.

OFF-BUDGET FEDERAL ENTITIES—Federal entities or programs that are excluded from the budget under current law. The administration is proposing legislation to shift them on-budget. In order to be consistent with this proposal, the 1986 budget treats them in all tables and presentations as if they were on budget for all years. These entities are all included in the Federal funds grouping.

OFFSETTING RECEIPTS—Collections deposited in receipt accounts that are offset against budget authority and outlays rather than being counted as budget receipts. These collections are derived from Government accounts (intragovernmental transactions) or from the public (proprietary receipts) through activities that are of a business-type or market-oriented nature.

OUTLAYS—Payments, normally in the form of checks issued or cash disbursed, net of refunds, reimbursements, and offsetting collections. Outlays include interest accrued on the public debt.

RECONCILIATION—A reconciliation directive is a provision in the concurrent resolution on the budget that calls on various committees of the Congress to recommend legislative changes that reduce outlays or increase receipts by specified amounts. A reconciliation bill contains these changes.

RESCISSION—A legislative action canceling budget authority previously provided by the Congress.

SEQUESTRATION—The Gramm-Rudman process of requiring specific automatic spending cuts if Congress and the president exceed the act's maximum deficit amounts.

SUPPLEMENTAL APPROPRIATION —An appropriation enacted subsequent to a regular annual appropriation act. Supplemental appropriation acts provide additional budget authority for programs or activities (including new programs authorized after the date of the original appropriation act) for which the need for funds is too urgent to be postponed until the next regular appropriation.

TAX EXPENDITURES—Provisions of the Federal income tax laws that allow a special exclusion, exemption, or deduction from gross income or provide a special credit, preferential rate of tax, or deferral of tax liability. Tax expenditures frequently have results similar to spending programs, loan guarantees, or regulations.

BOX 6–6 *Continued*

TRUST FUNDS—Amounts collected and used by the Federal Government for carrying out specific purposes and programs according to a statute or trust agreement and specified by law as being trust fund money, such as the social security and unemployment trust funds. Trust funds are not available for the general purposes of the Government. Trust fund receipts that are not needed immediately are generally invested in Government securities and earn interest for the trust fund.

SOURCE: *United States Budget in Brief, Fiscal Year 1986* (Washington, D.C.: Office of Management and Budget, 1985), pp. 80–81; and Stanley Collender, *The Guide to the Federal Budget: Fiscal 1988* (Washington, D.C.: Urban Institute Press, 1987), p. 164 (for "sequestration").

---

the CBO may be evaluating the economic assumptions developed in the executive branch for the budget two years hence and also evaluating aspects of the budget proposal for the next fiscal year. It is no wonder that so many people, including those who write newspaper headlines, are so confused about the budgetary process. But let's start at the beginning and try to explain the sequence for a complete budget from start to finish.

The development of the budget that will end September 30, 1990 (FY 1990) begins in earnest in the early spring of 1988. At that time, budget officers in the various departments and agencies ask their bureau chiefs for estimates of the funding they will need to operate their programs during the period from October 1, 1989 to September 30, 1990 (FY 1990). The bureau chiefs supply dollar figures and also a description of the policy assumptions behind their calculations of these amounts. For instance, a bureau chief might assume that a large increase in funding will be necessary if the number of clientele, such as senior citizens or veterans, of the bureau's program is rapidly growing. The agency or department budget officer examines and coordinates these requests from the bureau chiefs and begins to formulate a tentative budget. This activity is informed by OMB's instructions and policy guidelines, which reflect the president's assumptions as to the revenues that will be available and the size of the federal deficit or surplus that will be appropriate from the perspectives of fiscal policy. However, the Gramm-Rudman-Hollings Act places limits on the size of planned deficits. The remaining of these are FY 1989—$72 billion; FY 1990—$36 billion; and FY 1991—no deficit. (In practice, the act allows deficits of $10 billion over these limits, as will be explained later on.)

Next, OMB reviews the agencies' tentative budgets. It can augment or reduce their proposals, but—with rare exceptions—OMB pares agency requests down. The agencies proceed to revise their initial estimates and prepare "final" estimates of the funds they will need. The final estimates are submitted to OMB during the summer (1988, in the example).

OMB reviews these estimates. It holds hearings with the budget officers of the various agencies and departments. It may ask them to defend the policy assumptions behind their estimates and to submit new information. The "final" estimates may be substantially altered during this process. By some time in December 1988, OMB makes recommendations on agency spending to the president. Once the president approves the tentative budget, OMB prepares the final budget proposal that will be submitted by the president to the Congress. The president actually transmits the budget proposal to Congress sometime in early January (1989). Throughout their review process, OMB officials will often be in contact with the president's advisors in the White House Office, the Council of Economic Advisers, the National Security Council, and other Executive Office units. But the director of OMB, who is usually viewed as the president's chief budget officer, generally wields great influence in the formulation of the final budget proposal.

The budgeting process in Congress involves three main sets of actors.

- The *CBO* examines the assumptions of the president's budget and works out alternative projections of revenues and expenditures. It also provides an analysis of the budget's likely impact on the economy. It may engage in a discussion of the priorities inherent in the president's budget and how these may be at odds with its sense of Congress's desires.

- The *House and Senate Committees on the Budget* work with the CBO in examining the president's proposal. These committees formulate a budget resolution intended to establish the budget's maximum spending authority.

- The *Appropriations Committees in the House and Senate* develop and bring appropriations bills to the floor of each legislative chamber for consideration by the legislature as a whole. The appropriations committees work within a framework of requirements generated by the budget committees.

In brief, the congressional budget process works as follows.[11] The various legislative committees complete a review of the president's budget proposal by February 25. They submit their views and estimates of the actions they will take on budget items concerning programs and activities under their jurisdictions to the budget committees. The budget committees also receive the CBO's report on the president's budget (by February 15). During this period, the budget committees hold hearings on the proposed budget.

During the period from January through March, the budget committees develop a budget resolution, which must be submitted to Congress as a whole by April 1. The resolution presents Congress's alternative to the president's budget. It compares revenues to spending (budget authority) and provides a framework within which congressional committees dealing with taxation and appropriations can formulate policies and levels. The resolution must not surpass the maximum deficits allowed by the Gramm-Rudman-Hollings Act. The budget resolution may also include specific instructions as to how other committees should reconcile their actions with the limits it imposes. Gramm-Rudman requires Congress as a whole to approve a budget resolution by April 15. From then until mid-June, it should complete the process of reconciling the limits imposed by the budget resolution with the spending levels allowed for the government's activities during the coming fiscal year.

Before any of the money that agencies began discussing with OMB a year earlier can be obtained and spent, laws must be enacted authorizing agencies' actions and funding them. By September 30, Congress should have passed these bills, which are subject to presidential veto. If they are not enacted before the end of the fiscal year, some agencies will theoretically go unfunded. In the past, though, they have generally been allowed to continue their operations at existing levels.

But suppose Congress and the president are unable to comply with the maximum deficit levels established by the Gramm-Rudman-Hollings Act? Here the law calls for an innovative process called "sequestration," which requires spending cuts.[12] If invoked, sequestration begins in August, when OMB and CBO make assessments of the projected size of the deficit for the fiscal year about to begin. If the directors of these agencies disagree, their figures are averaged. Their projections are reported to a special joint congressional committee composed of the members of the House and Senate budget committees. If their forecast is for a deficit greater than $10 billion over the limit established by Gramm-Rudman, sequestration may occur. If it does, defense and nondefense programs will be cut in equal dollar amounts to bring the deficit within the limit imposed by Gramm-Rudman. However, with the threat of such cuts (which are mandated with considerable specificity in the law) hanging over their heads, Congress and the president may agree on ways to bring the deficit down to acceptable limits. If they can do so by mid-November (1989, in our example), sequestration will not occur.

The Continuing Saga of the Budget: Execution

As lengthy and complex as adopting the federal budget may be, its enactment is only the beginning. It must also be executed. Notice that the process that began in the spring of 1988 is intended to result in final approval by October 1, 1989 and continue in effect until September 30, 1990. Thus budgeting has at least three time frames: (1) formulation in the executive branch (about March–December 1988 in our example); (2) legislative action (January–September 1989); and (3) execution (October 1989–September 1990). The last stage, of course, is the one that most affects the performance of government and the economy, and in that sense it is the most critical. Yet execution is subject to all kinds of pitfalls.

First, suppose that for one reason or another the budget's projection of revenues falls short. Perhaps the economy has performed worse than anticipated and consequently revenues from income taxes have fallen off due to higher than anticipated unemployment and slower than anticipated growth in personal and corporate income. Consequently, if the government spends at the levels authorized by the budget, it may run a deficit that is considered too large and/or too inflationary. Under such circumstances, a president may want to reduce governmental expenditures. This commonly entails one of the following:

Hiring Freezes   A president can refuse to allow vacant federal positions to be filled through **hiring freezes.** This probably does not generally amount to much of a savings relative to the entire budget. However, it is a symbolic act that may be politically desirable. It is also true that agencies may not be able to spend the funds appropriated to them if their programs are drastically understaffed.

Impoundments   An **impoundment** occurs when the president refuses to allow an executive agency to spend the funds that have been allotted to it. Impoundments can take two forms. **Recissions** are terminations of funds for an agency or program. **Deferrals** are delays in the spending of appropriated funds. The constitutionality of impoundments has long been in doubt. The first impoundment occurred during Thomas Jefferson's presidency, but the exercise of impoundments seems not to have reached crisis proportions until recent times. In the early 1970s, President Nixon impounded some $12 billion earmarked for highway, health, education, and environmental projects. This provoked a number of lawsuits, most of which were lost by the president. It also encouraged the 1974 Budget and Impoundment Control Act. Under this legislation, the president was authorized to impound funds, but subject to congressional approval. However, the provision for deferrals relied on a type of "one house veto" that was declared unconstitutional in *Immigration and Naturalization Service* v. *Chadha* (1983).[13] Subsequently, several members of Congress and some cities brought suit against deferrals on the basis that Congress would not have granted deferral authority to the president had it known that it would not be able to exercise a legislative veto over his actions. As a result of this litigation, presidential deferrals are now considered unconstitutional.[14]

A second set of problems associated with the execution of budgets occurs at the agency level. Agencies need flexibility in administering their programs. They need to be able to respond to changes in the environments of their programs, to new demand levels, and to unexpected success in accomplishing their purposes. After all, one of the chief reasons for the creation of administrative authority is to enable government to react more rapidly and flexibly than is generally plausible through coordinated congressional and presidential action. So what happens when an agency has funds earmarked for one program that it feels should be spent elsewhere in view of new circumstances? Remember, the agency may have formulated its initial budget request two or more years earlier. Two devices are commonly used to shift funds around within agencies.[15] One is called **transfers.** Money can be transferred from one purpose to another if Congress has authorized this process in advance. Transfers are particularly common in the field of foreign affairs, where depending on regime changes abroad, government agencies may want to spend more or less on aid and military assistance. Closely akin to the transfer is **reprogramming.** Under this process an agency is not authorized in advance to switch funds from one program to another but rather must consult first with the relevant committees in Congress to obtain permission to do so. Despite all the attention paid to funding agencies at the stage of formulating the budget, relatively little is paid to these devices, which can result in the movement of billions of dollars from one purpose to another.

One additional process at the agency level bears mention. It is commonly assumed that if an agency fails to spend its entire appropriation it must return the leftover portion to the Treasury. However, some agencies are authorized to retain the money and apply it to next year's budget. Again, the sums accumulated in the "pipeline" of "no year" money can be substantial, reaching several hundred million dollars for the government as a whole.

When one puts all these elements together, it is evident that the budget as enacted may be at some variance from the budget as executed. Very substantial sums can be involved in recissions, transfers, reprogramming, and in the "pipeline." These procedures are often used to promote political ends, as apart from administrative economies. They open the prospect for continuing controversy over funding even after appropriations have been authorized. But this is only one of several problems associated with the federal budget process.

Constant Problem Areas

Among the major problems with the federal budget process that we have not yet emphasized are the following.

The Length of the Budget Cycle   Based on our example of developing the budget for FY 1990, it is evident that the entire budget cycle from start to finish takes about thirty months (March 1988–September 30, 1990). This has several problematic consequences. It often means that the assumptions about the economy and the needs of any given program that were present at the start of the cycle are inappropriate later on. This is one reason that flexibility in execution is so desirable. The interdependence of the United States and foreign economies, the rapidly changing character of international relations, and even the unpredictability of the weather's impact on agriculture and energy consumption all make even one-year predictions somewhat unreliable.

The length of the budget cycle has an impact on presidential transitions. A newly elected president, who may have run against the incumbent, spends January 20 to September 30 under the budget established by his predecessor (opponent) and already being executed by the agencies. The presidential budget proposal that would go through the next fiscal year (that is, from October 1 of the year of presidential inauguration to September 30 of the next calendar year) has already been worked on in the executive branch for some nine months or so. If timetables hold, it has already been transmitted to Congress as well. The new president is in a position to modify this budget proposal somewhat, but a radical refashioning is difficult, though possible, as the Reagan administration demonstrated in 1981. A new president elected in 1988, taking office in January 1989, will not be able to work with a budget of his own proposing until October 1, 1990—almost a full two years after the electoral campaign that may have given him a mandate for change. It is no wonder presidents often find administrative matters so exasperating. On the other hand, a positive feature of the length of the budget cycle is that it makes for administrative continuity. It is sometimes proposed that the government move away from the annual budget to a two-year budget, but while this might reduce the amount of effort per year that goes into formulating a budget, it would not alleviate the political problems associated with the long time frame.

Playing the Budget Game   Sometimes budgeting takes on the aura of a game, with the various agency players trying to increase their shares and elected officials trying, at least ostensibly, to keep taxes down and promote administrative economy. A number of agency strategies are common. One is to threaten to cut the most popular or politically desirable functions first. Thus a school district will frequently threaten to cease providing transportation to students if the voters do not approve higher taxes. So, too, do federal agencies threaten to cut out popular services unless their full funding requests are met. The National Park Service once even threatened to close the Washington Monument in such a game! Agencies also pad their requests in the expectation that they will subsequently be reduced. This promotes a kind of budgetary ritual that involves a lot of noise, activity, hand-wringing, newspaper headlines, and virtually no significant change. Agencies can play the "camel's nose" game and seek to obtain seed money—limited funds for a one-year program—with the expectation that, like a camel, once they get their nose under the budgetary "tent," more is sure to follow. Finally, **repackaging** is a common ruse used to seek increased funding. Under this approach, an existing program is explained in terms that seem to fit with a president's new priorities. Although it is difficult to become irate about these games, they are inherently dishonest and can hardly raise the levels of public debate and voter information about the way the government operates.[16]

Raising the Roof (Ceiling)   The federal government has never fully accepted the idea that long-term deficits are legitimate. There is something psychologically pleasing about the notion of a balanced budget. Consequently, it has been thought that there should be a statutory limitation on the size of the federal government's accumulated deficit (the federal debt). But Congress and the president have found it impossible or undesirable to live within the confines of these debt ceilings, so with routine frequency they simply vote to raise the ceiling and increase the debt. The point of this charade is probably best left to psychologists and psychiatrists to figure out—apparently the legislature finds security in fixing limits that really aren't there.

Uncontrollable Spending   Perhaps all these problems point in the direction of what seems to be the most serious problem with federal budgeting at the present time: to a very large extent, perhaps involving as much as 75 percent of the budget, federal spending is uncontrolled in the sense that funds are committed in advance for the foreseeable future. Such commitments take three main forms: First, there is payment of the federal debt, generated by the borrowing that accompanies deficit spending. Payment cannot legally or constitutionally be avoided and default by the federal government would surely spell disaster for the nation. Interest payments on the debt alone account for 14 percent of budget expenditures. A second kind of uncontrollable spending involves **entitlements**

(see Chapter 3). Entitlements arise out of governmental commitments to groups of citizens. Social Security, various welfare, Medicare, Medicaid, and veterans' benefits are examples. The expense of entitlements tends to rise over time as the number of people in the eligible group expands. For instance, as the proportion of the population that is elderly expands, so too expands the number of individuals entitled to Medicare and Social Security benefits. In addition, there is a tendency to raise the level of the benefits. Cost of living adjustments (COLAs) may be granted to beneficiaries to compensate for inflation. Especially as the size of the entitled group expands, pressure is put on members of Congress and the president to increase the amounts of payment to them. Finally, uncontrollable spending is derived from contractual obligations entered into by the government. Often these are multiyear and involve cost overruns and adjustments for inflation that become quite substantial. However, it should be borne in mind that despite the label "uncontrollable," all of these costs can be reduced over time. Indeed, as part of a general reaction to the "uncontrollable" problem, federal agencies now make five-year projections of the cost of their programs.

A BUDGET THEORY, OR THEORIES ABOUT BUDGETING?

For the most part, the difficulties we have been discussing are problems of practice. The mixing of political, economic, administrative, and legal concerns in the area of public budgeting makes it difficult to develop a budgetary process that adequately satisfies all of the government's needs. Although we have been focusing on the federal level, the same would be true for the states. The main differences are that states do not engage in countercyclical spending, though they may reduce taxes to stimulate economic growth, and that they are under greater pressure to avoid annual deficits. Interestingly, in the 1980s, many states had surpluses that stood in stark contrast to the federal government's huge deficit. As noted earlier, states make a distinction between capital budgets, which is money used for the building of projects, and operating budgets, which are the costs of running the governmental enterprise. Consequently, their surpluses are sometimes partly due to accounting techniques. Another difference is that the state legislatures tend to play a smaller role in budgeting than does Congress. They are generally deferential to the governor. Several states also differ from the federal government in that they use a biennial rather than an annual budget.[17]

One might look to the states as laboratories in which different approaches to budgeting might be undertaken. There is enough variation among them to provide a fruitful field of investigation. The ways in which they raise revenues differ widely, as do their spending patterns. Some states rely heavily on income taxes and fund huge educational programs or welfare programs, whereas others rely on sales taxes and provide a much reduced program of public services. The behavior of local governments also varies substantially with respect to raising and spending revenues. However, despite all these "laboratories" and variations, it is still true that the United States has not worked out a dominant theory of public budgeting that can answer what has long been considered the most basic question on the expenditure side: "On what basis shall it be decided to allocate x dollars to activity A instead of activity B?"[18] We can study the variety of budgetary processes, sources of revenue, and allocation of expenditures ad nauseum without finding an answer to this question. As usual, however, part of the reason for this is that different perspectives generate different answers. Those who view budgeting as a managerial endeavor stress one set of values, those who see it as political emphasize another, and those imbued with legalistic concerns still others. Therefore, there are theories of budgeting rather than a single budget theory. And, as in other areas of public administration, there is a vigorous contest among these theories for influence and dominance.

The Managerial Approach to Public Budgeting

The managerial perspective on public administration seeks to develop an approach to budgeting that promotes the values of efficiency, economy, and managerial effectiveness. It seeks to use budgeting to cut out waste, encourage the highest level of productivity, and strengthen managerial control over the operation of government.

The first major step in the development of a managerial approach to budgeting occurred in 1914, when the New York Bureau of Municipal Research called for the development of a performance budget. Later, in 1949, the influential First Hoover Commission called for the use of performance budgeting in the federal government. To understand the importance of the performance budget one must remember that it was predated by lump-sum appropriations and the **line item** budget. Lump-sum budgets simply gave agencies funds to expend more or less as they saw fit, with very little political control over how the funds were actually used or misused. The lump-sum approach was chaotic and left the activities of public administrators pretty much beyond the scrutiny of elected officials. The line item budget was adopted to rectify this situation. It requires that appropriations be linked to objects of expenditure. Although these objects could be defined in different ways, the tendency was to place every significant expenditure on a separate line in the agency's budget. For instance, the salaries of each employee might be listed separately, as might the cost of pencils, paper, pens, and so forth. The chief executive or legislature could then go down the list of agency requests for appropriations and cross out, reduce, or, as is less likely, augment the agency's funding request for any of the items. This obviously provides a great deal of control of *how* money is spent, but it tells elected officials very little about what is supposed to be accomplished by the agency. In other words, what are all those pencils for? What is it that the agency does? And how much does it cost? Enter the **performance budget.**

The Performance Budget   This type of budget seeks to answer these questions without losing control over expenditures. At a minimum, it involves:

1. "The *formulation* and adoption of a plan of activities and programs for a stated time period." In other words, what is the agency intending to do, why, how much of it, and when?
2. *Funding*, that is, relating program costs to resources, or determining what kind of agency performance can be obtained within the confines of the resources available.
3. *Execution*, or the achievement of the authorized plan, within the time frame, and resources allocated to it.[19]

Performance budgeting contains at least the seeds of all modern managerially oriented public budgeting strategies. It fits in well with specialized organizational designs, as the subunits of agencies could be considered the "activities" for which funding is targeted. For example, in a public hospital, "food service," "ward service," "X-rays," "surgery," and "housekeeping" might be considered activities and they might also form separate administrative organizational units. Performance budgeting promotes the managerial goal of allowing evaluation of administrative performance since it often requires "performance reports" to accompany budget requests. Consequently, performance budgeting has a concrete meaning to public managers: activities and organizational units tend to coincide; performance is measured and evaluated (in some fashion); and budgetary requests and appropriations are connected to performance levels.

The use of performance budgeting has made considerable headway in American government at all levels. However, even though most states use it in some aspects, only a few could be considered to adhere rigorously to the performance concept. Among the common complaints about performance budgeting are that: (1) it does not afford the legislature the same level of participation and control as does the line item budget, and (2) that it is not refined enough to deal with the complexity of administrative operations. Enter the **program budget.**

The Program Budget   Program budgeting is often considered interchangeable with performance budgeting, but there is a significant difference, at least in theory. Whereas performance budgeting concentrates on activities and tends not to overlap organizational units, program budgeting looks at the purpose (not activities) of governmental administration and seeks to relate funding to the achievement of these purposes. Program budgeting may tend to overlap administrative organizational units, but it does not necessarily do so. It is also prospective in the sense of seeking to adopt policies based on the prospects for the achievement of their goals at given levels of cost. In other words, it incorporates a cost-effectiveness approach, while exploring various administrative approaches to obtaining any given level of benefit at the lowest cost.

Returning to our example of performance budgeting in a hospital may help clarify the difference between these two systems of budgeting. Listing costs by activities does not provide us with an idea of what the purpose of a hospital is. It tells us what it does, but not what its ultimate goal is. Program budgeting, on the other hand, would identify the goals of the hospital and seek to relate funding to these. For instance, "housekeeping" might be redefined in terms of providing "sanitation," and an appropriate level of sanitation might be defined. Next, different ways of obtaining that sanitary level might be mapped out, along with their projected costs. Then the approach providing the desired level at the lowest cost would presumably be selected and funded. Such an exercise can involve interesting choices. For instance, if the hospital is concerned with sanitation in surgery rooms and if it must pay employees who sanitize the rooms a night-rate differential (higher wage rate), then, all other things being equal, the hospital might elect to schedule as much surgery as possible during the times (mornings and afternoons) when the rooms can be cleaned at a lower cost. Similarly, the performance budgeting activity of taking X-rays could be redefined in program budget terms as part of a wider objective of "diagnosing." The success of the operation of the X-ray department at this point would be related to the utility of using X-rays to diagnose medical problems and the cost of X-rays would be compared to the cost of other diagnostic techniques. This would have obvious implications for the purchase and use of different types of X-ray equipment and for the decision as to who should operate it, technicians or medical doctors.

Perhaps policing provides a more familiar example of the distinction between the performance budget and the program budget. "Patrolling" under the performance budget could become "crime control" under a program budget. Then different types of crimes could be targeted for reduction, and police officers and other resources could be assigned accordingly.

These examples should help clarify the difference between performance budgeting and program budgeting, but they are not intended to suggest that program budgeting is not without very substantial problems. These were made quite evident by the introduction of a particular kind of program budgeting into the federal government in the 1960s. The federal experience with the Planning Programming Budgeting System (PPBS) provides so many lessons that it should be considered in some detail.

PPBS was once hailed as a revolutionary approach to budgetary and administrative decision making with almost messianic qualities.[20] It promised to solve many of our budgetary problems, many of our administrative ones, and even our political conflicts over how governmental funds should be spent. It was used by Secretary of Defense Robert McNamara in the early 1960s in an effort that was popularized as getting more "bang for the buck." In 1965 President Johnson made it mandatory for most federal agencies. By 1971 it was discontinued as a requirement for all agencies. The essence of PPBS was the following:

1. The analysis of program goals in operational terms. For example, instead of saying the goal of a program is to promote highway safety, the goal would be presented as averting x number of deaths through traffic accidents, averting y number of serious injuries, averting z number of lesser injuries, and reducing property damage by w percent.
2. Analysis of the total costs of programs over one and several years.
3. Analyze alternative ways of achieving the goals. This would be done from a cost-effective approach. In the example above, how much does it cost to

avert a death through the use of seat belts versus the cost per death averted through better driver training?

4. Develop a systematic way of considering the costs and benefits of all government programs in a comparative fashion. In other words, what is the cost of a death averted through driver training versus the cost through public health activities or the cost through promotion of world peace? What are the total benefits of each approach?

At first glance, this sounds eminently reasonable. What does it cost the government to do what it seeks to do? How could it do it for less? Certainly these are important questions. However, PPBS was hard to apply and, even where applied, did not always determine how funds should be appropriated. Why did PPBS not work out in practice?

First, the goals of governmental programs may be unclear and lacking in any operational content. For example, how does one define "promoting world peace" in operational terms? To some this means avoiding the death of members of the U.S. armed forces in combat. To others, it might mean promoting U.S. control of foreign nations through the use of military force. Even more complicated is the situation where a program, such as food stamps, is put together by a coalition of diverse and economically antagonistic interests. Under such conditions an operational definition of the objectives of the program would threaten to destroy the coalition and the program along with it. While PPBS cannot work without operational goals, in some policy areas the U.S. political system may not be able to work well *with* them, since they exacerbate conflict and make it difficult to build majority coalitions.

Second, cost-benefit analysis can be exceedingly difficult even where goals are clear. This is especially true in governments where there are so many program overlaps. In addition, some costs and benefits cannot be quantified. Yet, at least in government, these may be of great political importance. For example, what was the cost of the Vietnam War in terms of the United States' self-image and international stature? What is the benefit derived from a public park? From a strong civil rights policy? How does one assess the costs and benefits of any specific course of activity on the reputation of the president and his ability to exercise the functions of that office effectively?

Third, projecting the costs and benefits of different administrative means of obtaining objectives can be highly speculative or even impossible. In short, often not enough is known about how government can achieve its goals to enable us to predict the consequences of one particular strategy versus another.

Finally, even where the analysis was undertaken with sufficient rigor, while the PPBS approach could inform political decision makers it could not necessarily resolve the key issues in choosing policy alternatives. Returning to our macabre example of deaths averted we can illustrate this point by drawing upon the work of Elizabeth Drew.[21]

In an article called "HEW Grapples with PPBS," she found that the Department of Health, Education, and Welfare (HEW) had programs intended to avert deaths caused by disease and through traffic accidents. The cost of averting a death by promoting the use of seat belts was $87; the cost of averting a death by attacking cancer of the uterine cervix was $3,470. In cost-benefit terms (assuming each death averted to be of equal benefit), the greatest benefit for the least cost would have had HEW allocate its resources to programs in the following order:

Seat belt use

Automotive restraint devices

Avoiding pedestrian injury

Motorcyclist helmets

Arthritis

Reduce driver drinking

Syphilis

Cancer of the uterine cervix

Lung cancer

Breast cancer

Tuberculosis

Driver licensing

Cancer of the head and neck

Colorectal cancer

Now suppose you have limited resources to give HEW for these worthy objectives (as taxpayers and legislatures do). Are you willing to allocate funds to motorcyclist helmets over cancer of the uterine cervix or breast cancer? What would the National Organization for Women say about a decision to follow the logic of cost-benefit analysis in this case? What would motorcyclists say about being required to wear helmets? What would philosophers say about the choice available to those who die in motorcycle accidents for failure to wear a helmet? What would they say about the "choice" available in getting cancer of the breast or cervix? Should these differences affect one's budget allocations?

The point here is not that PPBS cannot be useful in providing an indication of the costs and benefits of various programs. However, it should be evident that it cannot answer the classic question, "On what basis shall it be decided to allocate x dollars to activity A instead of activity B?" In fact, although conceived as a managerial system of budgeting, PPBS tends to illustrate the fundamentally political nature of budgeting. If one could actually use PPBS to resolve the matter of policy choice, then the political priorities of the nation would be clear and several political problems would be solved.

PPBS died in the federal bureaucracy largely for the reasons just discussed—

and also because it was very difficult to apply where programs overlapped several agencies, as is so often the case in the federal bureaucracy.[22] But that does not mean it is not appropriate for some kinds of budgetary decisions. It is used in some state and local governments, apparently with satisfactory results, for some functions. Still, its failure at the federal level sparked interest in other managerial approaches to budgeting. Perhaps most important among these has been **zero-base budgeting (ZBB)**.

Zero-base Budgeting   ZBB is intended to give budgetary decision makers a choice among different funding levels for different programs and activities. It starts from the intellectual premise that the budgeting process should be used to review the political desirability and administrative effectiveness of governmental programs. The concept of zero base is that existing programs and activities should not automatically be funded, but rather should have to justify their continuation as part of the yearly budget cycle. In theory, each program and activity is vulnerable to zero funding in each new fiscal year.

The main elements of ZBB are as follows:

1. The identification of *decision units*. These are the lowest-level organizational or programmatic units for which budgets are prepared.[23] Each decision unit must have a manager who is identified as responsible for the operation of that administrative entity as a whole.
2. The formulation of *decision packages*. These are derived from a comprehensive yearly review of each decision unit's purposes and functions. This review considers such questions as what would happen if the decision unit were not funded at all, what would happen with 50 percent funding, 75 percent, etc., how can its operations be improved, and can a greater benefit-cost ratio be developed? Once the review is completed, the decision unit's operations are divided up according to the perceived importance of its activities. Those activities of top priority are in the first decision package, those of secondary importance in a second decision package, and so on. The operations, costs, and benefits of these packages are presented in a comprehensive fashion to budgetary decision makers.
3. The ranking of decision packages by top-level managers. This establishes organizationwide priorities and seeks to coordinate the agency's choice of level of activity with the amount of funding that is likely to be forthcoming. The key to ranking decision packages is not simply choosing from among different activities, but also deciding upon different levels of activity within any given package.

Like other budget processes, ZBB is complex and difficult to understand in the abstract. Consequently, an example is in order. Peter Pyhrr, the developer of the ZBB concept, provided the following illustration.[24] For "residential refuse collection" in a city, the decision unit is the administrative operations responsible for collecting and transporting all residential solid waste for disposal. The decision package would evaluate different ways of performing this function and different levels of activity. Different means would include such approaches as:

1. Requiring residential users of the service to purchase plastic bags and place their garbage in them.
2. The use of neighborhood dumpsters.
3. Collection from garbage cans rather than plastic bags.
4. The use of "barrel" trucks rather than conventional trucks with the capacity to crush (compact) the garbage.
5. Contracting out to private firms for refuse collection.

The cost of each of these means would be assessed and this assessment would go a long way in dictating the choice as to which would be used.

Different levels of activity would then be considered. For instance, these might involve pickup once a week, or twice a week for garbage and different levels of activity for brush collection. When the decision packages were ranked, the most desired means would be linked with the most desired level of activity. In this fashion it might turn out that pickups twice a week could be afforded when dumpsters were used, but that otherwise pickups would have to be limited to once a week.

As in the case of virtually all known budgetary strategies, ZBB has some limitations. The analysis can become too complex or cumbersome to be useful. The identification of decision units runs into the problem of specifying objectives in clear operational terms. Assessing costs can be difficult or impossible. In addition, as the garbage example above suggests, shifting the cost of a function may pose difficult problems for analysis. Requiring residents to purchase plastic bags pushes some of the costs from the city onto the private citizens. Anytime this occurs there is likely to be an equity issue. Is the cost of plastic garbage bags substantial enough to pose an economic hardship for the city's poorest residents? Additionally, since plastic is a petrochemical, is there a significant cost to the nation imposed by requiring the use of scarce energy resources (petroleum) in this fashion? Of course, the city manager or council is unlikely to worry much about the latter, viewing it instead as a national problem subject to congressional attention. But if dumpsters posed a health problem for residents, it could not be ignored. When we try to apply ZBB at the federal level, such shifting costs from one program to another may be a more substantial problem.

Despite these problems, several jurisdictions have had success with ZBB or some adaptation to it. However, it seems to have been misapplied in the federal government during the Carter administration. The main difficulties were that (1) perhaps out of political and organizational necessity, decision units were identified to coincide with agencies and bureaus rather than programs and activities and (2) the ZBB approach was applied governmentwide, rather than selectively. Pyhrr called Carter's approach "absolute folly."[25] Others detected a note of shrewdness: ZBB became little more than an overlay on traditional budgeting processes; consequently it was easy to apply, engendered little controversy, and enabled Carter to take credit for a major reform!

PPBS and ZBB are leading examples of the managerial approach to budgeting. While they do improve the budgeting process and generate much information that is pertinent to budgetary choices, neither has been fully satisfactory thus far in reducing the budgetary process to a purely managerial endeavor. In truth, they are probably not intended to do so entirely; but they do tend to downgrade the political nature of budgets and the political choices inherent in budgetary decisions.[26]

The Political Approach to Public Budgeting

The political approach to public budgeting emphasizes several concerns: representation, consensus and coalition building, and the locus of power in allocating funds. **Incrementalism** has been the favored political approach to public budgeting in the United States. This approach tends to treat last year's appropriation to an agency or program as a base that should be diminished only under unusual and highly controversial circumstances. The base being more or less untouchable, the real discussion is over the increment that will be allocated to an agency or program during the next fiscal year. Moreover, incrementalism shies away from comprehensive analysis, the specifications of clear goals, and program evaluation. This approach is politically comfortable for several reasons but, at the federal level, it may no longer be able to withstand the pressures to reduce deficits and the national debt.

Incrementalism makes it possible to provide widespread representation to groups and interests in the society. Any socially and economically diverse society, including the United States, is made up of antagonistic interests. Incrementalism allows these sectors to be represented in government even though they are at cross purposes. This is true because it does not demand a comprehensive statement of the objectives of governmental activity and because it does not rigorously question the base appropriation to existing agencies and functions. Consequently, it is possible to have governmental programs that conflict with one another without giving serious consideration to the issue of whether the failure to make fundamental choices among them is in some sense irrational. For instance, the federal government has subsidized tobacco growers and at the same time tried to discourage smoking by the public.[27] The growers are represented in the Department of Agriculture. Public health interests are represented in the Department of Health and Human Services. Each can be funded in the budget process, and until deficits were considered a major problem, neither was very concerned about having its level of appropriation reduced from that of the past fiscal year. In this case, incrementalism worked as a kind of compensatory device for the tobacco growers, who stood to lose a great deal when it was concluded by the U.S. Surgeon General that "smoking is dangerous to your health." The representation of diverse interests and their funding allows public policy to be made through compromise: few, if any, interests that achieve formal representation in the administrative structure are threatened with immediate loss. Rather, change occurs over the long run as declining support for an interest is reflected in decreasing budgetary increments.

Another factor favoring incrementalism is that it allows the building of consensus and coalitions by providing funding to diverse interests. Some degree of consensus is necessary if the citizenry is to support governmental programs and, indeed, the government itself. Coalitions make it possible for political parties to exist and for politicians to be elected. Consensus is fostered where conflict is muted. And conflict can be avoided where the objectives of government are stated in terms that can be widely accepted. Again, "nutrition," "defense," "health," "justice," and "peace" are examples. Almost everyone in the society might agree that these are desirable governmental objectives in the abstract. However, the reaction may be quite different when they are translated into specific programs with specific objectives—to subsidize farmers, avert deaths in one way or another, deploy nuclear weapons and build bases, require school desegregation through busing, represent the interest of the fetus in court, and destabilize foreign regimes through covert activities. A primary difficulty with PPBS and ZBB is that they exacerbate conflict, break down consensus, and make it difficult for the political system to work well at the national level. Incrementalism, on the other hand, allows funding for a variety of activities that when left unanalyzed and ill defined enable different groups and citizens to define and conceptualize them in their own favorable terms.

Similarly, incrementalism enables parties and politicians to build broad coalitions by providing governmental funding to diverse and competing interests. The classic example of such a coalition was put together by Franklin D. Roosevelt. He was able to gain widespread support of southerners, unions, urbanites, and members of minority groups. This "New Deal Coalition" remained the backbone of the Democratic party well into the 1960s.[28] It was routine for Democrat to oppose Democrat on civil rights issues, but the basic coalition held together at least until the election of 1968. Of course, the typical legislator does not have to develop such a grand coalition. He or she has to be more concerned with voters in a specific district. One way of building a coalition there is to engage in "pork barrel" allocations, getting as much public funding into the district as possible. This promotes the economic health of the community and is likely to provide more jobs. "Pork barrelling" can be done without regard to ideology. For example, even communities in which there is strong support for reducing military appropriations generally are likely to want nearby military bases to be kept open. Incrementalism fits this approach to coalition building because it does not threaten existing governmental facilities and spending, but rather promises more and more. If a legislator's district is large and diversified enough, as in the case of senators from states such as California and New York, the incremental approach can also be used to support conflicting interests within the electoral constituency. It is not unusual for rural-urban conflicts to be diminished in this fashion in an effort to build statewide support. Simultaneous subsidies for mass urban transportation and spending for rural highway development are a common example.

Congressional support for the incremental approach also stems from the fact that incrementalism tends to place the locus of power for budgetary decisions in the legislature. Most of managerial approaches strengthen the executive's role in the budgetary process. Some of them, such as PPBS, have had a marked centralizing bias within the executive branch.[29] They have militated against administrative decentralization and administrative responsiveness to the legislature. Under such circumstances, the "budget bureau" displaces the legislative appropriations committees as the key organizational participant in the budgetary process. This also tends to place power over budgetary decisions in the hands of unelected administrators as opposed to elected legislators. If one views budgets as political statements, then incrementalism has the benefit of placing the locus of power in the hands of the citizenry's elected representatives. Presumably, legislators can be held accountable to their constituencies and presumably they will therefore be responsive to them at least in the areas where the electorate has identifiable and salient interests. In addition to potentially enhancing the representative qualities of government in this fashion, incrementalism helps to maintain the viability of checks and balances by maintaining the historic legislative role of the power of the purse intact.

The nature and advantage of incrementalism have been summarized by Aaron Wildavsky and Arthur Hammond in a passage that is worth quoting at length:

> Whatever else they may be, budgets are manifestly political documents. They engage the intense concern of administrators, politicians, leaders of interest groups and citizens interested in the "who gets what and how much" of governmental allocations. Participants in budgeting use its political components as aids to calculation. They drastically simplify their task by concentrating on the relatively small portion of the budget that is politically feasible to change. The previous year's budget, the largest part of which is composed of continuing programs and prior commitments, is usually taken as a base needing little justification beyond that offered in the past. Attention is normally focused on a small number of incremental changes, increases and decreases, calling for significant departures from the established historical base of the agency concerned. Parts of the total budget are given to various administrative agencies, appropriations subcommittees, Budget Bureau divisions, and other interested parties for special attention. This fragmentation is increased because all budgetary items are not evaluated together, but are dealt with in sequence by the various participants, so that only a small number of items need to be considered by any participant at any one time.[30]

However, although this approach maximizes important political values, it has limitations. Budgets are political documents, but they are also economic documents and managerial documents. Incrementalism makes it difficult to use the budget as a countercyclical fiscal tool. The natural tendency is to spend more and avoid cuts. At the same time, when the locus of power is in the legislature, raising taxes, which is so politically unpopular, will be particularly difficult. Consequently, the tendency is for the budget to be unbalanced and for deficits to grow. This promotes inflationary pressures, which may have to be countered by raising interest rates. The latter may hamper economic growth and affect international trade by increasing the dollar against other currencies. But even if taxes were raised to match the ever-continuing incremental increases in spending, it might cause problems for the economy. Eventually government might collect and reallocate a great deal of money from the private sector, which might seriously sap the economy's vitality and even the viability of capitalism as traditionally present in the United States.

By avoiding a clear identification of governmental objectives and priorities, incrementalism also makes public administration difficult. How do you manage an agency whose goals are unclear and contradictory? What does efficiency and economy mean in this context? More than one top-level administrator has found these questions frustrating in the extreme.

These problems of incrementalism are so profound that drastic measures are being considered to limit its negative impact on the economy. One such measure that has gained some credence in recent years has been the **balanced budget amendment.** This would constitutionally force the federal government to balance the budget on an annual basis, unless a clear emergency were present and an extraordinary majority of the Congress agreed to let it be unbalanced. Of course, to some extent, balancing the budget is a matter of accounting practices. The federal government would show a far lesser deficit if it used a capital budget. Programs such as Social Security can also be put "off budget" by converting them into trust funds (see the glossary in Box 6–6). Consequently, a constitutional amendment might fail to accomplish its purpose, while at the same time constituting an extreme response to the myriad difficulties of budgeting. The Gramm-Rudman-Hollings Act is a more moderate response to eliminating deficit spending. But it is subject to change through legislation whenever a majority of Congress (or two-thirds of each house in the case of a presidential veto) and the president decide to amend or abandon it.

Sunset provisions are another approach to keeping incrementalism in check. Sunset legislation provides for the termination of programs at some future date, often five years, unless they are reauthorized by statute at that time. This means that the programs will go out of existence if no legislative action is taken and, consequently, the burden is placed on those administrators and political actors who favor their continuance to justify the need for such programs. The sunset concept is incorporated in zero-base budgeting, since there is a presumption that each agency should justify all the budgetary allocations to it (not just the increment) on an annual basis. Thus far, experience with sunset provisions has been mixed. It seems to work least well in programmatic areas where there are narrow and strongly organized interest groups, such as occupational licensing administration. On the other hand, where there are broad and well-articulated conflicting interests involved, sunset provisions can promote better accountability and evaluation of the performance of agencies and programs. (Sunset provisions are discussed further in Chapter 8.)

The Legal Influence on Budgeting

Today, the courts also have an important influence on budgets. The legal approach to public administration seeks to protect the constitutional rights of individuals, assure their equal protection under the law, and promote procedural fairness and equity. In some instances, seeking to promote or maximize these values can lead to sizeable and identifiable costs for the political community. This is especially true where the judiciary finds that wide-ranging institutional reforms are necessary in order to protect individuals' rights. Such cases often involve prison reform, the reform of public mental health institutions, and school desegregation involving major changes in the operation of entire public educational systems.[31] Some courts have been involved in statewide reforms in each of these areas. As mentioned in Chapter 1, in the early 1980s, about half of Boston's budgetary appropriations were "presided over" by federal and state judges.[32] There are two key aspects of judicially fostered reforms of this nature. First, generally speaking, the courts do not actually *require* a legislature to spend money on a function such as incarceration or public mental health care. Rather, the judicial logic is essentially stated to the legislature as follows: "You don't have to run prisons, mental health facilities, or public schools, but if you choose to do so, then you must not violate the constitutional rights of prisoners, patients, and students in the process."[33] Thus, the legislature is given a way out—it does not have to maintain the function or appropriate money to bring it up to constitutional standards. But the choice is often a hollow one. States may curtail some public mental health care or educational programs, but they are highly unlikely to stop imprisoning or institutionalizing dangerous persons or to terminate a public role in education. Nevertheless, by framing the issue in this fashion, the courts avoid the necessity of forcing the states to budget funds for any specific function.

Second, the judiciary is cognizant of the costs of its decrees, but overall, it does not consider limited resources to be a legitimate excuse for failing to protect someone's constitutional rights. As one court put it, "Inadequate resources can never be adequate justification for the state's depriving any person of his constitutional rights."[34]

In the abstract this approach may not present any particular issues in terms of budgeting. However, in concrete terms genuine allocational problems do arise. For instance, one court decreed that the state's mental health facilities would have to have at least one shower or tub for each fifteen patients, at least one toilet for each eight patients, no single room with less than one hundred square feet of floor space, and a temperature range between 68 and 83 degrees Fahrenheit.[35] In addition it ordered that more staff be hired. These reforms cost money; where will it come from? This is a question that the judges do not have to address directly. They do not know if the funds will come from housing programs for the elderly, nutrition programs for malnourished elementary school pupils, or the taxpayers in general. By seeking to define the rights of some groups in isolation from all the competing potential claims on the public treasury, the courts do not have to balance the constitutional rights of some against the economic needs of others. In short, the courts do not consider the possible trade-off of more floor space for the insane leading to less for the elderly. This fits the judiciary's historic role in protecting members of the political community who are inadequately protected or represented by the other branches of government. But it also fragments the budgetary process even further, since in a practical sense the judges are allocating money for some groups of people without assessing their claims relative to those of other groups. The judiciary is generally inclined to rely on a contractarian, as opposed to utilitarian, basis for fundamental rights. The legislature, in turn, may victimize other politically weak groups who remain without meaningful judicial protection. This would occur, for example, if a state raised the temperature in its mental health facilities with money that previously would have gone into public housing for the elderly or poor. No doubt a public administrator in charge of such a housing program would find it frustrating to see appropriations earmarked for that function shifted to upgrading conditions in the mental hospitals.

Yet the judicial influence on budgeting does not have to be so dramatic. There are countless public administrative activities and programs that tend to spend more money in one neighborhood than another. Schools, streets, lighting, sanitation, building inspection, police, and fire protection are some of the leading examples. Would unequal allocations be unconstitutional in violation of equal protection where neighborhoods evidenced a great deal of residential segregation by race or ethnicity, by age, or by wealth? The answers to these questions depend upon the precise nature of the functions, the administrative intent in providing them on an unequal basis, and the nature of the social divisions among the neighborhoods. In some cases involving schools and public works, however, courts have found that the equal protection rights of the residents were violated by unequal spending. In such instances, judicial decisions force a reallocation of funds that can have a substantial impact on the budgets of local governments or even states.[36]

The judiciary may also have an impact on the raising of revenues through taxation. There is an issue of intergovernmental immunity, which may make taxes of the federal and state governments upon each other unconstitutional. State taxation of corporations doing business both within and outside of the state can also be the basis of complicated litigation. Indeed, judicial involvement in tax policy has been so extensive that the federal government was prevented by court decision from levying a progressive income tax until the Sixteenth Amendment to the Constitution was adopted.[37]

This is not the place to present a tome on tax law or judicial influence on the public budgetary process generally. It is enough to alert the student of public administration to the reality of judicial involvement in the budgetary process, to have identified the rationale for its activity, and to note some of the concerns associated with it. Above all, however, the public administrator must remember that the courts have become a partner in public administration and that their expanded role promotes justice, but also inevitably complicates budgetary processes and decisions.

CONCLUSION: THE SEARCH FOR A SYNTHESIS

It is evident that the managerial, political, and judicial approaches all identify important concerns in the area of public budgeting. It is also apparent that the approaches are at odds with one another at a number of points. What are the prospects for synthesis? At present, one would have to respond, "Not good!" The judicial influence does not seem to lend itself readily to integration with executive and legislative budgetary processes. Managerial and incremental budgeting can be combined to an extent, but performance and program budgeting appear to be inherently at odds with the incremental approach. Still, progress can be made if we avoid across-the-board approaches in developing budgetary strategies. Clearly managerial orientations are appropriate for some governmental functions, but not for others. Many of the functions of local governments are particularly subject to improvement through PPBS and ZBB approaches—and these strategies have been more successful at that level than in the federal government. On the other hand, incremental approaches are useful when it is politically difficult to establish clear objectives and priorities without denying some groups representation and weakening consensus and political coalitions. One approach to synthesis therefore is to "fudge" the issue somewhat. This appears to have been what happened with the federal experience with ZBB. Where ZBB's assumptions did fit the nature of programs and agencies, ZBB was used in a sensible fashion. However, where this managerial approach simply did not fit, whole agencies might be defined as decision units, objectives might be defined in vague, unoperational terms, and analysis might be perfunctory. This enabled such agencies to recast the incremental approach into the language and form of ZBB. Another possibility is to admit openly that there cannot be a single budget process and to treat different agencies and programs differently. The continuing federal budgetary crisis spawned the innovative Gramm-Rudman process. Experience with it may lead to other reforms and the development of new budgetary techniques. Whatever course is chosen in the future, however, one thing is certain—budgeting will remain an area of controversy and high interest to public administrators, elected officials, political executives, interest groups, commercial interests, and the public at large. The way in which budgetary questions are framed has a great deal to do with the outcome of contests for public budgetary dollars. Both the budget *process* and budget *allocations* are of critical political, economic, and organizational importance in the modern administrative state.

NOTES

1. Robert Lorch, *State and Local Politics*, 2nd ed. (Englewood Cliffs, N.J.: Prentice-Hall, 1986), pp. 302–303.
2. See Morris P. Fiorina, *Congress: Keystone of the Washington Establishment* (New Haven, Conn.: Yale University Press, 1977); Edward R. Tufte, "Determinants of the

Outcomes of Midterm Congressional Elections," *American Political Science Review*, 69 (1975): 812–826.

3. Gary Klott, *Complete Guide to the New Tax Law* (New York: Times Books, 1986), p. 30.

4. John Maynard Keynes, *The General Theory of Employment, Interest, and Money* (New York: Harcourt, Brace, and World, 1935).

5. See Tufte, "Determinants of the Outcomes of Midterm Congressional Elections."

6. A useful place to start on this issue is Charles Schultze, *The Politics and Economics of Public Spending* (Washington, D.C.: Brookings, 1968).

7. Klott, *Complete Guide to the New Tax Law*, p. 37.

8. Peter Kilborn, "Where the Reagan Revolution Went Awry," *New York Times*, November 8, 1987, sec. 4, p. 1. The facts reported in the paragraph are from this source.

9. Susan Tolchin and Martin Tolchin, *Dismantling America: The Rush to Deregulate* (Boston: Houghton Mifflin, 1983).

10. Jonathan Fuerbringer and Nathaniel Nash, "Seven Ways to Reinvent the Budget Process," *New York Times*, September 27, 1987, p. E-5, quoting Louis Fisher.

11. See Stanley Collender, *The Guide to the Federal Budget: Fiscal 1988* (Washington, D.C.: The Urban Institute Press, 1987), for a detailed discussion.

12. The technicalities of sequestration are very complicated. Part of the original process was declared unconstitutional by the Supreme Court in *Bowsher* v. *Synar*, 92 L. Ed. 2d 583 (1986). See Collender, *The Guide to the Federal Budget: Fiscal 1988*, chap. 7, for a more detailed discussion.

13. *Immigration and Naturalization Service* v. *Chadha*, 462 U.S. 919 (1983).

14. *City of New Haven* v. *United States*, U.S.C.A., D.C., No. 86-5319 (January 20, 1987).

15. See Louis Fisher, *Presidential Spending Power* (Princeton, N.J.: Princeton University Press, 1975).

16. For a comprehensive discussion, see Aaron Wildavsky, *The Politics of the Budgetary Process*, 4th ed. (Boston: Little, Brown, 1984).

17. Lorch, *State and Local Politics*, 2d ed., chap. 11.

18. V. O. Key, Jr., "The Lack of a Budgetary Theory," *American Political Science Review*, 34 (December 1940): 1137–1140.

19. Catheryn Seckler-Hudson, "Performance Budgeting in Government," in Albert Hyde and Jay M. Shafritz, eds., *Government Budgeting* (Oak Park, Ill.: Moore, 1978), pp. 80–93, especially p. 81.

20. Hyde and Shafritz, *Government Budgeting*, includes several works on this subject. See section III.

21. Elizabeth Drew, "HEW Grapples with PPBS," *The Public Interest*, 8 (Summer 1967): 9–27.

22. Allen Schick, "A Death in the Bureaucracy: The Demise of Federal PPB," *Public Administration Review*, 33 (March/April 1973): 146–156.

23. See Graeme M. Taylor, "Introduction to Zero-Base Budgeting," in Hyde and Shafritz, *Government Budgeting*, pp. 271–284, esp. p. 273; and Peter A. Pyhrr, *Zero-Base Budgeting* (New York: John Wiley, 1973).

24. Peter A. Pyhrr, "Zero-Base Approach to Government Budgeting," *Public Administration Review*, 37 (January/February 1977): 1–8.

25. *Houston Post*, April 8, 1977, p. 14A. See also Robert Anthony, "Zero-Base Budgeting Is a Fraud," *Wall Street Journal*, April 27, 1977.

26. Aaron Wildavsky, "The Political Economy of Efficiency: Cost-Benefit Analysis,

Systems Analysis, and Program Budgeting," *Public Administration Review*, 26 (December 1966): 292–310.

27. A. Lee Fritschler, *Smoking and Politics* (New York: Appleton-Century-Crofts, 1969).

28. For some of the dynamics, see Samuel Lubell, *The Future of American Politics* (Garden City, N.Y.: Doubleday Anchor, 1955).

29. Wildavsky, "The Political Economy of Efficiency," p. 26.

30. Aaron Wildavsky and Arthur Hammond, "Comprehensive Versus Incremental Budgeting in the Department of Agriculture," pp. 236–251, in Hyde and Shafritz, *Governmental Budgeting*, at p. 237.

31. David H. Rosenbloom, *Public Administration and Law* (New York: Marcel Dekker, 1983), and Donald Horowitz, *The Courts and Social Policy* (Washington, D.C.: Brookings, 1977).

32. Robert Turner, "Governing from the Bench," *The Boston Globe Magazine*, November 8, 1981, p. 13.

33. In one case, a Virginia county was required to maintain a public school system because in abandoning it, the county was seeking to prevent racial integration; Griffin v. County School Board of Prince Edward County, 377 U.S. 218 (1964). See also Richard Lehne, *The Quest for Justice* (New York: Longman, 1978).

34. Hamilton v. Love, 328 F. Supp. 1182, 1194 (1971).

35. Wyatt v. Stickney, 325 F. Supp. 781 (1971), et seq. See also "The *Wyatt* Case: Implementation of a Judicial Decree Ordering Institutional Change," *Yale Law Journal*, 84 (1975): 1338–1379.

36. Hawkins v. Town of Shaw, 437 F.2d 1286 (1971); San Antonio Independent School District v. Rodriguez, 411 U.S. 1 (1973); Lehne, *The Quest for Justice*; Horowitz, *The Courts and Social Policy*, chap. 4.

37. Pollock v. Farmers Loan & Trust Co., 158 U.S. 601 (1895). For a brief discussion, see J. W. Peltason, *Corwin & Peltason's Understanding the Constitution*, 7th ed. (Hinsdale, Ill.: Dryden Press, 1976), pp. 207–208.

ADDITIONAL READING

Burkhead, Jesse. *Governmental Budgeting*. New York: Wiley, 1956.

Fisher, Louis. *Presidential Spending Power*. Princeton, N.J.: Princeton University Press, 1975.

Hyde, Albert C., and Jay M. Shafritz, eds. *Government Budgeting*. Oak Park, Ill.: Moore, 1978.

LeLoup, Lance. *Budgetary Politics*, 3rd ed. Brunswick, Ohio: King's Court, 1986.

Lyden, Fremont, and Marc Lindenberg. *Public Budgeting*. New York: Longman, 1983.

Pyhrr, Peter A. *Zero-Base Budgeting*. New York: Wiley, 1973.

Wildavsky, Aaron. *The New Politics of the Budgetary Process*. Glenview, Ill.: Scott, Foresman, 1988.

STUDY QUESTIONS

1. Some advocate a constitutional amendment that would require the federal government to balance its budget on an annual basis. What would be the chief advantages and disadvantages of such an amendment? Do you favor it? Should such an amendment have a clause allowing an unbalanced budget in times of emergency?

2. What kinds of changes in U.S. government and politics would make program budgeting easier to apply? Would you favor such changes?

3. Think of a recent political campaign that involved the issue of government spending. Evaluate the candidates' remarks and positions on matters of spending, taxation, and budgeting. Whose position would you support, and why?

4. What are the fundamental differences between the budgetary process in the federal government and in the state where you reside? What are some of the major consequences of these differences?

CHAPTER 7 | *Decision Making*

This chapter reviews varied approaches to decision making, which many view as the essence of higher-level public administration. The managerial approach to decision making relies on bureaucratic organization to promote rationality. It favors rational-comprehensive decision making that specifies objectives and identifies the most satisfactory means of achieving them. Many believe that this approach does not fit the U.S. political system well. The political approach favors a kind of pluralistic give and take in decision making. This permits coalition building but generally leads to incremental decisions that modify past policies only relatively slightly. The legal approach favors an adjudicatory model. An approach called "mixed scanning" is a partial synthesis of these three approaches. No matter what approach is taken, however, there are important pitfalls to be avoided when making administrative decisions; a list of common ones is considered toward the end of the chapter. Finally, a major issue for the future is raised: How profoundly will the use of computers affect both our thinking about administrative decision making and the actual deciding?

Public administration involves the formulation and implementation of public policies intended to provide services and/or impose regulations upon individuals, groups, and organizations in the political community. Consequently, a large part of the job of some public administrators requires that they make decisions defining the objectives of public policies and choose appropriate means for achieving them. In essence, administrative decision making is simply the choice from among competing alternatives of the ends and means that an administrative program or organization will pursue and employ. But how should public administrators go about the business of deciding among these alternatives? How, in practice, do they actually decide? How can administrative decision making be improved? What are the inherent limitations on administrative decision making? These are important administrative questions that should be considered by students and practitioners of public administration. This chapter will address them by considering the managerial, political, and legal approaches to administrative decision making and by considering a technique that can serve as a partial synthesis.

THE MANAGERIAL APPROACH TO DECISION MAKING

The managerial approach to public administration stresses the need for rationality in decision making. It also seeks to enable public administrators to make rational decisions in the most efficient, economical, and effective manner. One way to introduce rationality into the decision-making process is to design a system that helps the public administrator choose from among competing alternatives by (1) reducing the number of alternatives that need to be considered, (2) reducing the number of values that must be assessed in making a choice from among the alternatives, (3) assuring that the administrator knows how to make a rational choice, and (4) providing the administrator with sufficient information to select from among the alternatives. In very large part, such an organizational design will be bureaucratic.

Specialization

Specialization is the preeminent means of reducing the number of alternatives that a public administrator can consider when making a decision. Jurisdictional specialization among public agencies confines the authority of public administrators to relatively well-defined areas of public policy. For instance, the public administrator in the Department of Agriculture does not have to be concerned with issues of national security under the jurisdiction of the Department of Defense. Nor do public administrators in different agencies need to determine the social value of the various programs they administer as compared to those implemented by other agencies. Specialization within agencies has a similar effect. Some public administrators will formulate policies and rules, whereas others will enforce them. Even though the two acts are obviously and intimately connected (or at least should be), the individual engaged in enforcement may be in a position to make some choices over means, but is generally not in a position to consider the objective of the rule or policy itself. For example, a public personnel administrator engaged in the enforcement of an affirmative action program may be able to make choices as to the content of goals for hiring and promoting women and members of minority groups. If resources are scarce, such an administrator may also have to decide in which agencies and at what grade levels such goals ought to be established and filled. A wide variety of additional decisions may also have to be made by such an official. However, being charged with enforcement, the public administrator in question will not have jurisdictional authority to determine that affirmative action is an inappropriate means of pursuing equal opportunity, or more drastically, that equal opportunity is not an objective with which public personnel administrators should be concerned. Of course, many cases are much more mundane, as when a public manager in charge of any particular unit is concerned solely with the internal operating efficiency and effectiveness of that unit. Specialization breaks up the functions of public agencies into manageable units; therefore, the questions, issues, problems, and alternatives facing any given individual public administrator will be limited accordingly.

Specialization also limits the values that a public administrator must take into account in making choices from among competing alternatives. Public administrators must be concerned with promoting the public interest as it relates to their authority. They are not free to choose from among policy alternatives in an unfettered fashion. For instance, the Department of the Interior is charged with promoting conservation of the nation's natural resources. It is not free to decide that conservation is a senseless public policy and that the agency should concentrate its efforts on assuring exploitation and consumption. Similarly, since the FCC is charged with regulating the nation's airwaves in the public interest, necessity, or convenience, it is not free to eliminate all television broadcasting on the grounds that if people watched less TV they would probably read more books and that would be better for the nation's intellectual health. Sometimes the political heads of agencies do try to depart radically from an agency's historic values, but this almost always causes turmoil in the administrative structure and is seldom fully successful. Thus, for the public administrator, the question in decision making is, "Within the set of values embodied in my official authority, what should and can be done?"

Answers may be narrowed by "premise controls." Specialization can affect the cognitive premises and thought patterns of individuals. Being socialized into and working in a bureaucracy, a skilled trade, or a profession often has an impact on the way people define situations. The decision maker "voluntarily restricts the range of stimulii that will be attended to ('Those sorts of things are irrelevant,' or 'What has that got to do with the matter?') and the range of alternatives that would be considered ('It would never occur to me to do that')."[1] The importance of premise controls varies not only with the nature of specialization but also with the character and level of work. Charles Perrow explains:

Premise controls are most important when work is nonroutine . . . and this is one reason scientists and other professionals have such latitude in organizations. Their premises are well set in their training institutions and professional associations. Premise controls are also most important near the top of the organization because managerial work there is less routine, [and] the consequences of decisions are hard to assess immediately. . . . But . . . premise controls exist at all levels, created and reinforced by schools, the mass media, and cultural institutions in general.[2]

Hierarchy

The hierarchical nature of bureaucratic organizations also narrows the range of choices available to decision makers. Hierarchy defines the authority of public administrators. Typically, those with less authority have more limited choices confronting them. Some public administrators make virtually no important decisions, but rather handle a large number of repetitive, routine cases. They simply determine whether the case at hand fits one category or another—and they do so without exercising any significant discretion. An example would be an employee in a motor vehicle department who administers an eye test. Criteria for passing are established elsewhere in the organization, and the employee at the testing station simply observes whether a particular individual has met those criteria.

However, even as one goes up the organizational ranks to positions with substantial authority over specific programs, hierarchy continues to limit the responsibility of officials and thus helps to define the values with which they must be concerned. This is not to say that mid-level public administrators have no difficult choices to make. But it is only when one reaches the very top levels of an organizational structure that it is typically necessary to consider choices from among a wide variety of competing and conflicting values.

To some extent, as this discussion suggests, specialization and hierarchy tend to overlap one another in the sense of limiting authority. But the distinction is within the kind of authority being limited: specialization limits jurisdictional authority, whereas hierarchy limits managerial authority. The difference is somewhat subtle but it can be conveyed in the distinction between the following two statements: "I'm not responsible for what they do in that operation" (specialization) and "I don't make the rules" (hierarchy). In sum, hierarchy enables those with superior authority to define and limit the value choices available to subordinates. Although this process has informal aspects, in bureaucratic organizations it is often maintained through formal requirements.

Formalization

Formalization is particularly important in facilitating decision making through reducing alternatives available by specifying precisely the factors and information to be taken into account in exercising choice. As the term "formalization" suggests, standardized forms may be used to solicit the information that is deemed by the public agency to be relevant to its decision making. Certain information is included; other information is excluded. The exclusion, in particular, tends to simplify decision making because it limits what must be considered. However, exclusions may prevent individuals from presenting mitigating information. For example, at one time, several states had long residency requirements for those seeking welfare benefits. These were intended to prevent individuals from moving into the states in order to receive benefits that were higher than those available elsewhere. But the application processes did not ascertain the individual's intent or reasons for migrating to the state, which could well have involved family matters such as moving in with one's parents or other relatives. Rather, the regulations and formal process assumed that newcomers were drawn by higher benefits and attributed this motive to all of them. Eventually such residency requirements were declared unconstitutional,[3] but they remain a vivid illustration of how formalization is used to assure that if the organization does not anticipate its relevance, some information will be ignored by it. In a case like the one just described, formalization is used to attain the goals of impersonality and procedural equality (see Chapter 1).

Formalization may also include a more direct statement of values. It can indicate to a decision maker the relative weight to be assigned to different factors when there is a potential conflict among them. A clear statement of this kind can be found in the U.S. Civil Service Commission's early set of instructions on affirmative action: "Agency action plans and instructions involving goals and timetables must state that all actions to achieve goals must be in full compliance with merit system requirements."[4] This clearly placed the value of merit above that of social representation in federal personnel administration. For those making decisions on the implementation of affirmative action, the CSC's statement of values acted as a constraint that substantially reduced the alternative courses of action permissible.

Merit

The managerial approach to public administration also affects the decision-making process by seeking to assure that public administrators have the technical ability to make the most rational choices. It also seeks to guarantee that they will use this ability free of partisan political considerations. The quest for technical expertise and nonpartisanship is embodied in the merit system. Competent employees are defined as those who are able to understand the jobs they are hired to do, who can process the information before them, and who can grasp such concepts as specialization and hierarchy. They are further expected to perform their functions efficiently. Their actions are to be governed by the agency's hierarchy, rules, and values, as well as by the rule of law. They are not supposed to take their personal political beliefs or affiliations into account when implementing the will of the legislature or of their superordinates.

The constraints of the managerial approach on decision making are frequently reinforced by the development of **agency cultures.** These develop as agencies begin to express a consistent set of values, as they recruit individuals for their highest career positions who reflect these values, and as the values become expressed through procedural mechanisms and formalization. According to Harold Seidman, for instance: "Each agency has its own culture and internal set of loyalties and values which are likely to guide its actions and influence its policies." Therefore, "institutional responses are highly predictable. . . ."[5]

In the ways described above, the managerial approach promotes an organizational design that has a very important impact on public administrative decision making. The approach necessarily accepts the reality of "bounded rationality" (see Chapter 4), since not all the consequences of a complex decision are likely to be known in advance. However, it attempts to enhance rationality through specialization, hierarchy, formalization, and technical competence.

The effort to structure decision making for rationality sometimes takes the form of "grid regulations" ("grid regs"). Grid regs display the intent of written rules in tabular form. Box 7–1 presents an example of the grid regs developed for the Social Security Disability Insurance (SSDI) program. The agency's rules make SSDI available when there is no job in the national economy that the impaired individual can perform on a sustained basis. The regulations in Box 7–1 categorize work as "light" (rule 202) and "medium" (rule 204). Age, education, and previous work experience are taken as the determinants of disability. Rule 202.01 states that an impaired worker of advanced age (55 and over), who has limited education and is unskilled should be considered disabled. By contrast, rule 202.03 places an individual of the same age and education but with transferable skills in the category of "not disabled."

Grid regs clearly reduce the discretion of individual administrators and hearing examiners in determining the status of the individuals whose cases are before them. They clarify policy and promote uniform treatment. They prevent decision makers from taking factors that the rules consider extraneous into account. At the same time though, the regulations make it difficult or impossible for hearing examiners to assess the personal situation of each claimant. Consequently, an individual closely approaching advanced age (50 to 54) will sometimes be treated differently from one who is 55, even though for all other intents and purposes there is no significant physical or mental difference between them. Consequently, the rationality of grid regs very much depends upon the appropriateness of the categories that they incorporate.[6]

The managerial approach to decision making can generate a number of techniques. MBO and PERT (discussed in Chapter 4), are examples. But most generally, the managerial approach favors what is known as the rational-comprehensive model of decision making.[7]

The Rational-Comprehensive Model

Determining Objectives   In simplified form, the rational-comprehensive model consists of the following steps. In making decisions, the public administrator must first determine what are the objectives of public policy. These objectives should be identified in operational terms, in ways that can be observed and, better still, measured. Again, equal employment opportunity (EEO) as applied

BOX 7–1 **Social Security Disability Insurance "Grid Regs"**

RESIDUAL FUNCTIONAL CAPACITY: MAXIMUM SUSTAINED WORK CAPABILITY LIMITED TO LIGHT AND MEDIUM WORK AS A RESULT OF SEVERE MEDICALLY DETERMINABLE IMPAIRMENT(S)

Rule	Age*	Education	Previous work experience	Decision
202.01	Advanced age	Limited or less	Unskilled or none	Disabled
202.02	do†	do	Skilled or semiskilled—skills not transferable	Do
202.03	do	do	Skilled or semiskilled—skills transferable	Not disabled
202.04	do	High school graduate or more—does not provide for direct entry into skilled work	Unskilled or none	Disabled
202.05	Advanced age	High school graduate or more—provides for direct entry into skilled work	Unskilled or none	Not disabled
202.06	do	High school graduate or more—does not provide for direct entry into skilled work	Skilled or semiskilled—skills not transferable	Disabled
202.07	do	do	Skilled or semiskilled—skills transferable	Not disabled
202.08	do	High school graduate or more—provides for direct entry into skilled work	Skilled or semiskilled—skills not transferable	Do
202.09	Closely approaching advanced age	Illiterate or unable to communicate in English	Unskilled or none	Disabled
202.10	do	Limited or less—at least literate and able to communicate in English	do	Not disabled
202.11	do	Limited or less	Skilled or semiskilled—skills not transferable	Do
202.12	do	do	Skilled or semiskilled—skills transferable	Do
202.13	do	High school graduate or more	Unskilled or none	Do
202.14	do	do	Skilled or semiskilled—skills not transferable	Do
202.15	do	do	Skilled or semiskilled—skills transferable	Do
202.16	Younger individual	Illiterate or unable to communicate in English	Unskilled or none	Do
202.17	do	Limited or less—at least literate and able to communicate in English	do	Do
202.18	do	Limited or less	Skilled or semiskilled—skills not transferable	Do
202.19	do	do	Skilled or semiskilled—skills transferable	Do

BOX 7–1 *Continued*

RESIDUAL FUNCTIONAL CAPACITY: MAXIMUM SUSTAINED WORK CAPABILITY LIMITED TO LIGHT AND MEDIUM WORK AS A RESULT OF SEVERE MEDICALLY DETERMINABLE IMPAIRMENT(S)

Rule	Age*	Education	Previous work experience	Decision
202.20	do	High school graduate or more	Unskilled or none	Do
202.21	do	do	Skilled or semiskilled—skills not transferable	Do
202.22	do	do	Skilled or semiskilled—skills transferable	Do
203.01	Closely approaching retirement age	Marginal or none	Unskilled or none	Disabled
203.02	do	Limited or less	None	Do
203.03	do	Limited	Unskilled	Not disabled
203.04	do	Limited or less	Skilled or semiskilled—skills not transferable	Do
203.05	do	do	Skilled or semiskilled—skills transferable	Do
203.06	do	High school graduate or more	Unskilled or none	Do
203.07	do	High school graduate or more—does not provide for direct entry into skilled work	Skilled or semiskilled—skills not transferable	Do
203.08	do	do	Skilled or semiskilled—skills transferable	Do
203.09	do	High school graduate or more—provides for direct entry into skilled work	Skilled or semiskilled—skills not transferable	Do
203.10	Advanced age	Limited or less	None	Disabled
203.11	do	do	Unskilled	Not disabled
203.12	do	do	Skilled or semiskilled—skills not transferable	Do
203.13	do	do	Skilled or semiskilled—skills transferable	Do
203.14	do	High school graduate or more	Unskilled or none	Do
203.15	do	High school graduate or more—does not provide for direct entry into skilled work	Skilled or semiskilled—skills not transferable	Do
203.16	do	do	Skilled or semiskilled—skills transferable	Do
203.17	do	High school graduate or more—provides for direct entry into skilled work	Skilled or semiskilled—skills not transferable	Do
203.18	Closely approaching advanced age	Limited or less	Unskilled or none	Do
203.19	do	do	Skilled or semiskilled—skills not transferable	Do
203.20	do	do	Skilled or semiskilled—skills transferable	Do

BOX 7–1 *Continued*

RESIDUAL FUNCTIONAL CAPACITY: MAXIMUM SUSTAINED WORK CAPABILITY LIMITED TO LIGHT AND MEDIUM WORK AS A RESULT OF SEVERE MEDICALLY DETERMINABLE IMPAIRMENT(S)

Rule	Age*	Education	Previous work experience	Decision
203.21	do	High school graduate or more	Unskilled or none	Do
203.22	do	High school graduate or more—does not provide for direct entry into skilled work	Skilled or semiskilled—skills not transferable	Do
203.23	do	do	Skilled or semiskilled—skills transferable	
203.24	do	High school graduate or more—provides for direct entry into skilled work	Skilled or semiskilled—skills not transferable	Do
203.25	Younger individual	Limited or less	Unskilled or none	Do
203.26	do	do	Skilled or semiskilled—skills not transferable	Do
203.27	do	do	Skilled or semiskilled—skills transferable	Do
203.28	do	High school graduate or more	Unskilled or none	Do
203.29	do	High school graduate or more—does not provide for direct entry into skilled work	Skilled or semiskilled—skills not transferable	Do
203.30	do	do	Skilled or semiskilled—skills transferable	Do
203.31	do	High school graduate or more—provides for direct entry into skilled work	Skilled or semiskilled—skills not transferable	Do

* Advanced age = 55 and over; closely approaching advanced age = 50–54; younger individual = 18–49.
† do = Ditto

SOURCE: U.S. Department of Health and Human Services, Social Security Administration; regulations in *U.S. Federal Register*, vol. 43, pp. 55368–55370, November 28, 1978.

to the public sector provides a good example. If the objective is defined as equal opportunity in public employment, then the objective will necessarily remain vague and difficult to implement. Equal opportunity may be undefinable. (Is it simply nondiscrimination, or equalizing opportunity by equalizing education, nutrition, housing, etc., or is it actually compensating for the disadvantages placed upon groups by the society?) Nor can EEO be seen or measured directly, though some surrogate indicators can be developed. If, on the other hand, equal opportunity is defined as the social representation of groups in the public sector work force, there will be an objective that can be readily observed and measured. Social representation is simply far more tangible than opportunity. It is important to stress, however, that as discussed above, the public administrator does not have a free hand in establishing objectives. He or she is constrained by authority, specialization, hierarchy, law, and political factors. If the legislature is completely clear about what it wants, it will severely reduce the alternatives available to the public administrator trying to interpret its will.

Considering the Means   Once the objectives of public policy are established, various means for accomplishing them must be considered. If the requisite comprehensiveness is to be achieved, virtually all the potential means that can be identified must be scrutinized. This may require heavy reliance on theory, since it is highly unlikely that all the potential means have at one time or another been tested and evaluated in actual practice. According to the rational-comprehensive model, in considering the potential means to the objectives, the public administrator is required to try to project *all* the consequences of each of the means on all the various areas of governmental concern.

Continuing with the equal employment opportunity/affirmative action example, several means could be identified. Assuming that the objective is defined in terms of social representation, as is actually the case, then the use of goals and timetables for the recruitment and promotion of members of specified minority groups and women can be viewed as one appropriate means. Similarly, protections might be afforded members of these groups in reductions in force. In addition, various special training programs to promote their upward mobility in the civil service could be developed. Other potential means include governmental programs, similar to those used by the military, to fund students' college and graduate educations in return for the students' commitment to join the civil service for a specified number of years. The elimination of veteran preference would be a means of promoting the employment of women. The objective of social representation could also be achieved by firing nonminorities (white males) to make room for blacks, Hispanics, women, and other affirmative action target groups. Another possibility would be eliminating competitive merit exams and the "rule of three" (see Chapter 5) in favor of pass exams and selection by race, ethnicity, and/or gender. One could go on and on identifying potential means in this context, and that is precisely what the rational-comprehensive model seeks to assure.

Choosing the Best Alternative   Once all the potential means for achieving an end are identified, it is necessary to choose among them. According to the managerial approach, this choice should be made so as to maximize efficiency, economy, and effectiveness. Where these three values are not in full harmony with one another, an appropriate balance is to be struck among them. Although the latter may prove difficult, there is no doubt that these values can serve as helpful guides. For instance, in terms of affirmative action, they would probably rule out establishing programs to pay for the higher education of women and members of minority groups in return for a commitment on their part to work for a relatively short period. Eliminating competitive exams and the rule of three could prove very expensive in terms of the mechanics of recruitment and selection. Affording large-scale training to minorities and women might also prove very expensive. Aside from potential political and legal problems, firing white males could lead to widespread demoralization and inefficiency. On the other hand, relying solely upon goals and timetables for recruitment and selection might prove ineffective in bringing about change. In order to chose the most desirable means under such circumstances, a program might be developed using goals and timetables, training, aggressive recruitment of women and members of minority groups, the modification of veteran preference, affirmative action preferences in reductions in force, and various personnel devices to relax the harsh effects of competitive examinations and the rule of three. The result, at least in theory, is a comprehensive program designed to operate within the confines of what is acceptable in terms of efficiency, economy, and effectiveness. Whether such a program can be applied in practice, given political and legal constraints, however, is another matter.

Critique of the Rational-Comprehensive Model

The rational-comprehensive model, derived from managerial perspectives on public administration, has some important benefits. It is comprehensive and provides a good deal of direction in the choice of potential means to identified policy objectives. It encourages the public administrator to think a problem through and to apply his or her technical expertise in identifying the best solution. If we look upon public administrative decision making as a problem-solving endeavor, then the rational-comprehensive model is often very useful. Nevertheless, in practice this model is not always suitable to the actual nature of governmental decision making. First, the objectives of governmental

By permission of Robbin T. Armstrong and The Daily Orange Corporation.

Comprehensive Irrational Decision-making Style

1° policies are not always clear. For instance, the Department of the Interior is charged with making sure that there is an "equitable" distribution of the benefits from nationally owned land and resources. But what does that mean? What is equitable in this context? What kind of technical expertise does the public administrator possess to define "equitable" in meaningful and politically acceptable terms? Similarly, many agencies are charged with doing one thing or another "in the public interest." Although it is probably necessary for the political community to believe that there *is* a public interest, it may be impossible to identify what the public interest requires in operational terms. This is because as soon as we become specific, we tend to generate conflict. For instance, veterans may agree that equal employment opportunity is in the public interest, but they are likely to disagree that, therefore, the public interest requires the elimination of preferences for their own group. In pluralistic politics, consensus is built by developing inclusive coalitions that tend to offer something to many significant political groups, without being very specific concerning the aims of a policy and the priorities within it. Looking at EEO in the federal government, we can see the effect of this tendency. The program was established with a clear focus on black employment; subsequently, women and Hispanics were included within its ambit; today, it includes not only these groups but also Native Americans, Pacific Islanders, Asian Americans, veterans, and the handicapped. In some localities, homosexuals have sought to be included within equal opportunity/affirmative action programs. This approach builds broad coalitions supporting the public administrators' programs, but it makes it difficult to say precisely what a program's goals are in operational terms or to establish priorities. Thus, veterans' preference has an adverse impact on the employment interests of women. Nor are the employment interests of blacks and Hispanics identical. Gains for one group are not necessarily associated with greater employment opportunity for the other.[8]

2° A second problem with the rational-comprehensive model is that it assumes that public administrators have the time to approach problems in a dispassionate way, to identify comprehensively all the potential means of achieving identified objectives, and to assess all these means in terms of efficiency, economy, and effectiveness. While circumstances in which the public administrator is truly proactive in this fashion may exist, many practitioners of public administration would find such a scenario quite alien to their work environment. To a very large extent, public administration in the United States is not proactive, but rather reactive. It requires that public administrators react relatively quickly to problems, deadlines, or crises. Many hardly have enough time to identify even one potential means toward an end, much less to try to identify all potential means and then determine which is best in terms of efficiency, economy, and effectiveness.

3° Another difficulty with the rational-comprehensive approach is that the very specialization of which it makes such strong use may also become a liability. We are all familiar with the image of the government's right hand not knowing what the left one is doing. This is because the hands operate in different spheres, under different time constraints, and with different objectives in mind. But modern government, of course, has more than two hands; it has almost countless tentacles. The public administrator operating one of these is bound, on occasion, to be at odds with the actions of another. This is how the State Department came to back one side in the 1971 India-Pakistan War while the Department of Defense backed the other.[9] Or how one agency seeks to preserve wilderness and wetland areas while another fights to develop it. Returning to our familiar EEO/AA example, an EEO office would probably oppose programs for comprehensive labor relations, since these would make priorities in reductions-in-force a subject for collective bargaining, in which the interests of minority workers might not be well protected.

To some extent, specialization also makes it difficult to assess the full costs of any particular governmental course of action. An agency making decisions in a complex policy area is likely to create new problems for other agencies. For instance, when the Department of Defense seeks to deploy a new advanced weapons system or NASA undertakes a new program of space exploration, it will inevitably have consequences for other governmental programs, including those concerned with exploiting and stockpiling strategic resources and programs dealing with scientific education. In terms of the rational-comprehensive model, the problem is that these costs are difficult to assess because they tend to get lost in the system of specialized jurisdictions. The problem is compounded by the fact that as the administrative state grows, less and less is truly external to governmental concerns, so even costs that are shifted from government to society tend to eventually become a public policy concern.

A final criticism of the rational-comprehensive model is that because it relies on theory and abstract expertise, it can produce decisions that are inappropriate in terms of practice. This allegedly is one reason why centralized planning has not worked out as well as anticipated in a variety of political communities.[10] It also partly explains why various budgeting techniques, such as PPBS and ZBB, have not worked out as well as anticipated in the United States (see Chapter 6).

THE POLITICAL APPROACH TO DECISION MAKING: THE INCREMENTAL MODEL

Critics of the rational-comprehensive model of decision making argue that it is unrealistic, that it does not fit the nature of contemporary administrative operations, and that it requires administrators to exercise a degree of rationality and comprehensive expertise that is beyond their ability. These critics suggest that another process is more suitable to the public sector in the United States—a process that has been dubbed the **incremental model**.[11] It is important to note that discussions of this model develop a dual argument. First, that the incremental approach is in fact the approach most characteristic of public administrative operations in the United States, and second, that it is the model that *should* be relied upon to the greatest extent. Its proponents claim that it fits the nature of United States politics and political institutions to a great extent and that it is a model that public administrators can actually apply. As will become evident, the incremental model is highly compatible with the political approach to public administration.

It is generally maintained that the incremental model recognizes the vagueness of many of the stated objectives of public policy. Such vagueness is considered endemic in a pluralistic political community and often seems to be the price of building a consensus strong enough to operate administrative programs at all. Politics, in this view, often requires that the objectives of public policy not be expressed in operational terms. Here is the difference between EEO and AA, for example. It is easier to build a consensus in favor of EEO, because in the abstract anyone can support the principle of equality of opportunity. However, when it is operationalized in terms of the use of goals and timetables for the purposes of creating a socially representative civil service, support for the program may decline drastically. Affirmative action identifies some groups as beneficiaries and others as those who will potentially bear a heavy burden. Consequently, some who can support EEO in the abstract are inevitably turned into opponents of an AA program. A similar phenomenon occurs in terms of agency missions to serve "the public interest" or assure "equity," and so forth. As long as these terms remain ill defined in an operational sense, a broad coalition can support the programs designed to administer them. (This point is illustrated by the case study of benzene in the workplace, presented later in the chapter.)

If the price of defining an objective is loss of political support and the demise of an administrative program, public administrators will be reluctant to express their missions or objectives in comprehensive and operational terms. Rather, they will prefer to move slowly, step by step toward a somewhat improved state of affairs, even though this may require some backtracking and constant modification of policies and means of implementing them. In other words, such an approach will be incremental and it will be considered by many to be in step with the style of U. S. politics.

The incremental model of decision making follows from the political approach to public administration. It stresses the need for public administrators to be responsive to the political community, to be politically representative of the groups that comprise it, and to be accountable to elected officials. Together, these values dictate that administrative decision making should involve public participation; that public administration should be based on the development of political coalitions and political consensus; and that it should allow nonexpert, political officials not only to give direction to public administrators, but also to exert pressure on them to decide in favor of one policy application or another.

The incremental model specifies the following general process for administrative decision making.

Redefining the Ends   Means and ends are not treated as distinct from one another. The model recognizes that policy objectives may be too unclear to serve as ends in any operational sense. Consequently, the ends of government policy are often defined by the means available to an agency for moving in some general policy direction. In the affirmative action example, for instance, this would require that, if used at all, goals and timetables would be in addition to merit exams, veteran preference, the rule of three, and so forth. It would be recognized that it is politically impracticable to reform the personnel system in one fell swoop but that eventually greater equal opportunity or social representation could be achieved by developing limited programs toward those ends. Since the means to achieve full social representation of all ethnic and racial groups in the society are not available without such major reform, the end of social representation itself may be redefined. Thus, it may become the proportional representation of minorities and women of working age. Since this too might be unattainable, the end might be further redefined as proportional representation of these groups in the work force. Such an objective might be further scaled down to be the proportional representation of such people in the work force in the occupations in which government personnel engage. A still further modification might be that any given agency's staff should be proportionally representative of minority groups and women in the work force in the occupations *and* in the geographic area in which the agency engages in recruiting. In such a scenario, the means available eventually determine what the end of public policy will be—at least until it is possible to employ other means or build a consensus for other ends.

Arriving at a Consensus   The test of a good decision is agreement or consensus in favor of the policy and method of implementation it develops. Means and ends are treated as packages that are more or less acceptable to relevant communities of interest. The package that is most acceptable—that has the greatest consensus behind it—is typically considered the "best" approach. In this sense representativeness and responsiveness replace efficiency, economy, and effectiveness as the values to be sought in choosing means. The traditional managerial values are not treated as inconsequential by the incremental model, but they are not weighed as preeminent. A program that does *less* and costs *more* may be more acceptable in the incremental model than one that is more economical and efficient. There are several additional points implied by this view:

1. Since the test of a good policy is the level of political support it generates, decisions are not actually tested against their impact in producing a change in a given area of social, economic, or political life. Rather, the test is the maintenance of political support, often expressed through increases in budgetary allocations. Consequently, even a program that is overwhelmingly *symbolic* and has no discernible impact on society other than generating support can be considered successful. Perhaps the U.S. Commission on Civil Rights could be considered an agency with predominantly symbolic functions.

2. Since the test of a good policy is not its impact on some target in the society but rather the support it generates, to oppose a program it is generally necessary to demonstrate what would be better. In other words, it is not enough to say that the program doesn't work, one has to indicate what *will* work. The latter, of course, is likely to be difficult and may very well be

politically infeasible because it threatens the coalition in support of the existing program.

3. This procedure for judging administrative decisions tends to be an obstacle to policy evaluation and to make performance appraisal difficult. Here again, therefore, the disjuncture between the political and managerial approaches to public administration is evident. (Policy evaluation is discussed in the next chapter.)

Making a Satisfactory Decision   In the process of incremental decision making, analysis tends to be more limited than in the rational-comprehensive approach. Administrative decision makers taking the incremental approach will consider a few means-ends packages and select one that is *satisfactory*. Little or no effort is made to reach an optimum decision that maximizes the pertinent values. Decisions are guided by past practice and tend not to rely heavily upon theory. However, a substantial degree of comprehensiveness may be built into the incremental decision-making model by encouraging the participation of relevant interest groups, other agencies, members of the legislature, and concerned individuals in the process of deciding upon a policy. To some extent this approach is found in the federal Administrative Procedure Act of 1946 and many similar state statutes. Under such legislation, when an agency is considering adopting a new policy it generally must publish its proposed rule changes and an explanation of them in a public forum. It may explain the rationale behind its proposals in considerable detail. Interested parties are given a chance to respond in writing or through legislative-style hearings, and the agency is supposed to take these responses into account before issuing its final rules. Often advisory committees are created or authorized to participate in agency policy making. By providing such pluralistic representation, a degree of comprehensiveness is developed in an agency's consideration of what can and should be done. Here is an area where the political approach's emphasis on pluralistic administrative organizational structure reinforces its approach toward decision making. Overlapping agency missions require the participation of several administrative units in making major decisions, and these units are likely to express differing perspectives. Compromises will be developed in the interests of maintaining cooperation and consensus. In general, radical departures from past practices and policies will be limited.

A Critique of the Incremental Model

It is obvious that the incremental approach has some major advantages in terms of representation and responsiveness. But its limitations are perhaps equally clear. First, it is inherently conservative to the extent that it may become extremely difficult for government effectively to penetrate the society in the ways it generally intends. Pluralism tends to be self-reinforcing. Every interest seeks its own governmental spokesman (bureau or agency). The more administrative units involved, the more difficult coordination becomes. Consequently, more and more interagency advisory committees are created. Policy judged by consensus will place a heavy emphasis on building and maintaining political support. As a result, conflict resolution and conflict avoidance will be stressed. Lawyers will work out acceptable lines of turf for the overlapping programs of different agencies or bureaus. Budgeters will seek to assure that relative levels of funding remain constant. Such an approach can even lead beyond conservatism to *immobilism*, as the description, in Box 7–2, of the Federal Trade Commission's experience with "Red Dye #3" indicates.

A second difficulty with the incremental model is that because it relies on the successive taking of small steps in modifying policy, it is possible eventually to end up with very undesirable and totally unforeseen consequences. In other words, the direction of the march being unclear, an inappropriate destination may be reached. One well-documented, outstanding example of this was the

---

BOX 7–2 **The Perils of Incrementalism—Immobilism at the FDA (1960–1985)**

On February 1, 1985, the Food and Drug Administration (FDA) postponed a decision to ban Red Dye #3 for the twenty-sixth time in twenty-five years. The dye is used in a variety of beverages, vitamins, cereals, dessert foods, and maraschino cherries. Based on animal studies authorized in 1977 and completed between 1981 and 1983, the FDA determined that Red Dye #3 is a carcinogen (at least in laboratory animals). Based on the Delaney Amendment (1960) to the Food, Drug and Cosmetic Act, any substance whose ingestion is believed to cause cancer in animals or humans must be banned for human consumption. The amendment is unequivocal; it does not require a risk assessment. But the FDA does not have final authority to ban products such as Red Dye #3. That authority is shared with the secretary of the Department of Health and Human Services, in which the FDA is located, and with the Office of Management and Budget, which has authority to oversee the issuance of regulatory rules by some agencies. The stakes are high, and so is the level of interest-group activity. The Public Citizen Health Research Group and other consumer advocates have lobbied and sued to have the dye banned. Several trade groups, including the National Food Processors Association, the Certified Color Manufacturers Association, and the Cosmetic, Toiletry and Fragrance Association, have actively lobbied over the years for modification of the Delaney Amendment. At least eight senators and thirty members of the House of Representatives lined up on the side of the trade groups. Many of these legislators represent states or districts where the proposed ban would have an unfavorable and substantial economic effect. The pressure on the FDA was so intense that, at one point, it completely reversed itself within a two-day period (April 11–12, 1984). In commenting on the deadlock over Red Dye #3, Congressman Ted Weiss (D-NY) said, "Ultimately, I think the courts are going to rule against the FDA and force them to remove the colors. But that is not the way this ought to be done. The American people deserve better than that." In the meantime, hold the cherry!

SOURCE: Marian Burros, "The Saga of a Food Regulation: After 25 Years, Still No Decision," *New York Times*, February 13, 1985, pp. C1, 8.

"Bay of Pigs" invasion of 1961. A military force of anticommunist Cuban exiles was formed and trained in the United States and some Central American countries. The force was created as a somewhat remote contingency that could be used in an effort to overthrow the regime of Fidel Castro. Step by step, the force was enlarged and strengthened. Eventually, President Kennedy was confronted with the question of what to do with it. He didn't want to turn it loose in the United States, nor were other countries willing to accept it. There seemed only one alternative, which was to let it invade Cuba. It did so, with the help of the United States, and was destroyed by the Cuban governmental forces. In writing about this sorry episode, Theodore Sorensen said:

> This plan was now or never, for three reasons: first, because the brigade was fully trained, restive to fight and difficult to hold off; second . . . because his only choice was to send them back to Cuba or bring them back to this country, where they would broadcast their resentment; and third, because Russian arms would soon build up Castro's army. . . .[12]

A related limitation of the incremental model is that it can produce *circularity* in policy making. Taking step after step with no clear and consistent policy objective in mind can lead administrators to repeat past processes and organizational arrangements even though at an earlier time these were modified because of their perceived defects. For instance, the federal government's EEO program was shifted into its central personnel agency twice and out of it twice. Each second shift was accompanied by a well-worn rationale.[13] In other words, the incremental approach is particularly susceptible to failure to maintain an "organizational memory." The rational-comprehensive model's effort to identify all possible means is likely to lead to a consideration of previous efforts (if any). Adjudication, which is discussed in the next section, also enhances organizational memory. It often involves an exhaustive search for past decisions that may be relevant to a present one.

Finally, the incremental model of decision making does not fit fundamental decisions intended to redirect the society or commit it to some large-scale venture. Despite its limitations in practice, centralized planning seems more appropriate in such cases. It is partly for this reason that societies seeking rapid economic development tend to avoid incrementalism. However, since incrementalism virtually requires a pluralistic political system and fragmented administrative organization in order to be comprehensive, rejecting incrementalism can reduce a political community's emphasis on developing and maintaining representative political institutions. Of course, much depends on the degree of heterogeneity in the society. To some extent, however, the debate over rational-comprehensive centralized planning versus incrementalism is also a controversy over the nature of political systems.

THE LEGAL APPROACH TO DECISION MAKING

The legal approach to public administrative decision making relies upon adjudicatory procedure in an effort to assure that individuals, groups, corporations, or other parties are not denied their rights or otherwise treated unfairly or arbitrarily in a way that adversely affects their interests. Adjudication is a special form of incrementalism, one bounded by an elaborate, formalized procedure and rules intended to identify (1) the facts of a situation, (2) the interests of opposing parties, and (3) the balance between these interests that best fits legal requirements or best serves the public interest.[14] It is assumed that by going through adjudicatory procedure in a large number of instances dealing with essentially the same area of public policy, it will be possible eventually to build a body of principles that define the public interest.

It is useful to think of adjudication as falling into two broad categories, prospective and retrospective. **Prospective adjudication** frequently involves requests by regulated utilities, transportation companies, radio and television broadcasters, and so forth for the right to modify some aspects of their service, such as their rates, routes, or programming. It may also concern requests for licenses to operate a business or provide a service in a regulated sector of the economy. Prospective adjudication, which often occurs when one applies for social welfare benefits, generally requires that the private party file a request for some kind of change and supply information and a rationale for its request. Typically, the public agency undertakes an analysis of the request. Assuming there is some controversy involved, such as whether the applicant is eligible or granting the request is in the public interest, a hearing before an impartial administrative law judge or hearing examiner will be held. During the hearing the party requesting the change will be afforded the opportunity to present more information relevant to the request. The staff of the regulatory agency may present countervailing information pertaining to its view of what the public interest requires, as outlined in the relevant statutes. Both sides will be able to present witnesses and confront and cross-examine witnesses on the other side. Third parties may be invited to submit statements either orally or in writing. The hearing examiner may play an active role in trying to clarify the issues, information, and opinions before the agency. This stage of adjudication will end when the hearing examiner renders a decision. Generally, the decision will be reviewed at a higher level in the agency, often by a "commission" of some kind. It may be ratified, rejected, or amended at this stage. The whole process will be legalistic in the sense of being bound by established rules of procedure (that is, the order of the proceeding, who can appear as a witness, the form cross-examination takes, and the nature of the information that can be presented at the hearing). Administrative adjudication makes use of adversary procedure, but it is generally more flexible than courtroom procedure, especially in terms of rules of evidence and the more active role frequently played by the hearing examiner.

A second type of administrative adjudication is **retrospective.** Here, an alleged wrongdoing comes to the attention of an administrative agency. This may occur through the filing of a complaint against an individual, corporation, or other party. Such a complaint may allege unfair competition, deceptive advertising, an unfair labor or personnel practice, or other form of behavior that violates law or agency regulations. Sometimes the agency becomes aware of the alleged wrongdoing through its own preliminary investigations, monitoring of reports, audits, and similar means.

Once a wrongdoing is alleged, the agency is likely to undertake an elaborate investigation to determine what actually occurred. If agency officials in a "prosecutorial" role believe that the situation warrants further action, notice is given to the party charged with the wrongdoing. That party is then afforded a formal opportunity to respond, either orally or in writing. In many cases, this response will be in the form of a hearing presided over by an administrative law judge or independent hearing examiner. Again, the hearing will resemble a judicial trial, although it is likely to be more flexible. The party charged with the wrongdoing may have a right to be represented by counsel, to present witnesses, and to confront and cross-examine adverse witnesses. Adversary procedure is used to establish the truth of what occurred and varying interpretations of the rules governing the action. The hearing examiner will render a decision, which will probably be subject to review at some later stage within the agency or by another governmental body.

Adjudication is an important means of making administrative decisions in several policy areas, especially regulation, personnel administration, and the granting or termination of social welfare benefits. Its overall advantages are considered to be that it enables administrative bodies to act in a judicial fashion that is detached from political pressures. This encourages them to develop an independent view of the public interest that is informed by their expertise, to make decisions in an incremental fashion supporting that view, and to develop a body of law or precedent that helps identify the public interest on a continuing basis. Adjudication is especially useful where the legislature cannot agree or establish a comprehensive policy, where there is a need to make adjustments on a continual basis, as in the setting of rates for public utilities, and where flexibility is desired. It is also a useful process where decisions must turn on idiosyncratic factors, such as the intent, financial status, or physical condition of a party, or the extent to which a party was acting in good faith. Adjudication is especially suitable where the enforcement of a rule, law, or policy requires the weighing of several criteria in the context of a specific situation.

A good example of the utility of adjudication occurs in the area of public employees' complaints of prohibited discrimination. It would be very difficult to identify, in the abstract, every personnel situation in which such an employee might be discriminated against. Indeed, prohibited discrimination ranges from dismissals, to scheduling of work hours and coffee breaks, to assessment of the performance of an employee and evaluation of his or her attitude. Such assessments of attitude, especially, can be incredibly subtle. Social stereotyping can cause "initiative" in one person to be labeled "aggressiveness" or "abrasiveness" in another who belongs to a different social group. Moreover, since discrimination is subjective and rarely openly stated nowadays, it is necessary to probe the behavior and motivation of a supervisor who has allegedly engaged in such a prohibited practice. This may require reviewing his or her past record in dealing with minorities, women, or men as a group. Adjudication is a useful vehicle for allowing one side to present a case and the other to defend his or her actions. An impartial weighing of the information (evidence) in a wide variety of cases can lead to the development of a body of principles identifying prohibited discrimination and helping to determine when it occurs. Presumably, such a body of principle will take into account the interests of individuals in being treated fairly as well as the public interest in enabling supervisors to manage their employees. It is difficult to imagine how equal employment opportunity policy could be enforced without at least some reliance on adjudication. The same is true for a variety of other areas of public policy.

By the same token, adjudication also has serious limitations. Adjudication is a peculiar form of incrementalism. It shares the major pitfall of that approach to decision making. It is possible to make a series of incremental decisions in a policy area without being fully cognizant of the resultant state of affairs toward which those decisions are ineluctably leading. One might find examples of this problem in several areas of adjudicative decision making. A case of intimate concern to public administrators involves the rights of public employees. Through a series of judicial decisions and administrative hearings, the constitutional and legal protections afforded public employees in adverse actions evolved from being minimal prior to the 1950s to being extremely comprehensive by the early 1970s. Decisions involving substantive rights, equal protection, and procedural due process built upon one another to the point where it appeared to many that the public service was becoming unmanageable, for sanctions could not be levied effectively against public employees whose performance or behavior was inadequate in some respect. President Nixon complained that the federal service was undisciplined and President Carter claimed that it was inadequately meritorious for this reason.[15] Whatever one's view, however, the point is that while each decision contributing to the trend of affording greater rights may have made sense on its own terms (as each *must* have to those making them), the ultimate result was something that was unplanned and unanticipated.

Adjudication has other limitations as well. It is time-consuming. It can lack uniformity, as when different hearing examiners reach different conclusions in similar cases. The content of the decisional **case law** (that is, the legal principles that can be derived by analyzing decisions in previous cases) is not readily accessible to the public or to interested outside parties. It may even be obscure to the public administrators who are governed by it. The adjudication of federal equal employment opportunity complaints and political neutrality cases are examples of the latter problem. In neither area is the content of the case law highly publicized nor particularly clear in its principles, yet supervisors and employees are supposed to abide by the content of the rulings. Adjudication also limits outside participation. Individuals and organizations can file the equivalent of "friend of the court" briefs under some circumstances, but there is no provision for the general, open participation of the public or interest groups in such proceedings. In addition, adjudicatory decisions can be tied to an eclectic set of facts that may tend to distort the principles underlying decisions. Hard cases make bad law precisely because there are at least two opposing and seemingly equally valid sets of principles upon which they can be decided. In such instances, decisions may turn more than usual on the way the cases are presented to the hearing examiner or judge, upon the personal sense of justice held by such officials, or even upon their biases.

A final criticism of adjudication is that it places public administrators and individuals or organizations in an antagonistic, adversary position where such a relationship is inappropriate to the public policy ostensibly being promoted. Examples of this are relationships such as public service supervisor and public employee, teacher and pupil, social welfare caseworker and welfare recipient. In each of these instances, cooperative and supportive relationships are generally considered more appropriate than hostile ones. Yet when such parties enter adjudication, their relationship becomes an adversary one. Moreover, adversary procedure encourages each side to present the strongest, most forceful case. This often results in exaggerated allegations that place the opposing party in the worst possible light. Behavior and motives are portrayed in black-and-white terms. This leads each party to distrust the other even more, and the conflict is exacerbated. Eventually, one will "win" and the other will "lose." A great deal of anxiety and emotional stress occurs. In the meantime and even afterward, the parties may have to continue working together in a relationship that can hardly be functional. For instance, in an EEO complaint, a supervisor will be accused by an employee of engaging in prohibited discrimination. Adjudication is likely to involve allegations that the supervisor is "racist," "sexist," "ethnically chauvinistic," or the like. Thus, the supervisor is portrayed as "immoral" and essentially unfit for his or her job. The supervisor, on the other hand, is likely to claim that the action of which the employee complained was taken because the employee is somehow inadequate in terms of capability, judgment, and/or personality. If carried to its logical extreme, adjudication of this sort can develop an air of absurdity: an allegedly inadequate employee versus an unfit supervisor, all within the confines of a "merit system."

THE CASE OF BENZENE IN THE WORKPLACE

We have been discussing the managerial, political, and legal approaches to public administrative decision making as though they are easily separable or come in distinct packages. In practice, public administrators are forced to combine these approaches in their day-to-day decision making. But sometimes, perhaps frequently, the decision making approaches converge in one area of public administration in a way that clearly highlights their advantages and disadvantages. The effort by the federal Occupational Safety and Health Administration (OSHA) to reduce the hazards of benzene in the workplace provides an excellent illustration.

The Occupational Safety and Health Act of 1970 states that the secretary of labor,

> . . . in promulgating standards dealing with toxic materials or harmful physical agents . . . shall set the standard which most adequately assures, to the extent feasible, on the basis of the best available evidence, that no employee will suffer material impairment

of health or functional capacity even if such employee has regular exposure to the hazard dealt with by such standard for the period of his working life.

Benzene is a rapidly evaporating, aromatic liquid produced by the petroleum and petrochemical industries for use in manufacturing motor fuels, solvents, detergents, pesticides, and other organic chemicals. It is known to be associated with leukemia, a cancer attacking white blood cells. No safe level of benzene, which is measured in its airborne state in parts per million (ppm), is known.

Following what he understood to be the legislative mandate, the secretary of labor issued standards reducing the allowable levels of benzene from 10 ppm to 1 ppm in the rubber, petroleum refining, and petrochemical industries. The costs to the industries were projected to range from $1,390 to $82,000 per worker (in physical plant changes and first-year costs). The secretary was sued by the American Petroleum Institute partly on the grounds that he exceeded his statutory authority, because the reduction from 10 ppm to 1 ppm was not feasible. The case reached the Supreme Court level under the title *Industrial Union Department, AFL-CIO* v. *American Petroleum Institute* (1980).[16] Part of the issue was what "feasible" meant in the context of the statute.

To answer this question, one might turn to the legislative record and attempt to discern the intent of Congress. Supreme Court Justice Rehnquist did this and concluded:

> I believe that the legislative history demonstrates that the feasibility requirement . . . is a legislative mirage, appearing to some Members [of Congress] but not to others, and assuming any form desired by the beholder. . . .
>
> In sum, the legislative history contains nothing to indicate that the language "to the extent feasible" does anything other than render what had been a clear, if somewhat unrealistic, standard largely, if not entirely, precatory. There is certainly nothing to indicate that these words . . . are limited to technological and economic feasibility. [Concurring opinion.]

The words "to the extent feasible" may not mean anything specific in the context of the statute, as Rehnquist argues, but the mirage they conjured up was crucial to Congress's decision making. They were offered as a substitute for the original language of the OSHA bill as a means of forming a coalition in support of greater regulation of workplace health and safety. The words may have had different meaning to different members of Congress, but they reduced opposition to the bill and generated greater support for it.

This is an example of incremental decision making. It is accepted that eliminating toxic substances from the workplace is a desirable policy objective. Such a policy is viewed as a step forward in improving American life. But it is a small and tentative step because the statute does not identify the substances deemed toxic and the standards for determining the feasibility of eliminating them. Were it to do so, it would face so much political controversy and opposition that it might be entirely impossible to move in the desired policy direction of creating safe workplaces. For example, identifying benzene as a toxic substance in the bill itself would have provoked opposition from the petroleum, rubber, and petrochemical industries, as well as their lobby organization, the American Petroleum Institute. Since benzene is used in pesticides, agricultural groups might also have become involved, and so on. But benzene would not be the only toxic substance identified in the bill, and consequently opposition from other industries and economic sectors would have been forthcoming. Members of Congress whose districts included the industries that would clearly be adversely affected (in the short run) might well oppose the bill. Politically, the way around this problem is to do just what Congress did, that is, to form a broad coalition in favor of a desired policy objective by avoiding taking any specific regulatory steps. The bill was neither comprehensive in its identification of toxic substances, nor particularly rational in its language. But it was passed and it did establish a process for making America's workplaces safer.

A more rational-comprehensive approach was left to OSHA and the secretary of labor. OSHA developed the following standard: "Whenever a carcinogen is involved, OSHA will presume that no safe level of exposure exists in the absence of clear proof establishing such a level and will accordingly set the exposure limit at the lowest level feasible." Feasibility here was defined in terms of the technologies available for eliminating the toxic substance, the devices available for measuring its presence, and the costs likely to be incurred. In the case of benzene, technology and measurement dictated 1 ppm. OSHA did consider the costs to the industries, but it "did not quantify the benefits to each category of worker in terms of decreased exposure to benzene. . . ." It reasoned that since the costs were bearable by the industries, the new standard was feasible. OSHA's assumption was that 1 ppm of benzene was the lowest level feasible and therefore the one that was safest. This assumption was a key issue in the subsequent adjudication in the federal courts.

Industrial Union Department, AFL-CIO v. *American Petroleum Institute* divided the Supreme Court so much that while it was able to reach a judgment, it was unable to formulate a single opinion to which a majority of the justices could subscribe. This is called decision by plurality, rather than majority opinion. Four justices, Stevens, Stewart, Powell, and Chief Justice Burger, expressed the view that the secretary's rule of 1 ppm was not supported by appropriate findings. At a minimum, they reasoned that before promulgating any standard, the secretary was required to "make a finding that the workplaces dealt with in the standard are not safe in the sense that significant risks are present and can be eliminated or lessened by a change in practices."

Chief Justice Burger issued his own concurring opinion in which he warned against the pitfalls of rational-comprehensive decision making in the regulatory area: "When the administrative record reveals only scant or minimal risk of material health impairment, responsible administration calls for avoidance of extravagant, comprehensive regulation. Perfect safety is a chimera; regulation must not strangle human activity in the search for the impossible."

Justice Powell also concurred separately. While he agreed with the plurality of the Court that OSHA failed to meet its statutory obligations, he emphasized that he did not think "the statute requires the quantification of risk in every case. . . . [N]either the statute nor the legislative history suggests that OSHA's hands are tied when reasonable quantification cannot be accomplished by any known methods."

Justice Rehnquist was the fifth justice to concur in the Court's judgment that the secretary's regulation was invalid. However, his opinion was based on a completely different line of reasoning. He considered the Occupational Safety and Health Act to be unconstitutional for at least three reasons: (1) It violated the separation of powers by delegating legislative policy-making authority to the executive branch; (2) it did so without "any guidance" to the secretary of labor; and (3) "the standard of 'feasibility' renders meaningful judicial review impossible."

Justice Marshall dissented in an opinion joined by Justices Brennan, White, and Blackmun. He argued that adjudication was an inappropriate model for determining whether the secretary had acted properly. If his rule were not in keeping with Congress's intent, Marshall suggested that Congress was free to rewrite the statute to correct the defective interpretation. But adjudicatory decision making could not adequately resolve the matter. In Marshall's words, which underscore the limitations of adjudication,

> three factors . . . in my view, make judicial review of occupational safety and health standards under the substantial evidence test* particularly difficult. First, the issues often reach a high level of technical complexity. In such circumstances the courts are required to immerse themselves in matters to which they are unaccustomed by training or experience. Second, the factual issues with which the Secretary must deal are frequently not subject to any definitive resolution. . . . Causal connections and theoretical extrapolations may be uncertain. Third, when the question involves determination of the acceptable level of risk, the ultimate decision must necessarily be based on considerations of policy as well as empirically verifiable facts. Factual determinations can at most define the risk in some statistical way; the judgment whether that risk is tolerable cannot be based solely on a resolution of the facts.

This case study of decision making concerning benzene in the workplace juxtaposes the rational-comprehensive approach, incrementalism, and adjudication, which is a particular variant of incrementalism, as noted earlier. It suggests that the legislature and the courts face serious institutional limitations in decision making. Public administrators are also constrained by institutional barriers, but sometimes their tasks are further complicated by the likelihood that their implementation of vague legislative mandates will be overturned by the courts. The case shows how the three styles of decision making can be opposed to one another—how what is acceptable reasoning under one is unacceptable under another. Combination is sometimes possible, but often is not. A better strategy is to try to overcome the shortcomings of each approach by introducing the corrective technique discussed in the next section.

---

* When reviewing administrative decisions, the courts are usually called upon to employ one of two standards: substantial evidence or preponderance of evidence. The former is a less rigorous test of administrative action.

SYNTHESIZING DECISION-MAKING APPROACHES

Each of the decision-making approaches reviewed here has advantages and disadvantages. None is fully suitable for all areas of public administration. Therefore, as in other aspects of public administration, it becomes necessary to try to develop a synthesis through which the advantages of each of the managerial, political, and legal approaches can be maximized while their limitations are minimized. To date, the most comprehensive approach to accomplishing this in the context of decision making has been the **mixed-scanning approach.**[17]

Mixed scanning attempts to combine incrementalism, including adjudication, with the rational-comprehensive approach. This approach to decision making was developed by Amitai Etzioni, who illustrates it as follows:

> Assume we are about to set up a worldwide weather observation system using weather satellites. The rationalistic approach would seek an exhaustive survey of weather conditions by using cameras capable of detailed observations and by scheduling reviews of the entire sky as often as possible. This would yield an avalanche of details, costly to analyze and likely to overwhelm our action capacities (i.e., "seeding" cloud formations that could develop into hurricanes or bring rain to arid areas). Incrementalism would focus on those areas in which similar patterns developed in the recent past and, perhaps, on a few nearby regions; it would thus ignore all formations which might deserve attention if they arose in unexpected areas.
>
> A mixed-scanning strategy would include elements of both approaches by employing two cameras: a broad angle camera that would cover all parts of the sky but not in great detail, and a second one which would zero in on those areas revealed by the first camera to require a more in-depth examination. While mixed-scanning might miss areas in which only a detailed camera could reveal trouble, it is less likely than incrementalism to miss obvious trouble spots in unfamiliar areas.[18]

Mixed scanning requires decision makers to differentiate between fundamental decisions pertaining to long-range goals and more limited decisions that are made within the context of those goals. This distinction between fundamental and limited decisions is akin to the distinction made by the managerial approach between politics and administration. However, Etzioni recognizes that public administrators may make both kinds of decisions and simply argues that they ought to be clear about what it is they are doing. Moreover, he believes that by clarifying the relationship between rational-comprehensive and incremental decision making, the shortcomings of each can be substantially reduced.

Several examples of the utility of mixed scanning can be found in federal administration in the United States. The Executive Office of the President, in particular, contains a number of units that are essentially charged with taking a long-range view of a particular policy area and evaluating policy options. The Council of Economic Advisers is responsible for analyzing the national economy and its various segments, advising the president on economic developments, evaluating governmental programs, and recommending policies for economic growth and stability. The National Security Council has somewhat more complex operating responsibilities, but its main function is to advise the president with respect to the integration of domestic, foreign, and military policies relating to the security of the United States. Presidential commissions in various policy areas, including Social Security, Central America, and nutrition, are also used as mixed-scanning devices. In addition, various administrative operations can include a mixed-scanning function, as when agencies make five-year budget projections that try to develop a realistic appraisal of where they should be headed. Any of these devices can serve as checks on administrative "drift" through incrementalism and on the overly complicated and unrealistic qualities of the pure rational-comprehensive decision-making model.

What to Avoid

Whichever administrative decision-making approach is employed, there are several pitfalls that should be avoided. As a public administrator, it is all too easy to make mistakes. There are many sources of pressure; time, interest groups, members of the legislature and their staff, the media, chief executives and their staffs, personal advancement, and personal goals are among the more common. Specialization may limit the public administrator's view and definition of reality, and administrative jargon may obscure matters. Furthermore, group decision making carries within it a tendency toward conformity, the stifling of dissent, and constant reinforcement of the agency's traditional view of matters. It is also difficult to know precisely when to decide and when to await further development before adopting new policies and new procedures.

Among some of the more commonly identified obstacles to sound administrative decisions are the following:

1. *Lack of clarity of goals.* As the incremental decision-making model suggests, sometimes the political price of having an administrative program at all is the absence of clear goals. Public administrators also display a tendency to confuse ends and means: the agency's continued existence and growth may become the true end, and its programs merely a means for justifying that end, rather than vice versa. The development of administrative ideologies touting the importance of the agency and its programs is often a sign of this ends-mean inversion. Where such ideologies are taken at face value by decision makers, misplaced priorities are likely to become a problem.

2. *Confusion of the public interest with that of a clientele group or constituency.* The nature of bureaucratic politics in the United States places emphasis on the formation of iron triangles among bureaucratic agencies, legislative (sub)committees, and interest groups. Such alliances can easily distort a public administrator's view of the public interest. There is also a tendency to confuse the reaction of interested parties (that is, constituencies) with the view of the public more generally. This has commonly been apparent in the decision-making process of regulatory agencies.

3. *Rigid conservatism in the sense of strict adherence to rules, procedures, and past practices.* For various reasons discussed in Chapter 4, bureaucratic organization—especially hierarchy—can cause public administrators to feel personally insecure. Under such circumstances, rigidity is often a favored course of action. It is less likely that one will be disciplined or affected adversely when "going by the book" than when taking risks to further one's vision of the public interest.

4. *Specialization causing public administrators to oversimplify reality.* It is likely that any social or economic problem is the result of several factors and will have several effects. Specialization may confine the vision of any group of public administrators to one or a few of these causes and effects and, hence, an appreciation of the whole problem is lost. For example, a former head of the U.S. Equal Employment Opportunity Commission, who was engaged in designing a better EEO *complaint* system, once told the principal author that "*all* racial and sexual discrimination in the federal service was interpersonal." Yet the evidence is overwhelming that much discrimination, probably most, was built into the system of examinations, position classification, and job design.

5. *"Overquantification" causing public administrators to deemphasize qualitative factors in making decisions.* Pressures for accountability, political neutrality, and job security, as well as an emphasis on objective technical expertise, make public administrators reluctant to exercise "subjective" judgment. Consequently, they seek quantitative indicators of qualitative performance. Sometimes these indicators are satisfactory, but at other times they lead administrators to decide in favor of what will look best in terms of quantity. For instance, a hearing examiner dealing with adverse action complaints or EEO cases may decide cases rapidly, since that can be quantified, rather than seek to render the highest degree of justice in each one. When emphasis on quantitative compliance detracts from qualitative performance—as it could in the above example—the relationship between the two is *pathological,* because it does not further the agency's mission.

6. *Reluctance to engage in policy and program evaluation.* It is axiomatic that decision makers need information about the impacts of their decisions in order to make improvements. However, largely for political reasons, administrative agencies may be reluctant to gather information and engage in analysis that makes their past decisions and program implementation look seriously inadequate. Such analysis also facilitates the ability of outsiders to review and understand an agency's operations. Consequently, there is sometimes a tendency to engage in only the most perfunctory and superficial kind of policy and program evaluation. Agencies also contract private firms to engage in evaluative studies, occasionally with the tacit understanding that a strongly critical review will make the agency unlikely to use that firm in the future. Administrative culture tends to be intolerant of internal and external criticism. Thus public administrators often fall into

a highly defensive posture when confronted with challenges to their internal hierarchies, past decisions, and present procedures.

The Future: Information

New technological developments in the use of information are occurring at a very rapid pace. Computers and management-information systems were considered exotic just a few years ago. Now they are common. Like other decision-making tools, computers assist in the process of gathering and organizing information. In the view of some, such as Herbert Simon, the advent of the computer and attendant information systems has the potential to revolutionize public administration.[19] These developments enable public administrators to cope with the complexity of the programs and policies they implement. Computerization makes the rational-comprehensive model more usable by enabling the public administrator to compare and project the likely consequences and costs of alternative means of implementing public policies. Eventually, computers may be able to "think" in nontrivial ways that are relevant to rational administrative decision-making.

Computers can also be beneficial to the incremental and adjudicatory models. Incrementalism is deeply concerned with making decisions that gain political support among relevant communities and constituencies. Computers can assist in this effort by making it possible to analyze rapidly information gained by public opinion polls, community surveys, and from voting results. They can also aid in the analysis of the limited means-ends packages under consideration. They can help provide a better "organizational memory" to incremental decision makers. Computerized legal information systems have already demonstrated their ability to bring previous decisions and principles to the attention of lawyers, who, in turn, may raise them in presenting their cases before judges and administrative law judges.

No matter which decisional approach is taken, computers and information systems can clarify thinking. They cannot resolve value conflicts among the managerial, political, and legal perspectives, but they can help us to foresee the consequences of choices made within the framework of these perspectives. As in the case of many new technologies, computers also carry some risks. They can be used to reduce individuals' privacy.[20] They sometimes promote excessive impersonality and reliance upon inappropriate quantifiable indicators of qualitative performance.

As in other areas of public administration, when considering decision making, the student and practitioner should avoid the once common tendency to believe that there is always "one best way" and that technological and organizational processes can automatically resolve policy conflicts over competing values. Certainly, the managerial, political, and legal approaches are all more useful in some circumstances than in others. The problem is to improve them and to determine when each should be used alone or combined with one or both of the others.

NOTES

1. Charles Perrow, *Complex Organizations*, 3rd ed. (New York: Random House, 1986), p. 129.
2. Ibid., p. 130.
3. Shapiro v. Thompson, 394 U.S. 618 (1969).
4. See David H. Rosenbloom, *Federal Equal Opportunity* (New York: Praeger, 1977), p. 113; Robert Hampton, Chairman, U.S. Civil Service Commission, "Memorandum for Heads of Departments and Agencies," May 11, 1971.
5. Harold Seidman, *Politics, Positions, and Power* (New York: Oxford University Press, 1970), p. 18.
6. The Supreme Court upheld the legality of grid-regs in Heckler v. Campbell, 461 U.S. 458 (1983).
7. See Charles Lindblom, "The Science of 'Muddling Through,' " *Public Administration Review*, 19 (Spring 1959): 79–88; Herbert Simon, *Administrative Behavior* (New York: Free Press, 1965 [originally copyrighted in 1945]); Alan Altshuler and Norman Thomas, eds., *The Politics of the Federal Bureaucracy*, 2nd ed. (New York: Harper & Row, 1977), chap. 3.
8. See Personnel Administrator v. Feeney, 422 U.S. 256 (1976) and David H. Rosenbloom and Peter Grabosky, "Racial and Ethnic Competition for Federal Service Positions," *Midwest Review of Public Administration*, 11 (December 1977): 281–290.
9. Peter Woll and Rochelle Jones, "Bureaucratic Defense in Depth," in Ronald Pynn, ed., *Watergate and the American Political Process* (New York: Praeger, 1975), esp. pp. 216–217.
10. For an interesting discussion from the perspectives of individual administrators, see David Granick, "The Red Executive," in Gerald Bell, ed., *Organizations and Human Behavior* (Englewood Cliffs, N.J.: Prentice-Hall, 1967), pp. 218–230. See also Alfred Meyer, *The Soviet Political System* (New York: Random House, 1965); Joseph LaPalombara, ed., *Bureaucracy and Political Development* (Princeton, N.J.: Princeton University Press, 1963).
11. Lindblom, "The Science of 'Muddling Through' "; Amitai Etzioni, "Mixed Scanning: A 'Third' Approach to Decision-Making," *Public Administration Review*, 27 (December 1967): 385–392, and reprinted in Altshuler and Thomas, *Politics of the Federal Bureaucracy*, pp. 139–146; and Etzioni, "Mixed Scanning Revisited," *Public Administration Review*, 46 (January/February 1986): 8–14.
12. Theodore Sorenson, *Kennedy* (New York: Harper & Row, 1965), p. 296.
13. See Rosenbloom, *Federal Equal Employment Opportunity*, chaps. 3 and 4.
14. For students of public administration, a useful discussion can be found in Peter Woll, *American Bureaucracy*, 2nd ed. (New York: Norton, 1977), chap. 3.
15. *New York Times*, July 20, 1974, p. 14; and March 3, 1978, pp. 1, 10. This is suggested in Alan K. Campbell, "Civil Service Reform: A New Commitment," *Public Administration Review*, 38 (March/April 1978): 102; see also Justice Powell's dissents in Elrod v. Burns (427 U.S. 347, 1976) and Branti v. Finkel (445 U.S. 506, 1980).
16. 448 U.S. 607 (1980).
17. Etzioni, "Mixed-Scanning."
18. Ibid., reprinted in Altshuler and Thomas, *Politics of the Federal Bureaucracy*, p. 143.
19. Herbert Simon, "Applying Information Technology to Organization Design," *Public Administration Review*, 33 (May/June 1973), esp. p. 276.
20. See Alan F. Westin, *Privacy and Freedom* (New York: Atheneum, 1967).

ADDITIONAL READING

BRAYBROOKE, DAVID, AND CHARLES LINDBLOM. *A Strategy of Decision*. New York: Free Press, 1970.

DIMOCK, MARSHALL. *Law and Dynamic Administration*. New York: Praeger, 1980.

DROR, YEHEZKEL. *Public Policymaking Reexamined*. Scranton, Pa.: Chandler, 1968.

JANIS, IRVING, AND LEON MANN. *Decision Making: A Psychological Analysis of Conflict, Choice and Commitment*. New York: Free Press, 1977.

LINDBLOM, CHARLES. "The Science of 'Muddling Through,' " *Public Administration Review*, 19 (Spring 1959): 79–88.

QUADE, E. S. *Analysis for Public Decisions*. New York: American Elsevier, 1975.

ROURKE, FRANCIS. *Bureaucracy, Politics, and Public Policy*, 3rd ed. Boston: Little, Brown, 1984.

SIMON, HERBERT. *Administrative Behavior*, 3rd ed. New York: Free Press, 1976.

WILSON, DAVID. *Top Decisions*. San Francisco: Jossey-Bass, 1986.

STUDY QUESTIONS

1. How are decisions made at the college or university that you attend? What values are maximized by this approach? What are its advantages and disadvantages, in your view?

2. How do you make decisions when:
   a. you think about your career plans?
   b. you are involved in a social activity?
   c. you are called upon to resolve some disagreement between friends, co-workers, fellow students, or relatives?
   Does your decision-making process differ in varied contexts? If so, how?

3. "Interactive TV" enables the viewer to send electronic signals instantaneously to the broadcaster. These signals can indicate agreement or disagreement with statements or propositions made on the TV program. Elaborate interactive systems would also enable the viewers to indicate the general level of intensity of their preferences.

   Some believe that interactive TV is a way of improving government decision making by allowing the public to register its preferences on matters of public policy. Do you think interactive TV would have any utility in improving public administrative decision making? Why or why not?

CHAPTER 8

Policy Analysis and Evaluation

Public administration's penetration of the economy and society has fostered concern with how well public policies work and how their implementation could be improved. This chapter focuses on two ways of judging policy implementation, namely, policy analysis and policy evaluation. Policy analysis considers the extent to which a policy achieves its objectives. It also assesses how the process through which the policy is implemented contributes to the achievement of such objectives. In the context of public administration, policy evaluation focuses on whether implementation maximizes appropriate values. The managerial, political, and legal perspectives tend to agree that implementation can be problematic if it allows too much discretionary authority to individual administrators. Each of these perspectives may be more suitable for evaluating policy in a particular area of public administration, such as overhead administrative functions or regulation.

Public administration is an activist part of government. It is a means by which government seeks to intervene in aspects of the economy, society, and polity. For example, public administration has been used to try to prevent imbalances in economic markets, protect consumers, prevent harm to the environment, and provide financial, medical, psychological, and other assistance to individuals who appear to be otherwise unable to care adequately for themselves in these respects. It also seeks to protect the civil, political, and voting rights of the citizenry vis-à-vis private groups and even some governmental jurisdictions. When called upon to be the arm of governmental intervention in these spheres of life, public administrators are required to *implement* policy. The question of how successfully public policy is being implemented inevitably arises. And, if the answer is, "Not successfully enough!" then is the problem with the implementation, the policy, or both? In essence, seeking answers to such questions is *policy analysis and evaluation.*

THE GROWING CONCERN WITH POLICY ANALYSIS

Although these questions seem normal enough, it has only been in recent years that public administrators began to pay serious attention to systematic policy analysis. In part this is because of a shift in the nature of administrative intervention in the 1960s that made public administration more salient in the workplace, in neighborhoods, in families, and in the society generally. President Lyndon Johnson's "Great Society" program, for instance, rested very much upon the premise that public administration could intervene successfully in a wide range of aspects of life to promote greater equality of opportunity among the citizenry. However, as discussed earlier, perspectives on public administration tend to follow what is known as "Miles's law"—"Where one stands depends on where one sits." What one person considers to be a *service* provided by public administration, another may consider to be a *constraint*. Thus, while an employee may view public administrative intervention to protect him or her from harmful substances in the workplace as a valuable governmental service, the employer may view it as an untoward administrative interference in legitimate business considerations. As public administration provides more services to people, it also engages in more extensive regulatory activities.

By the 1970s, it was evident that many individuals and groups thought that the administrative state had gone too far in regulating their activities. Many also thought it had the additional consequence of sapping individual initiative and sense of responsibility for making one's own decisions and taking care of oneself. Some policies for broad social change, conceived in optimism in the 1960s, appeared to fail. Perhaps even worse, they seemed to linger on well after their inadequacies were widely understood. In truth, many of the policies being implemented by public administrators were established by legislatures, but nonetheless opposition often focused on "the bureaucrats."

Seat belts provide an example of the kind of web of administrative implementation that many view as counterproductive and individually debilitating governmental intervention in the society. Originally, seat belts were an option one could choose to have installed in one's car. The federal government was dissatisfied with leaving this option up to the individual, since so many people opted not to buy seat belts. It then made seat belts mandatory equipment in new cars—with the cost being borne by the buyer. Even though new car buyers were required to have seat belts in their cars, they might still decide not to use them. Again the government's effort to protect motorists seemed frustrated. Next, new cars were required to be equipped with devices, such as buzzers, flashing lights, and ignition interlocks to prod people to use seat belts. No doubt, these policies had some success. More people were probably using seat belts and more serious injuries and deaths were probably averted. Nevertheless, many people still refused to use their seat belts—and many simply disconnected all those prodding devices. Daunted, but not yet ready to surrender, the federal government sought to require either that a different type of seat belt be installed—one that provides a passive restraint—or that automobile manufacturers install air bag safety systems to cushion motorists in the event of a collision. Subsequently, the National Highway Traffic Safety Administration sought to rescind these regulations. Its action resulted in litigation that reached the Supreme Court.[1] All this cost money: administrators had to be paid, automobile manufacturers had to engage in developing seat belts, air bags, and prodding devices, consumers had to buy the belts and devices, lawyers had to be paid when litigation ensued, and groups for and against these measures employed lobbyists to try to make their points with Congress and the National Highway Traffic Safety Administration. It also seemed to bother a lot of people who did not want to be required or to compel others to buy seat belts or air bags. The whole scene led many to ask, "Why not just leave it up to the individual whether he or she wants to use seat belts?" or "Why not just legally require all drivers and passengers to fasten their belts and fine those who don't?" There may be good answers to these questions, and finding them is much of what policy analysis is about.

Public administrative intervention in the economy, society, and polity makes policy analysis more salient. The more the administrative state intervenes in our lives, the more we want to know about the effects it is having. However, an additional development of far-reaching consequence for public administration coincided with this increased devotion of attention to the problems of the administrative state. This was the rapid development of analytic techniques, especially in the social sciences, that could be used to assess the impacts of administrative interventions and to ascertain the costs and benefits associated with public administrative implementation of policies. In one sense, the basic question is at least as old as Woodrow Wilson's call in the 1880s for a new study of administration that could "discover, first, what government can properly and successfully do. . . ."[2] The development of new statistical techniques and new social scientific methodologies gave impetus to the development of "public policy analysis" as an area of study and applied research. We will outline some broad aspects of these methodologies further on in this chapter.

By way of introduction, it should also be mentioned that in a practical sense policy analysis was strengthened by a number of related administrative developments. Among these were the congressional requirement that, in many policy areas, 1 percent of a program's budget be set aside for program evaluation; the enactment of the Freedom of Information Act of 1966, which facilitated greater public access to the information that would make policy analysis feasible; the development of program budgeting; and the growing tendency to place "sunset" clauses in enabling legislation. The latter provide that programs will be self-terminating after a period of time, often five years, unless the administering agency can convince the legislature that the program is effective and still desirable or necessary. Policy analysis can help in this regard by showing whether a program is having the intended impact in a cost-effective manner and with a favorable cost-benefit ratio.

In sum, a variety of political and technical developments coalesced in the 1970s to focus greater attention on policy analysis as a part of public administration. In fact, policy analysis may now be considered a true part of the core of contemporary public administration.

APPROACHES TO ANALYZING PUBLIC POLICY

It is sometimes useful to distinguish between two aspects of public policy. One is called **policy output,** the other **policy impact.**[3] These are obviously linked, but they can be separated for analytical reasons, to avoid confusion. The formulation of public policy involves establishing the objectives to be attained and at least sketchily outlining the general means to be used in seeking to achieve these. For instance, to return to a familiar example, if a legislature decides that equal employment opportunity is a desirable objective, it may enact a statute intended to regulate the behavior of employers so as to facilitate the achievement of this aim. The statute may also vest responsibility for implementing or enforcing its provisions in an administrative agency, such as an equal employment opportunity commission. Presumably, if the legislature is serious in its intentions, it will allocate sufficient budgetary and personnel resources to the administering agency and also grant it the legal powers to accomplish its mission. The formulation of public policy is often highly politicized and may involve hotly contested elections, votes in the legislature, and extensive lobbying activities. The outgrowth of policy formulation is the policy output—that is, an official statement of governmental intent, delineation of powers and methods, and allocation of resources. Policy outputs may be tangible or symbolic. For instance, statutes, congressional resolutions, presidential proclamations, the allocation of staff and funds are all policy outputs.

Policy Outputs   Policy outputs are extremely important in politics and administration. They are statements of the goals of the polity and are prerequisites to the attainment of these through administrative action. However, from the perspective of policy analysis, it is crucial not to confuse policy outputs with policy impacts. The outputs themselves do not tell us very much about actual performance or the achievement of stated objectives. The outputs are essentially *activities.* It is hoped that they are positively related to the effective achievement of a policy objective. But today, only a naive political observer would assume simply because a statute is enacted, an administrative agency empowered, or funds spent that a governmental purpose is actually achieved. We have learned too much about the limits of governmental action to assume that the output necessarily has the intended impact.

Policy Impacts   Policy impacts by contrast are concerned with performance: What effect is the policy output having on the intended target? Is the objective being achieved? If not, why not? If so, is achievement related to administration? At what cost? With what side effects? These are the types of questions that are most pertinent when we engage in policy analysis with regard to the activities of public administrative agencies. Unfortunately the answers we seek are sometimes very elusive. This is due partly to the limitations of analytic techniques, partly to problems of measurement, partly to lack of information, and to other problems.

Impact Analysis

Before the impact of a policy can be ascertained, it is necessary to identify the content of that policy in operational terms. In other words, the policy must have some specific content that lends itself to observation. Many policies do just that. For instance, a policy of reducing taxes to stimulate economic growth is something that can be analyzed. But many policies are too vague in their objectives or too resistant to measurement to be systematically observed. Policies to promote justice, equal opportunity, and peace are examples that tend to fall into this category. Such policies may be extremely important—after all, they are the stuff of which politics is made and over which wars and revolutions are fought—but their content may simply not be suitable for the policy analysis techniques and methods currently available to us. Still other policies fall somewhere in between these two categories. In principle their impact can be evaluated; in practice it becomes difficult to separate out the impact of the policy itself from other factors. In one well-documented example, an analysis of the policy of strict enforcement of speeding laws by Connecticut seemed at first to show that the policy did substantially reduce traffic fatalities.[4] On further consideration, however, it turned out that there were several other factors aside from the strict enforcement that were confounding the analysis. For instance, strict enforcement was only part of a larger safety campaign involving better driver training, safer cars, use of seat belts; even the weather was a factor. This type of problem is not inconsequential, for very often specific policy outputs are part of a larger concern with a general political, economic, or social problem. Thus, equal opportunity is part of a concern with equality in general, including the areas of education, housing, health, nutrition, etc. Even two such strange bedfellows as food aid and weapons shipments may be part of the same concern; "food for peace" is politically in much the same category as selling or providing weapons to unstable regimes. Which, if either, has a stabilizing impact?

Assuming that the objectives of the policy outputs are suitable for it, an

impact analysis may be undertaken. Impact analysis can be defined as being "concerned with examining the extent to which a policy causes change in the intended direction."[5] The basic idea behind impact analysis is causality. Does the policy cause change? Or is the change, if any, or some of it, independent of the policy?

Answering such questions can often be exceedingly complex in the context of public administration. This is not the place to review the subject in depth, but the student should be alerted to some of the major hurdles to policy analysis involving public administrative activity.

Limited Opportunities for Experimentation   One way to try to assess the impact of a policy is to apply it to one group but not to another composed of similar individuals. This is called an **experimental design** and has many variants. In the public sector, however, opportunities for experimentation are frequently limited by political, moral, and/or legal concerns. For example, suppose you are in the public health service and you want to analyze the impact of treating people for syphilis. Can you treat some while creating a control group by withholding treatment from others in similar condition even though ample resources are available to treat everyone? In essence, this was done over a period of three decades by the U.S. Public Health Service in Tuskegee, Alabama, and it was not a happy story (see Box 8–1).[6] What about constructing experiments to provide welfare, nutrition, medical assistance, police protection, education, or voting rights to some but not others in an effort to assess the impact of policies? Although some creative approaches to experimentation are politically, morally, and legally feasible in these areas, many technically appropriate approaches are ruled out.

The well-known "New Jersey negative income-tax experiment" is an example of both the utility and difficulties of experimentation. It was conducted from 1968 to 1972 in several cities. The negative income tax is a governmental payment to individuals having little or no income. It is designed so that the payment is reduced as an individual or family receives other income, presumably from employment. However, within the range of income that defines eligibility for the negative tax, the reduction in the payment is always *less* than the amount of the other income the individual or family receives. For instance, if the basic payment is $3,000 to a family with no income, a family that earns $1,000 would receive less than the $3,000 payment but more than a payment of $2,000, thus assuring that it would be better off economically as a result of its earnings. The scheme is intended to create an incentive to earn income. It is viewed as potentially preferable to conventional welfare programs because it encourages recipients to find employment. The family earning $1,000 might be eligible for a negative income-tax payment of $2,500, which would leave it with $3,500 instead of the $3,000 it would have received if it had no outside income at all.

A central question pertaining to the negative income tax is at what point the reduction of payments (the reduction rate) becomes a disincentive to seek or engage in paid work. Clearly, if one could receive $3,000 by not working at all and only $3,100 after earning $1,000 in an unpleasant job (due to a reduction

---

BOX 8–1 Experimental Research Design: The Case of "Bad Blood"

From 1932 to 1972, the United States Public Health Service (PHS) conducted a study on the effects of *untreated* syphilis on black men in the area around Tuskegee, Alabama. The "Tuskegee Study" involved 399 men with syphilis; 201 others were used as controls. The Public Health Service's primary interest was in learning about the impact of the disease on blacks in its final stages. They found that untreated syphilis can cause skin tumors and ulcers, mutilating bone destruction, heart damage, paralysis, insanity, and blindness. Apparently, the dominant view of the PHS was that, "There was nothing in the experiment that was unethical or unscientific." Once the experiment became highly publicized in 1972, much of the nation was not so sure.

According to James H. Jones, "Journalists tended to accept the argument that the denial of penicillin [to the untreated group] during the 1940s was the crucial ethical issue." Earlier forms of treatment were ineffective, painful, and in some respects as bad as the disease.

However, the men may have benefitted greatly from penicillin, and withholding it from them condemned the untreated men to a painful life with a very debilitating disease. But some observers thought a moral problem was inherent in the experiment from the outset. The *St. Louis Post-Dispatch* argued that, "The fact is that in an effort to determine from autopsies what effects syphilis has on the body, the government from the moment the experiment began withheld the best available treatment for a particularly cruel disease. The immorality of the experiment was inherent in its premise." Jones's book, *Bad Blood*, makes it clear that the study was also inherently racist.

Eventually, a lawsuit was filed on behalf of the untreated men and their heirs. The case was settled out of court, with the government agreeing to pay $37,500 to each of the "living syphilitics," $15,000 to the heirs of each of the "deceased syphilitics," $16,000 to each living member of the control group, and $5,000 to the heirs of each of the "deceased controls."

SOURCE: James H. Jones, *Bad Blood: The Tuskegee Syphilis Experiment* (New York: Free Press, 1981), pp. 8, 9, 217.

---

rate of 90 percent), one might decide not to work. As a matter of public policy design, the "best" reduction rate would reduce total governmental negative income-tax payments to the extent feasible while maintaining a satisfactory incentive for recipients to work. Experimentation would seem to be an excellent way of establishing what the best rate would be.

The New Jersey experiment was sponsored by the federal Office of Economic Opportunity and comprised 1,300 families. Half of these were in the experimental group and half in a control group that received no payments. Those in the control group were interviewed periodically, as were those in the experimental group. Several combinations of payment levels and reduction rates were tried among those in the experimental group. At first, the overall conclusion seemed to be that the negative income tax could be designed in a way that did not create a significant disincentive to work. However, upon subsequent analysis, it was found that six months after the experiment began, New Jersey *independently* changed its welfare policies by offering generous benefits to eligible families, including those in both the experimental and control groups. Once these new benefits were taken into account, analysis suggested that rather than establish an incentive to work, the negative income tax would inherently present a disincentive. This finding was precisely the opposite of what supporters of the negative income-tax policy had initially expected.[7]

The New Jersey negative income-tax experiment demonstrated the possibilities of using experimental design. It enabled policy-makers to test an idea without having to implement it on a statewide or nationwide basis. After the experiment was conducted and analyzed, support for the negative income tax waned and the concept was more or less abandoned. The experiment was expensive to carry out, but in the end it may have saved a great deal by forestalling the implementation of a misguided policy. At the same time, however, the episode demonstrated how difficult experimentation can be. New Jersey's decision to change its welfare laws while the Office of Economic Opportunity was sponsoring the experiment illustrates how unplanned events and external conditions can interfere with the logic of an experimental design. Here, the experimenters' painstaking care in establishing basic payment levels was rendered almost entirely irrelevant by New Jersey's action. Moreover, the initial conclusion derived from the experiment was subsequently reversed when the full import of the unplanned change was understood.

Assuming Causality in Nonexperimental Analyses   The limited opportunities for experimentation in the public sector force policy analysts to rely upon other approaches. Some of these can be convincing at best but misleading at worst. For instance, one can analyze the nutrition of children who receive school lunches through governmental programs. One might find that their nutrition is adequate; but one should not assume on that basis that this is due to the availability of the lunches alone. Perhaps other information could be brought to bear on the situation in an effort to ascertain causality. For instance, are the lunches the *only* food consumed by some of the students? What do the others eat? Still, without a control group, one cannot be sure what the students would do for nutrition in the absence of the lunch program.

A similar problem arises in what is called a **preprogram-postprogram analysis.** Here the condition of the target population prior to the implementation of the program is compared with the condition afterward. Comparison can be in terms of any number of criteria that seem relevant. For instance, if one wants to assess the impact of affirmative action on patterns of federal employment, one could look at the employment of a group, such as blacks, prior to the use of affirmative action. Salary, grade, and occupation could be some of the aspects of employment considered. The patterns observed could be compared with patterns after the implementation of affirmative action. One might find changes or the absence of change. And one might be tempted to attribute this to the use of affirmative action. Without further information, however, that could be a serious mistake. A wide variety of factors—including job-market conditions and demographic and general attitudinal change—could have contributed to changing employment patterns independently of the use of affirmative action. Moreover, even if there were no change, does this mean that the program does not work in terms of maintaining and preventing deterioration of the present level of equality of opportunity? Without more to go on, this question cannot be answered within the framework of the nonexperimental research design.

One way of improving on preprogram-postprogram comparisons is to establish the rate of change before the introduction of a new policy such as affirmative action. By projecting this rate of change into the postprogram period, we can obtain a rough idea of what would have been expected had the new policy not been adopted. Then the projection can be compared with the observed reality. Of course, this approach remains vulnerable to variations in confounding conditions. But in the absence of these, focusing on the rate of change may often provide a better basis for assessing the impact of an alteration in policy.

Quasi-experimental Research Designs   The opportunity for truly experimental research designs is often limited in public administration. Nonexperimental designs are not likely to be very satisfactory, especially in complicated policy areas where the political and administrative salience of solid policy analysis is often greatest. Sometimes it is possible to bridge this gap somewhat by developing a **quasi-experimental design.** Such designs often try to determine the impact of policies by contrasting performance between groups exposed to the policy and those not exposed while statistically controlling for confounding conditions. Federalism, which allows for such great variation among governmental policies, often facilitates such comparisons. For example, one state may enforce mandatory seat belt laws while neighboring states do not. Subsequently, one could compare motorist fatalities or serious injuries in these states. If the state enforcing the use of seat belts had fewer fatalities or serious injuries it would *suggest* that the policy was responsible. That is the general idea of quasi-experimental designs. However, elaborate precautions have to be taken in such research to assure that the conclusion is valid. For instance, in the foregoing example, it would probably be advisable to compare fatalities or serious injuries per mile driven on the states' roads, since one state may have a much greater number of drivers than the other. The topography of the state, the number of miles of roads in urban and rural areas, the nature of licensing procedures, the demographic character of drivers, such as average age, percent over 70 or under 20, and several other factors would probably have to be taken into account before being relatively sure that the seat belt policy was having the intended effect.

Interpreting Results   Taking so much into account obviously makes for a difficult analysis that may be very time-consuming and expensive. Moreover, the results of such a study may be equivocal. It is unlikely that analysis will lead to such conclusions as, "Spending *x* dollars to compel drivers to use seat belts saves *y* lives per year." In fact, one of the great problems of policy analysis is that so many studies are unable to ascertain what kind of effect, if any, a policy is having. It is important that the public administrator not draw the wrong lesson from this. Simply because the impact of a policy cannot be satisfactorily ascertained through our available methods of policy analysis does not mean that the policy is not working. It may be working, and even working well, even though we are unable to demonstrate, in an analytically satisfactory way, that it is doing so. By contrast, even where policy analysis suggests that a policy is working well, the public administrator should always bear in mind that there may be some factor that was not taken into account in the analysis that explains the seeming success. For instance, reorganizing and redeploying a police force may coincide with a reduction in crime rates. However, such a reduction could stem from a number of other factors, including a decline of the population in the area that is male and between the ages of sixteen and thirty, since this group is known to have a greater propensity to commit crimes.

Moreover, although policy impacts may be observable in the short run, strong policy analysis must also consider the long run. It must be concerned with the target group in the future, the policy's impact on nontarget groups ("spillover" effects), and the options created or foreclosed by the policy. For instance, a welfare policy aimed at providing aid to poor children may successfully accomplish that while simultaneously and unintentionally encouraging teenage pregnancy in poor families. It may also create a disincentive to remain employed among members of the "working poor," a nontarget group. If such a policy encourages a higher birth rate among the poor, eventually public policy addressing the health and educational needs of poor children is likely to cost more. Since resources are scarce, funds to do so will limit their availability for other purposes. Additionally, policy analysis should also be sensitive to the symbolic importance of governmental actions. Even if a policy has no discernible impact, it may be an important political indicator of a government's interest in dealing with a problem.

In practice one of the important issues in discussions of the results of policy analysis is "Who has the burden of proof?" Must public administrators demonstrate that their programs are having the intended effect, or is the burden on others to show that the programs do not work? Sometimes, shifting the burden of proof in such discussions is tantamount to determining the outcome of the debate or dispute. For instance, whoever has the burden of proof in demonstrating that civil service examinations predict on-the-job performance in white-collar occupations is likely to lose.[8] This is not necessarily because the exams do not actually predict performance, but rather because it is so difficult to *prove* that they do. Common sense may often be the best guide in these matters, but sometimes when political interests are at stake, common sense may be hard to find.

Process Analysis

Ascertaining the impacts of public policies is often difficult or impossible. However, policy analysis should not be confined to considering impacts; it can also be used to assess the *process* through which a policy is being implemented. **Process analysis** concerns the way in which a particular policy or program is implemented.[9] Its importance can be succinctly stated: "The content of a particular public policy and its impact on those affected may be substantially modified, elaborated, or even negated during its implementation. Obviously, it is futile to be concerned with the impact of a particular policy if it has not been implemented."[10]

Surprisingly, however, policy analysis often neglects process analysis. In part this may be because it calls for a different type of approach than impact analysis. Whereas the latter tends to deal with aggregate data, such as crime rates or traffic fatalities, process analysis requires that the analyst become intimately aware of the administrative process through which the policy is implemented. For instance, if the policy is mandatory use of seat belts, one would have to look at the process of getting people to buckle up. Do public relations approaches work? Do police officers issue tickets for nonuse? Are penalties applied? If so, are they substantial? Just as the enforcement of other traffic laws may vary widely, so might that be the case with a mandatory seat belt law. In that event, it would not simply be the policy but the enforcement also that one would expect to have an impact on the area of behavior (driving).

In recent years, much process analysis has taken the form of "implementation" studies. These have identified some key factors affecting the execution of policies. One is the number of points at which different administrators must make decisions concerning implementation. In general, the more decision points there are the less likely it is that the policy will be implemented as those who formulated it intended. Serious underfunding of programs is another barrier to successful implementation. Sometimes the goals or objectives of policies are so unclear that different agencies and public administrators adopt disparate approaches to defining and implementing them. For instance, during the early years of affirmative action in the federal personnel system, some agencies adopted goals and timetables that, if implemented, would have left their work forces *less* socially representative of the nation's working population. One agency even sought to increase occupational segregation by sex by establishing a 100 percent hiring goal for women in clerical positions. This may have provided more jobs for women, but it was a peculiar—though plausible—interpretation of the policy of using affirmative action to achieve equal employment opportunity.[11]

Implementation studies suggest that a process analysis may be the place to begin policy analysis. If the implementation is such that there is no logical reason to expect a policy to have much or any impact, then there is no need to go further. Nevertheless, process analysis is sometimes neglected because it may require access to public administrators and the ability to monitor aspects of their behavior over substantial periods of time. But such access can be perceived by administrators as a potential threat, for in the area of process analysis, evaluation of administrative behavior is seldom far beneath the surface.

POLICY EVALUATION

Policy evaluation depends upon policy analysis, but it is a different enterprise. In terms of public administration, the question is whether the implementation of the policy is appropriate, rather than whether it has the intended impact at all. Policy analysis may enable us to agree that a policy works. In part that is because we tend to share a certain analytical paradigm that we agree can make such things knowable. However, in public administration, as we have seen throughout this book, such a consensus on normative questions is often missing. Just as what we are likely to view as "good" public administration depends upon our perspective, what we consider properly executed policy will often depend upon whether we adopt a managerial, political, or legal perspective.

THE MANAGERIAL PERSPECTIVE ON POLICY EVALUATION

Assuming that a policy has some traceable impact in the intended direction on its target, how can we determine whether its execution is optimal, or whether it is "satisfactory" or "not good enough"? The managerial perspective toward public administration, by placing an emphasis on effectiveness, efficiency, and economy, tends to present a distinctive set of answers to this question.

Effectiveness

Effectiveness in this context will tend to focus on the process of implementation. Among the major questions likely to be asked are: Is the administering agency effectively (that is, rationally) organized? Is the behavior of the public administrators involved *predictable?* Are patterns of authority and responsibility clear? Is feedback within the agency sufficient? Is communication adequate? Are enough resources being devoted to the policy? In short, does the organization of the effort to implement the policy follow the notions of effective management with regard to structure, personnel, budgeting, decision making, and so on? From this perspective, some policies are more suitable for implementation than others. Those that are relatively unsuitable will not be considered to be policies that work well, even though they may achieve their intended objectives. They will not be considered "good" policies because their administrative costs will be judged excessive and they will be thought to be too resistant to "good" (effective) management.

From this perspective there are many policies that simply will not work well. Policies that require "street-level" interactions between administrators who are, at the time, unsupervised and clients or other individuals will inevitably have an unpredictable quality about them. For example, no matter how explicit the formal rules seem to be, one housing inspector, police officer, member of the border patrol, teacher, or other **street-level administrator** will treat very similar situations, cases, or individuals differently from another administrator.[12] The exercise of discretion is simply unavoidable in many of these interactions. Actions may turn on individual administrators' judgments of the motives of the people with whom they come into contact, or with assessments of their behavior.

What is "suspicious" behavior to one police officer may not appear so to another.

The unpredictability of these kinds of interactions presents a problem from the managerial perspective. Administrators may be acting in ways that deviate from the organization's formal guidelines. Consequently, the organization itself may be deviating somewhat from its intended role within the framework of the public policy being implemented. Teachers may be baby-sitting or controlling students rather than educating them. Police may be punishing suspects by using excessive force rather than simply arresting them and leaving punishment to the courts and prisons. Housing inspectors may be making judgments that have the tendency to allow some areas of a city to deteriorate far more rapidly than others. Moreover, since the individual street-level administrator is so difficult to supervise—and in fact is often the main source of information about his or her activities—the management of the organization may not even be aware of how discretion is being used or abused.

The managerial approach, in turn, will try to develop indicators of performance that constrain the street-level bureaucrat more to the formal guidelines and expectations of the organization. Where these indicators are indeed indicative of what it is the street-level administrator is supposed to be doing, this will be a helpful response. However, in many cases solid indicators cannot be developed. Sometimes, in fact, quantitative indicators of qualitative performance can be counterproductive, as when teachers pass students on to the next grade even though they have not shown satisfactory learning. (In other words, a teacher whose pupils fail to learn is likely to be judged a poor teacher. Consequently, he or she may exaggerate the students' achievements.)

Policies requiring or involving hearings of some sort to determine eligibility for a government program are also likely to be considered less effective from the managerial perspective. Again, the problem is largely one of predictability. Hearings lead to idiosyncratic assessments by examiners or administrative law judges and to unplanned allocations of resources. Their outcomes may be unpredictable and inconsistent.

Policies may also be judged as undesirable from a managerial perspective because their goals are too amorphous. The managerial emphasis on effectiveness favors policies with clear, identifiable goals so that formal organizational arrangements and guidelines can be formulated toward their achievement. In addition, the clearer the goal, the more likely it is that meaningful indicators of performance with regard to its achievement can be developed. From a managerial perspective it is difficult to have an effective implementation process unless there are clear objectives and indicators of performance.

The managerial approach favors techniques for evaluating policy implementation that allow investigations to remain under the control of an agency's hierarchy. Three common techniques of this kind are:

1. *Site visits* by teams of high ranking administrators and other experts in the agency's employ to assess operations at various installations. As Thomas Dye notes, "these teams can pick up impressionistic data about how

programs are being run, whether programs are following specific guidelines, whether they have competent staffs, and sometimes whether or not
'clients' (target groups) are pleased with the services."[13]

2. *Process measures,* such as the number of claims processed, pupils matric-
   ulated, or arrests made are often a useful gauge of activity on a year-to-year
   or month-to-month basis.

3. *Comparison with professional standards* is useful in some areas where such
   standards have been established independently by engineers, educators,
   health professionals, or others. For example, civil service examinations
   may be evaluated for "construct validity" (see Chapter 5) through comparison to standards set by professional organizations of psychologists or
   personnel specialists.

Cost-Effectiveness

Cost-effectiveness combines concern with efficiency, economy, and effectiveness. Its central question is, given that a policy achieves a certain level of success,
could another means achieve the same or a higher level at the same or less cost?
For instance, if the policy is to have clean streets, will it be cost-effective to use
mechanical street sweepers to replace human labor? Would adopting and enforcing antilitter laws be more cost-effective? If the policy is education, is the
presently favored school district system preferable in terms of cost-effectiveness to
voucher systems allowing parents or pupils to choose which school to attend?
Would vouchers foster better education by spurring greater competition among
the schools for students? In any of these areas, the managerial perspective is likely
to favor the approach that achieves the most output per unit of cost (input).

The managerial evaluation of public policy from the perspective of cost-
effectiveness can become quite complicated. The best policy may be considered
the one that is most cost-effective, but cost-effectiveness can depend on the level
of application of the policy. This is the matter of **marginal costs,** which is
embodied in the simple-sounding question "How much will it cost to treat one
more case?" Generally speaking, the marginal cost of treating the first case is very
high and then decreases until we approach a point where treating each additional
case theoretically becomes more expensive than treating the one immediately
preceding it. To place the principle in more concrete terms, suppose the public
policy is to immunize all children in the United States between the ages of two
and five against a variety of diseases. Suppose further that the policy is premised
on the use of public administration to administer inoculations (perhaps to those
children not provided with them by private doctors). In order to accomplish the
public goal an administrative capacity would have to be established. A public
health service of some type would be set up. It would occupy physical space,
employ medical practitioners as well as administrative staff to manage it in terms
of such functions as personnel, budgeting, and organizational design; it would
also have clerical staff to assist management and in recordkeeping. In addition,
staff for security and transportation might be necessary. These arrangements cost
money: for salaries and supplies of the front-line service providers (the medical

practitioners); for the physical plant; for administrative overhead. If such a system were put in place to treat only two or three cases, the cost per case would be very high. However, the cost per case would probably come down dramatically if thousands or perhaps millions of children were inoculated by the system. Here, economies of scale would result from the ability of the same medical practitioners to inoculate more children for the same salary, from the ability of relatively fewer managers (per case treated) to oversee the operation, and from relatively fewer clerical and other staff. No matter how well the system was designed, however, there would be some children who were difficult to inoculate. Perhaps they live in remote areas, drift around from place to place, live in urban slums where they are difficult to find, have parents who are opposed to inoculation for one reason or another. Tracking down such cases for inoculation is probably possible, but the costs of doing so would obviously be much greater than the cost for the majority of children who are brought into a public health center by a parent for inoculation. In other words, achieving 100 percent compliance would probably be *disproportionately* more expensive than achieving only 80 percent compliance. Indeed, depending on the precise circumstances, gaining compliance from the last 10 or 20 percent might cost as much or more than treating all the rest of the cases.

This is a common phenomenon in cost-effectiveness analysis and can be applied to a wide range of examples. How much will it cost to pick up the last ton of garbage that is scattered around in the form of litter in an urban area? How much will it cost to educate the slowest student to an eighth-grade reading level, as compared to the average student? How much more will it cost to achieve 100 percent seat belt usage as opposed to 50 or 80 percent?

The managerial approach *tends* to evaluate policy implementation as not working well, in terms of cost-effectiveness, if its marginal costs are *rising*. If they are decreasing, the managerial perspective may support the treatment of still more cases; if they are level, this perspective may look for additional ways to reduce them (by cutting administrative overhead, for example). However, if no means of saving are evident at the point that marginal costs begin to rise, the managerial perspective will tend to conclude that the policy is being applied to too many cases, that it is too comprehensive, and that another approach should be developed. For example, public health service inoculations can be augmented by activities of the public schools in identifying those who have not been treated or by treating them directly. Garbage collection can be augmented by antilitter laws and deposits on beverage containers. Alternatively, the managerial perspective may simply conclude that the policy itself is too comprehensive in its objectives and cannot be soundly implemented as a consequence. In a sense, the question here is, "How much is enough?" And the managerial answer is often, "As much as will reduce marginal costs to their lowest plausible level." An exception are cases in which universal or highly comprehensive treatment is necessary to make the policy work at all, as might be true in eradicating diseases such as smallpox.

The managerial approach raises a number of questions from political and legal perspectives. The criterion of cost-effectiveness may need to be augmented by cost-benefit analysis. Whereas the cost-effectiveness approach assumes the value of each unit or case treated is constant, cost-benefit analysis requires assessment of potential differences among these units or cases. It also assumes that greater or lesser application of a policy may have disproportionate benefits. For instance, who are those children not inoculated? Where do they live? What effect does not treating them have on the benefits derived from inoculating others? Additionally, those adopting a legalistic approach will augment concerns with cost-effectiveness with constitutional values. For example, what level of compulsion can be used to force those opposed to inoculation to have their children treated? Suppose the basis of resistance is "squeamishness," or suppose it is firmly held religious convictions. Does the application of the policy involve disparate treatment by race or gender? These are the kinds of issues that the analysis of cost-effectiveness in policy implementation does not satisfactorily address.

In short, when applying a cost-effectiveness approach, it is always necessary to remember that the cases or units for treatment must be identical. This was the problem we observed in relation to budgeting in Chapter 6. The cost of averting a death by promoting the use of seat belts or motorcycle helmets is less than by treating or curing cancer of the cervix. From a managerial perspective the "case" is the death averted, and aside from costs, it does not matter much how it is averted (by buckling up or treating cancer). From political and legal perspectives, however, it may matter a great deal *whose* death is being averted.

Economy

In addition to cost-effectiveness, the managerial perspective will consider a policy to be executed well when its administrative costs and loss through mistakes, fraud, or waste are minimal. For the most part, this aspect of the managerial approach to evaluating public policy is not controversial. It tends to focus on a process analysis, though it is also concerned with impact in the sense that ineligible people should not be treated by the policy and that the policy should not be constructed in such a way as to facilitate fraud by its beneficiaries. Sometimes, however, this perspective does raise interesting questions from political and legal standpoints.

Passing Costs on to Clients   One classic way of reducing administrative costs is to pass them on to the recipients of services. Often, this is very simple, and may involve no more than making would-be recipients apply for a benefit, rather than using the administrative apparatus to go out and find them. For the most part, this pattern is followed in welfare and Social Security programs. Those believing that they are eligible for benefits must apply for them at an administrative office. Sometimes the passing on of costs is more subtle and sometimes it can be quite serious in its consequences (see Box 8–2).

Making the potentially eligible apply for the benefit may deter some people. But even greater deterrence is accomplished by forcing applicants to wait in line for long periods of time under unpleasant conditions. For instance, those ap-

---

BOX 8–2 **Passing Costs on to Others**

WALTER LITTLE, Appellant,

v

GLORIA STREATER

452 US 1, 68 L Ed 2d 627, 101 S Ct 2202

[No. 79-6799]

Argued January 13, 1981. Decided June 1, 1981.

Decision: Connecticut's application of its statute charging costs of blood grouping tests in paternity suit to requesting party, to deny indigent putative father such tests, held violative of due process.

SUMMARY

An unmarried woman gave birth to a child, and, as a requirement of the Connecticut Department of Social Services stemming from the child's receipt of public assistance, identified the putative father. The Department then provided an attorney for the mother, who commenced a paternity suit against the putative father in a Connecticut state court. The putative father moved the trial court to order blood grouping tests on the mother and the child pursuant to a Connecticut statute. The statute provided, in part, that the costs of such blood tests shall be chargeable against the party making the motion. Although the putative father asserted that he was indigent and asked that the state be ordered to pay for the tests, the trial court granted the motion only insofar as to order the blood tests, but denied the request that the state pay for the tests. Consequently, no blood grouping tests were performed, because the putative father could not afford their cost. After hearing testimony, the trial court found that the putative father was the child's father, and ordered him to pay child support. The Appellate Session of the Connecticut Superior Court affirmed the trial court's judgment in an unreported per curiam opinion. It held that the statute does not violate the due process and equal protection rights of an indigent putative father, and found no error in the trial court's denial of the putative father's motion that the cost of blood grouping tests be paid by the state. The putative father's petition for certification was denied by the Connecticut Supreme Court (180 Conn 756, 414 A2d 199).

On appeal, the United States Supreme Court reversed and remanded. In an opinion by BURGER, CH. J., expressing the unanimous view of the court, it was held that the application of the statute to deny the putative father blood grouping tests because of his lack of resources, where the statute requires that the costs of such tests be chargeable against the party requesting them, violated the due process guarantee of the Fourteenth Amendment.

---

plying for welfare benefits at New York City's office in lower Manhattan must stand in a long line that snakes around a dingy, poorly ventilated corridor that can be very hot and crowded. It may take as long as four hours or more to move from the end of the line to the proper administrative official. Seating is virtually nonexistent and closing time is scrupulously guarded, thereby forcing some who may have waited considerable time to return again. Although it is impossible to say how many, certainly some individuals who are eligible for the program do not apply for it due to such conditions. In fact, it is believed that about one-third of the population eligible for a typical administrative service fails to utilize it for one reason or another, including unpleasant administrative conditions.[14] In theory, perhaps, those deterred most are those whose eligibility is most questionable. In practice, however, this may not be the case.

Another means of passing on costs is to rule people ineligible for benefits, such as Social Security disability, pending decision of an individual's appeal in an administrative hearing.[15] If the individual subsequently wins, retroactive benefits may not necessarily be awarded. In any event, many individuals elect not to pursue their opportunity for a hearing, even though they may be eligible.

Residency requirements are another potential way of passing costs on to would-be clients. For instance, until the Supreme Court ruled such an approach unconstitutional in violation of equal protection and the right to travel in *Shapiro* v. *Thompson* (1969),[16] several states had residency requirements for welfare benefits. Connecticut, for example, had a one-year requirement, which it argued would accomplish a number of laudable administrative objectives. It would facilitate planning the welfare budget; it would reduce fraud through multiple payments to individuals; it would encourage individuals to seek work (rather than welfare) upon arrival in the state; and it would assure that recipients of the benefits were bona fide residents of the state. Although the residency requirement may have made sense from a managerial perspective, the Supreme Court considered the cost passed on to the individual to be a sacrifice of an essential right and liberty.

Passing Costs on to Employees   Employees can also be made to bear some of the costs of implementing an administrative program. For example, employees may have to supply their own uniforms, their own transportation for official purposes, or their own continued training through refresher courses and the like as a condition for continued employment. More controversially, employees may bear the costs of occupational disease and exposure to harmful substances in the workplace. Recently, for example, public employee unions have been protesting against the continued presence of asbestos in public buildings.

Controlling Misuse   The reduction of costs may be quite controversial when it involves an effort by public administrators to assure that clients do not misuse funds allocated to them. For instance, if one wanted to assure that food stamps were used to procure a nutritious diet, the food items for which they could be used would be substantially limited. This would raise political pressures from agricultural interest groups hoping to have their products defined as acceptably nutritious under the program. It would also raise cries that the government is unduly paternalistic in telling people what to eat. What might the Potato Chip and Snack Food Association, a Washington-based trade association, have to say about such a plan? Similarly, efforts to assure that welfare funds to families with dependent children are actually used for the children's benefit can raise difficult issues. Can a case worker insist on entering a dwelling on pain of cutting off the funds?[17] Is advance notice necessary? Are unannounced "midnight raids" allowed?[18] Can a case worker insist that the child's bed be made? That the child have a bed? At what point does the recipient of an administrative benefit have a constitutional right to privacy that cannot be abridged because she or he receives the benefit?

Overlooking Latent Functions   In a classic essay on political corruption, Robert Merton pointed out that the political machine, though corrupt, did have some *latent functions* that were quite beneficial, especially to immigrants seeking employment and favors in exchange for votes.[19] Sometimes the term "welfare bureaucracy" is used as the antithesis of an administrative system that reduces operating costs. Here the bureaucrats themselves are considered to be on "welfare" as a result of administrative overstaffing. Yet if the object is to provide employment, as in the case of public works programs, then overstaffing may not be dysfunctional from a policy standpoint. Moreover, if overstaffing of administrative units is viewed as a way of assimilating social groups and enhancing their opportunities to enter the mainstream of American political, economic, and social life, then the fact that administrative costs may appear excessive may be somewhat beside the point. The latent function, such as assimilation and upward mobility, may be well worth the price from a political standpoint.

THE POLITICAL PERSPECTIVE ON POLICY EVALUATION

As we have been suggesting, a political perspective on whether a policy is being successfully implemented may differ from a managerial perspective. Again, assuming that the policy has been determined to have some impact, evaluating its execution will depend on how well it fits the values inherent in the political approach. For even if a policy achieves its objectives, the means it uses and values it embodies may be evaluated as either satisfactory or unsatisfactory.

Representation

The political approach tends to view a policy as appropriately executed, within the parameters of the policy actually having a discernible impact on the target, if it affords representation to those individuals and interests most affected by it. Perhaps the use of the value of representation to judge the working of public policy through administrative implementation can best by conveyed by considering it from two perspectives that are common in public administration.

Participation in Decisions About Implementation   Several administrative programs in the United States have emphasized the idea that those most directly affected by the program be granted a voice in deciding how it will be implemented. One well-known instance involved the Taylor Grazing Act of 1934.[20] The policy propounded by the act was to issue permits for the grazing of livestock on the federally owned lands in the West in an effort to prevent denudation (with its consequent dust storms) through overgrazing. The act stated that the regulation of grazing should be made "in cooperation with local associations of stockmen."[21] Eventually this concept was implemented through the election of advisors from among the local stockmen in the various grazing districts. During the first fourteen months, the advisors' advice was followed in roughly 98 percent of the decisions involving the allocation of 14,000 permits.[22]

Although the Taylor Grazing Act presented a somewhat extreme case of individual participation in administrative implementation, it is by no means unique. Similar ideas have long prevailed in other agricultural programs and public school education. The Federal Advisory Committee Act of 1972, as noted in Chapter 1, seeks to assure representation of interests through the participation of advisory committees in administrative decision making. During the 1960s, the poverty program sought to make use of local participation through the election of some members of community action agencies. The Model Cities Program of that same decade sought the representation of local communities in urban renewal and revitalization decisions. The poverty program went somewhat beyond other approaches by encouraging the participation of representatives of the local population directly in the implementation of policy.[23]

From the perspective of the political approach, a policy that fosters an administrative system that does not allow participation of those most affected by the program may be judged a policy that is undesirable because it does not provide a measure of self-regulation.

Representation of Demographic Constituency Interests   The political perspective is also concerned that public administrative implementation be deemed to be substantively in the interest of demographic groups in legislative constituencies. For instance, an immunization program that fails to include rural children or severely economically disadvantaged children in urban areas may very well be judged inadequate from a political perspective. This is true even though a cost-benefit approach might show that it is dysfunctional in terms of administrative efficiency to try to reach those groups. Similarly, an approach to picking up garbage that leaves some neighborhoods, with identifiable economic or social characteristics, relatively neglected is likely to be challenged from a political perspective. Passing on costs to an identifiable constituency may also be opposed. There are many regulatory and service activities of public administrators that may potentially affect demographic groups differentially. Indeed, it has even been argued by the attorney general of New York State that allowing a rise in the cost of telephone calls from pay phones would have a particularly adverse impact on poor people, who may have no other access to phones.

Responsiveness

The political perspective's value of responsiveness is related to considerations of representation. However, it sometimes goes beyond the representation of relatively specific interests to a sense of being in step with what the community as a whole seems to want. For instance, in the early 1980s, a grass-roots movement against drunken driving developed in several states. Mothers' and students' groups against drunken driving sprang up. Some laws were rewritten in response to the public's pressure. Police began enforcing "driving while intoxicated" (DWI) laws more stringently and vigorously. In some states, New York for one, police roadblocks, at which all drivers are stopped as potentially DWI, became common. This redeployment of police, and the inconvenience it creates, is criticized by some. However, it is probably responsive to the concerns of the majority of citizens who care about the matter.

Sometimes the issue of responsiveness acts as a check on administrative logic that, while internally sound, is simply not in touch with reality. In other words, it can be invoked to counteract the "tunnel vision" that sometimes develops as a result of administrative specialization. For instance, an official directive from the now defunct U.S. Department of Health, Education, and Welfare once sought to prohibit "mother-daughter" and "father-son" events at public schools on the grounds that they were manifestations of prohibited sex-role stereotyping and gender-based discrimination. Whatever one thinks of HEW's logic, the public just wouldn't stand for the rule and it was promptly rescinded. The minting of the Susan B. Anthony dollar coin in the 1970s was another example. Administrators in Washington, D.C., were convinced that the coin would be useful. Apparently, serious consideration was given to its size, shape, and design. But as far as the public was concerned, there was no need for the Anthony dollar and they would not use it. (See Box 8–3 for an illustration of responsiveness.)

BOX 8–3 Public Comment in Public Administration: What's the Beef?

In December 1981, the National Cattlemen's Association asked the U.S. Department of Agriculture (USDA) to change its standards for the grading of beef. The cattlemen thought that the public was interested in leaner beef. The USDA proposed new standards for the Prime and Choice grades by requiring less fat in the form of marbling. The department held hearings on the proposed new standards in Des Moines, Dallas, Atlanta, Washington, and Salt Lake City. According to a USDA spokesperson, they received "4,000 comments from various segments of the public, and almost 80 percent were against the changes. The strong common denominator was, rightly or wrongly, the perception that the new regulations would cause consumer confusion and destroy consumer confidence, neither of which would ultimately help the meat industry. And since we are concerned with industry profitability, the new proposals did not seem like a good idea." Consequently, the old standards were retained in response to the public's will as expressed through opportunities for public comment on the USDA's proposed policy change. This is just one illustration of the importance of the public's right to receive notice of administrative agencies' proposed regulations to have the opportunity to respond to them.

SOURCE: Mimi Sheraton, "Department of Agriculture Withdraws Proposed Changes in Grading of Beef," *New York Times*, September 21, 1982, p. A22.

Decentralization of administrative operations is another aspect of responsiveness that can lead the political and managerial perspectives to diverge on what constitutes proper implementation. It may often be cheaper for administrative agencies not to maintain a large number of field offices. Instead, individuals wanting something from the administrative agency or compelled to interact with it are required to travel to its headquarters or less conveniently located field offices. In the state of Vermont, for example, at one time at least, to register a new car brought in from outside the state, one had to travel to the capital, Montpelier, which might be a substantial distance away. There were no local offices in towns to deal with this administrative operation. From a political perspective, such an arrangement is not responsive to the needs of individuals who live in areas remote from the administrative offices. If these remote areas coincide with legislative districts, there is every likelihood that pressure will be placed on elected representatives to require the administrative agencies to maintain more convenient field offices in order to be more *responsive* to the needs of the legislators' constituencies. This is one reason why states with large geographic areas and low population densities tend to have more public administrators per capita than do other states.[24]

Accountability

Accountability is a final value that should be considered in addressing the political perspective's evaluation of the functioning of public policy. That perspective demands that public administration be held accountable to elected officials, particularly legislators. Accountability is addressed in greater detail in Chapter 12. Here, however, it is desirable to indicate how the execution of some policies can pose a challenge to it.

Sunshine   It was once said by Supreme Court Justice Louis Brandeis that sunlight is the best disinfectant. Since the late 1960s, federal policy and that of several states has emphasized the desirability of promoting "freedom of information" about the operation of administrative agencies. Some laws require that certain types of meetings and hearings within agencies be open to the public and the press. Although these **sunshine laws** hardly provide any citizen with a right to each and every bit of administrative information, they do serve to *open* the administrative process to public and legislative scrutiny to a very substantial extent. From this perspective, an administrative program that operates in secret may be judged not to be working "well," even though it achieves its objectives at a reasonable level and cost. Covert CIA operations have been opposed on this basis. In fact, Supreme Court Justice Douglas once said that if the public was not told how the CIA spent its money, "a secret bureaucracy is allowed to run our affairs."[25] Some of the administrative arrangements associated with the Executive Office of the President, especially during the Watergate period and the Iran-Contra affair, were criticized on this basis as well. To make the problem more concrete, suppose you were passed or failed on a driver's licensing exam on the basis of unknown criteria? Or were held back in school, with no inkling why that administrative decision was made?

Sunset   Sunset provisions, as noted earlier, are another manifestation of the desire to hold public administrators accountable. From a managerial perspective, all the reporting and justifying that are involved when agencies operate under a sunset provision (and desire to be continued) can be serious diversions from or barriers to efficient, economical, and effective operations. Yet from the political perspective, administrative programs that do not labor under such conditions may not be considered policies that work well. For the policy to work well, a review by the legislature at some fixed time is sometimes deemed essential.

General Legislative Oversight   Legislatures in the United States use a committee and subcommittee system partly to exercise "oversight" of administrative operations. They may also create administrative agencies of their own, such as the federal General Accounting Office, to engage in oversight. In general, a policy that eludes effective oversight, perhaps because it overlaps too many committee jurisdictions, may be judged a policy that does not work well. Even if its objectives are achieved, a policy that is inherently resistant to oversight may be evaluated as a poor means of using public power to intervene in the economy or society because such a policy would be largely beyond the control of elective officials.

Case Work   Legislative case work, discussed in Chapter 2, can be a means of promoting the accountability of public administrators to elective officials. Consequently, from a political perspective, a means of policy execution that prohibits the administrators from responding to case work inquiries could be judged undesirable. Of course, sometimes resistance to legislative involvement in administrative routines is understandable because it is desirable to insulate public administration from political pressures. For instance, the IRS may not want to divulge what triggers a tax audit. Other times, though, as when the IRS or Social Security Administration refuse to be bound by the advice that their own local offices give to taxpayers and applicants, the inability to use case work effectively may suggest a greater difficulty with the nature of public policy: namely, that the administrative rules are so complicated and difficult to understand, that the agencies themselves do not even trust their own subordinate officials to explain the rules or policies accurately![26]

THE LEGAL PERSPECTIVE ON POLICY EVALUATION

The legal approach to public administration also asks a distinctive set of questions in evaluating the operation of public policies. Its focus tends to be on equal protection, fairness (procedural due process), and protection of the rights of those individuals who come into contact with public administrative operations. Consequently, since the questions asked by the legal perspective differ from those asked by either of the other perspectives, the answers it reaches may also be different. It is obviously impossible to consider in detail all the fine points that the legal perspective would take in evaluating policy, but some of the more central aspects can be briefly reviewed.

Equal Protection

As we have seen, distributional issues often arise in the administrative implementation of public policy. Who shall receive a benefit and where? Who shall be subject to a regulation and will there be discernible patterns of enforcement? The managerial approach to public administration tends to address such issues from a cost-effectiveness or economizing approach. The political perspective considers them from the perspectives of representation of identifiable groups or constituencies and responsiveness to these groups. The legal approach adds yet another dimension.

It focuses more on whether individuals or groups are afforded equal protection of the law.[27] In other words, does the policy place members of some social groups at a disadvantage? If so, is the policy rationally formulated and executed to achieve a legitimate or compelling governmental purpose? Does the policy intentionally discriminate against groups that have historically been subject to discrimination and disadvantage in the United States?[28] Answers to questions such as these will determine whether the legal perspective will view a policy and/or its execution as appropriate or inappropriate.

In practice, two kinds of problematic cases arise. One is where public policy allocates resources differentially to different racial or ethnic groups. Here the issue is likely to be whether such a policy, even if otherwise rationally related to a legitimate governmental purpose, has an unconstitutional or illegal discriminatory intention. For instance, in one case, the town of Shaw, Mississippi, managed to pave streets, put in sewers, streetlights, and other improvements in the white section of town, but not in the black neighborhood.[29] Its actions were found to be unconstitutional by the federal courts. In another case, the school system in San Antonio, Texas, allocated far greater funds per student to a school attended primarily by "Anglos" as opposed to one with a large number of Hispanic students. The city argued that the classification, or basis for distribution of funds, was based on wealth, not ethnicity, and that it rationally served a legitimate purpose. The U.S. Supreme Court agreed.[30]

A second type of problem is the use of social characteristics, such as race, as proxies for some other attribute. One example, though decided under the Fourth Amendment rather than equal protection, concerned the U.S. Border Patrol. The function was to stop motor vehicles near the Mexican border to check on the citizenship or visa status of their occupants. The policy was to stop primarily (if not solely) those people who "looked Mexican." This practice obviously created a proxy—"looking Mexican"—for a condition, namely, being an "undocumented alien." The Supreme Court found the policy to be unconstitutional.[31] Consequently, stopping cars on the basis of the ethnic appearance of their occupants is unconstitutional. But from a managerial perspective of trying to make the most efficient, effective, and economical use of scarce personnel and other resources, would it make sense for the Border Patrol to expend time and effort stopping those who "looked 'Anglo' " or even Scandinavian? Here is an area where different approaches to policy evaluation stand in stark contrast.

Procedural Due Process and Protection of Individual Rights

The legal perspective toward public administration also favors providing those dependent upon administrative services or subject to administrative regulation with procedural protections against an adverse action. Thus whereas the managerial perspective might support immediately cutting off a benefit to a client who is suspected of fraud, the legal perspective might favor continuing the benefit until the individual is given the opportunity to answer the allegations that he or she had engaged in fraudulent behavior.[32]

The legal approach also takes an expansive position on the importance of individual rights and liberties. Consequently, it may view some administrative policies as not working well if they tend to infringe upon these rights. An example already mentioned is the imposition of residency requirements for eligibility for welfare benefits. Other intriguing instances have been such requirements as being available for work on Saturday, despite one's religious beliefs to the contrary, for unemployment insurance;[33] exclusion from extracurricula high-school activities for being married;[34] and a variety of "morality" impositions placed on residents of public housing. Because the legal approach has such a distinctive view of public administration, we will address its values more fully at a later point (Chapter 11).

UTILIZING EVALUATION

Policy evaluation is intended to be useful to politicians and public administrators. At the very least, it should contribute to knowledge about the effects and design of public policies. Ideally, evaluation would also lead to direct improvements in policy implementation in the short run. But there are barriers to the effective use of evaluation research. First, as Aaron Wildavsky observes, administrative organizations may not be set up to digest evaluation. He writes:

> Evaluation and organization may be contradictory terms. Organizational structure implies stability while the process of evaluation suggests change. Organization generates commitment while evaluation inculcates skepticism. Evaluation speaks to the relationship between action and objectives while organization relates its activities to programs and clientele.[35]

Second, even if administrative organizations were amenable to evaluation research, they would still face problems in interpreting such studies. Many evaluations are, quite simply, inconclusive. Some studies are unable to ascertain any significant impact of public policy. Others show very limited effects. The failure to discern impacts may lie in any of the following or some combination thereof: (1) the policy itself, (2) implementation, (3) the evaluation design and methodology, or (4) errors in carrying out the evaluation research.

When evaluation fails to find a policy impact, supporters of the program may argue that *more* funding and authority are needed to make the policy work. Opponents, by contrast, may assert that the policy is misconceived or that implementation is unworkable. Both can speculate about the likelihood of the policy working better in the long run. In essence, the political debates concerning public policies are frequently left largely unresolved by evaluation studies.

Perhaps experience with evaluation is still too limited. Utilization may become more systematic in the future if (1) the quality of evaluation research improves; (2) evaluation research becomes more institutionalized in agencies such as the federal Office of Management and Budget, General Accounting Office, and Congressional Budget Office; (3) evaluation research can be integrated with policy making in the legislative and executive branches; and (4) evaluation studies include specific plans for utilization.[36]

SYNTHESIZING THE PERSPECTIVES ON POLICY EVALUATION

For the most part, policy analysis is a straightforward endeavor. There is considerable agreement on the appropriateness of various methods in various applications. This is not to say that disputes do not sometimes occur over methods and findings, but rather that very often when these disagreements do occur it is because circumstances prohibit the use of methods that would be most suitable in a technical, research sense. Again, a leading example is experimentation, especially where it entails governmental action that deliberately harms individuals by withholding or withdrawing treatments or benefits from them. The more challenging issue is constructing policy that satisfies, as much as possible, the perspectives on public administration flowing from the managerial, political, and legal approaches.

We have contrasted the perspectives on policy evaluation stemming from these approaches for the sake of illustration. However, there is at least one element common to all of them that can serve as a guideline in identifying policies that are unlikely to be evaluated as working well.

Control of Administrative Discretion

The managerial approach to policy evaluation does not favor policies that rely heavily upon street-level interactions. The political approach also finds the unbridled administrative discretion that is often involved in such encounters to be undesirable. That is partly why citizen participation is favored in the form of school boards and, sometimes, civilian review boards of police actions. The legal approach is also opposed to such unchecked discretion. This is true even if no patterns of discrimination are evident. In fact, the Supreme Court has put forth this perspective in no uncertain terms. In *Delaware* v. *Prouse* (1979), it held that the police could not stop cars to check their registrations, licenses, or safety, without some articulated reason or preestablished plan for stopping any given car.[37] In other words, the police might stop a car if its headlights were not functioning at night, or they might stop every car, or perhaps every tenth car, but they could not constitutionally stop any particular car without a reason that could be explained.

The convergence of the three perspectives in this area of policy implementation suggests that certain features of contemporary public administration could be improved. The polity has been involved in such an effort, largely on this basis, in terms of two of the most common kinds of street-level administrators—police and public school teachers. The former have been subject to a range of legal, managerial, and political controls during the past two decades. Constraints have also been placed on teachers and school systems in an effort to reduce their discretion in dealing with individual pupils. Indeed, the Supreme Court has even held that a public school student has a minimal right to due process before he or she can be briefly suspended.[38] (On the other hand, the Court has placed only minimal restrictions on administrative searches of students in public schools.[39]) Still, there are additional areas where reduction of unbridled discretion can be achieved. One is the frustrating practice, mentioned earlier, whereby some agencies, notably the IRS and the Social Security Administration, do not consider themselves bound by the advice that their own employees give to the public. Certainly, if an agency places an employee in the position of giving advice, then the individual citizen who follows this advice should not be penalized for so doing at some later date—especially if the case is well documented (see Box 8–4).

When we move beyond this guideline, however, it becomes difficult to synthesize the three perspectives. Instead, it might be more satisfactory to consider the nature of the policy itself, and then try to apply one or another of the perspectives that is most suitable to it. However, since policies do not come in neat packages with labels, this may be difficult to achieve. Still, some ideas can be suggested as an example of how we might further clarify our thinking regarding policy evaluation.

Overhead Policy   Overhead policies are those concerned with keeping public administrative operations running on a day-to-day basis. They do not include levels of budgeting, the allocation of personnel, or the nature of missions. They *do* include disbursing and accounting for money, personnel functions such as compensating and retiring employees, and the maintenance and interior design of the physical plant of agencies. For the most part, managerial perspectives are most appropriate in judging the overhead policies. There is little doubt that

BOX 8–4 **Bearing the Cost of a Bureaucrat's Error**

Richard Schweiker, Secretary
of Health and Human Services
v.
Ann Hansen
450 U.S. 785, April 6, 1981

Ann Hansen met for about fifteen minutes with Don Connelly, a field representative of the Social Security Administration, and inquired as to her eligibility for "mother's insurance benefits." Connelly erroneously told her that she was not eligible and did not recommend that she file a written application or advise her of the advantages of doing so, even though the administration's thirteen-volume Claims Manual instructed field representatives to advise applicants of the advantages of filing written applications and to recommend to applicants who are uncertain about their eligibility that they file written applications. About a year later, Hansen learned that in fact she was eligible, filed a written application, and began receiving benefits. Pursuant to the regulations, she was entitled to receive benefits for up to twelve months preceding her application and she did receive retroactive benefits for that period. She contended that she should also receive retroactive benefits for the twelve months preceding her initial interview with Connelly, since he gave her erroneous information and failed to alert her to the desirability of filing a written application.

The U.S. Supreme Court held that Connelly's error did not prevent the Secretary of Health and Human Services from denying Hansen retroactive benefits for the twelve months prior to her interview with Connelly. The Court reasoned that the Social Security Administration could not be bound by the errors of its lower-level functionaries, since

. . . the Claims Manual is not a regulation. It has no legal force, and it does not bind the SSA. Rather, it is a 13-volume handbook for internal use by thousands of SSA employees, including the hundreds of employees who receive untold numbers of oral inquiries like [Hansen's] each year. If Connelly's minor breach of such a manual suffices to [prevent Schweiker from withholding the retroactive benefits sought], then the Government is put "at risk that every alleged failure by an agent to follow instructions to the last detail in one of a thousand cases will deprive it of the benefit of the written application requirement which experience has taught to be essential to the honest and effective administration of the Social Security Laws" [citation omitted].

But as Justice Marshall argued, in dissent, "the fault for [Hansen's] failure to file a timely application for benefits that she was entitled to must rest squarely with the Government. . . ."

Their fault, her loss. How would you have ruled?

efficiency, effectiveness, and economy have been valued here ever since the managerial perspective was developed.

Sociotherapeutic Policies   These policies—such as, for example, the war on poverty and the Model Cities Program—seek to treat an undesirable condition that has become associated with a particular group. The group could have various attributes: it could be racial, economic, urban, elderly, or rural, for example. To a very large extent, sociotherapeutic policy coincides with the idea "welfare" in the label "welfare state." Such policies seem to favor the political perspective in their administrative arrangements. The participation of their beneficiaries and responsiveness to their needs are of great importance in their relative success. Moreover, in the absence of participation and representativeness, these policies become paternalistic; they become regulatory in the sense of controlling individuals' behavior without affording them a voice in the process.

Regulatory Policy   Regulation through administrative action comes in many guises. However, some programs are clearly "regulatory" in a very classical sense. These are programs that are engaged in such functions as rate-setting for public utilities and common carriers; in zoning; in assuring purity or healthfulness of substances such as food, water, and air; and in promoting "fair" economic competition and eliminating deceptive marketing practices. Regulatory policies generally rely heavily upon a legal perspective. Since the rights of private parties are being determined through public administrative action, it has been considered highly desirable to assure the private parties protection against untoward infringements on those rights. In practice, this often means that an adjudicative hearing format is used. Due process is stressed, as is the impartiality of the hearing examiner. There are some good reasons why the legal perspective seems most appropriate to regulatory policy. Managerial perspectives could easily lead to the squelching of the rights of private parties and to harming their legitimate interests. The political approach's emphasis on responsiveness to the general public could easily facilitate a kind of "tyranny of the majority" against the interests and rights of the private parties. The legal perspective, by contrast, seeks to balance the public and private interests in each instance, affording adequate protection to both.

Perhaps this does not take us far enough. After all, there are many other types of policy, including those that emphasize foreign affairs, national security, macroeconomic policy, economic redistribution, energy, and distribution of the nation's resources. It is not possible in this volume to assess which of the perspectives, if any, would be generally most suitable in any of these areas. Quite possibly, different aspects of each of these policy types would most properly be organized according to one or another of the perspectives. Perhaps one perspective could even dominate a whole policy area. Still, without answering or even addressing these speculations, we hope that our suggestions for analyzing these problems will be helpful. The synthesis of the three perspectives in determining what can be evaluated as being "good" policy execution has inherent limitations, since the perspectives differ so much. Awareness of what they demand should help us to evaluate policy more sensibly and eventually may lead us to formulate better means of implementing policy.

NOTES

1. Motor Vehicle Manufacturers Association v. State Farm, 463 U.S. 29 (1983).
2. Woodrow Wilson, "The Study of Administration," *Political Science Quarterly*, 56 (December 1941): 481.
3. See David Nachmias, *Public Policy Evaluation* (New York: St. Martin's, 1979), chap. 1. Much of the discussion in the first part of this chapter is based on this source.
4. Ibid., pp. 57–61.
5. Ibid., p. 5.
6. James H. Jones, *Bad Blood* (New York: Free Press, 1981).
7. David Kershaw, "A Negative Income Tax Experiment," in David Nachmias, ed., *The Practice of Policy Evaluation* (New York: St. Martin's, 1980), pp. 27–41; Thomas R. Dye, *Understanding Public Policy*, 6th ed. (Englewood Cliffs, N.J.: Prentice-Hall, 1987), pp. 368–369.
8. David H. Rosenbloom and Carole C. Obuchowski, "Public Personnel Examinations and the Constitution," *Public Administration Review*, 37 (January/February 1977): 9–18.
9. Nachmias, *Public Policy Evaluation*, p. 5.
10. Ibid.
11. David H. Rosenbloom, *Federal Equal Employment Opportunity* (New York: Praeger, 1977), chap. 5.
12. Michael Lipsky, *Street Level Bureaucracy* (New York: Russell Sage, 1980); Pietro S. Nivola, *The Urban Service Problem* (Lexington, Mass.: Lexington Books, 1979); Eugene Bardach and Robert Kagan, *Going by the Book* (Philadelphia: Temple University Press, 1982).
13. Dye, *Understanding Public Policy*, 6th ed., p. 356. The remainder of this paragraph draws heavily from this source.
14. Daniel Katz, Barbara Gutek, Robert Kahn, and Eugenia Barton, *Bureaucratic Encounters* (Ann Arbor: University of Michigan, Institute for Social Research, 1975).
15. Mathews v. Eldridge, 424 U.S. 319 (1976).
16. Shapiro v. Thompson, 394 U.S. 618 (1969).
17. Wyman v. James, 400 U.S. 309 (1971).
18. Parrish v. Civil Service Commission, 425 P.2d 223 (1967).
19. Robert Merton, *Social Theory and Social Structure* (Glencoe, Ill.: Free Press, 1957), pp. 71–81.
20. See Grant McConnell, *Private Power and American Democracy* (New York: Knopf, 1966), chap. 7; Phillip O. Foss, *Politics and Grass* (Seattle: University of Washington Press, 1960); Wesley Calef, *Private Grazing and Public Lands* (Chicago: University of Chicago Press, 1960).
21. McConnell, *Private Power and American Democracy*, p. 203.
22. Ibid., pp. 204–205.
23. See Daniel P. Moynihan, *Maximum Feasible Misunderstanding* (New York: Free Press, 1970).

24. David H. Rosenbloom and Frank Bryan, "The Size of Public Bureaucracies," *State and Local Government Review*, 13 (September 1981): 115–123.
25. U.S. v. Richardson, 418 U.S. 166, 201 (1974).
26. Schweiker v. Hansen, 450 U.S. 785 (1981).
27. See Zobel v. Williams, 457 U.S. 55 (1983), for a concise recent statement.
28. Washington v. Davis, 426 U.S. 229 (1976).
29. See Hawkins v. Town of Shaw, 437 F2d 1286 (1971).
30. San Antonio School District v. Rodriguez, 411 U.S. 1 (1973).
31. U.S. v. Brignoni-Ponce, 422 U.S. 873 (1975).
32. Goldberg v. Kelly, 397 U.S. 254 (1970).
33. Sherbert v. Verner, 374 U.S. 398 (1963).
34. Cochrane v. Board of Education, 103 NW 2d 569 (1960); Starkey v. Board of Education, 381 P.2d 718 (1963).
35. Aaron Wildavsky, "The Self-Evaluating Organization," in Nachmias, ed., *The Practice of Policy Evaluation*, pp. 441–460, quoted passage from p. 443.
36. David Nachmias and Gary Henry, "The Utilization of Evaluation Research: Problems and Prospects," in Nachmias, ed., *The Practice of Policy Evaluation*, pp. 461–476, esp. pp. 473–475.
37. Delaware v. Prouse, 440 U.S. 649 (1979).
38. Goss v. Lopez, 419 U.S. 565 (1975).
39. New Jersey v. T.L.O., 469 U.S. 325 (1985).

ADDITIONAL READING

DYE, THOMAS R. *Understanding Public Policy*, 6th ed. Englewood Cliffs, N.J.: Prentice-Hall, 1987.

NACHMIAS, DAVID, ED. *The Practice of Policy Evaluation*. New York: St. Martin's, 1980.

PRESSMAN, JEFFREY, AND AARON WILDAVSKY. *Implementation*, 2nd ed. Berkeley, Calif.: University of California Press, 1973.

WEISS, CAROL. *Evaluation Research*. Englewood Cliffs, N.J.: Prentice-Hall, 1972.

WHOLEY, JOSEPH S. *Evaluation and Effective Public Management*. Boston: Little, Brown, 1983.

WILDAVSKY, AARON. *Speaking Truth to Power*. Boston: Little, Brown, 1979.

STUDY QUESTIONS

1. Can you think of a policy that is attaining its objectives, but through a kind of implementation to which you are opposed? Consider the use of police roadblocks to combat DWI.

2. During the early and mid-1980s, many states raised their drinking ages to 21, in response to federal prompting and as a means of promoting traffic safety. How would you go about analyzing the impact of this policy? What kind of approach would you take and what kinds of information would you seek and use? Suppose your analysis discerned no policy impact, how do you think different political groups would react?

The Convergence of Management, Politics, and Law in the Public Sector:

An Illustration

Chapter Nine | Regulatory Administration:
An Illustration of Management, Politics, and Law in the Public Sector

CHAPTER 9 | *Regulatory Administration:*

An Illustration of Management, Politics, and Law in the Public Sector

Regulation, the subject of this chapter, has become a major and controversial public administrative activity. Regulatory administration provides a good illustration of how the managerial, political, and legal perspectives can converge and conflict in a policy area. The roots of governmental regulation are economic, political, and social. Regulatory structure and process often involve a "commission" format and the combination of executive, legislative, and judicial functions. The challenges facing regulatory administration tend to parallel those of public administration more generally. There is a strong need to recognize the relevance of managerial, political, and legal concerns and also to strive for a synthesis of them that is in the public interest.

In recent years, regulation has emerged as an area of distinctive concern in public administration. Since regulatory administration encapsulates much of the challenge that contemporary public administration poses for the United States political system, it can be used to illustrate the convergence and clashing of different perspectives. It represents a very direct use of governmental power to penetrate spheres of life that were once left primarily to the workings of private social and economic forces. For instance, regulatory agencies are engaged in rate-setting for utilities and some forms of transportation; they seek to assure that products sold on the open market are not injurious to the health and safety of consumers; they have the authority to prohibit the use of industrial, mining, and agricultural processes that are deemed damaging to the environment; and they are involved in seeking to protect workers from discrimination and unhealthy or unsafe conditions in employment. Moreover, in general, regulatory administration tends to vest a great deal of power in the hands of agencies that are by design considerably independent of elected officials. These agencies also tend to combine legislative, executive, and judicial authority. They make rules that constrain the conduct of individuals, corporations, and other organizations; they implement or enforce these rules; and they often adjudicate the application of the rules should a challenge to them arise. As the scope of regulatory administration has grown, greater attention has been paid to its economic, political, and social costs and benefits—and many have come to believe that the costs are too high and that regulatory reform or deregulation is often desirable. In this chapter we will consider the development and growth of regulatory administration, the problems it presents, and managerial, political, and legal approaches toward seeking to improve the quality of governmental regulatory activities. Although the discussion will focus on federal regulatory agencies, the reader should bear two things in mind: First, that regulatory administration is illustrative of many of the broader problems and challenges confronting public administration today; and second, that a great deal of what takes place on the federal level is matched by the operation of state regulatory agencies. The latter are especially important in regulating utilities, occupational licensing, consumer affairs, and workplace conditions.

THE DEVELOPMENT AND GROWTH OF REGULATORY ADMINISTRATION

Today, a vast number of aspects of American economic and social life are the direct subjects of administrative regulation by the federal government. It is debatable when federal regulatory activity began in earnest. Some might date it from the 1850s, when the federal government created a Steamboat Inspection Service; others from 1883, when the Civil Service Commission was created to regulate federal personnel administrative practices; still others from 1887 when the Interstate Commerce Commission was created to regulate railroad rates and service. However, it is hardly debatable that until the recent trend toward reform and deregulation began in the 1970s and continued more forcefully into the

---

BOX 9–1 **Alphabet Agencies**

During the early part of the New Deal (1933–1937), a large number of new federal agencies were created. They were commonly referred to by their initials, such as NLRB, thereby giving rise to the term "alphabet agencies." But for the uninitiated, sometimes alphabet agencies need some unscrambling. The following is a key to the abbreviations used frequently throughout this chapter.

CAB Civil Aeronautics Board
CPSC Consumer Product Safety Commission
EEOC Equal Employment Opportunity Commission

EPA Environmental Protection Agency
FAA Federal Aviation Administration
FCC Federal Communications Commission
FDA Food and Drug Administration
FMC Federal Maritime Commission
FTC Federal Trade Commission
ICC Interstate Commerce Commission
NHTSA National Highway Traffic Safety Administration
NLRB National Labor Relations Board
NRC Nuclear Regulatory Commission
OSHA Occupational Safety and Health Administration

1980s, regulation had developed a very broad sweep. The table in Box 9–2 lists the main regulatory agencies that existed in the late 1970s, their subject matter, the date of their creation, and their location within the government's administrative structure. The table conveys a good deal of information to which we will be referring throughout this chapter. It should be noted, though, that some of these regulatory activities have fallen by the wayside in the movement toward deregulation. Especially notable in this context has been the demise of the CAB and deregulation of some aspects of banking, truck, bus, and rail transportation, and the natural gas and oil industries. Perhaps the most immediate question raised by the table is, "Why so much regulation?"

The general origin of federal regulatory activities is associated with the growing economic, technological, and social complexity of life during the past century or so. The increasing division of labor and greater specialization make us all highly dependent upon one another but less able to assess the predictability and reliability of each other's behavior. For example, we are dependent upon farmers, food handlers, and processors whom we do not know personally. Since they are anonymous, traditional channels (families, religious organizations, and communities) for exercising control over their behavior and assessing their reliability are unavailable to us. Of course, we can still exercise some personal judgments about the safety of foods, drugs, products, and modes of transportation. Private organizations such as the Consumers Union and Underwriters Laboratory might also help to inform us of dangerous or hazardous products. Yet we may want more certainty, especially when the consumption of products or the use of services can lead to disasters. We may also favor regulation when we are informed by private sources of how undesirable some industrial processes are,

BOX 9–2 **Some Regulatory Agencies of the Federal Government**

AGENCY[a]	PRESENT ORGANIZATION	YEAR OF ORIGIN	RESPONSIBILITY[b]
Comptroller of the Currency	Dept. of Treasury	1862	National banks
Fish and Wildlife Service	Dept. of Interior	1871	Preservation of fish and wildlife
Interstate Commerce Commission	Independent	1887	Prices, entry in rail, trucking, buses, and inland and coastal waterways
Forest Service	Dept. of Agriculture	1905	Management of resource use
Employment Standards Administration	Dept. of Labor	1913	Wages, hours, and discrimination in employment
Federal Reserve System	Independent	1913	Interest rates, national banks, and banking
Federal Trade Commission	Independent	1914	Consumer information, advertising, business practices
Coast Guard	Dept. of Transportation	1915	Ship safety, environmental protection
International Trade Commission	Independent	1916	International "dumping," industry relief
Food Safety and Quality Service	Dept. of Agriculture	1916	Food inspection, grading, and standardization
Federal Energy Regulatory Commission (formerly, Federal Power Commission)	Dept. of Energy	1930 (FPC)	Prices for natural gas, interstate electricity, oil by pipeline
Food and Drug Administration	Dept. of Health and Human Services	1931	Food and drug safety
Federal Home Loan Bank Board	Independent	1932	Interest rates and entry into savings-and-loan industry
Agricultural Marketing Service	Dept. of Agriculture	1932	Food inspection, grading, and standardization
Commodity Credit Corporation	Dept. of Agriculture	1933	Farm commodity pricing
Federal Deposit Insurance Corp.	Independent	1933	Insurance of bank deposits
Federal Communications Commission	Independent	1934	Entry into broadcasting, aspects of telecommunications
Securities and Exchange Commission	Independent	1934	Information and trading conditions of securities
National Labor Relations Board	Independent	1935	Labor contracts and collective bargaining
Agricultural Marketing Service	Dept. of Agriculture	1937	Aspects of farm commodity marketing
Civil Aeronautics Board	Independent	1938	Prices, entry into airline industry
Bureau of Land Management	Dept. of Interior	1946	Management of public lands
Federal Aviation Administration	Dept. of Transportation	1948	Airline, airport safety
Animal and Plant Health Inspection Service	Dept. of Agriculture	1953	Food inspection

BOX 9–2 *Continued*

AGENCY*	PRESENT ORGANIZATION	YEAR OF ORIGIN	RESPONSIBILITY†
Agricultural Stabilization and Conservation Service	Dept. of Agriculture	1961	Farm acreage allotments
Equal Employment Opportunity Commission	Independent	1964	Ending prohibited employment discrimination
Federal Highway Administration	Dept. of Transportation	1966	Truck and bus safety
National Oceanic and Atmospheric Administration	Dept. of Commerce	1970	Management of marine resources and protection of marine mammals
Federal Railroad Administration	Dept. of Transportation	1970	Rail safety
National Highway Traffic Safety Administration	Dept. of Transportation	1970	Motor vehicle safety & fuel economy
Environmental Protection Agency	Independent	1970	Environmental protection of air, water, and land
Postal Rate Commission	Independent	1970	Recommends prices of U.S. Postal Service; reviews post office closure decisions
Occupational Safety and Health Administration	Dept. of Labor	1970	Worker safety
Consumer Product Safety Commission	Independent	1972	Safety of consumer products
Bureau of Alcohol, Tobacco, and Firearms	Dept. of Treasury	1972	Labeling
Mine Safety and Health Administration	Dept. of Labor	1973	Miner safety
Economic Regulatory Administration	Dept. of Energy	1974	Petroleum pricing and allocation, coal conservation, temperature limits for buildings, energy standards for new buildings
Commodity Futures Trading Commission	Independent	1975	Information and trading conditions of commodity futures
Nuclear Regulatory Commission	Independent	1975	Licensing & regulation concerning nuclear reactors
Federal Grain Inspection Service	Dept. of Agriculture	1976	Grain inspection
Office of Surface Mining Reclamation and Enforcement	Dept. of Interior	1977	Environmental effects of surface mining
Merit Systems Protection Board	Independent	1979	Federal personnel administration

* Some agencies listed have been phased out in the movement toward deregulation.

† Some agencies have nondomestic regulatory or nonregulatory functions as well.

SOURCE: Derived from Lawrence J. White, *Reforming Regulation* (Englewood Cliffs, N.J.: Prentice-Hall, 1981), Tables 3-1, 3-2; pp. 32-33, 36-39.

even though they may pose no immediate danger. For instance, the publication of Upton Sinclair's *The Jungle* (1905), which described the filthy conditions in the meatpacking industry, was a catalyst in the framing of the Pure Food and Drug Act of 1906. The book turned President Theodore Roosevelt into an advocate of the regulation of some aspects of the food and drug industries.[1] To some extent the issue was not that the meat depicted in *The Jungle* was dangerous to one's health after being cooked, but rather that it was so filthy as to be repulsive—that is, even if it wouldn't hurt them, after knowing how it was handled people did not want to eat it. On the other hand, danger is often real. In 1938, drug regulations were expanded to require testing of new drugs *prior* to marketing after some 107 people were killed by "sulfanilamide," a new form of sulfa drug that had been initially hailed as very promising. Similarly, just as once the safety of steamboats was of great concern to passengers who were not in a position to make a sound evaluation, today few of us are able to evaluate the safety of different types of commercial airplanes or of railroad trestles and trackbeds. Consequently, we may turn to the government to assure the safety of these transportation services.

Regulatory administration to assure the safety of products, services, processes, and technologies is currently handled by the FDA, FAA, Consumer Product Safety Commission, National Highway Traffic Safety Administration, NRC, and a variety of other agencies. It is largely based on science and engineering and tends to rely on inspections and testing for enforcement. A special variant of this type of regulation involves occupational licensing, mostly at the state level, in a number of fields to assure the public that practitioners are competent.

But regulation is not just aimed at assuring safety. We are also economically interdependent and consequently may want some economic practices to be made predictable, reliable, and perhaps stable through regulation. Rate-setting is one example. In the 1880s, farmers in some areas were dependent upon railroads to transport their produce to markets. Some railroads sought to take advantage of their monopolies on various routes by charging rates that bore little relationship to the actual cost of transporting the farmer's shipments. If allowed to continue indefinitely, this would most likely have depressed the agricultural sector of the economy, at least in some geographic areas, and/or have driven prices for food in urban areas way up. It was also viewed as fundamentally unfair. In 1887, the ICC was set up to avoid these consequences by regulating rates in the public interest.

Regulation of this type is intended to create a surrogate for the market. It concentrates on setting prices (or rates) and/or controlling entry into a field of economic activity. It has been most common in transportation (rail, bus, trucking, shipping, and air), the field of public utilities, and some aspects of the FCC's regulation of radio and television broadcasting. In recent years, deregulation of some of these areas has been substantial. Surrogate-market regulation is characterized by economic analysis of costs, rates of return, and distribution of services. Sometimes it is used to subsidize an industry, as when past ICC regulations enabled truckers to compete with railroads on long hauls, even though their real costs were higher. More commonly, surrogate-market regulation creates **cross subsidies** through which one set of customers (such as long-distance callers) pay prices that are intended to subsidize another (users of local telephone service).

Regulation is also used to assure the proper functioning of markets. Antitrust and fair-trade regulations are preeminent examples. The Sherman Anti-Trust Act of 1890 was intended, in part, to assure that markets did not become noncompetitive through monopolization. The Federal Trade Commission Act of 1914 was also concerned with competition, but it became the basis of regulatory activity also intended to curb trade practices that distorted market forces, such as false advertising and price fixing.

The list of regulatory activities does not stop there. In recent decades there has also been great concern with environmental regulation. Like Upton Sinclair's *The Jungle,* Rachel Carson's *Silent Spring* (1962) helped crystallize demands for regulation by increasing public awareness of the long-term dangers confronting the environment through chemical pollution and various agricultural, mining, and building practices. Some of these dangers have already materialized, such as "air inversions" and dangerous levels of smog that can be factors in individuals' deaths. Others, such as acid rain, threaten eventually to wreak havoc on the ecology of vast geographic areas. Greater regulation of shipping practices has been a direct result of a number of spectacular oil spills by supertankers and a growing realization that the ecology of the oceans is vulnerable to pollution.[2] One reason why regulation of the environment appears sensible and desirable to many is that the forces of the marketplace do not always seem to work as an adequate check on the short-term practices of a broad range of economic concerns. For instance, in the short term, it may be cheaper for utilities and manufacturers in the Midwest to pass off sulfur dioxide pollution as an *externality* rather than to change their processes or install "scrubbers" to reduce it. An externality is an aspect of a product or its production that is not accounted for in the economic transaction between buyer and seller. In this case, it is a part of production that returns in the form of acid rain and is paid for by the Northeast and parts of Canada.

Environmental regulation relies on engineering, a host of sciences, and economic analysis. It makes use of "environmental impact statements," or analyses of the likely ecological effects of economic development, production processes, and product uses. Inspections and monitoring are also used as enforcement techniques. Today, environmental regulation frequently involves health concerns, as in the case of the disposal and cleanup of hazardous wastes.

Employment is another area of comprehensive regulatory activity. It has been felt that some economic and production practices have such undesirable and major social consequences that they should be prohibited through regulation. Child labor and unsafe "sweatshops" are classic cases. Collective bargaining practices, including union organizing, are regulated by the NLRB. The EEOC was created to prevent employment and union practices that illegally discriminate against individuals on the basis of race, color, religion, national origin (ethnicity), or sex. Discrimination based on age or handicapping condition are also under its current jurisdiction. Congress has considered discrimination along these lines to be not only *unfair but also as impeding interstate commerce and harming the nation's economy*. Occupational safety and health regulation has grown immensely since OSHA was established in 1970. In part, this has been a response to the growing awareness that the individual worker might be unable to make a sound judgment as to the safety of some substances, such as benzene or asbestos, found in the modern workplace. More specialized regulatory activities exist in some occupations, such as mining.

The regulation of employment practices is so broad and prone to overlap other forms of regulation that it necessarily involves a variety of techniques. The NLRB and the EEOC rely heavily upon adjudicatory processes. Accordingly, their operations are largely informed by legal analysis. OSHA, by contrast, relies far more on rule making and inspections. Much of its activity is based on health sciences and engineering.

Although these are the main types of regulatory administration in the United States, they do not encompass all of it. There is also the Federal Election Commission, which regulates some aspects of election campaigns for federal office. Several federal and state agencies are engaged in regulatory activity to protect individuals' civil rights in voting, in places of public accommodation, on common carriers, and in educational facilities. Some federal regulations pertain to state and local jurisdictions, as in civil rights and some aspects of employment and environmental regulatory administration. This creates a kind of "regulatory federalism," in which subnational *governments* are the regulated. Finally, it should be noted that a great deal of federal regulatory activity is augmented by state and local agencies, especially in the fields of health, safety, employment, the environment, and fair trade practices.

The scope and complexity of regulatory administration make it difficult to generalize about regulatory policy. Some analysts use categories such as "old style" or "economic" regulation (surrogate market and market functioning) in distinction to "new style" or "social" regulation (health, safety, environment, and employment).[3] Such simplifications are convenient for some purposes, but they must be used with caution: some environmental and health regulation is older than some forms of economic regulation, and it is not altogether clear why unfair-practice regulation, including discrimination, in employment should be considered "social" rather than "economic." Perhaps regulatory administration is best understood as part of a web of controls—economic, social, and legal—over activity that is considered antisocial or otherwise undesirable. Therefore, an important question is, given all the mechanisms for exercising such controls, how is the choice for different types of regulatory administration made?

Political Patterns

Regulatory administration is established as a political response to a problem, real or imagined, in the economy, society, or ecology. It will have costs and produce benefits that may be distributed in a variety of ways. Hence, inevitably there is a "politics of regulation."[4] In considering the origins of regulatory administration, James Q. Wilson has been able to identify several types of political conditions that are associated with the creation of specific regulatory agencies and statutes.

Majoritarian Politics   When the costs and benefits of a governmental policy or activity are widely distributed, we see **majoritarian politics** occurring. "All or most of society expects to gain; all or most of society expects to pay."[5] Wilson believes that the passage of the Sherman Antitrust Act (1890) and the Federal Trade Commission Act (1914) are examples. Neither was aimed at a specific industry; both promised to eliminate unfair, harmful, or unscrupulous economic practices without specifying what these were. Neither was strongly supported nor strongly opposed by business.

Interest Group Politics   When both costs and benefits are narrowly concentrated, **interest group politics** results. "A . . . regulation will often benefit a relatively small group at the expense of another comparable small group. Each side has a strong incentive to organize and exercise political influence. The public does not believe it will be much affected one way or another; though it may sympathize more with one side than the other. . . ."[6] Perhaps the best single example in the regulatory realm is the Shipping Act of 1916, which since 1961 has been administered by the Federal Maritime Commission. The competition was between those who shipped goods by sea and the shipping companies. Although the public interest was involved in a general sense, the public itself and others not directly or immediately affected were relatively uninvolved in the issues posed. The National Labor Relations Act of 1935 (Wagner Act), which created the NLRB, was another example. It pitted organized labor against industry.

Client Politics   At those times "when the benefits of a prospective policy are concentrated but the costs are widely distributed,"[7] **client politics** prevails. Here some relatively small and easily organized group stands to benefit, while the costs are "distributed at a low per capita rate over a large number of people." Consequently, there may be little incentive to organize forceful opposition. Wilson finds that the creation of the CAB and many public utility commissions at the state level more or less fit this pattern. He suggests that occupational licensing boards probably do also. However, he notes that sometimes opposition may develop to what would otherwise be a case of "client politics" when public interest groups become involved. Wilson also notes that despite the widespread distribution of relatively low costs, many business or other groups may become involved in discussion of the policy when it is first proposed.

The "client politics" model makes clear that despite the popular view that private enterprise thoroughly opposes government regulation, there is much reason to believe that some industries have sought to be regulated. Economist George Stigler developed an influential theory about this. In his view, "regulation is acquired by the industry and is designed and operated primarily for its benefit,"[8] This is especially true where the industry sees the opportunity of using governmental power to keep new entrants (would-be competitors) out. To accomplish its ends, the industry may seek to "capture" the regulatory agency, often a commission. Such a strategy was first propounded by Attorney General Richard Olney in the early 1890s, with regard to the probable future of the ICC. He wrote: "The Commission . . . is, or can be made, of great use to the railroads. It satisfies the popular clamor for a government supervision of railroads, at the same time that the supervision is almost entirely nominal. Further, the older such a commission gets to be, the more inclined it will be found to take the business and railroad view of things. . . ."[9]

The capture theory was also influentially stated by Marver Bernstein, who hypothesized that regulatory agencies go through predictable "life cycles."[10] At birth they avidly regulate the industries under their jurisdiction on behalf of consumers, rate payers, or the public interest more generally. Stage two is reached when the agency has either eliminated the worst abuses it was created to correct, or, alternatively, becomes frustrated with its inability to do so and the lack of public concern with its activities. At this point, agencies begin to compromise more with the regulated industries and begin to view the industries themselves as an important part of their constituency. In the final stage, the regulatory agency becomes protective of the status quo and often a de facto "captive" of the industry. In the latter case, the industry gains informal but real political control over the appointment of regulatory commissioners and uses the commission's public power for private gain.[11] Such a pattern is frequently descriptive of client politics, but is not necessarily confined to it.

Entrepreneurial Politics   When "a policy may be proposed that will confer general (though perhaps small) benefits at a cost to be born chiefly by a small segment of society,"[12] we encounter **entrepreneurial politics.** Wilson points to antipollution and auto-safety bills as examples. What is peculiar about this type of politics is the inability of the small segment upon whom the burden falls to block the regulatory policy at issue. Wilson attributes this primarily to the work of people he calls **entrepreneurs,** such as Ralph Nader, whose work was instrumental in the passage of the Auto Safety Act of 1966. An earlier example was Dr. Harvey Wiley, who helped mobilize support for the Food and Drug Act of 1906. This type of policy entrepreneur effectively represents groups that are not directly involved in legislative policy making.

In sum, Wilson concludes that the politics of regulatory policy "follows different patterns, mobilizes different actors, and has different consequences depending, among other things, on the perceived distribution of costs and benefits of the proposed policy."[13]

Wilson's scheme is very useful in gaining an understanding of regulatory policy. Although his categories do not coincide perfectly with the types of regulation discussed above (or any other typology, for that matter), some *tendencies* are evident. Client politics describes much surrogate-market regulation; entrepreneurial politics, much health and safety regulation; majoritarian politics, as noted, is associated with the regulation of the market's functioning; interest group politics is descriptive of much but not all employment regulation.

Wilson's discussion encompasses the politics and some of the economic bases of regulation. It is necessary to consider social factors, as well, in order to have a more complete picture of the growth of regulatory administration.

Social Factors

Sometimes the contemporary administrative state is referred to as the "welfare state," and it is alleged that government has placed a "safety net" underneath everyone in the population, to protect those who are unable to care for themselves. While some argue that the safety net is already too broad, others maintain that it needs to be enlarged to encompass some individuals and circumstances for whom or which there is currently inadequate protection. Whatever one's stance on the desirability of the "safety net," it does seem evident that as a society the United States has developed two characteristics in this regard that bear heavily upon regulatory administration and public administration in general.

First, this society has frequently sought to replace personal responsibility with government regulation. The variety of state mandatory seat belt laws provide an outstanding example. The federal government has long required that new cars sold in the United States be equipped with seat belts. There are now very few cars on the roads without them. So the belts are there for anyone to fasten. It is a simple matter of personal responsibility, requiring but a few seconds and little effort to accomplish. However, for one reason or another, the states reasoned that it was *their* responsibility to make sure that everyone buckles up. In many places it is now a regulation to be enforced by the police and courts— not something left up to the individual. The same tendency to use regulation to override (and actually diminish) personal responsibility can be found in consumer affairs. Here, state agencies and the FTC seek to protect the consumer from being deceived or cheated. Laudable though this may be, in the past that was the consumer's personal responsibility. Similarly, some of the OSHA regulations tend to treat workers as though they were incapable of judging how to use equipment safely and move about in the workplace.

Second, it has been observed that, "wholly aside from objective changes in risk, cultural changes in the past two decades have increased our *intolerance of risk*, resulting in greater expectations of security from physical hazards, illness, environmental degradation, and even from being cheated in the marketplace."[14] Greater affluence, sensitivity to power relationships and exploitation, and the growing concern with the quality of life seem to have coincided with the rise of the opportunities for entrepreneurial politics, as described by Wilson. Public interest groups and political entrepreneurs both in and out of government have taken it upon themselves to represent and mobilize support for what they perceive to be the public's interest in reducing risks. Indeed, in retrospect many readers may find it amazing that prior to 1938 there was no general requirement that drugs be tested before being sold to the public in large quantities. The growing intolerance of risk and reduction of personal responsibility is a factor in the shifting focus of much regulation from surrogate-market to environmental and health and safety (both generally and in employment).

THE STRUCTURE AND PROCESS OF REGULATORY ADMINISTRATION

Regulatory administration can also take several organizational forms. In the past, the commission format was most common. This approach to administrative organization was discussed briefly in Chapter 3. Its most distinctive feature is that it is headed by a number of commissioners, who form a bipartisan group and typically hold fixed and staggered terms of office. The purpose of this arrangement is to insulate the workings of the regulatory commission from electoral politics. It provides a degree of stability and continuity in the commissions and protects them from rapid changes in leadership when the partisanship of the presidency or majority in Congress changes. Political detachment of this type has been deemed desirable, as it is thought that the commissions' missions are to regulate sectors of the economy or aspects of commerce in the public interest in the long run. They are not intended to engage in rapid ideological shifts in striking balances among the competing interests they must consider. Rather, they are intended to develop a clear vision of the public interest by making highly specific rules and adjudicating cases that may arise under them. In this fashion, it is thought, they can determine what the public interest is in any given context.

When the ICC, the prototypical federal regulatory commission, was set up in 1887, Congress clearly believed that the policy area of railroad rate regulation ought to be taken out of partisan politics and that the commission was capable of ascertaining the public interest with little direct guidance from the legislature. Eventually, Congress established some commissions with very broad missions and virtually no genuine guidance as to what policies should be adopted. The FCC is perhaps the extreme in this regard. Its mission is to regulate the use of the nation's airwaves for broadcasts in the "public convenience, interest, or necessity." Such a broad mission leaves the commission a great deal of freedom to make policy. It also bespeaks of the legislature's unwillingness or inability to be more active in formulating policy in the regulated area. Coupled with their structural independence, this gives some regulatory agencies a substantial degree of autonomy.[15] The FCC has been able to embrace a rule guaranteeing a fair opportunity for individuals or groups to respond to broadcast editorializing *and* also, subsequently, to propose abandoning that rule.

In recent years, it has become more common for regulatory agencies to be placed within executive branch departments. For instance, as Box 9–2 indicates, this is true of OSHA, NHTSA, and some others. Agencies such as the EPA are placed within the executive branch, but not housed in another department. Agencies of this type are not headed by a commission, but rather by a director, who is appointed by the president, typically with the advice and consent of the Senate, and serves at his pleasure. These structural arrangements are intended to give the president greater influence or control over the policy-making and enforcement activities of the regulatory agencies. However, some relatively new agencies, including the EEOC and the MSPB (Merit Systems Protection Board), do retain the traditional commission form.

Regulatory administrators use several processes. As noted earlier, they make *rules*. For example, the FDA has made a number of rules regarding the labeling of drugs and foods. It requires that drug advertising include a statement of side effects, contraindications, and appropriate precautions and warnings. It has also issued rules for "standards of identity" of products such as fish sticks, ice cream, and hot dogs. In one celebrated case, it took two years or so to determine whether a new type of potato chip could be fairly called "potato chip." Some of these rules make rather odd reading: frozen fried fish sticks are defined as "clean, wholesome, rectangular-shaped unglazed masses of cohering pieces not ground of fish flesh coated with breading and partially cooked. . . . Frozen fried fish sticks weigh up to and including 1½ ounces; are at least three-eighths of an inch thick and their largest dimension is at least three times the next largest dimension."[16] Such a rule has its purpose—to prevent misleading of the consumer and to serve specific economic interests. In 1987, for instance, the National Milk Producers Federation and the Committee for Fair Pizza Labeling fought a minor political battle over whether pizza made without cheese should be required to carry a prominent label to the effect that it "contains cheese substitute."[17]

In fact, there is no doubt some rationale behind all the regulatory rules placed in the massive *Federal Register* in any given year. Thus, when OSHA decided to drop some nine hundred rules considered to be "nitpicking," it received some serious objections. While it is easy to poke fun at some of the regulatory agencies' rules, it must be remembered that they also deal with matters of true gravity, such as auto safety, airline safety, food poisoning, dangerous products, deadly pollution, and radioactive contamination of the environment.

Many regulatory agencies are also engaged in adjudication. Here an agency such as the FTC may charge a business with deceptive advertising practices, or one like the NLRB may be called upon to decide whether an employer or a union has engaged in an unfair labor practice. By and large, *adjudicatory procedure is regulated by administrative law and constitutional concerns*. We will address these topics further on in this chapter. However, there is a good deal of administrative flexibility as to how cases should be selected. This is a matter of *adjudicatory policy*.

In general, adjudicatory policy can be considered either reactive or proactive. Reactive strategies depend upon complaints being filed with the regulatory agency by private parties or other governmental agencies. Sometimes these are called **mailbag cases**. Agency employees respond to these complaints in several ways: some are dismissed as frivolous; some are routed to more appropriate agencies; some are acted upon in an effort to obtain some form of restitution for the complainant; some lead the agency to take action against the party who has allegedly committed a breach of proper conduct. Additional steps may include investigating, bringing formal charges and holding formal hearings within the agency, or litigating in the courts. Mailbag cases tend to concern matters of "conduct," that is, they involve allegations by an individual that some business enterprise has engaged in an unfair or illegal practice. For example, such complaints may be made by consumers against merchants or repair services, by employees alleging discrimination on the part of their employers, or by unions or employers (including public employers) alleging unfair labor practices. Sometimes such cases are also filed by businesses that believe their competitors are engaging in prohibited practices. By their nature, **conduct cases** pertain to relatively concrete practices and to specific sets of events.

Proactive cases are those developed by a regulatory agency through an investigation or study of some kind. Based on its observations about the practices of a business or group of private parties, the agency may conclude that some violation of law or its rules has occurred. Proactive cases initiated by field investigations often resemble conduct cases. The inspectors may find violations and issue citations, which can become the subject of adjudication. Housing inspectors, OSHA inspectors, and health service inspectors are examples. Many proactive cases, however, are of a different nature. These are called **structural cases,** and they do not arise from specific events, but rather are the result of patterns and broad practices that are deemed by the agency to be prohibited. For example, whereas a health inspector in a restaurant will stick a thermometer into the chili to see if it is too cold, a structural case is more likely to consider whether a chain of restaurants is mislabeling its products or engaging in unfair or anticompetitive practices. Rather than ask, "What temperature is the beef?" or even "Where's the beef?" the structural case will tend to ask, "What is the economic relationship of the seller of the beef to its franchisees and to the producers?"

But structural cases are often far more complicated than this. They deal with the structure of competition in whole industries, such as petroleum products, or patterns and practices of discrimination against members of minority groups or women by a large employer or even within an entire industry. Structural cases are often informed by theory. For example, to learn whether prohibited monopolization has occurred in an industry a regulatory agency will need to know how firms behave and how pricing operates. Assessing such matters may depend upon a theoretical understanding of the differences between the behavior of firms in competitive markets as opposed to monopoly markets. One dramatic example of a structural issue that has recently confronted public administration almost everywhere in the United States is **comparable worth** (see Chapter 5). Are women in the public sector systematically paid less than their "worth" because the public employer has taken advantage of social inequalities in calculating the salary structure for occupations, such as secretaries and nurses, that tend to have women as a very high proportion of their employees?

Although structural cases have the potential to regulate forcefully what the agency considers to be prohibited practices, they also have some important drawbacks. First, they are very difficult and time-consuming to adjudicate and litigate. The parties charged with the prohibited behavior often have great opportunity to delay these cases and drag them on for years. Second, they often involve new legal theories or new interpretations of existing theory. Consequently, administrative law judges and judges in the courtroom may require a great deal of convincing that the agency's interpretation is correct. Third, they tend to create a personnel problem because agency lawyers often want experience in adjudication and litigation as opposed to the lengthy preparation of cases. Conduct cases offer a far greater opportunity for this experience. Finally, structural cases can engulf very considerable amounts of an agency's resources. For instance, in fiscal 1978, one such case in the FTC consumed 12 to 14 percent of its entire antitrust budget. [18]

At this point, a word should be said about inspectors, who are functionally agents of rule enforcement that can lead to adjudication. Many regulatory agencies depend upon inspectors to implement their policies. Inspectors hold a very complex job. They are street-level bureaucrats who have a great deal of discretion, cannot be fully supervised or held accountable by the administrative hierarchy, and are highly visible and even intimidating to the businesses they inspect. They have the ability to make the regulatory process work well or very badly. Where inspectors provoke hostility on the part of the inspected and when they seek to enforce every rule in a highly technical way, regulation is not likely to work well. Private parties will be evasive; they may seek to require the inspector to obtain a warrant before entering the premises; they will try to fool or mislead the inspector. Where the inspector wins the confidence of those being inspected, the latter may strike a much more cooperative posture and try to take advantage of the inspector's expertise in eliminating dangerous, unhealthful, or other prohibited practices in the workplace. Since the object of regulatory policy in the first place is to evoke responsible social and economic behavior, cooperation and voluntary compliance by private parties with the spirit of regulation can certainly serve an agency's purposes.

Just as the effective police officer seeks to promote the safety of persons and property, rather than to write numerous tickets for minor traffic, noise, and other violations, the effective inspector seeks to promote substantial and voluntary compliance with the spirit of agency regulations and the specific letter of those requirements that protect against immediate dangers or seriously antisocial behavior. Consequently, the effective inspector must be technically competent, honest, tough-minded, and willing to exercise authority while also being empathetic and able to get along well with people. This combination of characteristics, needless to add, is not easy to find. Eugene Bardach and Robert Kagan describe the generalized interaction between a "good inspector" and the regulated businessperson:

> The inspector has three major things he can trade for greater efforts toward responsible social behavior. First, at a bare minimum, he can give the regulated businessman a fair hearing; he can treat him with respect and take his arguments and problems seriously. When he must insist on strict compliance, he gives reasons. In other words, he exhibits *responsiveness*. Second, the inspector can selectively negate, modify, or delay the enforcement of regulations when their literal application to a particular violation would be unreasonable or of secondary importance. In short, he can give *forebearance*. Third, he can provide *information* to the regulated enterprise that reduces the difficulty or cost of compliance, or at least makes the required compliance measures seem understandable and justifiable. [19]

One of the advantages to a regulatory agency of having "good inspectors" is that it may make their missions far more manageable. For instance, in the mid-1980s, New York City had seventeen health inspectors who attempted to inspect each of some 15,000 food establishments about once a year.[20] Voluntary compliance is crucial where there is such a huge workload.

Regulatory agencies also rely upon *testing* to implement their objectives. This is especially pronounced in the areas of health and safety, but it also pertains to some aspects of consumer affairs generally. Testing may be done by the regulatory agency itself or may be required of the private parties that produce and market a product. The FDA, for instance, relies heavily upon testing, but primarily by evaluating the tests done by drug companies and others. The EPA, by contrast, directly engages in monitoring and testing itself. Testing can be either pre-market or post-market. Drugs, food additives, and other substances for human consumption are likely to be tested in advance of being marketed because of their potential danger. In addition, however, post-market tests may be undertaken, especially if a suspicion develops that the product is not safe under certain conditions or if some reevaluation of the pre-market tests suggests that they were faulty in some way. Product recalls are often the result of post-market testing. In either case, the testing may be quite elaborate and costly to the producer and the agency. For example, a new drug application at the FDA may contain as many as two hundred volumes.[21] The FDA's pre-market testing procedure is likely to involve the following:

1. Preliminary assessment of therapeutic potential based primarily on small-scale animal studies;
2. short-term toxicity studies in animals to assess the danger to humans;
3. brief and highly supervised tests on humans for toxicity;
4. three-month animal studies to assess safety for humans;
5. two phases of clinical trials to confirm efficacy, hazards, and appropriate dosages; and
6. two-year animal studies to assess hazards of long-term treatment.[22]

Elaborate tests, such as those required by the FDA, can certainly serve to assure the safety of drug and food products. However, sometimes they can be misleading. For instance, if a product is dangerous to animals, should it automatically be banned from the marketplace? That question confronted the FDA when it was determined that saccharin causes cancer in laboratory animals. Under the existing statute, the "Delaney Amendment," the FDA seemed compelled to prohibit its sale. But products with saccharin were very popular with consumers. Eventually, through congressional intervention, a compromise was reached and warnings about saccharin's dangers to laboratory animals were required on the containers or labels of all food products, such as diet soft drinks, containing the substance. That was a political and economic compromise, but it left it up to the consumer to judge the scientific evidence as to whether saccharin was dangerous to his or her individual health.

PROBLEMS IN REGULATORY ADMINISTRATION

It is plausible that no aspect of public administration has been subject to as much criticism as regulation. It is inherently intrusive and consequently annoying to some, who are constrained by it or burdened heavily by its costs. But the case against regulatory administration goes much further and is illustrative of opposition to public administration as a whole.

Regulation Is Expensive

Nobody knows what the cost of regulation to a society may be. However, it is certain that simply adding up the budgets of regulatory agencies at all levels of government would not begin to tell the story. Regulation affects costs, productivity, and innovation. In a series of articles about the state of regulation in the 1970s, prior to relatively extensive deregulation by the federal government, the *Wall Street Journal* reported that "transportation economists . . . estimate that price-fixing and waste allowed under the Civil Aeronautics Board, Federal Maritime Commission and Interstate Commerce Commission regulations cost consumers between $8 billion and $16 billion."[23] One example of waste it reported was that "at any given time 40 percent of the trucks on the road are running empty because of government regulations that prevent them from carrying cargo on return trips after making deliveries."[24] This regulation, since abandoned, allegedly cost food retailers alone some $250 million a year. Moreover, at the time airfares were estimated to be 35 to 50 percent higher than would be the case if the CAB did not try to protect the least efficient carriers. In fact, since deregulation, fares declined 13 percent on average.[25]

Additional information on costs is reported by Bardach and Kagan, who reviewed studies indicating the following:

Water and air pollution: $26.8 billion (1978)

OSHA standards: $3 billion (1978)

Federal safety and pollution controls for automobiles: $500 per car (1976), or about $3.35 billion total.[26]

In addition, they found that meeting OSHA's regulations in iron and steel foundries accounted for more than 30 percent of all capital investment during the 1970s and that regulations could lead to massive declines in productivity per worker.[27] Even these massive costs do not seem to explain the full impact of regulation on the economy.

Regulation Dampens Economic Performance

It has long been thought that regulation has serious negative impacts on the productivity, growth, and innovation of the economy. In this context, regulation has been criticized for doing and not doing at once. Where it regulates competition by restricting entrance to an industry or by setting rates or fares, regulatory administration has been attacked for protecting weak companies or industries at the expense of consumers and others who use their products. The ICC and the CAB, as noted earlier, were criticized from this perspective. Public utility commissions are frequently criticized on this basis as well. Many maintain that surrogate-market regulation inevitably leads to the "capture" of the public regulatory agency by the private enterprises ostensibly being regulated. On the other hand, the FTC has been accused by some of being antibusiness, resulting ultimately in harm to the consumer; the Department of Justice's Antitrust Division has been criticized on the grounds that it vacillates between too vigorous and too lackadaisical enforcement, both of which fail to promote or protect economic competition.[28]

In terms of performance, the FCC has been viewed by some as holding back the nation's progress in communications, and the FDA has kept some useful and safe drugs off the market too long and has inhibited the development of new drugs by the pharmaceutical industry. Indeed, one analyst believes that if its current regulations had applied in the past, penicillin and aspirin would not have been made available.[29]

Regulation Produces Delay and Extravagant Red Tape

Another criticism of regulatory administration is that it is too slow. Some examples are legendary; for instance, it took the FDA a decade to develop standards of identity for peanut butter.[30] The process for seizing contaminated food can take at least sixty-five days (see Box 9–3). For thirty-three of its first forty years, the FCC was trying to resolve a dispute between radio stations DOB in Albuquerque and WABC in New York.[31] In some cases major responsibility for the delays can be attributed to the private parties involved, rather than to the agency, but nonetheless delay on the part of regulatory agencies can be frustrating. This is especially likely to be the case when an individual or firm requires a license or permission to perform a service, market a product, or open a place of business.

Red tape is endemic to administrative life and regulatory administration is certainly no exception. Sometimes the agencies create their own red tape. For instance, they write long inspection manuals in obtuse administrative terminology ("bureaucratese"), and require their employees, often inspectors, to fill out lengthy forms pertaining to their official activities. The Department of Transportation's Motor Carrier Safety handbook runs more than four hundred pages and the Department of Agriculture's instructions on the post mortem inspection of beef carcasses contains fifteen single-spaced pages of instructions for the inspector.[32] Perhaps Herbert Kaufman has best been able to convey the frustrations and costs of red tape in concrete terms:

A "Mom and Pop" store with a gross annual income of less than $30,000 had to file tax forms fifty-two times a year. A firm with fewer than fifty employees had to prepare

BOX 9–3 Federal Food and Drug Administration's Process for Seizing Contaminated Food—If the Consumer Doesn't Get There First

ACTION	Identify & confirm violation	Technical confirmation of violation	Review policy toward seizure	Review legal basis	File seizure order	Seizure of product
ORGANIZATIONAL UNIT	Investigator; Laboratory analysis; Compliance Director	Center for Food Safety & Applied Nutrition	Associate Commissioner for Regulatory Affairs	General Counsel	U.S. Attorney	U.S. Marshal
AVERAGE TIME	(District Level) 24 days		(Headquarters) 17 days		(Department of Justice) 24 days	

SOURCE: Cass Peterson, "Snail's Pace at the FDA," *The Washington Post National Weekly Edition*, October 29, 1984, p. 33.

seventy-five or eighty submissions a year for various agencies. A small securities broker-dealer sent thirty-eight submissions to seven different agencies in one year. A plant employing seventy-five people had two of them working half time solely to draw up compulsory plans and reports; a company with a hundred employees made seventy filings or payments each year to the Internal Revenue Service alone; a small radio station assigned two employees full time for four months to supply all the information specified by the Federal Communications Commission for license renewal, and another reported that its application for renewal weighed forty-five pounds. The chairman of the board of a large pharmaceutical firm claimed that his company prepared 27,000 government forms or reports a year at a cost of $5 million. ("We spend," he added, "more man-hours filling out government forms or reports than we do on research for cancer and heart disease combined.")[33]

Various agencies, at all governmental levels, have sought to reduce paperwork, but no doubt too much remains.

Incompetence

Although there have been many exceptions and signs that changes are occurring, over the years the regulatory commissions in particular have frequently been staffed at the top with political appointees of less than impressive qualification. As the *Wall Street Journal* expressed it, "Indeed, the Washington regulatory landscape is strewn with old friends of Presidents, unprepared for their assignments and largely uninterested in the industries they regulate. While some take the work seriously, many others simply slide by, attending hearings, flying around the country speaking to industry groups, and doing little to resolve the complex issues their agencies face."[34] One joke making the rounds back in the 1960s was that if Willard Deason, a close personal friend of President Lyndon Johnson, had given the president a pair of horses, rather than the famous pair of LBJ beagles, he would have been given a seat on the Supreme Court rather than on the ICC. Usually the incompetence is dispersed among the regulatory commissions in a way that is not disastrous to any single one. In recent years, however, it has been argued that a substantial part of the inadequacy of the Federal Maritime Commission results from the alleged fact that "the top people just aren't qualified people."[35] In fact, the FMC has developed a degree of notoriety for its top leadership. Lawyers who deal with the commission have referred to the commissioners as "semistupid," lacking a "full deck," and either ignorant, crooked, or politicos. One long-time member, Ashton Barrett, was widely known as "Ashcan."[36] During the mid-1970s, the CPSC was so mismanaged that only 43 percent of its staff thought that the agency was doing a good job.[37] However, in judging the competence of commissioners, it must be borne in mind that sometimes the regulatory missions and statutes are so confused that it would be difficult for even the most accomplished of appointees to develop sound policies.

Corruption

Regulatory commissions have long been criticized for developing cozy relationships with those they are charged with regulating. A former high-ranking Justice

Department official remarked that there are "incredible love affairs going on between the regulators and the regulated."[38] A federal judge, J. Skelly Wright, once asked publicly whether the CAB was not too oriented toward the interests of the industry it was designed to regulate.[39] There are several valid reasons for such "coziness." Some aspects of regulation require frequent contact with representatives of the industry. It is said, for example, that the FDA could not possibly do its job of drug evaluation without frequent personal contacts with the manufacturers. Exchanging information in writing simply would not work. Similarly, it can be useful for members of agencies such as the FCC, ICC, and FMC to be attuned to how the industries they regulate view the present and probable future state of affairs. This may require frequent contact with the regulated, but how else could a regulatory commissioner be expected to make sound policy? A second reason for the "love affair" is that regulatory commissioners are frequently drawn from the industry being regulated or law firms that work on its behalf. This too can be justified on the grounds that regulation requires regulators who are knowledgeable about the industries being regulated. Who is likely to know more than one drawn from such an industry? Sometimes, however, the contacts between the regulated and the regulators do appear to smack of too much coziness. This is evident, for example, when regulatory staff attend the annual convention of an industrial association or labor union and spend too much time socializing with other attendees. More problematic, scandals involving regulatory administration sometimes reveal favoritism in the enforcement of the law. For instance, during the early 1980s, some of the EPA's "superfund" money, which was earmarked for the cleanup of toxic waste sites, was disbursed on the basis of partisan motives. Congressional hearings indicated that "funding for the Stringtown site in California was delayed to avoid helping the Senate election campaign of Democrat Jerry Brown. Two sites in New Jersey were funded to help the campaign of Republican Millicent Fenwick."[40] Eventually, the EPA's director, Anne Gorsuch Burford, was forced to resign, as were some additional twenty high-ranking officials. Moreover, the investigations left no doubt that the EPA had defined the promotion of business interests, rather than the public interest, as its chief concern.

The Ever-Increasing Inclusiveness of Regulation

Another criticism of regulatory administration is that there is a tendency to write <u>overinclusive rules and then to expand them even further</u>. The problem of overinclusiveness is that it is generally difficult to write a set of comprehensive rules in advance that can be applied *strictly and reasonably* in a very wide variety of circumstances. For instance, consider New York City's effort to regulate some 15,000 restaurants. These establishments serve an amazing variety of foods in an astonishing range of settings. Some are among the fanciest in the world, others are run-down take-out shops. Yet all fall under the same rules: failure to pass inspection is automatic if cold food is more than 45 degrees Fahrenheit or if hot food is less than 140 degrees. In addition to these absolute requirements, the inspectors grade restaurants on additional criteria on a 100-point scale for which

70 is a passing grade.[41] It is implausible that a food one degree too hot or cold that has just been prepared to order in an otherwise hygenic establishment is dangerous; we have all consumed such food with no ill effects in our own kitchens. Yet once rules are written there are strong pressures on inspectors to enforce them rigorously, *even if unreasonably*. Failure to enforce rules can be viewed as corrupt—coziness with the regulated. Moreover, if an inspector mistakenly assumes that a rule violation is inconsequential to the safety of workers or the public, and a tragedy occurs, the inspector will face many liabilities—moral, legal, and professional. When one considers not just the fifteen thousand restaurants in New York but all the thousands upon thousands of workplaces under OSHA's jurisdiction, or all those personnel systems under the EEOC's, for example, the problem of overinclusiveness becomes self-evident.

What is less evident is the reason why regulatory agencies tend to add more and more regulations to their lists without deleting those that have become obsolete. This has been referred to as the **regulatory rachet**.[42] An example would be fire codes where as new technologies, such as sprinkler systems and fire-retardant construction materials, are required, no effort is made to determine whether older approaches such as fire doors are still necessary. Regulatory officials treat regulation as "additive" because there is little or no incentive to abandon older rules, despite their inefficacy. Reasons for this lack of incentive include that: (1) dropping a rule can be interpreted as a sign of backtracking or capitulating to the regulated; (2) deleting rules does not directly contribute to the agency's regulatory objectives; (3) there is sometimes a risk that in some remote instance a rule that is abandoned will make an important difference; and even (4) deleting rules is considered boring work.[43]

The Regulatory Process Is Out of Control

To a considerable extent, these criticisms amount to the indictment that the regulatory process gets beyond control. Originally, regulatory commissions were structured to be insulated from direct political or partisan control by the elected components of government. Like public administration generally, regulation was supposed to be nonpartisan and devoted to the public interest. Eventually, however, at the federal level the commissions were considered to be a true fourth branch of government, neither directly under presidential nor congressional control, but exercising executive, legislative, and judicial roles. The statutes under which some of them operate provide little direction. To ask an agency to regulate the use of the nation's airwaves in the "public convenience, interest, or necessity" is to provide it with very little guidance indeed. To charge another with regulating unfair and uncompetitive economic practices is not providing much more. Similarly, the FMC operates under a statute that is probably so broad as to justify virtually *any* decision it reaches on matters under its jurisdiction. Moreover, some of the regulatory agencies are charged with enormous tasks and not afforded nearly enough personnel or budgetary resources. The EEOC is an excellent example, though the missions of OSHA, CPSC, and the EPA are also thoroughly daunting.

Finally, there is no agreed upon standard as to levels of success. Economists prefer to consider the issue in cost-benefit terms, but the costs are sometimes economic while the benefits are social. For example, how can we determine what it is worth to us collectively to have more or less comprehensive inspections of elevators? It will do little to alleviate our apprehensions, irrational though they may be, to argue that inspections really don't make much difference because the potential of liability suits will make sure building owners keep their elevators in good repair. We know all too well that some building owners are likely to put their resources elsewhere if allowed to do so and to take a few chances (with our lives). Elevator maintenance companies may do the same. Even if such a statement only applies to 1 percent of the building owners, we might favor regulation in advance. We seek comprehensive protection, even though the costs per life saved may be very high or at least higher than placing reliance on liability suits. Similarly, the FDA may inhibit the development and marketing of new drugs, but it also has done a great deal to assure that the drugs actually available to us are not dangerous. We may be able to ascertain the costs of the EEOC's enforcement of antidiscrimination regulations, but how can we measure the benefits gained in the form of fairer treatment for minorities and women? How can the full costs and benefits of something like the FCC's fairness rule be accurately measured? OSHA regulations are expensive, but they do save lives and prevent injuries. At some point we may agree that they are *too* expensive. At some other point the society might favor spending more. But how can we arrive at an acceptable cost-benefit ratio in between?

Regulation, like many other aspects of public administration, confronts the society with some very difficult moral problems. If we agree to safety and antipollution regulation that adds $500 per car, perhaps it is because as a population we are asking the government to require us to do what we believe is good for us and society. If this is true, then we are recognizing that we will not do it as individuals, suggesting that we believe that for any single individual, in the absence of cooperation by others, the costs would be too great for the benefits obtained. This is the basic "collective action" problem. Some benefits to the society require widespread participation or cooperation of individuals whose personal economic incentive is not to join a group effort. (Why be the only one in the country whose car does not contribute to pollution? Why not be the only one whose car does pollute? What tangible difference will it make?) But if the benefits depend on near-universal cooperation or compliance, then how will we evaluate the regulatory problem? Clearly, cost-benefit analysis will not be wholly adequate, especially when assessed in per capita terms (e.g., the cost per vehicle equipped with antipollution devices). Nor do the aggregate costs alone tell us much more than that regulation is expensive.

Concern with the level of compliance raises a related problem. It is obvious that the marginal cost of enforcing regulations may often rise as administrators approach obtaining universal (total) compliance. This is true, for example, where regulation involves inspections of a large number of sites, some of which are very small (as in restaurant inspection) and, possibly, remote as well. The marginal benefits, whether calculable or not, of obtaining greater compliance are likely to decline when the few recalcitrant rule evaders are small establishments with limited capacity to do serious harm. A point might be reached where the marginal costs of more enforcement begin to exceed the marginal benefits. But this would not necessarily be a compelling argument for curtailing enforcement efforts. Legal principles, such as equal application of the law, and social concepts of fairness and risk elimination might well lead to the conclusion that an effort should be made to enforce the regulations in *all* the cases to which they apply.

Consequently, in discussions of regulation, an economically oriented approach such as cost-benefit analysis is often augmented by psychological, social, legal, and political perspectives. Government officials, interest groups, and substantial numbers of political activists generally argue that regulation should reduce individual anxiety and risk concerning the safety of foods, drugs, cars, jobs, motels, hotels, office buildings, elevators, new technologies, and so forth. They also feel that it is partly the job of regulatory administration to protect individuals' lives even when those individuals are reluctant to do so themselves, as in the case of mandatory seat belt laws. This is partly because other people are socially dependent on or socially connected to these individuals and consequently, it is argued, serious injuries or deaths will adversely affect the society as a whole. For example, if the use of seat belts can save the lives of parents, should they be optional in view of the social costs of orphanhood? From a political angle, many favor regulation for the safety of groups in the population who might otherwise be especially vulnerable. The regulation of child labor and nursing homes falls into this category. In this sense, regulation is a microcosm of all public administration. The question it addresses concerns the kind of society we want government to help establish and maintain.

Toward Regulatory Reform and Deregulation

Since regulation is so broad in scope, so varied in kind, so difficult to evaluate, and so problematic to implement, it is not surprising that many have favored regulatory reform and deregulation in recent years. Those taking this approach generally advance four main arguments other than that the costs of regulation are too high. One is that free markets can provide more benefits to the society than can regulated ones. This view applies primarily to surrogate-market regulation and some aspects of market-functioning and employment regulation. Deregulation of the airlines and the phasing out of the CAB serve as an illustration. Since deregulation occurred, there has been more price competition, with prices on many routes dropping dramatically. Service in many places has been increased, but in others, where ridership is low, service has been cut entirely. Safety, which is under the FAA's jurisdiction, has not been deregulated and it is unclear whether it has suffered. The economic pressures placed on airlines as a result of the new competition have severely hurt some while enabling others to flourish. From a free-market perspective, this was pretty much the way things should have been. But the consolidation of thirty-eight carriers, through mergers and acquisitions, has enabled the eight largest airlines to control 94 percent of the market. Consequently, there is growing demand for the application of antitrust regulations.[44] This is not a contradiction since both surrogate-market *deregulation* and market-functioning *regulation* have the same general objective—to promote market competition as the primary means of organizing and coordinating economic activity.

A second argument raised by those in favor of deregulation is that liability law can be used to assure safety in many aspects of life. For example, the potential of suits against automobile manufacturers can provide them with a great incentive to design safe cars. The same logic would apply to the drugs produced by pharmaceutical companies. Proponents of this approach generally believe that once the incentive is strong enough, the private sector can be innovative and responsible in designing safe products and in developing safe and healthful work processes. And they can do so without having to deal with the unproductive consequences of overinclusive regulatory rules and red tape. However, even if one accepts this view, there may be a dispute as to whether liability laws need to be rewritten in some areas to provide a strong enough incentive to market only safe products.

Another argument advanced against government regulation is that there is great potential for the private sector to engage in self-regulation. For example, many firms and unions do employ safety inspectors and take an active interest in establishing and maintaining healthful and safe conditions in the workplace. In some cases, public law may require enterprises to engage in self-regulation, as in the hazardous waste disposal business, trucking (at least in California), and the manufacture of intravenous solutions by pharmaceutical firms.[45]

Finally, proponents of deregulation sometimes argue that if business enterprises were required to disclose information relevant to the safety, healthfulness, and security of their products, services, or other offerings, then the public could act as its own inspectors. For example, tobacco companies print the tar and nicotine content of their cigarettes. Some states require used-car dealers to reveal known defects in the cars they sell, as did federal regulations for a time. Credit agreements indicate the yearly interest rate, and stock and banking offerings are subject to a number of mandatory disclosure regulations.

During the mid-1970s and early 1980s, the arguments for regulatory reform and deregulation coalesced into a broad, bipartisan effort to redesign federal regulatory administration. Reforms generally sought greater coordination, centralized review, and more thoroughgoing assessment of the impact of regulations, as well as their overall reduction. Early steps in these directions were taken by the Nixon administration, which initiated a regulatory review process. Authority was given to the newly created Office of Management and Budget (OMB) to conduct "quality of life" reviews of proposed regulations. These reviews considered the objectives of the regulations, their costs and benefits, and alternatives to them. Although the Nixon program focused mostly on environmental regulations, it established a precedent for future reforms.

The Ford administration, which was more concerned with inflation, followed the same general approach but required that agencies send "inflation impact statements" to OMB along with their proposed regulations. Under both the Nixon and Ford programs, agencies were able to establish final rules despite OMB's opposition to them.

The Carter administration promoted further regulatory reform. Carter created a Regulatory Analysis Review Group to review a limited number of agency proposals likely to cost industries at least $100 million per year. He also issued Executive Order 12044, which required that:

1. Proposed regulations should be as simple and clear as possible.
2. Meaningful alternatives must be considered and analyzed before an agency could promulgate a regulation.
3. The public should have a meaningful opportunity to participate in the development of agency regulations.
4. Agencies must publish an agenda of significant regulations under development at least twice a year.
5. An economic-impact analysis must be prepared for all significant regulations.
6. Existing regulations must be periodically reviewed to determine whether their objectives were still being met.[46]

OMB was assigned the responsibility of overseeing agencies' compliance with these requirements, though actual review was typically performed by the review group.

President Carter also moved significantly toward surrogate-market deregulation in airline, trucking, and railroad transportation. Some controls, deemed anticompetitive, were lifted on financial institutions and natural gas pricing. On the other hand, Carter embraced greater environmental regulation and strengthened the EEOC.

The Reagan administration went even further in promoting regulatory reform and deregulation. Its strategy was more complex and far-reaching than that of its predecessors, though its results were mixed. First, in February 1981, Reagan issued Executive Order 12291, requiring agencies, unless otherwise prohibited by law, to submit their regulations to a cost-benefit analysis. It also specified that the regulatory objectives were to be achieved by the means least costly to society. OMB had authority to review, at its discretion, any rules that would have a major impact on costs and prices or that adversely affect competition, employment, investment, productivity, or innovation. The order enabled OMB to demand a regulatory-impact analysis of both *existing* and proposed rules. Although the order did not apply to independent commissions, it placed OMB at the center of a great deal of regulatory policy making. For instance, in 1985, OMB reviewed 2,221 rules, taking an average of 43 days for major ones and 16 days for others.[47] Most of these were approved (71 percent), but there is no doubt that the review process forced agencies to draft rules in anticipation of OMB's response. In 1985, agencies were required to submit "draft regulatory programs" even before developing proposed rules. By 1986, considerable congressional opposition was directed toward the lack of public scrutiny of OMB's contacts with interest groups and industry representatives as part of its review process. Turning the tables on the budget-cutting agency, Congress threatened to reduce OMB's appropriation by $5.4 million (of a $40 million budget).[48] Subsequently, OMB announced a more acceptable policy!

A second aspect of the Reagan strategy for reforming and reducing regulatory administration was to appoint to important regulatory posts individuals who were committed to dismantling regulation. Among those prominently mentioned in this regard were Anne Gorsuch Burford at the EPA, Raymond Peck at NHTSA, and Thorne Auchter at OSHA, all of whom "have been generally viewed as being not only poorly qualified to run their agencies but also interested primarily in helping industry at the expense of the public."[49] Several appointees to the EEOC actually appeared to be unsympathetic to equal rights for women and minorities.

Finally, the Reagan administration promoted deep budget and staffing cuts in regulatory agencies, thereby making it more difficult for them to function effectively. By one calculation, the number of permanent positions in major regulatory agencies decreased from 90,000 in 1980 to 76,000 in 1984, or a decline of 16 percent.[50] Cumulative budget cuts also took a serious toll in several agencies, including the EPA, CPSC, and the ICC.

President Reagan's early successes notwithstanding, by the end of his second term it was clear that, for the most part, the movement toward deregulation had run its course. Deregulation was most successful where the objective of regulation had been to provide a surrogate for the market. Other areas, such as employment and market functioning, were "deregulated" by neglect and management that was unsympathetic to traditional regulatory goals. However, by the mid-1980s, some agencies, notably the EPA and OSHA, showed signs of resurgence. The deregulated airlines were facing serious calls for "reregulation" in the form of antitrust measures, better safety controls, and the elimination of deceptive scheduling practices. Pressure was on the FAA to do much more to assure passenger safety.

In all likelihood, the more lasting contributions of the past fifteen years will be in the area of regulatory reform. Regulatory-impact analyses can clearly be a valuable tool for fashioning and evaluating regulatory policy. Centralized review of regulatory rules and proposed rules can be invaluable in promoting coordination, elimination of duplicative or contradictory rules, and assurance that regulatory agencies do not view the public interest with tunnel vision.

Whatever specific reforms are developed, however, regulatory administration is likely to remain controversial for years to come. The regulatory-deregulatory pendulum is likely to swing back and forth and new reforms will be advanced. Since regulation will be a controversial part of public administration in the foreseeable future, it is incumbent upon public administrators to do their best to organize and implement it well. But when we turn our attention to the matter of what is "good" regulatory administration, we are also confronted by differences in perspective.

PERSPECTIVES TOWARD REGULATORY ADMINISTRATION

The Managerial Perspective

As in other areas, the managerial perspective toward regulatory administration emphasizes the values of effectiveness, efficiency, and economy. In terms of regulation, effectiveness has often been considered the avoidance of a major crisis or scandal. As James Q. Wilson observes, for agencies such as EPA, OSHA, and the FDA, "a major scandal would be a dramatic loss of life or catastrophic injury among people nominally protected by the decisions of the agency."[51] The CAB would have faced crisis or scandal if it had let a major airline go bankrupt, as would the FMC today if a major shipper did likewise. The Nuclear Regulatory Commission was scandalized by the Three Mile Island catastrophe in 1979. The FAA was severely criticized after the 1979 crash of a DC-10 airplane in Chicago that killed 250 passengers and crew members. Several tragic crashes and near misses in 1987 raised new concerns about the agency's adequacy. In the past, the EEOC was viewed as scandalously ineffective and in perpetual crisis because of its huge backlog of cases (about 130,000 in the 1970s). But how can regulatory administration be managed to avoid scandals and crises while also remaining efficient and economical?

First, the effort to be effective in the sense of avoiding crisis and scandal will dictate a conservative approach to rule enforcement and decision making. There will be a very strong tendency toward strict—even rigid—enforcement of the rules. This is because any exercise of discretion or departure from the rules that results in scandal or crisis will be severely criticized by the legislature, the media, and other political actors. It may trigger legal liabilities. An agency's failure to enforce its own rules that results in tragedy may even bring about a thorough administrative reorganization of its functions. Conversely, even if a crisis develops, when an agency has followed its own rules and when those rules are pursuant to legislation and have been previously tested in the courts, the agency may claim that it has done all it could within its power in the face of an unforeseeable future. It may even turn the crisis into a request for greater authority so that it can handle such events in the future. The FDA, for example, was given greater authority over the marketing of drugs as a result of the sulfanilamide scandal in the 1930s and the thalidomide scandal in the early 1960s, even though the latter, which resulted in the birth of children with misshapen limbs ("phocomelia," or "seal limbs"), was mostly confined to Europe and Canada. If nothing else, strictly following the rules tends to absolve an agency of any taint of corruption or inconsistency.

Second, as noted earlier, there will be a strong tendency to avoid deleting rules, even though it may appear that they are outmoded. Just as rules tend to be overinclusive, rescinding those that seem unnecessary may mistakenly overlook a single facility, work process, or economic relationship where the rule would make a difference. Should a scandal or crisis result due to the agency's dropping of the rule, the agency would be subject to massive criticism. When the FDA contemplated redirecting its emphasis vis-à-vis regulation of the food industry from poor sanitation to chemical and microbiological health hazards, it was severely criticized by *Consumer Reports* articles on the grounds that it had "casually dismissed" the problem of "filth" (see Box 9–4).[52]

Third, the development of new rules and application of new policies will be slow. Major departures from past approaches, such as widespread and immediate deregulation, are likely to be avoided since the results may be

BOX 9–4 **The Food and Drug Administration's "Rat Hair" List**

The following listing of "current levels for natural or unavoidable defects in food for human use that present no health hazard" was made public by the FDA in 1972. Out of sensitivity to the reader, the author will neither confirm nor deny that such a list is still in use. What did you eat today?

OFFICE OF THE ASSISTANT COMMISSIONER FOR PUBLIC AFFAIRS
FOOD AND DRUG ADMINISTRATION
ROOM 15B42
5600 FISHERS LANE
ROCKVILLE, MARYLAND 20852

Current Levels for Natural or Unavoidable Defects in Food for Human Use That Present No Health Hazard

PRODUCT	DEFECT ACTION LEVEL
Chocolate & Chocolate Products	
Chocolate & Chocolate Liquor	Average of 150 insect fragments per subdivisions of 225 grams or 250 insect fragments in any one subdivision of 225 grams. Average of 4 rodent hairs per subdivisions of 225 grams or 8 rodent hairs in any one subdivision of 225 grams. Shell in excess of 2% alkali-free nibs.
Coffee Beans	10% or more by count are insect infested, insect damaged or show mold.
Eggs & Frozen Egg Products	
Dried Whole Eggs Dried Egg Yolks	Decomposed as determined by direct microscopic count of 100,000,000 bacteria per gram.
Frozen Eggs & Other Frozen Egg Products	Two cans contain decomposed eggs; and subsamples examined from cans classified as decomposed have counts of 5,000,000 bacteria per gram.
Flours & Cornmeals	
Corn Meal	1. 20% of the subdivisions contain over 100 insect fragments per 50 grams or 2 insects of equivalent per 50 grams and an additional 20% of the subs show over 25 insect fragments per 50 grams or one insect or equivalent per 50 grams; or 2. 20% of the subs contains over 5 rodent pellet fragments per 50 grams and an additional 20% of these subs contain over 2 rodent pellet fragments or detached rodent hairs per 50 grams.

BOX 9–4 *Continued*

PRODUCT	DEFECT ACTION LEVEL
Fruit Olives	Pitted: average of 1.3% by count of olives with pit fragments 2 mm. or longer measured in the longest dimension,. exclusive of whole pits. Salad olives: average of 1.3 pit fragments per 300 grams, including whole pits and fragments 2 mm. or longer measured in the longest dimension. Salt cured olives: Insect: average of 15% by count of olives with 10 scale insects each, or, average of 25% by count of olives show mold. Imported black or green: average of 10% by count wormy or worm-cut. Salad type: Average of 12% by weight insect infested and/or insect damaged due to the olive fruit fly.
Grains Popcorn	1. One rodent pellet in one or more subs upon examination of 10/225 gram subs or 6/10 oz. consumer size packages and one rodent hair in other subs; or 2. Examination shows two rodent hairs per pound and rodent hairs in more than half the subs; or 3. Examination shows 20 gnawed grains per pound, provided that rodent hairs are found in more than half the subs; 4. Examination shows field corn in the popcorn exceeds 5% by weight.
Wheat	One rodent pellet per pint. 1% by weight of insect damaged kernels.
Jams, Jellies, Fruit Butters & Fig Paste Apple Butter	Microscopic mold count average exceeding 12%. Rodent: average of more than 8 rodent hairs per 100 grams of apple butter. Insects: average of more than 5 insects or insect parts (not counting mites, aphids, thrips, scales) per 100 grams of apple butter.

BOX 9–4 *Continued*

PRODUCT	DEFECT ACTION LEVEL
Peanuts & Peanut Products	
Peanut Butter	Average of 50 insect fragments per 100 grams; or, average of 2 rodent hairs per 100 grams.
	Grit: gritty to the taste and the water-insoluble inorganic residue is more than 35 milligrams per 100 grams.
Vegetables	
Asparagus, Canned or Frozen	15% of spears by count are infested with 6 attached asparagus beetle eggs or egg sacs.
Beets, Canned	Pieces with dry rot exceed 5% by weight in the average of the subs.
Broccoli	Over 80 aphids or thrips/100 grams in the average of all subs examined.
Brussel Sprouts (frozen)	Average is more than 40 aphids and/or thrips per 100 grams.
Corn (Sweet, canned)	Examination of 24 pounds (24 No. 303 cans or the equivalent) shows the following: two 3 mm or longer larvae, cast skins, larval or cast skin fragments or corn ear worm or corn borer, *and* aggregate length of such larvae, cast skins, larval or cast skin fragments exceeds 12 mm.
Tomatoes & Tomato Products	
Canned Tomatoes	10 fruit fly eggs per 500 grams or 5 fruit fly eggs and 1 larva per 500 grams or 2 larvae per 500 grams.
Tomato Juice	10 fruit fly eggs per 100 grams or 5 fruit fly eggs and 1 larva per 100 grams, or 2 larvae per 100 grams.
Tomato Puree	20 fruit fly eggs per 100 grams or 10 fruit fly eggs and 1 larva per 100 grams, or 2 larvae per 100 grams.
Tomato Paste, Pizza & Other Sauces	30 fruit fly eggs per 100 grams, or 15 fruit fly eggs and 1 larva per 100 grams, or 2 larvae per 100 grams.

unpredictable. The case of airline deregulation and the CAB illustrates this tendency. The CAB, which had resisted deregulation until 1975, waited until after 1977 before approving, on a step-by-step basis, measures that would enhance price competition. The CAB was mindful of the dislocations that might occur if the industry were subjected to immediate and thoroughgoing increases in competition.[53]

The major difficulty with these approaches from a managerial standpoint is that they can undercut efficiency and economy. Strict enforcement of additive rules and conservativism in responding to rapidly changing conditions and technologies can lead to the expenditure of an agency's human and economic resources on aspects of regulation that make no real difference in terms of safety, environmental quality, economic competition, and so forth. Enforcement of the rules for their own sake is the essence of a bureaucratic approach, in the worst sense of the term. The key to successful regulation is viewed by many as flexibility based on the sound exercise of discretion. Bardach and Kagan, for example, have considered at length how regulatory administration in several areas, including safety, health, employment, and some aspects of trade practices, can be successfully managed. Among their suggestions are:

1. Careful training of inspectors, so that their judgment is more reliable.
2. Specialization of inspectors, so that their knowledge of what they are inspecting is thoroughgoing.
3. Controlling the discretion of inspectors through such approaches as rotating the inspectors from site to site, reinspection by others, supervisory monitoring of their use of time and their issuance of citations to violators. Supervisors may also find it desirable to meet with inspectors on a regular basis to discuss hard cases and work problems in general.
4. The efficient deployment of inspectors and other personnel so that they are concentrated where the real problems are.
5. Attempting to resolve violations or complaints of prohibited practices informally, rather than through formal adjudication.
6. Exploring the possibilities for "piggybacking" the functions of different agencies in order to reduce the need for duplication of efforts in inspections, investigations, information gathering, and processing complaints.
7. Shifting some of the burden for complaints to complainants by requiring them to supply more of the information that will be needed for informal resolution or adjudication.
8. Encouraging self-enforcement and self-regulation by educating enterprises as to their obligations and the rationale for the regulations imposed on them. [54]

Management in the regulatory sphere will require a balancing of different concerns in different contexts. It will also require a realization that the approaches to regulatory administration informed by the political and legal perspectives may stress additional and competing values.

The Political Approach to Regulatory Administration

In the past, it was common for "political hacks" to be appointed to regulatory commissions. Their chief ethos appears to have been to seek reappointment by avoiding enemies rather than by making friends. [55] In practice, this dictated not upsetting the status quo. In consequence, many agencies did seem to be in the last phase of the traditional "life cycle," that of being captured by the industries ostensibly being regulated. Where this was the case, many of the politicos were assured cushy jobs in the industry after they stepped off the regulatory commissions.

Today, however, the situation seems quite different. The movement toward deregulation and regulatory reform, as well as the scrutiny of regulatory activities by public interest groups and legislators have transformed the political approach toward regulatory administration. Two key values are emerging.

One is greater attention to the full range of constituencies of a regulatory program, or expanded representation. In the past, after the life cycle went through its first phase, the constituency of the regulatory agency was often considered to be those groups being regulated. For the ICC, the constituencies were railroads and truckers; for the CAB, the constituency was the airlines; under the Taylor Grazing Act it was the stockmen; for the FMC, it is the shippers; under the Atomic Energy Act (1946), it was clearly the nuclear power industry; and so on. Today, however, the public, or segments of it, may often be viewed as an important constituency of the regulatory agency. Sometimes the public is presumed to be represented by public interest groups and spokespersons, such as Common Cause and Ralph Nader. In other cases, the agencies simply pay more attention to their mandates to serve the public interest. Thus, the FCC, long faulted for promoting anticompetitive practices in the broadcast industry and being oblivious to the quality of radio and TV programming, has recently shown an interest in getting some radio stations to agree not to play songs that promote or glorify drug abuse, and it has also paid more attention to the question of the public interest in granting renewals for TV stations. In other areas, segments of the public, such as the activist senior citizens called the Gray Panthers, have become politically mobilized to make sure that regulatory administration relevant to their interests, such as nursing homes, does in fact serve their needs rather than primarily the desires of the regulated industries. Consumers' groups have also mobilized in this way to gain greater protection of their interests. An important corollary of paying greater attention to the public is the establishment of procedural mechanisms for public participation in administrative decision making. This has been especially pronounced in the regulation at the state level.

William Gormley found the emphasis on representation so striking and pronounced that he called it a "revolution." In his words,

> The most striking finding to emerge from this review of the literature is that public representation in state regulation can promote substantive representation. Citizens' groups have effectively participated in coastal zone management hearings and water quality planning hearings. Ombudsmen have successfully resolved complaints by nursing home patients for whom the regulatory process has been disappointing. Proxy advocates have effectively championed consumer interests in rate relief and more liberal disconnecting policies.
>
> These successes are all the more remarkable because they have involved different settings, strategies, and goals. In environmental regulation, citizens' groups have converted community support and political pressure into formidable weapons. In nursing home regulation, ombudsmen have used technical expertise and jawboning to secure service responsiveness. In utility regulation, proxy advocates have utilized technical expertise, a knowledge of administrative law, and adversarial strategies to promote policy responsiveness.[56]

The second emergent value in the political approach toward regulatory administration is accountability. Although accountability has always been part of the political perspective toward public administration, it has been given a far greater emphasis recently in terms of regulation. Perhaps the best single example is the National Environmental Policy Act of 1969 (NEPA). The act cuts across a wide range of federal administrative activities, including regulation. The purposes are to promote a "productive and enjoyable harmony between man and his environment," to "eliminate damage to the environment and biosphere and stimulate the health and welfare of man," and to "enrich the understanding of the ecological systems and natural resources important to the nation." It requires that administrative agencies develop "environmental impact" statements. These must discuss any proposed action having a potential impact on the environment. They describe possible adverse environmental effects, alternatives, long-term consequences, and irreversible and irretrievable commitments. The impact statements are to be made available to federal, state, and local agencies dealing with environmental matters, to the president, to the federal Council on Environmental Quality, and, generally, to the public. Some of these statements can be highly elaborate and expensive, as the Department of the Interior's report on the trans-Alaska pipeline, which fills nine volumes and cost $25 million to prepare.[57] Although such a vast amount of information can be forbidding, many political actors, such as legislators, their staff, and public interest groups, frequently do devote enough attention to environmental impact statements to assure a greater degree of administrative accountability. The judiciary has also been active in reviewing procedures under NEPA. Where agencies' procedures include public hearings, the impact statements may become the basis for informed public participation in regulatory administration. In addition, the federal judiciary has been friendly to suits by individuals seeking to compel agencies to fulfill their obligations under the act.[58] It is not difficult to envision that, in the future, regulatory-impact analyses could be used in parallel ways.

The Legal Approach to Regulatory Administration

Regulatory administration in the United States has been highly legalistic in its approach, processes, and organization. The legalistic quality of regulatory administration is understandable, since regulation affects the rights of individuals, groups such as labor unions, and business enterprises. It also concerns the use and disposition of their property, including intangible property such as trademarks. Additionally, regulatory rules constrain the policies and operations of other administrative agencies and subnational political jurisdictions. Like the managerial and political approaches, the legalistic perspective places a distinct emphasis on certain values.

The Effects of the Adversary Procedure   At the stage of deciding how regulatory rules should be enforced, the legalistic approach tends to favor cases that place the agency or one party against another in an **adversary proceeding**. This follows from the view that regulation involves the definition of rights and obligations pursuant to statutes or agency rules. However, it has two important consequences that distinguish it from other approaches to regulatory administration.

First, the legal approach depends upon the *building of cases* for adjudication. This is true even though many conflicts are resolved by consent prior to going to formal hearings or court. Building a record entails uncovering violations. This places the agency in an adversarial role vis-à-vis the individuals, groups, or firms it is investigating. Whereas the managerial and political approaches often tend to view regulatory administration as oriented toward solving problems, the adversarial approach of the legalistic perspective tends to view it as developing, documenting, and winning cases. Moreover, in the adversarial mode, the agency, or part of it, becomes an *advocate* for a perspective. Consequently it may emphasize the information that supports its case and downplay information or reasoning to the contrary. From the point of view of those being regulated, this can be extremely frustrating. They are generally seeking to run an economic enterprise profitably and within the law, rather than seeking to build a record of winning cases. In practice, the difference in perspectives on this point can be quite striking. For instance, Terrence Scanlon, chairman of the CPSC under Reagan, stated, "We are stressing voluntary development of standards. We want to work with companies to solve problems, not against them."[59]

Second, the legal approach tends to favor relatively simple conduct cases where one party or the agency alleges that another has violated the law. It tends to shy away from the complicated structural cases that rest on theory and often depend upon novel interpretations of the law. Conduct cases fit the adjudicatory process better; simple conduct cases enable the agency to develop a strong record of winning. In the FTC, for example, there has been a competition between economists and lawyers based largely on the differing perspectives toward structural and conduct cases.

Neutrality and the Administrative Law Judge   At the level of adjudication, the legalistic approach relies on the adversary proceeding before an impartial administrative law judge or court. In practice, the neutrality of the administrative law judge stands in stark contrast to the managerial emphasis on control through hierarchy and the political perspective's stress on accountability.

Due Process Protection   The rights of the private party being charged with a violation or being sued will be protected through a set of formal procedural requirements. Such parties will often have constitutional protections at the stage in which the agency is gathering information and building its case. For instance, searches, wiretaps, bugging, and the surveillance of mail will be controlled by constitutional standards, although with the proper safeguards against abuse, they may be allowable. If the agency decides to press the case, the regulated parties must be given adequate notice of the charges against them, and of the agency's proposed action. Normally, the parties will be given an opportunity to respond, either in writing or orally. If the matter is serious enough, a hearing is likely to be afforded at some point; the regulated party may also have a right to take the case to court for judicial review of the agency's behavior. At either the administrative hearing stage or in court, the party will have the right to be represented by counsel, though the agency does not necessarily have to provide counsel for the party. Many of these rights are spelled out in the Administrative Procedure Act of 1946, as amended. At the state level, similar provisions generally apply.

Reasonableness   At the level of determination of the outcome of the case, the legalistic approach will stress fairness not only of procedure, but also in terms of the result. This often involves a judicial assessment of the reasonableness of the agency's action. Until recent years, the judiciary seemed far more concerned with whether a matter was under an agency's jurisdiction and whether proper procedures were followed than in the quality of the agency's decision in terms of its substantive content. Nowadays, however, in an effort to protect the rights and property of individual parties and to check abuses of administrative discretion, the judiciary is far more inclined to question the logic of the agency's decision. For example, in *FTC* v. *Sperry and Hutchinson* (1972), a case involving whether the redemption of S&H Green Stamps was being controlled in an unfair or deceptive fashion, the Supreme Court found that the agency had not done its adjudicatory job properly.[60] The court found that "the Commission has not rendered an opinion which, by the route suggested, links its findings and its conclusions." Thus the Court held that the case should be sent back to the commission for further consideration. An even more dramatic example of judicial review along these lines occurred in *Motor Vehicle Manufacturers Association* v. *State Farm Mutual Automobile Insurance Co.* (1983) in which the Supreme Court found that the National Highway Traffic Safety Administration "failed to present an adequate basis and explanation" for rescinding its earlier rule requiring the installation of passive-restraining seat belts on all new cars by 1984 or air bags by a later date.[61] Here the agency, which had the discretion to make the rule in the first place, could not withdraw it in the absence of a well-reasoned and publicly articulated explanation that was considered reasonable by the Court. Similarly, in an important 1971 Court of Appeals decision, it was reasoned that "courts should require administrative officers to articulate the standards and principles that govern their discretionary decisions in as much detail as possible."[62]

The courts have adopted this new line of thought to assure that as regulation reaches deeper into society, the personal and property rights of private parties are not undermined. At least one case demonstrates this emphasis with remarkable clarity. *Abbott Laboratories* v. *Gardner, Secretary of the Department of Health, Education, and Welfare* (1967) involved the intriguing question of whether the Commissioner of Food and Drug could, pursuant to a somewhat ambiguously worded statute, require that drug companies print the generic name for drugs, also having trade names, every time the trade name appeared on a label or in an advertisement.[63] In a surprising step, the Supreme Court agreed to determine whether the commissioner had the authority to issue the regulation before it was actually put into effect or applied to any drug company that might violate it. As the Supreme Court saw it, unless prior review of this kind was granted (within the bounds of the statute that governs such review, the Declaratory Judgment Act), the drug companies would lose regardless of whether they complied or not. If they did comply, the regulation would be treated as lawful and the companies could harm their business interests by printing the generic name. Doing so would require changing their labels, advertisements, and the promotion of their products. It might also encourage far greater price competition. Failure to comply would run the risk of prosecution. In the latter event, even if a company successfully argued that the FDA lacked authority to issue the rule, its public image could be seriously damaged in an area where the public's trust is an important factor in a firm's economic viability.

In sum, the legal approach to regulation emphasizes adversary relationships, the legal obligations and rights of the parties, procedural fairness, and reasonableness in terms of the substantive content of regulatory administrative decisions. Of course, these values and concerns are merely sketched out here; many volumes can be and have been written on the administrative law of regulation.

SYNTHESIS

It is once again evident that there are many conflicts and tensions among the managerial, political, and legalistic approaches toward regulatory administration. The managerial approach's desire for effectiveness, that is, focusing on the impact that regulation has on the regulated parties, is frequently at odds with the political approach's current emphasis on making regulation responsive to organized, broad constituencies, as suggested by the CAB's initial resistance to deregulation, for instance. Economy and accountability are certainly at odds, at least in the short run, over the requirement that environmental impact statements be developed and publicized. Efficiency is frequently at odds with adjudication and procedural due process, which require that agencies "build cases" and adjudicate them fairly (and also at some expense). Adjudication is also in conflict with the managerial perspective's desire to control administrative operations tightly; administrative law judges are not simply subject to direct hierarchical control by an agency's managers. The political perspective's effort to protect broad constituencies, such as consumers, can be in tension with the legalistic approach's emphasis on the protection of private parties' property and business interests. This was shown in the Abbott Labs case by the dissent of Justice Clark, who wrote, "Rather than crying over the plight that the laboratories have brought on themselves [by charging ten to twelve times too much for trade name drugs] the Court should think more of the poor ailing folks who suffer under the practice."

All these values are in competition in a very wide range of aspects of regulatory administration. Can they be synthesized through the development of a perspective that would enable at least some important priorities to be established?

One way of thinking about such a synthesis is first to identify the broad objectives of regulation and then to consider which of the perspectives is most suitable to it. In the past, there has been a tendency to view *all* regulatory administration from the point of governmental penetration of the economy and society. Consequently, some observers thought that *deregulating* surrogate markets while *strengthening* antitrust enforcement was contradictory, even though the objective of each policy initiative is to promote competition. Similarly, deregulation of surrogate markets is not necessarily inconsistent with greater health, safety, employment, or environmental regulation.[64] In the future, finer distinctions should be drawn. For the sake of illustration, the following approach is suggested.

The Public Interest   Where the regulatory administration involved concerns a very broad public interest, the political approach seems most suitable. Environmental regulation is a clear case. As NEPA recognizes, what happens to the environment will affect everyone in the nation now or in future generations. That is the justification for the environmental impact statement, even though it is costly and can reduce the short-term economic development. If we are all directly and more or less equally involved, then accountability becomes paramount. Otherwise the public loses control of its fate and democracy is very seriously compromised. Robert Dahl, a leading political scientist, has argued cogently that for the same reasons, the public must also be involved in decisions about nuclear weapons.[65] At times it will be difficult to determine when the public interest is so broad that regulatory administration should stress accountability over other goals. Yet the place to start is by considering each regulatory program individually on its merits from this perspective, rather than trying to prejudge everything at once on the basis of theory.

Balancing the Interests of Private Parties Against Each Other   Where regulation aims to strike a proper balance between two private concerns, such as monopoly producers and consumers or businesses and organized labor, the legal approach is most suitable. For example, the regulation of utility and other rates fits into this area. Rate-setting was a standard judicial function even before regulatory commissions and public utility commissions were created. The objective is to allow utilities or other regulated enterprises to earn a "fair" rate of return on their investment. Utilities tend to have monopoly status and therefore could gouge the public; conversely, if turned completely over to the political approach's emphasis on representing constituencies, regulatory administration in this area could result in unreasonable harm to the profitability of such enterprises. It could also lead to one group of rate payers absorbing the costs, perhaps unwittingly and unwillingly, of providing service to others. Adjudication of such matters enables a balancing among the competing interests with an acceptable compromise as the result. The adjudication of numerous and repetitive violations of fair trade practices and routine health and safety regulations also seems to protect private parties against harassment while enabling regulation to proceed vigorously. Assessing the fairness of various labor practices has also been largely accomplished through adjudication. In all likelihood, most antitrust activity would fall into the category of balancing rights against one another. However, cases might be so broad as to make the political approach more salient.

Protection Against Disaster   Where regulatory administration is aimed at protecting against disastrous events and accidents, as in the regulation of drugs and air transportation safety, the managerial perspective is most suitable. Here the point is prevention; inspections, voluntary compliance, and cooperation are desirable. Whereas all the legal approach demands is minimal compliance with law, the managerial approach seeks cooperation with the purposes of the regulatory administration. For instance, the FDA punishes violations, but it also tries to get the drug companies to engage in sound pre-market testing. Airlines engage in safety maintenance, but few would suggest they should merely comply with a checklist of FAA required procedures. Rather, they carefully consider any additional safety procedures that appear reasonable to them. In a similar way, OSHA is likely to be far more effective in preventing accidents in the workplace when its inspectors avoid a legalistic approach to violations and seek to help firms eliminate genuine safety risks. Until some measure of deregulation set in, banking was another area largely treated from the managerial perspective toward regulatory administration. The purpose was largely to prevent a collapse of a major bank or the banking system as a whole since that would bring economic disaster to the nation or a specific group of people.

Of course, it is necessary to stress once again that in the regulatory world, as in public administration in general, cases do not really come in such neat packages all the time. Many cases will be mixed and more difficult than those presented here. Some proponents of one or another of the perspectives will seek to promote it even where it is plainly inappropriate. But for the student and the practitioner of public administration today, integration and synthesis are the watchwords. Commitment to fundamental principles may be laudable, but administrative dogmatism is to be avoided.

NOTES

1. Paul J. Quirk, "Food and Drug Administration," in James Q. Wilson, ed., *The Politics of Regulation* (New York: Basic Books, 1980), pp. 191–235, at p. 194.
2. See Wesley Marx, *The Frail Ocean* (New York: Ballantine, 1967).
3. Lawrence J. White, *Reforming Regulation* (Englewood Cliffs, N.J.: Prentice-Hall, 1981), chap. 3.
4. Wilson, ed., *The Politics of Regulation*.
5. James Q. Wilson, "The Politics of Regulation," in Wilson, *The Politics of Regulation*, pp. 357–394, at p. 376.
6. Ibid., p. 368.
7. Ibid., p. 369.
8. Quoted in ibid., p. 358; originally, George J. Stigler, "The Theory of Economic Regulation," *Bell Journal of Economics and Management Science*, 2 (Spring 1971): 3.
9. Quoted in Grant McConnell, *Private Power and American Democracy* (New York: Knopf, 1966), p. 284.
10. Marver Bernstein, *Regulating Business by Independent Regulatory Commission* (Princeton, N.J.: Princeton University Press, 1955).

11. See McConnell, *Private Power and American Democracy*, chap. 8.
12. Wilson, "The Politics of Regulation," p. 370.
13. Ibid., pp. 371–372.
14. Eugene Bardach and Robert A. Kagan, *Going by the Book: The Problems of Regulatory Unreasonableness* (Philadelphia: Temple University Press, 1982), p. 12.
15. See McConnell, *Private Power and American Democracy*.
16. Quoted in Bardach and Kagan, *Going by the Book*, p. 260; (50 CFR 261.1).
17. Clyde Farnsworth, "Line-Item Pepperoni? Fiscally Sound Anchovies?" *New York Times*, June 29, 1987, p. B6.
18. Robert A. Katzmann, "Federal Trade Commission," in Wilson, ed., *The Politics of Regulation*, pp. 152–187, at p. 157.
19. Bardach and Kagan, *Going by the Book*, p. 130–131.
20. *New York Times*, July 15, 1984, p. A33.
21. Quirk, "Food and Drug Administration," p. 207.
22. Ibid., p. 219.
23. *Wall Street Journal*, October 9, 1974, pp. 1, 20.
24. Ibid.
25. Walter Adams and James Brock, "Why Flying Is Unpleasant," *New York Times*, August 6, 1987, p. A27.
26. Bardach and Kagan, *Going by the Book*, p. 26.
27. Ibid.
28. Suzanne Weaver, "Antitrust Division of the Department of Justice," in Wilson, ed., *The Politics of Regulation*, pp. 123–151, at p. 125; and Adams and Brock, "Why Flying Is Unpleasant."
29. Quirk, "Food and Drug Administration," p. 203. In 1983, an "orphan drug" law was passed by the federal government. It allows drug companies to market drugs to small numbers of people with unusual medical problems, without first requiring that rigorous and expensive premarket tests be undertaken.
30. Herbert Kaufman, *Red Tape* (Washington, D.C.: Brookings Institution, 1977), p. 20.
31. *Wall Street Journal*, October 15, 1974, p. 1.
32. Bardach and Kagan, *Going by the Book*, p. 36.
33. Kaufman, *Red Tape*, pp. 7–8.
34. *Wall Street Journal*, October 25, 1974, p. 1.
35. Edward Mansfield, "Federal Maritime Commission," in Wilson, ed., *The Politics of Regulation*, pp. 42–74, at p. 62.
36. Ibid.
37. Kenneth J. Meier, *Regulation* (New York: St. Martin's Press, 1985), p. 104.
38. *Wall Street Journal*, November 1, 1974, p. 1.
39. Ibid., p. 25
40. Meier, *Regulation*, p. 165.
41. *New York Times*, July 15, 1984, p. A33.
42. Bardach and Kagan, *Going by the Book*, chap. 7.
43. Ibid., pp. 195–196.
44. Adams and Brock, "Why Flying Is Unpleasant."
45. Bardach and Kagan, *Going by the Book*, pp. 224–225.
46. Larry Gerston, Cynthia Fraleigh, and Robert Schwab, *The Deregulated Society* (Pacific Grove, Calif.: Brooks/Cole, 1988), p. 46.
47. Judith Havemann, "Here's How You Get OMB's Attention—Cut Off Its Funds," *Washington Post National Weekly Edition*, June 2, 1986, p. 12.
48. Ibid.

49. Gerston, Fraleigh, and Schwab, *Deregulated Society*, pp. 54–55.
50. Ibid., p. 54.
51. Wilson, "The Politics of Regulation," p. 375.
52. Bardach and Kagan, *Going by the Book*, pp. 204–205.
53. Bradley Behrman, "Civil Aeronautics Board," in Wilson, ed., *The Politics of Regulation*, pp. 75–120, at pp. 104–120.
54. Bardach and Kagan, *Going by the Book*, chap. 6.
55. Wilson, "The Politics of Regulation," p. 378.
56. William Gormley, "The Representation Revolution," *Administration & Society*, 18 (August 1986), pp. 179–196, at p. 190.
57. Kenneth C. Davis, *Administrative Law and Government*, 2nd ed. (St. Paul, Minn.: West, 1975), p. 336.
58. Ibid., Chapter 21, and Students Challenging Regulatory Agency Procedures v. U.S., 412 U.S. 669 (1973).
59. Gerston, Fraleigh, and Schwab, *Deregulated Society*, p. 15.
60. FTC v. Sperry and Hutchinson, 405 U.S. 233, 248 (1972).
61. Motor Vehicle Manufacturers Association v. State Farm, 463 U.S. 29 (1983).
62. Environmental Defense Fund v. Ruckelshaus, 439 F2d 584, 598 (1967).
63. Abbott Laboratories v. Gardner, 387 U.S. 136 (1967).
64. See Gerston, Fraleigh, and Schwab, *Deregulated Society*, p. 45, for an opposing point of view.
65. Robert A. Dahl, "Controlling Nuclear Weapons: Democracy vs. Guardianship," Abrams Lecture Series, Syracuse University, March 1984.

ADDITIONAL READING

BARDACH, EUGENE, AND ROBERT KAGAN. *Going by the Book: The Problems of Regulatory Unreasonableness*. Philadelphia: Temple University Press, 1982.

BERNSTEIN, MARVER. *Regulating Business by Independent Regulatory Commission*. Princeton, N.J.: Princeton University Press, 1955.

DERTHICK, MARTHA, AND PAUL QUIRK. *The Politics of Deregulation*. Washington, D.C.: Brookings Institution, 1985.

GERSTON, LARRY, CYNTHIA FRALEIGH, AND ROBERT SCHWAB. *The Deregulated Society*. Pacific Grove, Calif.: Brooks/Cole, 1988.

HEFFRON, FLORENCE, WITH NEIL MCFEELEY. *The Administrative Regulatory Process*. New York: Longman, 1983.

MEIER, KENNETH. *Regulation*. New York: St. Martin's Press, 1985.

WILSON, JAMES Q., ED. *The Politics of Regulation*. New York: Basic Books, 1980.

STUDY QUESTIONS

1. Deregulation is currently an important political issue. Do you think the U.S. is "overregulated" in some areas of economic or social life? "Underregulated" in any? What criteria can you develop to help you decide?

2. Some economists are pretty adamant about regulation being treated from a cost-benefit perspective. Assuming it is technically possible to do a solid cost-benefit analysis, do you think such an approach is appropriate in all areas of policy? Where and where not? Why?

3. To what kinds of regulatory administration is your college or university subject? Assess their costs, benefits, and appropriateness (from your own perspective).

PART FOUR | *Public Administration and the Public*

CHAPTER 10 | *Public Administration and the Public*

The public interacts with public administration in several roles: as client, regulatee, participant, and litigant as well as in street-level encounters. Public administration penetrates the economy and society. The public's evaluation of public administration, which is explored in this chapter, depends on the context of the interaction. As citizens, people find it powerful, omnipresent, and problematical. As clients, they find it satisfactory; as regulatees, they see it as unsatisfactory. The managerial, political, and legal perspectives offer different views of the public. Participation is stressed by the political perspective and offers some possibilities for emphasizing the "public" in public administration. The perspectives can be synthesized to a certain extent by applying them to different areas of administration, such as service or therapy.

The development and growth of the contemporary administrative state has myriad ramifications for the public at large. Certainly, the public has benefited greatly from public administration. Public administrators are concerned with the provision of "public goods," such things as defense of the political community, roads, and public recreational and cultural facilities. They are also actively involved in providing justice, safety, economic security, health, education, and other benefits to the public at large, or segments of it. But the provision of these benefits has not been without important social, political, and economic costs. Too often in the past, public administration texts failed to address the place of the "public" in the public administrative state. In this chapter, we will explore this matter in some detail, for at the risk of seeming redundant, it is crucial that "every public administrator should always be aware of the public."

THE PUBLIC'S INTERACTION WITH PUBLIC ADMINISTRATION

Every person in the United States is affected by some public administrative actions all the time. For example, whether we are awake or asleep, in an urban metropolis or on a remote mountain peak, protecting each of our lives is in some sense the responsibility of public administrators in the Department of Defense. We are all generally affected by the activities of the Environmental Protection Agency, the Food and Drug Administration, and the U.S. Department of Agriculture's inspection and crop-related programs. If we listen to the radio or watch TV, the FCC is involved; wherever we are, some police department has formal responsibility for our safety and conduct. The list could go on and on. It would be an interesting exercise to keep track of how many of one's daily activities are in some way affected by a public administrative agency. But such a review of the extent to which public administrators affect our well-being and have an impact on the structure of our daily lives does not begin to tell the full story of the relationship between the public and public administrators.

The public interacts directly with public administrators in several contexts. For the sake of analysis, these can be placed into five main overlapping categories.

Clients   The public interacts with public administrators as *clients*. The range of possibilities in this context is quite extensive. One study, for example, found that over half (57.5 percent) of a sample of the general population had at least one direct recent contact with an administrative agency dealing with one of the following areas: employment, job training, workmen's compensation, unemployment compensation, public assistance, hospital/medical care, or retirement benefits.[1] If public education, postal service, and other functions such as contact with agencies dealing with consumer fraud and the like were added to the list, the percentage of the public acting as clients would escalate considerably. The essence of the client role is that the citizen seeks to obtain a benefit or service from an administrative agency. In many cases, the individual client will meet face-to-face with a public administrator.

Regulatees   The public interacts with public administrators as *regulatees*. For instance, four of the more common situations in which members of the public meet public administrators in the role of being regulated are vehicular licenses, traffic violations, income taxes, and police matters.[2] The full extent of interactions in these four categories is unknown, but it certainly does not fully indicate all the possible situations in which the citizen is a regulatee of an administrative agency. As pointed out in the first chapter, often service and constraint are combined. Thus, the client may also be a regulatee, as in the case of individuals seeking public housing, public assistance, and even public education. Moreover, some of the less fortunate members of society are housed in public mental health facilities and prisons. Such people are not merely *regulated* or *constrained*; they are *controlled* and/or *restrained*. In the early 1980s, there were some 483,000 prisoners, 249,000 parolees, 136,000 persons confined to public mental health hospitals, and about 123,000 in public facilities for the mentally retarded.[3] Additionally, many people are subject to legal constraints in the role of employee or employer, especially in terms of regulations of occupational health and safety, equal opportunity, and labor relations.

Participants   The public interacts with public administrators as *participants* in public administration. Many public administrative programs, especially in the realm of agriculture and education, provide for direct public participation. Public utility commissions, housing agencies, and other public agencies often hold public hearings as well. Members of the public respond to agencies' proposals to adopt rule changes. Overall, it appears that the level of public utilization of these opportunities to participate is low (as it is in politics generally), but nonetheless the opportunity is there. In fact, in some cases groups are so effective in using participation to make public administrators responsive to them that they are considered to be an agency's "constituency."

Litigants   The public interacts with public administrators as *litigants*. A very limited segment of the population seeks to *litigate* claims or complaints against public administrators. Litigation in this context may mean nothing more than a direct response to an agency's notice that it proposes to do something that will harm the individual, such as cutting off public assistance benefits. It may involve an appeal through administrative hierarchies, a hearing before an administrative law judge, or a suit in a state or federal court. Although the proportion of the public that engages in litigation is small, their cases are often numerous enough to place substantial burdens on agencies' and courts' ability to hear them. For instance, the Social Security Administration adjudicates about 250,000 cases a year. Moreover, the ramifications of a few court decisions on public administration can be very extensive. For instance, Supreme Court decisions requiring procedural due process in many administrative actions have forced welfare agencies, in particular, to change their processes and modify their structures extensively.

Street-Level Encounters   The public interacts with public administrators through *street-level encounters*. Street-level encounters, which were discussed in Chapter 8, are often a feature of the individual role of regulatee. However, sometimes they do not involve regulation per se, but rather an effort by the street-level bureaucrat to determine whether constraints should be applied or whether assistance should be rendered. Police are perhaps the best example. Their role involves both the application of constraints and the provision of assistance. Street-level interaction with them can be touched off in any number of ways, including simply asking them for directions, injuring oneself in an accident of some kind, or engaging in suspicious or prohibited conduct.

In sum, there is little doubt that the public is deeply affected by public administration and is frequently involved in direct interactions with public administrators. These are developments that are part and parcel of the evolution of the contemporary administrative state, developments that cannot help but have important impacts on the public's social, political, and economic environments.

THE INDIVIDUAL IN THE ADMINISTRATIVE STATE

The Individual in Society

Public administration thoroughly permeates American society. Many matters that were once left to families, communities, and religious organizations are now the subject of administrative activity. Examples would be education, provision for one's economic security and health in old age, welfare benefits (formerly charity), and housing. Even matters of marriage and family are affected by public administration in terms of welfare, social security, and taxation generally. Even though there is currently a tendency for government to rely on private, not-for-profit organizations to carry out some of its functions, historically, to a considerable extent, administrative services have replaced privately provided social services and administrative controls have replaced more traditional social controls exercised by families, communities, and religious organizations.

Equally important, public administration tends to be bureaucratically organized. This form of organization, in particular, is often in tension with traditional social values. Consequently, individuals may have to be socialized to interact well with bureaucracy, and in the process their own values may be modified. In this sense, many have concluded that the public is very strongly affected by public administration.

Following Max Weber, Ralph Hummel has explained that bureaucracy is at odds with society because it relies on "rationally organized action," rather than "social action."[4] Rationally organized action in this context means action that "is a logical means to a clearly defined end" and "is performed in such a manner that its means-ends logic is visible."[5] Hummel explains the differences between this kind of action and social action in practical terms:

> Social action is normally initiated by a human being who has certain intentions or purposes. The action is intended to convey such goals or purposes and is addressed to a social partner whose understanding of the action is a key part of the purpose. Social action, then, consists of a human initiator, the action itself, and a human recipient, or co-actor.
>
> Bureaucratic action is reduced to the action itself. It does not have a human originator in the sense of expressing the private will or intentions of a human being; it originates—and this is a key characteristic of bureaucracy as a system—in an office whether or not a specific human being fills the role of officeholder. (In automated bureaucracies, the action may originate in a computer.) Next there is the operation or function itself. What makes it an operation or function, however, is not primarily related to the logical end point which was the original purpose of the action. What makes it an operation or function is determined by whether or not the action meets the values and standards of higher offices charged with control.[6]

Hummel's last point about rationally organized action is very important. It gets at the "one-directional" aspects of bureaucracy and public administration in general. Commands flow downward through the hierarchy; information flows upward. The client or regulatee supplies information, but cannot give commands. This means the client or regulatee cannot sensibly ask the bureaucrat to modify his or her administrative behavior and routines. These can only be modified by direction from above in the bureaucracy. In essence, rationally organized action at the level of the client or regulatee tends to be a problem-*processing* activity, rather than problem-*solving* activity. The latter virtually demands two-way communication. The difference is as follows: "Let's discuss it" implies social action; "*We* (the agency) will need the following information from you (the client or regulatee)" suggests rationally organized action.

Hummel carries this line of thought at least two steps farther. On the level of the individual who works in a bureaucratic setting, he notes that emotional feelings of affection are transformed. In his view, which is intended to portray the impact of bureaucratization at its outermost limits, the individual in bureaucratic life is taught (1) not to attach "affect" (positive emotional feelings) directly to persons; (2) to attach affect to their own administrative functions; and (3) to attach affect to the exercise of power or authority. Note how far this diverges from ordinary social values. Society, in the normal sense of the term, cannot exist where people feel no affect toward one another; where they care primarily about the performance of their own functions, and when they exercise their own power to the exclusion of empathizing with other people or identifying with groups and individuals outside their workplace. In such a "society," there would be no sympathy, trust, love, or other emotional feelings between people. This may sound far-fetched, but thinking back on Chapter 4, how much sympathy, trust, love, hate, and so forth does one expect from a public administrator, even if one works as a colleague with one?

Hummel also maintains that as bureaucracy permeates society, it creates a tension between its own values and those of society at large. Inevitably, the values of *both* are modified in the process, but those of bureaucracy tend to make greater headway. Ask yourself what you think bureaucracy values most, and then what you personally think is of most importance in life. Hummel's list is shown in Chart 10.1.[7] In sum, he finds "the *cultural* conflict between bureaucracy and society is between systems needs and human needs."[8]

One does not have to agree with Hummel entirely to get the picture: public administration, bureaucratically organized, tends to be in tension or conflict with society in terms of styles of action, emotional feelings, and overriding concerns. The differences between societal and bureaucratic values, in short-hand form, are: social interaction versus administrative action; feeling versus doing; and belief, randomness, and emotionalism versus specialized expertise, systemization, and impersonality. These ideas are abstract. Perhaps by thinking about some of your own experiences with administrative agencies, they will become more concrete. They will also become clearer by considering how the tension between public administration and society affects the individual in the role of client of administrative agencies.

The juxtaposition between social action, with its values, and rationally organized action, with its own values, is often clearest when the individual is in the role of client. The client approaches the public administrator with an understanding of the society's culture. But the culture of bureaucracy can require behavior with which they are unfamiliar or ill at ease. As Victor Thomp-

Chart 10.1: Bureaucracy versus Society

Bureaucracy	*Society*
precision	justice
stability	freedom
discipline	violence
reliability	oppression
calculability of results	happiness
formal rationality	gratification
formalistic impersonality	poverty
formal equality of treatment	illness
	death
	victory
	love & hate
	salvation & damnation

son once pointed out, "The bureaucratic culture makes certain demands upon clients as well as upon organization employees. There are many people in our society who have not been able to adjust to these demands. To them bureaucracy is a curse. They see no good in it whatsoever, but view the demands of modern organization as 'red tape.' "[9] Such people do not possess "the aptitudes and attitudes needed to obtain reasoned consideration" of their cases by public administrators.[10] Their "low powers of abstraction" and "need to personalize the world" seem to be the most important barriers to their ability to deal effectively with public administrators.[11] Functional illiteracy is also a problem for some clients. Inability to function well in bureaucratic language ("bureaucratese") is a problem for many more. In fact, the entire client-public administrator interaction may be distasteful and threatening to many. As Alvin Gouldner explained, clients are likely to be critical of bureaucracy when they feel it challenges their egos. This commonly occurs in two ways:

> (1) A claim which he [the client] believes legitimate is not taken "at face value." He must either supply proof or allow it to be investigated. He is, as one remarked, "treated as a criminal"—he may feel his worth is questioned, his status is impugned. (2) Not only are his claims and assertions challenged, but other details of his "private life" are investigated. The individual enters the situation on "official," "technical," or "public" business, and feels that he ends up by being investigated as a person.[12]

The client role can be difficult for anyone. However, lower-class populations have been identified in particular as having acute difficulty in dealing with public bureaucracies. In part, this is because the agencies they deal with often provide a mixture of service and constraint, as in welfare and public housing programs. Moreover, members of the lower class may typically be heavily dependent upon public agencies and consequently feel at their "mercy." In addition, problems of literacy and the juxtaposition between social culture and administrative culture may be most severe for members of the lower class, who may not have been socialized to understand the workings of administrative agencies. In fact, the kind of socialization they receive may be dysfunctional when it comes to presenting their cases and claims, for it appears to emphasize the acceptance of hierarchical authority. As a result, some have even argued that "bureaucratic systems are the key medium through which the middle class maintains its advantaged position vis-à-vis the lower class."[13] For example, in some cities, an increasing number of teenage mothers are receiving public assistance benefits of one kind or another. In many cases, they are consciously seeking to switch from being dependent upon their mothers to being dependent on welfare agencies. In some cases being assigned a case worker and receiving one's own benefits is taken as a sign of upward mobility in terms of status and financial *independence*. It is equivalent to a middle-class teenager getting a job with a boss and a paycheck. But the net result is that such teenage mothers become subject to a great deal of control through public administrative action.

If part of the difficulty that lower-class individuals find in dealing with public agencies is due to their manipulation by administrators, then it stands to reason that members of other groups may be better at using administrative values and operating principles to obtain the treatment they seek. It has been found that the norms of the administrative culture tend to permeate mainstream culture in the United States to a very large extent. For example, it has been noted that public school education is typically hierarchically organized and that "the process of obtaining passes, excuses, and permission slips to be granted entrance or exit serves as a useful apprenticeship for dealing with the bureaucracies later in life."[14] Herbert Wilcox found that by the fourth grade children are able to understand something about hierarchical relationships and can read organization charts. By high school, many students are able to perform as well as college students and city managers on a test designed to ascertain understanding of organizational relationships. Based on these findings, Wilcox concludes that "[t]he principles of organization do constitute a cultural trait of high school students. . . . The most important period of acculturation in relation to the trait is prior to age eleven and possibly age nine."[15]

To the extent that administrative values, especially hierarchy and impersonality, replace traditional social values, they can pose a serious problem for the individual in the society. This is not simply that using public agencies effectively may be difficult; there is also the risk that each individual will deal impersonally with others and will feel isolated and relatively unable to achieve control over his or her environment. Sometimes this feeling is referred to as **anomie.** There are many aspects of American society that have become increasingly impersonal, as the traditional roles of family, community, and religious organizations have been partly superseded by public administration. For instance, day care, after-school care, and care of the elderly are increasingly an organizational as opposed to a family function, deterring and even reporting crime is increasingly a police function as opposed to a community one, and today charity is largely managed by impersonal public or private secular organizations. Even procreation can now be impersonal by "surrogacy" or other means. The focal point of one's existence in the administrative culture, as Hummel notes, is increasingly one's organization and organizational role, not one's community, church, family, or attachment to geographic place.

The Individual in the Political System

The individual's role in the political system also undergoes major transformations with the rise of the administrative state. Here again, a deep disjuncture between the principles and values of representative, democratic government and those of public administration is present. Indeed, the relationship between democratic government and public administration is viewed by many as the preeminent issue of contemporary government. Frederick Mosher expresses the problem succinctly:

The accretion of specialization and of technological and social complexity seems to be an irreversible trend, one that leads to increasing dependence upon the protected, appointive public service, thrice removed from direct democracy. Herein lies the central and underlying problem. . . . How can a public service so constituted be made to operate in a manner compatible with democracy? How can we be assured that a highly differentiated body of public employees will act in the interests of all the people, will be an instrument of all the people?[16]

According to Max Weber, who viewed the power of trained bureaucratic expertise as "overtowering," the answer to Mosher's question is that we may as well resign ourselves to being governed by public administrators rather than elected officials.[17] The conflict between the requirements of democratic, representative government and public administration are profound, as Chart 10.2 indicates.

For the individual in the contemporary administrative state, the main consequences of the tension between democratic values and principles and those of public administration seem to be: (1) a feeling that the political system is beyond control, and (2) a tendency toward nonparticipation in politics and governmental affairs. There are several indicators of these developments.

Americans widely believe that "the trouble with government is that elected officials have lost control over the bureaucrats, who really run the country."[18] Overall, 57 percent of the population subscribed to this outlook, according to a poll conducted in 1973. The view has spread to virtually all sectors: city, surburban, and rural residents; the highly educated and those with no more than primary school education; the relatively well-to-do and the poor; whites and blacks; and Democrats, Republicans, and independents. Thus for a majority of Americans, the political system seems beyond direct control through the ballot box. A majority also believe that the federal government has become too bureaucratic and a growing number seem to feel that there is little they can do about the adoption of specific policies.[19] For instance, in 1973, a majority (58 percent) thought there was something that they could do about an unjust governmental regulation, but back in 1960, some 77 percent felt they could do something about it.[20] In the view of at least one observer, Emmette Redford, the growing feeling of inability to control government is normal in the administrative state because the citizen becomes a *subject* of government, rather than a meaningful participant. In his words,

Chart 10.2: Democracy versus Public Administration

Democracy Requires:	Public Administration Favors:
equality	hierarchy
rotation in office	seniority
freedom	command
pluralism	unity
citizen participation	participation based on expertise
openness	secrecy
community	impersonality
legitimacy based on election	legitimacy based on expertise

The first characteristic of the great body of men subject to the administrative state is that they are dormant regarding most of the decisions being made with respect to them. Their participation cannot in any manner equal their subjection. Subjection comes from too many directions for a man's span of attention, much less his active participation, to extend to all that affects him. Any effort of the subject to participate in all that affects him would engulf him in confusion, dissipate his activity, and destroy the unity of his personality.[21]

As Redford indicates, a sense of loss of control inevitably is linked to a decline in political participation. If you truly believe that elected officials no longer control the government, then why participate with any vigor in electoral politics, or even vote at all? According to this view, the same "thrice removed" and "protected" bureaucrats will control the government and public policy regardless of who wins the election. There are other and perhaps more familiar and acceptable ways of putting essentially the same thought. For instance, try these: "The presidency has grown too big for one person to fulfill its responsibilities," "Congress has become too fragmented to accomplish much, and anyway, the staff are really in charge," "Single-issue interest groups are a threat to the electoral process," "It takes too long to get anything done through the courts, their dockets are too crowded." Political scientists and others have long been concerned about the long-term trend of declining participation in elections and have attributed it to a wide variety of factors. Among them, as a *New York Times* poll found in 1976, is that 58 percent of nonvoters believe that the political system needs more radical change than can be brought about through the ballot box.[22] Additionally, over 40 percent of voters felt the same way! In fact, at least one leading political scientist has urged "principled abstention" from elections to force the political parties and elected officials to change their approaches.[23]

For whatever reasons—and they are surely not all directly connected to the rise in administrative power—voter turnout in the United States has suffered a long-term decline. For instance, in 1952, 61.6 percent of eligible voters participated in the presidential election, while 57.6 percent cast ballots in elections to the House of Representatives. In 1976, the turnouts were 54.5 percent and 49.5 percent, respectively.[24] In the 1980 and 1984 presidential elections, the turnouts were about 53 percent. These figures not only show a decline, they indicate far more limited participation by eligible voters in elections than is typically found in other democratic countries and than was customary in the United States in the late nineteenth century. Elsewhere such rates of participation often exceed 80 percent. Even more disturbing, in the view of some, is that even these rates of participation mask the extent to which the individual has become a subject of government. As Hummel summarizes this view: "Bureaucratic power will replace political power; politicians will look more and more like managers or will be run by managers. Ideology and ideals will still play roles in political campaigns—but only apparently, as tools to be manipulated by campaign managers. People will no longer vote, they will be voted. The sense of alienation will increase because, though we will feel pressured psychologically to take part in politics . . . we will not have a sense that the political system into which we are impressed is in any sense legitimate."[25] Hummel's choice of the word *impressed* is worth noting, because sometimes it is urged that the United States adopt a system of *compulsory* voting to solve the problems of nonparticipation.

Voting, of course, is not the only means of participating in politics. Interest groups can be formed and used to lobby politicians, letters can be written to members of legislatures; official contacts can be exploited; protests can be staged. Despite the effective quality of some of these means of influencing government, the available evidence suggests that the vast majority of the citizenry is only marginally involved directly in politics. For example, a very comprehensive study authorized by the U.S. Senate, made public in 1973, found that in their entire lifetimes, only 33 percent of the public had written a letter to a member of Congress, 22 percent had spoken personally to their own congressman, 13 percent with their senator; 14 percent had visited a state legislator in the state capitol; 14 percent had been actively involved in presidential or congressional electoral campaigns, 11 percent in senatorial campaigns; 11 percent had picketed or taken part in a street demonstration, 2 percent had taken part in a demonstration where violence occurred.[26] The broad conclusion reached by this report was that "the hard fact is that by any measure, on any ongoing basis, less than a majority of the people are involved. Conversely, a majority of the public is essentially passive. . ." in politics.[27] The same report found that only 24 percent of the population had ever gone to their local government to get them to do something; only 13 percent had approached their state government, and only 11 percent had approached the federal government for the same general purpose of influencing the course of public policy.[28] Although the extent of public participation in some of these areas may have increased since 1973, nonparticipation and limited participation continue to characterize the public's involvement in politics.[29]

It is not possible to demonstrate, with available information, that the rise of the contemporary administrative state is the chief culprit in pushing the typical citizen into the role of "subject." However, indications that the administrative state has played an important role in this regard abound. Perhaps the most interesting of these concern Congress. Under the original constitutional design, Congress was intended to be the main proactive, representative, and policy-making branch of government. Thus, it could be expected that Congress's business would be composed of representing constituencies in the formulation of public policies. However, as Morris Fiorina argues persuasively, the rise of an activist federal government, with its attendant bureaucracy, has fundamentally changed the "mix of congressional activities."[30] "Specifically, a lesser proportion of congressional effort is now going into programmatic activities and a greater proportion into pork-barrel and casework activities."[31] "Pork-barrel" and casework both directly involve public administration. The former represents an effort to bring governmental largess back to the legislator's home district or state. Dams, roads, post offices, federal office buildings, military bases, and grants for housing, water, and other projects are examples. Remarkably, even in the current period of widespread concern with the size of the federal budgetary deficit, "pork barreling" remains a staple of legislative politics.[32] Often, the effort to obtain "pork barrel" benefits involves bargaining with public administrators, such as bureau chiefs. Casework, as mentioned in Chapter 2, is the legislator's intervention in some difficulty an individual is having with a public agency or help in obtaining a benefit for a constituent. Many of the letters individuals write to members of Congress concern casework rather than matters of public policy. A leading example is difficulty in obtaining Social Security benefits. Casework can involve virtually any federal administrative action that is directed at a specific individual. Casework has been routinized and institutionalized—members of Congress solicit casework letters from their constituents and agencies treat "congressionals" (inquiries forwarded through members of Congress) differently than other inquiries or letters. Available evidence suggests that pork barrel politics and casework have enabled members of Congress to "make relatively fewer enemies and relatively more friends among the people of their districts."[33] Consequently, many have been able to assure their reelection by taking advantage of the opportunities that large-scale public administration offers for winning votes. This is ironic, since electoral campaigns often ring with condemnation after denunciation of the "irresponsible, entrenched, incompetent bureaucrats." However, it is a logical extension of the individual citizen's role as "subject." The "subject" calls on the representative, not to fundamentally alter public policy, but to help him or her vis-à-vis an administrative agency. In other words, the development of large-scale public administration is associated with a change not only in the role of legislators, but also in the nature of individual involvement in governmental matters.

The Individual in the Economy

The contemporary administrative state also changes the character of the individual's place in the economic system. As public administration penetrates the society and economy to a greater extent, government inevitably gains greater control over the nation's economic resources. (In Chapter 6, we noted that the federal budget has increased as a share of the GNP.) Charles Reich explains this development in straightforward terms:

> One of the most important developments in the United States during the past decade [1950s] has been the emergence of government as a major source of wealth. Government is a gigantic syphon. It draws revenue and power, and pours forth wealth: money, benefits, services, contracts, franchises, and licenses. Government has always had this function. But while in early times it was minor, today's distribution of largess is on a vast, imperial scale.
>
> The valuables dispensed by government take many forms, but they all share one characteristic. They are steadily taking the place of traditional forms of wealth—forms which are held as private property. Social insurance substitutes for savings; a government contract replaces a businessman's customers and goodwill. The wealth of more and more Americans depends upon a relationship to government. Increasingly, Americans live on government largess. . . .[34]

Public administrative control or direction over a large share of the nation's economic resources has important consequences for the individual. First, it makes the individual dependent upon government for his or her economic well-being. If government controls access to resources, occupations, markets, franchises, technologies, and the right to operate such enterprises as utilities, broadcasting, and, until recently, air, truck, and rail transportation, then individuals cannot function in a wide variety of economic areas except upon the conditions established by government. In addition, when government takes on responsibility for individuals' economic security in terms of seeking to guarantee full employment, minimal inflation, fair labor standards (wages and hours), healthful and safe working conditions, pensions, adequate housing, health insurance, and so forth, it is inevitable that government becomes the focus of efforts to enhance one's economic status and well-being. Thus, political effort is directed toward obtaining economic benefits or advancement through the adoption of specific public policies. As Reich points out, this development is not new in kind, but rather in scope.

A second consequence of the accumulation of wealth in the hands of the administrative state is that the government gains greater leverage and control over the individual's life. This is a feature of the contemporary role of government to which political and economic conservatives have long been vehemently opposed. In Reich's words, "When government—national, state, or local—hands out something of value, whether a relief check or a television license, government's power grows forthwith; it automatically gains such power as is necessary and proper to supervise its largess. It obtains new rights to investigate, to regulate, and to punish."[35] This development tends to erode the protections private property once afforded the individual against the exercise of governmental power. Milton Friedman is among those who have noted the changing economic situation of the individual in the United States and who have protested the encroachments on traditional economic and political freedoms that it entails. In his words:

Economic freedom is also an indispensable means toward the achievement of political freedom. . . .

The citizen of the United States who is compelled by law to devote something like 10 percent of his income to the purchase of a particular kind of retirement contract, administered by the government, is being deprived of a corresponding part of his personal freedom. How strongly this deprivation may be felt and its closeness to the deprivation of religious freedom, which all would regard as "civil" or "political" rather than "economic," were dramatized by an episode involving a group of farmers of the Amish sect. On grounds of principle, this group regarded compulsory federal old age programs as an infringement of their personal individual freedom and refused to pay taxes or accept benefits. As a result, some of their livestock were sold by auction in order to satisfy claims for social security levies. . . .

A citizen of the United States who under the laws of various states is not free to follow the occupation of his own choosing unless he can get a license for it, is likewise being deprived of an essential part of his freedom. So is the man who would like to exchange some of his goods with, say, a Swiss for a watch but is prevented from doing so by a quota. So is the Californian who was thrown into jail for selling Alka

Seltzer at a price below that set by the manufacturer under so-called "fair-trade" laws. So also is the farmer who cannot grow the amount of wheat he wants.[36]

As Friedman suggests, not all of the freedom lost in conjunction with the government's larger role in the economy can be categorized as "economic freedom." The extent to which matters of personal life-styles, individual values, and political views can be subject to regulation by government through its control of economic activity can be truly astounding. Reich points to governmental efforts to use "largess" to regulate "moral character." Among his examples are the following: "The District of Columbia denied a married man in his forties a permit to operate a taxi partly because when he was a young man in his twenties, he and a woman had been discovered about to have sexual intercourse in his car. Men with criminal records have been denied licenses to work as longshoremen and chenangoes and prevented from holding union office for the same reason. A license to operate a rooming house may be refused for lack of good character. Sonny Liston [one-time heavyweight champion] was barred from receiving a license to box in New York because of his 'bad character.' Louisiana attempted to deny aid to dependent children if their mothers were of bad character."[37] As noted in Chapter 5, individuals were dismissed from or denied federal employment at one time based on their answers to such questions as "Does your wife have liberal viewpoints?" and "Do you support racial integration?"[38] Incidentally, at one time or another loyalty tests were applied to those seeking fishing licenses, unemployment compensation, driver's licenses, and governmental approval to engage in wrestling and piano selling.[39]

The increasing dependence of the individual on government for his or her economic well-being and the greater governmental power over individuals that is a by-product of this dependence are developments of fundamental importance to the polity. They have occurred in direct association with the rise of the administrative state. As noted in Chapter 2, the increasing penetration of the economy by government has been a major cause of the growth of public administration. Additionally, though, the existence of public administrative authority and capacity has made further governmental penetration feasible. Friedrich Hayek, in a well-known book, viewed the transformation of the United States economy in this regard as overly invasive of individual freedom and as an embarkation on "the road to serfdom."[40] If unchecked, it has been argued, virtually all important individual preferences will be replaced by governmental preferences and all economic and social questions will be transformed into political ones.[41] According to this view, this is the very essence of totalitarianism, because government becomes the total institution in society. It subsumes the roles traditionally played by families, religious organizations, private groups, communities, and private economic firms.

This argument is an extreme formulation of the transformation that has been taking place in conjunction with the rise of the administrative state in the United States. However extreme, it does pinpoint certain tendencies we can clearly recognize. For example, would you be surprised today to find a member of the public whose prenatal welfare was aided by government funds and care, who was born in a public hospital at public expense, who was raised in public housing with the assistance of public welfare funds, whose diet was subsidized through the food stamp program, whose education was in public school, whose income was augmented by public benefits, whose health care was subsidized by the government, and who will be the recipient of governmental benefits in old age?

Although some oppose the contemporary governmental role in the economy on the grounds that it makes the public too dependent upon government, much support for the modern welfare state is based on the belief that increased governmental power can be exercised humanely with proper regard for individual freedoms, value preferences, and liberties. In this view, government penetration of the economy is a very suitable means of protecting individuals from abuse by the economic power of other individuals and private firms. Governmental encroachment on traditional economic freedoms may be considered less troublesome than the lack of protection individuals had from boom-and-bust business cycles prior to governmental efforts to mitigate them. As in so many aspects of public administration, the overall picture is hardly so simple as the partisans of one or another particular viewpoint would have us believe.

THE PUBLIC'S EVALUATION OF PUBLIC ADMINISTRATION

It is not surprising that the public's evaluation of public administration is complicated and puzzling. If public administration generally tends to fall into three relatively distinct patterns that emphasize different values, structural arrangements, processes, ways of thinking about individuals, and methods of seeking knowledge, then perhaps it is to be anticipated that the citizenry is not quite certain just what to make of public administration. Moreover, when it comes to evaluation, the public does not speak with one voice. Members of the public have different political perspectives on government, they have different experiences with public administrators, and they are influenced by different sets of social and cultural values. In fact, polls of citizens' views of public administration often seem to yield inconsistent or ephemeral results. Nevertheless, by relying upon in-depth studies of public opinion regarding public administration, it is possible to identify three broad patterns in the public's general response to it.

Apprehensiveness

In order to make a meaningful assessment of the public's outlook on public administration, it is necessary to take note of a well-documented, long-term trend toward less confidence in government generally.[42] The information displayed in Box 10–1 substantially reveals the scope of this trend. It indicates that between 1958 and 1980, the public's perception was that government became more wasteful, more oriented toward a few big interests, less trustworthy to do what was right, and less responsive to ordinary citizens. Additionally, throughout the period, a majority agreed with the statement that "sometimes politics and government seem so complicated that a person like me can't really understand what's going on."[43] Overall, these findings indicate that the public is somewhat apprehensive about the government's orientation and performance.

Within the context of declining confidence in government, the public finds public administration or government bureaucracy to be quite important. The potency of public administration in the public's view has already been noted. No clearer statement of this view is likely to be found than that a majority of both the public and elected officials believe that bureaucrats "really run the country." A large proportion of the public finds public administration to be omnipresent in day-to-day life. Available information further suggests that, over time, the public is becoming more aware of the federal government's impact on their individual lives. For instance, between 1960 and 1973, the proportion of the public believing that the federal government has a great impact on their daily lives rose from 41 percent to 63 percent.[44] The presidential elections of 1976, 1980, and 1984 addressed this perception by hammering at the need to reduce the size, scope, and intrusiveness of the federal government in the public's daily life. At least in the abstract, the public seems to agree that government has become "too bureaucratic" and that it is losing its ability to improve the quality of life. Thus, in 1973, 73 percent of the public and 80 percent of a sample of elected officials agreed that the federal government had become too bureaucratic.[45] Only 16

BOX 10–1 **The Public's Confidence in Government, 1958–1980**

STATEMENT	PERCENT OF THE PUBLIC AGREEING			
	1958	1970	1974	1980
The government wastes a lot of money.	43	69	74	78
Government is run for the benefit of a few big interests.	24	50	66	70
You cannot trust government to do right most of the time.	23	44	62	73
People like me don't have any say about what the government does.	31	36	40	39
Public officials don't care much what people like me think.	25*	47	50	52

*In 1960.

SOURCE: Seymour Martin Lipset and William Schneider, *The Confidence Gap: Business, Labor, and Government in the Public Mind* (New York: Free Press, 1983), p. 17, figure 1–1; pp. 21–22, figure 1–2.

percent of the public and 12 percent of the elected officials disagreed with this perception. When it comes to the issue of the type of impact the "too bureaucratic" government is having, the results are disheartening: in 1960, 76 percent of the public thought the federal government's activities improved the quality of life, but by 1973 this figure had dropped to 23 percent.[46] At the same time, the percent of the public believing the federal government had made the quality of life worse increased from 3 percent to 37 percent. Similarly, an increasing proportion of the public considers itself to be personally worse off as a result of government regulation of the business practices of large corporations. In 1970, 43 percent of the public thought such regulation made them better off and 15 percent believed they were worse off due to it. By 1981, though, only 24 percent considered themselves to be better off, while 40 percent viewed government regulation of this kind as making them worse off.[47] Overall, in 1980, the public expressed limited confidence in the executive branch: 27 percent held positive views, 49 percent had neutral opinions, and 24 percent were negative in their responses.[48] Interestingly, the public expressed greater confidence in the military and the press but even less in Congress, big business, major companies, and organized labor.

However, despite its apprehensiveness concerning bureaucracy and its lack of confidence in the executive branch, the public clearly wants the government to go on providing services and even to take a role in assuring the provision of more services than now exist. In 1987, a New York Times/CBS News poll found: 60 percent were unwilling to have "the Government . . . provide fewer services, even in areas like health and education"; 71 percent of the public agreed that the federal government should "see to it that everyone who wants a job has a job"; 78 percent favored government guarantees of medical care for all people; 62 percent thought that it was the government's role to assure "that day care and after-school care for children are available."[49]

How can the view that government is wasteful and unresponsive be reconciled with the belief that it should maintain the services it already provides and shoulder the responsibility for assuring the provision of additional ones? Seymour Lipset and William Schneider offer a plausible explanation: "the public supports improving the existing bureaucracy over creating a new bureaucracy. And it prefers free enterprise and competition over bureaucracy altogether. But it will accept a bureaucratic solution if that is the only one offered."[50]

There is both encouragement and discouragement in these findings. On the one hand, the public is definitely aware of the existence of public administration and views it as an important aspect of political life. It expresses support for public administrative services. On the other hand, the public is apprehensive about bureaucratic power, and its overall confidence in government seems to have been declining ever since the 1950s. The view that the government has become "too bureaucratic" and that it can have a negative impact on the quality of life is clearly discouraging. These views can be examined further by considering the public's assessments of administrative service and regulatory activity in greater detail.

Clients Are Satisfied

There have been a very large number of surveys of individuals' evaluations of their interactions as clients with public administrators. The results have been summarized and analyzed by Charles Goodsell in a book called *The Case for Bureaucracy:*

> Citizens perceive their concrete experiences with bureaucracy in a generally favorable light. Usually the preponderant majority of persons asked describes their recollections or immediate experiences in highly approving terms. Most positive evaluation response rates are at least at the two-thirds level, and many reach beyond 75 percent. Disapproval levels are almost always in the distinct minority, and most fall well below one-third. The vast majority of clients of bureaucracy reports itself as satisfied with the encounter and transaction therein. In most instances bureaucratic personnel are described as helpful, efficient, fair, considerate, and courteous. They are, furthermore, usually perceived as trying to assist, ready to listen, and even willing to adapt the rules and look out for client interests. Also, the actual performance output of bureaucracy is usually praised. The picture presented by citizens in their assessments of bureaucracy appears, in sum, as an almost complete contradiction of the hate image depicted in popular media and academic writing.[51]

What accounts for this disparity between abstract views of bureaucracy and concrete interaction remains something of a puzzle.

One can point to three common explanations, though no doubt others can be developed as well. First, some have argued that the surveys of client evaluations of public administrative encounters are inherently unreliable. Among the pitfalls such surveys allegedly face are that (1) public expectations of bureaucracy are so low that any positive treatment is viewed favorably, (2) respondents to the surveys feel under social (or even political) pressure to answer favorably, and (3) the questions tend to be worded so as to evoke positive responses.[52] There is some truth to these criticisms, but how much is a matter of dispute that defies resolution in the literature of public administration.[53]

Second, Goodsell offers a commonsense approach to understanding why concrete interactions with public bureaucracy as clients tends to be viewed favorably at the same time that bureaucracy in general is viewed negatively:

> Perhaps bureaucracy should be thought of as not so much a terrible beast as a fairly good used car, quite old but well maintained and functioning not all but most of the time. It is those mornings when the car does not start—perhaps once or twice every winter?—that we recognize the machine's fallibility and then malign it furiously. For a fundamental feature of bureaucracy is that it continually performs millions of tiny acts of individual service, such as approving applications, delivering the mail, and answering complaints. Because this ongoing mass of routine achievement is not in itself noteworthy or even capable of intellectual grasp, it operates silently, almost out of sight. The occasional breakdowns, the unusual scandals, the individual instances where a true injustice is done, are what come to our attention and color our overall

judgment. The water glass of bureaucracy is quite full, and we have difficulty realizing it.[54]

This explanation of the discrepancy between the public's general evaluation of bureaucracy and its specific evaluations of individual encounters in the role of clients is supported by some comprehensive empirical analysis. In what remains the most complete research on the matter, Daniel Katz and associates propose in *Bureaucratic Encounters* that "closer examination . . . reveals that general evaluation is related to specific experience if the experience was negative, but not if it was positive. A negative experience with an agency lowers one's general evaluation of government, but a positive experience does not raise it."[55] In Goodsell's terms, those who experience the car's failure to start curse it forever; those for whom it does start seem to feel lucky and to consider themselves exceptions to a pervasive rule. In other words, despite their own good fortune with bureaucracy, a large share of the public may nevertheless feel that it usually does not work so well.

A third possible explanation is that "general evaluations of bureaucracy may tap the ideological level, and specific evaluations of experiences may tap the pragmatic level" of an individual's thinking about public administration.[56] It is easy to see how this could work. We may be very satisfied with the courteous, prompt, and fair treatment we receive at the Motor Vehicle Department or the post office and still think, as a matter of public policy, these departments and public bureaucracies generally are too expensive for the society to support and too distracting for elected officials to control while performing their policy-making and representational functions as well. Moreover, we could believe that the services we use personally are worthwhile, but those that pertain to other people are undesirable: those who benefit from the FAA's regulation of airline safety and those who benefit from public welfare programs may be two very distinct groups of people. In other words, in pragmatic terms we may like what *we* get from public administration, while we begrudge what it gives to others. In short, we like our subsidies but hate our taxes. As a result, legislators find a larger constituency for spending than for cutting back on expenditures or raising more revenues. This is part of the tendency toward deficit spending. But rather than attack the deficit head-on through reducing popular spending or raising taxes, politicians are prone to suggest that budgets can be balanced by tough management that eliminates bureaucratic waste and fraud. Hence, the "bash-the-bureaucrat" syndrome, used with some success by Jimmy Carter and Ronald Reagan, among others.

Each of these explanations for the disparity between the public's general and specific evaluations of public bureaucracy is plausible. Presumably each explains *something* about the disparity and consequently each provides a basis for trying to improve the public's understanding of and interaction with public administration and to improve public administrators' thinking and dealing with the public. Before we develop this theme, however, it is desirable to turn to another kind of public interaction with public administration—that involving direct regulation.

Regulation Is Opposed

Although the constraints and services implemented by public administrative agencies are often mixed, individuals sometimes find themselves in the situation of being directly regulated by a bureaucratic agency. In such an instance, the individual is likely to be summoned to the agency, to have some anxiety at the potential of having his or her interests injured and being subject to constraints on his or her conduct, and, in general, will find the whole episode distasteful. There are important distinctions between seeking a benefit from a public agency and being called to an agency to face penalties of some kind. In the latter case, of course, the transaction is not voluntary on the part of the individual. The agency is very much in control. The individual is treated not as a client but rather as a miscreant of some kind who presumably has done something that is perceived as illegitimate. Subtle burdens may be shifted to the individual that, when considered in total, may be frustrating and make the individual highly critical of the administrative encounter. For example, the administrative officials may be less polite than when dealing with clients; since the individual is compelled to be present, lines and waiting time may be longer; additionally, more probing questions may be asked of the individual and less credence may be given to his or her explanation of some event. To the extent that individuals find themselves in the role of regulatee, therefore, the public's evaluation of public administration may be highly critical.

Katz and associates explored the public's reaction to **constraint agencies** in some depth. Among these were agencies dealing with drivers' licenses, traffic violations, taxation, police matters, and miscellaneous other regulatory activities. The public's general evaluation of these agencies stands in rather stark contrast to its views of agencies when interacting with them in the role of client.

> A majority of the constraint agency respondents felt negatively about the procedures used by those agencies. One-fifth of the constraint group stated that they had been subjected to threats and pressures, although there was wide variation across the four constraint areas. Half of the respondents with police and traffic violation experiences reported such treatment, compared to 13 percent of those who had been called in for tax problems. . . . Approximately one-third of the respondents felt that the constraint experience had created some difficulty, and about two-fifths felt that the agency had created a great deal of difficulty. Furthermore, almost one-half of the constraint agency ["regulatees"] felt that agency personnel had made the problem worse by the way they had handled it. [57]

Thus, the public is rather critical of the administrative operations and behavior of constraint agencies. Very significantly, the public also raises a fundamental political complaint about the way such agencies operate. Katz and associates observe:

> On the question of equitable treatment, a much lower proportion of constraint agency respondents than service agency respondents felt that they had been treated fairly (45

percent as opposed to 76 percent). In addition, almost two times as many constraint agency ["regulatees"] perceived constraint bureaucracies as operating on a preferential basis. Moreover, the constraint agency respondents who thought that differential treatment existed were in considerable agreement as to who received better treatment. *The rich and those who knew someone* were seen as being in a more advantageous position.[58]

These findings indicate that another plausible explanation emerges for the gap between the public's general negative evaluation of public bureaucracy and individual's satisfaction with their own specific encounters with public agencies as clients. It is quite possible that when asked to evaluate public bureaucracy in the abstract, the public tends to focus more on its distasteful interactions with constraint agencies than on its other encounters with public administrators. In other words, unlike Goodsell's explanation that it is the random breakdowns in an otherwise smoothly functioning public bureaucracy that stick in people's minds, this explanation suggests that *routine* subjection to regulation by public administrators is an important source of discontent with public bureaucracy generally. To the extent that this is true, improving attitudes toward public bureaucracy may require more genuine administrative change and less public relations than Goodsell's explanation suggests.

The public's evaluation of public administration raises some puzzling issues. The public's general attitude toward public bureaucracy is more negative than its actual experiences as clients suggest it should be. Its experiences with constraint agencies is more in keeping with its overall evaluation of bureaucracy, but encounters with such agencies appear to be less frequent than with service agencies. Additionally, comprehensive assessments of the public's evaluation of public bureaucracy are relatively new and consequently we have little idea of how positive or negative we should expect them to be. As Katz and associates observe, "A majority of satisfied clients may leave a sizable minority dissatisfied. Even a 75 percent level of satisfaction may be low for some programs in which 90 percent or higher is desirable and feasible. In a population of 200 million, small percentages are large numbers."[59] Almost all observers agree that public administration should be more attuned to the public in order to facilitate and improve public bureaucratic encounters. How this should be done tends to vary with one's perspective.

PUBLIC ADMINISTRATIVE PERSPECTIVES ON THE PUBLIC

The Managerial Approach to the Public

From a managerial perspective, interaction with the public should maximize the values of efficiency, economy, and effectiveness. The overwhelming tendency of the managerial perspective, as we noted in Chapter 1 and elsewhere, is therefore to depersonalize the client or regulatee by turning him or her into a "case." But sometimes this engenders resistance that can frustrate the attainment of these values. In such instances, the managerial approach may seek to take special steps to educate the public in a variety of ways so that its members can deal more effectively with a particular administrative agency. For example, the IRS now runs a taxpayers' information service to help individuals fill out their tax returns. Agencies also engage in public relations not only to generate greater political support for their activities but also to help clients, regulatees, and others to understand what they do. Educational efforts can be important, as it has been thought that one reason for the public's generally negative view of public administration is that "the policy makers are remote and their basic goals are not understood."[60]

Another managerial approach for dealing with the public is to institute **ombudsman** arrangements of some sort. In a traditional sense, ombudsmen are independent agents of the legislature who are empowered to investigate specific complaints by individuals alleging maladministration of some kind. Such agents can criticize, publicize and make recommendations, but they cannot reverse the administrative action at issue. Ombudsmen of this kind originated in Sweden in 1808 and can be found in other Scandinavian countries and several other nations. In the United States, Alaska, Hawaii, Iowa, and Nebraska have used ombudsmen at the state level. Several cities also employ them. However, in some cases, the ombudsmen do not fit the traditional concept completely because they are attached to the administrative agency or executive branch, rather than the legislature. Moreover, in the United States, individual members of state legislatures and Congress are inclined to function as ombudsmen for their constituents, although here the function is referred to as **constituency service** or casework. In any event, the ombudsman concept is useful from a managerial perspective because it acts as a genuine check on the poor administrative and public relations practices by subordinate public administrators. Even rudeness on the part of the latter can be the basis of an individual's complaint to an ombudsman. The ombudsman is useful in dealing with complaints that would otherwise be channeled through an agency's own hierarchy. Ombudsmen also help to educate the public concerning agencies' missions and procedures.

The managerial approach also dictates doing whatever is cost-effective to improve the quality of the public's interaction with public administrators. This may involve using higher levels of technology, such as computers, to process such things as tax returns and drivers' licenses. Or it may involve such mundane procedures as positioning waiting lines so as to be as pleasant as possible. For example, whereas in the New York State Department of Motor Vehicles offices it was once necessary to wait on one line for any eye test and then another to pay for a driver's license, now the whole transaction can take place at one window.

Finally, those pursuing the managerial approach should be wary of its tendency to shift the burdens of cost and time to individual members of the public. For instance, long lines and convoluted steps in an administrative encounter, such as being shunted from clerk to clerk, are sure to be bothersome to a sizable share of the public. So is placing the burden on individuals for supplying information that the government already has in some other office, or requiring individuals to supply multiple copies of pertinent documents as is sometimes done by consumer protection agencies. Appeals processes should also be as simplified as possible, while still being fair. In general, where investigations are necessary to determine eligibility for benefits of some kind, it is best to use the least intrusive methods. Certainly predawn raids on the homes of welfare recipients are unlikely to lead to positive attitudes on the parts of those recipients.[61] Interactions involving constraints present a complicated problem in this regard, since it sometimes may be less expensive, more efficient, and more effective to *violate* individuals' constitutional and legal rights. Consequently, public managers of policing functions must take special care to avoid any violations of this kind.

Dealing with the public is an area where the managerial values of economy and effectiveness may frequently be at odds with one another. Although it is often cheapest to follow the impersonal approach by treating individuals as cases, this approach may be inappropriate to the function being served. This is particularly true in therapeutic functions, such as mental health care and social work. "Corrections" of prisoners may also be frustrated by too much reliance on impersonality. It is more expensive to treat each individual on a personal, individual basis in these areas. However, by now the record is clear that failure to do so makes it nearly impossible for the administrative function to be performed effectively. In the area of mental health the courts have sometimes required that each patient or resident of a state facility be provided with some amount of individual treatment.[62]

In view of the tension between social values and those embodied in the managerial approach to public administration, there is no doubt that public administrators should be concerned with the public in all facets of their work. Historically, however, public administrative theory and practice paid inadequate attention to some aspects of dealing with the public. One result has been marked *underutilization* of services provided by public administrative agencies.[63] This, in itself, would tend to make the administrative state less satisfactory in intervening in the society and economy to promote the public interest. According to proponents of a "new public administration," a fundamental shift in public administration is needed to make it "client-centered," as is discussed in the next section.

The Political Approach to the Public

The political approach to public administration emphasizes the values of representation, responsiveness, and accountability to the public. This often dictates that the public be afforded means for *participating* in public administration. Public participation of some kind is viewed as contributing to the ability of public administrators to understand and respond to the public's concerns. It also requires that the administrators explain their actions, policies, and so forth to the public and is seen as a means of more completely incorporating the citizenry into the governing of the administrative state. Specifically, it is argued that:

1. A lack of citizen participation in modern governance reduces the capacity of the political system to be representative and responsive.
2. Nonparticipation also erodes the quality of citizenship in democratic nations by reducing the citizen's sense of moral and political obligation to take part in governance.
3. Nonparticipation promotes ignorance about the way government functions; participation, on the other hand, promotes understanding.
4. The absence of meaningful channels for citizen participation in government leads to alienation on the part of the public. Without participation, the public feels no sense of "ownership" or responsibility for governmental actions. On the contrary, the citizenry believes that it is acted upon (that is, subject) rather than being an actor in government. Participation also reduces alienation by providing the public with a greater sense of control over its environment.
5. Participation promotes a sense of political community and political integration. It helps individuals to see the relationship between what they personally want from government and what others, with conflicting viewpoints, are seeking. Ideally, participation enables everyone to understand and respect each others' political perspectives. Rather than promoting conflict and competition, participation is viewed as promoting cooperation.
6. Participation promotes the sense that government is legitimate and fosters compliance with its decisions. It is important to remember in this context that bureaucracy has been viewed as a means of inducing citizen compliance with "rational-legal" regulatory functions.[64] Its expertise, specialization, and impersonality have been considered particularly important in this regard. However, as noted above, impersonality, in particular, may not be well suited to some administrative functions involving service and therapy. In these areas, individuals are thought to be more apt to comply with administrative decisions, procedures, and directives if they are allowed to participate in their formulation and implementation.

There is a large body of literature and thought behind each of these propositions concerning the desirability of citizen participation in public administration.[65] Each proposition remains debatable, but for the most part, the political approach to public administration is committed to finding means of expanding citizen participation so as to achieve the state of affairs embodied in these propositions. As William Morrow observes,

Contemporary politics . . . has been marked by a revolution seeking more direct participation by citizens in policy-making. In contrast to the tendency for institutions to represent organized interests, this resurgence of participatory democracy seeks direct access to decision centers and involvement in decision-making regardless of any connections or affiliations that the participants might have with organized interests. In fact, the participation movement has stressed representation of unorganized publics that have been given only casual concern in policy arenas.[66]

Direct Participation   Although there has been a tendency among some to dismiss the political approach's interest in participation as idealistic, it should be noted with emphasis that there are some outstanding examples of long-term citizen participation in public administration. Public school governance is one example. It has strongly emphasized the need for local control and accordingly there has been great diversity in teacher qualifications, curriculum, extracurricular activities, class size, school calendar, extent of collective bargaining, and grouping of pupils in schools by age. Citizen participation has also been an important aspect of agricultural administration for many decades. More recently, New York State's citizen-participation specialists have been effective in facilitating public participation in dealing with environmental problems such as toxic waste sites and water pollution.[67] Participation through organized interest groups is also prevalent, as noted in Chapter 2, and has been institutionalized at the federal level by the Advisory Committee Act of 1972.

These examples of workable citizen participation in public administration notwithstanding, there have also been some remarkable failures. Both the Economic Opportunity Act of 1964 and the Model Cities Act of 1966 sought to incorporate citizen participation in federal programs dealing with the needs of the poor, especially the urban poor. The Economic Opportunity Act was the basis for the "poverty program." It sought to incorporate citizen participation through representation on the governing boards of community action programs. These boards also included public officials and representatives of private social service agencies. The representatives of the poor were to be elected by the poor themselves. Participatory community action agencies (CAA's) were also relied upon by the Model Cities Program. In both cases, the drive for citizen participation was frustrated. For one reason or another, the poor simply did not participate. As Daniel Patrick Moynihan observed, "The turnouts [in elections to CAA's] in effect declared that the poor weren't interested: in Philadelphia 2.7 per cent; Los Angeles 0.7 per cent; Boston 2.4 per cent; Cleveland 4.2 per cent; Kansas City, Mo. 5.0 per cent. Smaller communities sometimes got larger turnouts, but never anything nearly approaching that of a listless off-year election."[68]

Moynihan claimed that these low turnouts were reflective of the fact that participation is a middle-class value of little interest to the lower class. The poor, in his view, needed money, jobs, housing, and many other things much more than they needed "identity," "a sense of community," and "control over their destiny." Others have argued that representation of the poor was even further compromised by the tendency of their elected representatives to be coopted and to have sometimes docilely allowed the middle-class representatives on community action agencies to direct funds toward the real clientele—not the poor but the city's businesses.[69]

Client-Centered Administration   On balance, therefore, it is reasonable to conclude that participation can work in some programs and among some groups of the citizenry, as in the case of public school governance, farmers, and a considerable range of advisory committees representing economic and social interests. On the other hand, it clearly does not work among all programs and groups, as experience with the Poverty and Model Cities Programs indicates. Advocates of greater citizen participation in public administration have argued that, consequently, administrative agencies dealing with clients who for one reason or another are unable to represent themselves effectively should be **client-centered.**[70]

Client-centered agencies would seek to treat clients as individuals rather than in groups or as abstract "cases." This would require agencies to be flexibly structured around the needs of clients, more or less as defined by the clients themselves, rather than according to the needs of administrative organizations as institutions. Combining housing benefits, health programs, and nutritional programs would provide an illustration. Where programs dealing with these areas are placed in different agencies even though they are directed toward many of the same clients, the client is apt to face redundancies in filling out forms and to be required to encounter public administrators in three agencies rather than just one. More importantly, because no one agency has full responsibility for the client, each is likely to be responsive to other interests which may be in conflict with what the client is seeking. Housing agencies may be more responsive to construction, banking, and business interests; health agencies to medical and pharmaceutical interests; and nutritional programs may be placed in agricultural agencies, as is true of the federal food stamp program. Yet it would be hard to argue that health and nutrition are not related, or that housing is not relevant to programs seeking to promote client's health and nutrition. If all these programs were placed in the same agency, the argument goes, it could not help but see the client as the center of things and the other interests as peripheral. The case of "Bad Blood," discussed in Chapter 8, in which the Public Health Service failed to treat people for syphilis in order to aid medical knowledge rather than the health of the patients, is a dramatic example of what can go wrong when agencies are not client-centered. A more mundane benefit of client-centered organization is that it helps eliminate catch-22's and may make service delivery easier.

Coproduction   In some ways, **coproduction** is the opposite of client-centered public administration. Client-centered administration seeks to create organizational structures and programmatic arrangements that focus on the client's interests, since the client is believed to be unable to assert these directly. Coproduction assumes that the public can understand its interests and cooperate with public administrators in performing functions. Coproduction is "the joint provision of public services by public agencies and service consumers."[71] Everyday examples are parents of children in public schools helping them with their homework, residents carrying garbage out to the curb for collection, and participants voluntarily organizing recreation programs using public facilities. Other possibilities include community-based crime prevention groups; a statewide "green-up" (that is, clean up litter) day, as has long existed in Vermont; and groups such as "friends" of the library, parks, or symphony. Even placing a "totfinder" on a window to help firefighters identify the bedrooms of young children is an act of coproduction of public administration.

The simplicity of some aspects of coproduction should not obscure the political importance of this approach to public administration. It puts forward a different model of administrative service delivery. By being a joint venture, the citizen is a participant, not merely a consumer or subject. Citizens are therefore jointly responsible for productivity and the quality of services. Consequently, they may learn about how a public administrative function is organized and operated. One cannot help a child with homework without learning something about what goes on in the school. Nor can a citizen-based crime prevention organization fail to learn more about the problems faced by the police and how they cope with them. Moreover, some believe that coproduction can help "to build in citizens a *loyalty* to place, neighbors, and their community."[72] This loyalty results from "face-to-face contact and an investment of energy in the improvement of neighborhoods and communities."[73]

Public Interest Groups   Public interest groups are another vehicle for increasing the participation of citizenry in public administration, albeit somewhat amorphously.[74] In Chapter 2, we noted that public interest groups seek collective goods that do not selectively and materially benefit their membership. While recognizing that the distinction between this type of group and a traditional interest group may at times be blurred, there is a difference in emphasis. Public interest groups seem concerned with "representing the people against the special interests."[75] Common Cause, Consumers Union, the League of Women Voters, and a variety of groups associated with Ralph Nader are examples. These groups often interact with public administrators in an effort to promote the groups' views of the public's interest. They have made considerable use of the opportunity, afforded by the Administrative Procedure Act of 1946, to participate in administrative rule making by submitting information, views, and/or testifying before agencies. They have also made use of the National Environmental Policy Act of 1969 in this regard. Such groups provide an important counterbalance to traditional interest groups in the realm of bureaucratic politics. The average citizen has neither time nor inclination to monitor what agencies are doing, to challenge their proposed rules, or to present his or her perspective to agencies. But the public interest group does, and through constant attention to agency proposals in the *Federal Register* and equivalent volumes in the states, these groups can have an important cumulative impact. In fact, the main issue is less whether they have an impact than whether they actually represent their members in any meaningful sense. There is no way of ascertaining this. Insofar as is known, to the extent that such groups represent the public, it is broad middle-class interests upon which they focus.

The Legal Approach to the Public

The legal approach to the interaction of the public with public administration seeks to assure that individuals' constitutional and statutory rights are protected. This concern has been reflected in a number of changes in constitutional doctrine and administrative law practices over the years, especially since the New Deal. Together, these changes have led to the judicialization of many public administrative practices and greater judicial review of public administrators by the courts. Thus, administrative hearings before administrative law judges are now a standard feature of public administration in the United States. In most instances, the individual member of the public is entitled to be represented by counsel, provided at his or her own expense, at such a hearing. A very considerable body of constitutional rights for clients, regulatees, and litigants now exists. Street-level encounters are also regulated by constitutional law. The opportunities and rights of individuals to participate in public administrative activities are defined by statute, but once established by law they cannot usually be denied to a specific individual without due process of law. The individual's ability to bring actual litigation has been enhanced by a number of developments, including the enactment of the National Environmental Policy Act and the development of judicial doctrines that make it easier to have "standing"* to litigate an injury to an interest caused by some aspect of public administration.[76] Moreover, in recent years, many federal judges have shown a far greater inclination to exercise oversight of public administrative activities dealing with the public. Judicial involvement in public schools, zoning, mental health care, prison management, and public housing are examples. Concomitantly, the judiciary has greatly expanded the liability of public administrators who violate individuals' constitutional or statutory rights.

In sum, the legal approach has sought to create a network of rights to protect the public against arbitrary, capricious, invidious, or discriminatory administrative action. It has further sought to assure that the treatment of the individual by an administrative agency is fair and that individuals have access to litigation should they be injured by administrative action. Moreover, the judiciary has given public administrators an incentive to protect individuals' rights strictly: if they fail to do so, they may be personally liable for monetary damages in a civil suit initiated by the individual whose rights were violated. We will address some of these developments in greater detail in the next chapter.

---

* Standing is the ability to show sufficient stake (e.g., personal injury) to bring suit in a justifiable controversy.

SYNTHESIS: PUTTING THE PUBLIC BACK IN PUBLIC ADMINISTRATION

The growing concern with "the public" is one of the most important developments in American public administrative theory and practice. In the past, public administration paid lip-service to the concept of the "public" and the existence of a public. The notion that somehow the public must be the focus of public administration seemed too threatening and too irrelevant to expert, politically neutral public administration. Many dismissed the concept of a public as too ambiguous, too romanticized a notion, too politically oriented, and too much an aggregation to be of serious use at all.[77] In an effort to make the notion of the public more concrete, the managerial approach tended to focus on the public as clients or regulatees, who were processed as cases. The political approach tended to aggregate them into social and economic interest groups. This was an effort to promote the values of representativeness, responsiveness, and administrative accountability through greater opportunities for citizen participation in public administration. Thus, the citizenry were considered in terms of such categories as "farmers," "the poor," and so forth. The Federal Advisory Committee Act of 1972 affords the opportunity for participation through organized interest groups to a wide range of groups of people with whom federal bureaucratic agencies are involved. The legal approach views the public as a collection of individuals who possess certain constitutional and statutory rights that must be protected against administrative encroachment. It regards the protection of these rights as obviously in the public interest.

For the most part, these perspectives are so broad that a synthesis is possible. However, the conflicts among their values and approaches for achieving these values should not be underestimated. In the past, the managerial perspective considered citizen participation to be inefficient and ineffective because it brought amateurs into public administration, which was seen as the domain of professionals and experts. Citizen participation was also viewed as too expensive. Those imbued with the managerial perspective would admit, though, that the citizenry could legitimately act as "authoritative critic" of administrative actions, to use Woodrow Wilson's term.[78] Certainly, the "citizen-subject" or "citizen-consumer" of administrative action could develop a legitimate and informed opinion about it. The trouble was that the citizenry seemed unclear in its evaluation of public administration. In the abstract the public was critical, in the area of services it was generally positive, in the area of constraint, negative.

The managerial approach was also at odds with the legalistic one. The main conflict here has been "judicialization" of public administration, which has the tendency to fragment administrative authority and to be time-consuming. No doubt those committed to the managerial view that administrative legitimacy flows from technical expertise were also opposed to the increasing scope of judicial review and oversight of administrative action.

Finally, there is plenty of potential for the political and legal approaches to clash over the very basic question of "Who is eligible to participate?" Very many categorizations of people for participation in public administration run the risk of violating the constitutional requirements of equal protection.

Despite these conflicts among the three perspectives, matters pertaining to the public and public administration have tended to sort themselves out by *function*. While recognizing that the categories are broad and imperfect, the following patterns have emerged.

Service   The managerial perspective toward the public has been relied upon where the function is service of a nontherapeutic nature, such as retirement benefits, unemployment compensation, and workers' compensation. For the most part, these services involve routine handling of numerous individuals who fall into similar categories (e.g., reach the age of retirement). Treating them as "cases" is efficient and apparently does not seriously offend the clients, as is suggested by the public's evaluation of such activities.

Therapy   Therapeutic service and regulation for the purpose of providing therapy, as in public mental health facilities and prisons, tend to require a more client-centered and/or participatory approach. Prisons and residential mental health facilities come close to being totally client-centered in the sense that all the ostensible needs of the client (or regulatee, in this context) are met there. Welfare and some health programs also tend to be client-centered to a considerable extent. Therapy requires individualized attention. This is obviously true in medical and psychological terms, but it is also pertinent in a social sense. It is not an accident that "social workers" deal with their clients on an individual basis and in a face-to-face context. Social work may involve visits by the public administrator to the home of the client, and a plan of therapeutic action may be developed for each client, based on his or her needs. A basic notion here, though perhaps a somewhat paternalistic one, is that those subject to therapy are unable independently to assert their own interests.

Regulation   Regulation not involving therapy tends to be organized along the lines of the managerial perspective but is also strongly influenced by legalistic considerations of rights and procedures. Examples would be regulation by police, tax agencies, and motor vehicle departments. Agencies engaged in these functions treat individuals as cases and seek to process them as efficiently and economically as possible. However, since some very fundamental rights are involved, the legalistic perspective has been asserted to a considerable degree as a means of protecting individuals.

Litigation and Street-Level Encounters   These kinds of interaction between the public and public administrators are largely informed by the values of the legalistic approach. The rights of the individual are specified in some detail and certain procedures are required to assure that these rights are respected. This has gone so far that it may now be considered unconstitutional for the police to approach an individual walking on the street and ask who he or she is and what he or she is doing—unless there is at least a reasonable suspicion that the person has actually done or is about to do something illegal.[79] The courts have been particularly active in defining the constitutional limits on "stop and frisk" operations by police. Litigation, of course, is the full realization of the legalistic perspective.

Participation   Individuals also participate in public administration. This role is dictated almost entirely by the political perspective, and the values associated with it overlay some of the practices found in the realm of service delivery and therapy. Participation is also dictated in subsidy programs. It is prevalent in federal agricultural policy and was an important value in the Poverty and Model Cities Programs. The regulation of economic concerns and activities, though not of individuals, also tends to emphasize participation by organized interest groups, as we saw in the previous chapter. But participation is so fundamental a political process for obtaining representativeness, responsiveness, and accountability that it has worked its way into many aspects of public administration. For instance, coproduction is a means of participation in service delivery. Client-centered administrative operations are viewed as a means of representing and responding to the interests of individuals who otherwise might not be able to assert their interests well. Mental health patients are a clear example. At a broader level of economic regulation and subsidization, client-centered agencies become "clientele" agencies, such as the U.S. Departments of Agriculture, Commerce, and Labor. Here the political approach is followed in imputing the same sets of interests to all members of a categorical group, such as organized labor, which is seen as the political constituency of the agency. Public school governance is another manifestation of society's overriding concern with the values of the political approach to public administration.

Of course, the association of these approaches and values with different administrative functions in different degrees does create tensions for day-to-day public administration. Yet as long as the society seeks conflicting goals—greater administrative efficiency, public participation, strict protection of an individual's constitutional and legal rights—the balance already reached in terms of the public's interaction with public administration seems reasonably sound. No doubt adjustments can be made, but once again, no fundamental changes are likely unless conflicts among the values and goals of public administration can be fully resolved. There is, however, one aspect of the public and public administration that virtually all analysts are agreed upon—the public would benefit from a better understanding of public administration, and public administration would benefit from a public that knew more about its functions, concepts, values, and processes. Let us conclude this chapter by returning, once again, to Woodrow Wilson, who began the self-conscious study of public administration in the United States.

> The problem is to make public opinion efficient without suffering it to be meddlesome. Directly exercised, in the oversight of the daily details and in the choice of the daily means of government, public criticism is of course a clumsy nuisance, a rustic handling of delicate machinery. But as superintending the greater forces of formative

policy alike in politics and administration, public criticism is altogether safe and beneficial, altogether indispensable. Let administrative study find the best means for giving public criticism this control and for shutting it out from all other interference.[80]

NOTES

1. Daniel Katz, Barbara Gutek, Robert Kahn, and Eugenia Barton, *Bureaucratic Encounters* (Ann Arbor, Mich.: University of Michigan, Institute for Social Research, 1975), Table 2.1, p. 20.
2. Ibid., pp. 101–116.
3. U.S. Department of Commerce, *Statistical Abstract* (Washington, D.C.: Bureau of the Census, 1986), pp. 99, 100, 172, 173.
4. Ralph P. Hummel, *The Bureaucratic Experience* (New York: St. Martin's, 1977), p. 20.
5. Ibid., p. 27.
6. Ibid., p. 29.
7. Ibid., p. 57.
8. Ibid., p. 56.
9. Victor Thompson, *Modern Organization* (New York: Knopf, 1961), p. 170.
10. Reinhard Bendix, *Nation Building and Citizenship* (New York: Wiley, 1964), p. 129.
11. Thompson, *Modern Organization*, pp. 172–173.
12. Alvin Gouldner, "Red Tape as a Social Problem," in *Reader in Bureaucracy*, ed. by R. K. Merton et al. (Glencoe, Ill.: Free Press, 1952), p. 413.
13. Gideon Sjoberg, et al., "Bureaucracy and the Lower Class," in *Bureaucratic Power in National Politics*, 3rd ed., ed. by F. Rourke (Boston: Little, Brown, 1978), p. 40.
14. Katz, et al., *Bureaucratic Encounters*, p. 193.
15. Herbert G. Wilcox, "The Cultural Trait of Hierarchy in Middle Class Children," *Public Administrative Review*, 28 (May/June, 1968): 222–235, at p. 231.
16. Frederick Mosher, *Democracy and the Public Service* (New York: Oxford University Press, 1968), pp. 3–4.
17. Max Weber, *From Max Weber: Essays in Sociology*, trans. and ed. by H. H. Gerth and C. W. Mills (New York: Oxford University Press, 1958), p. 216.
18. U.S. Congress, Committee on Government Operations, Subcommittee on Intergovernmental Relations, *Confidence and Concerns: Citizens View American Government* (Washington, D.C.: Government Printing Office, 1973), part 2, p. 115; part 3, p. 61.
19. Ibid., Part 2, p. 114; part 3, p. 60.
20. See David Nachmias and David H. Rosenbloom, *Bureaucratic Government, U.S.A.* (New York: St. Martin's, 1980), p. 245, table 9–7.
21. Emmette S. Redford, *Democracy in the Administrative State* (New York: Oxford University Press, 1969), p. 66.
22. *New York Times*, November 16, 1976, p. 33.
23. Theodore J. Lowi, "A 'Critical' Election Misfires," *Nation*, December 18, 1972.
24. See Nachmias and Rosenbloom, *Bureaucratic Government, U.S.A.*, p. 250, table 9–10.
25. Hummel, *The Bureaucratic Experience*, p. 193.
26. U.S. Congress, *Confidence and Concern*, part 1, pp. 83–84.

27. Ibid., part 1, p. 85.
28. Ibid., part 2, pp. 297, 307, 317.
29. Stephen Bennett, *Apathy in America, 1960–1984* (Dobbs Ferry, N.Y.: Transnational, 1986).
30. Morris P. Fiorina, *Congress: Keystone of the Washington Establishment* (New Haven, Conn: Yale University Press, 1977), p. 46.
31. Ibid.
32. Ward Sinclair, "It's Not the Size of the State . . . It's the Seat on the Appropriations Committee," *Washington Post National Weekly Edition*, November 23, 1987, p. 16.
33. Fiorina, *Congress*, p. 46.
34. Charles Reich, "The New Property," *Yale Law Journal*, 73 (1964): 733.
35. Ibid., p. 746.
36. Milton Friedman, *Capitalism and Freedom* (Chicago: University of Chicago Press, 1962), pp. 8–9.
37. Reich, "The New Property," p. 747.
38. See David H. Rosenbloom, *Federal Service and the Constitution* (Ithaca, N.Y.: Cornell University Press, 1971), Chapter 6.
39. Ralph S. Brown, Jr., *Loyalty and Security* (New Haven, Conn.: Yale University Press, 1958), pp. vii, 18, 377.
40. Friedrich A. Hayek, *The Road to Serfdom* (Chicago: University of Chicago Press, 1944).
41. Ibid.
42. Seymour M. Lipset and William Schneider, *The Confidence Gap: Business, Labor, and Government in the Public Mind* (New York: Free Press, 1983).
43. Ibid., p. 21, figure 1–2. In 1952, 71 percent agreed and in 1980, 70 percent agreed, but in 1960, only 59 percent agreed.
44. U.S. Congress, *Confidence and Concern*, part 2, p. 61; and Gabriel Almond and Sidney Verba, *The Civic Culture* (Boston: Little, Brown, 1965), pp. 46, 47.
45. U.S. Congress, *Confidence and Concern*, part 2, p. 114; part 3, p. 61.
46. See Nachmias and Rosenbloom, *Bureaucratic Government, U.S.A.*, p. 243, table 9–4.
47. Lipset and Schneider, *The Confidence Gap*, p. 228, table 8–3.
48. Ibid., p. 95.
49. *New York Times*, December 1, 1987, p. B24.
50. Lipset and Schneider, *The Confidence Gap*, p. 251.
51. Charles T. Goodsell, *The Case for Bureaucracy* (Chatham, N.J.: Chatham House, 1983), p. 29.
52. Ibid., p. 31.
53. Ibid., chap. 2.
54. Ibid., p. 37.
55. Katz, et al., *Bureaucratic Encounters*, p. 186.
56. Ibid., p. 187.
57. Ibid., p. 116.
58. Ibid.
59. Ibid., pp. 114–115.
60. Ibid., p. 188.
61. Parrish v. Civil Service Commission, 425 P2d 223 (1967).
62. Wyatt v. Stickney, 325 F. Supp. 781; 334 F. Supp. 1341 (1971); 344 F. Supp. 373; 344 F. Supp. 387 (1972); Youngberg v. Romeo, 451 U.S. 982 (1982).
63. Katz, et al., *Bureaucratic Encounters*, chap. 2.

64. Weber, *From Max Weber*, chap. 8.
65. See Samuel Krislov and David H. Rosenbloom, *Representative Bureaucracy and the American Political System* (New York: Praeger, 1981), chap. 5, for a brief review.
66. William Morrow, *Public Administration* (New York: Random House, 1975), pp. 189–190.
67. Richard Schwartz, "Public Participation and Democratic Decisionmaking: Clean Water for The Empire State?" Presented at the Annual Meeting of the Society for the Study of Social Problems, Chicago, August 14, 1987.
68. Daniel P. Moynihan, *Maximum Feasible Misunderstanding* (New York: Free Press, 1970), p. 137.
69. See Morrow, *Public Administration*, p. 198.
70. This term gained currency in the movement for a "new public administration." See Frank Marini, ed., *Toward a New Public Administration: The Minnowbrook Perspective* (Scranton, Pa.: Chandler, 1971).
71. Charles Levine, "Citizenship and Service Delivery: The Promise of Coproduction," *Public Administration Review*, 44 (Special Issue, March 1984): 181.
72. Ibid., p. 185.
73. Ibid.
74. See Krislov and Rosenbloom, *Representative Bureaucracy*, pp. 170–175.
75. Ibid., p. 172.
76. Kenneth C. Davis, *Administrative Law and Government* (St. Paul, Minn.: West, 1975), esp. p. 72.
77. David Mathews, "The Public in Practice and Theory," *Public Administration Review*, 44 (Special Issue, March 1984): 120–125.
78. Woodrow Wilson, "The Study of Administration," *Political Science Quarterly*, 56 (December 1941): 498.
79. Kolender v. Lawson, 461 U.S. 352 (1983).
80. Wilson, "The Study of Administration," p. 499.

ADDITIONAL READING

FREDERICKSON, H. GEORGE, AND RALPH CLARK CHANDLER, EDS. "Citizenship and Public Administration," *Public Administration Review*, 44 (Special Issue, March 1984): 97–204.

GOODSELL, CHARLES. *The Case for Bureaucracy*, 2nd ed. Chatham, N.J.: Chatham House, 1985.

KATZ, DANIEL, BARBARA GUTEK, ROBERT KAHN, AND EUGENIA BARTON. *Bureaucratic Encounters*. Ann Arbor: Institute for Social Research, 1975.

KAUFMAN, HERBERT. *Red Tape*. Washington, D.C.: Brookings Institution, 1977.

LEWIS, EUGENE. *American Politics in a Bureaucratic Age: Citizens, Constituents, Clients and Victims*. Cambridge, Mass.: Winthrop, 1977.

REDFORD, EMMETTE S. *Democracy in the Administrative State*. New York: Oxford University Press, 1969.

STUDY QUESTIONS

1. Consider a recent interaction you had with some aspect of public administration. How would you describe your role? What approach did the agency or official take toward you in that role? How satisfactory or unsatisfactory was the experience?

2. Do you find yourself to be like the public generally in expressing both criticism and praise of public administration? If so, how would you explain your evaluations of it? If not, what is your personal evaluation of public administration? How did you come by that evaluation?

3. How realistic do you think greater citizen participation in public administration is? Do you favor or oppose it? Why?

CHAPTER 11 | *Public Administration and Democratic Constitutionalism*

This chapter explains why public administrators must understand constitutional values and discusses the nature of those values. Among the constitutional values considered are the separation of powers, legitimacy, diversity, liberty and freedom, property rights, procedural due process, equal protection, individuality, and equity. This chapter does not attempt to teach constitutional law per se but rather to explain the nature of these fundamental values in the context of public administration.

Our discussion of public administration's development, core functions, and processes makes it evident that there are times when the values of managerially and politically oriented public administration may be in pronounced conflict with the values and principles of democratic constitutionalism. There have been many instances in which public administrative action, taken in good faith and seeking to maximize values inherent in the managerial and political approaches, has been declared unconstitutional by the courts. So deep does the tension between constitutional arrangements and contemporary public administration run, that on one occasion the Chief Justice of the U.S. Supreme Court observed that, from the perspectives of the modern administrative state, "The choices we discern as having been made in the Constitutional Convention impose burdens on governmental processes that often seem clumsy, inefficient, even unworkable. . . ."[1] Looking at the same problem of the tension between public administration and democratic constitutionalism from the perspective of public administration, Dwight Waldo has contended that "It *cannot be solved*—acceptably, workably—given our constitutional system, our constitutional history, and our democratic ideology. All we can hope for is piecemeal solutions, temporary agreements."[2] The objective of this chapter is to provide the beginnings of such a piecemeal solution by imparting an understanding of the nature of the conflicts and tensions between public administration and democratic constitutionalism. A comprehensive appreciation of these conflicts and tensions is an absolute prerequisite to determining how to take public administrative action that both is constitutional and maximizes appropriate managerial and political values. Our approach to this subject will emphasize the fundamental principles and values of the Constitution rather than present interpretations of its specific clauses or the historical development of its doctrines.

WHY PUBLIC ADMINISTRATORS MUST UNDERSTAND THE CONSTITUTION

Until recent years, it would have been rare to find a chapter in a text on public administration devoted to a discussion of "democratic constitutionalism." It was frequently taken as a given that Woodrow Wilson was correct when he observed that for the most part the concerns of public administration were far removed from the concerns of framing and amending the Constitution. He saw the two endeavors as so separate that he claimed it was getting to be harder to run (that is, administer) a constitution than to frame one.[3] Today, however, judicial involvement in public administration is so pronounced and the legal approach so strong that the need for public administrators to understand the Constitution is almost self-evident. There are three aspects of the relationship between public administration and the Constitution that should be emphasized in this regard.

First, as Woodrow Wilson indicated, the "principles on which to base" a sound public administration in the United States "must be principles which have democratic policy very much at heart."[4] But public administration cannot be based on these principals unless it understands them and appreciates their worth.

It is difficult to contest seriously the view that the ultimate object for public administration in the United States is a combination of the values of the managerial and political approaches that is fully compatible with constitutional principles and values. This is something that all public administrators should be working toward.

Second, many, perhaps most, public administrators take an oath to support the Constitution. Cynics may dismiss this as a pro forma requirement, utterly devoid of any significant content. However, they may be dismissing this requirement too easily. Upholding the Constitution might be considered more important than routine administrative functions because it is connected to the moral principle that a public office is a "public trust." Moreover, the polity is unlikely to judge administrative action that violates the Constitution as desirable (see Box 11–1). The Iran-Contra affair (1986–1987), in which some members of the National Security Council and other officials placed achievement of their policy goals above adherence to the constitutional rule of law, provoked a great deal of legislative and public wrath. A breach of the oath can constitute perjury, which may be punishable by criminal or civil penalties.

Third, as discussed earlier in Chapters 1 and 5, many public administrators are now personally liable in civil suits for damages when they violate the constitutional rights of individuals or groups. Their action violating such rights may also subject them to punitive damages. These damages may be assessed at the amount a jury considers adequate to punish the public administrator and to deter others from taking similar action.[5] In the process of redefining the liability of public administrators at all levels of government, the Supreme Court has arrived at the general standard that the public administrator can be personally sued for damages if he or she knew or reasonably should have known that his or her action would be in violation of others' constitutional rights. Reasonable knowledge of the constitutional rights of the people upon whom public administrators act has become a key aspect of the public administrator's job and competence in the eyes of the judiciary. If for no other reason, public administrators need to understand the Constitution in order to protect their pocketbooks from civil suits for damages.

Unfortunately, understanding the Constitution is easier said than done. We alluded to this problem in Chapter One. As far as the public administrator is concerned, the Constitution must be considered a set of values and principles that far exceeds the specific holdings found in past judicial decisions. The *case law* provides only part of the understanding that is necessary, because the Constitution is largely a document of the imagination. Its current requirements go well beyond its specific language. Rather, those requirements are derived from legal, philosophical, moral, and political considerations as to how the Constitution should be applied in a variety of contemporary circumstances very much unforeseen by the Founders. For example, some of the principles we will consider in this chapter are the notions of "chilling effect," "least restrictive alternative," and "two-tier test" pertaining to equal protection. Each of these principles is absolutely critical to an understanding of the Constitution today, but none can actually be found in the words of that document. In addition, some

BOX 11–1 **Putting Constitutional Values in Public Administration: A Right to Disobey?**

57 Cal.Rptr. 623
Benny Max PARRISH, Plaintiff
and Appellant,
v
The CIVIL SERVICE COMMISSION OF the
COUNTY OF ALAMEDA, etc., et al.,
Defendants and Respondents.
S. F. 22429.

Supreme Court of California,
In Bank.
March 27, 1967.

Mandamus proceeding to compel reinstatement of county social worker after his discharge for insubordination. The Superior Court, Alameda County, Wayne P. Burke, J., entered judgment denying petition, and petitioner appealed. The Supreme Court, Tobriner, J., held that where county failed to secure legally effective consent to search homes of welfare recipients, through early morning mass raids to determine welfare eligibility, and, even if effective consent had been obtained, county could not constitutionally condition continued receipt of welfare benefits upon giving of such consent, such raids, in which county directed social worker to take part, transgressed constitutional limitations, and thus social worker, in light of his knowledge as to scope and methods of projected raids, possessed adequate grounds for declining to participate and could not properly be found guilty of insubordination warranting his discharge.

Reversed and cause remanded with directions.

McComb, J., dissented.

Opinion, Cal.App., 51 Cal.Rptr. 589, vacated.

John R. HARLEY
v.
SCHUYLKILL COUNTY et al.
Civ. A. No. 78–861.

United States District Court,
E. D. Pennsylvania.
Aug. 23, 1979.

Discharged prison guard filed civil rights suit against county and warden, alleging that his discharge was wrongful in that it was a deprivation of his liberty interest without according him due process, constituted a violation of his First Amendment rights, was based on his refusal to perform an unconstitutional act, and constituted a violation of rights secured under the Pennsylvania Constitution. On a defense motion to dismiss, the District Court, Huyett, J., held that: (1) the right to refuse to perform an unconstitutional act is a right "secured by the Constitution" within the meaning of the Civil Rights Act of 1871; accordingly, in the instant case, prison guard had the right to refrain from performing an act, ordered by the warden, which would have deprived prisoner of his constitutional rights, and (2) a county is liable for acts of its employees which violate Article 1, Section 1 of the Pennsylvania Constitution, where those employees are acting within the scope of their official duties.

Motion denied.

very fundamental constitutional rights, such as the right to privacy and the right to travel among the states, are derived from the principles and values of the Constitution, rather than specifically enumerated within it.

The broad and unspecific quality of the Constitution can be quite frustrating to those who seek to understand it and model their administrative conduct accordingly. Sometimes it is best to think of the Constitution as a body of values and principles that are inherent in the nation's political culture, social ethos, and history. These values and principles are not articulated all at once. Rather, the courts declare what they are when the proper occasions arise. Such an occasion is one that presents the circumstances in a framework that is suitable for adjudication and develops the constitutional issues with adequate clarity. In most cases where there is a real and protracted dispute over what the Constitution requires, the Supreme Court will be the final judicial arbiter. Its members will follow their consciences and philosophical and political views in interpreting what the words, principles, values, and previous constitutional decisions require in any particular set of circumstances. Perhaps Justice Frankfurter expressed the idea best, with due attention to its abstract qualities:

> There is in each of us a stream of tendency, whether you choose to call it a philosophy or not, which gives coherence and direction to thought and action. Judges cannot escape that current any more than other mortals. All their lives, forces which they do not recognize and cannot name, have been tugging at them—inherited instincts, traditional beliefs, acquired convictions; and the resultant is an outlook on life, a conception of social needs, a sense in James' phrase of "the total push and pressure of the cosmos," which, when reasons are nicely balanced, must determine where choices shall fall. In this mental background every problem finds its setting. We may try to see things as objectively as we please. None the less, we can never see them with any eyes except our own.[6]

At the same time, of course, the justices and judges are not free to "rewrite" or even reinterpret the Constitution at will. There are checks on the courts and the questions they address are framed by the litigation before them, just as the answers they provide are partly framed by past precedents and previous considerations of the nature of constitutional values and principles. Few judges and constitutional scholars truly believe that the Constitution should (or could) be interpreted solely from the perspectives of the Framers' "original intent." But, by the same token, few believe that the "original intent" is irrelevant to present interpretations.

Constitutional law derived in this way has certainly had its oddities over the years. Sometimes one decision is overturned by another within a period of but a few years.[7] Sometimes the incremental declaration of constitutional requirements leads to peculiarities. For instance, in the public administrative realm, from 1983 to 1985, Congress was constitutionally prohibited from regulating wages and hours for state employees but allowed to prohibit a state from forcing some of its employees to retire at age fifty-five. The first case (wages and hours) was viewed as an infringement on state sovereignty under the Tenth Amendment, while the second was not. Consequently two aspects of the same employee's employment were subject to regulation, but only by two separate governments! (In 1985, the Court changed this anomalous situation by overruling its previous decision on wages and hours.)[8] However, the great virtue of the system of constitutional law that has been developed in the United States is that it enables the polity to adapt the fundamental values and principles of an eighteenth-century document to continually changing political, economic, social, international, and environmental circumstances. Moreover, it helps the society maintain a good deal of political consensus on those fundamental principles and values. As a result, rather than trying to govern itself through the "dead hand of the past," the United States has a written, but also a "living" constitution. And, without a doubt, public administration is now a part of this.

We now turn to a discussion of those fundamental principles and values that are most salient to public administrators.

ADMINISTRATIVE STRUCTURE AND CONSTITUTIONAL STRUCTURE

Both public administrative and constitutional doctrine advocate the separation of functions among different structural units, such as agencies, bureaus, or branches of government. However, there are crucial differences. When following the managerial approach, public administrative agencies place different functions in different units for the sake of specialization and the efficiency, economy, and effectiveness that is derived from the division of labor. When the political approach dictates the organization of agencies, it is likely that the separation of functions goes by policy area or clientele group and is intended to enhance administrative representativeness and responsiveness. The Constitution, on the other hand, seeks to separate powers—legislative, executive, and judicial—for the sake of creating checks and balances that safeguard against authoritarian or tyrannical government. As James Madison explained in the *Federalist Papers*, the combination of legislative, executive, and judicial power in the same hands could be considered the very essence of tyranny. He also explained that the system of checks and balances was intended to provide "great security against a gradual concentration of the several powers in the same department [i.e., branch of government] . . . [by] giving to those who administer each department the necessary constitutional means and personal motives to resist encroachment of the others."[9] Hence, the different terms of office and modes of election or appointment of members of each house of Congress, the president, and the judiciary. But, as Chief Justice Burger pointed out, it is precisely this system that sometimes makes the federal government seem cumbersome and even unworkable in the contemporary administrative age.

In an effort to try to overcome the slow and cumbersome quality of government according to the separation of powers and checks and balances, since the 1930s the United States has increasingly vested combinations of legislative, executive, and judicial functions in individual administrative agencies. In other words, there has been a tendency to *collapse* the functions of the three constitutional branches into the federal bureaucracy. Regulatory commissions are the clearest example of agencies that engage in legislative functions (rule making), executive activities (implementation and enforcement), and judicial roles (adjudication). Although many criticize bureaucracy for its slow and lumbering qualities, historically public administration has been viewed as more flexible than government strictly according to the constitutional separation of powers as originally designed. For instance, agency rule making and recision of rules is far simpler, and generally much quicker, than Congress's legislating. Unlike the House and Senate, individual agencies are unified and coordinated by hierarchy to a very large extent. Agency adjudication is usually faster and more flexible than litigation before the judiciary.

The "collapsing" of the separation of powers into the administrative branch has both administrative and constitutional consequences. Among the most important is that public administrators can be held responsible to each of the three constitutional branches. Aside from serving the public, many federal administrators serve three masters, not one: Congress, the president, and the federal judiciary. Since public administrators exercise functions originally assigned to each of the three constitutional branches, it is to be expected that each of those branches will be concerned about the way those functions are performed. Consequently, whereas it is common to think of public administration as being hierarchically organized, top-level public administrators can be held accountable, for certain aspects of their jobs, to three sets of political actors (the legislature, chief executive, and courts). Moreover, as Madison noted, each of these sets of actors has a different term of office, a different constitutional role, and different interests. Sometimes this has the effect of complicating public administration to the point of exasperation.

One concrete example of this problem was presented in the case of *American Federation of Government Employees* v. *Phillips* (1973).[10] Phillips was acting director of the Office of Economic Opportunity (OEO). Upon hearing the president's budgetary message, which indicated that the president intended to eliminate OEO and would not seek any additional funding for it, Phillips began to cut back on spending the appropriations previously granted for the then current fiscal year. (Remember, the budgetary message is for the next fiscal year, and does not directly affect the current one.) In Phillips's view, it seemed wasteful and administratively inappropriate to spend money for a program that was likely to come to a screeching halt at the end of the fiscal year. Some of the funds had been earmarked for projects and perhaps equipment that were intended to be of long-run utility. Sinking more funds into start-up projects with no future would be pointless. However, Phillips's cutbacks were opposed by the American Federation of Government Employees, a labor union, because they would eliminate the jobs of some of its members. Intended beneficiaries of some of the previously planned projects also opposed the cutbacks. But Phillips considered himself to be responsible to the president and to be engaging in sound, economizing, public administration.

Phillips's view was deemed inappropriate by a circuit court of appeals. It reasoned that Phillips should not have defined his responsibilities so narrowly. First, he had a legal obligation to spend funds already allotted by Congress. His responsibility was to the law and legislature in this regard. Second, since the president's budgetary message was only a *message*, having no binding quality upon Congress, Phillips was wrong to take direction from it. After all, Congress could allocate funds to OEO even though the president was opposed. The separation of powers and checks and balances gives the legislature a critical role in budgeting—that of passing bills authorizing the spending of federal funds. Congress has different constituencies from the president, and it might have a different political outlook on the desirability of OEO. The constitutional world of public administration was far more complicated than Phillips thought.

On the one hand, it is easy to see Phillips's mistake. On the other, was he really wrong in not wanting to spend money for projects that were likely to be abandoned and were unlikely to do much good unless continued for a long period of time? One lesson here is that "democracy is not cheap."[11] The costs of the separation of powers may seem irrational in terms of managerially oriented public administration, but from a constitutional perspective they are thought to be fully justified.

Phillips tried to twist the Constitution to enable him to be a good public manager. At times, Congress or the president has tried to twist the Constitution in order to avoid the limits that the separation of powers places on their ability to direct aspects of public administration. Perhaps the most outstanding example here is the **legislative veto.**

Contemporary public administration in the United States frequently involves the exercise of powers delegated to administrative agencies by the legislature. For instance, regulatory commissions exercise such powers. They are authorized by the legislature to make rules having the force of law for the regulation of the conduct of private parties. From a generic perspective, this is legislation, even though it is done outside the legislature. The legislature does not provide public administrators with free rein of legislative powers. Rather, it establishes general or specific guidance as to what the content of the administrative rules should be. But even where highly specific, such guidance may be viewed as an inadequate control by the legislature. Hence, the legislative dilemma: on the one hand, it feels unable or unwilling to enact detailed legislation on all the matters now regulated by governmental activity, and consequently, it delegates this task to administrative agencies; on the other, since the legislature is delegating *its* own power, it wants to retain strict control over its use. The legislative veto was considered a promising resolution of the dilemma.

The legislative veto is a logical procedural device that enables the legislature to block an administrative exercise of delegated powers to which it is opposed. The veto requires that the administrative agency inform the legislature of the rules or actions it is proposing and that the legislature have an opportunity to prevent those rules or actions from being put into effect. Sometimes the veto was by one house of Congress, sometimes both houses were required. Sometimes it required that the legislature express approval of the proposed rule or action, other times legislative action took the form of disapproval. Generally, there has been a time limit attached to the exercise of the legislative veto, such as thirty, sixty, or ninety days from the time the administrative rule or action is proposed.

The first legislative veto provision passed at the federal level appears to have been in 1932. By 1983, when the Supreme Court ruled at least one type of veto unconstitutional, there were some 295 federal legislative veto provisions in 196 statutes.[12] The bulk of these were adopted after 1970, as the legislature sought to take a greater role in controlling the operations of the executive branch.

Notwithstanding the popularity of the legislative veto in Congress, in *Immigration and Naturalization Service* v. *Chadha* (1983), the Supreme Court found the one-house type veto to be an unconstitutional shortcut for attempting to control administrative discretion. As the Court saw it, this type of veto places one house essentially in a position to legislate. It negated the checks and balances provided by bicameralism. It also failed to afford the president opportunity to intervene with a veto of his own, since unlike an act of Congress, the legislative veto is not presented to the president for approval or veto. In essence, the problem with the one-house veto was that it distorted the Constitution and bent its separation of powers and checks and balances out of shape. In the Court's words:

> The bicameral requirement, the Presentment Clauses, the President's veto, the Congress' power to override a veto were intended to erect enduring checks on each Branch and to protect the people from the improvident exercise of power by mandating certain prescribed steps. To preserve those checks, and maintain the separation of powers, the carefully defined limits on the power of each Branch must not be eroded. To accomplish what has been attempted by one House of Congress in this case requires action in conformity with the express procedures of the Constitution's prescription for legislative action: passage by a majority of both Houses and presentment to the President.[13]

Again, the lesson is that public administration is not responsible under the Constitution to merely one master, and the assertion to the contrary by one house of Congress was unconstitutional. The Supreme Court's ruling on the one-house veto in *Chadha* seems broad enough to encompass the two-house veto as well. The demise of the legislative veto requires that if Congress seeks to assert control over administrative activities, it does so through its traditional constitutional means, including the power to establish agency missions, appropriations, organizational arrangements and staffing, and the power to engage in oversight.

In *Phillips* we saw that a public administrator should not consider himself or herself responsible solely to the president; *Chadha* stands for the principle that one house of Congress, and probably Congress as a whole, cannot constitutionally seek to make public administrators solely responsible to it. It is often true that the courts fare no better in practice when they try to assert unilateral dominance over administrative operations. As Alexander Hamilton argued in *Federalist Paper* No. 78, the judiciary "has no influence over either the sword or the purse" and consequently depends upon the other branches of government to implement its decrees. One example at the federal level was presented in the litigation in *Hobson* v. *Hansen* (1967).[14] The case involved the equalization of spending of funds on schools and pupils in the District of Columbia. It was decided against the backdrop of trying to untangle the effects of a history of racial segregation in the Washington, D.C., public schools. Although assessments may differ, one comprehensive analysis of the litigation concluded that the federal District Court's efforts to achieve equalization of spending in the school system, which is also part of the federal government, failed.[15] In part, the failure could be attributed to limitations placed by Congress on the use of federal funds to achieve racial integration.[16] The main consequence was that without Congress's support, the objectives of the judiciary's decision were thwarted because the school administrators were prohibited from using funds for reforms that would help achieve those objectives. But under such circumstances, what were the Board of Education and the superintendent of schools supposed to do? Again they were required to be responsive to more than one master—which had the potential to lead them in different directions.

The separation of powers complicates public administration by frequently making it responsible to more than one branch of government and by pulling it in different directions at once, as in *Phillips* and *Hobson*. These tendencies often make it difficult for agencies to maximize the values of the managerial or political approaches to public administration. The unity of structure and control sought by the managerial approach is easily frustrated by the effects of the separation of powers. The representativeness and responsiveness sought by the political approach become muddled when more than one constitutional actor, each having different motives and interests, becomes involved in public admin- istration. The effect may be frustrating from virtually all perspectives. For as Peter Woll explains, the need for coordination among the three constitutional branches to control public administration sometimes means that the exercise of administrative authority slips through the cracks in the separation of powers.

> What the framers [of the Constitution] clearly failed to predict was the demise of local interest groups and the development of groups with a national orientation. . . .
> . . . The separation of powers system, by placing Congress in the position of an adversary of the President, motivates the legislature to place a significant portion of the administrative branch outside the legal sphere of presidential control. In this manner, the separation of powers idea, instead of limiting governmental power, results in the relative independence of the administrative branch by displacing the most natural focal point of control. Because of the attachment between private clientele groups and public bureaucratic interest groups, the constitutional separation of powers often leads to an increase of "faction" in government.[17]

As discussed in Chapter 2, these factions or interests often take the form of "iron triangles" that seem impervious to presidential direction and resistant to control by a legislature as a whole.

The irony of constitutional structure is that by placing several masters over public administration, in practice it may provide public administrators with none. The efforts of the constitutional branches of government to control the administrative branch are sometimes frustrated by the Constitution itself. But it is the very same Constitution and system of separation of powers and checks and balances that also can frustrate administrative action that is informed by sound administrative values and theories.

There are different conclusions to draw from this irony. One is that public administrators should try to play one constitutional branch off against another in a quest for independence and autonomy. Another is that since the Constitution itself does not establish a fully adequate system of practical control by the constitutional branches over public administrators, administrators' obligations to the Constitution must be augmented by a more direct responsibility to uphold its fundamental values and principles. Indeed, this is precisely what Article VI of the Constitution requires: "The Senators and Representatives before mentioned, and the Members of the several State Legislatures, and all executive and judicial Officers, both of the United States and several States, shall be bound by Oath or Affirmation, to support this Constitution. . . . ." Once again, the need to understand constitutional principles and values is evident.

CONSTITUTIONAL VALUES

Legitimacy

There is a stark contrast between the bases of legitimacy upon which democratic constitutionalism rests and those values in the managerial and political approaches that are seen as legitimizing public administrative activity. Legitimacy in this context can be thought of as the belief on the part of the population that public administrators have a right to help make and implement public policy and to exercise political authority and discretion. Legitimacy is extremely important because it strongly fosters voluntary compliance or obedience to administrative directives and decisions. In its absence, the political community would have to rely more upon authoritarian or highly coercive processes, often involving the use of physical force or terror by the government against the population.

According to the managerial approach, the legitimacy of public administrators' authority is derived from their politically neutral technical competence, their specialized expertise, and the rationality and law-bound quality of their processes. Following Max Weber, sometimes this is referred to as legitimacy based on the rational/legal quality of administrative operations.[18] The political approach seeks to base administrative legitimacy on the representativeness, responsiveness, and accountability of public administrators and agencies. The Constitution has a somewhat different emphasis. It promotes the principle that governmental legitimacy, including that involving the exercise of administrative power, rests upon the consent of the governed. The Founders provided that the Constitution itself would have to be ratified by special conventions in the states, rather than by the state legislatures. This would assure that the Constitution rested on popular consent, rather than on the consent of state governments. It also guarantees that each state will have a republican form of government. But consent, in this context, is not merely the agreement of a majority. An extraordinary majority may be required, as in the case of amending the Constitution or approval of treaties by the Senate. Moreover, constitutional principles and values seek to protect the fundamental rights of minorities from encroachment by majorities. In this sense, consent of the governed is intended to include even those groups or individuals that find themselves at odds with the majority of citizens. Their consent, too, is to be valued.

At this juncture, the differences between constitutional theory, on the one hand, and the managerial and political perspectives, on the other, are profound and reach to the very center of the concepts upon which the political system is based. Constitutional theory views the government as an outgrowth of a *contract* formed by "We the People." The contract, which is the Constitution, fixes limits on governmental power, as in the First Amendment's prohibition on "an establishment of religion." The managerial and political perspectives are less contractarian than utilitarian in their fundamental premises. They tend to favor the legitimization of governmental action on the basis of the greatest good of the greatest number, or upon a similar formulation of that principle which is often incorporated into their conceptions of the public interest. In practice, they tend to view legitimacy as based on performance rather than on adherence to the contractual terms of the Constitution alone. For the managerial perspective, such performance is efficient, economical, and effective government. For the political approach, performance is viewed in terms of the representativeness, responsiveness, and accountability of government to organized constituencies and/or to a majority of the people.

West Virginia State Board of Education v. *Barnette* (1943)[19] can serve as an example of these fundamental differences regarding legitimacy. The case involved a public school system's requirement that all students salute and pledge allegiance to the flag. The political and administrative rationale for the regulation was that it would promote feelings of loyalty toward the United States and a feeling of political community among students. The regulation was enforced with a two-pronged strategy. Students who refused to salute and say the pledge were expelled. If they were not placed in suitable private schools, their parents could face criminal charges for the truancy of their school-age children. This was obviously a heavy-handed strategy, but it could be considered effective and efficient. Given the potential penalties, it was likely that the pupils would at least say the pledge and possibly develop the proper feelings of patriotism. Politically, the measure was probably quite popular. It was wartime, patriotism and loyalty were considered desirable if not essential sentiments, and a majority of the state's population no doubt strongly supported the promotion of such feelings in the schools. Moreover, refusal to salute the flag and say the pledge could be taken as a sign of disrespect for the nation, the majority of citizens who supported it, and the armed forces who were risking their lives and sustaining heavy casualties to protect its liberty and independence. However, one group of citizens was opposed to the salute and pledge. These were Jehovah's Witnesses, who believed that engaging in the salute and pledge showed disrespect for their God and therefore violated their religion. Despite a decision just three years earlier to the contrary, the Supreme Court held that the compulsory flag salute and pledge violated the rights of a minority not only in terms of their religious freedom, but also because it tended to compel their support (consent) for the political system. In Justice Jackson's eloquent words, "If there is any fixed star in our constitutional constellation, it is that no official, high or petty, can prescribe what shall be orthodox in politics, nationalism, religion, or other matters of opinion or force citizens to confess by word or act their faith therein. If there are any circumstances which permit an exception, they do not now occur to us." The compulsory salute and pledge were unconstitutional because they compelled consent, something wholly antithetical to the Constitution's approach to governmental legitimacy.

Diversity Among the Citizenry

One of the most outstanding conflicts between managerially oriented public administration and constitutional values concerns the desirability of uniformity as opposed to diversity. The managerial perspective strongly supports uniformity in a broad range of administrative contexts. It relies on impersonality among public employees to assure that individual diversity in interpreting regulations and implementing programs is eliminated to the extent practicable. Max Weber saw this as the special virtue of bureaucracy and, accordingly, viewed bureaucrats as "cogs."[20] In related fashion, clients are turned into "cases," which can often be treated impersonally, and therefore, with relative uniformity. These aspects of the managerial approach were discussed in greater detail in Chapter 1. By contrast, the Constitution values diversity to a great extent. In some ways, the entire design of the constitutional scheme rests on the desire to maintain and promote diversity. Thus, in *Federalist Paper No. 10*, James Madison argued that a large, extended republican form of government would necessarily include so much social and economic diversity as to preclude the development of a majority faction, or a majority political group that was united by a common interest that was adverse to the good of the nation as a whole. In fact, he considered fostering diversity to be the first object of government. Additionally, the Constitution incorporates diversity in the sense of federalism, bicameralism, separation of powers, different modes of election and appointment for the constitutional branches, and different terms of office. This is partly intended to assure that the government will not be subject to complete overturn at the hands of a majority united only for a brief time by a common interest or passion.

The political approach to public administration tends to fall in between those two poles on the continuum from uniformity to diversity. It favors diversity to a considerable extent, but has a tendency to try to eliminate groups thought to be disloyal to the nation or subversive of its policy objectives. It also attempts to silence individuals whose opinions are considered dangerous to the political system. For example, the Communist party and its members have been subjected to a number of regulations and restrictions in public employment, labor union affairs, and other aspects of life that have never been even considered seriously as appropriate to apply to the Democratic or Republican parties or their members. On the other hand, the political approach seeks diversity in public administration as a means of providing representation and responsiveness to politically "acceptable" groups, such as farmers, union members, social groups, and trade associations.

Many Supreme Court decisions emphasize the constitutional value of diversity. For instance, in the Barnette case, discussed above, the Supreme Court pointed out that although the promotion of national unity is permissible, "individual freedom of mind" should be given preference to "officially disciplined uniformity" because history shows that "[t]hose who begin coercive elimination of dissent soon find themselves exterminating dissenters. Compulsory unification of opinion achieves only the unanimity of the graveyard." *Keyishian v. Board of Regents* (1967) presents another example.[21] There, a complicated New York State scheme for excluding persons with subversive ideas from its educational system was under challenge. The U.S. Supreme Court held that the regulations were too imprecise to withstand constitutional scrutiny because they excluded individuals who were not subversive as well as those who were. In the course of its ruling, the Court pointed out that

> Our Nation is deeply committed to safeguarding academic freedom, which is of transcendent value to all of us and not merely to the teachers concerned. That freedom is therefore a special concern of the First Amendment, which does not tolerate laws that cast a pall of orthodoxy over the classroom. . . . The classroom is peculiarly the "marketplace of ideas." The Nation's future depends upon leaders trained through wide exposure to that robust exchange of ideas which discovers truth "out of a multitude of tongues, [rather] than through any kind of authoritative selection."

According to this articulation of constitutional values and principles, diversity is absolutely critical to the nation's future. (See Box 11–2 for another test of constitutional values, this one involving freedom of religion.)

One of the serious problems with New York's regulations was that by following a combination of managerial and political concerns, the regulations allowed administrators to impute subversive ideas to individuals based upon their organizational affiliation rather than upon what those individuals actually said, wrote, or did. However, basing judgments on individual behavior as the Constitution preferred in this case could be expensive, since investigations and elaborate hearings might be required. Assessing an individual's behavior could also present difficulties for the political approach, as it could require a clear definition of "subversive." In the late 1940s and early 1950s, federal employees were considered loyalty or security risks on the basis of such beliefs as favoring racial equality, opposing the institution of marriage and female chastity, and agreeing that communism had some good features.[22] By the end of the 1960s, though, a definition of subversive that could cost one a teaching job would obviously have to be far more specific and lucid. Because the state would have difficulty coming up with such a definition, it followed the political approach in assuming that membership in a group gave all individuals similar beliefs and interests. Hence, membership in the Communist party was considered evidence of subversiveness. But, as the Court pointed out, this is impermissible, because it bars the employment of those who are members of the Communist party but personally do not support any of its alleged illegal or subversive objectives. Consequently, the regulatory scheme infringed on the exercise of legitimate First Amendment rights of belief and association.

BOX 11–2 Putting Constitutional Values in Public Administration: Public School and the Santería Faith

The Santería faith is a centuries-old African religion that originated with the Yoruba tribe of Nigeria and was brought to the Caribbean by slaves. About 50,000 people in southern Florida practice the religion, which involves initiation rights lasting three to four weeks. Initiation as a priestess takes place when the high priest determines it is time; it does not depend on age. A schoolgirl, whose age was given as eight or nine, missed a month of public school to undergo initiation rites. The Dade County (Florida) School Board has a policy that five or more unexcused absences in a semester precludes granting a student credit for classes. The school board first questioned whether the Santería faith could be considered a religion and then whether the pupil could be given initiation during the summer when classes were not in session. It received a legal opinion from an attorney to the effect that, "In this instance, the compulsory attendance laws must give way to the freedom of religion laws. We have concluded that an absence of up to a month is a religious necessity when a person is being initiated into the priesthood of the Santería." The board decided to excuse the absence and allow the girl to make up the schoolwork she missed. As another school board attorney put it, "You can't change Christmas to the weekend just because it doesn't fall on Sunday."

SOURCE: "School Case Backs an Ancient Ritual," *New York Times*, December 9, 1984, p. 84.

Freedom and Liberty

Constitutional values obviously place a very great emphasis on individual freedom and liberty. According to one view of constitutional theory, perhaps the dominant view, individual freedom and liberty are antecedent to the Constitution. Since freedom and liberty existed prior to the creation of the constitutional government in 1789, they are provided both specific and general protections against governmental encroachment in the Bill of Rights. The Ninth Amendment in particular makes this point: "The enumeration in the Constitution, of certain rights, shall not be construed to deny or disparage others retained by the people." Rights to freedom and liberty therefore do not come from the Constitution, they are merely recognized by it as aspects of life that lie outside the legitimate realm of the exercise of governmental power. This is not to say they are "absolute"; they can be abridged or infringed when the government has an overriding, compelling need to do so. But the burden will fall upon the government to show that it does, in fact, have such a need and that the means chosen are the least damaging to the exercise of protected constitutional rights.

This approach is frequently at odds with public administration in either the managerial or political perspectives. Public administration, as we have seen, provides both services and constraints. It is often involved in direct or indirect regulation and consequently enforces limits on the freedom and liberty of individuals. Such constraints, of course, are considered in the public interest, as they are generally intended to promote the public's security, safety, health, welfare, and/or the political and economic viability of the nation. The conflict between constitutional values and principles on the one side and public administration on the other, therefore, is typically over means, not ends.

There are many dramatic examples of this conflict. The Keyishian decision, reviewed above, is one. There, the Supreme Court had little quarrel with the state's overall objective of barring subversive teachers from the public educational system. The issue was over the means, which the Court found inappropriate because they compromised individual freedoms and liberty too much. A very intriguing additional example can be found in *Shelton* v. *Tucker* (1960).[23] There, the Supreme Court declared unconstitutional an Arkansas statute requiring every teacher, as a condition of employment in a state-supported school or college, to file "annually an affidavit listing without limitation every organization to which he has belonged or regularly contributed within the preceding five years." The state's purpose in seeking this information was somewhat unclear. The act was based on the desire "to provide assistance in the administration and financing of the public schools" and to help resolve problems involved in responding to the Supreme Court's school desegregation decisions. There was no stated desire to fire teachers based on their organizational affiliations, and it appears that only refusal to submit the affidavit would be clear cause for action against the employee. In other words, on the face of it at least, all the state wanted was to know to which organizations its teachers belonged. On the other hand, there was some reason to believe that teachers belonging to the NAACP might be victimized as a result of the regulation. While recognizing that the state had a legitimate interest in promoting the fitness and competence of its teachers, the Court found that the act placed too much of a strain on the right to freedom of association which, in the Court's words, "lies at the foundation of a free society." This was because the "breadth" of abridgement of constitutional rights "must be viewed in the light of less drastic means for achieving the same basic purpose." Less drastic and more appropriate means, in this case, for promoting competence and fitness would have been to ask certain teachers or even all teachers about *certain* of their organizational affiliations, or about the number of organizations to which they belonged. But to ask *every* teacher about *every* organization was simply too great an impairment of teachers' freedom of association.

The Shelton case is pertinent because it illustrates three constitutional principles relating to freedom and liberty that serve as constraints on public administrative action:

1. *Chilling effect.* Although the regulation involved did not prohibit or punish association, it had the tendency to deter the free exercise of the right to association. This was particularly true because the statute did not prohibit public disclosure and placed heavy "pressure upon a teacher to avoid any ties which might displease those who control his professional destiny. . . ." In other words, the teacher's ardor for freedom of association would be "chilled."

2. *Overbreadth*. As noted above, a regulation that abridges or chills one's exercise of constitutional rights must be narrowly drawn so that it does not unnecessarily infringe upon legitimate activity. A regulation is overly broad if, in the process of legitimately constraining some activities, it gratuitously infringes upon others protected by the Constitution. In *Shelton*, for example, if the state were concerned that some of its teachers belonged to so many organizations that they did not have enough time left to devote to the proper performance of their professional duties, it could have simply inquired about with how many associations the teachers were affiliated. If the state were concerned about membership in certain organizations, it could have asked directly about those. Its scheme, however, had the tendency to deter membership in legitimate organizations for fear of public disclosure or reprisal by the state's educational system.

3. *The least restrictive alternative*. Overbreadth deters the exercise of legitimate rights upon which the government has no compelling need or reason to place restrictions. The least restrictive alternative principle accepts the state's legitimate need to deal with an area of behavior, but requires that the state do so in the fashion that constitutes the least practicable infringement upon protected rights. In other words, in *Shelton*, could the state have found a means of promoting competence and fitness that was less of an invasion of constitutionally protected freedom of association? From the managerial perspective, the answer is "yes, but"—it could prove to be expensive, inefficient, and time-consuming. For instance, one alternative that would be very much less restrictive would have been to identify teachers whose competence and fitness were marginal, and then inquire of those teachers only whether they had extensive organizational affiliations that were diverting their attention from their professional performance. To do so, however, would require elaborate administrative means of measuring fitness and competence and hearings or investigations to ascertain the amount of time and nature of commitment a teacher devoted to his or her organizational memberships. From the managerial perspective toward public administration, it was more satisfactory to achieve this in reverse: find out to which organizations every teacher belongs, and then identify teachers whose performance might be improved if they abandoned some of their affiliations.

The principles of "chilling effect," "overbreadth," and "least restrictive alternative" have emerged in a great number of cases involving the constitutionality of public administrative action. Consequently, it is important to emphasize that for the public administrator who seeks to adhere to constitutional values, they are guides rather than barriers to effective action. They do not prohibit the attainment of legitimate ends through public administrative action. Rather, they stand for the general view that freedom and liberty are so valuable that they should not be compromised more than is absolutely necessary to accomplish such an end.

Property Rights

Property, like liberty, is highly valued by the Constitution. In fact, the due process clauses of the Fifth and Fourteenth Amendments rank life, liberty, and property alongside one another and afford them all protection from arbitrary, invidious, or capricious governmental encroachment. Like liberty, property has frequently been considered anterior to the formation of the constitutional government. Property and property rights existed prior to 1789 and the adoption of the Constitution is not typically seen as infringing upon them. On the contrary, the Constitution is generally viewed as affording them governmental protection. In the past, political theorists sometimes considered "liberty" and "property" as almost interchangeable or codeterminate. For example, James Madison once wrote that property exists not only in land and possessions but also in opinions, religious principles, and general liberty.[24] Moreover, he viewed property as an important factor in the development of individual personality and political preferences. As in the case of liberty, though, property rights are not absolute: private property can be taken for public use, although just compensation should be provided. Similarly, searches and seizures of personal property can be undertaken by government, but only after a warrant is issued or the circumstances are such that there is constitutionally sufficient reason for them.

Historically, public administration has from time to time encroached upon established property rights. But it has only been during the past two decades that the concept of property became a serious limitation on a wide range of public administrative activity. During the 1960s and 1970s, the idea took hold that governmental benefits (or largess), such as welfare payments, occupational licenses, and public housing, should be considered a form of "new property" and afforded constitutional protection.[25] Perhaps no case made this clearer than *Goldberg* v. *Kelly* (1970).[26] The issue was whether New York City could terminate welfare benefits to an individual without first affording him a full evidentiary hearing. The city did provide seven days' prior notice and an opportunity to respond in writing. For a majority on the Supreme Court, however, more due process was required. In the course of its opinion, the Court observed that "it may be realistic today to regard welfare entitlements as more like 'property' than a 'gratuity.' Much of the existing wealth in this country takes the form of rights that do not fall within the traditional common-law concepts of property." The emergence of this "new property" interpretation is made clear by Justice Black's vigorous dissent: "The Court . . . in effect says that the failure of the government to pay a promised charitable installment to an individual deprives that individual of *his own property*, in violation of the Due Process Clause of the Fourteenth Amendment. It somewhat strains credulity to say that the government's promise of charity to an individual is property belonging to that individual when the government denies that the individual is honestly entitled to receive such a payment." Black went on to observe that "the procedure required today as a matter of constitutional law finds no precedent in our legal system."

The current constitutional concept that governmental benefits or largess, including much of public employment,[27] are a form of "new property" to be afforded constitutional protection is an example of how the Constitution can be adapted to changing circumstances. The more dependent individuals became on the largess of the administrative or welfare state, the more they needed protection from arbitrary, invidious, or capricious treatment by it. By considering largess to be a form of property, the individual who receives or is entitled to it has a constitutional right to due process if the government seeks to withhold it. From a managerial perspective, due process is an expensive, ineffective, and inefficient means of organizing and implementing public administration. Nevertheless, due process is now required in a wide range of administrative actions dealing with the distribution of benefits or largess.

Procedural Due Process

As noted many times throughout this text, procedural due process is fundamental to the legal approach to public administration. It is also a constitutional value of great importance. Although it requires different kinds and amounts of procedural protections for individuals, depending upon the nature of the governmental action involved and the individual interest at stake, procedural due process seeks to assure fundamental fairness when the government is taking action that will injure a specific individual. It has been described in many ways on different occasions by the Supreme Court. One such statement in the administrative context was presented in *Greene* v. *McElroy* (1959):

> Certain principles have remained relatively immutable in our jurisprudence. One of these is that where governmental action seriously injures an individual, and the reasonableness of the action depends on fact findings, the evidence used to prove the Government's case must be disclosed to the individual so that he has an opportunity to show that it is untrue. While this is important in the case of documentary evidence, it is even more important where the evidence consists of the testimony of individuals whose memory might be faulty or who, in fact, might be perjurers or persons motivated by malice, vindictiveness, intolerance, prejudice, or jealousy. We have formalized these protections in the requirements of confrontation and cross-examination. They have ancient roots. They find expression in the Sixth Amendment. . . . This Court has been zealous to protect these rights from erosion. It has spoken out not only in criminal cases, . . . but also in all types of cases where administrative . . . actions were under scrutiny.[28]

But since procedural due process is a flexible concept, it can require more or less protection depending upon the administrative context. This can be quite frustrating for public administrators, who may be uncertain as to what kinds of procedures to establish in different circumstances. However, some constitutional principles appear to be reasonably well settled:

1. The individual whose interests are likely to be injured by the governmental denial or cutoff of benefits, such as welfare, social security, public school attendance, or public employment, is entitled to advance *notice* of the proposed action.

2. The individual will have a chance to *respond* in writing or orally.

3. Depending on the nature of the action, the individual may have a right to a full-fledged *administrative hearing* prior to governmental implementation of the proposed action. The test here is likely to be threefold: (a) The ability of the individual to pursue the hearing after the benefit is cut off is considered. In *Goldberg* v. *Kelly*, it was reasoned by the Court that an individual whose welfare benefits were cut off *prior* to a hearing was deprived of the means to live while pursuing his appeal; but in *Mathews* v. *Eldridge* (1976), the Court reasoned that someone receiving Social Security disability benefits was not entitled to a hearing prior to termination since the benefits were not based, strictly speaking, on financial need or distress.[29] (b) A prior hearing is more likely when there is a high risk that without it the deprivation of benefits will be based on erroneous judgments or purported facts. (c) The extent of financial and administrative burden thrust upon the government by prior hearings in the category of cases at issue is considered.

4. The individual generally has a right to a post-termination hearing, if no prior hearing is afforded.

5. Depending on the interests at stake, the individual may have the rights to *confrontation*, *cross-examination*, to be represented by an *attorney* (at least, at one's own expense), and *to bring witnesses* on one's behalf before an *impartial governmental decision maker*, such as an administrative law judge or hearing examiner. In some instances, due process may require that the hearing be open to the press and public. It is important to remember, however, that an administrative hearing is required only where there is a question of fact involved. If both parties agree on the facts, a hearing is not necessary, since its primary purpose is to establish the truth about some set of circumstances.[30]

The constitutional principle that procedural due process of some degree applies to deprivations of the "new property" has been a major factor in the "judicialization" of much of public administration. Welfare and public housing agencies, Social Security Administration, occupational licensing boards, and many other types of agencies have had to revamp their administrative procedures to accommodate this constitutional value. Public personnel administration has also been deeply affected by it (see Chapter 5). Moreover, accommodating due process has been expensive and sometimes inefficient and ineffective as a means of reducing fraud, preventing the distribution of benefits to individuals who are legally ineligible to receive them, and removing unfit public employees. The Supreme Court has not been oblivious to the administrative costs but, on the whole, has sought to protect individuals from harm through arbitrary, capricious, invidious, or patently unfair administrative actions.

Equal Protection

The Fourteenth Amendment provides that no state shall "deny to any person within its jurisdiction the equal protection of the laws." It has been held that *equal protection* is within the meaning of the "liberty" protected in the Fifth Amendment and therefore applies to the federal government as well.[31] The original purpose of the Fourteenth Amendment's equal protection clause, ratified in 1868, was, at least, to protect freed slaves and blacks generally in the South. Whether those who drafted it expected more is now a moot point. Today, constitutional values and principles dictate broad application of the clause. An elaborate scheme for determining what is required has been developed.

Classifications   It is often desirable or necessary in matters of public policy to classify people according to economic, social, demographic, or other characteristics. For instance, taxpayers may be classified by the amount of income they earn; individuals may be classified by age, veteran status, education, and geographic residence, citizenship, or alienage. They can also be classified by race, color, religion, gender, or national origin (ethnicity). Over the years, the Supreme Court has developed a "two-tier" approach to dealing with classifications of individuals. Some classifications are called "suspect" because, on their face, they appear to be used to deny individuals equal protection of the law or to discriminate invidiously against them. When a classification is suspect, the burden of proof is on the government to demonstrate that the categorization serves a compelling state interest or is not invidious, that is, not intended to demean or harm a group.[32] This is difficult though possible to do, and the courts will apply very "strict scrutiny" to the state's rationale in order to assure the classification is fully appropriate. At present, classifications based on race, religion, or ethnicity (though not necessarily citizenship) are generally suspect. For example, a law specifically barring members of a racial group from public employment or a profession would be suspect. Other classifications are "nonsuspect"; there is no apparent reason to believe that they violate equal protection. Here all the state has to do, when challenged, is to show that there is a "rational basis" for the classification. Age is an example. Compulsory education laws may apply to children between ages of, say, six and fourteen. The states may afford others the opportunity for public education, but they are not *required* to attend a state-approved school. Age-based mandatory retirement laws in the public service have also been treated as nonsuspect classifications and subjected to the rational basis test.[33]

As cultural and political values change, it is possible for a classification that was once considered "nonsuspect" to be treated as "suspect." It appears that this is occurring with gender-based classifications today.[34] Previously, legislation treating women and men differently was common. Often the purpose was allegedly to "protect" women, but the result was to place barriers in the path of their employment, property rights, and educational and other opportunities. Society is now far more cognizant of unequal treatment of women, and the courts have begun to take a deeper look at gender-based classifications. In particular, the courts have "invalidated statutes employing gender as an inaccurate proxy for other, more germane bases of classification."[35] Eventually, such classifications may be considered just as suspect as those based on race, and require a compelling state interest and be subject to strict scrutiny.

Discriminatory Purpose   Many governmental regulations do not actually establish classifications, but they tend to have a harsher impact on one social group than another. For example, the Supreme Court speculated that this may be true of "a whole range of tax, welfare, public service, regulatory, and licensing statutes that may be more burdensome to the poor and to the average black than to the more affluent white."[36] Such regulations are not considered in violation of equal protection unless a discriminatory purpose can be shown. In the Court's words, "Our cases have not embraced the proposition that a law or other official act, without regard to whether it reflects a racially discriminatory purpose, is unconstitutional *solely* because it has a racially disproportionate impact."[37] Rather, a purpose to discriminate must be present if the regulation is to be found in violation of equal protection. Such a purpose does not have to be "express or appear on the face of the statute" and it "may often be inferred from the totality of the relevant facts, including the fact . . . that the law bears more heavily on one race than another."[38] In short, the disproportionately harsh impact of a regulation on members of one racial or other social group is not enough to demonstrate a violation of equal protection. This was made evident in *Personnel Administrator of Massachusetts* v. *Feeney* (1979), in which the Supreme Court found that a veterans' preference system in state employment strongly favored males over females but did not actually establish a gender-based classification, either overtly or covertly, and was not intended to discriminate against women.[39] Consequently, the preference was not considered unconstitutional.

In terms of public administration, there is more to the equal protection clause than may be immediately apparent. The constitutional values and principles of equal protection tend to establish a different kind of "rationality" than that inherent in either the managerial or political approaches to public administration. This was perhaps best illustrated by the case of *Craig* v. *Boren* (1976).[40] In an effort to promote traffic safety, Oklahoma adopted a statute that prohibited the sale of "3.2 percent" beer to males under the age of twenty-one. Females could purchase it at the age of eighteen. The state's rationale was that statistical evidence indicated that males in the eighteen-to-twenty age bracket were more prone than females of the same age to be involved in alcohol-related driving offenses. These statistics were not overwhelmingly convincing—one survey found that of all those arrested in Oklahoma for driving while intoxicated, 0.18 percent of the group were females aged eighteen to twenty, whereas 2 percent of the group were males in the same age bracket. Nevertheless, this finding seemed to support what was taken to be common knowledge: namely, that males of this age were more of a threat on the road than their female cohorts. From a managerial perspective, therefore, the regulation appeared sensible. It would be more expensive, inefficient, and less effective to arrest intoxicated eighteen- to twenty-year-old males for driving offenses than simply to seek to reduce the likelihood that they would be driving while drunk at all by making it more difficult for them to obtain the 3.2 percent beer. Similarly, the political perspective supported the notion of aggregating all the males of this age into a group, and then addressing the circumstances of the group as a whole through legislation. From both perspectives the regulation was considered in the public interest because it promoted the public safety, especially that of the eighteen- to twenty-year-old males.

In assessing the regulation from the perspectives of constitutional values and principles, the Supreme Court reached a startlingly different conclusion. In a key paragraph, the Court's majority opinion attacked both the managerial and political approaches: "Proving broad sociological propositions by statistics is a dubious business, and one that inevitably is in tension with the normative philosophy that underlies the Equal Protection Clause. Suffice to say that the showing offered by the [state] does not satisfy us that sex represents a legitimate, accurate proxy for the regulation of drinking and driving." Here we see two very important constitutional principles at work. First, "sociological propositions" that create or are derived from social classifications, such as male/female or black/white, are disfavored by the equal protection clause because they inherently tend to suggest that public policy should treat different social groups differently. In other words, they suggest that different opportunities should be afforded to or different restrictions imposed on distinct social groups. Ideally, the principle of the equal protection clause would be that no such classifications should be made in the public sector because the classifications themselves are too broad to guarantee equal protection to each and every individual within them. Justice Stevens made this point in a concurring opinion in *Craig* when he protested against the unfairness of treating all eighteen- to twenty-year-old males "as inferior to their female counterparts." Certainly, there must be some males in that age group who could handle both 3.2 percent beer and driving. Moreover, some males of that age do not have driver's licenses and do not drive. Why should eighteen-year-old female drivers be afforded the right to buy 3.2 percent beer while it is denied to twenty-year-old male nondrivers? The latter are clearly less threatening to traffic safety than the former.

The second constitutional principle evident in the Court's opinion is that the legislative or administrative classifications based on social groups must at least be accurate proxies for the regulation of the behavior with which the state is concerned. In particular, relying on stereotypes as the basis for such regulations is unacceptable under the equal protection clause. For example, it is not enough to assume that everybody knows teenage males in Oklahoma are wild "cowboys." If the state wants to treat them differently than teenage females, it has to demonstrate that the quality of being male is substantially related to the achievement of particular legitimate public policy objectives. Here, then, is a place where solid policy analysis and constitutional law demand the same thing— an accurate understanding of the behavior of the target group. In fact, the Supreme Court suggested that such social classifications would have to rest on "predictive empirical relationships." Of course, even then, the classification could be unconstitutional if it were invidious to a racial, religious, or ethnic group.

Thus, the constitutional values and principles associated with equal protection provide public administrators with a difficult challenge. In a nation with a heterogeneous population, such as the United States, the classification of social groups has long been deeply ingrained in the culture. Private individuals and public policy have traditionally used such classifications as proxies for knowing how to act and what to do. For instance, in *Baker* v. *City of St. Petersburg* (1968), a police chief used the race of police officers as a proxy for being able to get along with citizens of the same race and to engage in efficient and effective police work.[41] In *U.S.* v. *Brignoni-Ponce*[42] (see Chapter 8), "looking Mexican" was taken as a proxy for the likelihood of being an illegal alien. Consequently, what the Supreme Court is saying in *Craig* v. *Boren* is nothing less than that the equal protection clause demands that we change our style of thinking. Classification by social group is viewed by the Constitution as inherently undesirable. What is the alternative?

Individuality

Constitutional values and principles prefer to look at individuals as individuals per se rather than as members of legislative classifications or categorical statistical groups. Class-action suits are entertained by the courts, but judges sometimes go to considerable pains to assure that such a class actually exists and that the individual or organization litigating the suit is truly a representative of it. Perhaps public sector mandatory maternity leave cases best illustrate the constitutional emphasis on individuality in the public administrative context.[43] School systems, acting on the basis of managerial values, sought to establish a systematic procedure for replacing pregnant schoolteachers. In particular, the schools wanted ample notice of when the teachers would no longer be able to fulfill their professional responsibilities. This would enable principals to plan ahead for the hiring of permanent substitutes or other replacements. Allowing the pregnant teacher to determine when she was no longer able to teach classes might provide too short notice to make adequate arrangements for the continuation of her classes. The regulations at issue in the cases reaching the Supreme Court required pregnancy leaves to begin in the fourth and fifth months of pregnancy. The Court found that these regulations infringed upon the constitutionally protected liberty to make personal choices regarding matters of marriage and family. It also found the regulations to be irrational because if the fourth or fifth month of a teacher's pregnancy occurred toward the very end of the school year, then mandatory maternity leaves would actually disrupt the continuity of teaching, since many teachers would be medically able to continue well beyond that time. The infringement on liberty and the irrationality of the regulations, when coupled together, violated constitutional values and principles in the Court's view. Rather, it suggested, either mandatory leaves should commence very late in the term of a normal pregnancy (during the eighth month) or leaves should be based on an *individualized* medical determination of a pregnant teacher's ability to perform her professional responsibilities. In either event, of course, the school systems might not receive adequate notice of when the teacher's leave would begin, but the Court stressed the importance of treating the individual as an individual, rather than part of a group, in these circumstances. In short, in many cases, the constitutional value of individuality is likely to outweigh the administrative burdens it imposes.

Equity

Equity is a final constitutional value that should be mentioned. It is generally thought of as "the power to dispense with the harsh rigor of general laws in particular cases."[44] In other words, where following the law to the letter would result in an obviously unfair or unreasonable resolution of a case, equity allows an exception to be made. Equity also enables the judiciary to develop *remedies* for breaches of constitutional rights, even though such remedies are not specifically provided for in any statutes. For example, the federal judiciary has ordered "forced busing" as a means of desegregating school systems that unconstitutionally separated students by race.[45] It has also fashioned "quota" hiring and promotional systems to remedy racial discrimination in public personnel administration.[46] Although the Constitution provides that the judicial power shall "extend to all cases, in law and equity," it is sometimes now contended that the judiciary has used its powers in equity to virtually transform the Constitution into "an omnibus piece of legislation."[47] Such criticism notwithstanding, public administrators should recognize that contemporary constitutional values are unlikely to tolerate harsh and unfair results in particular cases dictated by rigidly strict adherence to laws and precedents. Administrators may prefer to "go by the book" and avoid making exceptions, even when they seem appropriate. The Constitution, however, is less willing to do so. When combined, equity and the value and principles of procedural due process dictate procedures and substantive results of public administrative action that are considered fundamentally fair. This is true even if these procedures and results cause inefficiency, added expense, hamper effectiveness in some sense, or are politically unpopular. Perhaps the best example is quota hiring in the public sector as a remedy for past racial discrimination. For those espousing the managerial perspective, this is a breach of merit principles that is viewed as promoting inefficiency by bringing less qualified individuals into the civil service. Politically, such quotas have been a matter of contention for over a decade. Yet they have been widely imposed through the federal courts' powers in equity.

SYNTHESIS: AN ONGOING PARTNERSHIP

Constitutional values and principles have often stood at odds with those of public administration. Today, however, both the judiciary and public managers are more frequently realizing that there is a need for them to develop an ongoing partnership.[48] More searching judicial review of administrative action and the development of far greater personal and agency liabilities for public administrators who violate individuals' constitutional or legal rights have forced public administrators to be aware of and responsive to constitutional values and principles. As judges have become more involved in administrative activity themselves, through overseeing the management of public institutions, such as schools, mental health facilities, and prisons, they have recognized the worth of some public administrative values and the practical constraints of administrative action. It was once taken virtually for granted by judges that they could bring these institutions up to constitutional standards by issuing decrees or directly involving the court in their day-to-day management. In retrospect, most would probably now recognize that this attitude was too optimistic.[49] Their decrees and redesigns of public school systems have sometimes been frustrated by "white flight," or the withdrawal of white students from the school systems. Their orders for reforms of prison and mental health facilities have likewise foundered upon the very unmanageability of those institutions. Thus, after a decade or so of a relatively high degree of confrontation between public administrators and judges, both sides are now gaining a greater appreciation of the values and perspectives of the other.

This can be clearly seen in the cases of public administrators who seek to avoid liability. Just one example from the judiciary makes the point as well. In *Mathews* v. *Eldridge* (1976), Justice Powell, joined by Justices White, Blackmun, Rehnquist, and Chief Justice Burger, wrote:

> Financial cost alone is not a controlling weight in determining whether due process requires a particular procedural safeguard prior to some administrative decision. But the Government's interest, and hence that of the public, in conserving scarce fiscal and administrative resources is a factor that must be weighed. At some point the benefit of an additional safeguard to the individual affected by the administrative action and to society in terms of increased assurance that the action is just, may be outweighed by the cost.[50]

He also argued that calculations of the public interest must be aware of any serious "administrative burden" they impose.

The remarkable feature of American constitutional law is its adaptive quality. The Constitution is a living document. Drafted in the horse-and-buggy age, it has survived through the Industrial Revolution, the rise of the contemporary administrative state and the consequent transformation of governmental structure and role, and continues with us into the postindustrial era. There is little doubt that its values and principles will be more completely synthesized with those of public administration in the future. Public administrators and judges have no choice but to make their partnership work, and they have the means to do so—for it depends primarily upon both exercising their powers of reason.

NOTES

1. Immigration and Naturalization Service v. Chadha, 462 U.S. 919 (1983).
2. Dwight Waldo, *The Administrative State*, 2nd ed. (New York: Holmes and Meier, 1984), p. xviii.
3. Woodrow Wilson, "The Study of Administration," *Political Science Quarterly*, 56 (December 1941): 481–506, at p. 484. (Original copyright, 1887.)
4. Ibid., p. 504.
5. Smith v. Wade, 461 U.S. 31 (1983).
6. Quoted in Walter Murphy and C. Herman Pritchett, *Courts, Judges, and Politics* (New York: Random House, 1961), p. 27.
7. Minersville School District v. Gobitis, 310 U.S. 586 (1940); West Virginia State Board of Education v. Barnette, 319 U.S. 624 (1943).
8. National League of Cities v. Usery, 426 U.S. 833 (1976); Equal Employment Opportunity Commission v. Wyoming, 460 U.S. 226 (1983); Garcia v. San Antonio Metropolitan Transit Authority, 469 U.S. 528 (1985).
9. *Federalist Paper No. 51*, in Clinton Rossiter, ed., *The Federalist Papers* (New York: Mentor, 1961), pp. 321–322.
10. American Federation of Government Employees v. Phillips, 358 F. Supp. 60 (1973).
11. Governor Snelling of Vermont, quoted in the *Burlington Free Press*, July 24, 1983, p. 1.
12. Immigration and Naturalization Service v. Chadha, 462 U.S. 919 (1983).
13. Ibid., at pp. 957–958.
14. Hobson v. Hansen, 265 F. Supp. 902; 269 F. Supp. 401 (1967). For an analysis, see Donald Horowitz, *The Courts and Social Policy* (Washington, D.C.: Brookings Institution, 1977), chap. 4.
15. Horowitz, *Courts and Social Policy*, chap. 4.
16. Ibid., p. 116.
17. Peter Woll, *American Bureaucracy*, 2nd ed. (New York: Norton, 1977), p. 34.
18. Max Weber, *From Max Weber: Essays in Sociology*, trans. and ed. by H. H. Gerth and C. W. Mills (New York: Oxford University Press, 1958), chaps. 4 and 8.
19. West Virginia State Board of Education v. Barnette, 319 U.S. 624 (1943).
20. Weber, *Essays in Sociology*, p. 228.
21. Keyishian v. Board of Regents, 385 U.S. 589 (1967).
22. See David H. Rosenbloom, *Federal Service and the Constitution* (Ithaca, N.Y.: Cornell University Press, 1971), chap. 6.
23. Shelton v. Tucker, 364 U.S. 479 (1960).
24. See John Rohr, *Ethics for Bureaucrats* (New York: Marcel Dekker, 1978), p. 213.
25. Charles Reich, "The New Property," *Yale Law Journal*, 73 (1964): 733–787.
26. Goldberg v. Kelly, 397 U.S. 254 (1970).
27. See Cleveland Board of Education v. Loudermill, 470 U.S. 532 (1985), for a recent Supreme Court interpretation.
28. Greene v. McElroy, 360 U.S. 474, 496 (1959).
29. Mathews v. Eldridge, 424 U.S. 319 (1976).
30. Codd v. Velger, 429 U.S. 624 (1977).
31. Bolling v. Sharpe, 347 U.S. 497 (1954).
32. Morton v. Mancari, 417 U.S. 535 (1974).
33. Massachusetts Board of Retirement v. Murgia, 427 U.S. 307 (1976).
34. See Craig v. Boren, 429 U.S. 190 (1976).

35. Ibid., at p. 198.
36. Washington v. Davis, 426 U.S. 229, 248 (1976).
37. Ibid., p. 239.
38. Ibid., pp. 241–242.
39. Personnel Administrator of Massachusetts v. Feeney, 442 U.S. 256 (1979).
40. Craig v. Boren, 429 U.S. 190 (1976).
41. Baker v. City of St. Petersburg, 400 F.2d 294 (1968).
42. United States v. Brignoni-Ponce, 422 U.S. 873 (1975).
43. Cleveland Board of Education v. LaFleur; Cohen v. Chesterfield Co. School Board, 414 U.S. 632 (1974), argued and decided together.
44. Gary L. McDowell, *Equity and the Constitution* (Chicago: University of Chicago Press, 1982), p. 5.
45. Swann v. Charlotte-Mecklenburg Board of Education, 402 U.S. 1 (1971).
46. See David H. Rosenbloom and Carole C. Obuchowski, "Public Personnel Examinations and the Constitution: Emergent Trends," *Public Administration Review*, 37 (January/February 1977): 9–18, United States v. Paradise, 55 *Law Week* 4211 (1987).
47. Henry Abraham, Foreword, in McDowell, *Equity and the Constitution*, p. xi.
48. David L. Bazelon, "The Impact of the Courts on Public Administration," *Indiana Law Journal*, 52 (1976): 101–110, and David H. Rosenbloom, "Public Administrators and the Judiciary: the 'New Partnership,'" *Public Administration Review*, 47 (January/February 1987): 75–83.
49. See Donald Horowitz, "Decreeing Organizational Change: Judicial Supervision of Public Institutions," *Duke Law Journal*, 1983 (1983):1265–1307; Horowitz, *The Courts and Social Policy*; and M. Kay Harris and Dudley Spiller, Jr., *After Decision: Implementation of Judicial Decrees in Correctional Settings* (Washington, D.C.: Government Printing Office, 1977).
50. Mathews v. Eldridge, 424 U.S. 319, 348 (1976).

ADDITIONAL READING

BARRY, DONALD, AND HOWARD WHITCOMB. *The Legal Foundations of Public Administration.* St. Paul, Minn.: West, 1981.

CARTER, LIEF H. *Administrative Law and Politics.* Boston: Little, Brown, 1983.

COOPER, PHILLIP. *Public Law and Public Administration*, 2nd ed. Englewood Cliffs, N.J.: Prentice-Hall, 1988.

DAVIS, KENNETH CULP. *Administrative Law and Government*, 2nd ed. St. Paul, Minn.: West, 1975.

FREEDMAN, JAMES O. *Crisis and Legitimacy.* New York: Cambridge University Press, 1978.

ROSENBLOOM, DAVID H. *Public Administration and Law.* New York: Marcel Dekker, 1983.

WARREN, KENNETH. *Administrative Law in the American Political System.* St. Paul, Minn.: West, 1982.

STUDY QUESTIONS

1. Can you identify a few public policies that use a social attribute as a "proxy" for some behavioral or economic tendencies? How are you personally affected by such policies?

Are there any associated with age or gender that you find particularly desirable or undesirable from the perspectives of equal protection?

2. Do you think the development of "new property" and the greater emphasis on procedural due process have gone too far in protecting the interests of those receiving government assistance such as welfare benefits? Why or why not?

3. Should judges become involved in the management of: (a) prisons, (b) public mental health facilities, (c) public schools? If the answer is yes, what forms should their involvement take? In addressing these questions, what political and administrative aspects of such judicial involvement seem most troublesome to you?

CHAPTER 12 | *Accountability and Ethics*

Public administrators may be seen as the "guardians" of the contemporary administrative state. This raises a very fundamental issue in political thought: "Who guards the guardians?" Public administrators must be held accountable because there are aspects of their jobs that can lead to misconception of the public interest, corruption, and subversion. But there are also many aspects of public administration that make it difficult to attain a satisfactory level of accountability. This chapter will consider managerial, political, and legal perspectives on accountability and ethics. Ethics can be considered a form of self-accountability, or an "inner check" on public administrators' conduct. The various approaches are in many ways complementary to one another: the legal approach tends to favor the inner check; the managerial approach, a check that is external to the individual but internal to the agency; and the political approach, a check that is external to the agency and exercised through outside oversight of some kind. Many consider a new sense of professionalism, including perhaps a "code of ethics," to be a sensible means of helping the "guardians" to guard themselves.

Public administration has become an important locus of political power and influence in the United States. Public administrators, sometimes individually, but generally collectively, play an active role in the formulation of public policies. They also have a great deal to do with the style, pace, and tone of the execution of those policies. Out of this set of conditions arises a fundamental problem. If public administrators are in fact the "permanent branch" of government, the guardians of the long-term public interest, and the keepers of the public trust, then who guards the guardians? Or as Frederick Mosher puts the same question, "How does one square a permanent civil service—which neither the people by their vote nor their representatives by their appointments can replace—with the principle of government 'by the people'?"[1] To many concerned citizens and political authorities in nations throughout the world, this is the fundamental *political* issue presented by the development of the contemporary administrative state. However, it is also a central issue of modern management. As Victor Thompson has noted, the increasing specialization and technical expertise of subordinate employees have created a severe imbalance between the formal hierarchical authority and responsibility of high-level administrators, on the one hand, and their actual intellectual capacity to manage their "staff," on the other.[2] Accountability is also a legal matter. It concerns such questions as, "Who is liable for what?" and "What kinds of conduct are illegal?"

This chapter tackles the issue of assuring that public administrators do not violate their public trust. It discusses managerial, political, and legal perspectives on accountability and ethics. Ethics are considered an internal, personal check; accountability is the process of applying external checks on public administrators. Since the accountability of public administrators is truly a worldwide concern, it is worth taking some time to consider precisely why public administrators might abuse their public trust and act in ways not considered by the citizenry and/or political authorities to be in the public interest.

WHY THE GUARDIANS NEED GUARDING

Although American public administration is generally considered exceptionally honest and able by world standards, one can point to three main types of factors that can impel public administrators to violate their public trust. One concerns misconception of the public interest; another, corruption; and the third, subversion.

Misconception of the Public Interest

There are several forces frequently at work in public administration that could lead civil servants to misconceive or misconstrue the public interest. First, there are social forces. Public administrators, especially in the higher-level, more complex, and typically more politically influential jobs, may not constitute a social group that is representative of the nation's population as a whole. At the very least, they are likely to be disproportionately drawn from the ranks of the middle class.[3] They may, in some cases, as was true in the United States during the early years of the present republic, come heavily from the upper class. The social class basis of the civil service is important because it colors perceptions of how people live, what their problems are, and what they want and need. It also is an important element in the creation of individual and group values and norms of proper behavior. To a very considerable extent, one's world view is likely to be influenced by one's social attributes. As Seymour Martin Lipset notes, "The behavior of government bureaucrats varies with the nongovernmental social background and interest of those controlling the bureaucratic structure."[4] Importantly, in this regard there are rarely neutral categories: one is born female or male; to one race or ethnicity or another; to a social class. Overall, in comparison to the nation's general population, public administrators in the United States are thought to be disproportionately middle class, and in the upper levels of public services, to be disproportionately white and male.[5]

A second factor that can lead public administrators to misconceive the public interest is an artifact of their specialization. In the simplest sense, public administrators—like others who perform a highly specialized function—may eventually develop a very narrow outlook concerning the public interest. They may tend to exaggerate the importance of what they do and downgrade the importance of what others do. They may also develop ways of thinking that make it difficult to understand alternative approaches or to recognize the dominance or even the legitimacy of competing values. There are many well-known instances of this in American life. Lawyers, for example, sometimes successfully defend individuals who they know are guilty of horrible crimes. Their rationale is that everyone is entitled to the best defense possible and that our system of justice cannot properly function otherwise. For the layman, however, it may be somewhat more difficult to find a moral distinction between one who, for example, aids a child rapist to escape from the scene of the crime and the lawyer who uses the technical rules of evidence to get him off after an arrest has been made. Similarly, public health administrators, imbued with professional values emphasizing economy, have been known to authorize the routine nighttime drugging of patients to reduce staffing costs. Although such practice is medically undesirable and potentially dangerous, it can be seen as desirable from narrow administrative perspectives concerned with cutting costs. Public administrators who deal with a particular type of client or population may eventually come to view them as truly representative of the population as a whole or of "human nature" in general. Police in urban settings are so accustomed to dealing with hard-core criminals, prostitutes, and sexual and other deviants that they may develop a distorted sense of the public.

These are familiar patterns that affect the thinking of individuals in some specialized job settings, including those in the civil service. They are augmented by various kinds of socialization at work. In bureaucracies socialization is often thought to be an extremely important mechanism of inculcating values in employees and consequently influencing their on-the-job behavior. For instance, Anthony Downs argues that bureaucracies develop **bureau ideologies** that tout their virtues. He maintains that every bureau ideology:

1. Emphasizes the positive benefits of the bureau's activities and de-emphasizes their costs;
2. indicates that further expansion of the bureau's services would be desirable and any curtailment thereof would be undesirable;
3. emphasizes the benefits that the bureau provides for the society as a whole, rather than its services to particular "special interests";
4. stresses the high present level of the bureau's efficiency; [and]
5. emphasizes its achievements and future capabilities and ignores or minimizes its failures and inabilities.[6]

Moreover, in his view, these ideologies are imparted to the bureaucracy's key employees because "all officials exhibit relatively strong loyalty to the organization controlling their job security and promotion."[7] When taken together, administrative specialization and socialization can be extremely important in coloring the public administrator's world view. Thus, we are all accustomed to educators, military officials, and urban development, health, and other public administrators considering their functions to be the most crucial to the future welfare of society.

A close relationship with a particular clientele group or constituency is another factor that can lead public administrators to misconstrue the public interest. As noted in Chapter 2, the development of the American administrative state was partly an outgrowth of clientelism. Different economic interests and social groups sought the establishment of government agencies to promote their interests. Sometimes, however, this process has led the agency to confuse the interests of the clientele or constituency with the public interest and to act as an advocate of those interests. Moreover, public administrators in such agencies may mistakenly consider the interest groups with which they deal to be wholly representative of all individuals in the economic sectors or social groups involved. Joseph LaPalombara has referred to this condition as a "clientela"[8] relationship in which "an interest group, for whatever reasons, succeeds in becoming in the eyes of a given administrative agency, the natural expression and representative of a given social sector which, in turn, constitutes the natural target or reference point for the activity of the administrative agency."[9] In the United States, relationships along these lines often form the basis of "iron triangles" among interest groups, administrative bureaus, and legislative committees that may view the public interest with acute tunnel vision.

The pressures of social background, specialization by function and bureau, and clientele relationships can have an important impact on the world view of public administrators in a wide variety of settings. They may lead public administrators to misconceive the public interest. However, they become acutely problematic if they develop into obsessions that tend to drive other, more balanced, perspectives out of administrative decision making and implementation. When this occurs, the violation of public trust may be very substantial. Examples are so numerous as to make the need for constant attention to accountability obvious. One outstanding case occurred in conjunction with the testing of nuclear weapons in Nevada from 1951 to 1963. The Atomic Energy

Commission persisted in such tests even though "enough was known by scientists, engineers, and policymakers in the AEC to indicate that there was some danger to animate things that came into contact with the effects of the blast" from these tests.[10] Impelled by its limited perspectives and overwhelming commitment to the development of nuclear weaponry and power, the AEC endangered people and farm animals with its tests. Furthermore, it lied and engaged in a cover-up to the extent of perpetrating a "fraud" upon a federal court hearing a suit against the federal government for damages due to the alleged killing of thousands of sheep in Utah by radioactive fallout. The AEC maintained that the sheep deaths were the result of "unprecedented cold weather" and natural diseases—even though its experts knew better.[11] In the context of the Cold War, perhaps the AEC and nuclear weaponry were reasonably perceived as the guardians of the nation against "the communist threat," but who guards the guardians? More recently, the Iran-Contra affair revealed that high-ranking officials in the Executive Office of the President were so committed to funding the Contras that they were willing to violate the law in order to do so. They saw themselves as guardians of the national interest, which they thought Congress had misunderstood. In the end, though, their actions harmed and embarrassed the United States.

Corruption

Corruption can be defined as a betrayal of the public trust for reasons of private interest. By many accounts, corruption in public administration is virtually a worldwide phenomenon and limitation on the ability of public administrative systems to accomplish some of the tasks assigned to them. To mention only a few examples, during the Vietnam War, forces in both North and South Vietnam publicly complained that "bureaucratic corruption" was hampering their efforts; in both the Soviet Union and the United States, the "bash the bureaucrat" syndrome prevails, and examples of administrative corruption are ferreted out by the press and publicly denounced by officials; in many countries throughout the world, corruption in the form of bribery and the use of personal contacts has literally become institutionalized, and "baksheesh," "la mordida," "la bustarella," "speed money," "dash," and "protekzia" are considered as common a way of dealing with bureaucrats as filling out forms.*

The main reason for the worldwide presence of public administrative corruption is that public administrators have something to allocate that other people want. As Michael Johnston explains:

> The demand for government's rewards frequently exceeds the supply, and routine decision-making processes are lengthy, costly, and uncertain in their outcome. For

---

* "Baksheesh," a "tip" or bribe in the Middle East; "la mordida," "the bite" in Latin America; "la bustarella," "the little envelope" in Italy; "speed money," used in India to expedite the processing of forms and requests; "dash," a tip or bribe in Western Africa; "protekzia," exploitation of personal contacts to achieve favorable treatment in Israel.

these reasons, legally sanctioned decision-making processes constitute a "bottleneck" between what people want and what they get. The temptation to get around the bottleneck—to speed things up and make favorable decisions more probable—is built into this relationship between government and society. To get around the bottleneck, one must use political influence—and corruption, which by definition cuts across established and legitimate processes, is a most effective form of influence.[12]

Although the source of corruption is similar in all public administrative settings, precisely what is considered a betrayal of public trust and corrupt activity on the part of administrators varies among political cultures.[13]

Every country has norms and values that define the legitimacy of different kinds of **political exchanges.** Political exchanges can be thought of as quid pro quo relationships involving government and politics. For example, if a candidate for Congress says, "You vote for me and I'll reduce your taxes," it constitutes a political exchange. So does the plea to a traffic officer, "Let me go with a warning this time and I won't speed again." Trading votes and support for one another's positions in legislatures, in the drafting of political party platforms, and in the recruitment of party candidates for public office are all examples of political exchange. Obviously, no political system could operate without political exchanges of some kind. But not all kinds of political exchanges are considered legitimate in all societies. For example, in the United States a candidate for Congress may say, "Vote for me and I'll reduce your taxes," but if he or she says, "Vote for me and I'll give you $20," it becomes a crime. A public administrator may be requested to expedite a case involving congressional case-work, but if the same case were speeded up because the private individual concerned paid the administrator to do so, it would be a criminal offense. One of the difficulties in understanding administrative corruption, therefore, lies in determining precisely which kinds of political exchanges are considered acceptable parts of political life.

In the United States, defining administrative corruption has largely involved a contest between the norms and values of two types of political cultures. One is the **boss-follower,** or **political-machine-based** culture. The other is generally referred to as the modern **civic culture.** These were represented in the epic contest over political ethics presented by the nineteenth-century civil service reform and the early twentieth-century Progressive movements, on the one hand, and political machines, on the other. In the machine-based political culture, political exchanges were generally between citizens and the boss or his agents and between the machine and businesses. Votes were traded for jobs and favors; money for licenses, franchises, and public works contracts. For the most part, these exchanges were not considered illegitimate, though sometimes they were termed "honest graft." Similarly, it was commonplace and acceptable for administrative officials to deviate from administrative rules or laws in minor ways to benefit supporters of the machine or friends. Public officials might also accept gifts from clients and others for the purpose of generating generalized good will. Public employees were expected to take part in electioneering and to pay assessments to the political party in power. On election day, they would be expected to help "get out the vote" (among party loyalists), while being paid from the public treasury. Public officials might also legitimately profit from "insider" knowledge, as in the case of knowing in advance where a new road or building was to be located. In general, the purpose of politics in this system was not to accomplish any ideological or policy goals, but rather to make personal gain by trading political support and money for the granting of governmental largess.[14] (See Plunkitt's description of "honest graft" in Box 12–1.)

The "civic culture" has a radically different outlook. Its essence is "community-regarding" in the sense of promoting public, rather than merely private, interests. It is also impersonal. Government is not looked upon as a means of dispensing largess and favors. It is viewed as an organization capable of advancing the general welfare of the community. Rather than considering the "boss" as the protector of individuals' interests, the civic culture holds that this is the role of the state, as embodied in a written or unwritten constitution. In such a system trading votes for jobs is considered illegitimate. Offering money for licenses, franchises, and contracts is also considered corrupt. These benefits are to be allocated according to impersonal and community-regarding rules, such as contracts to the lowest competent bidder. Public administrators are forbidden to use their "inside" information for private gain, and conflict-of-interest laws are adopted to prevent them from so doing. They are also prohibited from taking part in a wide range of partisan and electioneering activities. Rules are applied

---

BOX 12–1 "Honest Graft"

Everybody is talkin' these days about Tammany men growin' rich on graft, but nobody thinks of drawin' the distinction between honest graft and dishonest graft. There's all the difference in the world between the two. Yes, many of our men have grown rich in politics. I have myself. I've made a big fortune out of the game, and I'm gettin' richer every day, but I've not gone in for dishonest graft—blackmailin' gamblers, saloon-keepers, disorderly people, etc.—and neither has any of the men who have made big fortunes in politics.

There's an honest graft, and I'm an example of how it works. I might sum up the whole thing by sayin': "I seen my opportunities and I took 'em."

Just let me explain by examples. My party's in power in the city, and it's goin' to undertake a lot of public improvements. Well, I'm tipped off, say, that they're goin' to lay out a new park at a certain place.

I see my opportunity and I take it. I go to that place and I buy up all the land I can in the neighborhood. Then the board of this or that makes its plan public, and there is a rush to get my land, which nobody cared particular for before.

Ain't it perfectly honest to charge a good price and make a profit on my investment and foresight? Of course, it is. Well, that's honest graft.

SOURCE: From William L. Riordan, *Plunkitt of Tammany Hall* (New York: Knopf, 1948), pp. 3–8.

impersonally, without regard to partisanship, and bribery is strictly forbidden.[15] In fact, even offering a bribe may be illegal.

Part of the problem of identifying administrative corruption in the United States is a result of the coexistence of norms of each of these two political cultures. Political machines have dwindled, become fragmented, and are now much weaker than in the early part of the century. This has been an intended consequence of the civil service reform and Progressive movements. However, the norms, values, and some of the practices common to machines in the past still play a role in partisan politics. Some positions, those denoted "political executive," are still allocated on a partisan basis. Government largess is still used to manipulate votes, though its distribution in the form of "pork-barrel" projects is aimed at winning support from whole communities or states, rather than from specific individual beneficiaries only. Contracts for governmental supplies, ranging from pencils to very expensive military hardware, may be allocated, under political pressure, on a regional basis. But contemporary public administration is nonetheless imbued with the norms and values of the civic culture. It looks down upon the intrusion of partisan politics in administration as an unhealthy perversion of the need to be community-regarding and to operate in accordance with impersonal rules. Some very important legislation is aimed at minimizing the extent to which such intrusions can occur. Political neutrality statutes and merit systems are leading examples.

Since public administrators are engaged in the allocation of governmental benefits, they are sometimes pulled or pushed in opposing directions by the machine-based and civic culture-based approaches to government. This is part of the tension commonly found between political executives seeking to implement an electoral "mandate" of some kind and career public administrators who seemingly are intransigent in clinging to what they regard as established procedures for promoting community-regarding, impersonal administrative activity. In fact, as discussed in Chapter 5, the modern civil service is based on the civic culture approach. The divergence between the machine-based and civic culture-based approaches is sometimes reflected in legislation. For instance, conflict-of-interest statutes may prohibit public administrators from quitting the public sector to work for private corporations with which they had official dealings. Yet there are no equivalent regulations on the future employment of members of Congress, and some have left the legislature to work for firms and lobbying organizations whose interests they previously promoted in an official capacity. Similarly, candidates for public office, including incumbents, may accept funding from political action committees ("PACs"), and may hold economic interests in firms with which the government deals. But public administrators are often under a very strict standard, requiring them to eliminate altogether even any *appearance* of impropriety or wrongdoing.[16]

The juxtaposition of these two political cultures can place substantial pressures on public administrators to do what is considered corrupt from a civic cultural perspective and may also weaken the norms and values of that perspective as they apply to public administration. The Watergate scandal of the early 1970s provided many examples. One was the creation of a political "enemies list" in the IRS. Here, with direction from the White House, the head of the IRS was urged to single out vocal critics of President Nixon for unfavorable tax treatment. A second was in the Civil Service Commission, which provided favorable and expedited treatment to federal job seekers having White House connections. When one considers that the CSC was a creation of the nineteenth-century civil service reform movement and was intended to police the federal personnel system against precisely such patronage incursions, it is not surprising that the CSC's activities during the Nixon administration were an important cause of the agency's demise.

Definitions of "corruption" vary with political cultures, but within any political or administrative system there will be several types of corruption. One useful way to organize thinking about corruption is to consider the mode of execution and the purpose of the corrupt activity.[17] Execution can involve a single individual or agency and be **unilateral** in the sense that it does not involve a direct exchange with another individual or corporate entity. For instance, an individual administrator may cover up his or her mistakes. So may a unit of an agency or even the agency as a whole. Individuals and agencies may also falsify data and records in order to make it look like they are doing a better job. In these examples, the purpose of the individual or agency is to retain, augment, or attain authority of some kind. But unilateral corruption can also be aimed at obtaining material benefits. Here, theft, embezzlement, and use of official resources for private gain would be leading examples.

Corruption can also be **transactional,** involving a direct exchange of some kind. Where concern is enhancing administrative authority, such behavior might take the form of extremely strong clientela relationships. In return for support from the clientele group, the individual administrator or agency grants it benefits that are not even arguably in the public interest. The routine payment of "cost overruns" and extraordinarily high prices for common items by the Department of Defense of the United States *may* constitute an example. It was precisely because the potential for such perversions of the public interest is present that President Eisenhower once warned the nation about the possibility of the "military-industrial complex" extracting too much wealth from the society. Transactional executions of corruption can also be for the purpose of obtaining material benefits. Bribery, extortion, kickbacks and so forth are clear examples.

Subversion

Public administrators might also betray their public trust by engaging in subversion. This has been a serious fear at many times in United States history, particularly in wartime. The clearest and most recent example occurred in the late 1940s and early 1950s. Since the loyalty-security program of that period was discussed in Chapter 5 only a few additional points need to be mentioned here. One is that the fear of subversion was real, though actual instances were hard to find. For instance, the 1952 Republican party platform charged that the Democrats had "permitted communists and fellow travelers to serve in many key agencies and to infiltrate our American life."[18] Second, the potential for actual damage to the public interest from subversive civil servants is considerable. Finally, although it is common to think of subversion in terms of efforts, instigated by foreign governments, to weaken or destroy the government, conscious subversion of administrative programs can occur for several reasons. For example, it can be the result of unilateral or transactional corruption for private gain. It can also be due to extreme discontent with one's position in the public service.

WHY IT IS DIFFICULT TO GUARD THE GUARDIANS

It is clear that public administrators should be held accountable for their actions, especially as there are such broad prospects for them to abuse their trust. However, finding satisfactory means of establishing accountability has been difficult in the United States and other countries. Several reasons for this are discussed below.

The Accretion of Special Expertise and Information   Public administrators are often expert at what they do. Outsiders are unable to match their knowledge or properly second-guess their decisions and activities. Public administrators also have information available to them that others have difficulty obtaining; it may be information that the administrators themselves decided to generate. This information is often the basis of decision making. Other information could lead one to make different decisions, but the initial decision as to what information to gather is frequently left up to the administrators (see Chapter 8). Since public administrators have such special expertise and access to information, at times it may be beyond the ability of those charged with oversight to hold the administrators accountable.

The Advantage of Full-Time Status   For the most part, public administrators do their jobs on a full-time basis. Outsiders who would hold them accountable typically are engaged in other activities and cannot devote sufficient time to watching the public administrators. For instance, this is true of congressional oversight of administrative activities. Members of Congress have a great deal more to do than look over the shoulders of public administrators. Moreover, the incentives to engage in forceful oversight on a routine basis are often weak. For Congress, the net result is that most oversight activity is left up to the congressional staff. But since it is not an activity of high priority to their bosses (that is, members of Congress), there is a tendency to concentrate on other matters.

The Protective Nature of the Personnel System   Public personnel systems in the United States and elsewhere tend to afford public administrators a great deal of job security. Discipline and dismissal are possible, but cumbersome and difficult. Consequently, petty infractions, such as using public resources of limited value for private purposes, are likely to go unpunished. However, the cumulative impact of such infractions can be significant. If each federal employee used a dollar's worth of public property for private purposes, the total cost would be about $3 million. Similarly, deviation from administrative rules or their misapplication may not be deemed worthy of discipline unless the consequences are severe and, possibly, public.

The "Law of Counter Control"   It takes bureaucracy to control bureaucracy. Anthony Downs has maintained that there is a "Law of Counter Control": "The greater the effort made by a sovereign or top-level official to control the behavior of subordinate officials, the greater the efforts made by those subordinates to evade or counteract such control."[19] But the greater the efforts in either direction, the more staff that are likely to be needed to try to secure accountability. The greater the number of staff, the more likely the effort to control one bureaucracy will result in another. For instance, to a large extent one could describe the history of expansion of the Executive Office of the President in these terms.[20]

The Problem of Coordination   In the United States, the separation of powers complicates the quest for accountability. The president is charged with the faithful execution of the laws, but congressional involvement is necessary to create, fund, staff, and empower administrative agencies. Without coordination between the president and Congress, accountability is very difficult to obtain. But since both branches of government have different constituencies, roles, incentives, and interests, coordination is not a simple matter. Historically, there have been times when one branch has impeded the efforts of the other to hold public administrators accountable. For instance, in the Iran-Contra affair, Congress criticized Attorney General Edwin Meese's failure to protect some documents from being shredded.

The Lack of Political Direction   Politics in the United States does not provide comprehensive political direction to public administrators. Political parties are fragmented and elections do not convey clear mandates. Undoubtedly, most public administrators would follow clear mandates, if they existed, but in their absence, political direction of public agencies is uncertain. This is exacerbated by the relatively short tenure of political executives, which is generally in the range of two to three years. Coupled with the protective nature of personnel systems, the absence of clear mandates and short tenure of political executives provide career public administrators little incentive to depart substantially from their views of the public interest and the interests of their agencies. Many political executives have complained bitterly about the difficulty of changing the directions of the career service.

The Fragmentation of Agency Structures and Functions   The structure of public agencies in the United States is often fragmented and missions are often overlapping. Fragmentation and overlapping responsibilities, addressed in Chapter 4, have their sources and benefits. However, they may make it difficult to pinpoint responsibility for any given administrative action. Agencies can be quite dexterous in obscuring and shifting the blame for even the clearest of agency failures.

The Large Size and Scope of Public Administration   On average, the federal government spends over $34,000 per second every second of the year. Some administrative departments and agencies employ over a hundred thousand employees. The Department of Defense employs more than one million civilians. The Postal Service employs more than 700,000. The *Federal Register* had some 47,000 pages in 1986. In 1940, when the federal service was only about half its current size in terms of personnel, there were almost 19 million vouchers covering government expenditures.[21] Even with advances in computer technology, who can keep track of all these dollars, people, regulations, forms, and so forth? Unless there is some reason to suspect that public administrators or agencies have deviated from the public interest in some way, there is little possibility of using routine audits to find serious infractions. Rather, the scandal must break first—and by then it is too late to prevent whatever damage the infractions have caused.

These barriers to holding the "permanent" civil service accountable in a systematic fashion are so formidable that the formal theory of accountability in democracies is clearly at odds with the reality. In the formal theory,

> power emanates from the people and is to be exercised in trust for the people. Within the government each level of executive authority is accountable to the next, running on up to the President or the Cabinet. The executive authority as a whole is accountable to the Congress or Parliament, which is assisted in its surveillance of expenditures by an independent audit agency. Officials are required to submit themselves to periodic elections as a retrospective evaluation of their performances and to receive a new mandate from the people.[22]

However, as the authors of the above passage point out, perhaps inevitably, "accountability gets lost in the shuffle somewhere in the middle ranges of the bureaucracy."[23] How can we find and retrieve it?

PERSPECTIVES ON ACCOUNTABILITY AND ETHICS

The Managerial Perspective

The basic tenets of the managerial approach to accountability and ethics are probably fairly well known to those who have had several dealings with public administrative organizations. As mentioned in Chapter 10, there has been a tendency for some managerially oriented norms to work their way into the cultural values of the American middle class. Specifically, however, in keeping with its emphasis on efficiency, economy, and effectiveness, the managerial approach stresses the need for organizational unity as a means of establishing accountability and as a guide to ethics.

First, the managerial approach emphasizes that authority and responsibility must be clearly assigned. Overlapping functions, which tend to obscure responsibility and consequently to frustrate accountability, should be reduced to a minimum. The lines of hierarchical authority should be clear and comprehensive. Ideally, they should culminate in a single position, rather than a commission of some kind. Plural agency heads are frowned upon because they can muddle the lines of authority and cloud issues of responsibility. They can also divide the loyalties of subordinates.

Second, this approach emphasizes the need for strict subordination, which is the other side of the coin of hierarchy. Underlings must strictly obey the directives and commands of superordinates. This is necessary for organizational effectiveness and accountability. An act of disobedience, termed insubordination, is a substantial offense against the organization, according to this view. It is often punishable by dismissal. Logically, this is viewed as necessary, for otherwise superordinates would be officially responsible for behavior that is beyond their control. Accordingly, under the managerial approach a public administrator who is unwilling to follow orders is expected to leave his or her organization, either through transfer or resignation.

Third, concern with strict subordination dictates a limited span of control. The span of control, it will be recalled, is the number of subordinates directly responsible to a superordinate. Orthodox public administrative theory paid a great deal of attention to determining the proper span of control. Discussions were oriented toward effective management, but concern with accountability was built into the concept. Just as plural leadership was considered inappropriate, too many subordinates per superordinate was also viewed as a problem.

Fourth, subordinates are encouraged to be loyal to the organization and to their superordinates. Loyalty is generated in several ways. One is through organizational socialization that attempts to inculcate the importance of the agency's mission and the need to work toward it with a high degree of unity. Another is through occupational specialization that makes it difficult for employees to find equivalent work elsewhere; firefighters are a good example of this. A third approach is to make the employees materially dependent upon the organization to a great extent. Aside from pay, pensions and conflict-of-interest regulations have an important role here. Sometimes pension plans create a strong incentive to remain with an organization. Conflict-of-interest regulations may seek to make the employee dependent, economically, on the organization. The employee may be required to divest himself or herself of economic assets that could create conflicting interests or loyalties. Attempting to "close the revolving door"—preventing public employees from taking private employment with firms they previously dealt with in their official capacities—is a related effort to make them dependent upon and loyal to their public employers. At the federal level in the United States, both traditional conflict-of-interest statutes and anti-revolving door regulations are currently very comprehensive. [24]

Fifth, the managerial approach relies on formal disciplinary systems to enforce accountability and subordination. These systems seek to identify breaches of proper conduct. As already noted, insubordination typically ranks high on the list of misbehavior. Other matters may range from very broad prohibitions on "immoral and notoriously disgraceful" conduct to specific considerations of misuse of agency authority or property. For example, using stationery with the agency's letterhead for personal purposes is sometimes considered a serious breach of ethics. It violates the concept of unity of authority within the agency, since it is unauthorized, and also suggests that government property is being misused for private purposes. John A. Rohr points out in *Ethics for Bureaucrats* that some agencies develop elaborate codes of conduct intended to impart a sense of what is to be considered ethical or unethical behavior.[25] Some of the examples he cites are drawn from the U.S. Department of Agriculture. They concern the use of office equipment (including telephones) for personal business, the use of government automobiles for personal purposes, and whether the agency can take action against employees who fail to pay personal debts. Rohr evaluates this approach as reducing ethical behavior to "staying out of trouble," and empha-sizing, "meticulous attention to trivial questions."[26] In fact, in his view, "These exercises provide a clear example of the worst aspects of the mentality that continues to dichotomize politics and administration."[27] For example, they are more concerned with a personal phone call than whether the administrator engages in behavior that abridges someone's constitutional rights to due process (see Box 12–2).

The type of disciplinary system the managerial approach prefers in enforc-ing these codes of conduct and organization norms is one that is simple and always under the control of the agency's own hierarchy. Otherwise unity and hierarchy are weakened—and these are the very goals of the codes of conduct in the first place. However, pressures for the fair treatment of employees have often led to collective bargaining agreements that seriously reduce managerial author-ity to discipline employees. In addition, the legal perspective's concern with protection of the constitutional rights of public employees has promoted both more elaborate adverse action hearing systems and judicial review of managerial disciplinary decisions and procedures.

Sixth, the managerial perspective's concern with fiscal regularity and em-ployee performance places emphasis on the use of internal audits. Audits can be a strong deterrent to corruption or other abuse of the public trust. Sometimes they are performed by a unit within an organization, as the managerial approach prefers. Sometimes, however, it is thought that an outside auditing body is more desirable, such as the U.S. General Accounting Office, which is an agency of Congress. Sometimes a compromise is adopted: the audit bureau is within the agency, but independent of its hierarchy. Audits can be concerned with general fiscal matters of performance and management, or matters of reporting, such as the number of cases closed. Some agencies use "inspectors general" as a kind of internal policing mechanism having authority to engage in investigations and audits in a broad range of circumstances.

All of these approaches are important in promoting accountability ande-thics. They are all found in a vast array of contemporary public and private organizations in one form or another. Their main limitation, as Rohr points out, is their narrow focus. They are concerned with protecting managerial values more than protecting the public from a breach of trust in a more political sense.

The Political Perspective

In contrast to the managerial perspective, the political approach emphasizes the need for developing mechanisms for accountability that are *external* to public administrative agencies. In the past, this was done primarily through political control of public personnel through patronage appointments. Nowadays, however, the political approach must rely on other means. Among some of the more familiar are the following.

Legislative Oversight   Legislative oversight is exercised by members of the legislature, their staffs, and legislative agencies, such as the federal General Accounting Office and the Congressional Budget Office. Depending on the incentives facing the legislature, oversight can be a forceful means of promoting accountability of public administrators. The congressional Watergate hearings in the early 1970s and the Iran-Contra hearings in 1986–1987 presented spectacular examples of the use of legislative oversight to hold the executive branch accountable.

Budgetary Control   Historically, the "power of the purse" was considered an extremely important legislative check on the executive's "power of the sword." While legislatures in the United States retain a great deal of the power of the purse, they tend to share the budgeting function with the executive to a very considerable extent. Nonetheless, agencies can be held accountable, to some degree, by the need to win legislative approval for their routine, year-to-year funding.

Rotation in Office   The political approach has long stressed the need to rotate public administrators from office to office or in and out of the public service altogether. This is a matter of preventing misperception of the public interest due to too much specialization in one agency or function. In the 1840s and 1850s, rotation was through the spoils system, while today it is accomplished in a number of ways in modern public personnel systems. For instance, the creation of the Senior Executive Service in the federal civil service reform of 1978 was intended, in part, to enable top-level career civil servants to move from bureau to bureau or agency to agency in the hope that they would consequently develop a broader perspective on the public interest. The federal Intergovernmental Personnel Act authorizes public administrators to move temporarily from positions in the federal government to the states and vice versa. Political executives are routinely rotated out of office when a new president takes office, especially if he is of a different party than his predecessor.

Representation and Public Participation   Just as rotation is aimed at reducing misconception of the public interest, encouraging pluralism within public administration can subject public administrators to a greater diversity of perspectives and interests. A socially representative public service is likely to be more diversified, in terms of values and political perspectives, than a homogeneous one. Allowing public participation and interest group representation in admin-

---

BOX 12–2 **General Services Administration's Code of Conduct: Some Examples**

---

§ 105-735.210 Indebtedness.

GSA personnel shall pay their just financial obligations in a proper and timely manner, especially those imposed by law, such as Federal, State, or local taxes. For the purposes of this paragraph, a "just financial obligation" means one acknowledged by the employee, or reduced to judgment by a court. In a dispute between GSA personnel and an alleged creditor, GSA will not undertake to determine the validity or amount of a disputed debt.

§ 105-735.211 Gambling, betting, and lotteries.

GSA personnel shall not participate, while on property owned or leased by the Government or while on duty for GSA, in any gambling activity, including the operation of a gambling device, participating in a lottery or pool, participating in a game for money or property, or selling or purchasing a numbers slip or ticket, except as otherwise lawfully authorized.

§ 105-735.212 General conduct prejudicial to the Government.

GSA personnel shall not engage in criminal, infamous, dishonest, immoral, or notoriously disgraceful conduct prejudicial to the Government.

§ 105-735.213 Intermediaries.

In any relations with the public, GSA personnel shall not recommend or suggest the use of any non-Government person (individual, firm, corporation, or other entity) offering service as intermediary, consultant, agent, representative, attorney, expediter, or specialist for the purpose of assisting in any negotiations, transactions, or other business with GSA.

§ 105-735.214 Lending or borrowing money.

GSA personnel shall not lend money for profit to other GSA personnel or lend money for profit to any other person on Government premises. A supervisor shall not borrow money from a subordinate under any circumstances. This prohibition is not applicable to recognized employee credit unions or employee welfare plans.

§ 105-735.218 Purchase of real estate.

GSA personnel, whose official du-

---

istrative processes further brings public administrators into contact with the views of the public, or at least segments of it. The Administrative Procedure Act of 1946, the Federal Advisory Committee Act of 1972, and the Civil Service Reform Act of 1978 all contain provisions, mentioned earlier in this book, that encourage representation and participation.

"Going Public" The political perspective holds that it is proper and ethical for public employees to inform the public or its representatives, such as legislators, of misconduct by public administrators and of violations of the public trust or interest by agencies. In other words, they are expected to use their voices to protest administrative activities that they consider illegal and/or immoral. Public resignations and whistleblowing are viewed as appropriate, and often highly moral acts. Whistleblowing is now statutorily protected at the federal level. In addition, the federal government has institutionalized a fraud, waste, and abuse

---

BOX 12–2 *Continued*

---

ties are in any way related to the acquisition or disposal of real estate or interests therein or to the maintenance or improvement of real estate, shall not, directly or indirectly, purchase any real estate or interest therein except for occupancy as their personal residence unless a full disclosure of the proposed transaction is made in writing to the appropriate supervisor who shall consult with the Special Counsel to the Administrator for Ethics (regional counsel in a region), and the prior written approval of the appropriate supervisor is obtained. A copy of the approval shall be promptly furnished by the supervisor to the Special Counsel to the Administrator for Ethics. Surplus real property may not be purchased under any circumstances. (See § 105-735.217.)

§ 105-735.219 Use of intoxicants.

GSA personnel shall not use intoxicants habitually to excess (5 U.S.C. 7352). GSA personnel shall not use intoxicants on U.S. Government-owned or leased premises except upon occasions and on property as to which the

Administrator or Regional Administrator has granted an exception in writing or, in the case of property occupied by another agency, except as authorized by the head of that agency in accordance with law.

§ 105-735.220 Use of Government vehicles.

GSA personnel shall not use or authorize the use of Government-owned or leased motor vehicles or aircraft for other than official purposes (31 U.S.C. 638(c)) and shall operate such vehicles or aircraft in strict compliance with all applicable laws.

§ 105-735.221 Use of official telephones.

GSA personnel shall not use Federal Telecommunications System or commercial telephone facilities for long-distance calls unless authorized to do so.

§ 105-735.222 Use of Government documents.

GSA personnel shall not knowingly, willfully and unlawfully conceal, remove, mutilate, falsify, or destroy any Government document or record (18 U.S.C. 2071).

SOURCE: Office of the Administrator, General Services Administration, "Revisions to GSA's Standards of Conduct Order," November 29, 1983 (Washington, D.C.: General Services Administration, 1983).

"hot line," whereby employees or others can anonymously report instances of misconduct to the General Accounting Office for further investigation. Some of these hot line tips have resulted in the removal of public administrators from the federal service.[28] More important, though, is their deterrent effect. Where whistleblowing and "hot lining" are regarded as virtuous activities, loyalty to the agency and superiors, in the managerial sense, is inevitably undermined. Indeed, agencies have sometimes issued "gag" orders to prevent employees from going public. But cover-ups are now more difficult, and individual acts of corruption are riskier. Today, federal employees who engage in whistleblowing are afforded considerable statutory protection.[29] These protections reach beyond reporting mismanagement and fiscal abuse to speaking out on specific and substantial dangers to the public health or safety. Public employees at all levels of government also have some constitutional protections in speaking out on matters of public concern. One of the thornier issues in this area is when anonymous or secretive "leaks" to the press are appropriate. Sometimes the unauthorized disclosure of information can prematurely foreclose an agency's policy options or adversely affect the behavior of the public, as would be the case if someone in the Federal Deposit Insurance Corporation announced that a certain large bank was nearly insolvent.

"Sunshine"   The political perspective holds that open, public dealings are an important means of securing the accountability and proper conduct of public officials. Consequently, it has promoted a number of approaches to fostering "sunshine" in public administration. These range from the requirement that some hearings and meetings be open to the public to the Freedom of Information Act's creation of a right for members of the public to obtain many categories of federal administrative documents.

Conflict of Interest   The political approach agrees with the managerial approach that conflicts of interest ought to be eliminated. It also holds that the "revolving door" should be watched carefully, though not sealed altogether, since it does make agencies more responsive to the economic interests with which they deal. The rationale here is less to bolster hierarchical authority within agencies than to eliminate the temptation to misuse positions of public trust for private gain.

The political approach to accountability emphasizes the need for external checks on public administrative conduct. Unlike the managerial perspective, it is not content to allow the maintenance of accountability to be largely the purview of the administrative heirarchy itself. There has long been debate over how efficacious this approach can be. Max Weber maintained that outside (extra-agency) checks on public administration are inherently inadequate. Even if they functioned very well, they would militate against the maximization of the values of the managerial perspective for efficiency, economy, and effectiveness. But relying exclusively on checks within agencies themselves has obvious limits. The world is too familiar with self-serving administrative action and corruption to expect the guardians alone to guard themselves. Moreover, both the political and managerial approaches rely primarily on enforcement mechanisms that are *external to the individual*. This may seem inappropriate because "responsible conduct of administrative functions is not so much enforced as it is elicited."[30] In other words, the desire to engage in ethical behavior must spring, to a large extent, from within the individual public administrator. Similarly, the strongest system of accountability would be self-imposed.

From the perspectives of ethics as an inner, personal check on public administrators' conduct, the managerial approach's emphasis on loyalty is regarded as being sound, but too narrow. John Rohr observes that it must be enlarged to encompass a broader sense of professionalism and to include dedication to **regime values**.[31] Combining these two concerns and adding some of the externally oriented approaches of the political perspective can provide the beginnings of a synthesis in terms of ethics and accountability in contemporary public administration. We will return to this prospect after mapping out the legal perspective, which stresses the concept of "regime values."

The Legal Perspective

We have noted at many points throughout this book how constitutional values and requirements can be at odds with the perspectives of the managerial and political approaches to public administration. Presumably in response to this disjuncture, the federal judiciary has articulated a number of constitutional rights that are viewed as protections of individuals against certain administrative actions. Moreover, the judiciary has adjusted the standards of public administrators' liabilities for causing unconstitutional infringements of these rights. In the process, the courts have intentionally provided public administrators with a strong and *personally internalized incentive* to protect, or at least avoid abridging, the constitutional rights of the individuals upon whom they act in their official capacities. John Rohr notes that what the courts have done is tantamount to articulating a set of regime values to which public administrators should be accountable. Moreover, these regime values provide ethical guidance to public administrators.

More specifically, Rohr notes that the regime-values approach rests on three considerations: "(1) That ethical norms should be derived from the salient values of the regime; (2) That these values are normative *for bureaucrats* because they have taken an oath to uphold the regime; (3) That these values can be discovered in the public law of the regime."[32] To a very considerable extent, the regime values of the United States can be found in its constitutional law, and adherence to the values it articulates can be the internalized guide for public administrators' ethical behavior and broad accountability. As noted in Chapter 11, some courts have even embraced the concept that public administrators have a right to *disobey* unconstitutional orders.

Since we have already discussed the nature of pertinent constitutional values in the previous chapter, little more needs to be said here with regard to the legal perspective. However, it should be remembered that this approach does not rely entirely on the individual guardians to guard themselves personally. By holding that they can be liable in civil suits for damages, the federal judiciary takes on an important role in guarding the guardians. Moreover, although the legal perspective may be at odds with the other perspectives on occasion, it is not intended to preempt them entirely.

SYNTHESIS: AN INTEGRATED APPROACH TO PUBLIC SERVICE PROFESSIONALISM

In recent years the American public administrative community has shown a considerable interest in questions of ethics and accountability. Much of the recent discussion has moved well beyond traditional concerns with matters of organizational structure and legislative oversight. Today much more attention is being paid to the obligations and responsibilities of public administrators, as individuals, to engage in ethical behavior and to maintain their public trust. To a substantial degree, the current approach focuses on whether a new definition and sense of professionalism for public servants can instil the proper ethical values and conduct and prompt public administrators to hold themselves more accountable to the public interest.

In a sense, there is nothing new about bringing the issues of ethics and accountability back down to the level of the individual administrator. In terms of the way we posed the matter earlier in this chapter, this approach merely argues that, to a large extent, the guardians must individually guard themselves. In a book called *The Frontiers of Public Administration*, published in 1936, John M. Gaus wrote: "Certainly, in the system of government which is now emerging [i.e., the administrative state], one important kind of responsibility will be that which the individual civil servant recognizes as due to the standards and ideals of his profession. That is 'his inner check.' "[33] The main difference now is that the concept of public administrative professionalism is being expanded to be more inclusive of the values of the political and legal perspectives.

From the civil service reform movement of the nineteenth century to the early 1930s, the "professional" obligations of the public employee were very largely those mapped out by the managerial approach. Efficiency and economy were treated as the major moral virtues for public administrators, and it was thought that they would be promoted by having a politically neutral and technically competent civil service. The merit system, the principles of scientific management, and those of classical organization theory were thought to create the proper morality and means of accountability in the public service.

By the 1940s, as it became more evident that public administrators had a role in the formulation of public policy, more concern arose with working political values into the concept of ethical behavior. A very important debate in public administration started in 1940 when Carl Friedrich wrote that "the responsible administrator is one who is responsive to these two dominant factors: technical knowledge and popular sentiment. Any policy which violates either standard, or which fails to crystallize in spite of their urgent imperatives, renders the official responsible for it liable to the charge of irresponsible conduct."[34] However, Friedrich may not have appreciated the complexity frequently posed when public administrators seek to integrate technical competence with considerations of political responsiveness and representativeness. More recently, the "new public administration" movement and a number of important books and articles have wrestled with this problem. [35]

By the mid-1970s, after the Supreme Court had substantially redefined the legal liabilities of public administrators, adherence to the letter and spirit of constitutional values was added to the categories of concern that could define public administrators' ethical obligations. In the future, it seems likely that not just law, but public administrative theory concerning ethics and accountability will demand that public administrators be individually and collectively responsive to these regime values.

The need for public administrators to be guided, at least in part, by an "inner check" now seems settled. Nor can there be much dispute that this inner check must reflect the values of each of the three perspectives toward public administration that have been discussed throughout this book: management, politics, and law. To one who is considering public administration seriously for the first time, this may by now sound incredibly obvious. However, a struggle has been involved in each step of the process of legitimizing these three approaches and the concept of the inner check. Now the major step confronting the public administrative community appears to be developing a public administrative *professionalism* and meaningful codes of ethics that can suitably advance ethics and accountability in the public service.

The rationale for developing a public administrative professionalism that imparts a sense of ethics has been expressed as follows:

> Although one might quarrel with certain self-serving aspects of the codes of ethics developed by the medical and legal professions, there is little doubt that it is the high sense of professional definition among physicians and lawyers that accounts for the relatively clear ethical standards of their professions. They have some understanding of what it is that makes them *different* from everyone else. Ethical norms of behavior are then deduced from these differences. Government managers might well follow a similar course.[36]

From this perspective, the problem becomes identification of precisely what does differentiate the public service from other professions. One answer, as we have seen, is its commitment to uphold regime values. But this may be too limited an approach. For instance, it tends to assume that regime values and morality will coincide. In the past, however, regime values condoned slavery, racial segregation, and the denial of full political rights and equal protection of the law for women, despite opposition on moral grounds from many quarters.

Since public administration is characterized by several perspectives and a plethora of functions, perhaps its sense of ethics and accountability should be developed around its need to integrate so many diverse points of view and considerations. For instance, York Wilbern indicates that public administrative ethics should address the following types of considerations: (1) basic honesty and conformity to law, (2) avoidance of conflict of interest, (3) service orientation and procedural fairness, (4) democratic responsibility, (5) public policy determination, (6) compromise and social integration.[37] Debra Stewart takes a related view with respect to ethical standards in some aspects of public personnel management. She argues that the public manager in this area must (1) consider competing interests, (2) exercise informed moral judgment regarding the balance of these interests, and (3) purposefully use the premises underlying that judgment as the guide to administrative action.[38]

Still other approaches could and no doubt will be developed. At present the public administrative community is seriously considering the problem of ethics—from the point of view of the contemporary administrative state—and that in itself is an important point. The American Society for Public Administration has developed the code of ethics presented in Box 12–3. Perhaps it is only a

---

BOX 12–3 Code of Ethics of the American Society for Public Administration

---

The American Society for Public Administration (ASPA) exists to advance the science, processes, and art of public administration. ASPA encourages professionalism and improved quality of service at all levels of government, education, and the not-for-profit private sector. ASPA contributes to the analysis, understanding, and resolution of public issues by providing programs, services, policy studies, conferences, and publications.

ASPA members share with their neighbors all of the responsibilities and rights of citizenship in a democratic society. However, the mission and goals of ASPA call every member to additional dedication and commitment. Certain principles and moral standards must guide the conduct of ASPA members not merely in preventing wrong, but in pursuing right through timely and energetic execution of responsibilities.

To this end, we, the members of the Society, recognizing the critical role

of conscience in choosing among courses of action and taking into account the moral ambiguities of life, commit ourselves to:

1. demonstrate the highest standards of personal integrity, truthfulness, honesty and fortitude in all our public activities in order to inspire public confidence and trust in public institutions;

2. serve the public with respect, concern, courtesy, and responsiveness, recognizing that service to the public is beyond service to oneself;

3. strive for personal professional excellence and encourage the professional development of our associates and those seeking to enter the field of public administration;

4. approach our organization and operational duties with a positive attitude and constructively

---

beginning, but, clearly, ethics have now been firmly placed on the issue agenda of public administration in the United States.

If we consider ethics to be mainly an inner check or self-accounting (accountability to oneself), then the pattern for synthesis of the perspectives of the managerial, political, and legal perspectives in this area becomes relatively clear. Professionalism will require the individual public administrator to integrate several aspects of the three perspectives within the specific context of his or her function, job, and tasks. Loyalty, responsiveness, and adherence to regime values are matters that are of particular concern to public administrators as individuals. The inner check stemming from a new concept of professionalism and ethics can be augmented by mechanisms for promoting accountability that are external to the individual. Both the mechanisms that are found within management structures themselves and those that involve oversight by outsiders fall into this category. While there is little doubt that problems of ethics and accountability will always be with us, if interested parties along these lines work toward a synthesis of the three perspectives, as much as is practicable in any given situation, the guardians are likely to be guarded better.

BOX 12–3 *Continued*

support open communication, creativity, dedication and compassion;

5. serve in such a way that we do not realize undue personal gain from the performance of our official duties;

6. avoid any interest or activity which is in conflict with the conduct of our official duties;

7. respect and protect the privileged information to which we have access in the course of official duties;

8. exercise whatever discretionary authority we have under law to promote the public interest;

9. accept as a personal duty the responsibility to keep up to date on emerging issues and to administer the public's business with professional competence, fairness, impartiality, efficiency and effectiveness;

10. support, implement, and promote merit employment and programs of affirmative action to assure equal opportunity by our recruitment, selection, and advancement of qualified persons from all elements of society;

11. eliminate all forms of illegal discrimination, fraud, and mismanagement of public funds, and support colleagues if they are in difficulty because of responsible efforts to correct such discrimination, fraud, mismanagement or abuse;

12. respect, support, study, and when necessary, work to improve federal and state constitutions, and other laws which define the relationships among public agencies, employees, clients and all citizens.

Approved by National Council April 8, 1984.

SOURCE: American Society for Public Administration, 1120 G Street, N.W., Suite 500, Washington, D.C. 20005.

NOTES

1. Frederick Mosher, *Democracy and the Public Service* (New York: Oxford University Press, 1968), p. 5.
2. Victor Thompson, *Modern Organization* (New York: Knopf, 1961).
3. Samuel Krislov and David H. Rosenbloom, *Representative Bureaucracy and the American Political System* (New York: Praeger, 1981), esp. chap. 2.
4. Seymour M. Lipset, "Bureaucracy and Social Change," pp. 221–232, in R. K. Merton, et al., *Reader in Bureaucracy* (Glencoe, Ill.: Free Press, 1952), p. 230.
5. Kenneth Meier, "Representative Bureaucracy: An Empirical Analysis," *American Political Science Review*, 69 (June 1975): 526–542; David H. Rosenbloom, *Federal Equal Employment Opportunity* (New York: Praeger, 1977); V. Subramaniam,

"Representative Bureaucracy: A Reassessment," *American Political Science Review*, 61 (December 1967): 1010–1019.

6. Anthony Downs, *Inside Bureaucracy* (Boston: Little, Brown, 1967), p. 279.

7. Ibid., p. 276.

8. Joseph LaPalombara, *Interest Groups in Italian Politics* (Princeton, N.J.: Princeton University Press, 1963).

9. Ibid., p. 262.

10. Howard Ball, "Frauds upon the Court: Some Implications of Administrative Deception in a Federal Court," paper presented at the 1983 meeting of the American Society for Public Administration, New York, N.Y. (April 17–20, 1983), p. 3.

11. Ibid., p. 4.

12. Michael Johnston, *Political Corruption and Public Policy in America* (Monterey, Calif.: Brooks/Cole, 1982), p. 3.

13. Arnold J. Heidenheimer, ed., *Political Corruption: Readings in Comparative Analysis* (New York: Holt, Rinehart and Winston, 1970).

14. For a concise discussion, see Edward Banfield and James Q. Wilson, *City Politics* (Cambridge, Mass.: Harvard University Press and the M.I.T. Press, 1963), chap. 9.

15. Heidenheimer, *Political Corruption*, Introduction.

16. Robert N. Roberts, "Lord, Protect Me from the Appearance of Wrongdoing," in David H. Rosenbloom, ed., *Public Personnel Policy: The Politics of Civil Service* (Port Washington, N.Y.: Associated Faculty Press, 1985), chap. 11.

17. See Johnston, *Political Corruption*, pp. 11–12.

18. *New York Times*, July 11, 1952, p. 8.

19. Downs, *Inside Bureaucracy*, p. 262.

20. See David Nachmias and David H. Rosenbloom, *Bureaucratic Government, USA* (New York: St. Martin's Press, 1980), chap. 4.

21. Bruce Smith and James Carroll, eds., *Improving the Accountability and Performance of Government* (Washington, D.C.: Brookings Institution, 1982), p. 21.

22. Bruce Smith and D. Hague, *The Dilemma of Accountability in Modern Government* (New York: St. Martin's Press, 1971), pp. 26–27.

23. Ibid.

24. Carolyn Ban, "The Revolving Door: Have We Shut It Too Tightly?" Paper presented at the 1984 Annual Meeting of the American Political Science Association, Washington, D.C. (August 30–September 2, 1984). See also Robert N. Roberts, "Conflict-of-Interest Regulation and the Federal Service: The Legacy of Civil Service Reform," in David H. Rosenbloom, ed., *Centenary Issues of the Pendleton Act of 1883* (New York: Marcel Dekker, 1982), chap. 7.

25. John A. Rohr, *Ethics for Bureaucrats* (New York: Marcel Dekker, 1978), pp. 51–55.

26. Ibid., p. 54.

27. Ibid.

28. *New York Times*, September 30, 1984, p. 21.

29. Robert G. Vaughn, "Statutory Protection of Whistleblowers in the Federal Executive Branch," *University of Illinois Law Review*, vol. 1982 (1982): 615–667.

30. Carl J. Friedrich, "Public Policy and the Nature of Administrative Responsibility," pp. 333–343, in Alan Altshuler and Norman Thomas, eds., *The Politics of the Federal Bureaucracy*, 2nd ed. (New York: Harper & Row, 1977), p. 340.

31. Rohr, *Ethics for Bureaucrats*, esp. chap. 2.

32. Ibid., p. 59.

33. Quoted in Friedrich, "Public Policy and the Nature of Administrative Responsibility," p. 339.

34. Ibid., p. 338.
35. Frank Marini, ed., *Toward a New Public Administration* (Scranton, Pa.: Chandler, 1971); Louis Gawthrop, *Public Management Systems and Ethics* (Bloomington: Indiana University Press, 1984); Ralph Clark Chandler, "The Problem of Moral Reasoning in American Public Administration: The Case for a Code of Ethics," *Public Administration Review*, 43 (January/February 1983): 32–39.
36. Rohr, *Ethics for Bureaucrats*, p. 10.
37. York Wilbern, "Types and Levels of Public Morality," *Public Administration Review*, 44 (March/April 1984): 102–108.
38. Debra Stewart, "Managing Competing Claims: An Ethical Framework for Human Resource Decision Making," *Public Administration Review*, 44 (January/February 1984): 14–22.

ADDITIONAL READING

COOPER, TERRY. *The Responsible Administrator: An Approach to Ethics for the Administrative Role*, 2nd ed. New York: Associated Faculty Press, 1986.

HEIDENHEIMER, ARNOLD, ED. *Political Corruption*. New York: Holt, Rinehart, and Winston, 1970.

JOHNSTON, MICHAEL. *Political Corruption and Public Policy in America*. Monterey, Calif.: Brooks/Cole, 1982.

ROBERTS, ROBERT N. "Conflict-of-Interest Regulations in the Federal Service: The Legacy of Civil Service Reform," in *Centenary Issues of the Pendleton Act of 1883*, ed. by David H. Rosenbloom. New York: Marcel Dekker, 1982.

ROHR, JOHN A. *Ethics for Bureaucrats*. New York: Marcel Dekker, 1978.

SMITH, BRUCE, AND JAMES D. CARROL, EDS. *Improving the Accountability and Performance of Government*. Washington, D.C.: Brookings Institution, 1982.

VAUGHN, ROBERT G. *Conflict-of-Interest Regulation in the Federal Executive Branch*. Lexington, Mass.: Lexington Books, 1979.

STUDY QUESTIONS

1. Can you identify a case of public administration with which you are familiar where the official violated his or her public trust, in your view? If so, what seems to have been the cause? How was the breach of trust discovered, and how was the issue resolved? Do you feel the resolution was the best one possible?

2. How realistic do you think the notion of an "inner check" on administrators' conduct is?

3. Do you think public administrative corruption is a serious problem in the United States, relative to corruption among elected officials? If you see a disparity here, what might account for it? What can it teach us about accountability?

CHAPTER 13 | *The Future: Building a New Administrative Culture*

As public administration in the United States moved from relative simplicity to greater complexity, it outgrew some aspects of its earlier values and practices. The older assumptions that public administration is (1) a single process, (2) based in management rather than law, (3) an art being transformed into a science, and (4) at the heart of the problem of modern government must be reevaluated or elaborated upon. The emerging new administrative culture values recognizing the complexity of contemporary public administration, accepting personal responsibility for the exercise of official functions, seeking to protect the constitutional rights of individuals, representativeness, participation, and the sharing of information.

Today, public administration can be considered to be in a state of prolonged and slow-moving crisis. Intellectually, as noted at the outset of this book, it lacks a coherent paradigm or conceptual framework.[1] The study of public administration covers a vast area of human concerns, ranging from trash collection to the exploration of outer space, from managing the most developed postindustrial economies to helping some peoples to move beyond the most rudimentary forms of subsistence farming. The field of public administration is so broad that some do not believe that it can be studied as a single coherent entity. An alternative is to break it down into its constituent parts, such as health administration, social welfare administration, regulatory administration, developmental administration, and defense administration. But this approach would deny or disguise the common principles that underlie most public administrative activity.

Public administration has proved equally perplexing as an area of practical activity. Although all modern nations have well-developed administrative components, these are typically considered politically problematic. The United States is no exception. Electoral campaigns continue to focus on issues related to the costs and performance of public bureaucracies. "Doing" public administration, it seems, is just as difficult as thinking about it.[2] But before one falls into projecting a "doom and gloom" scenario of public administration in the future, it should be forcefully stressed that in the United States, at least, great progress has been made in both doing and thinking about public administration. There is every reason to believe that many of the challenges posed by contemporary public administration will be successfully met in the future.

It should always be borne in mind that in the United States the development of the contemporary administrative state is a relatively new governmental phenomenon. It is also one to which the polity is still adjusting. The federal government did not develop a large administrative component until the 1930s. It was not until 1939 that the presidency was significantly restructured, through the creation of the Executive Office of the President, as an adjustment to the changing role of federal administration. Congress did not undergo reorganization for the purpose of dealing more effectively with the growing executive branch until the late 1940s. Only during the past two decades or so has the judiciary developed forceful checks on public administration. Administrative growth came even later at the state and local levels, the 1950s to the 1970s being the period of greatest expansion. Yet despite the extent of the changes in government brought about by the growth of public administration, and the relative newness of these changes, great progress has been made in assimilating them into effective democratic government.

Although problems remain, much more is known today about how to think about and carry out public administration than was the case in the 1930s. As an intellectual field, public administration has moved well beyond the reliance on simple proverbs and nearly obsessive concern with efficiency and economy that characterized the discipline in the 1930s.[3] In practice, great gains have been made in organizational design, personnel, budgeting, decision making, and policy evaluation and analysis. It is partly because public administration has successfully moved from relative simplicity to complexity that it now faces so many challenges. So we have made great progress—but where do we go from here?

THE OLD ADMINISTRATIVE CULTURE

Wherever we are going, surely we will not advance without expanding upon the public administrative assumptions, values, structures, processes, and technologies of the past. Consequently, we must go further than the bounds of the classical or orthodox public administration that developed in the United States from the 1880s to the late 1930s. For the most part, this orthodoxy is deeply embedded in the managerial perspective, as discussed throughout this book. To the extent that this orthodoxy dominated American public administrative practice and theory, it formed an **administrative culture,** or set of shared values and common structures and processes for achieving them.[4] One way of reviewing the old administrative culture is to reconsider the assumptions of the first major textbook on public administration published in the United States. This approach also offers an opportunity to see how these assumptions must be modified in view of the challenges and problems of today's public administrative theory and practice.

Leonard D. White's *Introduction to the Study of Public Administration* (1926) strongly influenced education and thought in public administration and was an important contribution to the development of the orthodox approach.[5] It was based on four explicit assumptions, each of which provides a key to understanding how public administration has changed over the years and helps suggest what it might look like in the future.

"A Single Process"

White assumed that "administration is a single process, substantially uniform in its essential characteristics wherever observed," and that therefore it is unnecessary to study municipal administration, state administration, or federal administration individually. Today, most would probably disagree with this assumption. Let us consider some important challenges to the notion of a "single process."

The Cultural Context   Since the 1950s, a vast and vigorous literature on comparative public administration has developed.[6] One lesson it holds is that the cultural values, patterns of thinking, and characteristics of political exchanges that pertain to public administration vary widely from society to society. Some nations embody the modern "civic culture" model referred to in Chapter 12; in others, "boss-follower" or kinship relationships define the character of political obligation, exchange, and public administration. Political culture also defines what is considered an appropriate task for public administration. Much of the world is divided on the basic questions of what kinds of enterprises should be managed by governmental administrators: railroads? telecommunications? agriculture? industrial enterprises? Cultural relationships also help define the character of administrative authority.

The Political Context   Culture and politics are related, of course, but White's concept of a "single process" leaves out consideration of the bureaucratic politics involved in different aspects of public administration. White was proceeding from the then dominant perspective that politics and administration were very much separate endeavors. This approach was a direct legacy of the civil service reform movement of the 1870s and 1880s. Whatever the truth of that point of view in the past, today few, if any, observers would seriously argue that politics is not involved in public administration. Public administrators are often direct participants in the formulation of public policy. Their perspectives are welcomed by legislatures. They are identified as important political actors by interest groups. In addition, public administrators often make policy choices in the implementation of programs. But the important challenge to White's idea of a "single process" in this context is that the kind of politics involved in public administration may differ from level to level of government and among policy areas. For instance, urban politics is different from national politics. State politics also has distinctive characteristics. Moreover, cities differ from one another, just as do states. Although some administrative characteristics will be similar from government to government, administrative processes are sure to vary widely with the different political contexts. Many believe that this is also true with regard to policy areas. For example, different types of politics having different impacts on public administration can be identified in the policy areas of distribution, redistribution, regulation, foreign policy, and maintenance of the political system.[7] Administration in the area of distribution is characterized more by interest group participation and legislative involvement than are the other areas. Regulatory administration has distinctive organizational structures and processes that are partly related to the political context, as discussed in Chapter 9. Consideration of bureaucratic politics has taught us that there is a great variety in administrative processes involving the formulation of public policy.

The Functional Context   Culture and politics are important in defining the functions in which public administrators will engage. However, the functions themselves are so varied that it is difficult to consider the administration of them to be a "single process." One of the themes of this book is that different perspectives are more apt for different kinds of administrative functions. Overhead functions, such as accounting and supply, are often best served by the managerial perspective. Regulation has frequently been organized around the legal perspective. Distributive programs tend to follow the political approach. Even finer distinctions can be developed as one considers these functions in greater depth. For instance, in our discussion of regulation, we concluded that the managerial perspective was well suited to regulatory administration aimed at preventing specific dangers to the health and safety of the public. The legal perspective was considered more appropriate in areas such as rate-setting for public utilities. The political approach is useful in understanding regulatory activities involving broad questions of the public interest, such as environmental regulation. Looking at functions in another way, street-level administration clearly involves processes that differ from much other administrative activity.

Resources and Technologies   The availability of resources and technologies also has immense bearing on public administrative processes. The resource and technological bases often determine the extent to which public administration will be labor-intensive. Poorer nations often lack the human and material resources and technological capacity to perform administrative tasks in the ways that they are performed in richer nations. Even at a relatively mundane level, for example, the administrative process through which one obtains a driver's license will vary broadly with the availability of computers. So will taxation. The process of a public education will also vary widely with the availability of human resources and transportation technologies. Any number of examples could be advanced to show how the process of providing the same type of function varies with the availability of resources and technologies. Administration is a "single process" only in the sense of making do with the resources that one has to provide a given function.

In sum, public administrative thinking has departed considerably from White's assumption that public administration is a "single process." Today, the emphasis is on the variety of administrative processes found worldwide, and the differences among them. In 1926, the "single process" idea fit in well with the then prevailing "scientific management" notion that there was one best way to accomplish virtually any task. In the United States today, as the discussion throughout this book indicates, there is little agreement that there is one best way to organize and carry out public administration. Rather there are three major competing perspectives on what public administration is all about. In fairness to White, however, it must be remembered that he was writing in an era of much smaller-scale and less complex public administration. Moreover, there *are* common aspects of public administration in a large variety of settings. It is just too great an overstatement to consider it a "single process" on the basis of these similarities.

"Management, Not Law"

White's second assumption was that "the study of administration should start from the base of management rather than the foundation of law, and is therefore more absorbed in the affairs of the American Management Association than in the decisions of the courts." This assumption must also be adjusted in view of developments over the past several decades.

The Public ***in Public Administration***   Over the years, and continuing to the present time, many have argued that management is a "generic" endeavor, that is, in essence public and private management are the same. Such a perspective largely depends on perceiving a traditional dichotomy between politics and administration. As soon as it is admitted that public administration involves making policy choices that legally allocate public resources and determine rights and statuses, then the political perspective becomes important. And since this political perspective values representativeness, responsiveness, and political accountability, it differentiates the public sector dramatically from the private sector. The public interest, however defined, and organizational structures and processes geared to the values of representativeness and responsiveness become paramount. Legislative involvement in public administration is also legitimized by the political perspective, as is public and interest group participation. In practice, the world of public administration is often so different from that of private management that executives going back and forth between the two may undergo a kind of "culture shock." Executives entering the public sector for the first time are especially prone to the disorienting differences between the two. They are very likely to find administration frustrating as a result.[8] In short, *public* administrators today may find the affairs of the American Management Association interesting, but contrary to White's assumption, most high-level administrators today would be wary of becoming absorbed in them to the exclusion of broad political values embodied in statutory and constitutional law.

Law and Public Administration   White adopted his assumption well before constitutional and administrative law played a major role in public administration. It is a moot point whether the foundation of public administration can be found in law. However, today no one can seriously deny that the decisions of the courts on the constitutional rights of the citizenry are extremely important to public administration in a variety of contexts. So are the judiciary's decisions on the liabilities of public administrators and administrative agencies. There has been a revolutionary change in the relevance of the Constitution to public administration, and judicial decisions have been the basis for changing a great number of administrative processes. Especially important has been the growth of due process in administrative actions. Similarly, the federal Administrative Procedure Act of 1946 and equivalent state statutes have made administrative law far more central to many public administrative operations. Based on contemporary constitutional and administrative law, the courts have been very active in a wide range of administrative activities, including providing access to information, providing equal protection and due process, and operating public institutions such as schools, mental hospitals, and prisons. In fact, today the judiciary is a full-fledged partner in public administration.

Once again, the problem is less with White's assumption as a reflection of his times than that developments now have overtaken the relative simplicity of public administration then prevalent. As public administrators became more involved in the formulation of public policy and as public administrative actions penetrated the society and economy to a far greater extent, politics and law became more relevant to public administration. Equating public management with private management simply provides too narrow a focus for today's times.

"Art and Science"

White's third assumption was that "administration is still primarily an art but [his book] attaches importance to the significant tendency to transform it into a science." This assumption might be more controversial now than it was in White's day, even though the thrust of public administrative thought since 1926, as White predicted, has been toward developing a science of public administration. Such a science would be a social science that could explain and predict how individuals and organizations behave in public administrative settings. There has been a protracted controversy over the extent to which this objective can be realized. However, by using scientific approaches, our knowledge of many aspects of public administration has been expanded and deepened. Yet practitioners still tend to view public administration as an art (or even a craft).[9] They welcome any advances in the quality of practice that can be brought about by scientific approaches, but tend to remain convinced that because public administration is so people-oriented and intensive, public management will remain predominantly an art for some time to come.

The discussion in this book also suggests that although there are gains to be made through the scientific approach, at some point public administration depends very heavily upon values that cannot be dealt with effectively through contemporary scientific methods. For example, it does not seem plausible that a scientific approach can resolve such contemporary public administrative issues as a contest among values such as efficiency, public participation, and due process. The thrust of this book has been to show how different value perspectives lead to disparate ways of thinking about, organizing, and performing many tasks of public administration. This does not mean that public administration cannot be studied from a scientific perspective, but rather that it will often be impossible to make fundamental administrative choices solely on the basis of scientifically derived knowledge of public administrative behavior.

"The Heart of Government"

White's final assumption was that "administration has become, and will continue to be the heart of the problem of modern government." Of this, today, there seems to be very little room for debate. The only potential challenge would seem to come from those who view the central problem of modern government as keeping the world safe from nuclear war. But, self-evident though White's fourth assumption may appear, its implications for public administration in the future are vast indeed.

MOVING INTO THE FUTURE

In the future, the theory and practice of public administration will have to encompass far more complexity than can be contained within White's assumptions. It may be that as late as twenty-five years ago White's framework was "still perhaps the best concise statement of the foundations of the discipline of public administration."[10] But during the past two decades it has become clear that the framework is far too limiting. Ironically, this is evident in White's correct, but underdeveloped, assumption that public administration is now the heart of the problem of modern government. Modern governments must have well-developed and effective administrative components in order to serve and regulate the society and economy. But because of this, it is no longer useful to draw a sharp distinction between politics and administration. The structural characteristics of public bureaucracies present substantial challenges to the *political* organization of virtually all nations. These challenges are clearly evident in democracies, as we have noted at various points throughout this book (especially in Chapters 10 to 12). In short, if government is to be democratic, then the public administration at its heart cannot be organized solely according to the dictates of orthodox or traditional public administrative theory.

One of the great failings of the traditional approach was its inability to recognize its inherent politically repressive and antisocial tendencies. Its political theory was explored and exposed by Dwight Waldo's great work, *The Administrative State* (1948).[11] Waldo showed that the classical approach was inherently opposed to the separation of powers and other aspects of American democracy. Other works have shown that its reliance on hierarchy and the "unity of command" are repressive of the constitutional rights of public employees and militate against popular participation in government.[12] By claiming that public administrators' participation in government was justified and legitimized on the basis of their politically neutral, technical expertise, the classical approach viewed as illegitimate any serious discussion by outsiders of the character of public administration. Politicians were viewed as inherently likely to pursue goals that would detract from administrative efficiency. The public was considered too untutored in matters of public administration to be sensibly afforded a direct role in the discussion of administrative methods, processes, and decisions. Some critics also viewed traditional public administration as inherently antisocial in its reliance on impersonality and specialization. For instance, Elton Mayo argued that impersonality and specialization have the tendency to break down society's ability to exercise social controls over individuals.[13] The result, in this view, is that government must step in to replace these controls with some of its own. This has a "snowballing" effect—soon a great number of controls are governmental—and government, rather than being just one organization in a society, begins to eclipse the others.

The politically repressive and antisocial characteristics of orthodox theory were one important impetus for the development of the contemporary political and legal approaches to public administration. In the future, the task is to integrate or synthesize these approaches with a modern managerial perspective wherever possible, and to create a useful dynamic tension among the three outlooks where they cannot be successfully combined. Of course, as we have seen in our analysis in this book, this is easier said than done. If it were easy or self-evident, combining the three approaches would be neither a problem nor a challenge.

Still, some ideas can be advanced. The task for the future is to create a new public administrative culture that is better suited to democratic constitutionalism as practiced in the United States. This will help resolve the "heart of the problem of modern government," in White's terms. A public administrative culture consists of the values inherent in the dominant approach to public administration, and the structural, procedural, and technological approaches relied upon to promote those values. As noted earlier, the managerial approach to public administration, in its classical form, was once the dominant public administrative culture in the United States. In the future, though, this approach is likely to prove too limiting. Rather, what seems to be evolving is an administrative culture that emphasizes the following.

Recognition of Complexity   The task of public administration is less likely to be construed as being public management or technical specialization in the future. Rather it will be recognized that the essence of public administration is dealing with relationships among political, economic, social, organizational, managerial, legal, scientific, and technological values and systems at both micro- and macrolevels. Public administration will be seen as a process of coordinating and directing these relationships. It will need to recognize them, understand them, reconcile conflicts among them, and make choices among the competing prospects and values they offer. Even to begin to do this successfully, the public administrator must be well versed in at least the three perspectives discussed in this book.

Personal Responsibility   The complexity of public administration must alter the traditional notions of accountability and responsibility. Reliance on hierarchical authority and external oversight for these purposes must be augmented by the concept of individual administrative responsibility. The opportunities for public administrators to do harm are now so great that they can no longer simply plead they are "just following orders." Administration should not be "rule by nobody."[14] "The buck" should stop everywhere, not just at the top of the hierarchy or formal chain of authority. Today, public law recognizes this to a greater extent than ever before. Public administrators can be held personally liable if they violate an individual's constitutional rights. They have something of a right to disobey unconstitutional directives.[15] And opportunities and protection for "whistleblowing" create a moral obligation to expose various kinds of maladministration. It is important to note, from the perspective of a public administrative culture, that the newer legal approaches to personal responsibility are diametrically opposed to the earlier organizational proscriptions concerning insubordination, disloyalty, and "going public" with information damaging to one's public employer.

Protection of Constitutional Rights   Traditionally, the "heart of the problem" of democratic government was often considered to be how to strike the proper balance between governmental authority and individual rights and how to assure that tyranny of the majority would not emerge. For a time in the United States, public administrative theory and practice seemed to place too much emphasis on governmental authority and consequently, though perhaps inadvertently, to diminish the importance of protecting individual and minority rights. A variety of newer laws and constitutional interpretations have sought to redress this balance. In the future, public administrators will have to be considerably more cognizant of individual rights and limits on governmental authority. However, the basis for this change should not simply be because it is required by the judiciary; the emerging public administrative culture should stress the desirability of accomplishing administrative ends within the framework of constitutional rights and values. This is true not only in terms of dealing with clients and regulatees, but also of the rights of public employees. Since roughly 15 percent of the work force is in public employment today, a commitment to democratic constitutionalism requires that the rights of this segment of the population not be sacrificed for the sake of administrative convenience, as construed by the orthodox approach.

Representation   The public administrative culture of the future will not legitimize administrative activity solely on the basis of politically neutral, technical expertise. The representative quality of public administration will also be emphasized and fostered. This change, stemming from the political approach to public administration, has already been written into some important statutes. The past two decades have witnessed a struggle between principles of merit and representation in the realm of public personnel administration. The same kinds of disparate concerns have become more evident in other areas, such as protection of the environment and even the development of nuclear strategy. This society is no longer willing to allow the claims and plans of technical experts to go unchallenged. Rather, the public, or a segment of it, wants to be represented in administrative decision making that can affect it in concrete ways. The rise of public interest groups is one manifestation of this desire. Ideally, the new administrative culture will appreciate the importance of representation along these lines and will not resent it as meddlesome or illegitimate.

Participation   Participation is a direct avenue for representation, but its dynamics go beyond simply the *opportunity* to raise issues and have them considered. Participation requires structural arrangements as well. Public administration in the United States already relies on participation in a variety of subsidy and sociotherapeutic programs, in public education, and in the regulation of public utilities. The federal Administrative Procedure Act and similar statutes at the state level encourage public response to proposals to change administrative rules. Despite what are judged as some spectacular failures of participation in the Great Society programs of the 1960s, the trend in the future will be to accept the legitimacy and desirability of public participation in public administration, but also to try to find the best structural and procedural arrangements for it.[16] Again, the new administrative culture will move away from the "single process" and "one best way" approaches in seeking to develop different arrangements for different kinds of programs and concerns.

The new administrative culture will also emphasize more participatory work arrangements for public employees. Collective bargaining is one manifestation of this. However, many see a broader trend toward worker participation in public and private organizations. Although such participation could take a wide variety of forms, the basic notion is that management will have to be more consultative with employees and that employees will have broader opportunities to structure their work and to participate in policy decisions. In terms of political theory, public employees' participation is sometimes viewed as necessary because if democracy is politically desirable, then it should be viewed as desirable within government itself.[17] If there are special reasons why this is not the case, the burden of proof should shift to those opposed to such participation to show that it is undesirable. Importantly, from a political perspective, claims of efficiency, economy, and administrative convenience are not likely to be judged adequate grounds for denying worker participation. Going beyond political theory, however, many are convinced that worker participation is desirable even from a managerial perspective. For instance, Robert Dahl observed that based on a broad range of studies it can be concluded that "participation by workers in decision-making rarely leads to a decline of productivity; far more often it either has no effect or results in an increase in productivity."[18] Shan Martin has argued that "managing without managers" is not only feasible but highly desirable in the public sector. She believes that it is quite possible that "saving public money and improving the quality of working life are synergistic objectives that, when achieved, seem likely to result in improvements in the public service."[19]

From the perspectives of a new administrative culture, the most important aspect of participation is that it be viewed as legitimate and desirable *in principle*. This will require a new definition of management. In the past, managerial authority was largely justified (or rationalized) by the claim that managers were indispensable contributors to the welfare of the planet. For instance, Peter Drucker, perhaps the preeminent management theorist in the United States, wrote, "The emergence of management in this century may have been a pivotal event of history."[20] In a similar vein, Herbert Mintzberg has written, "No job is more vital to our society than that of the manager. It is the manager who determines whether our social institutions serve us well or whether they squander our talents and resources."[21] The new administrative culture will have to develop a different view of management. Perhaps managers will be seen as coordinators and facilitators rather than directors or superiors, co-workers rather than "bosses." It has become evident that traditional hierarchical approaches to authority and nonparticipation in the workplace will have to undergo substantial change as more public employees fall into the various categories of being highly educated, professionals, union members, and users of highly specialized, advanced technologies.

Information   Perhaps most problematic, the new administrative culture will be less inclined to value secrecy. Rather, the public's right to know will be emphasized, as it already is in the federal Freedom of Information Act, the National Environmental Policy Act, and similar statutes at the state level. Legal and constitutional protections for whistleblowers also legitimize the sharing of much information about public administration with the public. Information is the basis for informed participation and consequently will be doubly important in the evolving administrative culture.

In many ways the administrative culture that we consider to be evolving is a synthesis of the three perspectives toward public administration that have informed the discussion throughout this book. That culture could go a long way toward integrating the values of these perspectives. Efficiency, economy, and effectiveness would not necessarily be compromised by movement toward recognition of complexity, personal responsibility, representation, participation, and less secrecy. There is a considerable literature that argues that we need to move in the directions outlined here precisely in order to maximize further these managerial values.[22] For instance, it is immediately plausible that (1) efficiency and economy are not served by oversimplification, (2) personal responsibility would reduce alienation and enhance commitment to serving the public interest, (3) representation and participation would promote administrative effectiveness by keeping administrative decisions in tune with the segments of the society that are most affected by them, and (4) sharing information about administrative activities can serve as a check on ill-conceived administration.

There is a certain internal dynamic to the administrative culture we foresee that gives it a good deal of coherence. Recognition of complexity suggests that notions such as the "unity of command" are out of date simply because no one individual can master that complexity. Representation helps clarify the competing concerns in a complex administrative world. Participation is an extension of representation. It enables members of the public to become more directly involved in administrative decision making. Providing the public and public employees with greater legal and constitutional rights provides protections against their viewpoints being squelched through administrative threats and intimidation. Greater access to information enhances the potential effectiveness of representation and participation. Guaranteeing rights further protects the pursuit of information. Holding public administrators personally responsible for the legality and constitutionality of their actions serves as further protection of the rights of others. It creates a liability for public employees that can be balanced in some respects by the protection of some of their own rights, such as the right to whistleblow or disobey, and by affording them greater opportunities for participation in defining how agencies should go about their business. No doubt other connections could be found as well.

The new administrative culture might emphasize a different mix among these attributes in different functional and policy areas. This is part of its recognition of the complexity of public administration. While we would expect its values to be found in all areas of public administration, they might be developed differently in programmatic areas as diverse as agriculture, urban development, and defense.

At times, of course, there will be intractable conflicts among the perspectives embodied in this new administrative culture. But it is important to recognize that such tensions can be dynamic and stimulating. Part of the problem of public administrative theory in the past was that it failed to recognize the dynamic quality of the competition among the managerial, political, and legal perspectives. Instead it sought to suppress the political perspective by asserting that public administration had (and should have) very little to do with politics. It also paid little attention to the question of what the rights of clients and regulatees should be. In the future, as we move away from the "single process" and "one best way" ideas, there will be greater recognition that an effort to balance competing concerns can lead to valuable solutions to administrative problems. This has already occurred in some areas. For example, the convergence of the three perspectives in the policy area of equal employment opportunity/affirmative action in public personnel administration has clearly stimulated an effort to develop sounder merit exams, to eliminate violations of equal protection, and to promote greater social representation in the public sector work force. It would be hard to argue seriously that public personnel recruitment, selection, and promotion procedures have not benefited immensely from this convergence. Yet if those who were inclined to view "merit" as the only legitimate approach, or if those viewing "representativeness" in the same fashion, were allowed to have their way, the result would have been far less satisfactory. Tolerance of competing concerns should characterize the new administrative culture as it comes to grips with the true complexity of public administration.

This is the future we see emerging. But prediction is difficult and frequently wrong. Hence, for our concluding words we will retreat to safer, but no less relevant ground, and quote Dwight Waldo:

> Whatever the future, excepting only oblivion—*no* future—public administration will have an important role in it. Public administration joins two major forces, government and administrative technology. Together they have been an integral part of the enterprise of civilization. They will not disappear unless and until civilization disappears, through decay or destruction, or through transformation into a new human condition.[23]

NOTES

1. Vincent Ostrom, *The Intellectual Crisis in American Public Administration* (University, Ala.: University of Alabama Press, 1973).
2. Nicholas Henry, *Doing Public Administration* (Boston: Allyn and Bacon, 1978).
3. For this perspective, see Luther Gulick and L. Urwick, eds., *Papers on the Science of Administration* (New York: Institute of Public Administration, 1937). See Herbert Simon, *Administrative Behavior*, 2nd ed. (New York: The Free Press, 1957), and Dwight Waldo, *The Administrative State*, 2nd ed. (New York: Holmes and Meier, 1984), for critiques of the earlier approach. Simon and Waldo both appeared in first editions in the 1940s.

4. On the concept of administrative culture, see David Nachmias and David H. Rosenbloom, *Bureaucratic Culture* (New York and London: St. Martin's Press and Croom Helm, 1978), and Gerald Caiden, *Israel's Administrative Culture* (Berkeley, Calif.: Institute of Government Studies, University of California, 1970).

5. Leonard D. White, *Introduction to the Study of Public Administration* (New York: Macmillan, 1926).

6. For an overview, see Ferrel Heady, *Public Administration: A Comparative Perspective*, 2nd ed. (New York: Marcel Dekker, 1979).

7. See, among others, Grant McConnell, *Private Power and American Democracy* (New York: Knopf, 1966).

8. Marver Bernstein, *The Job of the Federal Executive* (Washington, D.C.: Brookings Institution, 1958), and Hugh Heclo, *A Government of Strangers* (Washington, D.C.: Brookings Institution, 1977).

9. George E. Berkeley, *The Craft of Public Administration* (Boston: Allyn and Bacon, 1975); Simon, *Administrative Behavior*.

10. Herbert J. Storing, "Leonard D. White and the Study of Public Administration," *Public Administration Review*, 25 (March 1965): 38–51, at 39.

11. A second edition with "New Observations and Reflections" was published in 1984 by Holmes and Meier Publishers, New York and London.

12. Ralph Hummel, *The Bureaucratic Experience* (New York: St. Martin's Press, 1977); Frederick Thayer, *An End to Hierarchy! An End to Competition!* (New York: New Viewpoints, 1973).

13. Elton Mayo, *Human Problems of an Industrial Civilization* (New York: Viking Press, 1933).

14. The phrase is Hannah Arendt's. See Owen Fiss, "The Bureaucratization of the Judiciary," *Yale Law Journal*, 92 (1983): 1442–1468 for a discussion of its implications in an American context.

15. Robert G. Vaughn, "Public Employees and the Right to Disobey," *Hasting Law Journal*, 29 (1977): 261–295.

16. Mary Kweit and Robert Kweit, *Implementing Citizen Participation in a Bureaucratic Society* (New York: Praeger, 1981).

17. See Robert A. Dahl, "Democracy in the Workplace," *Dissent* (Winter 1984): 54–60.

18. Ibid., p. 60.

19. Shan Martin, *Managing Without Managers* (Beverly Hills, Calif.: Sage, 1983), p. 176.

20. Quoted in ibid., p. 17.

21. Quoted in ibid., p. 19.

22. See ibid., and the sources cited therein.

23. Dwight Waldo, *The Enterprise of Public Administration* (Novato, Calif.: Chandler and Sharp, 1980), p. 189.

ADDITIONAL READING

BERNSTEIN, PAUL. *Workplace Democratization*. New Brunswick, N.J.: Transaction Books, 1980.

EWING, DAVID W. *Freedom Inside the Organization: Bringing Civil Liberties to the Workplace*. New York: McGraw-Hill, 1978.

MARTIN, SHAN. *Managing Without Managers*. Beverly Hills, Calif.: Sage, 1983.

THAYER, FREDERICK. *An End to Hierarchy and Competition*, 2nd ed. New York: Franklin Watts/New Viewpoints, 1981.

WALDO, DWIGHT. *The Enterprise of Public Administration*. Novato, Calif.: Chandler and
Sharp, 1980.

STUDY QUESTIONS

1. Assessing public administrative organizations with which you are familiar, do you see signs of the "old administrative culture"? Do you see any evidence of the "new administrative culture" emerging?

2. If the "new administrative culture" emerged as described here, how well would its pieces fit together? What might be some of its defects, and can you think of ways of avoiding or eliminating these?

3. What kind of public administrative future would you like to see, and what could you do to help bring it about?

Index

About the Author

David H. Rosenbloom is Distinguished Professor of Public Administration at the Maxwell School of Syracuse University. He received his Ph.D. in political science from the University of Chicago in 1969. In 1970–71, he was an American Society for Public Administration Fellow. His publications include *Federal Service and the Constitution* (Cornell University Press, 1971); *Federal Equal Employment Opportunity* (Praeger, 1977); *Public Administration and Law* (Marcel Dekker, 1983); *Bureaucratic Government, USA* (St. Martin's, 1980; with David Nachmias); *Representative Bureaucracy and the American Political System* (Praeger, 1981; with Samuel Krislov); and *Essentials of Labor Relations* (Reston/Prentice-Hall, 1985; with Jay Shafritz). Professor Rosenbloom is currently co-editor-in-chief of *Policy Studies Journal*. In 1986, Professor Rosenbloom was elected to membership in the National Academy of Public Administration.